Companions of the Heart

A Treasury of Inspiration and Encouragement

by

Alan Cohen

Including the complete books:

The Dragon Doesn't Live Here Anymore

Rising In Love

The Healing of the Planet Earth

To order *Companions of the Heart:*

Personal Orders:

For a free catalog of Alan Cohen's books, tapes and workshop schedule, write to:

Alan Cohen Publications and Workshops
P.O. Box 450
Kula, Hawaii 96790

Bookstore Orders:

New Leaf
5425 Tulane Drive S.W.
Atlanta, Georgia 30336
(1-800) 241-3829
toll-free number for stores only

By Alan Cohen

BOOKS

The Healing of the Planet Earth

The Dragon Doesn't Live Here Anymore

Rising In Love

The Peace That You Seek

Have You Hugged a Monster Today?
with illustrations by Keith Kelly

Setting the Seen

Companions of the Heart

CASSETTE TAPES

Miracle Mountain

Peace
with music by Steven Halpern

Deep Relaxation
with music by Steven Halpern

I Believe in You
with songs & music by Stephen Longfellow Fiske

To you, the reader,
for giving me healing
by accepting it for yourself.

The Dragon Doesn't Live Here Anymore

Loving Fully
Living Freely

Alan Cohen

The Dragon Doesn't Live Here Anymore
by Alan Cohen

Title Page Art by Jack McKiernan.

Photography by Alan Cohen: pg. 93, 159, 167; Gene Dillman: pg. 3, 197, 217, 225, 249; Joel Friedman: pg. 309; Judy Marlow: pg. 225.

The author wishes to express his appreciation to the following authors, artists and publishers for their kind permission to print their copyrighted material:

For the reader's reference, these addresses are given for sources referred to by the author:

A Course in Miracles: Foundation for Inner Peace, P.O. Box 635, Tiburon, California 94920

The autobiography and writings of Paramahansa Yogananda: Self-Realization Fellowship, 3880 San Rafael Avenue, Los Angeles, California 90065.

To Bless and to Heal,
The Godly purpose of all
who have dedicated themselves to
the love and service of humanity

Lay down your burden
Lay it all down
Pass the glass between you
Drink it up
Place the Light before you
Come through the door
The dragon doesn't live here anymore

Sing with the choirs that surround you
Dance to the music in your soul
Look into the eyes that really see you
Place all that you have into that bowl

O lay down your burden
Lay it all down
Pass the glass between you
Drink it up
Place the Light before you
Come through the door
The dragon doesn't live here anymore

— "Lay Down Your Burden" by Colleen Crangle

About two years ago, my good friend Barbara Cole went to well-known psychic Vincent Ragone for his counsel. As he was speaking to her about the path of her life, he stopped and said, "Tell Alan to write." This was quite surprising to her, since she had not mentioned my name or told him anything about me. His advice did not make much sense to me, either, as I was not interested in writing, and typing was one of my least favorite things to do. So I just filed away his suggestion in the back of my mind, in hopes that one day I would understand what he meant.

Then, one December morning a year later, I awoke to hear a gentle voice within me whisper, "Sit down and write." It was not a voice that spoke in words, but an intuitive prompting. As I sat down and began to record whatever ideas came to me, I was fascinated to see how thoughts that I have been considering for years came together with almost ancient memories to form themselves into integrated units with themes and direction. I continued with this process until somehow, without my ever planning it, a few hundred pages later I had a book in my hands.

There is more to the story. During the first few weeks that I was writing, I had a pleasant picture in my mind of doing this work in some quaint secluded cottage, surrounded by fragrant trees and the simple song of the birds. I set out to find such a place, but no matter what people I contacted, advertisements I posted, or affirmations I declared, such a place did not materialize, and I wrote off the idea as just a writer's romantic fantasy.

The weeks of writing turned into months, and it became clear to me that I would need to devote a full-time effort to bring the final form of the book into focus. Then, into my mind flashed the thought, "*The Cenacle*," the name of a spiritual retreat center staffed by a sisterhood of Catholic nuns. I had driven past the place literally thousands of times, but I knew next to nothing about it.

I telephoned the Cenacle and asked if they had a quiet room in their house where I could write for a few weeks. The director, Sister *Barbara*, told me, "I'm afraid we don't have such a place in our house, but we do have a little secluded cottage amid some trees . . . Would you like that?"

It was not long before this Sister Barbara was walking me down a winding path lined with delightfully scented spruce trees, to a cozy ivy-covered cottage on a hill overlooking a park and a river. As she opened the door, I could hardly believe my eyes. Before me was a wooden desk with paper and pencils laid out on top of it, a big comfortable easy chair, and almost exactly the room I had envisioned months before — plus a color TV and a little refrigerator. (God gave me my wish plus interest!) As Sister Barbara handed me the key to the cabin, so ended any doubts that I ever had about God's ability to perform the impossible. I figured that if He could get a Jewish guy named Cohen into a convent, He can do anything.

After working there a few days, I decided to take a break, and I went out to a local barn theatre to see a production of *Joseph and the Amazing Technicolor Dreamcoat*. As I was sitting in the lounge during intermission, I felt extremely comfortable in this place, and I wondered why. As I looked up at the low sloping ceiling with its century-old rough-hewn beams, I realized that this room reminded me of the Upper Room as it was portrayed in the movie *Jesus of Nazareth*. This was the room where Jesus gave the disciples His parting blessings, and where He returned to them after the resurrection to tell them, "I am always with you." This scene is one of the most powerful and touching I have ever experienced, and I have often thought how much I would love to be in that place, receiving the Master's Blessing and His charge to live for Love, Healing, and Service to all. The Upper Room has a special place in my heart.

The next day, I was sitting in the Cenacle garden with one of the nuns, sharing our ideas and aspirations, when I felt moved to ask her, "What does 'The Cenacle' mean?"

"Oh, yes," she kindly explained, " 'Cenacle' is the French word for 'The Upper Room.' "

It is experiences like these that make me feel that there is a great plan of Guidance and Direction working within our lives, a purpose deeper and more powerful than we usually recognize. I feel privileged to have participated in the process of this book, and its birth is a testimony to the Truth that God is everywhere, that He is constantly seeking to work with us and through us, and that He is always willing to share the miracle of Love with us, as we are willing to accept it and express it.

One P.S.: When the book was complete, it turned out to be a series of short lyrical essays, and I took it to my friend Barbara to share with her. As I did, she played for me the tape recording of her original interview with Vincent Ragone, one which I had never heard. When the tape came to the moment at which Vincent said, "Tell Alan to write," there was another statement which Barbara had not told me about. He said, "I think a series of short lyrical essays would be very good."

I hope that you will enjoy the book and that you find value in it.

Alan Cohen

There is a story about a man who left this earth and was taken on a tour of the inner realms. He was shown a room where he saw a large group of hungry people trying to eat dinner, but because the spoons that they were trying to eat with were longer than their arms, they remained frustrated. "This," his guide told him, "is hell." "That's terrible!" exclaimed the man; "Please show me Heaven!" "Very well," agreed the guide, and on they went. When they opened Heaven's door, the man was perplexed to see what looked very much like the same scene: there was a group of people with spoons longer than their arms. As he looked more closely, however, he saw happy faces and full tummies, for there was one important difference: the people in Heaven had learned to feed each other.

The coming together of this book has been a miracle at every step of the way. People, materials, and connections have all seemed to be in just the right place at just the right time. Most inspiring to me has been the Divine support and help I have received from my friends who have demonstrated themselves to be nothing other than selfless sisters and brothers. All of the words in this book could not express my appreciation for their support. I hope that this page will capture the thought of my gratefulness.

I would like to humbly acknowledge my mother and father, who have taught me the meaning of unconditional love, Hilda, who has shown me the Miracle of Grace, and B.C., who has given me the precious gift of friendship. I am equally grateful to my family on the Land, the sisters of The Cenacle, Valerie Ginther and Dorene Yonelunas, Jack McKiernan, Gene Dillman, The Roses, Karolyn Kempner, David Crismond, Jeff Woolley, and all of the many others who have contributed in many ways to this work. I wish to express, as well, my deep appreciation for the dedicated music of the Paul Winter Consort and the angelic voice of Susan Osborn, whose sincere offering of "Lay Down Your Burden" captures all the Love and Light this book is intended to express.

It is my further hope that all of the masters, saints, yogis, and loving teachers who have helped me in my own growth will be honored through the blessing of all who read these words. Truly God loves us through each other.

PART I:
THE JOURNEY

PART II:
THE HOMECOMING

PART I:
THE JOURNEY

"I want to learn to fly like that," Jonathan said, and a strange light glowed in his eyes. "Tell me what to do."

Chiang spoke slowly and watched the younger gull ever so carefully. "To fly as fast as thought, to anywhere that is," he said, "you must begin by knowing that you have already arrived . . ."

The trick, according to Chiang, was for Jonathan to stop seeing himself as trapped inside a limited body with a forty-two inch wingspan . . . The trick was to know that his true nature lived, as perfect as an unwritten number, everywhere at once across space and time.

— Richard Bach, *Jonathan Livingston Seagull*

Starting Points

ONE STORY

Love is the way I walk in gratitude.
                                        — A Course in Miracles

At an early age, I remember saying to one of my Little League pals, "Gee, Johnny, wouldn't it be funny if we were all dead, and we were just dreaming that we are alive?" Then, as my childhood visions of playing centerfield for the Yankees were lost to a mad idea that dreams do not come true, I settled for a place in a world where the aspiration for love and freedom is written off as an impossible wish. Now, however, I have come full circle, and what I told Johnny is, ironically, pretty much what I believe now — that the life we live is something of a dream. The only difference is that now I believe that we are all alive, and dreaming that we can die.

When I was in second grade, I came down with pneumonia, and Doctor Bernie Friedenthal came to my house to tell my mother to sponge me down with cold water. As she continued to do this through the night, the thought occurred to me that I might die. I remember that at that time I did not fear death. The idea of dying seemed as matter-of-fact to me as the end of the school year. I asked my mom, "What will happen if I do not get better?" "Don't worry, honey," she told me comfortingly, "You'll be alright." But I was not asking out of fear — I was more curious than afraid.

Somehow, sometime after that, I learned to be afraid. I began to believe in a fearful and threatening world. I came to think that there were monsters out there, merciless dragons who could devour a

5

helpless me. I forgot how to feel beautiful and I learned to feel ugly. Somewhere along the line, I traded in my sense of "O.K. Kid" for a self-image that seemed always to be somehow less than others. I was overweight, awkward, and the only Jewish kid in the neighborhood. I thought that there was something wrong with me, and that there was something I had to do (like be skinny, athletic, and Protestant) to be like the gang of popular kids.

Since that time, however, as I have gotten to know more and more of the popular kids, I have had a startling discovery: *they felt the same way.* They, too, felt that there was something different about them, and that they had to be popular and acknowledged to earn love. Just like me, they thought that there was an "in crowd," and they were out.

This gave me something very interesting to think about: if everyone felt out, who, then, was "in?" As it turns out, there never really was any "in crowd," except in the eyes of those who thought they were out — which was just about *all* of us.

And so we are not so different after all. As we begin to share our stories, it becomes clear that we all learned to fear and feel separate and alone. We can see, too, that it is only the details of our stories that are different, and that the heart of our separate stories is really the same. What we thought were different stories are really One Story — our story.

When I arrived at Miss Greenberger's kindergarten class at Washington School, I was quite self-conscious and embarrassed about my weight. More than anything in the world, I dreaded the event of having to go down to the nurse's office to get weighed with my class, because the nurse would call each weight out loud. As I would step onto the scales, a great hush would come over the spellbound class, as if it were the final drawing of the Irish Sweepstakes, and the moment my weight was announced, all the normal kids would go wild, and their eyes would bug out, and they would grab each other and say, "Wow! Did you hear that?" They had a blast. As for me, I just wanted to blast off into some remote corner of the universe.

Well, one day, the awful announcement came: it was time for us to all go down to the basement to be weighed. I wanted to run out the door and hide, but since I couldn't, I marched down the stairs with all the skinny kids, praying all the while that the nurse wouldn't say my weight out loud. It sounds funny now, but at the time, it was a horror story. When we got to the basement, an honest-to-goodness miracle happened: there, waiting for me were my mom and dad, with a big birthday cake with five candles, lots of ice cream, and party hats for everyone. The weighing story was just a ruse to get me downstairs for a surprise birthday party! (Talk about being saved in the nick of time!) I was glad they decided to surprise me, but they could have at least picked a more compassionate ploy! But they did not know the private hell I was going through, and it was really an act of love.

I tell this story now, as it has come to symbolize to me the story of our fears in life. We hold horrible catastrophic fantasies of what is to come — fears based on learned unworthiness and misunderstanding. When we are forced or choose to confront these fears, however, we learn that there was never anything to be afraid of, after all. The fear is like that of the boogeyman who supposedly lived in the basement, but who turned out to never really be there when we turned on the light.

There is a sequel to the story. Years later, when I was pledging a fraternity in college, we pledges were continuously warned about the ominous *Hell Night*. When I would pass some initiation test during the pledge period, the brothers would say, "That's pretty good, pledge, but just wait until Hell Night . . . Then we'll see who really makes it!" I couldn't imagine it being any worse than some of the stunts they had us do during pledging, such as the night we had to line up outside the basement door and be called downstairs, one by one, to face the weird brotherhood-at-large. As I sat there waiting my turn, all I heard were crazed and ghoulish screams from the depths below. During those minutes at the top of the basement stairs, every Vincent Price movie that I had ever seen flashed through my mind, and I was sure that they had hired him to conduct the evening's program. When I finally got down there, however, I found that it was just the brothers making those noises to scare us.

When Hell Night, the final trial-by-fire of the pledge period came, we were told to arrive at the fraternity house at 6 p.m. on Saturday with no money, no identification, and to tell no one where we were going. (Luckily, I was in a Jewish fraternity, and because I observed the Jewish sabbath, they were kind enough to postpone Hell until 7 p.m., after dark.) And I must confess that I cheated. I stashed a $5 bill in the sole of one of my penny loafers. (I must have had great faith to think that $5 could save me from Hell!) But please don't tell anyone, or they might take back my fraternity pin.

When I arrived, we were lined up and told that we would have to go through a series of dangerous adventures to prove ourselves worthy of the final test. The path to this test, we were told, was a cleverly designed scavenger hunt. Our pledge class was then divided into two groups and told to wish each other well, as there was no guarantee that we would ever see each other again.

Our first clue led us to a locker at a bus station, where we found one-way tickets to New York City. Then, behind a *Time* magazine billboard in Manhattan, we found an envelope with subway tokens, which took us to our next clue on the George Washington Bridge. And then to a restaurant in Chinatown, where a message was hidden in the duck sauce. And then we were directed to walk through Central Park and whistle a certain tune, which would draw to us our next instruction, delivered by a well-known prostitute (who was actually a very innocent coed drama major, put up to the job by the conniving brothers). Her message led us to a specific subway platform in Greenwich Village, where, emerging from another train coming from a different direction was: the other group of our pledge brothers! (All paths lead to the same place.) There we were met by a brother who gave us outlandish costumes and party hats and marched us through the streets to the front of the Fillmore East Theatre. Here we did not feel conspicuous in our silly outfits, since most of the people in line to get into the *Canned Heat* concert were dressed weirder than we were.

Then the Pledgemaster appeared. This was the one known for his uncompromising ruthlessness and sheer joy at seeing pledges cringe. He lined us up and told us: "You have successfully conquered your trials to this point. Your final test now stands before you. In a few minutes, you will be taken to a room in which a group of people will be waiting for you. There, you will be asked to perform an action that you have not previously experienced. If you want to be initiated into this fraternity, you must do anything that you are asked. You have the right at any time to withdraw your request to be a brother in this fraternity. Am I making myself clear?"

Too clear. We pledges looked each other in the eye like the Little Rascals on a windy night's camping trip. But we knew that we had gone this far, and we were not about to quit now. And so we were marched down the street, in our little party hats and funny costumes, wondering what diabolical scheme, extracted from the repressed subconscious of a crazed fraternity pledgemaster, was waiting for us. Then we were stopped and directed to enter into a certain bar, which, as we passed through the door, one of my pledge brothers whispered to me, was gay. I had no idea what to expect. My mind was going in circles, and the word "faith" took on new meaning for me.

We were ushered into a back room, and there, waiting for us, was indeed a group of people. It was all of our fraternity brothers, with big smiles on their faces, singing the fraternity song, and adding the verse, "and we are so happy to welcome you to our fraternity." That was it! The task that we had to do was to accept our welcome into the brotherhood! At that moment, my "big brother" in the fraternity came over to me, gave me a big handshake, and walked me over to the refreshment table, where I proceeded to enjoy one hell of a party. And I didn't even need to use the $5.

Sometimes, however, we have to wrestle with a paper tiger for a while before we realize that he is a fraud. By the time I was getting to be a teenager, my feelings about myself had dropped below freezing. I was six feet tall with a size twelve shoe, and I had to bring a birth certificate to get in to the movies for the children's price, since no ticket seller in her right mind would believe that I was a child. To make things worse, pimples were beginning to sprout on my cheeks and one morning I woke up with braces on my teeth. On top of it all, I became interested in girls, which seemed to magnify every pimple, oral twinkle, and extra pound.

Perhaps it was out of necessity that, when I was twelve years old, I undertook my first act of determination in this life: I put myself on a weight-loss program. I went on a strict diet of raisin bread and jelly. It was not exactly a regimen that Adelle Davis might go for, but it worked. Within a few months, my weight was normal, and with the pounds went an old idea of "me."

A few years (and a lot of raisin bread) later, I received in the mail an invitation to attend a Sunday morning brunch for teenagers at my synagogue. Though I put the letter aside, the event held a strange fascination for me. This fascination I later came to know as the loving Voice of God, gently prompting me to come home to His open arms. I call it the Voice of God because it led me to a teacher that would guide me for a time on my path. Later, that very same voice was to draw me away from the forms of organized religion.

Out of what I believed to be curiosity, I went to this brunch. I had no rationale for going; in fact, after my Bar Mitzvah, I expected to steer clear of the synagogue forevermore. My parents were not affiliated with the temple, and there was no reason on earth for me to go — but there was a reason in Heaven.

When I got there, I met a man, Stuie, who was to become my spiritual guide for seven years. He was a dynamic, sincere, and open-hearted man, his life dedicated to the love of God. When he spoke that morning, his words touched a chord inside of me that had long been painfully silent. It was the chord of the awakening of my soul. My mind began to be intrigued with questions that I had long since put aside for lack of anyone to share them with, questions like "Why am I here?" and "Who is God?" More important, my heart flew open with the possibility of the reality of love and happiness and a purpose for life. I was on my way home.

Like a big brother, Stuie took me under his wing and gave me love and guidance in a way that I had not experienced in years. He respected me. He saw worth in me that no one else acknowledged. I felt accepted and whole, nurtured and good — feelings that I had nearly given up believing. My relationship with God was rekindled; I began to see positivity in life and wonder in the mysteries of the universe. I had stepped out of the loneliness of isolation and into the warm sun of a life worth living.

The years with Stuie and the temple youth group were ones of transformation and learning, and I shall always be grateful for them. I became very involved in Orthodox Judaism, strictly observing the sabbath, eating kosher food, and following the detailed laws and customs. Though I had to make some "sacrifices" in my outer life, such as quitting the track team and missing the Junior Prom, I did not care. I had found something within me that could not compare to that frightening outer world in which I had been struggling. I remember going to sleep one night wearing my prayer shawl, clutching its fringes, with such a love in my heart that I felt I was cradled in the arms of God Himself.

I decided to attend Yeshiva University, a college for Jewish studies, where I could continue my pursuit of God. There I had the good fortune to study with an exciting, inspired rabbi who made the

Bible more alive than anything else I was doing. He would come to class each morning and stand on the desk and literally yell about how wonderful is God! His love of Truth was so great that I felt drawn face to face with Abraham. There was something magical about the Truth brought to life. And there was something very warm and deep in the community of Judaism.

I would not be allowed to stagnate, though. After two years at the college, I no longer felt inspired. The laws and customs ceased to hold their magic for me, and I found myself performing rituals mechanically. I wanted to do other things; to live again in the world. I had extracted all that I could from Judaism, at that state of my evolution, and God had other plans for me.

There was a turning point. One holiday, a fast day, I found myself fasting and resenting it. I persevered and persevered, but it was not a perseverance of the heart — it was a clinging to a form that I had outgrown. I realized that I was fasting because I was afraid not to; I feared going off the path of Judaism (which I had been taught was a tragedy); I feared losing God's love and special favor; and I feared facing feelings of guilt and badness. At that moment I decided that fear was not a good enough reason to do a religious act, and it was certainly not a good enough reason to live a life, and I would rather take my chances in the world than live in fear. So I ate a piece of cake, and thus began the next stage in my unfoldment.

I transferred to a state college, joined my fraternity, and proceeded to whoop it up for two years. I lived out all the desires that I had repressed and missed during my Jewish years. Looking back on that time now, I see that I had to work through those desires and learn the ways of the world. Perhaps my evolution could have proceeded no further in a cloistered life. I certainly did not reason it out like this at the time; I was just busy having a good time; and that is exactly what I did. And I believe that in the long run the experience served my growth.

The summer after college, I went to Europe, and I had my nose rubbed in the world. A friend and I set out to have a two-month blast, but we soon found that life on earth is not always a fraternity party. Within one week of my trip, I had all of my belongings stolen, purely out of my own irresponsibility (I went to a rock festival and left my goods unattended), and this gave birth to a major lesson in my growing up.

I was not willing to accept responsibility for the world stealing from me. I felt the world owed it to me to make up the loss. So I decided to cash some travelers cheques and to fraudulently report them stolen. This way, American Express — and not me — would take the loss. I cashed several hundred dollars' worth of cheques with a sloppy signature to uphold the claim I would later make. The next step was for me to walk down the street to the American Express office to file the phony claim. But something stopped me. A quiet, but very real, still, small voice within me whispered, *"No — don't do this — no good can come of it."* This voice seemed new to me, yet astonishingly familiar. I stood in front of the door of the American Express office, thought quietly for a few moments, and then turned about and walked back to my hotel. I believe that then and there, in front of American Express, amid my raving desires and pounding emotions, I received grace from a guardian angel giving me gentle guidance to help me avoid further difficulties in the world, for, in truth, no good could have come of the act.

I returned to America to enter graduate school. How I got into the right graduate school is a miracle story, if ever there was one. I was pretty much a sleepwalker. Although I thought I was making choices, I now see that God was guiding me at every step of the way. What I thought were my reasons were really His Reasons. His Plan for me, you see, was much bigger than my little plan for my little self.

In college, I was a psychology major. Although I did not realize it, I was reaching out for a deeper understanding of the inner life. One night, at a local YMHA, I was hypnotized by an amateur hypnotist. I became intrigued with this process which led to another realm of experience and pointed to the possibility of states of consciousness beyond the one I usually experienced. Immediately I took up the study of hypnotism. I read all the books I could find on the subject; I mailed for pamphlets and began to hypnotize my friends; I entertained at fraternity parties, and had my fraternity brothers recite their Bar Mitzvah prayers, to the amusement of all.

I relate this now to show how the process of reaching out for God is one of homing in on target. At first it is gross and clumsy. In hypnotizing for fun, I was grasping on to a higher element of reality for which I yearned. At the time, it was the best — and the only — way that I knew how to touch God. Now I would not use mental power for entertainment, but then it was the best that I could do with what I knew or had.

Before long, I came upon the book *The Search for Bridey Murphy*, the true story of an amateur hypnotist who, through hypnotic age regression, took a woman into what she reported were a number of previous incarnations, for which documentation was later discovered. I became fascinated with the idea of reincarnation, and excited at the prospect of exploring it through hypnosis. It was not long before I was trying hypnotic regression to previous lives on any friend or student of mine who was game enough to try. I was obsessed with it. I even did it in some risky situations, such as with high school students when I was substitute teaching. I was crazy to do it as I did, but now I see that these experiments were really just attempts to know God. I was fortunate that I did not get into trouble over it. I like to believe, though, that my intentions were pure, and I was able to do what I did without harm of it.

Now, since I was also a finagler, I decided that I might as well get college credit for my treasure hunts into the subconscious. So I took a psychology senior research course and got to use the college laboratory for a hypnosis experiment which set out to verify the truth of hypnotic age regression. As it turned out, the study did not verify anything, but I did succeed in getting a pretty blonde coed to follow a post-hypnotic suggestion to call me up at midnight one night.

The professor of this senior research class was a very hip and transcendental sort of character. My first contact with him was an education in itself. I had just transferred from Yeshiva University, a very straight institution, as far as institutions go. When I came to Rutgers, I had to get my schedule approved by a certain Dr. Green, who, I was told, could be found in his office at the top of the stairs of an old house used as the psychology department. So I trod up a long stairway, knocked on the door, and heard a deep voice resonate, "Come on in!" There, sitting below a huge day-glow "Peace" poster, was this incredibly tall hippy with the longest arms and legs I have ever seen. His face was covered with a huge black beard and hair longer, it seemed, than his arms. He was sitting nonchalantly with his mile-long legs up on the desk, reading a magazine. He looked straight out of a *Fabulous Furry Freak Brothers* comic.

"Excuse me," I interrupted, "Could you tell me where I can find Dr. Green?"

THE DRAGON DOESN'T LIVE HERE ANYMORE

"That's me, man . . . come on in!"
I had most definitely left Yeshiva University.

Dr. Green and I became good friends. I signed up for his Psychology Seminar, in which he told about his LSD experiences, threw around words like "karma," and assigned us to read Carlos Castenada's *Teachings of Don Juan*. The first day of class, Dr. Green wrote on the blackboard this quotation, which he told us was from Don Juan:

> *Each man is different;*
> *Each man must find his own path.*
> *Each man is the same;*
> *Each man must find his own path.*

I was about to graduate from college, and the natural thing to do seemed to be to go to graduate school. I must report that I never gave a moment's thought to why I should go to graduate school, or whether it was the best choice of action, and it never really occurred to me that there might be something else to do, like join the Peace Corps or go to work. I had gone to school all my life, and as long as there was more school to go to, I guessed that I was supposed to go to it. On one level, it was a very unconscious decision, my being seemingly pushed along like a leaf floating on a river. But, as it turned out, there was a deeper plan for me — a downright Divine plot — one which I never could have guessed.

When I applied to graduate schools, there was no method to my madness. I just mailed applications to whatever schools sounded romantic or were well-known. It had very little to do with any reasoning. On my applications, where I was asked to state my career interests, I wrote down subjects like hypnosis, the placebo effect, and dream therapy. I was not seriously interested in anything, but now, as I consider what I wrote, they were all fields of inquiry that pointed toward discovering the inner knowledge — the wisdom of the higher self. My inner being was yearning for a deeper understanding of life, and I was trying to get at it in the academic realm of psychology.

It was no wonder that I was rejected from eight of the nine graduate schools that I applied to. And the one that did accept me, I didn't want to go to. I just did not feel as if I had found my place.

Then a friend suggested that I try Montclair State College. I knew nothing about this school, except that it was a state teachers' college, and I certainly was not interested in teaching. But I felt attracted to it for some unknown reason, and so I decided to check it out. The moment I stepped on the campus, I felt at ease and very much at home. There was something that just felt right about it. At the time, I thought it was because there were lots of attractive girls on campus, but, as it turns out, the girl that was really attracting me was the Divine Mother.

I went into the admissions office and asked, "Do you think I can get into this school?"

The admissions officer asked me about two questions, and said, "Sure! — Would you like a scholarship?"

"Sure!" I replied, and about a month later, I received a letter in the mail telling me that my tuition was waived, and that I was now the Graduate Assistant to the Dean of Students and the recipient of a very generous salary. I have a feeling God wanted me in that school.

I entered the program for Guidance Counseling, which was not really what I wanted, but it was the best thing on the menu, and so I took it. In my first class, a short, grey-haired professor with smiling eyes walked into the room, plugged in a tape recorder, and announced, "This is my course in a nutshell." As the "play" button clicked, I heard Sammy Davis Jr. singing, "I Gotta Be Me." I sat there thinking, "This teacher's weird," and then I began to listen to the words of the song. What did he mean, "I gotta be me?"

The book for the course was Carl Rogers' *On Encounter Groups*. I knew about encounter groups only what I had read in *Newsweek* magazine. I thought it was interesting and kind of nice for people who liked to sit naked together and be honest and cry. "This is good for those with problems," I thought, "but I am already honest and open." Nothing could have been further from the truth. I was living a phony, closed, and uptight life. As I read through the book, even as I read the first paragraph, something marvelously thrilling happened inside of me. I felt as if a warm and wonerful sun was rising in my chest. The words went right into my heart. The spirit of the book appealed to a deeper and more satisfying level of my being than I had experienced since I was a little child. All Dr. Rogers was saying was that his life was much more satisfying when he was open, honest, accepting, trust-

15

ing, and loving. And that was all I needed to hear to remind me of a hunger in my soul for truth and simplicity, two of the very important elements of happiness that I had not known in many years. Even when I was in Judaism, I was so busy being Jewish that I forgot to be me. And now I was being offered the opportunity to once again know myself.

I responded with more enthusiasm than I have ever felt for anything in this life. In the book, Dr. Rogers spoke of "human relations laboratories," planned workshops for practicing trust, honesty, and communication. "God, would I like to find one of these," I thought. I would do anything to get involved in something like this.

All I had to do was to walk, the next day, through the college student center lounge, for there, to my astonishment, was a poster: "Human Relations Laboratory, October 4-7." I flew to the sign-up table and registered as fast as my little unconscious hand could write. There was nothing, I tell you, *nothing* that could keep me from that workshop. Don't ask me why. At the time, I couldn't really tell you. I just knew it was for me.

The workshop turned out to be all that I wanted, expected, and needed — and more. It was, if it is possible to say, the turning point of my life. For the first part of the weekend, I was uptight and phony. My ego, you see, was threatened. It knew it was about to die, for I would have to give up my old way of being, and that is something the ego does not easily relinquish — even if the old way of being is empty. In my heart of hearts, however, I knew that this death was but a birth into a new and more wonderful way of living.

Late one night, in our workshop group, someone confronted me. "Alan," she said, "You don't seem like you're really with us. How are you feeling?"

"Comfortable," I lied, "and confident." (Not only did I lie, but I swore to it.)

"That's funny," someone else commented, "you don't seem very comfortable or confident to me."

"Nor to me," another agreed. "I see you the same way," said another, and another, and yet another — all in a loving and supportive way.

At that moment, something happened inside of me that was perhaps the most profound experience of my life. It was as if a little light went on in my gut, or something like a door to a dark room

16

being opened to admit morning sunlight. If I could give it a voice, it would have said, "It's O.K., Alan. You can let go, now. It's O.K." It was a moment so subtle and quiet that no one else could ever know it was happening, yet so spectacular that a new life sprang from it. It was nothing less than the transformation of a human being.

"Maybe you're right," I spoke, not believing that these words were coming out of my mouth. "I have not been feeling very confident; maybe I have been acting kind of phony."

When I finished these words, I felt as if a ten ton weight had been lifted off my shoulders. It was as if I could breathe again, as if the "me" that had been so long hidden under a burden of expectations and pressures had been freed to live once again in open daylight. I had found the key to unlock myself from a desolate tower of lonely isolation, and I began to dance down the stairs into a new world — a good world — in which I could allow other persons into my heart, and where I could share myself with them. I no longer had to be afraid of people, of my feelings, of opinions. I knew that I was alright, and that there was something wonderful in store for me if I could just make heart-to-heart contact with others. It was the end of my exile, and the beginning of a life that I could cherish.

I began to experience fantastic changes in my life. I literally threw away my contact lenses, for I knew I was loveable even *with* eyeglasses, and if someone would not have me with glasses, well, that was too bad for them. I began to write poetry and to be turned on by people. I could touch others, physically and emotionally. I spoke truth in my relationships. My life was evolving at a fantastic pace.

My old friends dropped away, as they had no idea what I was raving about. Some of them just stared at me and said, "That's nice," but I knew that they were just being polite, and our relationship was all but over. But new and more exciting and more fulfilling relationships blossomed in my life almost overnight. I just wanted to live, and to grow, and to experience this wonderful feeling of being that seemed brand new to me, and yet strangely familiar. I was in love with life, and life was in love with me. It was the very best kind of love affair.

Just around that time, I began to be interested in psychedelic drugs. When Dr. Green turned me on to Castenada and *Don Juan*, I became intrigued with the possibility that there were yet deeper realities. There was something temptingly mystical about Don Juan's teachings. It rekindled deep within my soul a memory of a realm of being in which *all* of life made sense. We were also assigned to read Aldous Huxley's *Doors of Perception*, in which he described his eye-opening experience with the drug mescaline. Huxley said that he became aware of a great "Mind at Large" — a universal intelligence which guides and knows and sees all things in wonder and delight. He had tuned in to God's Infinite Mind. That sounded pretty exciting to me. If this drug could reveal such a splendor, then I wanted to try it.

And so I did. A friend got me a small amount of mescaline, and I was in for quite an experience. I felt a tremendous surge of power pulsating through my body; not a physical power, but the release of a tremendous mind energy. It was wonderful, and frightening. At one point, I felt a great charge of love and peace, and all I could do was to smile at first, and then burst into uncontrollable laughter. Unfortunately, I and my friends were in a Chinese restaurant at the time. Fortunately, I was able to maintain some semblance of decorum, and I contained myself just long enough to retreat to the restroom, where the moment the door closed behind me, I burst into hysterical laughter. There I remained until this episode was over.

When I later "came down," the overall experience had had a jarring effect on my way of looking at the world. I had touched feelings and tapped energies that made the things that I had been taught to value seem empty. I had had a very brief taste of expanded consciousness, and after such a taste ("The first time the tiger tastes blood," described Claudio Naranjo), many of the activities that I was used to enjoying now seemed shallow and unfulfilling. I began to feel a little depressed and confused, for I did not know how to integrate my experience and new perceptions with my former way of life.

I felt a need for some kind of guidance, but I did not know anyone who could offer it. Then, a little voice inside of me kept gently repeating, "Go see Jim . . . Talk to Jim." Why it picked Jim, I had no idea. Jim was a strange and powerful man who had been in my wonderful, tranforming group on the human relations laboratory. I did not like him; his lifestyle, his manner, and his words seemed very foreign to me, and I felt threatened by him. I certainly did not understand him. There was something very unusual about him. When this little voice within me, a voice that I had never heard before, but that I trusted, told me to seek him out, I was perplexed. I put it off, and put it off, but my confusion was now being amplified by thoughts that I had lost my mind or gone crazy.

I had to talk to him. One evening I saw him at a workshop and I took him aside. "Jim," I asked reticently, "do you know anything about acid (psychedelic drugs)?" The moment he heard the question, his eyes begin to bulge, and I thought I saw mesmerizing whirlpool patterns begin to swirl in his eyes, the kind they show in the movies to indicate that someone is traveling through time into another dimension. "Acid?! . . . Did you say 'Acid'?!" (By this time I thought his eyes were going to pop out.) . . . "I am acid!!!" Boy, did I ask the sixty-four dollar question. I felt like Dorothy standing before the Wizard of Oz.

We sat down together, and Jim began to explain to me all of his understanding of acid. As you may have gathered, he was a little on the dramatic side. I wanted to be reassured that I was O.K., and that nothing horrible had happened to me as a result of taking this powerful drug. "Do you think I can go back to being happy doing the same things I've been used to doing?" I asked, half hoping that he would give me a simple "Sure," and that would be the end of it.

"Oh, no! You can't go back now!"

I was getting a little anxious, but I was magnetized to hear him out. "Do you know why?" he continued.

"Why, Jim?"

"Because now you are a *mutant!*" Chills of horror ran through my entire body. "Oh, no!" I thought, "I don't want to be a mutant . . . anything but that!"

"And do you know what else?" He didn't flinch one bit. (I could hardly wait to hear.) ". . . That's the best thing that could ever happen to you, because you are now a part of the next step in the evolution of mankind on the planet." I had no idea what he was talking about, but it was starting to sound good. He went on for a long time on the same theme. When he was done, I was still confused, perhaps even more so, but I was also encouraged and optimistic. I felt that there was a wonderous realm of understanding and a new awareness of life calling me. I had no idea what the next step would be; I only knew it would be exciting.

A few weeks passed. Then, one evening, Jim invited me to listen to what he described as an amazing tape that he had of a man named "Baba Ram Dass." The tape and the name had little appeal to me until Jim told me, "This guy knows a lot about acid." My ears perked up.

19

"You should really hear this tape . . . He gave four hits of acid to this guy in India, and nothing happened to him! . . . This guy was higher than acid!"

"Higher than acid? Wow!" I thought, "This guy must be *really* high!" I wanted to hear this tape.

So Jim and I got together and took some LSD and turned on this tape. The tape was four hours long, and it turned out to be the longest four hours of my life.

On the tape, Baba Ram Dass told the story of his spiritual awakening. He started out as a sort of neurotic high-achieving Jewish psychologist. I could identify with that. He got turned on to LSD, and he began to see the universe in a new way. I could identify with that. He went to India to find out what LSD was. I could identify with that, too.

By this time in the trip, I began to experience everything that Baba Ram Dass was saying as if it were literally the story of my own life. It was as if I had stepped right into his consciousness; I felt as if I was listening to *my* story being told by *my* voice on the tape. It was as if I knew everything he was going to say before he said it, like an ancient memory bank was made open for me.

The story came to when Ram Dass met his Guru, Neem Karoli Baba. After a long and depressing trip, Ram Dass found himself at the feet of Neem Karoli, who revealed to Ram Dass that he knew everything about Ram Dass' life. He told him facts that were known only to Ram Dass and God. "At that moment," told Ram Dass, "I let go completely . . . I fell at his feet and cried and cried and cried. The only way to describe the feeling was, 'I'm home.' "

At that moment, since I was totally identified with Ram Dass, I felt the exact same experience — and more. I felt that I had died — literally died; left my body; like my life was over. The thing that surprised me the most was that I was still here! Though I had died, I was still alive! The feeling of exhilaration and peace that I felt is not describable in words. What I saw was that death is not real; I had died, but yet I lived! Along with this ecstasy, I saw how ridiculous had been my fear of death. I looked back on my life and saw all the things that I had foolishly worried about, and I saw how silly I was to have ever feared anything. I saw the world as pure illusion. I saw death as illusion, and eternal life as real. I saw pain and suffering and starving children as illusion. It all seemed like a movie that had no substance. All I could do was to laugh and cry at the same time. I felt that I was home, and that the veils of ignorance had been lifted from my eyes. I saw that I never needed to ever worry about anything again, and I kept saying, dazzled and amazed, "There's nothing left to do now but to have a good time." I felt like I was in Heaven. Perhaps I was.

Well, this heaven lasted only a few hours, and then I went through the painful process of "crashing." Can you imagine entering the Holy Kingdom, and then being asked to leave? And then imagine not wanting to leave, but being compelled to. Christ told of this in the parable of the man who entered into the wedding feast without an invitation. "Bind him hand and foot and cast him into the outer darkness." I had crashed Heaven's party, but I had not earned the right to stay, and so back down I went.

The climax of the trip was over. The tape was over. Morning had come. Jim put on his jacket and left for his dentist's appointment. (How he could go to the dentist in that condition, I still do not understand.) But I was not the same person who turned on the tape player ten hours earlier. I called up a friend at seven o'clock in the morning and told her that I had just been to Heaven and that I had just seen God and that there is no death and that all is illusion. It was quite a wake-up story for her. She politely listened, but I began to see that I had been to a place that would be very difficult to describe.

Some kind of knowledge had been made available to me. It was as if some circuitry in my brain had been hooked up to a deep, deep memory bank, something like Aldous Huxley's "Mind at Large." That morning I went to the college cafeteria and had some coffee with a friend who was studying for an exam. Casually he asked me, "Do you know anything about Jung's anima and animus?" Somehow, my mouth opened and out came a discourse on the anima and animus, though I had but heard these two words and I knew next to nothing about them. Despite this, I gave him quite an explanation. My friend was amazed and he may have even taken notes. I don't remember. I was even more amazed than he was. Where I got the explanation from, I don't know. I don't know now what those words mean.

A few weeks later, I was substitute teaching for a seventh grade science class. Casually, I picked up a book on Einstein's theory of relativity. I understood exactly what he was talking about. I knew what his symbols meant. The equation made sense. "Of course he's

21

right," I said to myself. E = MC² seemed like child's play to me. It just seemed so logical. "Old Albert was on the right track," I thought. Don't ask me now what it means. I couldn't tell you.

I was hooked. Not on LSD. On God. Yes, for a while I worshipped LSD, but I soon learned that the experience I had was possible without drugs, which can be dangerous. At the bottom line, it has to be us and God, with no intermediaries. More than anything else, I wanted that experience again. I wanted to see God. I wanted to feel Heaven. I wanted to know all the time that there is no death. I wanted to know that all is illusion. I was prepared to do anything for it. The tiger had tasted blood.

Jim became my mentor, my home-made Guru. Everything he said, I listened to with open ears. Everything he did, I did. I walked like he did. I talked like he did. I laughed like he did. I didn't have to, of course, but I idolized the guy; he was my connection to God. He and I developed our own language that no one else could understand. But we understood each other, and that was enough.

We decided to take a trip cross country. (Actually, he decided, and I went along, because I did everything he did.) It was a fun trip, a crazy one, and at times a grueling one. It was a pilgrimage. We went to the St. Louis Planetarium and looked at Venus with a troop of cub scouts. We went to the Indian caves and meditated on the moon. We went to Arizona and Jim lived out his life's fantasy of throwing a tennis ball into the Grand Canyon. It was quite an event for him.

Along the way, Jim taught me about the great philosophers, like Socrates, Hegel, and Marcus Aurelius. I had tremendous faith in this guy. Once, for example, while I was doing the driving through the mountains of Pennsylvania, I saw a hand reach over my shoulder from the back of Jim's '62 VW bus, and in it were about a dozen pills of assorted colors, shapes, sizes, and inscriptions. Along with the hand came Jim's voice: "Here, take these."

"What are they?" I had to ask.

"Vitamins! . . . They're really good for you."

So I took them. About five minutes later, I felt my face start to burn as if every cell had swallowed a handful of chili peppers; when I looked in the mirror, it was as red as a Pacific sunset. At the same time, I felt thousands of tingles prickling up and down my spine, and I had to look in the mirror again to see if my ears were shooting steam. I felt like one of those hot dogs that gets roasted from the inside out.

"Say, Jim," I nonchalantly asked (to seem cool), "what was that you gave me, anyway?"

"Oh, that was niacin . . . I take it every day . . . It really gets you cookin', doesn't it?"

Cookin' was not the word. Microwavin' was more like it. I thought for sure that we could make it to California just on the energy I was feeling between my ears. And so I just kept my eyes on the road, my hands on the wheel, and I kept driving. And I survived. For all of his craziness, Jim was a very pure soul with a very big heart, and he knew exactly what he was doing on the inside, no matter how weird he looked or acted on the outside.

One California morning, Jim asked me if I'd like to go to a Zen monastary, and although I knew nothing about Zen, I said, "Sure," and off we went. We traveled about four hours over treacherous hair-pin mountain roads, and finally we arrived at a most peaceful little community. Jim instructed me to say that we were experienced Zen students so we could get in for the student rate. What he didn't tell me was that as students we would have to do what the students did, which was meditate about three hours a day in lotus position. Now I had never meditated before in my life, and I didn't know much more about meditation than what I had seen on *Kung Fu* or heard on *Sergeant Peppers' Lonely Hearts Club Band*. Nevertheless, the next morning I found myself sitting at a cold 5:30 a.m., facing a grey wall and watching my breath for an hour and a half. You might say it was a crash course in meditation. We stayed there about four days, and by the time we left, I had learned a lot about how many thoughts the mind can think in an hour and a half, and a little about meditation. It was very good.

From there we went to Esalen Institute, where everyone walks around naked and acts real. At the desk, the receptionist asked us what program we wanted to sign up for. Jim explained, "We came for IT!"

"It?" she queried.

"Yes, you know, IT!" (Like I said, he was a little dramatic.)

"Well, which 'It' would you like to sign up for? We have encounter, and rolfing, and Gestalt, and . . ."

"You don't seem to understand," Jim politely explained. "Me and my friend here came for IT!"

Well, this went on for a few more rounds, and we soon found ourselves registered for a new program — Arica Training. It was a system of exercises, meditation, and philosophy brought back from a mentor in Chile. It was esoteric, mystical, and new age, and so Jim and I found ourselves quite comfortable in it. It really was "IT!"

There, I began to come into contact with people from all walks of life, people that I would never have met elsewhere. My roommates were a Guatemalan pianist who played chess and did Gestalt therapy on the side, and a retired Air Force Colonel. (I shall never forget the conversation in which I tried to convince the colonel that there is no real competition in nature.) There, too, I met a gay construction worker and an Egyptian psychiatrist, two personages I never would have come in contact with at Yeshiva. And it was at Esalen that I read for the first time the words of Jesus Christ. Someone handed me a Bible with the words of Christ in red, and, though I was Jewish (and orthodox at that), the words of Jesus seemed to jump off the page and burn in my heart like an eternal flame. Something wonderful was happening in my life. New doors were being opened to me daily. I was being shown realms of spiritual Light with incredible speed and intensity. I was given much grace. I can't think of anything I did to deserve it. I feel as if God was reaching out to me and kindly taking me by the hand into His Garden. I thank you, God, for this.

After Esalen, we headed back east, where it just seemed so strange to me that people walked around with clothes on. After a period of adjustment, though, I carried on with my life.

Now, I was still very much in love with and devoted to Ram Dass. I knew nothing about him, except what I had heard on his tapes and read in his book *Be Here Now*. The book became my Bible. I thought about Ram Dass, talked about him, dreamed about him, and more than anything else, yearned to make contact with him. I had no idea where he was or how to get in touch with him; all I knew was that I wanted to connect with him, for, to me, he meant God.

One evening, weeks after I returned from California, I went to a very coarse punk rock concert at an outdoor stadium. I won't even say what the concert was like. After the concert, there was a massive traffic jam in the parking lot. Cars were just not moving. I began to pop the buttons on my radio to see what was on. On one station, I heard a beautiful young woman's voice, a little like Judy Collins', and I liked the sweet words she was singing. Then a male voice came on the air, and it began to give a spiritual rap, using some of the words and expressions that Ram Dass used. "Hey," I thought, "this guy must be into Ram Dass." To my ecstasy, not only was he into Ram Dass, but he *was* Ram Dass. A few moments later, the announcer took the microphone and told, "We're here with Ram Dass for four nights from midnight to dawn."

I had pressed the right button at about five minutes past twelve on the first night of the four. In the parking lot of a raunchy concert. This remains to me a shining example of God's Grace. We are told that "the teacher will find you." He sure did. My dream had come true. I called out for God, and God answered.

The next four nights were something wonderful and enchanting to me, the kind of gift that one receives only at the bestowal of angels. I felt as if I had been waiting lifetimes for these moments. I listened keenly and absorbed as much as I possibly could. Those four nights changed my life. I was given many answers, not only in the words, but in the quietness and the love that Ram Dass gave to each of the listeners. I was being given a very beautiful *darshan* — the experience of sitting in the presence of a teacher of Truth. Nine years later, I am still assimilating what was offered on those four very special nights.

During the days, I was working at a Seven-Eleven kind of grocery store. Strange, someone with a recent Master's Degree would work as a clerk there, but that was the only job it felt right to take at that time. As a result of Ram Dass' talks, I wanted very much to learn more about meditation, but again, I did not know where or how. At the time, one of our customers was a pleasant young woman who came in regularly to buy honey. One day she asked me, "Do you know anyone who wants to learn meditation? I'm an instructor." Bull's eye. I didn't know how to make the connection, but God knew.

The final Grace I shall designate as the conclusion of this one episode of this one story. It is really the end of one era and the beginning of the next.

On Ram Dass' radio show, someone asked him if he knew where a lady named "Hilda" was. "Right here in the studio," he answered. Over the next few months, her name began to pop up again and again in my life. I was standing in the record department of Korvette's, for example, and I overheard from the other side of the rack a familiar voice talking about his visit to Hilda's class. Then I saw her name in a magazine that came my way. And then, at a party, another person would be talking about this "Hilda." Finally, as Grace and Destiny would have it, someone invited me to go to one of her classes. Curious, I went.

Walking into a homey back room of a church in Greenwich Village, filled wall-to-wall with people, my eyes fell on a pleasant, vibrant lady in a *sari*, which turned out to be Hilda. Next to her was a sweet looking girl singing some very beautiful songs. I recognized the voice from somewhere, but could not place it. Then, in a flash, I remembered: it was the voice I had heard on the Ram Dass radio show. Her name was Mirabai. I was in ecstasy. It seemed as if all the threads of my newly found spiritual life were being woven together into a very lovely tapestry.

That is the story of what I had gotten from life until I came to Hilda's class. What did I get from Hilda? The rest of this book is that story.

THE RIGHT PLACE

One morning, a friend and I decided to go to a concert of flute and harp music. It was only a few hours before the concert that we made up our minds to go, and we started late. We got caught in traffic, and then couldn't find a parking space. We arrived at the theatre quite a while after the concert began, and the only seats left were way up in the back of the balcony. As I took my seat, I found myself sitting next to a smiling little elderly Black man wearing wire-rimmed glasses. He seemed to be enjoying himself immensely, munching on handfuls of gumdrops that he kept picking out of a paper bag. As I was getting myself settled, it occurred to me that he, too, had probably just arrived. I turned to him and complained, "Gee, it's too bad we got stuck way back here." He just sort of twinkled back and replied, "Oh, it's absolutely perfect; we just get what we earn by right of consciousness! . . . Would you like a gumdrop?"

Yes, we were in our right place, one which we had earned. Though my friend and I knew about the concert for months, we vacillated in our decision to go. Our interest in the concert was uncertain, and so we got seats where our view of the concert was uncertain. Those who were sitting up front were certain that they wanted to be there; they had probably gotten their tickets well in advance.

The right of consciousness. It's something to think about. One of my favorite stories is that of Joseph and his brothers. Joseph's eleven brothers were jealous of him because he was having prophetic dreams and their father, Jacob, was especially fond of him. So they threw Joseph in a pit and sold him into the slave market, where he was bought in Egypt by Pharoah's chief advisor, Potiphar. Joseph did so well as a servant that Potiphar made him his top aide, until Mrs. Potiphar also took a liking to Joseph and attempted to seduce him. Although Joseph was guiltless, Potiphar had Joseph thrown in the dungeon, where he successfully interpreted two other prisoners' prophetic dreams. When Pharoah began to have some disturbing dreams of his own, he called in Joseph, who had developed something of a reputation by then. Joseph's counsel to Pharoah was borne true, and Joseph was made Prime Minister of Egypt.

On a superficial level, Joseph's story is an exciting drama with a happy ending. Upon closer inspection, it is an example of how we are where we are because of our consciousness. Joseph was obviously a very deep and wise soul. It was no accident that Jacob took a special liking to him. Nor was it chance that his dreams were threatening to his brothers: his spirituality challenged their belief system. And because Joseph had something going for him, he was attractive to Potiphar (and his wife!) as a ranking servant. Then it was Joseph's prophetic ability that got him out of the dungeon and won him the favor of Pharoah, who could have made any one of millions of people Prime Minister of the Egyptian dynasty. The teaching is especially powerful because Joseph kept working his way out of horrible predicaments, like Flash Gordon or the characters in *Star Wars*. He was in a pit, in slavery, and on death row — but it was always his consciousness that saved him and put him in the place that belonged to him.

We are all, right now, in the place that belongs to us — for it is the one that we have earned by our consciousness. It may seem like a good place, and it may seem like a bad place, but it is always the right place. Actually, it is always good, because we are in the right position to learn the lessons that we need to bring us to a new and more fulfilling stage of personal growth.

We can attempt to mock up (or mock down) where we would *like* to be, but because we cannot mock up our consciousness, we will always be returned to where we *belong*. When I was in college, it was very popular for students to march on and take over the administration building. The yippies and friends would put on old army shirts, break into the college president's office, turn over a few file cabinets, and then get their picture in the newspaper, showing them smoking pot with their feet up on the president's big wooden desk. Then they would issue proclamations about how they were now going to be the

University administration, and how they would initiate credit courses in The Grateful Dead, and so on. This would go on for a day, or two, or three, but sooner or later they would somehow be ejected, the regular president would regain his office, and things would go back to normal (– well, almost normal). Though the yippies tried to establish their place as the leaders of the university, they had not earned it, and so they lost it.

I remember, too, a man who wanted to earn some money heard of an opening as a department manager in a well-known chain store. Though he had no experience in the work, he told his interviewer that he had, and he "fudged" his references. He was given the job, but it was not long before he was overwhelmed because he just did not know what he was doing. His department was losing money and he was losing sleep. So he accepted a demotion to assistant manager, a position in which he could learn. He remained assistant manager for a year or so, and then he was promoted to manager in a related department, a position in which he is now doing well – because now he has earned it.

Neither can we minimize our consciousness. We cannot make believe that we are less than we are. There are many great yogis and gurus who attempt to avoid students, but, because the teacher has something very valuable, the students somehow find him or her. The great Nithyananda went off to the jungle to meditate, and people found him and built a city around him. I know, too, of a simple man who lives on a remote mountain and holds a humble job as a pipe welder. Though he does not seek students, many people are willing to drive through snowy mountain roads to receive his counsel. And Hilda, who has no desire for fame or recognition, receives requests from people (like Barbara Walters) who want to do TV shows and books and movies about her. She came back to this country from India with the intention of staying for just a few weeks, but friends began to ask for her help, and she decided to stay as long as people sought her support. That was fourteen years ago. She started out with one or two people coming to visit her in the living room where she was staying, and then they brought their friends, and they theirs, until now three or four hundred come to see her each week in the Cathedral of St. John the Divine. She has never solicited any students, advertised, or taken any payment for her work; in fact, she never even wanted to be a teacher. But she has no choice; she is where she is by right of her consciousness, or in this case — the responsibility of her consciousness.

Despite all the questions raised by our meandering minds, we *are* in our right place, doing exactly what we need to be doing, at exactly the right time. Because life is a school, we are always in the class that we have chosen to learn the lessons we need to master. Sometimes it is fun, and sometimes we have to work at it a bit, but is is always appropriate. I was speaking to a woman who was struggling with questions about the direction she should take in her life. When I shared with her my enthusiasm about the perfection of the right of consciousness, she looked at me with a combination of surprise and relief, and asked, "You mean I'm in my right place?" I chuckled and responded, "Where else could you be?"

"Because God is perfect and just, so is your position in life. This is the source of peace of mind, as fears of ill and error can find no home in a world seen through the eyes of Perfection.

Your place is assured. You cannot be other than where Love has placed you to learn its holy lessons. It is only the restless mind that seeks to impose disorder where there is alignment, and chaos where there is serenity. Because thoughts do not leave their source, thoughts of chaos come only of chaotic thinking, and the Vision of Tranquility is born of the quiet self.

Trust frees you to see the wisdom of the moment. The goodness of life is invincible, and in Justice is your assurance of success. The laws of consciousness work consistently for your highest good. They offer you consolation and guidance. You now embody the choice to earn your goal, which is at hand.

The rights that you once rigorously strove for are now replaced by the Right that has always belonged to you. When you accept your attunement, you accept Truth. Injustice has finally been replaced by awareness, and the end of all questioning is accomplished."

TAKE WHATCHA GOT AND
MAKE WHATCHA WANT

A young Kansas City artist, struggling to realize his dream of drawing cartoons for a living, was turned away from every newspaper he approached for a job. "Forget it," the editors told him, "you have no talent . . . Find yourself another career." Rejection followed rejection, until one day he found himself holed up in an old, dilapidated, mice-infested garage, penniless, seemingly without a hope for success.

Having no shortage of time on his hands, he began to sketch the garage and the mice in it. He became fascinated with the little creatures, and he curiously developed a friendly relationship with them, especially one little fellow.

Little did the man realize at the time just how important this relationship would be for him. The man's name was Walt Disney. The mouse's name turned out to be "Mickey," and Walt and Mickey went on to become two of the most successful entertainers in the world, bringing happiness and joy to countless numbers of children.

If Walt had given up when the editors turned him away, he may have taken some other job, and his dream might have faded into a memory. But Walt had enough faith in himself to continue, and in so doing, he made an even greater discovery: God's infinite possibilities are *everywhere*, and success is always at hand — even at what seems to be the end of the road.

In a *Star Trek* adventure, Captain Kirk finds himself on an island planet, pitted against an especially creepy character — *the Gorn*. He is given the unenviable task of having to defeat this foe to save his life — and his ship. The challenge, he is told, is a test of creative ingenuity.

He is given no materials, but it is hinted that whatever he needs to save himself is available to him right on the planet. He must be clever enough to find what he needs and use it. The Captain suffers setback after setback, until he is battered and almost defeated, sprawled nearly helpless on the alien ground. Prospects look pretty dim for our hero.

At this critical moment, Kirk sniffs a familiar aroma — sulfur! Though he has seen it throughout his trials, he did not recognize it for how he could use it. Quickly he manufactures some rudimentary gunpowder, and (as you can guess) he soon overcomes the Gorn. Simply, the Captain took what he had, and made what he wanted.

One sage said, *"There is no invention — only discovery."* The people who succeed are those who adapt, combine, create, and make the best use of what they have been given to work with. George Washington Carver, for example, was a God-inspired genius of the highest caliber. When most of us look at a peanut, we see a peanut. When he looked deep into the peanut, Dr. Carver, with the all-seeing eye of God, saw over 300 uses for the tiny legume, including washing powder, shaving cream, bleach, salve, paper, ink, synthetic rubber, axle grease, linoleum, shampoo, wood filler, coffee, and pickles. He also discovered 118 uses for the sweet potato. In short, he accepted what he was given, recognized its preciousness, and served the world through it. Dr. Carver put into action the maxim that *"What you are is God's gift to you; what you make of yourself is your gift to God."*

Another one who made a gift of himself was St. Francis of Assisi. In his Divine simplicity, Francis was a misfit in a system of rigid religion. His heart yearned for the lofty freedom of the birds and the warm blessing of the sun. The inner voice whispered to him, "Francis, rebuild my church!" Symbolically, he took a small, abandoned, and unloved church, and, at first alone, place brick by brick, stone by stone, one upon another, bound together mostly by love. Before long, his sincerity and his purity attracted to him friends and followers in a new order of spirituality that has multiplied and gathered force for nearly one thousand years. The love of this gentle saint has won the hearts of millions, more books have been written about him than about any other saint, and he has recently been named the patron saint of the environment. St. Francis started right where he was, and God accepted him just as he was.

Just as we are now, each of us has all that we need to succeed.

TAKE WHATCHA GOT AND MAKE WHATCHA WANT

You and I are thoughts in the mind of God, and everything that we do, God does. God cannot be defeated. No matter what our past, our troubles, or our limitations, there is always a way for us to turn seemingly futile circumstances into splendid success, like the alchemist who knew how to transform lead into gold. There is, for example, a famous woman in Maine who lost use of her arms and legs — but she refused to be beaten. She put a paint brush in her mouth and began to draw the lovely country scenes she saw from her porch. Now she sells many of her beautiful paintings as Christmas cards. Her business is extremely successful — in more ways than one.

The aspect of human beings that sets us off from all other creatures is that of imaginative wisdom. Animals see things as they are, but we see them as they *can be*. We have been given the Divine ability to transform. I have never seen anything give a person as much energy as a vision that he or she is working to bring into reality. I have seen people forsake sleep, food, and comfort for the sake of a project that they love. There is something very holy about a human being dedicated to a purpose, something more precious than I can attempt to put into words. It is the miracle of creation.

It is exactly this miracle which enables us to transcend circumstances. Any circumstance is a good starting point for God. Dr. Carver was the child of slaves, and Francis was the son of a wealthy businessman; yet both of them found their way to God. The same energy that moved the Carvers, the Einsteins, and the Edisons to change the world, is within us. The alchemical power to activate Divinity is always speaking to us, if we are but willing to *listen* and *do*. It is none other than the Voice of God, beckoning to us to acknowledge the Divine Spark and to draw it into expression, that it may be shared by all.

"*Genius is God's gift to all, though it is accepted by few. Within you lie riches and talents far greater than you have recognized and expressed.*

The acknowledgement of your capabilities bears a double blessing. As you grow into your own evolution, you serve the world. The purposes of the individual are one with those of humanity, and the unfoldment of one marks the growth of all.

There is no limitation, Children, upon what you can do. God is incapable of containment or restriction. So, too, are you free, for you are Divine in nature.

Look at your lives with open eyes. If you see closed avenues, it is because you are looking with closed eyes. Do not be distracted by the small-mindedness of men. The child of man sees mountains where the Child of God sees skies. Choose your goal, and allow God to succeed through you."

ENOUGH IS ENOUGH

"There are three kinds of people," said the philosopher: "Those who complain, 'Too much! Too much!'; those who argue, 'Not enough! Not enough!'; and those who smile, 'Ah! Just right.' "

Really, these three symbolic groups can be distilled to two: *those who practice contentment*, and *those who do not*. Saying "Too much!" and saying "Not enough!" are really two sides of the same coin, for too much of what we don't want means not enough of what we do want. We are always practicing the Presence of God or His absence. No middle ground.

Contentment is an experience that we can cultivate through practice. Abraham Lincoln said that "most people are about as happy as they make up their mind to be." Like gratefulness and positivity, contentment is not usually handed to us as a gift, although it is always ours for the asking. We need only to align our thoughts with appreciation, for contentment is not so much a state of *affairs* as it is a state of *mind*.

If money could make us happy, millionaires would rest complete after their first million. If sex could fulfill us, those who enter relationships or marriages based upon sex would roam no further. If power were the source of peace, heads of state would be the happiest people in the world. But we all know that persons with much money, sex, or power are not the happiest; in fact they are often among the most unhappy. Why? Because anyone in a state of *seeking* can never be happy. Only those who are constantly *finding* are fulfilled. And finding is not something that happens to us — it is something we *do*.

THE DRAGON DOESN'T LIVE HERE ANYMORE

For the past few years, I have been practicing a very powerful mantra: "Perfect!" It is not the kind of mantra that is to be said sitting with eyes closed, although we certainly can do that. Instead, it is a mantra for daily life. It is a mantra that turns troubles into blessings. It is a mantra that gives encouragement and support. It is a word that heals. It is a statement of the truth.

Not long ago, I went to a concert by an elementary school band. As the director raised his baton, I sat back and for some reason expected to hear a beautiful symphony. To my surprise, I heard, instead, a horrid cacophony of squeaks, honks, upbeat notes on the downbeat, and a march that sounded like a 45 r.p.m. record played at 33. "This is terrible!" I thought, as I shriveled inside. And then I heard a gentle voice speak within me: "*These are children; they are learning; they are doing very well.*" The voice, of course, spoke truth. I was judging them according to my expectations, not accepting that they were all expressing according to their ability. At that moment, the music became so lovely to me. I sat back and thoroughly enjoyed every remaining moment of the concert, and I think I cheered the loudest at its finale.

When we see life in clear focus, it is always giving us enough. We have to get our minds tuned into contentment, even work at it a little bit, to win at the game of living. One evening, for example, I had a pot luck dinner, and everyone brought a main dish. Desserts were conspicuously absent. "Perfect!" we decided. "Here is our chance to cut calories and lose some weight." Several weeks later, everyone brought only dessert. "Perfect!" we declared, "This is our opportunity to celebrate!" Celebrate what? I don't exactly remember. We just celebrated.

It's not so much what we do that counts, but *what we think* about what we do. We can take any seeming failure, and find some way to turn it into a success. There was a man in South Africa who sold his farm for a pittance because the earth was too rocky and hard to till. Those who bought the property examined the land more deeply, and today it is the famous Kimberly diamond mine.

When we dig deeply enough into our own lot, we find that we are well taken care of. We must learn to distinguish between *needs* and *desires*. I often hear an "I want" masquerading as "I need." Our needs are so simple. St. Francis said, "I watch the sparrow enjoy just a little sip of water. How free are the birds who need so little and yet soar so high!" It is only when we think that we need more than we do that we lose sight of our aspirations.

A student went to his guru and asked to be enlightened. "Very well," said the teacher, "find yourself a nice cave, sit naked, and meditate. Then you will surely attain your goal." "That sounds fine," thought the student, and off he went. He decided, however, to take with him just one possession — a small loincloth.

The young yogi set out easily enough on his venture. He found a good cave and began to experience deep meditation. His loincloth, however, required occasional washing, after which he would hang it on a tree to dry. One day he noticed that mice had nibbled some holes in it, so he went into town to ask what to do. A kind lady advised him, "What you need is a cat to keep the mice away," and (since she just happened to have a litter of kittens) she gave him one.

Things went along nicely, until the yogi realized that the cat required milk. So he returned to town and begged for milk until the townspeople got fed up and told him, "Why don't you buy yourself a cow? That would provide for all your needs." So he took a few weeks off from his meditation to earn some money to buy a cow.

As it turns out, cows need grassy land on which to graze. So he left his cave for a longer period, this time to buy a small patch of pasture. Now, of course, he had to feed the cow and tend to its needs, so he took a wife who could care for the animals while he practiced being enlightened. (This was in pre-liberation days.) With marriage came children, and within a few years he had a *bona fide* family to support. As you can imagine, he soon found himself the busy manager of a small farm, and he just couldn't seem to find the time for even a moment's meditation.

One day years later, the guru happened to be passing through town, and finding the yogi's cave deserted, he ironically came to the man's house to inquire if anyone knew what had become of the yogi.

"That yogi was *me!*" the farmer told the teacher.

"What happened?" asked the guru.

"I took a loincloth with me," was the explanation.

We have ideas, concepts, and opinions about how things would be better if we had this or that, or if we were there instead of here. Often, however, our ticket to satisfaction is in mastering the job at hand. If we do well with what we have, we do not need to figure out how to advance; God, the best Manager of all, will take care of us. Martin Luther King, Jr., in a stirring address called "Remaining Awake During a Great Revolution," told the people:

> *It does not matter what you do. What does matter is that you do it the best. If you are a street sweeper, then be the best street sweeper that there ever was. Do your work with pride, and do it with dignity, and in so doing it, you will be doing it with greatness!*

This lesson was proven to me when I worked as a cook in a health foods restaurant. While I found the job very rewarding, some people did not think it was a very important job to do. (One fellow called me aside one day and asked, "So, Alan, what do you do in real life?") But because I saw God in that place, I used it to practice love, positivity, and mastery, and in so doing, I found great enthusiasm and commitment for the work. It was there that I was shown the principle of advancement through right use. Although the store was financially ailing and the owner turned down the other employees' requests for raises, he approached me one day to tell me that he was giving me a raise — one that I did not even ask for!

"There is enough of everything for everyone," explained Patricia Sun. It is only when we begin to *fear* lack that we *create* it. Wars, famines, and shortages occur only when someone feels afraid that he or she will not have enough, and a person, or a group, or a nation begins to act out of fear. God and Mother Earth (God's symbol for Abundance) have never withheld sustenance. Famines do not occur by happenstance or Divine Decree. They are always a result of war, economic turmoil, and political unrest — all created by us *people*. I learned that in the Bengla Desh famine there were shiploads of food that rotted in the ports because political bickering in the war-torn country held up the process of delivering it to the starving people for whom it was earmarked. We cannot blame God for withholding providence from us; it is *we* who must be prepared to *accept* it. If we can just hold on long enough not to act on fear of lack, abundance on earth would be manifest in the fullness that was originally intended.

Thoughts of "too much" are also out of the flow of life. In our struggle to realize the true meaning of spiritual living, we sometimes confuse non-attachment with unnecessary self-denial. In the early stages of treading the path, some seekers believe it is spiritual to shun money, or to denounce possessions, or not to bathe, or to starve, in the name of renunciation. Real renunciation is being able to take it or leave it, according to what is necessary. (The great Paramahansa Yogananda said, *"What comes of itself, let it come."*) I used to avoid money, gifts, experiences, and people, in fear of being selfish or attached. My mistake was that I was attached to not being attached.

I don't believe that God sent us here in exile. I think He sent us here for education. If a wealthy father sent his son to a boarding school, would he not send with him clothing, money for food and transportation, and even some "pin money" for an occasional movie or ice cream soda? Of course he would. Our Heavenly Father is no different. In fact, He is even more compassionate than most earthly fathers would be. You see, it is *we* who have chosen to run away from home to attend a school in a far country, and even in light of our rebelliousness, God lovingly provides for us as if He had sent us Himself.

One evening Hilda told us, "Take care of God's business and He'll take care of yours." That same night, a friend asked me for a ride home, quite a bit out of my way. This was during a gas shortage, and I knew that if I took her home, I would have to find an open gas station for me to make it home myself. But since she needed a ride, I decided to take care of God's business. As I dropped her off, the needle on the fuel gauge was leaning on the bottom of the big red "E." I knew that I would have to find an open station before I turned onto the Garden State Parkway. It was after midnight as I drove down Bloomfield Avenue, and every single station that I passed was closed. I was down to just a few blocks before the parkway. Then, on the very corner where I had to turn, there was an open station. Very late at night. Very unusual in a gas shortage. Yet there was no shortage of God. His tanks were full.

"*Children of Plenty, you are heirs to the riches of the universe. It is God's good pleasure to give you His good gifts.*

Thoughts of lack are empty musings, expressive not of the Truth, but of a limited consciousness which you have outgrown. Hold fearlessly to thoughts of fullness, and so shall your experience be confirmed as whole.

Remember that you are worthy of abundance. Know your spiritual riches, and material good shall be yours as well. There is a right amount for you. Trust the Creator to uphold and support you in your material life. He will not abandon you. This is the promise proven by your willingness to trust.

Stand with open arms to receive His riches. Extend your hands, as well, to allow blessings to flow forth in service to a waiting world. Be a comforter to your brethren. Uphold not thoughts of emptiness, but hold fast to your meditation upon the source of all. When you see all as full, you see all as God created it."

IF NOT NOW, WHEN?

Dr. Leo Buscaglia tells a sad story of two college students who were unexpectedly killed while walking across their campus. They were young, vibrant, in the mainstream of life, with many unfulfilled dreams. They had no idea they would be cut off so soon. "This," tells Dr. Buscaglia, "led me to realize that every moment of life is precious." He went back to his very unique "Love" class and asked the students to write an essay on what they would really like to do if they had the time. Some wrote, "I would take a long walk on the beach at sunset." Others wrote of shining aspirations: "I would leave college and devote all my time to playing music," and yet others wrote, "I would call up my Dad and resolve our strained relationship." In big red letters, across the bottom of their papers, Dr. Buscaglia wrote, "WELL, WHAT ARE YOU WAITING FOR? WHAT ARE YOU DOING HERE? WHY DON'T YOU DO IT NOW?" He says, "If you don't like what you are doing, then get out — quick — and fulfill your dream now."

We never really know how much time we have to do what we want to do. We act as if we have a hundred years, when we may have but a minute. If we ponder on these sobering thoughts, they must lead us to but one conclusion: *Now is our only moment to live.*

A few years ago, I attended a conference on the predictions of earth changes that have been prophesied to occur in the coming years. A diversified group of psychics, scientists, and spiritual teachers told of earthquakes, food shortages, economic and political collapse, and all kinds of holocausts, which they all agreed would culminate in a

43

new era of peace and unity on earth. The peace and unity sounded great to me, but the holocaust predictions were rather unnerving, especially when all of the speakers concurred that a large portion of the earth's population would be wiped out. The thought occurred to me that I might be one of those who went down, and I lost my cool. I wrestled with this fear for several days, trying to figure out how to escape and save myself. Then, one morning I woke up and my fear had vanished; I was resigned to my death. I just felt that it would not be so terrible if I did go down, for I knew that God would take care of me anyway. So I took the attitude that I had just a few months or years to live, and I began to look at life from this point of view.

I think that the few months that I held that outlook were the freest and most joyous in my life. I didn't worry or care about anything. All of the foolish little concerns that had occupied my attention became meaningless to me, and I saw that they really didn't matter after all. My meditations were the deepest and most powerful that they had ever been, and I found new appreciation to enjoy my friends. The teaching was that in learning how to die, I learned how to live.

There are many similar stories of persons who are diagnosed as having terminal illness, who confute their diagnoses by learning to live in the present. I have heard of a number of people, who, upon being told that they have just a few months or a year to live, let go of their businesses, boxes, and burdens, and go out to enjoy all the things that they have been putting off until retirement. They take the camping trip to the mountains that they've been dreaming of; they hop into the car late in the evening and drive to Friendly's for that hot fudge sundae they've been denying themselves; and they spend the money that they've been fearfully saving for some unknown need. The result is that they have such a good time enjoying life in freedom and ease that the dis-ease disappears, and they live long and fruitful lives. They learn to *live in the moment,* and in so doing, they learn to *live.*

There are three expressions which I have learned not to believe: "I will *try* to be there"; "*Maybe* I will do it"; and "I will do it *later.*" All are polite but irresponsible ways of saying "No" or "I don't want to." "I will do it later" is especially seductive because we use time as an excuse to avoid making a stand in the present. This is sad because, as anyone who has ever dieted or stopped smoking knows, *there is no later.*

The ancient Jewish *Ethics of the Fathers* puts it very succinctly:

If I am not for myself, who will be for me? If I am only for myself, what good am I? If not now, when?

Harvey Freeman tells the story of Joe, a man who is familiar to all of us. Joe is a pretty regular fellow, never really quite satisfied. In high school, he knows that he will be happy just as soon as he gets his driver's license. He gets it, but now he needs to get into a certain college to feel really fulfilled. Well, he is accepted, but now he very much wants to marry a special classmate. And so on. Then it's a child that will really do it, and then he just needs to be promoted to vice-president of the company. And then Joe begins to live vicariously through the children. And then he is just waiting for grandchildren, and then he begins to count the years until retirement, when he can *really* relax. Finally, Joe retires and sets out on his long-planned dream fishing trip in the Smokies. Joe rows out into the middle of the lake, casts out his line, and keels over, dead. Joe's moment of happiness never came; it was always just around the next bend.

Jesus spoke of the present. "Take no thought or worry for tomorrow," he instructed. "Look at the lilies of the field; they neither spin nor toil, and I tell you that Solomon, in all his glory, was not arrayed like one of these. If God takes care of the grass, which is here one day and gone the next, will He not all the more care for you, His Children?" The Master also explained, "The evil of the day is sufficient unto itself." In other words, just do what you need to do for today, and tomorrow will take care of itself.

Ram Dass, in *Be Here Now*, describes his training with a yogi who taught him the meaning of living freely in the moment. Ram Dass would ask, "Say, did I ever tell you about the time that I saw white light?" and the yogi would respond, "Don't talk about the past — just be here now." And then Ram Dass would ask, "When do you think we'll get to Madras?" and the teacher would interrupt, "Don't worry about the future — just be here now." The message was this, explains Ram Dass: "If you can live fully in the Now, when 'then' becomes 'now,' you will be perfectly taken care of and know exactly what to do."

Stephen Gaskin put it in another way. He said, "The here and now is always heavy (full and complete). If it's not heavy, you're not tuned in."

The process of this writing has been, for me, an education in living in the moment. At first, I planned only to write a short pamphlet on stress reduction and relaxation for the workshops that I conduct. This, I thought, would have to be a very scientific document that would appeal to professionals. As I began to write it, I noticed that I was staying away from "spiritual" topics, and especially avoiding the word "God." I knew in my heart, though, that I really wanted to write something that would express my deepest beliefs, which most certainly are God and the spiritual life. So I decided to write two separate works — first the secular stress reduction pamphlet, and then something about God. I got about two pages into the stress pamphlet, and I thought, "Wait a minute! What am I doing? What I really feel and want to do is to write something that expresses *all* of me, not a diluted version of me. Why am I putting second that which is first in my heart? How can I write about living in the moment when I am postponing my dream? I will write what I feel. If some people do not read it because it is too spiritually oriented, I cannot worry about that. At least I will be able to sleep at night, knowing that I have been true to myself and to God. I am not writing to please people; I am writing to express God." With that, I sat down to write a few chapters, and of those seedlings grew a book. I don't know if it will be a best seller, but my heart is satisfied, and that, to me, is the best seller of all.

Too many dreams are cast by the wayside in deference to opinion and tradition. Too many ambitions have been postponed for the wrong reasons. Too many lives have been lived for a tomorrow which never came. Ask yourself now, "If I had only a few months to live, what would I be doing?" Do not dwell on the fear, but consider your opportunities! Then do it. Can any of us afford to throw away one moment of life?

One of my favorite times in this life was the late 1960's, the early years of what is called the Age of Aquarius. It was a time when people from many different lifestyles were awakening to new and exciting possibilities of what life on earth can be about. It was a time when the Beatles took the world by the hand and led it from "*Money*" to "*A Little Help From My Friends*," and when Peace became more than just a catchword. It was a time that gave permission to young people to give away flowers on the street corners of San Francisco, and when young and old became one in an action to stop a war which just not enough people believed in. It was a time when a new wave of spiritual understanding began to sweep the planet in the seed-lights of new age communities and appreciation for the sacredness of our home, the earth.

Now I sometimes hear people make fun of that era. (The other day someone accused me of being a flower child — but I took it as a compliment.) Perhaps the brightness of those days has become overshadowed as we have moved into a time which requires more concrete social action. This is a serious time on earth, and I am willing to be serious to face it, but those days of the late 60's have a special place in my heart, and I refuse to compromise my appreciation for their wonder. In fact, I believe that that time was a taste of things to come; perhaps now we have to earn it.

I share this with you now because during that era, one early summer day I found myself in a little crafts shop in Denver. I remember the place for the bright rainbow painted over its faded brick wall facing an empty lot. In that shop was a poster with a caption which I shall never forget, one which has become my mantra for life:

TOUCH EVERY MOMENT OF LOVE

"*Dear ones, live for all that you would live for. Search your heart for your purest ideals, and set your life around your noblest vision. In the years to come, when the institutions that you know crumble around you, only your deepest aspirations will carry you through outer change. Live now for your heart's ambition.*

Think, beloveds, and think clearly. What do you truly want from your life? Why, in all earnestness, have you come to earth? Who do you now live for? Are you beholden to the misdirected vanities of the world, or do you respect your inclinations from a source resonating deep within your Self? Answer these questions for yourself, beloveds, and live the answers you find.

Time has been given you for a purpose. Learn to use it for your benefit, but do not be a slave to it. Make it work for you. In your awareness of the purpose of time is your mastery of it.

Set your priorities. Do not delay that which is most important. You can know God now, but you can never know Him tomorrow. Your enlightenment is the one thing that you cannot postpone. God is now."

Overcoming Limitations

BREAKING MOLDS

"It just makes me so mad when my husband squeezes the toothpaste from the middle of the tube!" reported a woman in one of my classes. ". . . Everybody knows you're supposed to squeeze it from the end!" Just for the fun of it, we took a class survey to see whether, in fact, everybody *does* know that you're supposed to squeeze it from the end. As it turned out, about half of the class knew that you're supposed to squeeze it from the end, and the other half knew that you're supposed to squeeze it from the middle.

The truth is, of course, that you're not supposed to squeeze it from any particular place; what you're supposed to do is get the toothpaste onto the brush, and it doesn't really matter how it gets there. If it matters, then it is a matter that we have created with our mind.

To live — to really be alive — we must allow ourselves to flow with the people and events around us. We cannot afford to confine ourselves to any rigid picture of who we are, or how things should be done. An oriental sage said that the secret of happiness is to "cease to cherish opinions."

Hilda calls these set ways of acting "molds." "We stuff ourselves into little habitual ways of doing things in a certain way," she explains, "and then if we do not get to do it our way, or if someone comes along who wants to do it a little differently, we get irritable and we become a nuisance to ourselves and those around us."

When I have shared the idea of "molds" with my yoga classes, the students have confessed to some delightfully zany molds. One woman would get upset if she found the toilet paper put on the roller in the "wrong" way. She liked it when the paper rolled from the wall side of the roll. Another person had to get "his" exact parking space when he left his car at the train station each morning. If someone else took that spot, he would think, "I am just going to have a terrible day." And another man would get irritable if his jogging socks were not folded in a certain way.

"The way to really be free, kids," explained Hilda, "is to find out what your molds are, and then break them: drive to work by way of a different street one day; wear a new hairstyle; rearrange the furniture in your room; do anything you can to keep from getting stagnant."

I suggested to the man who thought he had to have a certain parking space that he try, for one day or one week, purposely parking in a different spot, and see what happened. The next week he came to class smiling and beaming. "I tried what you suggested," he reported, "and I even had some great days! I see now that I was binding myself with my own thoughts. Now I am free to park wherever I like!"

I remember when I first discovered the power of breaking molds. I had a mold of a cereal bowl. Every morning I would take the same blue bowl and make myself the same breakfast of granola, milk, and one banana. This was my routine and my mold. One day, I went to take "my" blue bowl from the cabinet, and it was not there. A dilemma! When I looked and saw that someone else was using it for their breakfast, I got annoyed. "How dare he take *my* cereal bowl for *his* breakfast!" I thought. I had become the slave of a blue bowl. (If that is not selling out my freedom, I don't know what is.) Fortunately, I remembered Hilda's lesson and I thought, "O.K., this is my chance to get free of a binding mold . . . I can just as easily use another bowl." I did, and to my amazement I enjoyed my breakfast just as thoroughly as if I had that old blue bowl. After that, I was free of bondage to a bowl.

We are all free spirits and we are not bound to anything unless we think we are. We are all free to park wherever there is a space and to enjoy our granola out of any bowl. There was an old Three Stooges routine in which Larry would cry out to Moe, "I can't see! I can't see!" Moe would rush to Larry's aid, asking "Why not?" Larry would then smile and proclaim, "Cause I got my eyes closed!" (And then, of course, Moe would bop him on the head.) It is sometimes a good idea to think about what it is that we are not seeing because we have our eyes closed (before we get bopped on the head). We need to consider whether it is life that is penning us in, or *we* who confine ourselves with small thinking. Our happy realization is that we cannot be tied to anything, and that the only way we can be bound is with our own thoughts.

There is a relationship between freedom from molds and being young. I am not speaking of a number of years, but of the vitality, exuberance, and aliveness in a person's way of being and growing. Childhood lasts as long as we allow ourselves to think expansively, act freely, and be new. The secret of youth is open and adaptive thinking. We are eagles.

Scott and Helen Nearing left their city life in the 1930's and moved to the Green Mountains of Vermont, where they built a homestead of stone houses, made a lush garden out of soil that would at first yield only radishes, and became popular and beloved folk heroes. After about thirty years in Vermont, they decided to escape the growing commercialism, and the two started all over again in Maine, where they built more stone houses, set up a sun-heated greenhouse, and established a completely new self-sufficient farmstead. Scott is now about 98 years old, and Helen in her late 70's. I had the great privilege to meet them a few years ago, and they are two of the youngest people I have ever met. Helen said, "Flexibility increases with experience."

When I first saw Hilda, she appeared to be an older woman. After spending about five minutes in her presence, however, I felt no sense of age in her at all. She is as fresh and young as a little child. Someone gave an affirmation that perfectly describes Hilda: "I am as old as God, and as young as the morning." When Satya Sai Baba (a revered saint in India) would ask her, "How old are you, Hilda?" she would answer brightly, "I was never born and I shall never die!" This pleased Baba to no end. She is a beautiful and fascinating person to look at. Though she has spent a good number of years on earth, there are none of the lines or wrinkles in her face that tell of worry or resistance. In one of her lectures, Hilda was speaking of trends of years ago. She started to say ". . . but that was in my time," when she caught herself, stopped, thought for a moment, and explained, "I can't really say 'That was my time,' kids; my time is *now*."

The time for all of us is, of course, now. There is no need for anyone to wither in an unfulfilling and mechanical pattern of life. Routines cannot bind us unless we believe in them. Patterns were given to serve us — not for us to live for them. The Fountain of Youth is not a mysterious hidden well in Florida, but an ever-invigorating, ever-refreshing stream of life that is constantly flowing through us, bubbling up to renew us when we are but willing to make space for it and drink of it.

Behold the turtle, who makes progress only when he sticks his neck out.

"You are a Child of the Living God, and it is only your awareness of your True Identity that sustains, nourishes, and heals you.

Restriction and age are human inventions. They are born of limited seeing, and so bear fruits of like nature. You who would aspire to express your immortal heritage must remain free of narrowness. Those who would be grandiose must be grandiose. Those who would live must accept life. Those who would be immortal must love what is eternal.

Habits have been given for your strengthening, but they cease to be purposeful when you become subservient to them. Be masterful in approaching your activities. Consciously decide for free ways of being. No one is a master who is a slave to his own inventions.

We guide you to your next stage of evolution. The transition requires a surrender of the tools which served you in your earlier work. No more can you rely on forms for your strength. The time has come for you to rely on God and God alone."

FISHBOWL TO BATHTUB

If you wish to live in freedom, you've just got to become Divine.

— *David and Jamil*

One morning, Eve decided it was time to clean her fishbowl. Unable to find a container in which to put her two goldfish, Yin and Yang, while the bowl was being cleaned, Eve let about two inches of water into her bathtub, and lovingly placed the little creatures there. When she finished scrubbing the bowl and putting the ceramic deep-sea diver in a new position, Eve returned to find Yin and Yang engaged in a very thought-provoking behavior: the two goldfish were swimming around in one little corner of the bathtub, in a circle no bigger than the fishbowl!

In many ways, we humans are like the goldfish. We develop our patterns, our habits, and our taught lifestyles (which we have adopted from families, friends, and television commercials), and then, when we have the chance to go beyond them to discover a new and freer dimension, we prefer to remain in our tiny corner of the world, though it offers us little joy, a lot of anxiety, and no expansiveness.

Most people are sleepwalking. Many wander through life in a sort of semiconscious state, having some idea of what they do, but not really sure why they are doing it. Mostly, we do what other people do, for we have made gods of popular opinions, beliefs, and actions. We worship the masses instead of the mass. For a long time, I depended on the world to tell me who I was and what to do. After wandering through my life like this for years, I realized that this kind of unchosen living just doesn't work.

When we live in attempt to fulfill the dreams and desires of others, we may (for a while) succeed in convincing ourselves that we are happy, but sooner or later we must admit that we have our own calling in life. I know a young man who suffered through medical school because his parents wanted him to be a doctor, and they had almost convinced him that was what he wanted, too. He stayed in medical school for a while, mostly out of guilt and fear, for his father had taken out a second mortgage on their house in order to buy his son's way into an accredited school. But, alas, how long can one live a lie? The young man eventually became ill, quit the school, and got a job teaching science in the Virgin Islands, a position in which he now feels comfortable and fulfilled.

My friend's story reminded me of that of Zumbach the Tailor, which symbolizes the predicament in which many of us have found ourselves. A man went to Zumbach the Tailor to be fitted for a new suit. When the suit was ready, he stood before the mirror with the tailor, for final alterations. The man noticed that the right sleeve was just a bit short. "I think the sleeve is a little too short for my arm," he told Zumbach; "You may have to lengthen it."

"The sleeve is not too short," answered the tailor. "Your arm is too long. Just draw your arm up into the sleeve a bit, and it will look fine."

Reluctantly, the man did so, but this threw the collar of the jacket into disarray. "Now the sleeve looks alright, but look at the big gap between my neck and the jacket!"

"There is nothing wrong with the jacket," Zumbach defended. "What you need to do is raise your left shoulder a few inches."

The man again complied, but now the rear of the jacket was lifted far above his posterior. When he showed the tailor this misalignment, he was instructed to "lower your head and lean forward, and there will be no problem!"

Finally, the man walked out of the shop, convinced of its proper fit. (Unfortunately, he had to walk in a most contorted and uncomfortable position.)

He stepped onto a bus, and the man next to him laughed, "I'll bet you got that suit from Zumbach the Tailor!"

"How did you know that?" asked our friend with the suit.

"Because only Zumbach the Tailor could fit a man as crippled as you!"

God did not intend for any of us to be crippled. It is we who cripple ourselves with small thinking, ideas of limitation, and fear. Let's consider for a few moments what the average person might believe is stifling or preventing him or her from being all that he or she wants to be: lack of skill . . . lack of money . . . too much or too little age . . . too many or too few people . . . not enough physical energy . . . bad luck. These are not reasons for failure; they are the excuses that many people hold to justify a "victim" position that they are not even aware they are holding.

Not one of these circumstances has any power to withhold our highest good from any of us. This was an idea that took me a long time to accept, but I have now seen too many people break through these mirage barriers for me to believe in them any longer.

Let us take lack of skill, for example. I know a girl who was failing ninth grade; her counselors told her she was not school material, and so she dropped out. She worked for a while, traveled, and two years later passed a high school equivalency test, entered college, and completed her freshman year of college before her former classmates graduated high school.

Neither can the physical body bind us, unless we let it. Lack of physical energy is a lack of mental enthusiasm. I used to believe that I needed eight hours of sleep every night to be rested and effective. When I began this writing, however, I had so much enthusiasm for what I was doing that I would sleep for four hours or less, and awake fresh and energetic.

Nor has money ever stopped anyone from doing anything. If our intention is clear and our faith strong, the money will come. Howard Johnson started out with a tiny ice cream stand in Brooklyn. John Kraft and his wife sold cheese out of a pushcart. Louise Berlez had a dream to go to France, but not a penny. She made up her mind that she would be in Paris in six months. Five and a half months passed, and there was no sign of any trip. Then, unexpectedly, her supervisor called her into his office and asked her if she would like to go to Paris on business, all expenses paid. And so she did.

Faith is a magnetic force that draws to us as much good as we are open to accept. A few years ago, a friend and I took a vacation to Puerto Rico. Just before we were about to leave, our return airplane tickets were stolen. Although I thought that we could have them reissued at the airport, when we got there the ticket agent told us, "I'm sorry; you'll have to apply for replacements. Here are the forms; it takes only about thirty days." Thirty days! Well, that did not quite suit us, as our flight was scheduled to leave at 7 a.m. the next morning. My friend became very upset and worried, but I was not. I said, "I just know that we are going to be on that plane at seven tomorrow . . . I can just see those clouds below us, now!" I didn't know how; I just knew. Several hours later, two friends — people that we had met only a few days earlier — gave us their plane tickets (worth hundreds of dollars and their way home), trusting us to wire them new tickets. Their kindness was a twinkle in God's eye and our safe arrival His wink.

Confidence in God's ability to meet our needs is returned with Providence that laughs at chance. Eric Butterworth, the insightful and prolific Unity minister, tells that once, while he was on a cross-country airplane trip, the plane was forced to land for repairs. The passengers were sent into the terminal and told that there would be a twelve or more hour delay before another plane would be available. Nearly all the passengers became angry, grumbling and complaining to the airline personnel. Dr. Butterworth, however, realizing that disappointment is Hisappointment, remained relaxed and was attracted to the one other passenger who was serene and unruffled, a man who sat calmly looking through a picture magazine. The two men got together and were enjoying a pleasant conversation when an announcement came over the loudspeaker: "Attention passengers of flight 721 to New York: a replacement flight is now available. The substitute airplane is, however, smaller than your original one, and only a limited number of passengers will be able to leave immediately. These passengers will be selected by lottery." A hush came over the crowd as the names were about to be chosen. The first two names announced were those of Dr. Butterworth and his friend.

I often remember these two airplane stories when my faith starts to waver. They remind me that there is a much bigger scheme to life than most people see from the ground floor of the airport. We must observe our departures and arrivals from the control tower, and not the waiting room. We must listen with our hearts, and not our ears. We must have confidence in our Self.

A while back, I quit a well-paying government job with a certain amount of power and prestige, and I took a job in the Magic Garden Health Food restaurant. One day, while shopping in Foodtown, I ran into Mrs. Rothman (an old friend of my mother), somewhere between the cauliflower and the eggplant. When I told her of my job change, she asked me, "So, are you happy now?" "I am, Mrs. Rothman," I reported sincerely. "I love my work; I feel creative and alive; I enjoy the people I work with; I'm free of the pressures of working for the government; I'm happier than I've ever been!"

"Don't worry, dear," she told me, with a consoling look on her brow — "you'll find yourself."

The irony, of course, was that I was already found. And we are all already found, but it is each of us that must find our own self, and it is only within our own heart that we can know it. Once we align ourselves with a direction from within, no one in the world can convince us otherwise, for our Source of acknowledgement is far more powerful than any that the world could offer or any challenge the world could pose.

There was a cartoon about a fairyland that was oppressed by a dark tyrant called the "Shadow." All the fairies, elves, and animals in the kingdom fled in terror of the Shadow, until he was about to turn the entire kingdom into one huge shadow, and light would never again be seen. There was but one day of light left before darkness would rule completely. One brave little boy, armed with nothing but one single candle, decided to challenge the Shadow by heading straight for the evil one's lair. Unafraid, he entered the Shadow's chamber and lit the candle. That was the end of the Shadow, for, you see, the moment the light shined, it revealed that the Shadow had no substance.

Our learned limitations are our shadows, and, like the little boy in the story, we can rid ourselves of them only by facing them with a little light. Each of us must ultimately conquer our own shadows. Until then, our Divine Self remains penned in a little corner of a frightening world while we are acting happy, but really knowing that there is more, for we are more. Once we begin to see that we can be anything we want to be, our limits reveal themselves to be as illusory as the glass of a fishbowl that doesn't exist.

"You now stand on the brink of a vast realm of unlimited, eternal, and infinite space. You are free to enter it and to recognize the purpose for which you were created, a recognition which has too long lain covered with unsubstantiated thoughts of forms with empty powers.

For too long have you wandered through the mazes of narrow thinking and hopeless hopes. You have drawn your own boundaries and then given them homage as if they were Divinely ordained. You have made your own hell and resigned yourself to it.

Now before you is the answer to the dreams that you have denied as fantasy, but which your memory of the Divine has fanned and kept alive like an inextinguishable ember. Here is your moment, Children of Light. Here is found the long-lost portal to your ancient Home. Here is your Self.

Step forward, free of fear or hesitation. Your Heritage of Spirit must offer you more than you could ever offer yourself. It would gladly take from you your sufferings and disappointments, and lovingly replace them with living dreams that cannot be shattered by the vicious winds of

ephemeral chaos. Here, beloveds, is your dream, offered to you freely, recognizable only by the absence of conditions or guilt bargains for its return. It is given to you without barter, for it has always been yours for the asking, held in trust for you by an all-forgiving Father who is incapable of the kind of judgement that you have created to justify your learned guilt.

Here is the Answer to the questions that you learned to ask, but never fully believed. Here is the resolution to the problems that you were taught to worship, but never truly suffered. Here is the goal that you came to seek, but never really needed. Here is God.

Would you turn your back on All, for the sake of some? Would you trade your Heritage for hell? Would you remain in prison when the gate stands open?

Your taste of the Divine has ensured your acceptance of its blessings, and has so undone any need for fear. You cannot fail. In this happy fact is the assurance of your success, and the redemption of every soul that is carried into the Light because you are.''

THROWING AWAY CRUTCHES

Quietly sitting in the glow of a crackling campfire overlooking a peaceful mountain valley, I told the teacher what was bothering me. Two friends of mine had undergone a parting of the ways. They had been working together for spiritual service, but for reasons which I did not understand, they dissolved their partnership and set off on different paths. I told the teacher, "I am feeling a lot of pain about this separation."

"Come sit near me," he invited, with a strength in his voice that could come only of deep understanding. He gently placed his hand on my shoulder and explained, "What kind of happiness is that? You have let their actions determine your happiness. They were together, and you were happy. Now they are apart, and you are unhappy. What will you do if they get together again? . . . Be happy? Do not invest your happiness in the outside world, which is constantly changing and can never bring you real peace. Why not place your happiness in God, the unchanging, Who will never let you down?"

Although I had heard these ideas before (and had mouthed them myself many times), at that moment they rung in my heart like a mighty bell. I knew the truth of his thoughtful counsel, and my pain was resolved, never to disturb me again.

Another student, a paralytic, came to another teacher for healing. "Take up your bed and walk!" commanded the Master, and the man was healed. There is great grace in this lesson. Jesus was speaking not only to the paralytic, but to each one of *us*. Though we may not be physically paralyzed, we paralyze ourselves with mad ideas of experiences, people, and objects that we believe we need to keep us happy, and then we "lean out" on them in a false dependence that only keeps us sedated into believing that we are less than We Are.

We return to earth time and time again, we are told, to fulfill desires — thoughts that there is something "out there" that will satisfy our soul. We believe that a man, a woman, a cigarette, or a job will be the end of our seeking. The irony, or the joke, is that our soul is already satisfied, except for the *thought* that we need something else to fill us in. We must live out our desires in a painful evolution of disappointment until we realize that we are — and always have been — whole.

This process of disillusionment may sound callous and be difficult to accept, but life on earth is callous. No one in the world can escape the bumps and bruises of life. (Even Hilda was given a $50 summons for letting her dog off its leash for just a few moments.) Buddha said, "All life has in it the potential to bring suffering; when we give up craving, or attachment, then and only then does the pain stop." A woman came to Buddha with an appeal to restore her dead father to life. The Buddha gave her an empty cup and told her, "Fill this cup with sugar from a house where there has been no death, and I will restore your father's life." The woman eagerly went from door to door, but alas, there was not one person who was free of the pain which she sought to avoid. Buddha was not negative or cynical; he is called "The Compassionate Buddha" (Enlightened One). He knew that in the momentary pleasure of passing sense-objects, there is the possibility of pain when the object is lost.

We must be brutally honest with ourselves in assessing what brings happiness and what brings sadness in our lives. We must clearly discern between *fleeting* happiness and *real* happiness. People, objects, and experiences can make us "high," but the high is not whole, because we believe that it is the thing that has given it to us. We would give God's power to a thing. Satya Sai Baba says that drug experiences are "false grapes"; they look just like the real thing, but the moment we bite into them, we realize that they are imposters. The problem is not in the experience of a high, for we were made to be high; the error is in the association between the thing and the high. Believing that something can take us to Heaven means that we have left Heaven, and the only way we have left Heaven is in consciousness, and not in Truth. Because we are the Children of God, we carry God within us. If we believe that someone or something can give us God from outside, we have denied that She is already inside. No one can sell you the Brooklyn Bridge. If you live in New York City, you already own it. Buying it from someone means that you agree that it is not already yours and that someone else has the right to sell it to you.

I recently read that scientists believe they have found the cure for the common cold. Unfortunately, it is a rare enzyme from the stomach of a whale that can only be found in certain Arctic waters at a particular time of the year. This would mean that the Creator is so cruel, and that He so hated His creations, that He would plague them with a disease and then hide its cure in a remote and inaccessible place!

I prefer to think of the story of mankind, instead, as that of the musk deer, who searches the earth for the source of a beautiful aroma, only to find it emanating from within its own body. We tend to live on the periphery of our beings, seeking outside solutions for *inside* problems. When we believe that a degree, a raise, or a house can clinch our security, we sooner or later find that there is no more — or less — security outside than there is inside. And we see, too, that disillusionment is the best thing that could happen to us, for disillusionment means that illusion is over, and Reality is obvious.

Most of the dramas that we create over things in our lives are disguised attempts to feel spiritual peace; we have confused things with Spirit, and mistakenly equated acts with Love. But because we are spiritual beings, nothing less than spirit will satisfy us. I once sat through a long, drawn out court case of a woman who made a complaint against her next door neighbor, who had cut down a branch that was hanging onto her property from a tree that the plaintiff claimed belonged to her. The judge and lawyers argued the principles of the case in such microscopic detail that the judge finally decided to adjourn court and to have all the parties involved (including himself) go to the tree to see who was the rightful owner of the branch! The issue, of course, had nothing to do with trees and branches — it had to do with *people*. Before the incident, the two neighbors had been bickering for a time over some insulting things that one of them had supposedly said, which touched off a series of tit-for-tats, separation, and divisiveness, which led to the legal complaint over a broken branch. As I saw it, it was more of an issue of broken hearts than broken branches. People were feeling hurt and unloved, and the physical world of trees, branches, and fences was used as a means to manifest these hurt feelings. What I heard these women saying — screaming — in disguised ways was "I want to be loved! I want to be acknowledged! I want to feel connected!" All else, sadly, is the commentary of unskillful attempts to feel love.

Spiritual practices can be misused as crutches, too. We can become so attached to a teacher, to meditation, or to a diet that we lose sight of the fact that it is really *God* that we want, and not a habit. A teacher or a discipline ceases to serve its purpose if it becomes a dead end of devotion to a form. Stopping at vegetarianism or a particular form of meditation is like hanging out on Boardwalk and forgetting to pass "*Go.*" In the end, all forms must go.

When necessary, however, it can be very helpful to accept the support of a discipline, a person, or a group that can further our spiritual growth. If a man injures his leg, a crutch is very much in order, and a great blessing, at that. When the leg has healed, though, the crutch must be relinquished. At a stage of the journey, it may be very valuable to become attached to a teacher, to a physical practice (such as yoga, tai chi, or a good diet), or to a spiritual community. These positive crutches give us the momentum to free ourselves of old, destructive habits such as smoking, laziness, or negative company. These spiritual crutches are habits that lead to *no* habits, which is our real destination.

The reward of the adventure of life is freedom. The irony of the adventure is that we were free before we set out, but we needed to learn that freedom was not to be found where we fantasized it to be. We needed to learn, like our old friend Dorothy from Kansas, that there's no place like home, because there is no place *but* Home. When we learn that God is everywhere, that Love fills all space, and that Truth is the very Ground of our Being, we may surely release the little to embrace the All.

To be free, to be able to stand up and leave **everything** *behind — without looking back. To say "Yes" —*
—Dag Hammarskjold

"You can — and must — stand firm and whole as you are. Nothing in form can offer you more than what has already been given. That which is whole can never be made complete by addition to it. You only burden yourselves with thoughts of emptiness. Dwell in fullness, and providence is proven.

How long can you search the outer world for fool's gold? Do you not realize by now that the world is a house of mirrors with no foundation? Are you not weary of hunting for fulfillment in a land where none is to be found?

We remind you of choice. There is no choice as to the outcome, but you may realize your goal quickly by your own willingness to be complete. We ask you to release only that which brings you pain, for your freedom is without cost. We have no conditions for peace, for we know ourselves to be Peace. Surrender your crutches, and see that you never, in Truth, had any need for them.

You are close to the end of your journey. Were you not, you would not be drawn to these words. Allow God to offer you His final — and only — gift. You know the outcome of your journey. So close to the summit, who here would tarry? Accept guidance, and light shall the way be made. It is easy to release all when you have already released much.

Take up your bed of self-created sorrow, and walk. This is not a command, but a promise of the Divine possibility for yourself that you are now just beginning to see. The full Reality of that vision is your right and your promise."

ARTICHOKES AND ROCKS

The best form in which to worship God is every form.

—Neem Karoli Baba

One day, an African tribesman was sitting on a rock by a stream, eating an artichoke and enjoying the dance of the sunlight through the green leaves of the forest. Suddenly, as if a flash of lightning burst forth in his brain, he saw the truth, the wonder, and the glory of creation. He realized that he was born of God; he saw the marvelous perfection of the great plan of the universe; and he was filled with a sense of peace that made him complete right down to his toes.

He returned to the village to tell of his wondrous insight, and before long, crowds of his fellow tribesmen began to gather around him. They realized that he knew something great that they, too, yearned to know. When he told them of their wholeness and their perfection, someone asked him, "How did you find this wonderful knowledge that makes your face so bright and your heart so full?"

"I'm not exactly sure," he admitted. "All I know is that one morning I was just sitting on a rock by the stream, eating an artichoke, and all of a sudden the Truth was revealed to me!"

The next morning, this wise man awoke to find the village empty. Puzzled, he began to search for his brothers and sisters, but they were nowhere to be found. After hours of looking in huts and calling their names, he gave up his search and decided to rest for a while down by the stream. There, to his amazement, he found the whole tribe, huddled together on that rock, all eating artichokes!

We too often mistake the form of an experience for its essence. We worship the physical manifestation of the Holy Spirit, and not the Spirit itself. The tribesmen had confused the circumstances of one man's enlightenment with enlightenment itself. If they truly understood his message, they could have gone about their business and left the rock and the artichoke to their one brother, for it was *his* destiny to awaken in that spot, and not theirs.

Enlightenment is not something that we can acquire through an action. It is a deep inner knowing from which successful action proceeds. Rituals, which are very powerful and necessary, can also be misunderstood, and function as a distraction. For a long time, I had a long list of rituals that I believed I had to do before I could make contact with God. I thought I had to get up at a certain time in the morning, take a cold shower, do a certain number of yoga postures and breathing exercises, perform a certain preparation for meditation, and then (I believed) I could go within and experience my inner peace. And it worked. I grew tremendously from this practice — but there was a flaw in the way I was doing it. My mistake was that if I was occasionally unable to perform my rituals, I would feel frustrated and unfulfilled. I felt as if I was not prepared for the day, as if I had missed something. I had the mistaken notion that my happiness depended on these exercises. I believed that God is something that could be accomplished, when it is a Presence that needs only to be recognized.

On certain days, however, something very interesting would happen. I would have only ten minutes to meditate, and I would say a little prayer or affirmation to myself, like "O.K., God, I only have ten minutes to be with You now, so I will really concentrate and just dive right in to my Source." Then I would imagine that I had done all of my rituals and preparations, and I would go into a lovely state of meditation. And it worked. This led me to the important realization that all the ceremonies were not necessary to do all of the time — my intention and concentration were more important.

This lesson was made obvious to me on the tennis court. My partner and I would bike up to a court in a lovely spot overlooking a valley of patchwork farmland and play for a few hours. For the most part, our volleys would last three or four returns. Toward the end of the session, I or my partner would say, "Let's just play out these last three balls and then go home." At that point, an amazing phenomenon occurred: our volleys would go on for ten, fifteen, or more returns! Our skill level increased about two hundred percent! I would think, "Well, I have just a few minutes left; I'll really pay attention to what I am doing and see how well I can do." One day it occurred to me that I could probably do that well *all the time* if I would just concentrate, and that I certainly did not need to wait until the last five minutes to begin to play up to my potential!

We all have a potential for succeeding at the game of finding inner peace; we need only to let go of the idea that there is something that we need to do first to be peaceful. The way to be peaceful is to be peaceful. We can never find peace through war or strife; it just doesn't work that way. The only way it works is to start out where we want to end up, to begin by knowing that we've already arrived, and to recognize all as wholly Divine.

When we realize that God is everywhere, it becomes easy to see and love Her in all that we do. Every word becomes a prayer, every action a spiritual ceremony, and every morning a holi(Holy)day. We can read Her words in the funny papers and experience communion through Fig Newtons. Hilda tells how some of her house guests began to scrutinize a box of cookies that she offered them, to see if there were any eggs in the ingredients. "I don't eat eggs," she once told a large audience, "but I'm not afraid of them, either!"

Hilda also tells of a time when she climbed to the top of a mountain in the Himalayas to find a remote ashram (retreat) for yogis who had renounced the world. As she approached the monastary, she heard (to her amazement), "Give me my pillow!" with another voice retorting, "No! — it's *my* pillow!" The first voice came back: "That's the pillow that I use for meditation!" Second voice: "Well, I'm using it now!" and so on, into the night. These yogis had supposedly renounced everything in the world. Perhaps all they owned was a loincloth, if that. Yet the seeds of attachment to a form lay within them, sprouting at the first opportunity. They gave their power to enter the Kingdom of Heaven to a pillow.

You might like to take a few moments to ponder if there are any forms with which you bind yourself. Are there any spiritual rituals, practices, ceremonies, or disciplines which, if you were interrupted from performing by, let's say, a friend in need, would leave you angry, annoyed, or frustrated? If there are, you are perhaps confusing your priorities. Reconsider the importance of your practices and see whether or not you are giving them power over your happiness.

There are very few people in the world who think originally. Most people act like puppets, mimmicking the latest trends in fashion, voicing the popular opinions, and catching the same diseases, thinking, at the slightest sniffle, "I must be coming down with the flu that's going around." The few people who do think originally and have the courage to act on their inspiration are hailed as geniuses, trend setters, and saints. We are all geniuses, through God's wisdom. We can each set a trend toward God in our own lives, even if no other person ever follows (and probably they will follow if we are sincere in our own striving). And a saint, as Hilda has said, is "nothing other than an ordinary person, living the life that God intended." Saints, I believe, have no special dispensation; their portion of God is no greater than yours or mine. They just recognize the God within, and live it without.

There is a lovely story from the Jewish Hasidic tradition that I would like to share with you. Rabbi Zusya, a pious and revered sage, was lying on his deathbed, weeping. His students stood by him, perplexed.

"Rabbi, why do you weep?" one of them ventured to ask. "Surely, if anyone is assured a place in the Kingdom of Heaven, it is you."

The sage turned his head toward his beloved students and began to speak softly: "If, my children, when I stand before the Heavenly court, I am asked, 'Zusya, why were you not a Moses?,' I shall have no hesitation in affirming, 'I was not born a Moses.' If they ask me, 'Why, then, were you not an Elijah?' I shall speak with confidence, 'Neither am I Elijah.' I weep, friends, because there is only one question that I fear to be asked; 'Why were you not a Zusya?' "

"Know ye, Children of Light, that each of you is dear to God in a unique and individual way. To follow the path of another is a fruitless search in the thicket of shadows. God dwells within your very heart, and you need never look outside yourself to find Light.

Honor the words of those who have remembered their Divine Heritage, for, as your heart understands, they speak the very Truth. It is more important that you follow the example of their Love than the personality of their mannerisms.

You are created in the image and likeness of God. You are creators, according to your lineage. The hallmark of creativity is freshness and aliveness, not stagnation or imitation. Those who follow the path of forms are rewarded in their own way, for they are expressing according to their right evolution. Those who can hold lightly the way of forms are free to hold all forms with equal appreciation. We invite you to discover your own God Self in the way that most pleases your heart, for your joy is God's fulfillment. God holds no limitation over you.

Your path, Children, is one of ever-expanding freedom. Tarry not in modes and practices. Ceremony has been given to you as a stepping stone to communion. Let it be as such. The Light welcomes those who stand beyond the stricture of ritual. Be not afraid to come freely, for it is in freedom that you are accepted. Acknowledge yourselves in the selfsame awareness, and you will clearly understand the role of form in your journey into God."

THE EXCEPTION

We live in a world that is based upon *agreement*. If enough people agree on something, it seems to be true. We then act as if it were true, and our experience tends to recreate itself as true. This will occur even if what we agreed upon is not true, and it will continue until someone demonstrates the fiction of the original idea. Then everyone will agree to a new idea, whether or not it is true. *"As ye think, so shall it be."*

Consider, for example, the notion that the world is flat. Everyone agreed that this was so, and since everyone believed that if you set off toward the horizon, you would fall off the edge of the earth into space, nobody tried it. Everyone lived a lie, for that was the experience that they created with their thoughts. They all agreed, and that made it *practically* true.

Then along came Columbus (or perhaps, as some say, someone before him), who did *not* agree. This was a very rash and bold thing to do — not to agree with what everyone else believed. Very threatening. Downright heresy, some would say. Well, you know the story from there. He challenged the agreement, proved that the agreement was fiction, and now everyone agrees that the world is round. Maybe it is. Maybe it isn't. But we all agree that it is, and that seems to be good enough for most of us.

It only takes one demonstration of one freedom-thought to break agreement. This is very important to know, because all of our thoughts of limitation are upheld only through *absence of challenge*. In order to discern Truth from limitation, we must challenge the agreements we believe in, to which we add power through mass thinking.

THE DRAGON DOESN'T LIVE HERE ANYMORE

For many years, to run a mile under four minutes was considered impossible — beyond the capability of a mortal man. It was simply unheard of — basically, because it was *unthought* of. Then, one day in May, 1954, one man, Roger Bannister, did it. He just went out and ran a mile in three minutes and fifty nine point four seconds. Basically, because he did not agree that it was impossible. He was one person who did not subscribe to mass thinking. Now it is fairly commonplace for good runners to run the mile in under four minutes. Roger Bannister trampled down the weeds of limitation, and everyone ran down the path behind him.

Jesus demonstrated the possibility for the fullness of humankind. He showed us who we can be — and are — when we cease to think of ourselves as small and limited. "Even greater things than I, shall ye do," He said. While most people in the western culture are not aware of it, there are many yogis and mystics in the East who have performed "miracles" such as walking on water or raising the dead, like Jesus. They would not call them miracles, however; they simply describe them as the intelligent use of the natural powers of mind that God gave to all men and women. More important than the miracles, however, is the force of love and forgiveness that Christ released on earth. He shattered the agreement that we must take "an eye for an eye and a tooth for a tooth." He demonstrated that it is possible to be crucified and to forgive at the same time. That is breaking a very big agreement that humans commonly hold to be true — that we cannot forgive. But He did it — He really did it. And we can all do it.

Agreement is safe. It is comfortable. It is easy to continue, for when we agree to limitations we fit right into the mold of mass thought and action. All that it takes is one original thinker — of which there are few — to change or reverse a whole trend of culture. When the Beatles first emerged in the early 1960's, they were mocked for their long hair. They were considered by some to be freaks and heretics. Before that time, I would be reprimanded if my hair was even slightly longer than "it should have been." Within just a few years, however, long hair — and even very long hair — became stylish, and anyone sporting short hair was considered to be an oddball. Now the pendulum has swung in the opposite direction, and shorter hair is in fashion. All arbitrary. All agreement.

We have got to challenge the agreements that we hold to be true.

We must boldly ask, "Do I believe this because I really believe this, or because everyone else does?" I am amazed to find out how much of our belief systems are unfounded, adopted from the norms of others. So often I see children taking on the beliefs, values, and expectations of their parents or some figure that they idolize. They are living out someone else's thoughts. This usually brings reinforcement from the world, for other people just love for us to do what they do. Challenge them in the slightest, and see their friendship fade. A true friend is one who supports you in standing for what *your* heart tells you is True.

If you have an inspiration for a project that seems to fly in the face of agreed-upon reality, then test it! Those who laugh at you or criticize you do so only out of misunderstanding or a sense of threat; you may demonstrate the fragile nature of the values which they hold dear. Assume that God Himself is showing you a new possibility, and if He is, your venture will be borne out. Who ever heard of a burning bush talking, anyway?

"To know the Truth, you must extricate your consciousness from trends of thought. Too often, you mistake the power of popular belief for the power of Truth.

When the student of Truth sets out on his venture to discover what is Real, he may at first be met by opposition, derision, and loneliness. This challenge is, however, temporary. The spirit of Truth will nourish you far more deeply than any comfort that is offered you by the agreement of the world. In the end, only Truth stands triumphant.

There are wayshowers — those who would mark the path for those who would follow. You, My Children, must accept the responsibility of showing the way for others, for, beloveds, if you do not do it, who will? Know your Source, and know your Destiny.

Set your foot firmly upon the path of all that you wish to be, for in Reality your aspirations are but a memory of that which you already are. He will light your way. Tremble not, dear ones, for this is the path to your very Home. You must turn your back upon that which you have called home, for it is already disintegrating in a world of confusion.

At the edge of the woods is light. This is the Light of our Love for you, the all-encompassing Joy of the Father, who would have His Children live happily in the Home He makes for them. Turn away from the agreement of men and know the Love of the Father, which bears no need for agreement. Dare to live as a true Child of the One, and all of your inspirations will be upheld by the ranks of all the beings of loving kindness that guide you ever homeward."

THE MARGIN OF GREATNESS

What makes someone great in the eyes of the world? Are our heroes supermen and women who have come from another planet with exceptional powers? Or are they human beings, like ourselves, who have used just a bit more of the potential for greatness that is shared by all?

I was very surprised to learn that many of the saints had rather ordinary childhoods. St. Theresa of Lisieux, for example, describes herself as a terror of a child; her mother had to tie her in bed to keep her from throwing tantrums. Yet, as she grew into God, she learned to master her emotions through little acts of humility and positive thinking. Once, when a fellow nun returned a pitcher that St. Theresa had loaned her — Theresa's only valued possession — with a crack in it, St. Theresa was overjoyed. "Thank you, God," she thought, "Now I have no more ties to things!"

Swami Satchidananda, one of the most poised and one-pointed men that I have encountered, has a similar story. I used to think that this eloquent and accomplished yogi emerged from the womb six feet tall, in flowing orange robes and a long white beard. But this was not the case. Swamiji started like the rest of us: he had a family, he was an auto mechanic, and he smoked cigarettes. Little by little he used his life to develop mastery, self-control, and peace. He tells this story:

I used to meditate and pray a little, but my mind was on the market and the cinema. I used to go to the Himalayas, sit in front of the Ganges, close my eyes, and start meditating, but I would be meditating on the cinemas of New Delhi. I would be sitting in a cave but my mind was in the city. I repeated all the prayers correctly, and people who heard them said they sounded wonderful. They admired how I would sit quietly for hours and hours in meditation. But nothing came to my heart. I didn't feel or realize anything... Then I learned to pray for the sake of prayer and not for anything else. I would not be satisfied with anything but God. If our prayers are that sincere and our interest is only in God and nothing else, then God cannot sit quietly somewhere. He has to run to us. If we need help, it is always waiting. All we need to do is ask sincerely. *

The swami's story inspired me to work a little harder. I had a yoga teacher who told our class, "*You can always do a little more than you think you can.*" I have experimented with this principle, and I have found it to be true. In fact, we must continually apply this truth, or else we cease to be alive and grow. Accept limitations, and they confirm themselves. Challenge them, and they disappear.

Let's take a contemporary example of the margin of greatness, a very insightful one, told by Eric Butterworth. In professional baseball, most batters hit for an average of about .250, which means that they get one hit for every four times at bat. This is considered a respectable average, and if a hitter is also a good fielder, he can expect to enjoy a secure career in the major leagues.

Anyone who hits .300 — three hits out of ten at bats — is considered a star. By the end of the season, there are only perhaps a dozen players (out of hundreds in the leagues) that have maintained a .300 average, and these hitters are honored as the great ones. They get the big contracts, the acclaim, and the shaving cream commercials.

What is the difference between the greats and the ordinaries? *One hit out of twenty!* A .250 hitter gets five hits out of twenty, and a .300 hitter gets six hits out of twenty. In the world of baseball, one hit out of twenty is the margin of greatness! To me, this seems miniscule.

This slim margin of greatness symbolizes the dynamics of greatness in life. When we actualize just a tiny bit more of our potential — a miniscule amount — we become outstanding human beings.

*Swami Satchidananda, *Beyond Words,* Holt, Reinhart and Winston, *New York, 1977.*

The purpose of being outstanding is not to win acclaim or glory, but to be more of what we can be — and until we live up to all that we are, we shall never be satisfied.

It takes so little to make a difference in our lives and in the world. We humans are very easily influenced creatures. One day, for example, I was feeling a little grumpy and someone called on the telephone for one of my housemates. As I took his message, he spoke in such a sincere and polite way that it changed my whole attitude. He did not tell me that I was wonderful, or that he loved me, and he did not offer me a million dollars. He just spoke with a little kindness in his words, and that, to me, made a big difference.

I remember, too, when a friend once called me up to give me a suggestion on how I could improve my singing. She didn't have to do it. It was even a toll call for her. But those five minutes were precious to me. It was a real act of friendship on her part, and I shall not forget it. And it seems that wherever I go there is one person whose smile is just a little brighter, or whose welcome is just a little warmer, or whose hug is just a little more genuine than the others. These are the people that I really appreciate, who inspire me to try a little harder to give a little more and to make a difference in the lives of the people around me. Their extra effort makes me want to be like them, and to pass along what I have received.

It is the "little" acts such as these that have given me the encouragement to carry on when the path seemed steep. Many of these kindnesses are actions which most people would overlook, but which my heart remembers. I am sorry to say that I have not always acknowledged these kind deeds, but I hope that these words will be a source of encouragement to those who do not always see the fruits of their given love.

These quiet and unacclaimed acts are, to me, the real margin of greatness. Greatness is not in popularity, wealth, or long life, as most people believe. Real greatness is in simplicity and supportive words. It is in firm encouragement and gentle patience. It is in finding God in the midst of the turmoil of the marketplace, and remembering His goodness during hardship. No, greatness is not always found in those whom the world calls its heroes, but in the unheard of saints who unselfishly serve their families, lend a kind ear to a friend in despair, and lovingly see the Best in those who have become too accustomed to seeing themselves as mediocre.

"You, within whom greatness lies dormant like a sleeping saint, arise to your hidden spendor! We do not ask you to be world leaders or heroes, but to do what you have been given to do, with loving care and your best ability. There is much, much more that you may know, that you may do, and that you may be. Seek out your highest calling and respond with your all. Do a little, if you wish, but do it well.

Seek not greatness in the eyes of the world, for the world loves its own, and would have you be a part of it. When you serve God, you serve the world, for the world knows not how to serve itself. It believes it can serve itself, but only encumbers itself with thicker delusion. Seek worth in the eyes of God, who would have you be great through humility. Meekness is the refuge of the mighty which the arrogant cannot enter.

Be not deluded and blinded by the small thinking of men. Their goals are as foolish as the paths they take to reach them. You are living in a world of erroneous thinking. You must break out of the patterns of thought that bind men to themselves. Begin your liberation with a few small changes in thought, and you mark for yourselves the right to walk the entire Kingdom."

DETERMINATION

"*A saint is a sinner who never gave up,*" said Paramahansa Yogananda. This potent statement is, to me, a promise of the power of determination to make our dreams come true. We must push on relentlessly toward our goal, no matter what thoughts of unworthiness or failure attempt to dissuade us.

Let us consider the original apostles that Jesus chose to spread His message of Love and Light. There was a tax gatherer, some fishermen, a prostitute, and a doubter, among others. We are told, as well, that Jesus spent a good deal of time preaching in the taverns. Surely these, chosen by Jesus, are not our idea of saintly beings. They were, however, human beings who *grew* into sainthood. They did not descend on a silver cloud from Heaven; they rose from the dust of the earth. Jesus paid no attention to their outer garb of sin. He saw within them the Divine spark of greatness that He could fan into splendor, that those in the world might recognize their own Divine potential.

One of the early companions of St. Francis asked him, "Why you, Francis? Why you? Why did God choose you as a lighthouse to bless the world? You are not learned, you are not handsome, and neither are you wealthy. One would think that He would choose one who is attractive and successful to be exalted for His work. But you are none of these. Why you?" St. Francis smiled and replied, "Why me? I'll tell you why me. Because there could hardly be anyone who has made as many mistakes as I have! I have done and been everything you can think of that is abhorrent and unholy. I have absolutely nothing to offer to the world. That is precisely why God chose to glorify me! — to give hope to people who feel they have nothing to give, for if the Holy Spirit can work through me, it can work through anyone!"

These examples have given me the courage to keep going in the face of failure, to persevere in the absence of recognition, and to remain true to my Goal even when I seem to have fallen. Never allow yourself to feel that your spiritual work, your striving, or your discipline is not paying off. Even if you do not see the results immediately, or if you are not acknowledged by others, your actions are never for nought. If you are chopping down a tree, you may hack away for hundreds of blows and not see the tree move a millimeter. It is only when you make the final cut that the tree falls. Although you saw no apparent progress, each and every one of those blows was equally necessary to accomplish your goal.

There is no one who is so far from God that she or he cannot succeed. Star Daily was a convicted murderer and a criminal of the toughest order. He was so arrogant that the warden threw him in "the hole" — solitary confinement — to break him. He did not break, though, and he was near death when Christ appeared to him in a glorious Light and filled him with the Spirit of Peace. He walked out of that "hole" a new man, not broken by the warden, but transformed by the Grace of God.

Sometimes things come easily in life, and sometimes they don't. Sometimes we are given the gift of growth, and sometimes we have to work for it and earn it. There is a marvelous motto that encourages me to keep on keeping on when things do not seem to be flowing my way: "When the wind is not blowing — row!"

The people who succeed are the ones who are willing to hold steadfast to their dream, even in the face of apparent or temporary failure. When I first took a job as a coordinator of an agency, I met with several other men who were in similar positions. One of them gave me priceless advice: "There are going to be rewarding days and there are going to be days when you just want to quit. They are all part of the job. On the tough days, just keep plugging away." I never forgot his words. He was quite correct. Whenever I had a rough day I remembered his advice, and I gained the confidence of looking at the job from a broader perspective — and that made all the difference.

It is said that "Character is the ability to follow through on a *project long after the mood has passed.*"Often, we must stick to a task even if the goal does not seem to be at hand. Thomas Edison put up with over nine hundred failures in his effort to produce an electric light, before he hit on the right formula. He had quit school at the age of eight, after only three months of education; his teacher labeled him "backward." Ronald Clark, Edison's biographer, tells us, too, that "Leonardo da Vinci, Hans Christian Anderson, and Niels Bohr were all singled out in their youth as cases of retarded development; Newton was considered a dunce; Einstein's headmaster was to warn that the boy would never amount to anything."* But deep within their souls was engrained a spirit and a confidence to persevere, a faith that carried them over all obstacles to achievement.

Like these successful men, when we make an inner commitment to realize a clear-cut goal, a great force of Will wells up within us. It is a Will bigger and stronger than our little will; it is like a wind from the great Will of God that comes to fill the sails of the ship of determination, the mast of which we have hoisted with our commitment to succeed. We can do nothing by ourselves, but when we declare our firm intention to accomplish a task and we ask for support from God, we are given the strength, the wisdom, and the means to succeed.

One summer, years ago, I travelled cross country with a friend who was extremely determined and positive. I was driving through the Texan desert late one night when I noticed that we were very close to being out of gas. I began to feel anxious about running out of gas in the middle of nowhere. We came to a gas station, closed for the night. I decided to just pull into the gas station and wait until it opened the next morning. My friend, who was sleeping in the back seat, woke up and asked, "What's happening?" I explained my plan to him. With a masterful combination of will and compassion, he urged, "Oh, come on, we'll find a station that's open!" Sure enough, not far down the road, we did.

The force that opposes determination is *inertia*. Inertia is not a static thing; it is a *dynamic force*. Like any force, it tends to magnify itself and gain momentum until or unless it is superceded by another force stronger than itself. If you jog every day, and then stop for a day, and then two days, and then three, the momentum of inertia will

*Ronald Clark, *Edison — the Man Who Made the Future*, G.P. Putnam & Sons, 1978

make it more and more difficult for you to re-initiate your practice. This is how we can get sidetracked from our dreams. We slip into the undertow of inertia, and then forsake our commitment. It takes a strong will to buck inertia, but overcome it we must. When we refuse to be intimidated by unchosen habit, and we do just one act of our practice again, the momentum of the *practice* will increase, and it will be easier and easier, and not harder and harder, to continue. It's all a matter of vectors and dynamic momentum.

The secret to maintaining a disciplined practice, I have found, is to always continue to do *at least a little bit*, even when I don't feel like it. When pushing a car, the hardest part is to get the car rolling, for an object at rest tends to remain at rest unless acted upon by an outside force. Once the car is moving, it is easier to keep it moving than it was to start it, for an object in *motion* tends to remain *in motion* until it is acted upon by another force. So, if I don't feel like doing a lot of exercises one day, I just do one or two, which keeps the discipline alive and, in a sense, keeps the door open for further practice. And sometimes those one or two exercises feel so good that I want to continue and do more.

To mobilize will and determination requires practice. Hilda has taught us a "1,2,3" method for developing will. "If, in the morning, you do not feel like getting out of bed, but know that you must, say to yourself, 'I am going to count to 3, and when I reach 3, I will get out of bed. '1' . . . '2' . . . '3!' and then you get out of bed!" You have to. There are no two ways about it. Your whole life depends on it. It really does.

As we make determination our own, there is yet a more subtle teaching that calls for our mastery. We must be determined, but not *headstrong*. We must have faith that God will help us reach our goal, but we must hold a greater faith that if we have chosen a goal that is not in our best interest, there will be a good reason for our not accomplishing it. We must take the attitude of high school shop students: our teacher will give us all the materials and methods for improving our skills, but if he sees us heading for an accident, he will turn off the electricity at the master switch. We must hold firmly to determination, but be ready at any moment to let go of our goal if we discover that our plan is not God's Plan. Our challenge is to distinguish between inner guidance and outer thoughts of limitation.

Hilda illustrates this distinction with two stories. Once, she was traveling with a yogi, on their way to visit a sick person. They had car trouble and Hilda remarked, "Maybe this is God's way of telling us that He doesn't want us to go." The yogi admonished her, "Don't be silly! We will go!" Off they went, and the person who was ill was healed.

On another night, Hilda was driving up into a mountain canyon when she got a flat tire. As she repaired it, she felt as if the flat was given as Divine guidance and she turned around to go home. Just at that moment, out of the canyon emerged a gang of sinister-looking men. Her setback was a blessing in disguise, and she chose well in not bucking it. Intuition and inertia, you see, wear the same garb; it is for us to distinguish between the two.

Determination is the very opposite of "chance." When we practice determination, we take our destiny into our hands. The determined person refuses to surrender to the random winds of circumstance. Determination is mastery, and chance slavery. If we rest our fate in the hands of fortune, sometimes we shall succeed, and sometimes we shall fail, but always shall we be weak. When we practice determination, we live up to our identity as masters of destiny. In so taking charge of our fate we shall succeed most of the time and fail some of the time, but we shall always be strong. We shall have no regrets about our life, for we know that we gave it all we had to give.

George Bernard Shaw said,

> *I want to be thoroughly used up when I die, for the harder I work, the more I live. I rejoice in life for its own sake. Life is no "brief candle" to me. It is a sort of splendid torch which I have got hold of for a moment, and I want to make it burn as brightly as possible before handing it on to future generations.*

Be determined. Be tough. There was a sign that I saw in a gym: *"When the going gets tough, the tough get going."* Seize on opportunities to practice mastery and determination. Meet your tests with enthusiasm, knowing that through conquering your challenges you are bound to become stronger. Remember that you will never be faced with a challenge that you cannot overcome, and that you and God are a majority.

"There is a special place in our hearts for you who are determined to succeed. The force of God rushes to your support with enthusiasm and encouragement. While there are few gifts that you can offer to God, determination is one of them. It is the soul's way of demonstrating sincerity of aspiration.

Hold fast to your dreams, Children, for they are the stepping stones to the success for which you yearn. Do not make a distinction between determination to succeed in the world, and that to succeed in God, for it is the quality of steadfastness that is to be developed, more than the object of determination.

Know, as you strive, that there are and will be resting points - oases - where you may replenish your strength. Do not seek them or wait for them, but in the midst of your disciplines, know that when you have need of them, they will be shown to you.

We urge you to continue with your will to grow. No effort, however small, goes unnoticed or unrewarded. Call upon the higher forces within you, and they shall most certainly give you their blessings in great measure. Your faith will carry you through your travails. Your commitment to God is answered with His commitment to you."

The Mind

THOUGHTS ARE THINGS

"I was meditating on Love," explained a woman after she shared in a group meditation, "and I saw a rich, vibrant rose as a symbol. I held that lovely image in my mind, and soon my whole field of mental vision was filled with red roses."

"That explains it!" exclaimed the woman sitting next to her, with a broad smile of surprise. "I was meditating on Light when, all of a sudden, a bouquet of red roses appeared in my mind. They were beautiful, but I could not understand where they were coming from. Your roses came into my meditation!"

Thoughts are, most assuredly, things. They are conceived in the mind and they travel through time and space like ripples in a pond, affecting all that they touch. Thoughts are the building blocks of our experience; the world that we see is the one that we have created with our thoughts. Edgar Cayce said, "Mind is the builder." We think a thought, attach a feeling to it, and a circumstance in our life is attracted to it. If we want to see how we got to be where we are in life, we need only to trace our experience back to our thoughts.

Hilda once told this story: "I went to the country last weekend, and as we drove up a hill, I looked down at all the cars driving to and fro on the highways. What do you think was driving those cars, kids?" No one knew. "Thoughts! That's what was driving them! Someone woke up that morning and had a thought, 'Let's go see grandma today,' and off the family went. Or, 'I have to go fix my country house before winter,' or 'I'm gonna have a real good time fishing,' or some other thought of like nature. Each car was being led by a thought. You thought gasoline was powering the cars, but gasoline was only serving a thought!"

Everything we see, in fact, is serving — is a result of — thoughts. *"Your body is your thoughts in a form you can see,"* said Jonathan Livingston Seagull. This is easy to understand if we use a house as an example. Every house came only after an idea for it. Can you imagine a house being built before someone had a thought to construct it? No, houses always come from blueprints; never the reverse. In the same way, our circumstances are always a result of the mental blueprints — thoughts — that preceed them.

When Swami Satchidananda came to America, he was asked by his students to pose for a book of photographs of yoga postures. Although he had not done this kind of physical yoga in fifteen years (I am told), he went into the most difficult positions with ease. It was explained to me that his physical body had no tightness in it because his mind remained fresh and easy going. A calm mind pictured a relaxed body.

If there is any stress, resistance, or limitation in the mind, it will be manifested in the body. In yoga classes, for example, I see that most of the people who cannot do the headstand are prevented not by their body, but by their *mind* and by their emotions. Most of them are physically capable, but one little thought of "I can't" dams up the whole river of physical power. That little imp of a thought drags with it the emotion "I'm afraid" and the two together form a deadly duo that can effectively immobilize a muscular two hundred pound man. I could do the headstand only when I ceased to *think* of myself as "someone who cannot do a headstand" and began to *think* of myself as "someone who can."

To demonstrate this relationship between thoughts and the body, I did a simple muscle testing experiment in one of my classes. I asked a strong fellow to resist my pressing down on his outstretched arm while he thought of a stressful situation in his life. His arm became so weak that I was able to press it down easily, though he was trying hard to keep it up. I then asked him to think about his most refreshing and enjoyable vacation while I pressed on his arm again. This time the arm was so strong I could hardly move it. His mental stress had weakened his physical body, and his mental ease strengthened it. His body was a mirror of his thoughts.

There is more to our story of thoughts. Because they are things that are constantly, dynamically emanating from us, they create a subtle environment around us, like a force field or even a weather pattern. Although thoughts are not visible to the physical eye, we are always aware, on a subtle level, of the thought fields, or auras, of those around us. If I come into contact with someone who has just experienced emotional upset, for example, I feel or sense some kind of disturbance about them, even if there are no obvious physical signs. We all sense these kinds of energies. You may have had the experience of walking into a room where two people have just been arguing, and even though the people may have left the room, the air or atmosphere feels turbulent or muddy. By contrast, if you are in a room when a positive, happy person enters, you may begin to feel light, clear, and effervescent. I think we all know someone who makes us feel good just to be in their presence. Such a person is radiating thoughts of strength and positivity, and when we are near them we receive the benefit of their dynamic thought energy.

The reality of thoughts and the power they have to create and to change the world around us brings with it a supremely important realization: *we can bless and we can heal.* Blessing and healing are not mystical secret powers reserved for a special few. They are the God-given right — and responsibility — of every single human being, and as soon as we admit to ourselves that we can really be instruments for God's healing Love, we can begin to make the kind of changes in our lives and in the world that we always wanted to make, but did not feel that we were worthy or capable of offering.

A friend of mine arrived early to work one day, and while waiting for the store owner to arrive to open up, he decided to silently send out thoughts of good will to each person who passed by him on the street. After he was doing this for a few minutes, a shabbily dressed man walked up to him and told him, "What you're doing with your mind is good."

Such is the reality of thoughts. We must respect the power of thoughts, for they can make us or break us. We do not create our lives from nothing, but we certainly set into motion the events that create circumstances. By the time we see a circumstance, we are seeing the effect of a series of events that began with a thought long ago. This is why it is so ineffectual to attempt to improve life by manipulating circumstances. Any change in circumstances is due only to a change in the way we think. If we want to change our circumstances, we must

97

change the way we think. We cannot allow ourselves the luxury of an "idle" thought, for there is no such thing. Every thought is a seed. What we plant in our mental garden will grow. This is the Law of Mind.

> *Sow a thought, reap a word;*
> *Sow a word, reap a deed;*
> *Sow a deed, reap a habit;*
> *Sow a habit, reap a character;*
> *Sow a character, reap a Destiny.*

"You have been endowed with a great and marvelous gift. Your thoughts are the key to your freedom. You who would reclaim your Divine Inheritance must do so through your thoughts, for it is only in thought that you have strayed from the path, and only through thought that you regain it.

The power to change the destiny of humankind is in your hands. There is no nobler charge that is given you than that of the salvation of the world. And there is no lesser task that is worthy of your participation.

Attune your consciousness with the Good, the Beautiful, and the True. Be a light to your sisters and brothers. Your Love is more powerful than any negation. Your faith can overcome all doubts. Your Divinity will awaken Itself in your brethren. You will certainly beautify the world, for those who know the miracle of thought know the secret of blessing."

THE LAW OF ATTRACTION

A young woman burst into my office one afternoon and pleaded, "You've got to talk to my brother — he's going to kill himself!" I went out to her car and I sat down with the young man, who did not particularly want any counsel. After a long conversation, it was clear to me that his intention to take his life was strong. I attempted to work with him in the clearest way that I knew, but it seemed that there was nothing that I could say that would change his mind. We parted, and I knew that prayer was our only chance.

That night at Hilda's class, I told Hilda, who interrupted the class to pray for him. We all sent him our love and our intention that he would choose to continue to live. When I next saw his sister several days later, I eagerly asked what had happened. "He's in the hospital," she reported. I was disheartened. "Could it be that our prayers failed?" I thought. "But it was not from attempting suicide," she went on. "The most amazing thing happened: That night, though his plan seemed set, he suddenly changed his mind and decided not to go through with it. A few days later, though, he slipped in the shower and hurt himself seriously."

This, to me, is a strikingly clear demonstration of the Law of Attraction. We attract to us that which we think. If we think and see goodness and prosperity, they shall come to us. If we dwell upon negativity and suffering, that is what we will find. Although this man renounced his foolish plan, he had to reap the results of his morbid thoughts of self-harm, in the form of experience.

"As ye sow, so shall ye reap," said the Master. "Cast your bread upon the water and it shall return to you." The man's fall in the shower was no accident, nor did he purposely do it. He was simply facing his own thoughts in a form that he could see.

Every thought is a prayer. Each thought that we think is like an order that we place with God, who is prepared to give us all that we ask for in the form of our thoughts. The more we dwell on any thought, the more likely we are to see that thought manifested in our experience. We can make this principle work for us by focusing our minds on the thoughts that we would like to see turn into events and experiences. Hilda put it in plain language: "If you keep after God enough, He'll get so tired of your bellyaching that He says, "Let's give that one what she wants, and shut her up, already!" She once told someone, "If I had a goal like that, I'd pound the ethers until it came to pass!"

Actually, we do not need to talk God into anything She doesn't want to do, because there is no difference between our will and Hers. Resolution comes when we realize that there is no will outside of the one that God gave us to use. We are "co-creators" with God. We point the bow, and She shoots the arrow. A beautiful young boy once asked his father, "Daddy, who loves me more, you or God?" The father thought for a moment and answered, "God loves you *through* me, sweetheart."

We are encouraged by shampoo, deodorant, and handcream advertisements to be attractive. Actually, we are already as attractive as could be! We are constantly attracting to us people and conditions that mirror exactly our patterns of thought. There is no getting around it. Every element of our lives is where it is through very lawful placement. *We may see the events in our lives as being unlawful, but that is only because we do not yet understand the laws of mind that are operating behind the scenes of our daily dramas.* Once the laws are clear to us, we can see that "random" or "accidental" events are actually the result of a very intelligently designed system of justified relationships. What we think is what we get.

I saw this principle strikingly illustrated in a film that I saw on the laws of sound. A handful of iron filings was placed on a thin sheet of metal, and a certain musical tone was played near the sheet. Wonderously, the filings arranged themselves into the form of a snowflake! They were conforming to the vibrational pattern of the tone that was being played. Another tone was sounded, and the filings rearranged their formation, this time into a star pattern! Every sound had its own pattern, and the visible filings demonstrated the invisible pattern of the sound.

Our thoughts are like the sound, and the circumstances in our lives the iron filings. The filings had no volition or will of their own. They simply fell into the vibrational pattern of the sound. In the same way, automobiles, money, food, jobs, and relationships have no particular will of their own. Their nature is to follow the direction of the waves of thoughts that we send out.

Some say, "Look what I created!" but another way to say it is, "Look what I *attracted*." The word *circumstance* neatly depicts the process: *circum*, around, *stance*, stand. Circumstances are the conditions that stand around us, magnetized to us by the central core of our thought-forms. Change the thoughts at the center of the magnetic field, and you change the conditions that stand around you.

This ability to draw conditions to us has tremendous practical implications. It means that we can use our thoughts to make our life. It means that we can really change for the better. It means that *things no longer hold power over us*, for we realize that they are *just the expression of our thoughts*, and nothing more. Our bodies, for example, look just like we have made them with our thoughts. They have no mind of their own; they depend on our mind for direction. One yogi said, "Your physical body is made up of pizza pie and ice cream . . . Pizza pie has never made anyone overweight — but *thoughts* have. It is the mind that says, 'I need pizza with double cheese . . . Hand, pick up the pizza . . . Mouth, chew it!' The mind is the general and the hand and the mouth are the privates in the corps — or the *corpus!*"

"By their fruits shall ye know them" is a teaching that we usually take to describe the effects of a spiritual teacher or path. A pure teacher will bring about peacefulness in the hearts of his or her disciples, and an impure teacher will give rise to troubles. Perhaps there is yet a deeper meaning to Jesus' words, as I believe there always is. The Master spoke in parables because they describe the *inner dynamics* of life as well as the outer events. The "fruits" can mean the events and conditions in our lives. The "them" is our thoughts. To paraphrase, "By the events shall ye know the thoughts." If you want to know what is the nature of someone's thought patterns, just look at the conditions in his or her life.

THE DRAGON DOESN'T LIVE HERE ANYMORE

Harmonious living tells of harmonious thinking. A turbulent life reveals some kind of inner turmoil or lack of resolution. We may believe that we are positive, settled people, but if we notice troubles or conflicts in our outer conditions, we must look *within* to see what inner negativity is bubbling, or bubbled at some earlier time. If you want to know what's in your subconscious, you don't have to go to a psychiatrist or a psychic. Just look at the condition of your bedroom, your car, your house, your health, and your relationships. They are photographs of your subconscious. *Outer events are simply the skin and bones of inner thoughts, and to really take control of our lives, we must treat them as one.*

This is why we cannot be a "victim of circumstances," for it is none other than *we* who have brought about the circumstances in our lives upon which we would like to blame our unhappiness. We have attacted to us, for better or for worse, the conditions that were born of our very thoughts. When I was seventeen years old I drove my car through an unmarked intersection and collided with another car. I cannot blame my car or the other driver, nor could I sue the city for not having marked the intersection. I can only hold myself responsible for being careless and not proceeding with caution. My car, you see, looked like my consciousess at that time — a little battered and misshapen. Before the "accident," I had had a mental and emotional collision with a girlfriend. The car was repaired, but my consciousness was not. Two months later, I had the *exact* same "accident" in the parking lot of a department store thirty-five miles away. My car was damaged in *exactly* the same spot, this time with slightly less damage, by a smaller car. (You can imagine the look on my father's face when he came home and saw the car in the garage, damaged again!) Let's face it: I was in collision consciousness. The universe taught me, through two very solid collisions, to proceed with caution. An expensive lesson, but a valuable one.

The principles of attraction work between like-thinking people, as well as within each person. We are attracted, in deeper ways and through more subtle channels than we may be aware of, to persons who vibrate in harmony with us. Last year a friend of mine invited me to accompany her on a long ride that she had to make to a remote town in the mountains of Pennsylvania, where she was going for a job interview. I had no idea how I would occupy myself for the few days that she had to be there, but I felt that it might be nice to go with her.

When we arrived on a Sunday afternoon in the middle of winter, we felt like taking a ride to a nearby college that she thought she might like to attend if she took the job. It was a blustery, below zero day, and there was hardly anyone on the frozen campus. Hardly anyone, that is, except a dark-skinned man walking just ahead of our car, a man conspicuous only by the orange robe rippling in the wind just below the hem of his overcoat.

"I must find out who this man is!" I told my friend, and we pulled over to ask him.

"My name is *Gunaratana,*" he told us. His eyes were deep set and they spoke of tranquility. "I am here to lead a meditation retreat. Would you like to join us tomorrow?"

And so, the next morning, when my friend went to her interviews, I took her car and went to meditate with Gunaratana, who I learned was not only a very advanced yogi, but the teacher of two of my very dear friends in New York. There is no way I could have planned that one — but the Law of Attraction knew a way.

At another time, I received a letter from a friend of mine in New England, who had just returned from a convention in Canada, where she met a man named Stan, who was looking for someone to teach yoga in his program in New Jersey. My friend wrote me that she thought he and I might work well together, and she suggested that I contact him. He and I discussed the idea through a few letters, but his program was a little too far from my home, and our correspondence ended. Several months later, I went to a psychology conference in Atlantic City. In the first workshop of the program I met a man with whom I felt a strong connection. As this was a non-verbal workshop, we did not speak, but there was an unspoken bond between the two of us. We saw each other in passing during the weekend, but simply exchanged a warm hello.

The last workshop of the conference was a very dramatic and powerful one. Those who chose this workshop were asked to role play the successive stages of a human life. We were to act out and experience birth, youth, growth, clustering in families, maturity, and death. Toward the end of the workshop, we were told to choose families in which we would feel comfortable "dying." I went from group to group, interacting with many different individuals and clusters of "families," but none felt like home. I met, for example, two friendly women who invited me to be a part of their family, but my intuition told me not to stay. Though I very much wanted to find a place, there was none that seemed right for me. I began to feel lonely, and a bit of panic set in, for I feared dying alone and unsupported. All the others were with families, and I had no one. At that exact moment, on the verge of despair, I looked up — and there, walking toward me, also by himself without a family, was the very man with whom I had established such a strong connection in the first workshop. It seemed as if we were the only two people without a family in a workshop of a hundred or more persons. He, dramatizing the part of an old, crippled man, limped toward me with open arms, tears streaming down his cheeks. I felt a great wave of love well up within me as I approached him. We embraced each other like two ancient kindred spirits, and there, in each others' arms, we "died," our family — and our intuition — fulfilled. It was a very moving scene.

After the workshop, we introduced ourselves. His name was Stan. He was the very man about whom my friend had written me, and with whom I had corresponded about working with him. My friend was from Vermont, she met him in Canada, and I met him in Atlantic City. Attraction.

And the two women who had invited me to be a part of their family? Months later I met them again at Hilda's class. A year later they bought a house, and a few months after that, I moved in. In the end, I accepted their invitation to join their "family" — two years after they offered it — but the Law of Attraction is not always concerned about time — just results.

These lessons of attraction demonstrate that our thoughts *do* make a difference in how our life turns out. Where we are now is always a result of what we have thought, and where we will be will be a result of what we think now. If we wish to find ourself in a state of success, it will not be by accident; it will be only by our drawing success to us by thinking success-thoughts. By the same rule, we can condemn ourself to failure by concentrating now on what is wrong. The way of conditions is prepared by ideas.

This is why we must take care to think and attract to ourselves only that which is in harmony with our highest aspirations. If we think on or pray for something that is a passing desire, we may be forced to face the object of our desire long after the thought that spawned it has faded into obsolescence. Hilda has said, "Be careful what you ask for, kids, because you just might get it . . . You pray and pray and beseech God for a certain person or experience, and then when it comes to pass, you wish God wouldn't have listened to you!"

The "*Fantasy Island*" television show is very much about this teaching. There was an episode in which a man who always wanted a lot of money came to Fantasy Island with his wife, and there learned that he had just inherited one million dollars. Immediately all of his friends began to use him for his money, and he became very insensitive to his wife. He got caught up in a vicious cycle of inflated self-importance and decreased depth of his relationships, until he had no real friends and his wife was ready to leave him. Finally, his life was such a mess that all he wanted to do was to get rid of his money and return to his simple, peaceful lifestyle. Fortunately, Ricardo Montalban arranged for his inheritance to be discontinued, and the man and his wife left Fantasy Island with one more breath of happiness and one less fantasy.

I can think of jobs, relationships, and automobiles that I yearned and prayed for (through dwelling on them in my thoughts) that came to me long after I ceased to want them. I then had to deal with them. If I was strong, I would let go and say "No" when they came. If I was weak, I would accept them, living in a sort of dream world of memories that had outlived the desires that created them, until I would be forced to admit that the object of my desire was more a part of my past than my present.

As some persons begin to discover the relationship between thoughts and events, they begin to be afraid of thinking negative thoughts, worrying, "Oh no! I just had a thought of something bad happening to me . . . That means I will attract it!" This anxiety comes from an incomplete understanding of how thoughts attract events. There is no need to be concerned about stray thoughts of disaster or failure. They have no power unless we feed them with fear. We are thinking many, many thoughts per second (Buddha said trillions) and we are also catching the thoughts of those around us. Occasional thoughts of negativity or failure may creep into our consciousness, but if we "throw them off" before we indulge in them, they cannot harm us. It is thought *habits* that count. Continually dwelling on the same thoughts, feelings, and mental pictures begets conditions. Keep your thought *patterns* positive, and little negativities shall have no power to penetrate your established force field of positivity. We are told that there are many little disease germs in our bodies, but our overall health and strength of resistance holds them at bay.

If you now have negative circumstances in your life, cease to dwell on them mentally, and they will leave you. The best way to get rid of an unwelcome guest who lingers at your home is to empty the refrigerator. He'll be forced to seek refuge elsewhere. When we stop feeding our bad habits and conditions with thought and feeling energy, they will drop off like an old scab. If we pull out the plug from an electromagnet, all of the scraps of junk metal that cling to it fall off instantly. Refuse to water a weed, and die it must. Negative circumstances cannot survive when we refuse to sustain them with emotional energy.

Simply put, we are undeniably responsible for our lives. Wed to this responsibility is the freedom to use the laws of life in whatever way we choose. We can create Heaven or hell for ourselves through our thoughts and our actions. Do not wait for the world to stop "socking it to you." Start generating as many positive thoughts as you can, and you will bear witness to miraculous changes in your life. Think love, success, and happiness, and sooner or later these blessings are sure to be yours. Concentrate on that which you would become, not that which you now believe you are, and you will enter a new realm of consciousness — one of *chosen* good.

The realm of consciousness that most people tend to live in is a mental world. We see life more in the way that we *think* it is, than in the way that it actually is. Instead of stepping onto the porch to feel the air, we turn on the radio or the T.V. to learn what the temperature is. I found some wild spearmint growing in the woods, and my first thought was, "Wow! This smells just like chewing gum!" We ask, "What time is it?" to find out whether we should eat, instead of asking our stomach whether or not it is hungry. We devise and discuss elaborate systems of psychotherapy, and yet we fail to give our children a smile or a hug when they need it. Fritz Perls said that real psychotherapy is "losing your mind and coming to your senses." We experience ourselves as mental creatures, and the world of ideas has become an all-too comfortable place for us.

Perhaps we have entered this realm in order to learn to master it. As explorers in consciousness, we must learn to conquer, through

"Make your lives an offering, Children. It is within your ability to mark your own destiny. We would have you mark it for the highest good. How profound and pervasive are your quietest thoughts! As you realize their magnitude, you relinquish any notion of idleness.

Those who have been shown a moment of vision of the inner mechanics of the mind bear a great responsibility, greater than you currently understand. You hold within your hands the evolution and the destiny of all. Choose wisely, beloveds. The ramifications of your choices are being made known to you more rapidly, now. The energies of creation are multiplied as they are drawn from a place close to the center. Indeed, fathoming the intricacies of the mind is a final lesson in earth teaching. You must remain true to your most cherished principles in making application of the energies that you command. This is the greatest test of all. It is, after all, the only test of Christ Jesus after His baptism. He was challenged not for Himself, for He was already free. It was for all that He demonstrated the impotence of illusion. You need only to remember that what is free can never be bound.

We beckon you to offer the world Light while remaining in its midst. Those who serve mankind in this way are strong and blessed, indeed. A life transformed is more precious than a life escaped. Whatever your path, tread it well.

The Truth that gives you life is for you in all places. Make no distinction between degrees of Truth. All is Truth."

understanding, the mind which creates our destiny — *our own min*
The principles, like tools, have been set before us, and it is our charg
to take these tools and to use them with wisdom and integrity. We ar
told that previous civilizations on earth, such as Atlantis, unlocke
the secrets of the mind and proceeded to misuse them, which led to
their demise. We are also told that we have once again reached the
point at which we can free ourselves or destroy our civilization
through the use we make of the powers of the mind. It is a decision of
great responsibility, one which we all share, and one which we cannot
afford to take lightly.

We cannot deny the powers of mind that we all hold, any more
than we could deny a speeding car in which we find ourselves at the
wheel, with no power to stop it, but complete power to steer it. Our
thoughts are continually creating, or attracting the world of the next
moment. We do not have any choice as to *whether* we will create, but
we always have a choice as to *what* we create.

Harnessing the power of attraction opens the door to what some
would call the "secret" of living, although there is nothing hidden
about it. *We can change our lives simply by changing the way we
think!* We do not need to go through the cumbersome and impossible
work of fighting, struggling and attempting to manipulate the conditions in our lives. We need only to begin to think in new and more
productive ways, and the conditions will — must — reflect our way of
thought. The principle seems hidden or secret because most people do
not believe that thoughts are real, or that what we think has an effect
on the way our lives work. If people really believed in the power of
thought, our world would be a picture of harmony and perfection. It
would be a portrait of God.

Choice is in our hands, as always it has been. We may hesitate to
accept our power, for we have been taught to believe that there is a
world out there bigger and more powerful than who we are, but the
irony of this view is that the world "out there" *is* who we are. Align
your thoughts with the Truth, and all that is True will be attracted to
you. Believe in illusion, and your life will be clouded with experiences
that confirm lawlessness, only because you refused to see reality in
your original thought. Life blossoms for those who see the flowers in
their experiences. We are free to draw to us the life of our own choosing. Indeed, all that we see is the offspring of chosen thoughts.

REFLECTIONS

*Weapons will do you no good in that cave, Luke . . . You
will find only what you bring with you.*   — *Yoda*

One night I had a dream about Sasha, a dog I used to know. In
the dream, Sasha was whining for attention, and she just kept whining, no matter what I did, until I became very annoyed. I began to
raise my voice and command her to be quiet. She continued, and I became angrier until, in this dream, I began to hit her. Worked into a
furor, I awoke and found the whining I was fighting was nothing more
than my own wheezing in my sleep, from a stuffy nose.

Although the story is in one way funny, it was a precious teaching for me. It symbolized what has been taught throughout the ages by
all the great teachers of wisdom: All life is One; all that we see is our
own self; the experience of separation is a dream.

Jesus taught, "Love thy neighbor as thy self," and "Do unto others
as you would have them do unto you." He taught this because thy
neighbor *is* thy self, and when we do unto others, we *are* doing unto
ourself.

There is nobody out there. All that we see are reflections, or mirror images of our own self. When we talk, we are only talking to our
Self. When we fight, we only fight our Self. When we love, we are
only giving love to our Self. There is only One Being in all the
universe, and It is Us.

Several years ago, I traveled cross country with a friend. On this

111

trip, she and I spent a great deal of time bickering. We both grew enormously from it, but at the time we were engaged in mental Star Wars. We came to Wyoming, which, in this particular area, is a vast desert. If you have ever been there you know you can travel for hours, for hundreds of miles, and see hardly one person or green living thing. It's desolate.

We finally arrived at a public campground that was so remote, there was not even a ranger to take campers' money for the night's stay. There was just an old weathered wooden box with a few registration cards, a pencil, and a slot to put your money in. It was all on the honor system, this place was so far off the beaten path. We hiked to where the lake was supposed to be, only to find it dried up and arid. I mean this place was like another planet.

At least there was some living vegetation, so we decided to set up our tent and spend the night. We had just settled down when we heard, from just over the hill, a loud shrieking voice that made us jump, yelling, "How dare you do this to me?! I wish I'd never met you!" and so on, to which another equally enflamed voice shouted back, "Whaddya mean 'me?!' It's *you* who . . . !" and so on. I stealthily sneaked around the bend and found a man and his wife drinking and having one of the loudest, bawdiest quarrels I have ever heard. In the middle of nowhere. No water. No ranger. Just us and them. Just us.

All that we see is but a reflection of our own self. Through our bickering, my friend and I attracted that couple to us. We created that couple. We deserved that couple. We *were* that couple.

This lesson in the desert taught me a powerful method to short-circuit judgements and irritations that I feel about someone else. If I am annoyed at another's action, I ask myself, "Do *I* do that, myself?" If I am very honest, the answer is usually "Yes." Most of the time, the trait against which we are reacting in another is something within ourself that we do not accept. If you make a list of the positive and negative traits of someone you don't like, you will probably find a striking number of similarities between them and yourself. This requires a great deal of honesty, but if you can do it with a high intention, you will grow tremendously from it.

This may raise the question, "But people *do* have faults; am I supposed to be blind to the shortcomings of others?" No, this would be foolish. To believe that everything that everyone does is good would be irresponsible misuse of our Divine gift of discrimination. Earth is, in fact, a school for learning what to do and what *not* to do.

The key to knowing what is ours and what belongs to others is in understanding the difference between *observation* and *reaction*. I may *observe* that a room is untidy, that a word is misspelled, or that a person has a poor habit of interrupting others when they are speaking. If I can see it clearly, *without an emotional charge* on it, I am executing the very necessary faculty of discrimination, and such an observation is probably to my benefit as well as to the one doing the action. If, however, I become *upset* when I see the person doing what I don't like, and I lose my peace, then I am *reacting* to it, and it is most likely a trait within *myself* that I am refusing to accept. This method requires extreme honesty, and in order to benefit from it, we must want to grow more than we want to be right or to hold on to judgements and opinions.

Carl Jung called it the "Shadow." We project onto others what we do not want to see in ourselves. We have a need to deal with our non-acceptance of a certain trait, and it must be brought to the surface, as our purpose in life is to make the unconscious conscious, and to grow into loving it all. If, through our ego, we block ourselves from seeing the unwanted trait within ourselves, we project it onto another and we identify with the opposite of the trait, which we believe is "good," or we can accept. But the name of the game is to destroy thoughts of separation through exposing them to the light. As soon as we separate ourself from another and say, "*I* am this and *you* are that"; "*I* am good and *you* are bad"; "*I* am neat and *you* are messy," we have created a lie of separation, for we are *all everything*.

The way to get rid of the shadow is to *own*, or accept as part of ourself, that which we do not like or will not accept in another. Once we see that we were not reacting to another, but really to *ourself*, it immediately eliminates the conflict in the relationship, for we free the other person from the burden of our projection. We then do not have to change the entire world of others to fit our mold of what they should be like. We need, then, only to change ourself, which is much easier than reforming others or the whole world. We cannot, in fact, reform the world unless we first reform ourself.

Understanding this principle makes clear the reason why many social reform groups or movements are not successful. Actions or campaigns that are performed from a position of emotional self-righteousness have little power to bring about real and positive change, for those who would wage them are only reacting to an aspect of themselves, in the form of an outer shadow. By contrast, those who see a problem in society and can work against evil or injustice while at the same time loving and respecting the persons who are part of the problem, are much more likely to effect real and lasting change than those who see the problem as "them." Any time there is an "us" and a "them," a "good guys" and a "bad guys," a "criminal" and a "victim," there is a shadow. The extreme example of shadow-making is Hitler, who took all of the fears and guilts and angers of a whole culture and projected them *en masse* in a huge shadow onto a whole race, believing that he could purge a nation by annihilating people. We must beware, however, lest we deny our fears of evil within ourselves, and project them onto Hitler. Difficult as it may be to accept, unless we can love Hitler, we are only continuing to perpetrate the hatred and non-acceptance for which we hold him guilty.

Interestingly, the principle of the "shadow" can create separation even in the realm of "good." If you are inclined to worship, idolize, or prostrate yourself before any guru, teacher, or master, you have created a sort of "white shadow" which also must be reconciled. In such a case, you have refused to accept within yourself a good quality, such as wisdom, love, or kindness. By projecting it onto your guru, believing that he or she has it and you do not, you are creating another separation, denying that wisdom, love, and kindness are within you. Any real teacher of Truth reminds the students that all they would seek in the teacher is already within themselves. I once wrote a teacher a devotional letter, telling him that all I wanted to do was to hang out with him. He wrote me back a short reply, beginning with "no groupies . . . no students . . ." This was the kindest thing he could have done for me, for he did not allow me the luxury of separating myself from my own Divinity and projecting it onto him.

Perhaps the whole lesson of reflections can be summarized in an experience that I had while staying at a country house. At this house was a cute little pet white duck who would sit outside the kitchen door and quack whenever someone passed by. One morning I sat on the porch and watched several people respond to the duck as they entered the house. One woman, a professional singer, greeted him, "Why, Pete! How nice of you to sing me a morning song!" Five minutes later, an overweight man walked by and chided, "Oh, Pete! . . . There you go again, always quacking for more food!" And right after him came a rather intellectual fellow who replied to Pete's quacks with, "Always questions, Pete, always questions . . . perhaps we'll get you another duck to give you some answers." And so on. Meanwhile, Pete just went on quacking.

I am remembering, too, the tale of Narcissus, who lost awareness of himself when he became fascinated with his own reflections in a pool of water. While we usually take this as a lesson against vanity, it has much deeper implications. If, when we see others, we are actually seeing only ourselves, we, too, have been mesmerized by our own reflections, like Narcissus. The only way to break the spell is to begin to see ourselves, and not our reflections. The dream is over when we realize ourself to be all of the actors in the play.

"Divine ones, cease your continuous misidentification with the forms that you have created with your very own minds. Return to your true home within your Self. All that you see outside of you is a dream. In Truth, there is no separation, except that which you have made by your refusal to accept your own wholeness. Shadows exist only when you turn your back to the Light.

Courageously destroy all that you have made outside of yourself. Renounce your striving against that which you would not admit. Prostrate yourself before no man, but only before God, who dwells within you now.

Love the Divinity within all, and you free yourself of the slavery of artificial distinction. See the Perfection behind imperfection, and you behold the true being of your brethren and yourself. Those who teach Truth can do so only because they see Truth. Those who teach separation see divisions where none exist.

Strive to know yourself. Be unrelenting in your quest to discover what belongs to you, and to distinguish your true Self from that which has been taught to be yours. We tell you this with certainty: That which is yours can never be taken from you, and that which is not yours can never have belonged to you. Know this distinction — the only true distinction — and you free yourself of the tyranny of reflections."

ARE THESE MY THOUGHTS?

My housemate, Bill, had just gotten engaged to be married, and he was exuberant. One day around that time, I came home and I began to feel a little gloomy and depressed. My energies seemed to be dulled, and I did not understand why. Bill asked me for a ride to school, and as we drove along I felt a strange lethargy. The moment he stepped out of the car, I felt buoyant, light, and free. It was as if a cloud of smoke had flown out the window. I suspected that I had not been feeling down on my own account, but that I had been picking up some negative thoughts and feelings that he was experiencing, and taking them on as my own. I am not speaking of my relationship with him or my feelings about him, for we got along very well. I suspected that I was tuning into some disturbance within him. I could not understand it, though, because he had just been overjoyed to be engaged.

When I got home that evening, my answer came. Another housemate told me that Bill's engagement had just been broken. That explained it. Though he said nothing to me, Bill was feeling downhearted. I was not prepared to feel negativity from him, and as I left myself open, I assumed that the thoughts that he was emanating were my own.

Thoughts are catching. At times, such as in this case, we can feel thoughts (and the emotions that come with them) from other persons, and, if we are not careful, believe that they are ours. We are all generating a huge amount of thoughts and feelings all the time. If we are to remain strong, clear, and effective, we must understand and master thought energy.

THE DRAGON DOESN'T LIVE HERE ANYMORE

There has recently been a great deal of scientific research to demonstrate the reality of the transference of thoughts and feelings. In Peter Tompkins' *The Secret Life of Plants,* we are told of experiments in which a man measured his plants' reactions to his thoughts. He found that the plants to which he sent loving and positive thoughts grew much more favorably than those to which he sent no thoughts or negative thoughts. It has been demonstrated, too, that thoughts are independent of physical distance. In a documented study, a woman in Georgia sent thoughts at a predetermined time to seedlings six hundred miles away, in Baltimore. By the next morning, the plants had grown 84% faster than a control group.* Since I read about this study, I talk to my plants, which are twice as healthy as they used to be.

In another experiment (a cruel one which I regret having been done, but from which we can learn), a litter of baby rabbits was taken in a submarine to a depth beyond which radio waves could penetrate. Their mother remained on the land, monitored by an electronic sensor. One by one, the little rabbits were killed. At the moment that each baby died, the mother registered a strong reaction. Even on the animal level, we are all tuned into the Universal Mind, made of thoughts which are very real.

I recently attended a lecture at which a high-ranking physicist from the NASA space program described current scientific findings of very subtle particles that all of us emit. These particles vibrate in accordance with the thoughts and feelings that we generate. In other words, we are always sending out little bits of our experience and we "bombard" the people around us with these tiny but powerful particles. In essence, we are always in a big "soup" made up of the thoughts and feelings of those who share the space in which we happen to be. We are constantly mixing, blending, and merging with them. Those around us take on some our our particles, while we take on theirs.

Mystics and yogis have known and taught this for thousands of years. One evening Hilda told us, "No one will walk out of here the same as when you walked in. Just by sitting with each other, we take on each others' energies. Our auras tend to blend. I will take home a bit of you, and you will take home some of me."

The agreement of Hilda's teaching with that of the NASA scientist

---

*Peter Tompkins & Christopher Bird, *The Secret Life of Plants,* Harper & Rowe, 1973.

reminded me of a quote that I heard not very long ago: "When the astronomers finally make it to the top of the mountain, there they will find the theologians waiting for them, laughing heartily."

"Sympathetic vibrations" are not unfamiliar to us on the physical level. I once had two female dogs who, before they lived together, went into heat at different times. When they moved into the same house, they began to go into heat at exactly the same times. I am also told that women who live together, and mothers and daughters often begin to menstruate in synchronism.

As we come to understand the implications of the transference of thoughts and feelings, we can use the principles to our advantage. Until we do, we may feel like a leaf in the wind, at the mercy of the rampant energies of those around us. There are three ways in which we can capitalize on our understanding of how thoughts work:

1. *Seek to be in the presence of positive people who share your ideals; place yourself in environments that support your spiritual growth.*
2. *Keep your clear, calm center when you are in the midst of negative thoughts and feelings; do not compromise your awareness of God's Perfect Presence.*
3. *Be a generator of positive and loving thoughts and feelings, so that you will enhance, and not detract from the experiences of those around you.*

All of the great spiritual teachers and religions have placed a high importance on keeping good company. We are told to spend time in good fellowship, or to seek *satsang* — the company of Truth: those who are dedicated to thinking and living in a Godly way. There is much to be said for keeping good company. Through it, we give and receive support to reach our highest goals, and to remain strong in the face of adversity. It is a way to keep our spiritual batteries charged. It is the true purpose of community. Swami Kriyananda said, "If you have just one or two spiritual friends with whom you can share your highest aspirations, you should consider yourself richly blessed."

There are many spiritual communities that have grown up in recent years. They are like lighthouses in a dark world. If you have contact with spiritually-oriented people, whether or not you live in a formal community, you are very fortunate. I thank God each day for the friends that She has sent me along this path, for I truly receive much from them. I met a woman who was on a brief visit to this country from Yugoslavia, where she is not permitted to worship God or gather with others to do so. She sat in on one of Hilda's classes and drank it in with an appreciation far greater than the regular students, who sometimes take the experience for granted. Perhaps hers is the kind of enthusiasm and appreciation that we need to have all the time if we are to realize our spiritual aspirations.

If you are fortunate enough to have the benefit of sitting in the presence of a real spiritual master, one who teaches in Truth and Love, you are very fortunate, indeed. Such a teacher can offer Grace that can remove obstacles, lessen suffering, and save a great deal of time from your path — lifetimes, perhaps. Cherish any opportunity you receive to be with a real teacher, as well as any group gathered in the name of God.

If you are required, as we all are, to be in the presence of people or environments that are generating negative energy — anger, fear, uncontrolled emotions or words — you must learn to hold firm and remain confident of God's Presence even — and especially — in the face of thoughts, words, or news of "evil." You can do this by meditating regularly, cultivating positive thinking, visualizing and feeling a brilliant aura of light or positive energy all around you, and by controlling your words and actions that would react *in kind* to negativity. It is of the utmost importance to *not* go into agreement or align yourself with the turbulent feelings that another is experiencing, or you yourself will enter a disturbed state of consciousness from which you, like them, will have to extricate yourself.

If you want to help someone who is experiencing worry, fear, or depression, you must stay centered in peacefulness. This is the most effective position from which you will be able to truly serve them. A friend of mine is a psychologist in a mental health clinic. When he first began the job, he was a mess; he took on the problems of many of his clients. He was headed for "burnout." It was only when he developed an ability to emotionally detach himself from his clients' lives that he really became effective. Many other mental health professionals have told me that they made the same discovery for themselves.

I would like to share with you several case histories that illustrate this principle. A man that I know has devoted his life to the selfless service of people who live in the ghettos of New York City. He gets them food, clothing, organizes activities for children, and does all that he can to help them out of whatever troubles he finds them in. He works with many alcoholics, drug addicts, and others whose lives are steeped in suffering. Once, he explained to Hilda, "The other night I came home late and I began to meditate before I went to bed. I felt horrible — as if there were some negative force all around me. I had to meditate and pray as hard as I could to get rid of it. Finally I regained my clarity, but I do not understand what happened."

Hilda explained, "You know, you work in some pretty heavy environments. You are subject to some tough vibratory rates. If you had been working hard all day and felt tired, your aura may have broken down a bit, and you may have absorbed some of the 'muck' (negative thoughts and violent feelings) from those you work with. Perhaps you needed to cleanse yourself of the negativity that you had taken on. Keep up your work, but be sure you get enough sleep, and do not overwork yourself."

Another friend of mine was ill for several days. She began to feel better, but all of a sudden she started to feel lonely and rejected, though she could not understand why. Her son then approached her and confided that he was feeling put down by his peers, and that he felt like he had no friends. Through her experience of illness, her consciousness of wholeness had broken down, and she assumed the lonely feelings of her son. She talked it over with him in a loving way, and they both felt better.

Does this mean that we should avoid or cloister ourselves from the world? Certainly not. Running away from negativity is not usually helpful. I used to use "bad vibes" as an unconscious excuse to separate myself from others. My idea of peace was to be off meditating somewhere by myself. That idea still sounds good to me, but now I see, too, that finding peace amid chaos is more valuable for our growth — and service — than finding quiet amid quiet. Jesus said, "Resist not evil, but overcome evil with good." Light is always more powerful than darkness. Evil, when confronted with love and positivity, flees like a thief in the night.

I learned this important lesson when I worked in an office with a woman who spent a lot of time complaining over the telephone. Once, when I was the only one in the office, her phone began to ring, and I began to pick up another extension, in fear of "catching" all the bad vibes on her phone. But then I thought, "This is ridiculous! What am I afraid of? If I am centered in Truth, thoughts of negation are meaningless. I refuse to be intimidated by nothing." So I used her phone, and, of course, no great disaster occurred. What did happen, though, was that I proved to myself that my own awareness of God is always more powerful than anything in the world.

Because our thoughts and our awareness are powerful, we have a responsibility to the people, the things, and the world around us. Just as we would not want anyone to empty a trash can of negation upon us, we must take care not to disturb others with our thoughts. A man at a yoga retreat came to Swami Muktananda, raving, "Swami! Swami! A terrible injustice has been committed! You must find me a new roommate. The man that has been assigned to my room smokes cigarettes. This inconsiderate oaf is polluting my room with his foul habit. You must remove this ignorant man and correct him!"

The swami thought for a moment and responded, "Yes, you are correct; an injustice has been committed. I shall transfer you to another room. But not because he is polluting the physical air with his cigarettes; it is because *you* are polluting God's air with your thoughts of judgement and your anger. He may be committing an injustice to his body, but you are committing a greater injustice to him and to your soul!"

We are constantly creating and recreating one another through our thoughts. This can be a vital key to improving troubled relationships. Relationships suffer when we hold negative pictures of each other. *If you want to bring a difficult relationship into the light of love, make up your mind to change your image of who both of you are.* Realize that the relationship will continue in a rut and you will tend to live out each other's negative expectations until one of you sees both of you as Godly. You do not have to wait for the other person to change; *you have the power to change the relationship for both of you.* As soon as you let go of your ideas of limitations about the other person or yourself, you set both of you free, and the relationship is likely to improve.

I once had a friend who believed I was clumsy. Now, I am not the great ballet dancer Nijinsky, but I am not particularly clumsy. When I was around this person, though, I found myself making foolish blunders, and he would harp on them and criticize me for them, and I just felt awkward around him. One day I realized that in being open to him in an undiscerning way, I was unconsciously tuning into and living out his thoughts of who I was. (And he was probably mirroring some of my unconscious thoughts that I am awkward, as well.) The moment I saw this whole pattern, I decided to maintain my inner clarity in his presence, and to stay centered and graceful no matter what he thought or said to me. At that moment, the relationship changed dramatically. I saw that I could help both of us by refusing to accept limiting thoughts about me, whether they came from him, from me, or from anywhere. By my holding to my innate O.K.-ness in the presence of thoughts of Not-o.k.-ness, those thoughts of limitation eventually dissolved, and I have since ceased to feel, think, or act limited in his − or my − presence.

Creating each other with our thoughts works for upliftment, as well. Why does it feel so good to be in the presence of someone who loves us? They are blessing us with their thoughts that we are beautiful and wonderful and loveable. We catch those thoughts, and as our thoughts vibrate in harmony with theirs, we begin to love and accept ourselves, too. This is the way to really make thoughts work for us. *We can create lovely and loving people around us just by tuning into the qualities that we would like to enjoy in them.*

I find that it is extremely important to remember that, because our real nature is one of Goodness and Godness, *any* thoughts to the contrary are not our own. At first, it may appear that they belong to other people, but as we realize that we are all One, it is clear that they cannot belong to anyone else either. Who, then, do they belong to? To a force of negation that belongs to no one, but has been kept alive in consciousness only by belief in it, like an old theatrical costume that keeps appearing in different plays only because actors are willing to put it on.

Which thoughts, then, really *do* belong to us? Those that are Divine; those that are born of Love; and those that shine with effulgent Light. We can believe that negation belongs to us only if we believe that we are less than Divine. Yet, said one who knew His − and Our − Identity, "You are the Light of the world." And the only thought that can belong to the Light is Light.

"What you imagine to be your thoughts are merely echoes of the voice of the world, a voice which bears no relation to your true identity with Light. Constantly meditate upon your true nature, and you will easily discern between that which is of Love and that which belongs to error.

This teaching is but an elementary training in separating yourself from that which you have imagined to be your own. Your growth is marked by freedom from the effects of misdirected musings of the mind. Be not dismayed at negative consequences of your past actions, for you are occasionally required to bear out the unfoldment of earlier thought patterns before the fruits of your present work make themselves visible.

It is of the utmost importance to be an ardent worker for the force of positivity. You bless your sisters and brothers by cultivating strong and loving thoughts about them. In so doing, you serve the transformation of their lives as well as your own.

Be peaceful in your work, and Peace shall find a home in you. That which is other than Truth cannot bind you, for you have been given dominion over the world. Share not the delusion of mortality. Cease to cling to ownership of illusions, and illusions shall cease to retain the image of binding you.

Freedom is your name."

THE MIND AS THE
SLAYER OF THE REAL

Facts, my dear Sancho, are the enemies of the Truth.
    — Don Quixote, Man of La Mancha

A young seeker trekked over treacherous mountain roads to find a certain teacher who, he was told, could answer the question that had long been gnawing at him. After days of searching, asking local villagers for clues, and depending on little more than intuition and faith, the pilgrim found the one whom he sought.

"Master," the earnest young man immediately asked, "How can I know what is Real?"

The sage was silent for a few moments, but not because he needed to think. Then he spoke. "If you want to know what is Real, then you must realize what is the nature of the mind that you ordinarily use to look at your life."

The student was not satisfied. "But how can this understanding show me what is Real?"

"Because," the teacher explained, "the mind is the slayer of the Real!"

What did the wise man mean? How can the mind slay the Real? If something is Real, is it not impervious to threat? What is the mind, anyway? And aren't facts necessary to discover the Truth?

No, the mind could never mar one iota of Truth. The Truth is eternal, and it is not in any way assailable. *Our perception* of Truth is, however, vulnerable, and it is too easily distorted by the web of

125

ignorance, spun by the crafty spider of the rational mind. In order to know the Truth, we must learn to recognize a Source other than facts.

Jesus and His small band of disciples were sharing a quiet retreat time by a clear, cooling stream in the mountains. The disciples were discussing who the people thought He was.

Thomas spoke first: "You are Jesus; of this only can I be sure."

"You are a great teacher," offered Judas, ". . . perhaps the best."

Peter stood up under the bough of a mighty tree and looked the Master boldly in the eyes. "I say you are the Christ — the Messiah — the Son of the Living God."

"And I say you are truly blessed, Peter," immediately responded Jesus, rising as He answered, "for this you could not have learned from any mortal man, but only from my Heavenly Father Himself. Your faith is the rock upon which I shall build my church."

We all have Thomas and Judas and Peter — and certainly the Christ — within us. Thomas is the over-thinking, inconclusive part of us which refuses to believe anything until it is proven "beyond a shadow of a doubt." The thinking mind is not willing to accept anything as proven, for then it would have thought its way out of a job, and it loves its job dearly. Think about it now, with your reasoning mind: What do you know, for *sure*? Can you not see two sides to every argument? If we pursue Truth with our mind, as soon as we come close to proving anything, some evidence for the opposite point of view is rushed into the courtroom. It never really reaches a satisfying resolution.

Judas is the betrayer of the Truth — the slayer of the Real. He represents the fearful aspect of us that sees threat where there is good will and finds a way to take blessings and negate them. In a sense, this way of thinking hands over our spiritual experience to the kangaroo court of the rational mind. It believes that it can win salvation by delivering the Christ in us to the judgement of the senses. It is sincere, but mistaken.

And Peter? Peter stands for the direct knowing of the heart, the blessedness of spiritual intuition, and the eternal knowledge of what is Real. He stands for an awareness of Truth that is independent of the judgements and opinions of men. Now ask your *heart*, "What is True?" You will not get an answer in words, but you will feel the eternality of the Truth in your soul. In the mind there are no answers; in the heart there are no questions.

At a certain point in our evolution, we seem to be inundated with questions and doubts. It would appear that our awareness of what is Real has been betrayed and delivered to the never-ending trial of worldly confusion. The thought may even cross our mind that there is no God, or that if there was, He is dead. But remember that there is one more personage in our story: Jesus, who represents the Truth ("I am the Way, the *Truth*, and the Life"). Though He was crucified, Jesus was resurrected as the Christ, in final demonstration of the incorruptibility of the Real.

If our vision of the Truth is clouded in any way, we must discover how the mind maintains its veil of ignorance. We must learn to observe how our errors in thinking tend to create unhappiness in our lives.

There is a famous story which gives us a lucid clue about how pain and suffering are unnecessarily created. A man walks into a dark room and sees the form of a deadly snake coiled at his feet. He becomes so frightened that he collapses and falls to the floor, dead. A few minutes later, another man walks into the same room, turns on the light, and finds the first man lying there with a coil of heavy rope at his feet.

In this parable, there was no real threat — but the *perception* of a threat was strong enough to bring about the same result as if the threat were real. This is the story of suffering in our lives. We see snakes, where, if we were to simply turn on the light, we would find a harmless rope. Think for a moment. What have been the snakes in your life that turned out to be ropes? How many things have you worried about that never came to pass? And if they did come to pass, were they as horrible as you imagined them to be? Probably not. One man actually kept track of all that he worried about. He discovered that of all his worries, 92% of them never came to pass, and of the 8% that did, he was somehow given the strength and the ability to deal with them successfully. Our worries are paper tigers.

A great statesman said, "We have nothing to fear but fear itself." The experience of fear is usually more debilitating than the event that we fear. ("A coward dies a thousand deaths, a hero only one.") Fear is always the result of the absence of the awareness of Truth. When we know and feel the Truth, it is not possible to hold fear.

I would like to share with you a little snake and rope story of my own. One day I was sitting outside a grocery store, eating a muffin. Just then, a car pulled up, and I saw my first girlfriend, whom I hadn't seen in many years, get out and walk into the store. To my amazement, I became very edgy. "Should I talk to her?" I wondered, " . . . Maybe it's better if I just say nothing!" I hadn't really resolved my feelings about her, and my mind and emotions jumped about like school children at recess. My heart was beating rapidly, and I was gulping down my muffin. In new age spiritual terms, I had "lost my center."

A few minutes later she emerged from the store, and I just sat there and watched her get in her car and drive away. As the car turned the corner, I got one final look at her. And do you know what? It wasn't even her! It was just someone who looked like her. It was a rope that I made into a snake. (And even if it was her, it would have still been a rope.) Meanwhile, I had wasted precious minutes of my life, being nervous, pumping poisonous chemicals into my body, and improperly digesting a good muffin that I could have been enjoying. I felt pretty foolish, but at least I had a good laugh at myself.

Our experience will tend to bear out any thought that we believe, even if the thought is not true. This is how ignorance perpetuates itself. There was a period of time when I took a vacation from Hilda's classes. At the time, I did not know that it was a vacation; I thought that I was leaving her teachings. I began to find things wrong with Hilda and her way of teaching. The rational mind, which is incapable of holding two opposing ideas, had to make her "wrong" so I could be right. It was real insanity.

One night I returned to one of her classes and found that her chair had been placed on a small platform so she could have a full view of all the people in the class. My mind thought, "Look at this Guru Trip. She must have an ego, to be put up on a stage like that!" I sat there through the evening, bored, and I looked at the clock more in those three hours than I have in all the years I have been with her. As I write my experience now, it just seems so obviously ridiculous, for Hilda's intentions with the platform and the chair were born only of the humblest purity, which I later came to realize. But my mind needed to uphold my position of not attending classes; it needed to find a reason for what I was doing. So it created Guru Trips, egos, and boredom where none existed. Meanwhile, I missed out on an excellent class. I did, however, learn a good lesson about the inadequacy of the mind as a judge. Truly, the mind is the slayer of our *awareness* of the Real.

It is also true that a little knowledge can be worse than none at all. At around the same time, there were two people coming to the healing sessons at Hilda's classes, for healing of glaucoma. We prayed equally for both of them. One was healed and the other was not. The one who was healed was a simple (perhaps uneducated) woman. Ironically, the man who did not get healed was an optometrist by profession. "Do you know why the woman got healed, and the optometrist did not?" Hilda asked us one night. "Because," Hilda explained, "she did not *know* that the disease was incurable, but he *did*."

On another night, Hilda offered us a game to play: "I am going to concentrate on a number. See if you can guess it." Many people raised their hands, but they were all incorrect. Finally, after a long time, someone shouted out, "13," and Hilda answered, "That's right!" She went on, "How many of you thought, '13,' but didn't say it because you thought it was too 'negative' of a number for me to think?" Quite a few hands went up. "The mind is the slayer of the Real," she explained.

The story of the world is essentially that of the *Emperor's New Clothes*. As I remember the story, the Emperor's tailors made some kind of blunder which resulted in their failure to have the Emperor's new suit ready for the big parade. So they convinced him that he was wearing a beautiful new garment that he could not see. He ultimately agreed that it was very beautiful and set out to lead the big parade, wearing no more than his long johns. The people of the kingdom were convinced, as well, of his full attire, and the parade proceeded with everyone agreeing to this big lie. Everyone, that is, except for a little innocent child, who exclaimed, "Look, Mommy! The Emperor doesn't have his clothes on!" at which point everyone realized that they had been fooling themselves, and the Emperor was very embarrassed.

The mind has a way of teaming up with our desires, in a sort of tag team of illusion. We get a new car, a new guitar, a new girlfriend, and for a few days or weeks or months, we feel satisfied. Then, inevitably, a little voice begins to speak to us: "Wouldn't you like a better one? Or maybe another one? A bigger one would be nicer, you know!" and so on. From the vantage point of the mind, happiness is always *there*, never *here*. As soon as we move to Oregon, or have our first baby, or get that raise, everything will be alright. But that is not how it works, really, for as soon as we get Oregon, the baby, or the

129

raise, there is always something else that we need to *really* make us happy. A friend of mine called it "the mythical ten percent." This is, as he explained it, "the ten percent *more* that if we had, we know would really satisfy us . . . Only problem is, it's always ten percent *more* than we have — no matter what we have!"

There is a tale about a man whose car gets a flat tire on an old country road. Seeing a farm down the road, he decides to ask the farmer to borrow a jack. As he walks toward the farm, he begins to think, "I hope he has a jack . . . Oh, he probably will . . . But what if he doesn't want to lend it to me? That would be pretty selfish . . . Well, if he doesn't, maybe he would do it for a few dollars. How much would be fair? . . . I'll offer him three dollars . . . But what if he wants five? I'll just have to give it to him! I have no choice. Even if he wanted ten, I'd have to pay it! What nerve! What if he wants more? He knows I'm stuck . . . I'm at his mercy! What if he wants all the money I have? . . . Let's see, now, I have about forty-five dollars in my wallet . . . If he wanted it all, I would just have to give it to him! That's downright robbery! What kind of man would take advantage of me like this?!"

As the man approaches the farmhouse, he becomes angrier and angrier. By the time he reaches the house, he is downright irate. He rings the bell, and the farmer answers the door with a friendly "Yes?" Red in the face, our friend spouts, "You know what you can do with your jack?! . . ." slams the door, and storms away.

Although the story is somewhat exaggerated, can you not think of experiences in your own life when you allowed the thinking mind to blow a situation so much out of proportion that you lost your ability to deal with it effectively? I can think of too many such instances in my own life. Our mind can be our best friend, but, uncontrolled, it can work against our best interests.

Our mind can confuse us to the point where actions bear no relation to reason. We do things for the wrong reasons, and we are not even aware of what we are doing or why we are doing them. A friend of mine once asked her brother, who was always rushing through yellow traffic lights, "What will you do with those extra few seconds that you seem to gain by speeding through yellow lights?" "Gosh, I don't know," he replied, with a blank expression on his face. "I never really thought about it."

This seems to spring from the same sort of unquestioning attitude which has escalated America's arms race with the Soviet Union. America and Russia have spent trillions of dollars to develop the most sophisticated weapons that, we are told, can destroy our planet fifty times over. It's called, in military terms, "overkill." To me, it is the same as "The Emperor's New Clothes."

The Truth is so simple. Some of the happiest people that I have known are the retarded, and the elderly in a nursing home I have visited. I am certainly not denying their difficulties, but I do see a peace in many of these people that I do not find in the normal thinking population. Like little children, many of these people have a refreshing innocence about them. "Let the little children come forth. Lest ye be converted, and become as little children, ye shall not enter into the Kingdom of Heaven."

It has been said that "the rational mind is a wonderful servant, but a terrible master." We must *use* the mind, instead of giving it free rein to run wild. The thinking mind helps us to organize our world and to create technology that makes our lives easier and safer. If we do not control the mind, however, it will team up with the mouth and the tongue, and together they will get us into trouble.

We can stay out of trouble, and in the light, by thinking with our heart. I am not speaking of the emotions, but of the wisdom of the soul. Our heart will never lead us astray, or slay our perception of the Real. The heart *is* the Real. It cannot be misled, because it does not confuse facts with wisdom. It does not doubt, because it lives in God. And it cannot be slain, because it is Eternal.

"In your heart is etched the Truth of Existence. Thoughts that lead you away from that Truth are but delusion.

We encourage you, nay urge you to use your faculty of discrimination. Be not afraid to challenge the illusions that you have been taught. The Truth shall never fail to be revealed to you, for ignorance cannot stand the scrutiny of inspection.

Suffering is born of wrong thinking. The root of pain is error in perception. There can be no error in Truth, only errors in the perception of Truth. If you yearn to end human suffering, know, then, what is Real, for this Knowledge is the only source of invincible faith.

What is Real can never be slain; it can only be hidden from the mortal eye. To see the world rightly, you must look from the viewpoint of immortality. This is the only perspective that can bring meaning to a meaningless life. Thoughts of mortality are the only veils that can shield the Truth from view.

March on like true soldiers of Love. Annihilate illusion with the sword of discrimination, and the Reward of all quests is yours. We tell you this: the Real is your only salvation. Nothing that is Real can ever harm you, and nothing other than the Real can ever bring you the Peace that you seek. Acknowledge God, and welcome your Self."

THE NECESSITY OF
POSITIVE THINKING

To think positive is to think with God. This must be true because God is positive and God can do anything. When we think with God, we can do anything.

The key to success in life is to know without a doubt that God is our Mother/Father who wants only the best for us. All failure stems from the mistaken thought that we do not deserve the best that life has to offer. We are Divine Children of God. We were created to be magnificent. We were created to be great.

I have grown to have such a faith, such a belief, and such a confidence in the never-failing power of positive thinking that I believe it to be an absolute prerequisite for all success in life. We've all got to believe in ourselves. We've got to believe in our families, our friends, and our businesses. We've got to know the rightness of our hopes, our aspirations, and our dreams. God is desperately looking for people who will trust in the dreams He gives to us. There are so few people who are willing to take the inspiration that God breathes into them and hold tenaciously to it until the possibility becomes a reality. The world is numb to imagination, to creativity, to life. The neon lights of the cities block our view of the stars. The world has settled for second best, and in so bargaining has settled for nothing.

There is a story of a man who comes to the outskirts of an ancient city. There he finds a gatekeeper sitting quietly. The traveler tells the gatekeeper that he has just left his old city, and that he is thinking of moving here. "What's this city like?" asks the traveler.

"What was it like in the city you came from?" returns the gatekeeper.

"It was a rotten place. People were unfriendly, there were no jobs, and the government was crooked."

"Well, that's pretty much what you'll find here," explains the gatekeeper, and the traveler moves on in search of a better city.

A few hours later, along comes another man with a suitcase, also seeking a new home.

"What was it like in your old town?" asks the gatekeeper.

"Oh, it was quite a nice place," tells this second traveler; "lovely people, nicely kept; a shame I have to relocate on account of my job."

"Well, that's pretty much what you'll find here," reports the gatekeeper, and the man happily enters the city.

How we use our mind is crucial to our finding and getting what we want out of life, and giving what we want to it. Success, love, and abundance are not given to a privileged few by the whim of a capricious God. Those who enjoy happiness do so because they have earned it with their thoughts. They have the faith that God is working for their good, and that every moment of life is a precious gift. By so thinking, they open the door to goodness and success.

The foundation of positive thinking is this truth:

TO THINK IS TO CREATE

If we want to make it in life, we need to *start* with our goals clearly in mind; we need to decide what it is that we want, and then get a sharp mental picture of it. Then we must hold steadfast to our goal until it is realized. Refuse to be distracted by thoughts of failure; The Beatles were turned down by several recording companies before they were accepted by one. We've got to believe that if God gave us an idea to do something, He'll find a way for us to get it done.

We cannot allow temporary setbacks to be a cause for disappointment. God often has a bigger plan for us than we have for our little selves. Recently I was working on making a tape of deep relaxation exercises for my classes. I had the hardest time getting it done. First the microphone didn't work, and then the recorder short-circuited, and it seemed that one thing after another went haywire. A project that I expected to take no more than a few hours turned out to take weeks. I did not understand it, but I persevered. Finally the tape was finished, and I eagerly sat down to listen to the final product. It didn't turn out! All that I had recorded had mysteriously disappeared from the tape! I really couldn't figure that one out.

In desperation, I telephoned an electronic engineer friend of mine to ask his advice. "Why don't you come to my house and use my equipment," he offered; "I'll be glad to help you with it." I was delighted! There he gave me use of very expensive and sophisticated recording equipment, plus his expertise in pushing all the right buttons at just the right time, the sum total of which produced a recording far superior to any that I could ever have done by myself. While God was saying a temporary "No" to me in my earlier attempts, He was actually saying "Yes!" to a much bigger idea.

"Yes!" is the most dynamic word in the English language. It is the symbol of affirmation, acceptance and positivity. It makes me feel happy and strong just to look at the word.

When I went to visit a beautiful, Christ-like teacher named "Freedom," he asked me, "Do you want to be happy?"

"I sure do."

"Then say 'Yes!' " he advised me, with much love in his voice. "Say 'Yes!' to God, say 'Yes!' to life, say 'Yes!' to Love, say 'Yes!' to your Self. Then you will be happy."

Too often we miss opportunities because we do not live in the expectation of goodness. We believe that something is too good to be true, when, in fact, blessings are the only things *good enough* to be true.

Norman Vincent Peale, one of the most dynamic and enthusiastic people there has ever been, tells of two salesmen at an outdoor sports exposition, selling motorboats in booths adjacent to one another. Sales were slow and customers few. An Asiatic gentleman with sunglasses approached one of the booths and, after a few pleasantries, told the salesman, "I would like to purchase one million dollars worth of your boats."

The salesman was annoyed. "Listen, friend," he grumbled, "it's been a bad enough day without a comedian . . . Come back some other time when I'm in a mood for a laugh."

"Very well, sir," the customer replied, "Good day."

The man with the dark glasses went on to the next booth, and told the salesman, "I would like to buy one million dollars worth of your boats."

This salesman did not bat an eyelash. "Yes, sir!" he smiled, "Which models would you like?" and he began to fill out an order form. To the astonishment of the first salesman, the customer took out his checkbook, wrote a deposit check for $100,000, shook the hand of the salesman, and went on his way. The buyer was a wealthy Arab executive, and the salesman received his standard 10% commission — in this case $100,000!

Understood on a more subtle level, abundance is not something that we create, but that we *accept*. The second salesman made the deal only because he was *willing to accept it*. We can look at God, consciousness, and man through the symbol of the hourglass. God's infinite abundance is above us, waiting to flow down, and we have the space to hold it all. At the meeting point, at that skinny little juncture of the upper and lower vessels, is our mind. It regulates how much can come through. If our mind is small, tight, and fearful, a few meager grains will flow through. If the mind is open, free, and expansive, all of God's riches can pour through. We receive as much as we let in.

Ernest Holmes gives a good illustration of this principle. He asks us to imagine three people praying for jobs. In his last job, A earned $100 a week, B earned $200, and C, $500. All of them use the same prayer or affirmation, and all of them get new jobs. The results: A's new job pays him $100, B's job, $200, and C's, $500. Each of them put positive thinking to work, but each one was rewarded only to the level of his expectation. There is no reason for this confinement, except in the subconscious thoughts of limitation held by each person.

Real positive thinking means learning to look at *all* of life from a positive viewpoint. It does not mean just making money, gaining health, and finding the right spouse (although these are all valuable demonstrations). Real positivity means seeing the blessedness in *everything*. It requires a complete revision of the way we look at life. It means tearing down our judgements and opinions of what is good and what is bad, what is right and what is wrong. It means owning up to the truth that God is and lives in everything, and there is not one thing that exists, or one event that occurs that is not blessed by the Light of God. Simply, it means being willing to give up our mortal limited opinions.

When we let go of these binding concepts, we are initiated into a new level of evolution: the realm of God consciousness. This simply means that we see all as God and all as Good.

Learning to see God in all requires effort, creativity, courage, and love. Our old thought patterns of lack and failure will kick and scream, and they will find the subtlest and craftiest ways to retain their hold on our consciousness, for, in truth, their very life is being threatened. And that is the very best thing that could happen to us, for their life is founded on erroneous thinking and illusion. To break out of this old way of thinking, we must at first make a determined effort to deny the ranting and raving of our old mind which tells us that something is wrong. When negative thoughts assert themselves, we must challenge them with the light of Love, and dare to live the truth of goodness. Many people believe that it is courageous to live through a negative life. I believe that to live a life dedicated to happiness, freedom and forgiveness is the most courageous of all.

Overcoming negation with love is a matter of attunement. We must concentrate on that which is Good, Beautiful, and True. If there seem to be 999 negative attributes of a situation, and one positive aspect, we must seize on that one good thing, bless it, hold to it with determination, meditate on it, be grateful for it, exaggerate it, and glorify it. We will find that our tiny trickle of goodness has opened into a rushing stream, and then into a mighty river which pours into the ocean of God's storehouse abundant.

There was a woman who found herself lying in a hospital bed, paralyzed throughout her entire body, except for one of her little fingers. For a long time she bemoaned her fate, nearly lost in melancholia. Then she started to concentrate on that little finger. She began to acknowledge it, bless it, and move it. Then, one morning, she was thrilled to find that she could move another finger, and then her whole hand! She kept praising God for the parts of her body that she *could* move, until her whole body became flexible and healthy. She was a living example of the biblical promise, "To him that hath shall more be given."

We can let go of any notion that we have that God wants us to suffer. Jesus was one of the most positive thinkers of all time. He knew that our potential for happiness is unbounded, and that we can all go beyond our limited notions of how good it can be. He knew that every one of us has a great deal to offer, and that we too often sell ourselves short. And he knew that we all have a right to the very best in life. It was for this reason that he told us, "It is the Father's good pleasure to give you the Kingdom."

Life is showering its gifts upon us at this very moment. There is a force of love and light that is streaming, rushing, pouring toward us from all angles at all times. All we have to do is to let it in. Blessings are being offered to all of us without condition or limit. It's all already given to us. The keys to the Kingdom are ours whenever we are willing to accept them. What we have to lose is fear, lack, limitation, and sorrow. What we have to gain is peace of mind, success, health, and love. We do not need to become anything that we are not already. We need only to say "Yes!" to what the universe would just love to give us. We need to think with God.

"*Positive thinking is the acceptance of Truth. When you open your mind to the possibility of the goodness of God, it allows Him the opportunity to pour blessings of Love and Light into the chalice of your life. When you align the thinking mind with the Creative Mind, you make available to yourself a power which you do not completely understand, but are fully capable of using for the upliftment of all.*

We cannot overstate the importance of right thinking. It is your key to abundance and strength. Your habit of erroneous thought can be reforged into a powerful tool for the benefit of all humankind. Make your life a pillar of positive being. You have the opportunity to see the Light in all things, for, in Truth, the Light is in all things.

What you call "negative" thinking, we do not call bad or evil, but a blockage, or obstruction to the outpressing of Truth. It is simply a distorted view of reality, and it is corrected only by a clear vision of what is. When the Truth is seen, ignorance can hold no power over your life.

Your responsibility to the expression of Truth in the times to come is great. We ask only that you accept Love. Think in harmony with God, and the secrets of creation, which have never really been hidden from you, shall be clearly revealed. When the dreamer awakens, the dream is exposed to be nothing. Align your thoughts and actions with wakefulness, and you shall laugh at the dream of your former patterns of being. We salute you and we love you."

The Emotions

THE THREE BODIES

A friend of mine took a course in juggling. The first lesson of the course, he told me, was this: You have to remember that there is always one ball in the air.

This, to me, is pretty much the story of life: There is always one ball in the air. The moment we think we have really gotten life nailed down, there is something new that calls for our immediate attention. When will it ever end?

I don't know if it ever really will end. I don't think we can ever find real peace in the world. If we want to be satisfied, we have to tune in to the Spirit, in which we are Whole, Complete, and Perfect. In God are all of our problems resolved, for God has no problems. A yogi was once asked, "Why did illusion come into existence?" He answered, "It never did!"

In the meantime, dealing with life — from within life — requires us to take care of our physical, emotional, and mental selves. In a way, they are each like a separate body, each having their own needs which we, the custodian of the bodies, must handle. We cannot always pay attention to all of the bodies all of the time, so we must give each one our attention as it calls for it. Our job is something like that of a mother nursing triplets, or, to symbolize our spiritual journey, we are like mountain climbers with three baskets to carry but with only two hands. We have to alternate which baskets we carry, leaving one basket at a time behind, and then catching it up. Mastering life means keeping all of our bodies "caught up" and balanced.

We are all familiar with the physical body. It likes to eat, sleep,

143

have sex, and enjoy sensory pleasures. On a deeper lever, it has the very important function of being a learning device to help us understand the lessons which we came to earth to learn. Those lessons are deeply connected to learning how to make peace within the body. We learn, though experience, how to work with the body. Sometimes we overindulge it, and that doesn't feel too good, and sometimes we underindulge it, if we take a path of asceticism, and that doesn't feel too good, either. Eventually, we must find a comfortable middle path for the physical body. This we know.

What many people are not aware of, however, is that the emotional body works in a similar way. Instead of eating, sleeping, and sexing, it fulfills itself though feeling emotions and different forms of excitement. Emotional energies are necessary for our journey up the spiritual mountain, and in the same way that we learn to master physical life, we must learn the proper way of caring for our emotional self. Our challenge is that the emotional body does not really care what it feels; it enjoys stimulation of any kind. It will feel nourished through joy, sorrow, exuberance, anger, surprise, disappointment, and even fear. Like the physical body, we must learn to keep it in harmony.

If we are not careful, we can overindulge the emotions with uncontrolled energies. Perhaps you know someone (really all of us, more or less) who is like an "emotional yoyo." One day they are on top of the world, laughing boisterously, happy, jumping, and singing. The next day they are somber and sullen, down in the dumps. As exuberant as they were yesterday, that's how melancholy they are today. They have fallen from the peak of elation into the valley of despair. And tomorrow, they might just as easily be at the peak again.

A friend of mine, for example, was in a roller coaster relationship with a woman, which was like many male-female relationships that I have experienced and seen. (Hilda calls it "love, fight, love, fight, love, fight, etc.") They were alternately together and apart over a long period of time. When I saw my friend one night, he seemed as if he was dancing on air. "I am so happy!" he exclaimed. "Betty and I just spent the day together, and we had the greatest time! Boy, things are really working out fine between us! I feel terrific!"

I smiled and said, "That's wonderful!" but I could hear in the way that he was speaking that he was floating on an emotional bubble — one that could break at any moment. I certainly did not want to burst it, so I kept my mouth closed, but I knew that it would not be long before the other side of the coin would show its face. (An Oriental sage once said, *"The bigger the front, the bigger the back."*)

I saw him the next night, and sure enough, his song had changed. His face was long and his demeanor cloudy. "What's happened?" I asked. "I don't know," he morosely explained. "I just talked to Betty, and things just aren't so good." The pendulum had swung the opposite way, and he had swung with it.

When we ride the pendulum of emotions, we are sure to swing from one end to the other. Intense emotional happiness is almost always followed by intense unhappiness. This is so because *if we allow our emotions to be tied to the events in our lives, we have given the power of our happiness to the changing tides of circumstances.* This is not real happiness, but transient happiness. Until we find an inner contentment, a peace that is not connected to the good and bad in our daily lives, we shall continue to ride the roller coaster of worldly events. Jesus said, "A Peace I give to you that the world cannot give." He was speaking of a Peace that does not depend on people, things, or events.

Emotions are Divine gifts that can take us to God when we use them for their highest purpose. It is wild, uncontrolled emotional indulgence that is harmful, for such intensity is bound to take its toll on our emotional and physical systems and "play us out." In so indulging, we do a disservice not only to ourselves, but to the people around us, for in our negativity we tend to sap energy from them and render ourselves unavailable to fully be with them in a community. *"You are the light of the world; a light under a basket cannot shine."* The world needs you and me, our love, our strength, and our positivity.

What to do, then, with our emotions, which are a very natural part of our lives? This is a wonderful challenge that each of us must master. Let's take a look at our options.

There is a school of thought that says that to handle emotions properly, they must be discharged immediately by intensely expressing them to those around us, especially to those with whom we are angry. I have experimented with this method (and had it experimented on me), and I have not found it to work very well in the long run. Yes, it is necessary to take out our garbage, but we do not need to dump it on our neighbor's lawn. And if we manage our household efficiently, we will have less garbage to take out.

145

THE DRAGON DOESN'T LIVE HERE ANYMORE

It was in an encounter group that I had a breakthrough realization about the place that emotions have in our lives and how we can use emotional energies for or against ourselves. In this group, Bruce was angry at Nancy for something, and he told her so. At that point, Bob became irritated with Bruce, because Bob did not feel that Bruce's reason was good enough to be angry about. This annoyed Sara, since she felt that Bob was jumping on Bruce unnecessarily, while Jo was hurt because she felt akin to Nancy, who was the object of Bruce's wrath. You can see the pattern. A vicious cycle of negativity built up, filling the room with a thick emotional smog, until some intelligent person yelled, "Now wait a minute! We're all so busy relieving ourselves of our angry feelings that we've forgotten one basic element of human communication: old fashioned common courtesy!" He was right. I suggested that we stop what we were doing and, for a change, tell what we liked about each other. The transformation was amazing. The air cleared, hearts opened, and communication was once again possible. That moment was the end of any belief that I had that we can help ourselves or each other by expressing our angry feelings without forethought or consideration of the feelings of others. Some may not agree with me on this matter, but I have had a lot more success telling my angry feelings to God than I have had through telling them to other folks.

There are many very satisfying ways to nourish our emotional bodies. Music, song, dance, poetry, walking in nature, sharing a cup of tea with friends, theatre, all of the arts, and a thousand other activities are uplifting and joyous to the soul. If I feel bottled up emotionally, I pick up my guitar and begin to play and sing. Before long, that energy has been transformed into creativity. Physical exercise is also very practical for the emotions. Yoga, jogging, or any other constructive physical activity is great. I am not suggesting that we will never feel any negative emotions, for they inevitably arise. I am suggesting that there are many constructive ways of dealing with them that will keep our bodies in equilibrium and harmony, and free our friends from the burden of our negation.

Hilda has explained that when we get angry, our emotional body is upset for twenty-four hours or longer. That's how long it often takes to get back into focus. As my emotional body has become more and more peaceful over the years, any negativity that I indulge wreaks havoc on it. I say "I indulge," for there are inevitably little irritations or upsets that could jar me if I feed them with my thoughts and feelings. If, however, I let them go before they bury roots like weeds, their effect is negligible. In this world, we are bound to be subject to upset. If we do not create it ourselves, we can pick it up from others. The trick is to let it go in *forgiveness* the moment we become aware of it. In this way, we can keep our emotional self in healthy shape.

At the other extreme, emotional starkness is akin to physical starvation. We cannot deny the sweet symphony of life. If we do, we become dry, dreary, and empty. This is not God's pleasure, either. I remember going through a period of this kind of unnecessary asceticism. I became too rigid and uselessly stark. One evening I was going through some old papers to throw them out (to detach myself from my past!) when I came upon an old poem, written to me by a dear friend. As I read it, my heart flew open and I felt a flow of healing love, like a soothing balm, fill the cracks in my emotional body. I had become arid, and my emotional body had become parched like a prairie in a drought. The poem was so full of love that I instantly felt nourished and fulfilled, like a starving man given a loaf of fresh, warm bread. It was a wonderful lesson for me. From this experience I learned to maintain a fulfilling balance in my emotional self — not too wild, not too stark, but somewhere in the middle, where it feels just right. I still have the poem.

The mental body works on the same principle as the physical and emotional bodies, and we must keep it in balance, as well. The mental body just loves to think. It does not care what it thinks, as long as it is thinking something. It is really quite indiscriminate. It is we, the master of the bodies, who must control and decide what we want to feed to our mental body. Just as we would not put poison into our physical form, we would also not want to feed our mind with garbage. Most people, however, do not realize that thoughts are things, and they will digest thoughts that result in a mental stomachache, also known as a "headache."

It is really true that the mind is like a thought junkie. It is addicted to thinking. I realized this for myself when one evening I was sitting on the toilet and I found myself reading over and over again the instructions on a can of Drano. Now, I know very well how to use Drano; I've used it many times. And even if I hadn't, one reading of the label would have been sufficient. But the real clincher was that, on

147

this particular evening, I had absolutely no use for any Drano. There were no clogged pipes, and I was not taking a chemistry course. I was simply sitting on the toilet. My mental body, however, was not sitting anywhere; it just wanted to think something, and Drano was good enough for it.

This experience showed me that the rational mind, if allowed to run unbridled, will indulge itself to a ridiculous extreme. There is an old story about two psychologists walking down a hall to the laboratory, when they pass one of their colleagues, who greets them with a smiling "Hello!" One of the psychologists turns to the other and ponders, "I wonder what he meant by that?" Thinking is great, but, like all other activities, it is best used in moderation.

I have discovered, as well, why sleep is such a marvelous gift. It is because, for a number of hours, we get our mind to shut up! Just think of how wonderful we feel after a good night's sleep. Our body is refreshed; healing has taken place; our emotions are smooth, and our thoughts clear. This is only because we have escaped the tyranny of the mind! Even so, the mind will follow us into the private realms of sleep, bugging us with useless memories of bits and phrases of the day's events, the rug that Aunt Mildred gave us for Christmas, how to ask the boss for a raise, and the moldy cheese that we must return to Grand Union before lunch tomorrow. It is only when we dive, purely out of self-survival, into the abyss of deep delta-sleep that we can escape this cosmic nudge of a mind, and have a few moments of peace and quiet! When Jesus said, "The evil of the day is sufficient unto itself," He certainly knew what He was talking about!

It is very difficult to get the mind to be quiet. One yogi said that if you could get your mind to stay on one thought for two minutes — just two minutes! — you would be a very advanced soul, indeed. This is why meditation is so valuable. To simply sit quietly for even twenty minutes, and to allow the mind to settle down somewhat, bringing it under conscious control, bringing it to one point, is a very valuable experience. It is, in fact, a real blessing.

As long as we're thinking most of the time, we might as well put into our mind the kind of thoughts that will lead to joy and freedom, and avoid those which lead to confusion. The world of thoughts is similar to that of emotions — there are thoughts that bring liberation, and thoughts that bring bondage. Whenever we read something, for example, we are making a deposit into the bank of our consciousness. We can choose which thoughts we will think. I usually like to read a little bit before I go to sleep. I find that the autobiographies of saints are more soothing to me than murder mysteries or stock market reports. But I can speak only for myself; you may find something else very calming. I was once at a retreat where I saw a woman reading *Emergency!* magazine, stories of ambulance calls, just before going to bed. "Jo!" I exclaimed, "How can you read such junky stuff before you go to sleep?" "Oh, I don't find it junky at all," she explained, ". . . In fact, I find it quite relaxing . . . I work on the rescue squad, and this gives me some good ideas!"

If any one of the three bodies goes unchecked, it can interfere with the proper functioning of the other two. They are like three roommates who share common living space. If one leaves its clothes lying around, it is a nuisance to the others. I went through a period when I believed it was not good for me to eat peanut butter or dairy products, nor should I eat before I go to sleep. There may or may not have been wisdom in these practices, but I carried them to an extreme.

My lack of moderation came to a head when, one evening, I took a short walk down the road from my house, and I began to feel very faint. I turned back toward home, feeling weaker and weaker with each step; I was not even sure if I would make it back to the house. Somehow I did make it, and the moment I walked through the front door, a fascinating process took over in my body. *Without any thought,* I found myself literally charging the refrigerator, grabbing the cream cheese and peanut butter, and devouring it as fast as I could stuff it into my mouth. I had no idea why I was doing this; I certainly didn't think about it or decide to do it, and I wasn't even hungry in the sense of my stomach wanting a meal; I just sort of stood by and watched the whole movie unfold. By the time I polished off the cream cheese and peanut butter, I felt fine and went off to an excellent night's sleep.

Now this may seem like something of a gluttonous act, but here is how I understand it: through my mental zealousness in denying myself certain foods, I may have created some sort of protein or vitamin deficiency. At some point, my physical body had been pushed about as far as it would be, and it had no choice but to break out in open defiance of its mental roommate and say, in effect, "O.K., buddy, you've had your fun, but I have needs too, so out of my way, for I want to survive, as well." A more polite way of describing it would be "cooperative co-existence."

This brings us back to our analogy of our climb up the mountain with our three baskets — the physical, emotional, and mental aspects of ourself. We must learn to strike a comfortable balance in meeting the needs of the different aspects of our being. A whole person is a balanced being. At the top of the mountain, we realize ourself to be the master of the three bodies — and all life. We have learned the meaning of balance, and in so learning, we reflect the balance of the entire universe. And even if there *is* one ball in the air — or one planet, or one sun, or a million galaxies — we've got it handled. We have to. We're created in the image and likeness of God, and God has everything handled.

"We seek strong and well-rounded persons to work with. Well-balanced persons are able to implement the Teachings with power and effectiveness. The energies of inner awakening must be channeled productively, and not dissipated through purposeless thoughts and emotional indulgence. We speak to you strictly on these matters, as they are vital to your progress, and your progress is of the greatest concern to us. We urge you to use common sense in your upward journey. Temper your lofty ideals with practicality and wisdom. A true disciple is a master on all levels. The challenges may now seem difficult or complex, but their necessity shall be made clear to you as you come to understand them more fully. Wisdom shall be given to you to deal with any matters on which you seek guidance with earnestness and sincerity."

THE WAY OUT

Captain Kirk and Mr. Spock were trapped behind an invisible but impenetrable wall. Their friend, Dr. McCoy, was being mercilessly beaten before their eyes, but there was nothing they could do to save him. Kirk's angry frustration increased with each precious moment. "We've got to do something!" screamed the captain, "We can't just let him die while we stand here and watch!"

Spock, the voice of reason, spoke with clarity and firmness: "Perhaps there *is* something we can do, Captain, but I believe it may not be exactly in the way that you are thinking."

"What's that?"

"I wonder if this wall that is stopping us is one of your own creation?"

"What are you talking about, Spock? . . . Out with it!"

"This force field that binds us may be a result of the wild emotional energy that you are generating. It appears that the angrier you get, the thicker the wall becomes. Perhaps if you relaxed and let go of your sympathizing with the doctor's pain, the wall might weaken, and we could then go to our friend's aid."

"Alright, Spock, it's worth a try. What shall I do?"

"Simply put your emotions aside for a few moments. Understand that we cannot help the doctor by anxious worry about him. Enter a clear state of mind in which emotions have no hold over you. This, I believe, is our only avenue of escape."

The captain closed his eyes and began to comply with Spock's suggestion. As he did, the force field began to weaken and diminish.

"It's working, Captain . . . Please continue," encouraged Spock. Within a few moments, the wall disappeared and the crew was free to release their comrade.

Our emotional energies are gifts from God. We have it within our power to bless the world or wreak havoc in it. Like all power, we can use it *for* or *against* our best interests. Our emotions can uplift us or entrap us. They are like the electricity which can light a light or build a bomb. Uncontrolled emotions are the most destructive force on earth; consecrated ones are the most healing.

One of my favorite stories is that of a Samurai warrior who came to a Zen master for instruction. "Master, I would like to know if Heaven and hell really exist," asked the Samurai.

The teacher heard his request and broke into mocking laughter. "*You* would like to know about Heaven and hell?! . . . Don't be ridiculous! Just look at you: you're fat, you're uneducated, and you're uncouth! What teacher in his right mind would invest his time in the likes of you?! . . . Go back to your camp and practice your silly exercises!" With that, the teacher turned his back on the man and ignored him.

The Samurai became enraged. His face turned red, he began to breathe heavily, and he drew his sword, ready to chop off the master's head with his next breath. Just as the sword was about to fall, the master turned around smoothly, and calmly told him, "That, sir, is hell."

The Samurai stopped cold and realized the profundity of the master's teaching. He saw instantly how he had created his own hell through pride and anger. Immediately, he fell at the master's feet in humble reverence.

The master looked down at him, lifted the Samurai's head, and quietly said, "And that, sir, is Heaven."

Our emotions can take us to God or they can take us to hell. They can save us or drown us. As the popular slogan reminded us, we can make love or we can make war. It's all in how we use our energies.

The "binding," or counterproductive emotions are fear, anger, guilt, worry, resentment, jealousy, pity, loneliness, lust, envy, pride, unworthiness, hatred, and all the other variations on these themes. They do not feel good, they make our life energy go haywire, and they release a huge amount of physical poisons into the body. A friend of mine in medical school showed me a picture of all the toxins that are spread throughout the body of a person who becomes angry, and I want to tell you that it was an ugly picture. It certainly made me think twice about anger. Beyond the physical damage these emotions do, they distort our perception and disturb our ability to enjoy loving, fulfilling relationships. In addition, uncontrolled emotions stir up a smog of confusion around us that tends to muddy the clarity of persons near us who are susceptible. In short, they do not serve us or the world.

There is no evil, wrongness, or badness in experiencing these emotions, nor need they be any cause for guilt. They are simply a natural carryover from an earlier state of evolution that we all share. At some point in our personal growth, however, we realize that these emotions do not really serve a life of harmony and inner peace, nor do they help us to make the kind of contribution we would like to offer to the world. It becomes clear that loving and calm words and actions work, and chaotic ones do not. At that point, the old binding emotions begin to drop away by themselves because we no longer believe in their usefulness.

Two friends of mine took up zen. Whenever they became upset or had a problem, they would go to the *roshi* (teacher), tell him all their troubles, and ask him what to do. His advice to them was always the same: "More *zazen* (meditation)!" No matter what they told him: "More *zazen!*" He was not telling them to run away from the world, or to deny or negate their turbulent feelings. He was telling them that they could only be effective in the world when their minds were clear and their emotions calm. Otherwise, they would just be making more trouble for themselves.

Once, Hilda was answering telephoned questions on a radio program. I was amazed at how violently people reacted to her talking about God. People would call up and argue, "But what about war?!" or "There's too much crime to waste time praying!" or "Instead of meditating, why don't you go out and do something!" and so on. She met each one of them on a point of agreement, saying, "Yes, you're absolutely right; this is a time for action and service to the world. The best way we can serve the world is by starting from our calm center. When we make contact with the Peace within ourselves and we find our Inner Source, we are then in a perfect position to go out and make change; until then, we only contribute to confusion. Meditation without action is a cop-out, but action without meditation is fruitless."

Hilda has given us yet one more teaching about the nature of emotion: when we indulge or express any emotion, we tune into, or open ourselves to all of the energies of that emotion that are now being expressed or have ever been expressed. This is a very powerful statement, and an even more potent lesson in practical living.

If we become impatient, for example, we align ourselves with all the impatient thoughts and feelings of every tired commuter in every traffic jam, every college student in a long registration line on a hot day, and every hungry person in a crowded restaurant. Because thoughts and feelings are things, when we generate them they linger in the air like flourocarbons in the ozone layer. When we tune in with a certain emotion, Hilda explains, we make a little wedge in our aura for all of those energies to come in at our unconscious invitation. It's a little like buying a McDonald's franchise. Because you make a commitment to the organization, you get to wear the same color uniform, advertise through the same signs, and eat and serve the same hamburgers as thousands of other McDonald's employees. You become identified with McDonald's, and in so identifying yourself, you tune in with all the thoughts about McDonald's by every other McDonald's worker and customer that there ever was — 35 or 40 Billion, to be exact. If you like McDonald's energy, then you are in your right place. If not, you might do better to align yourself with an organization that comes closer to the energies that you want to feel and express, like Pizza Hut or maybe even Howard Johnson's.

These are light examples, but there is a great promise in the principle of attunement: *we can link our energies to those of our ideals, and so reap the benefit of all those who have lived for what we aspire to.* If we desire to live for Truth, every time we act with integrity, we tune in with and receive the grace of all those who have lived for Truth. In so doing, we actually join Ghandi in his march to draw salt from the ocean for the liberation of India. When we think a thought or do an act of faith, we stand with Moses on the shore of the Red Sea. And when we love, we literally join Jesus at His Sermon on the Mount. Put even more directly, when we love, we become the Christ.

This is the promise of Grace. When we cultivate the higher emotions of joy, peacefulness, appreciation, devotion, and enthusiasm, we lift ourselves up on the magic carpet of the accumulated thoughts and deeds of all who have ever loved goodness and loving kindness. As we open our arms in appreciation, we are blessed by a power greater than that of our seemingly small action.

Every act of love is infinitely powerful, and so is every thought or feeling that we cultivate in Love's Name. The world is in the sorry state that it is because we have underestimated the tremendous significance of what we think and feel. And the salvation of the world will come through the acceptance of every tiny deed as a way to see and express God.

Once again we find choice before us. Because our emotions are simply gross extensions of our thoughts, the secrets of emotional transformation are the same in nature as those of thought. Destiny is consistently in our own hands. We did not create the choices, but we certainly have the power to exercise them. We did not make God, but we can certainly know Him. We did not make Love, but we can certainly become It.

"It is now for you to reevaluate your emotions and come to a new understanding of the nature and the purpose of the energies that you experience. Love is your key to finding Peace. As you remain calm and quiet, God instantly fills your heart. His willingness to abide with you is constant. It is only emotional turbulence that stands between you and your knowledge of His gentle Presence.

There is infallible guidance available to you through the door of purified emotion. We speak not of the occult, for Love is not occult. Nor do we speak of mediumship, for you are inseparably One with God. We speak only of the realization of your Divine Heritage, which is an ever burning Light on the altar of your heart.

In calling you to emotional mastery, we do not ask of you anything of which you are incapable. You are most certainly able to control your emotional energies to a degree of quietude beyond your current expectation. In such serenity, you hear His simple bidding. You are the master of your destiny. As you claim this identity, your effort is rewarded with the vision of Truth.

We do not encourage unnecessary starkness. Enjoy life while you are learning. All of the elements of your Self are created for the expression of Divine Love. Learn to raise your emotions to this Holy end. Nothing more is required of you than the Peace that you seek. Thus is your redemption made easy for you through your awareness of your own Divinity."

The Body

HEALTH, WHOLENESS, AND HOLINESS

All the lessons of living are about allowing healing to take place. Health is the easiest thing in the world, and dis-ease the hardest. We do not need to add anything to our lives to be healed. We need only to tune into our own flow — the very flow that God is always whispering in our ear. Health is our natural condition, and it will always manifest itself when we attune our thoughts and actions to the guidance of our still, small voice, ever calling us to our own Peace.

There is a legend about a butcher who used the same knife for twenty years without having to sharpen it once. The townspeople were astounded, and one day one of his customers asked him, "How can you do so much cutting and keep the blade sharp?"

"It's really very simple," the master explained. "I do not try to cut through gristle or bone. Where I feel resistance, I move the knife slightly, and make the necessary adjustment. My knife is always speaking to me, and I work in harmony with it."

The physical body speaks to us in the same way, and if we are willing to listen to its messages, we can avoid disease. If we experience illness or its warning signs, it is God's way of showing us — through the physical body — that we need to make a course correction in something that we are doing *and* a way that we are thinking. Illness is *not* a *punishment*, but a *message* to us from a loving God, telling us what we need to do to stay healthy and happy, which is exactly that way She likes to see us. How cruel would God be if She allowed us to continue without correction in a way of life that is fraught with anxiety and struggle. It is only out of loving compassion that She sometimes jolts us a bit to head us away from a way of living that we will not admit is not working for us.

I learned this principle for myself — the hard way. One day, as I was merrily driving along in my wonderful Honda, I saw lit on my dashboard a red light which I had not noticed before. It said "BRAKES." I tested my brakes, and they seemed fine. I assumed that there must have been a short circuit in the lighting system, and since the car was running well, I left it as it was. Sometime later, however, my front brakes began to grind, and they sounded dangerous. When I took it to the repair shop I was told that the brakes had worn down to the metal, and due to the front wheel drive construction of my car, it would be a major job to repair. If I had caught the problem earlier, I would only have needed to replace the lining at a cost of about thirty dollars. Since I had let it go so long, however, a lot more parts and labor were required, and I ended up paying over $200 for the job. I could not blame the car, the mechanic, the light, or God. I could hold no one accountable but myself. Had I but read the owner's manual to see what the light was all about, I would have seen that it was a warning sign of things to come, and I could have saved myself some money. An expensive lesson, but a good one.

When we understand that disease is a teaching, we can begin to *learn from it* instead of simply being intimidated by it. There is a connection between our body and our mind. Health — and disease — begin in the mind (the way we think), expand to the emotions, and are finally expressed in the physical form. *The physical body is the last place we see the signs of illness;* by the time disease appears in the body, we are seeing the result of a long process that began with a pattern of thought. That pattern of thought brought about a series of emotions which eventually created a change in the physical patterning of the body, which we call "illness." If we can be sensitive to the messages we are being given through the experience of mental or emotional unrest, we can make the changes we need to make *before* the message is manifested in the physical body.

But because most people do not believe that there is a relationship between the way we think and the way our body feels, when disease appears they seek only to get rid of the symptom, and do not look any deeper to find the problem. Someone with a headache, for example, may be inclined to take an aspirin to remove the discomfort. This may be helpful, but the most helpful medication would be to learn to relax, let go of worry, and not to think so hard. When we take an aspirin or any other drug, we are simply masking the symptom that is a message to us from our higher self, calling our attention to what we need to do to make our life work better. The idea is, of course, to make the symptom go away, for all forms of pain are, according to their nature, not the way we were meant to live. The crucial issue is not *whether* to make the hurt go away, but *how* we do it. Too often we are prone to cover it up with a bandaid and hope that it will go away, or to remove the organ, as if the organ were the cause instead of the effect.

But because disease is a teaching for our *spiritual* growth, it will not go away until we learn the necessary *spiritual* lessons. We cannot, in the long run, sidestep doing what we need to do by avoiding the cues that remind us of what we must learn.

Eric Butterworth tells a marvelous story that neatly illustrates this very important principle. The copilot of a large airliner approached the pilot and told him, "Bob, I just saw the red warning light under 'LANDING GEAR MALFUNCTION' flashing on and off."

"So, what did you do?" quickly asked the pilot.

"I unscrewed the lightbulb!"

I do not know if this is a true story (I hope it isn't), but it certainly symbolizes the approach that many of us have taken toward ailments. A more effective approach would be to take a clear and honest look at the way we are living our life, and see how we can change, *from inside out*. It is easier to take a pill than to change. Real growth, however, requires change, and life is, in fact, pretty much about making the changes that lead to our greatest good.

Let's be a little more specific. Because the body is a symbol of the thoughts and the emotions, each organ of the body corresponds to a different and specific thought pattern. Where the physical body ails is the key to the mental, emotional, or spiritual work that we need to do.

I knew a scientist, for example, who was very fixed and rigid in his thinking. He had a case of arthritis. The arthritis did not cause the thinking; the *thought pattern* was *pictured* in the arthritis. What he needed to do was to loosen up and take life a little easier. Another friend had a skin eruption (rash) that cleared up when she discovered what in life she was reacting (erupting) against. In the case of constipation or problems of the eliminative organs, the question might be, "What is it that I am not letting go of? What am I holding onto tenaciously?" When we find an answer to the question, we will probably find the organ healed, as well.

Because the mind is the source of all of our experience, we can always trace our required lessons back to a pattern of thinking. When we discover the pattern of thought that needs to be changed, the physical symptom will disappear, for its function as the communicator of a lesson is no longer needed. Our bodies, like our lives, are not haphazard, and neither are they beyond our ability to understand their teachings and to see how healing can be accomplished.

At this point I want to make clear that I do have a tremendous respect for doctors, hospitals, and modern medicine. I believe that God heals through pills, machines, and surgery. I have seen doctors save lives that herbs could not, and I believe that antibiotics and painkillers save us time and energy that we could put to good use in other ways than to struggle with disease. To deny the blessing of medicine would be limited thinking. God doesn't limit Herself in the ways She is willing to express Herself. The important issue is *appropriate* use of medicine. There is a time for "natural healing" and there is a time for natural healing *through* medicine. We must be big enough to allow God to be big enough to heal us through whatever method She sees fit. If She gave someone an idea for a vaccine or an appliance, there must be a place for it. God doesn't waste any ideas.

No matter what form through which we accept healing, we must always remember that God is the only healer and that health is our only birthright. We cannot be healed if we believe we deserve to be ill. We must understand that because God is 100% God, we deserve to be 100% healthy. This chapter is called "*Health, Wholeness* and *Holiness*" because all of these words come from the same root, from the same idea in the Mind of God. When we remember we are holy, we are wholly healthy. If we are not healthy, we have missed the mark somewhere. As the poet Leonard Cohen put it, "If you're not feeling holy, your loneliness says that you've sinned." The Grace that supercedes sin is that all we need to do to get healthy is to get clear.

We need to give up our ideas that we deserve to suffer, to be ill, or to be punished. These thoughts are of an old way of thinking that is no longer useful to one who knows him or herself to be a reflection of Godly Light. To such a one, ease is a natural way of being, and health the natural way to express it.

A sign posted at a highway construction zone:

THE INCONVENIENCE IS TEMPORARY.
THE IMPROVEMENT IS PERMANENT.
THANK YOU FOR YOUR COOPERATION.

"God's Love is the only force that can heal you, and yet is it the very one that you have denied. You are annointed with the Holy Spirit of the living God. Your Destiny is to know yourselves as children of effulgent Light.

Yes, beloveds, you are whole. Accept no destiny less than Holiness. The world would have you agree with its dismal dream of limitation, but the Light would have you soar like the eagle of your sacred visions. In limitation is only sorrow, and in wholeness serenity. Choose wisely, for when you choose for yourself, you choose for all.

You have believed that your health is a function of your body, but we say to you now: Look deeper. There is no aspect of your experience that is unrelated to Spirit. See lessons in your physical experience, and you discover the Voice of God speaking in your life. The Spirit is eternally whole. In this principle there is no compromise. Believe only in Spirit, and you believe in God. Believe in chance, and you are lost. Choose wisely, beloveds.

The healing that you seek is available to you now. The Love that you ask for is freely given in this moment. You are a chalice of Universal Life, and the fulfillment of your journey is the consummation of His purpose for your existence.

All blessings be upon you."

The Flow of Life

LETTING GO

One evening I discovered some scrumptious-looking peanut butter cookies in the pantry of the house where I was staying. I really like cookies. (My mother used to give me cookies and milk every day when I came home from school, and I have only the fondest memories of the unbeatable combination of chocolate chip cookies, milk, and *Superman*.) I started to take one of these cookies, but my conscience began to wriggle a bit, since they were not mine. I knew that I could probably snitch one or two, and everyone would think that they were eaten by the rightful owners. But I decided to ask first. When I did, the person who baked them brightly replied, "Oh yes, sure, you can have them all! No one else likes them. Consider them yours!" (This is one of the advantages of being into health foods — no one else wants what you like.) I gave it up, in asking, and I got it all back. Yum.

I have given a lot of thought to the teaching, *"Give it all up and you get it all back."* I believe that this is an immensely potent formula for finding freedom and joy in living. Every time I have put this principle in action, it has worked. Whenever I have let go of something, God has either given it back to me, or given me something better, or shown me that I'm better off without it. More and more, I have come to see that God is always giving us exactly what we need for our highest good, and at no cost to anyone.

One evening, for example, a friend and I went to see a production of *Godspell*. Due to an error in the ticket office, two sets of tickets had been issued for our seats. We found ourselves potentially at odds with two other people who felt they had a right to the same seats. My friend said to me, "Well, we were here first, so let them find other seats." I saw that the other folks were getting a little upset, and I remembered Jesus' teaching, "If someone wants your coat, give them your cloak as well." So I said to my friend, "Let's let them have the seats; I think we'll be alright." And so we gave them the places. When I went to the ticket office to explain our predicament, the manager was very kind. He gave an usher two more tickets for us, and we were shown to two seats much closer to the stage, in a far better location.

The idea that "He who humbleth himself shall be exalted," is one of the most powerful and practical truths that I have ever encountered. It speaks of the miraculous principle that we do not need to "power-trip" our way through life; we will come out better in the long run if we allow God to take care of us.

Ironically, we can have only that which we are willing to give up. What we are not willing to let go of becomes a source of anxiety and threat. What we resist, persists. The second part of Jesus' teaching was, "He who exalteth himself will be humbled." The rabbis in *The Ethics of the Fathers* taught the same truth in a strikingly similar way: "He who seeks to gain reputation shall lose it; he who does not seek reputation shall win it." When I hear these proverbs, I usually think of the political figures involved in the Watergate scandal. It seems that the more they tried to gain or hold onto power, the more it backfired on them and resulted in their fall.

This principle applies to people and relationships, as well. A relationship based on clinging, possessiveness, or attachment cannot work. There is constant worry, fear, and threat. The moments of satisfaction in such a relationship are deceptive, for they lead only to pain. If "I have him/her" can bring joy, then surely, "I am losing him/her" will bring sorrow. *It is only when we hold people and things lightly that we can enjoy them fully.* Life is a constant flow of coming and going. Things and people come into our lives and they leave, just as sure as they came. Sometimes they stay for a moment, sometimes for a lifetime. We never really know how long it will be. Nor do we have any real control over how long we will share the path with someone. Our key to happiness is to enjoy a relationship while it lasts, allowing the person and the relationship complete freedom to evolve in the highest way for them, according to God's plan. Clinging never feels good. It brings hardship to the one who would possess, and to the one he or she would possess. Possession may be nine tenths of man's law, but it is not even one tenth of God's law.

If we feel pain at the loss of a relationship in our lives, it is not due to the loss of the person's presence; it is due to our *clinging*. When we stop clinging, the pain ceases. God may have been responsible for the loss, but we are responsible for the pain. This may sound stark, but it is true. In the long run, we are much better off for letting go. Is it not better to be free and happy than to be attached and in pain?

When a relationship ends, it is an opportunity to apply the principle of "Let go and let God." This means to accept that God is working for our highest good, and never against us. In such a situation, I would assume that He would not stop this relationship unless He had a good reason, and that this ending is really a beginning. Perhaps there is something or someone better in store. Perhaps we have given and received and shared and learned all that we could, for the time being, and now it's time to grow into a new and better space. That has to be the way it is; God wouldn't make a mistake with His child's life.

We must release the old to make room for the new. A friend of mine was praying and praying for a bigger and better apartment which she needed for herself and her family. But she was not doing anything about it. One day she was evicted by her landlord, and she was forced to find another place. The place that she found was the one that she had been praying for all along! She could not receive it, however, until she gave up the old one.

There is a lovely Zen story that delightfully describes this principle. A man came to a teacher for enlightenment. "Sit down," invited the teacher; "Let's have some tea." The teacher began to pour tea into the man's cup, but instead of stopping when the tea reached the brim, he continued to pour the tea, causing it to run over the cup, onto the table, and onto the man's legs.

Startled, the man jumped up and exclaimed, "What are you doing?! Can't you see that the cup is full?!"

"You have just learned the first lesson in Zen," explained the master: "You must make yourself an empty cup in order to learn. One who thinks that he already knows, cannot be taught anything new."

Put in other words, it is only when we stop trying to hold onto the past that we are able to fully accept the blessings that the present can offer us. Clinging (in reminiscence or bitterness) to a thought or an experience is the same as clutching to a person or a thing. It takes us out of our here-and-now center and detracts from our experience of the fullness of this moment. Too often we hold onto memories of "The Good Old Days," when we were "really happy," and when things went just right. If they were *really* good, then we would not feel pain in missing them now, for what is good is liberating, and if we are bound to the experience, it certainly did not liberate us very much. The *real* good old days were those which showed us that we are free to live fully in *any* moment, including — and especially — *now*. If I enjoyed something in such a way that I feel sorrow for its absence, I enjoyed it in the wrong way. I enjoyed it in a way that led to suffering, and not to freedom. I enjoyed the mortal, changing element of the person or the thing, and that element can never bring peace. Only when we enjoy the eternal, Godly, inner aspect of an experience can it bring us real happiness. When I look back on the experiences that I cherish, I feel no sense of loss whatsoever, for those were the experiences that made visible to me the Light that is within me now. That Light was there then, It is here now, and It will be here tomorrow. It is not the person or the experience that counts, it is the *spirit* that is precious, and spirit is present in all experiences. People and events are like teacups — vessels — through which God gives us love and loving lessons. Though teacups may fade, crack, or be lost, the God that gave them to us in the first place is always present, with an endless supply of new vessels in His Divine pantry.

When we cling to someone in resentment, we bind ourselves to him or her by our thoughts and memories. The river of life would have us flow to the ocean, but we would cling to the rock upon which we dashed our foot. We cannot change the events in our past, but we can always change *the way we look at* those events. Those who seemed to bring us pain and hardship were our teachers who presented us with challenges which helped us to grow into greater personal strength. When we realize that the problem was not in them, but in the way we were *looking at* them, we free ourselves as well as them.

We fight life only because we do not perceive our own best interests. It is rare that we can know how any particular experience will fit into the whole plan of good in our lives. Often there is a difference between what we think is good for us, and what God *knows* is good for us. The story of Joseph is a magnificent illustration of this truth. When we left the story, Joseph, whose brothers had sold him into slavery, had become Prime Minister of Egypt. Soon after that, famine struck the region, and Joseph's brothers were driven to seek food from

Egypt, the only land that had a reserve. They found themselves face to face with Joseph, though they recognized him not. In forgiving love, Joseph gave them food and revealed his identity to them. When they felt sorry and wept for their misdeed, Joseph consoled them: "Do not feel bad; you meant it for evil, but God meant it for good."

I like to believe that God means everything for good. This is difficult to see from a limited point of view, but easy and natural to see from the grandest point of view. It is said that "Prayer is the contemplation of the facts of life from the highest point of view." When we look at our experience through Divine eyes, we can see the essence of goodness in all experiences, and letting go is no longer a trial to be feared, but to be embraced as an opportunity to be filled in with something wonderful.

The famous Prayer of St. Francis affirms:

> *It is in giving that we receive*
> *It is in pardoning that we are pardoned*
> *It is in dying that we are born to eternal life*

Some have paraphrased the last line, "It is in surrendering that we are born anew." When we surrender all to God, we are not failing, or being weak, or losing anything. To the contrary, we are making ourselves available to be filled with the Holy Spirit, which is the strongest power in the universe, and all the Love that we ever really wanted.

We eventually see that it is not *things* that we must let go of, but our *attachment* to them. We can remove ourselves from things, but if we keep mental ties to them, we might as well be with them; in fact, we would probably do better to be with them, for then we could learn to let them go. There is a story of a yogi who went off to a cave for many years to renounce the world. The day he returned to the village, someone accidently bumped into him and he got angry. What good did all those years of "renunciation" do for him? He would have served himself and the world better to live in the city until he no longer got flustered when someone bumped him. Then he would have been a real renunciate, free to live in the city, or in a cave, or anywhere his heart guided him.

Attachments take the form of thoughts of *"mine."* A mine is

173

something that blows up when you step on it. I was once experiencing the pain of being attached to someone. I went to a lecture by a beautiful Buddhist monk who said, "All of our troubles are in the mind. That is where our problems start and that is where they end." His words changed my whole outlook! There were no physical chains binding me to the person; the chains were forged in my mind and the lock was fastened with my thoughts. The key to freedom was in the thoughts, as well. If a thought can bind, a thought can free.

When I leave this world, I do not want to be bound to anything — not to any object, any person, any philosophy, any unfulfilled desire. I want to head straight for the Light, with no delays on the local track. My prayer is to drop all of my luggage and to leave my arms free to embrace God and God alone. I don't want to have to come back for anything, unless I am to serve. I have never found any real or lasting pleasure in any physical object or person. Ironically, the more I have given up attachments to things and people, the more I am able to love and enjoy them.

In the end, we must give up our striving, as well. One sage said, "*Give up your lust for growth.*" Striving for growth is a necessary stage of the path, but finally we must accept fullness from a Source *within* ourselves and renounce the illusion of seeking or reaching out. As long as we see God, Peace, or Consciousness as *outside* of ourselves, we shall never know Him completely. The moment we find God within, our searching comes to an end, for we realize that He has been within us all along, and ever shall there remain.

The great yogi Tat-Walla said, "The last thing to go is God." He did not mean that God goes, for where could He go? What Tat-Walla meant to go was our *thought* of God as "Him," "Her," or "It," which creates an artificial separation between us and God. If we really want to be One with God, we cannot relate to God as an "other." We must relate to God as Self. When Ramakrishna was asked to describe God, he went into silent ecstasy. There was nothing he could say in the state of God. Who could he talk to? Lover and Beloved had become One.

So "God" must go, too. Some would call this blasphemy, but they called Jesus a blasphemer when He declared, "I and the Father are One." Loving God, serving Him, fearing Him and worshipping Him come to an end when we *are* Him. Neem Karoli Baba said, "Even better than having the *darshan* (sitting in the Presence) of Christ is to *become* the Christ."

> *All that I am*
> *All that I do*
> *All that I'll ever have*
> *I offer now to you*
>
> *All that I dream*
> *All that I pray*
> *All that I'll ever make*
> *I give to you today*
>
> *Take and sanctify these gifts*
> *For your honor, Lord*
> *Knowing that I love and serve you*
> *Is enough reward*
>
> *All that I am*
> *All that I do*
> *All that I'll ever have*
> *I offer now to you**

*"All that I am" by Sebastian Temple, Copyright © 1977, Franciscan Communications, Los Angeles, California 70015. Reprinted with permission.

"There is a freedom that befalls you who are willing to trust in God. You once attempted to gain security, power, and life through fearful clinging, yet to what avail? Your observation of those in your midst who are at peace with themselves has revealed that sharing is the very source of joy.

Because the values of the world are founded on distorted perception, you have been taught to believe that accumulation is success. That belief has all but departed from you now, as you have discovered that fulfillment cannot be found in things, but only in Spirit. The realm of selfless sharing extends to you its Holy invitation, awaiting only your acceptance of its joyous welcome.

Your happiness is completely dependent on your confidence in God's ability to give you that which you cannot give yourself. Your admission of the impotence of your striving self is the condition for your realization of the infinite power of your Divine Self. Release the goals that you have made for yourself and allow them to be replaced by the Goal that God has always had for you, one of total union with your Divine nature.''

GO WITH THE FLOW

I remember the summer I graduated from high school. Around the end of August, just about when I was getting ready to leave for college, I felt a sense of being lost in space with no one place I felt was home. Most of my old friends had gone away to college or were getting ready to be married, and I did not know anyone who was going to the college I was about to attend. I knew that there would be good friends awaiting me when I actually arrived, but I knew, too, that the time was not yet ripe. I felt as if I were in a kind of vacuum.

There is a stage like this on the spiritual path. Many sincere aspirants experience a period of seeming emptiness in which the old has lost its appeal, but the new has not yet arrived. It is a time when old friends, activities, and interests are no longer attractive, but new ones have not come along to replace them. Many students on the path say, "I don't feel like doing the things I used to enjoy, and I have the feeling that there is something good in store for me — something better than what I was used to — but I don't really know how to find it."

Hilda has described this in-between state as a "corridor between rooms." We have left our history, but not yet claimed our Destiny. This is a normal, natural, and necessary process, and it is, in fact, a very good sign. It means that we have completed — graduated from — one era of our growth, and we are now ready for something new and better. (Losing our old friends means that we are on the right track; it's when we hang out with the same people all of our lives that we know that we are in trouble!)

What we need to do during such a transitional time is to mobilize

177

faith and to realize that it is only a matter of time until our aspiration becomes our Reality. If you are moving from an old house to a new one, you are bound to spend a certain amount of time on the road between the two. This can feel a little insecure, especially if you've sold all of your furniture to make your transition lighter. While you are traveling, it is the vision of your new home that gives you the strength to keep on driving, and the expectation of a new and better way of living that makes the trip worthwhile.

If we can just let go and trust in the process of our advancement, we can appreciate the miracle of the flow of life. If, during our turbulent periods, we keep ourselves dynamically balanced like a skilled surfer, the waves of our experience will guide us smoothly to the shore. We may fear that the waves will drown us, but it is actually the waves that *move* us.

Steve is a dear friend of mine of many years. We met during our teens and shared an era of experiences. We stayed up late at night, involved in ponderous discussions of the nature of the universe; we laughed; we were inspired by the same great teachers of Truth; we traveled together and enjoyed the changing of the seasons around us. Steve and I supported each other, challenged each other, shared, and grew as brothers in life. Eventually we lived together for several years, in harmony and cooperation.

Gradually, Steve and I drifted apart in interests and activities. I sensed our growing separation, and inwardly I resisted. "Steve is my best friend," I thought; "He always has been, and always will be." In my heart, though, I knew that our paths were diverging.

Steve became involved in a relationship with a woman which was a painful one for him. I sensed Steve's hurt and I attempted to let him know that I was feeling with him and that I supported him. Strangely, he was not receptive, and I felt disappointed. It was then that I realized that Steve had to fulfill his own destiny, and that his life was taking a new direction. And there was nothing I could do to hold back the tide of life.

Several months later, Steve announced that he was moving out to live with this woman. At first I felt a little empty to hear this, for it signified to me that a very special era in my life was coming to an end. When I looked a little more deeply into myself, though, I discovered a very peaceful sense of relief and freedom, for I admitted to myself that it was O.K. for us to travel in different directions. I realized, too, that our sharing of interests was not what it used to be, and that I had been foolishly clinging to a picture of the past. At that moment I was free to wish Steve well and to offer him my blessings for his chosen path.

Now Steve and I are very dear to each other. We have since traversed our own peaks and valleys and we are both the richer for it. We do not spend as much time together as we once did, but we love and respect each other as fully as we ever did. I shall always value the early years of our friendship, as I do the moments we now share. And I am especially grateful for the lesson of letting go.

An oriental sage taught, *"That the yielding is more powerful than the resistant is a fact known by all and practiced by none."* To change one's mind or to humble one's self is considered by many to be a sign of weakness, although the most humble among men are the most exalted. We are taught to subjugate, manhandle, and mold the world to conform to our expectations. But power is a word that very few people understand. The power that we gain in the world is like a bubble on the Ocean of God. Sooner or later it pops and we once again find ourselves to be the ocean.

I was talking to a man just a few days ago who had been to the top of the ladder of success in the business world — and then to the bottom. When I last saw him about ten years ago, he held a very prestigious position in a major department store chain. He wore $300 suits, owned a few Cadillacs, and he and his family enjoyed all of the finest things in life. Then, almost overnight, his firm went out of business and he lost his job. His wife became ill, and he was faced with medical expenses. He remained out of work for five years. By God's Grace, he took it all in stride and remained positive during his trials. He has since gotten another job, his wife has recovered, and his attitude is excellent. As he told me his story, I felt no bitterness or resentment from him. He was able to flow with the changing circumstances of his life. I know another man who had a similar turn of events, but he was set back by it. As it was harder for him to take it in stride, he went through some depression and illness before he came out on the other side. Yet his seeming misfortune was actually God's Grace, for he was saved from the plight of the five men who preceded him in his job, all of whom died of heart attacks.

It is said that the willow tree enjoys longevity because its boughs can bend to relieve itself of the burden of heavy snow and ice which would break the branch of a more rigid tree. Master Sivananda, a great and revered yogi, well understood this principle when he gave his students a very practical mantra:

> Serve, love, meditate, purify,
> Be good, do good, be kind, be compassionate,
> *Adapt, adjust, accommodate,*
> Bear insult, bear injury, highest *sadhana**

There is an American guru who teaches these same principles. His name is Arthur Fonzarelli, affectionately known to his many disciples as *"The Fonz."* The Fonz is a master of what Hilda calls "quick adjustment of the mind." He knows how to take a challenge and immediately turn it into an asset. Once, for example, Ritchie was pledging a fraternity, and as part of his initiation, he has to go to a high school dance dressed as a girl. At the same dance, of course, is The Fonz, who (unaware of the disguise) takes a liking to Ritchie and asks him (her) to dance. As they are slow dancing, The Fonz begins to blow in Ritchie's ear and kiss him on the neck. Ritchie feels compelled to reveal his identity and begins to whisper, "Hey Fonz, it's me, Ritchie! — I'm just dressed up like this for my fraternity initiation!" The Fonz gets an incredibly startled look in his eye for about a half a second, but, in his invincible style, he does not lose his cool. He doesn't even miss one step in the dance. All he does is move just a few inches away from Ritchie and tell him, "Oh yeah, oh yeah . . . I knew it all along . . . I just wanted to help you with your initiation . . . Did you think that The Fonz would let you down?" and the dance goes on. Quick adjustment of the mind.

Adapting, adjusting, and accommodating are qualities that we in western culture sometimes have a hard time understanding or putting into action. I recently heard a wonderful talk by a Native American Indian gardener. She pointed out that many gardeners approach growing food and living things in a very aggressive way: we say "I'm going to *make* that garden grow." We attack the mother earth with chemicals and disrespect, pillaging her for instant gain, disregarding the long-range effects of our impetuousness. The great dust storms of the 1930's, she said, were largely a result of short-sighted overplowing, upsetting the balance of rooted living plants. The Native

*"sadhana": spiritual path

American way, she explained, is one of planting, cultivating, and harvesting in harmony with the natural flow of the land, always appreciating the bounty of the earth, and replenishing the soil with any precious nutrients that are removed. There is a great respect, she pointed out, for working *with* the seasons, never *against* them.

One way that we buck the seasons of our growth is by running away from situations we have not yet mastered. If the fire gets too hot in a challenging relationship or job, we may be tempted to take off to find an easier one. Unfortunately, as a friend of mine put it, "If an ass goes out to travel, it won't come back a horse." In other words, if you run away from a tough scene, you have succeeded only in avoiding the stimulus which presses your buttons, which is probably exactly what you need to understand and master in order to grow. Besides, we are sure to face the same challenge in another form somewhere else, probably to a more intense degree. So, we are better off sticking it out where we are, because if we run elsewhere, the fire will be even hotter. If you are tempted to leave husband 1 because he squeezes the toothpaste from the wrong end, you might as well work it out now, because husband 2 will probably leave the cap off the tube, as well!

When, then, are we free to leave a situation which we feel is not for us? We can leave when, in our heart of hearts, we are certain that we are not running away in hopes of finding a better replacement. If we hold an *emotional charge*, any anger, irritation, or resentment about the situation we would like to leave, it remains a golden opportunity for us to grow through resolving it, and we would probably benefit tremendously by staying. If, on the other hand, we feel satisfied, complete, and clear about the job we have done, and we *honestly* feel that it is no longer challenging or productive, we may very well be done with our spiritual work in that place. If we hear a very strong *inner* (not emotional) urge to make a change, and we feel in the *flow* (and not in *reaction*) with the change, then, perhaps, a change is very much in order.

Life in the flow does not guarantee any recipes; there are no cut and dried, pre-packaged rules of thumb. Sometimes the answer is in one principle; sometimes it is the opposite. Eric Butterworth has said, "It's not doing what you like that's important — it's liking what you do!" On the other hand, Patricia Sun was once asked, "Why am I so tired all the time?" Her answer: "Because you don't like what you're doing . . . Why not try doing something you like?" Who was correct?

Both of them. Each challenge requires a unique solution. We have to *feel* our way through life. We must be flexible enough to know what needs to be done in the moment, even if it was not what needed to be done a moment ago. Mahatma Gandhi said, "I am committed to Truth — not consistency."

I once was offered a very nice job working with retarded people. As I needed some money at the time, I took the job. I fell in love with the "clients," many of whom were very joyous and loving people and from whom I learned many valuable lessons. As time wore on, however, I began to feel unfulfilled in my work. I was over-sleeping, my physical health was not up to par, I was arriving to work late, and I began to look forward to holidays and to look for ways to get out of work.

I was yearning to express my creativity in a different way. I feel especially fulfilled teaching yoga, playing music, writing, traveling, and working on human relations workshops. This job seemed far afield from the kind of work I do best and enjoy the most. So, knowing the principle of "take whatcha got and make whatcha want," I attempted to introduce my skills into the program. I started to teach the clients yoga, I played music during lunch hour, and I started an incense-making business at the center. These programs were successful, but I was still trying to stuff a round peg into a square hole.

I very much felt inclined to leave the job, but here is how my mind acted as "the slayer of the real": it said, "You are running away. You are avoiding a lesson you need to learn. You must not be a quitter. You must stay until you learn the lesson." So, although I had no idea what the lesson was, I decided to stay and to give myself until Memorial Day to learn it.

Well, Memorial Day came and it went, and I still didn't know what the lesson was, but I was determined not to be a quitter and to learn that mysterious lesson, which I just knew would be revealed to me, probably now by the Fourth of July. So came and went Independence Day, and I still didn't get the lesson, and more and more all I wanted was to be independent of this job.

Now the mind — the little mind — has a very clever ability to team up with the emotions. I was afraid to quit the job because I would probably feel guilty about leaving these poor retarded people; "After all," I thought, "they really need *my* love!" (Meanwhile, the fellow who replaced me after I finally did leave, did a much better job than me.) I reasoned, too, that perhaps I had been retarded in some previous life, and now I had to pay off my karma by serving these people as some kind soul had served me. Or perhaps I had some other great karma that I could work out in this unhappy lot.

So I continued, day after day, week after week, until I finally decided to quit and take my chances with the lords of karma. And did it feel right and good to leave! The great lesson that I was waiting to learn was that I did not belong there.

I went on to develop my work with yoga, music, human relations, and writing. Now I look forward to awakening each morning, to creating in my own way, and to serving people according to my own bent. God gave me skills to express in a unique way, as He gave every person a special role. While I thought it was "wrong" or a "sin" to leave a job where I could render valuable service to humanity, now I feel it may be more of an error for any of us to deny the calling we are given, and an even greater sin to withhold our God-given inclinations from humanity, out of fear or guilt. If we have faith that God is guiding us, He will lead us to where we can serve in our own way — which is *His* own way.

Years later, Hilda explained a principle that brought the whole experience into light. She explained, "If you do something because you think you have karma to work out — in that moment, *by that thought* (of 'I have such and such a karma'), you are *creating* the karma." My thought of "I must stay in this job to work out karma" may have been the very karma that kept me there.

And so it is only the mind that can stand between us and the flow of life. And so it is the heart that reconnects us with its music. There is a moment which all musicians know, aspire to, and perhaps live for. It is that precious moment when the music takes over and the musicians become the instruments. It is the instant when the thought of separate players dissolves into the song, and there is only one energy, one idea in the room. In this moment, there is no thought, no history, no expectation. There is only now, and now proves itself to be very real, indeed. It is as if the rivers have merged into the ocean, and the many have become The One. The old, the parent of now, assumes its rightful role as servant of Life, and graciously gives birth to the new. And so a Child is born.

"You who would master the art of living, dance gracefully. Move lightly through your postures, and each will show you your way to the next. Your guide calls from within, pointing your path through evolution. Bend this way, now that, and give full confidence to the promptings of your soul.

Renounce the thinking mind as the final arbiter of your understanding of life. At times your mind bears witness to the Truth, but often it confounds you. We tell you to give full authority to your simple teacher, for it exists only for the releasement of the God that is you. The quiet wisdom of such a teacher is your only salvation.

The greatness that you are promised is not the grandeur that you have been taught to value by the world. The guide offers you the Kingdom of Heaven, which is already yours, though you remember it only faintly. The world offers you itself, which you know well, but not well enough to know that its end is emptiness. We show you the end of your strivings. Your attempts to find a resting place in the world have come to naught. This you can now see, and you are nearly ready to admit. Your growing inclination to turn about to your Father's House is the yearning which will surely bring you Peace."

SEASONS

A few evenings ago, I spoke with a lovely but sullen young lady. She was feeling guilty because she had let go of her spiritual discipline for a while. She told me that for a long time she had been going to church every day, meditating and praying for hours. During that time she felt very fulfilled, in her niche. She then stopped going, and felt sinful for it. Now she wanted to start again, but she feared that she had fallen away from the path, and she felt too unworthy to take up her practice again. "What good is it?" she asked, "if I start toward God, and then quit? I might as well not even start!"

But I didn't see her stopping as quitting. What she had needed, as I saw it, was a breather. She had done some very intense spiritual work, and she probably needed some time to absorb and integrate it. It might have been counterproductive to force herself to continue to sit for hours in that church, before her experience was gelled within her. I told her that I certainly did not consider it sinful to take a temporary rest from intense spiritual striving, and, in fact, such a "vacation" might have been exactly what she needed to get her ready for the next step of her growth.

Upon hearing this, she looked at me, almost startled, and asked, "You mean I haven't fallen from God because I stopped?" Of course she hadn't. In truth, she had never left the spiritual path. The form of her work had just changed. There is no such thing as falling outside of God, for this would mean that there is somewhere that God is not. The only place we can fall is in *consciousness*, and as soon as we rise back into God-consciousness, we see that He was with us always; we were just not looking at Him. This young lady loved God very much. Who she wasn't loving was herself.

There are seasons of our growth. When we flow with them and enjoy them, we accept their full blessing; when we buck them or attempt to deny them, we miss a rich treasure. *"To everything there is a season; a time for every purpose under Heaven."* There is a time for discipline, and a time for letting go; an occasion for pushing on, and one for surrender; a purpose for tears, and one for laughter. Everything in nature has a reason for living, in its right place.

I often feel awed by the change of the earth seasons. Ferlinghetti had an idea which I adapt to speak for me: "I am continually celebrating the rebirth of wonder." It is just such a mystery to me how each spring, trees that seem to be dead give birth to life in the form of little green buds. This miracle reminds me of what Jesus told the family of the little girl that He healed. "Don't be alarmed, the girl is not dead . . . She is just sleeping." In the heat of the summer, it is hard to believe that in just a few months the ground will be covered with snow, and the chill wind will blast us. If we can just look at these simple patterns of our earth, a world with which we are inseparably one, we can learn great lessons that we can use for our upliftment.

In the practice of hatha yoga physical exercises, for example, it is very important to stop after every few exercises and rest for a little while to integrate and absorb the effects of the movements. The real payoff of the exercises is the deep sense of relaxation and well-being that comes after completing the stretches. Students are required to lay down and rest for a period of time at the end of class, and it is during these moments that the healing effects of the exercises make themselves known. Both the activity and the resting are equally necessary and important. We cannot enjoy the full benefit without a combination of the two. In accepting *all* of the aspects of the process, it becomes one meaningful integrated whole.

People go through seasons that require us to look deep to understand them. There is a beautiful man who was very close to Hilda and our spiritual community. I felt great esteem and respect for him, as he has a great deal of spiritual wisdom and love to offer. One day I noticed that he had not been coming to our gatherings for a while, and I later learned that he had withdrawn himself from the classes. This troubled me, for I thought that he might have lost his spirituality or stepped onto the wrong road. I felt a sense of loss.

I did not say anything to anyone about this. Then, one day, Hilda took me aside and explained, "You know, J. never really left our group. He was just going so high in his meditation, and his spiritual growth was happening so fast that he was losing his ability to function effectively in the world. Out of wisdom, the inner guides, who want well-rounded workers, strong in practicality as well as spirituality, pushed him back into the world for a while. He is as much a part of our group as ever. Whether or not he comes to the classes, he has not lost his spirituality. He is just learning lessons in a different place."

There are lessons, in fact, to be learned in every place. The mark of spiritual mastery is the ability to remember God wherever we go, and through whatever we experience. A friend once sent me a greeting card that said, "We are living in a world of permanent change." Everything changes, and the more firmly we have this understanding imbedded in our consciousness, the easier it is to remember God as we go through all of the transformations that are necessary for our total evolution.

I am reminded of King Solomon's request to his counselor to tell him "something that will make me happy when I am too sad, and make me sober when I feel too happy." A few days later, the advisor gave the king a ring with these words inscribed on it: "This, too, shall pass."

I had a marvelous lesson in letting "this, too" pass. For many years, I was given to the practice of deep meditation. It was my greatest joy to sit, sometimes for hours, and dive into my deepest Self. I cannot describe in words the satisfaction that I experienced. I did not do it as a discipline or a practice. I did it because I loved to do it, and I grew tremendously from it.

Then, one morning I woke up and the desire to meditate had left me. I was not resisting it or running away from it. I just did not feel a need to meditate. At first, my mind was very uncomfortable with this new feeling. I thought, "You really should, you know, even if you do not want to." But the truth was that I wanted to, but did not feel the need to. And then I thought, "Well, you've been meditating every morning for eight years; what will you do if you don't?" and "If you don't meditate, you will have an awful day, and you will be sorry you didn't." But my inner voice told me to honor my intuition. So I carried on without lots of deep meditation, and, to my amazement, my days were wonderfully complete! I found I had a fantastic amount of time and energy to be creative, to be with others, and to contribute to the world in a new and different way.

At the time, I thought that I was finished with meditation, but there was an even more profound lesson in store. At a later date, the seasons of my growth made a full circle, and I resumed regular meditation, but this time without clinging to it. I now see that my retreat from my regular practice was actually a preparation for a new level of consciousness, one which would allow meditation to be an asset to my happiness, and not a dogmatic institution. That season of no meditation was required to show me that although I find God in meditation, I cannot afford to make a god of it. Now meditation is even more useful to me, as it blends with the overall flow of my life.

We must honor the natural rhythms and cycles in our nature. As I look around me, I see the great tapestry of the universe woven with a magnificent ebb and flow. We are told that the entire cosmos is pulsating like our hearts and like the microcosmic atoms vibrating within us. To feel the rhythm of life is to dance to the greatest symphony of all, and to deny its pulse is to miss the essence of all expression. Life is about changes, rhythms, growth, retreat, activity, rest, unfolding, delving inward. And when the seasons of our life have left us with all the teachings they bear, there is but one lesson that remains, ever beyond the effect of passing opposites: There is one unchanging life that breathes in and through us, and in which all seasons humbly come to resolution in seasonless Serenity.

To everything there is a season,
a time for every purpose under heaven:
a time to be born,
a time to die,
a time to plant,
a time to reap,
a time to kill,
a time to heal,
a time to tear down,
a time to build up,
a time to weep,
a time to laugh,
a time to mourn,
a time to dance,
a time for casting away stones,
a time to gather them;
a time to embrace,
a time to refrain from embracing;
a time to find,
a time to lose,
a time to keep,
a time to throw away,
a time to tear,
a time to mend,
a time to be silent,
a time to speak,
a time to love,
a time to hate,
a time for war,
a time for peace.

—Ecclesiastes 1-9

"You who would find your place and your purpose under Heaven, accept your goodness in His eyes. See the perfection of all things, and know that all in creation has a right and good purpose.

For too long have you denied the seasons of your life and the intelligence thereof. Now is your time to acknowledge your freedom to live, a right which you richly deserve. The era in which you are about to enter is ruled by the wisdom of the heart, not the meanderings of the mind. The mind has been sufficiently developed. There must be a balance. Hold Love in one hand and Wisdom in the other, and so you have the tools with which to build a new age.

Your work is that of attunement. You can no longer depend on form and imitation for your livelihood, for these would only serve to weaken you. In meekness there is mastery. This great truth was the cornerstone of the ancients, but ignorance of it is the fault of the present civilization.

The task, one which you have already accepted, is the wise merger of the ancient wisdom and the knowledge you have cultivated. Those who would deny one for the sake of the other do not see fully. You see fully, and so you are charged with the demonstration of this grand principle to those who have need to learn it.

Peace is to be learned through observation. Watch the peaceful and emulate its essence. Open yourself to the serene and accept it as your teacher. In this way, you gain conscious awareness of the seasons of your being, and in so learning, you make them God's gift to humanity."

THY WELL BE DONE

We have not correctly understood the Will of God. Somewhere along the way, we adopted the mistaken notion that God's Will is something to be feared. If, when we hear, "Thy Will be done," we begin to shiver and shake with a sense of impending doom, we do not know Who God Is. If we believe that if God really got to do His Will on us, we would be chastised and smitten, we do not know Who We Are. And if we think that God does not already love us with an everlasting Love, we do not know what Love Is.

The Will of God is the most wonderful thing that could ever happen to anyone. It is not to be feared, but embraced. The Muslim word for God is *Allah* — *"The Friend."* A friend of mine was walking in the park one day when be began to think of the things in his life that he was resisting. One by one he analyzed them, and soon he saw that the plan for his evolution was one of great Love and Beauty, and so it had always been. He saw, too, that in fighting the Will of God, he was really fighting his own best interest. As he explained it, "What I was afraid of was pure love, and, after all, I have nothing against pure love!"

We have been afraid to love. We have been afraid because we have felt hurt by what we thought was love. Love cannot hurt. Love can only heal.

Another friend of mine telephoned me to invite me to participate in a human relations workshop, the theme of which, she told me, was "Love."

"How wonderful!" I exclaimed, "I'm glad you picked such a

positive theme!"

"I don't know how positive love is," she countered; "I've been hurt by love too many times."

I knew her pain, but I could not agree that love could injure. "I, too, have felt the hurt that you say came from love," I told her. "And as I have let love become my friend, I see that it was not love that hurt us. Our hurt came from images, from expectations, from clinging. The Real Love that I have discovered has brought me only happiness."

Pain is not the offspring of love, nor is it the Will of God. We ascribe pain to love because we ascribe pain to God, and neither of these ideas is correct. Because God *is* Love, He could never bring pain. All we did was to dream an empty fantasy and then rail against it because it would not give us what it is impossible for a dream to give. God could never allow a dream to give us more than He can, or else He would not be God.

Love is the balm that heals all the wounds that we have ascribed to love. What else but love would heal the hurt that has been mistakenly blamed on itself?

Life is supposed to go right. I went to a lecture on esoteric astrology at which the lecturer told us, "People receive an answer to a prayer or experience a miracle and they come to me and exclaim, 'The most amazing thing just happened to me!' Actually, prayers are *supposed* to be answered and miracles are *supposed* to happen. God is real and His Love is true. Frankly, the most amazing thing to me would be if miracles *didn't* happen!"

Hilda taught this lesson in a very practical way. Once, when she learned that a cat at her house was injured due to someone's lack of paying attention, Hilda sharply chastised everyone present. "You've ruined my evening!" she chided. "There's no need for any cat or any animal or any person to be hurt! . . . If you would have paid attention, this would not have happened!" Hilda was not reacting in anger, but teaching a lesson: *There is no need for things to go wrong.* If we are living in the flow of God, things go right. Mishaps occur only when we step out of the flow, and healing is natural when we once again find it.

As we begin to see that God is really working *for* us, we see that Her only purpose is our happiness. Her commitment to our well-being is so unconditional that if we veer from that purpose and step out of the flow, She is right there to guide us back into it. We must know that for every brake about to wear out, it is God's Will to flash that little red light. But it is *we* who must mobilize our will to follow up the guidance with action. We must "pray with our feet moving." This is the alignment of the Will of God and the will of man. This is when *my* will becomes *Thy* Will, and the two are One.

The teacher "Freedom" once told me, "Life is easy. Love is easy. God is easy. It is *we* who make them complicated." When our intentions are attuned with the Will of God, we experience life as smooth sailing. Somehow our ship is guided around the reefs, and our course is straight for the port. When our seeing is out of focus with God's vision of Perfection, we experience conflict and turbulent waters. We cannot buck God. We can try, but as the popular play affirms, "Your arms are too short to box with God." Actually, if we really knew that God is always working for our happiness and peace, why would we want to box with Him in the first place? If we quit trying to grab His arms, we might just find Him hugging us.

"It is time for you to understand the purpose of your life. You are a chalice for God's Love and a vehicle for Him to bless the world. Realize your Divine purpose and your will is aligned with His.

Goodness is the theme of all life. See the Perfection in your life and you recapture your Childhood Vision. As you give up patterns of evaluation and cynicism, you accept the benevolence of God. Pain is born of resistance, and joy is a function of the acceptance of God's whole and Holy Love for you. Find purpose in your joy, and you find purpose in God.

We join you, in equal status, in looking out upon the marvels of the universe. We stand with you in awe at the mystery and the magnanimity of creation, miraculous beyond speakable understanding. The limited mind interprets vastness as intimidating, but wisdom reveals grandeur as a mark of your identity. As you release your fears, you are free to embrace the whole of the cosmos.

If there is any reason for sadness, it is the erroneous thought that the Father would work against the needs of His children. This idea is inconceivable to God and to those who know Him. 'If a man's son asks for a loaf of bread, would he give him a stone?' To the extent that we are saddened to see earth children deny their Divine Heritage, we are jubilant to see you accept it."

PART II:
THE HOMECOMING

"He arose and came to his father. But when he was yet a great way off, his father saw him and had great compassion, and ran, and embraced him and kissed him.

And the son said to him, 'Father, I have sinned against Heaven and in your eyes, and I am no more worthy to be called your son.'

But the father said to his servants, 'Bring forth the best robe, and put it on him . . . and let us eat and be merry, for this, my son, was dead, and is alive again; he was lost, and is found.'

And they began to be merry."

— Luke, Chapter Fifteen

The Vision of Freedom

BE THOU PERFECT

Our freedom depends on our willingness to see Perfection. The imperfection that we have been taught to see has led only to suffering. The world's belief that God is dead has made death a god, and Love a romantic fiction. Such a way of seeing takes a photograph and frames the negative as a portrait for all to worship as a dark standard. It is a standard that sees nothing and glorifies bitterness.

There is another way of seeing, a way that honors Perfection. It is a way of seeing all persons and things in the Light in which they were created, the Light of God. It is a way of seeing that restores Beauty and Wonder and Goodness to our lives and affirms that we are real because God is real.

Perfection is not a standard to be achieved, but a truth to be acknowledged. *It is not the difference between us and God, but the hallmark of our unity with Him.* And the honoring of Perfection is not a sin of vanity, but the humble acceptance of our identity as offspring of the Eternal.

If you do not now experience your Perfect Self, it is due only to an error in *awareness*, not in reality. We arrived on earth in purity and bliss. Our Innocence united us with the wonder of God's Love. We had no self-image, no self-consciousness, no thoughts of limitation. We lived in the Garden of Eden.

Then we gradually learned to not love ourselves. As pure children, we were open and receptive to harsh beliefs and vibrations. If mom was annoyed or angry about having to arise in the night to attend to our needs, or if older brother was fearful of our new place in the family, we incorporated those jagged feelings into our sensitive body. We cannot blame mom, dad, brother, or teacher for their negative feelings, for they were loving us in the best way that they knew, according to their level of evolution. They, too, learned not to love themselves in the same way. Simply by being born into the world, we take on a huge amount of unconsciousness. It is from this point that each of us began the noble task of learning to love ourselves in a world that denies Love.

Our learning to *not* love ourselves is what the bible describes as the fall from the Garden of Eden. Hilda has said many times that the Garden of Eden is not a place, but a *consciousness*. The story in the bible is not a distant, remote, and unrelated fable. It is *our* story, and it describes the evolutionary unfoldment of each and every human being. When Adam and Eve ate from the "tree of knowledge of good and evil," they began to cut the fruit of life into thoughts of worthiness and unworthiness. They entered into the illusion that it is possible to do things that will make us unlovable. They began to label actions as *evil*, or outside of God.

Since it is you and I who are Adam and Eve, each of us ate from the tree of "good" and "evil" when we accepted the belief that we were good if we did what mommy wanted us to do, but if we did not, we were bad, and punishable by being cast out of the garden of providence and protection. We accepted conditional human love in place of ever-forgiving Divine Love.

We can re-enter the Garden of Eden (in *consciousness*) by remembering that warm and blissful experience of being wholly loveable, the feeling that was so natural to us before we were taught that we had to do something before we could be enough. In the beautiful motion picture, *Brother Sun, Sister Moon*, Pope Innocent tells St. Francis, "In our obsession with original sin, we have forgotten Original *Innocence*."

The key to our entering back into the Garden is to locate the point where we left it. This requires a clear and bold look into our personal history. One evening, in a meditation class, I was guided to mentally return to my childhood to explore how I learned to feel unworthy and fearful. In a flash, a long-submerged memory was revealed to me: As a child, I drank milk from a baby bottle until a few years after the age that most children stop. My mother would continue to give me bottles, but she was very concerned that no one else know about it. It was O.K. for me to drink a bottle around the house, but if we went out I could only do it in secret. Once, we accidentally left a bottle at my aunt's house, and when she discovered it, my aunt made fun of me, and my mother was terribly ashamed.

As you can imagine, I absorbed these feelings of shame and embarrassment, which I most likely did not have before, and I began to think that there was something wrong with me; that I was less than other people; that I was unworthy; and that I had to hide what I did. This, perhaps, was my personal fall from the Garden of Eden in this life.

When, in my class, I saw this whole sequence clearly, I felt the exhilirating freedom of refound Innocence. I saw, as if a light had been turned on in a dark room, how my unworthiness was *learned*, and how it consisted of nothing more than my accepting a set of thoughts and feelings that other people believed in. I realized the joy that the lovely Patricia Sun described as her own self-discovery. She said that she had always felt that there was some awful, terrible thing inside of her that would just devour her if she ever looked at it. When, one day, she actually looked within, she saw that there was absolutely nothing there, and her fears were all based upon a hoax, a joke, — an illusion.

My experience after that realization was one of deep peace and contentment. I realized that there is nothing to do in life but just to *be*. I saw that all of this world (which Ramakrishna called "a mansion of mirth") is based upon desire, which is itself based on the illusion of "need." That night I knew, in my deepest heart of hearts, that I did not, in Truth, need anything, that I actually never have needed anything, and that I never shall. Nor has anyone on this earth ever, in Reality, needed anything. Indeed, we come on earth to learn that what we desire can never really make us happy. I saw, too, that all of our business — busyness — is just scurrying about in vain attempts to fulfill needs that we have created by thinking we need this or that to be happy.

There was an illuminating *Star Trek* episode in which Captain Christopher Pike is captured by a group of mentally powerful beings on another planet, and held prisoner in a glass cage of illusion, which his captors have created with their minds. He begins to suspect that his prison is not real, and in an effort to prove the truth, he captures one of his guards. The frail guard suddenly turns into a huge and horrible monster, about to maul Pike, who nevertheless maintains his hold on the guard-monster. Pike points a ray gun to the monster's head and demands, "You seem to be a monster, but I say you are not real — I say you are an illusion! Reveal yourself, or I'll blow your head off!" The monster disappears, the weak and fragile form of the guard reappears, and the captain escapes, free.

The monsters in our lives are the constructs of mass thoughts of limitation that we have accepted as true. When we point the ray gun of Truth at them, they, too, vanish like nightmares in the morning light.

The night of my insight, I was given the grace to see the flimsiness of the illusory fears that I once felt. These exposed boogeymen were powerless to touch me in this clear consciousness. Someone came at me with harsh criticism, and I, resting in this calm center, handled it easily. Nothing could disturb me in my Garden. The same night, someone invited me to play some music with a group, but it was just not in my heart to do so at that moment. At some other time, I might have agreed out of fear of saying "No," but this night, this very special night, my confidence in my enoughness was too strong to be seduced by fears of rejection. I felt so serene and secure that I did not care whether I lived or died.

Before retiring for the night, I thought whether to meditate and pray as I usually do. But how could I sit down to practice remembering who I am, when I already know? And how could I pray to Jesus, when I know myself — and all — to be one with the Christ? There was simply nothing to do. The falsehood of becoming had given way to the miracle of being.

Jesus said, "Be thou perfect, even as thy Father in Heaven is perfect." This was not a command, but a statement. He was telling us how it is. He was telling us Who We Are. He was telling us the Truth. Jesus was reminding us of our forgotten identity; He was showing us an aspect — *the* Aspect — of ourselves that we do not see. We do not need to attain perfection; we could not do that, even — and especially — if we tried. We just need to see it.

A teacher once told a group of us, "You are all already liberated!" Puzzled, I asked, "If we are all already liberated, then why do we fall?"

"Because," he explained, "you do not believe that you are free, and you push and you push and you push, until you fall."

Patricia Sun said it in another way:" It is impossible for you to

LEARNED SELF IMAGES

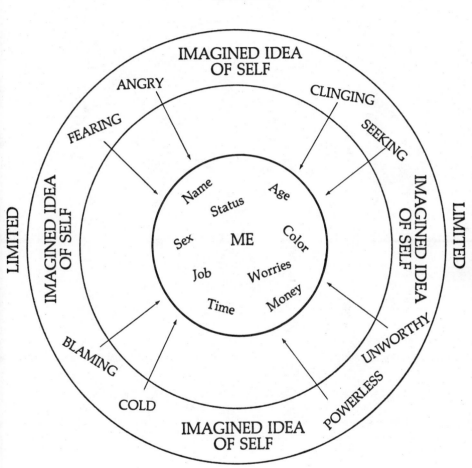

OUR REAL SELF

FREE

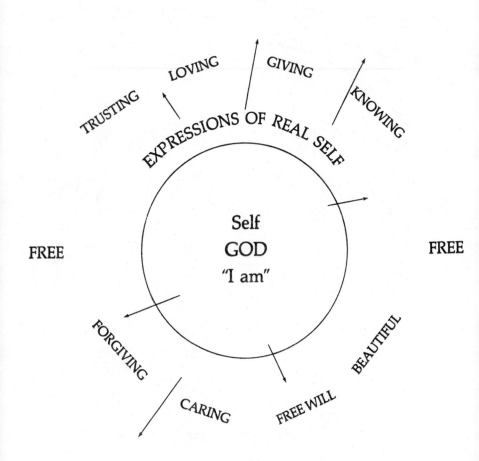

FREE

FREE

FREE

become good by doing something, because the act is based on the assumption that you are not *already* good!"

We must not confuse Perfection with Hollywood. We can have a bump on our nose, we can dial a wrong number, we can make a mistake, and still we are perfect. The Perfection that I am speaking of is not the kind that is ambitiously sought after in the world. God's idea of Perfection is much broader than the little mind's idea. Mother Nature is big enough to absorb a few jagged edges. Trees do not grow in straight rows. Lettuce can be very delicious and nutritious even with a few holes in the leaves. And scientists have told us now that the earth is not exactly round; it is just slightly pear-shaped. Seen from the highest perspective, the grand tapestry of nature is entirely perfect. All the little imperfections disappear and blend into the magnificence of the whole.

To claim our Perfection is not a delusion of the ego; to deny it is the real sin. Owning our Perfection means that we can and do have an important role in the unfoldment of humanity's destiny of Good. It means that we do not have to wait until we are 21, 30, or 65, or until we get married or a Ph.D. to be O.K. We can live up to our potential now. Sometimes our calling is as simple as a smile. Whatever our path, we must always remember that we are fully endowed by God to do what She gives us to do, and to do it well — even perfectly.

"The key to your freedom is the acceptance of your heritage of Perfection. Would that you were as ready to admit your Perfection as you are to identify with your flaws.

Your Perfection is your salvation. There is no middle ground between limitation and Perfection. Children of Light, adhere to your wholeness with all of your heart. It shall never fail you, for its very nature is eternal Fullness.

We stand ready to see you mature into the full understanding of your rightful place in the cosmos. Relinquish forever your dream of beggarhood. Those who struggle in the mire of earth see not beyond their own mind. Those who reach upward for Divine Knowledge dream a dream of kingship, one which bears fruit in the garden of His Truth. Emptiness is but a passing fantasy. Indulge not in lack, for lack is born of ignorance and must always be renounced for the inheritance of the Kingdom.

You who would aspire to the full understanding of your Destiny, shall know it, for in the asking is the promise of the answer. Ask your question, and renounce your search. Prepare a place for your wholeness by surrendering your concepts of oppression. So invited, shall Peace surely come.

There is a serenity that befalls the one who sees the simplicity that is God. Pain and despair are no more. Ponder upon these ideas until you realize them to be your own. In that realization, the lover has become the beloved, the seeker, the sought, and the man, the God. Nothing less shall ever satisfy you, and nothing more is ever possible."

UNDOING UNWORTHINESS

God has not condemned me. No more do I.
— A Course in Miracles*

Unworthiness is the subtlest of obstacles that stand between us and our Good. It is a crafty thief that masks itself in the garb of guilt, false humility, and even pride, and robs us of the full expression of our potential as Godly beings. It uses doubt as a weapon to create confusion of the lower mind, and kidnaps healers from the ill and lovers from the beloved. Unworthiness is responsible for the withholding of talent, service, and wisdom from a world which so desperately yearns for upliftment. If there is a devil, it is the *thought* that we are sinful, evil creatures. And because there is a God, the debunking of that thought is ensured with the realization that we are Divine.

Unworthiness is simply a case of mistaken identity. It seems formidable only when we shrink from it. Our freedom from unworthiness is bought only by awareness of Light. Like any other impediment to Self-knowledge, lack of self-appreciation is but a form of ignorance, and it is immediately overcome by simple clear seeing.

Several months ago I began to experience abundant success in my work. Creative and challenging projects, ideas, and money began to come my way with a powerful flow that I had not experienced before. I had the feeling that "this is too good to be true." But nothing is too good to be true. God is true and God is good.

*For information on *A Course in Miracles*, see reference on copyright page of this book.

THE DRAGON DOESN'T LIVE HERE ANYMORE

Around the same time, I began to feel that I was soon going to die. I had the strange sense that I did not have much time left on earth. When I held this notion up to the light of discrimination, I knew that it was not so — that my feeling was coming from a source other than intuition or Truth. But where?

I delved into this issue in meditation, and I discovered that what was indeed in the process of dying was a *concept of myself* as a mediocre person. I had never thought of myself as very successful, wealthy, or desirable. When these situations began to manifest themselves in my life, I did not know how to handle them. They seemed to be the kind of things that happened to other people — *successful* people — but not to *me*. In order for me to accept these positive changes in my life, I would have to let go of my picture of myself as someone who doesn't have very much to offer, and accept a new image — one of value and worthiness. I realized that it was not "me" or the body that was dying, but an old and non-productive idea of who "I" am.

"Let it die, then," I thought, "with my blessings." And so it did.

There is a story of a woman who sold fish all her life and knew little else. One spring she was invited to the king's palace for a royal festival. When she was shown to her room, she found it filled with colorful flowers and sweet incense. She was repulsed. "How disgusting!" she complained; "Please let me go back to sleep near my pile of fish." She chose the foulness of her fish, solely out of familiarity.

We, too, cling to our hurts, our grudges, our illnesses, our sorrows, and our angers as if they offered us comfort or serenity. In truth, all they offer us is the solace of familiarity and the surety of a self-image that we can hold onto in the face of the insecurity of a changing world. We accept the meager rewards of sympathy, agreement, self-righteousness, and attention, which are not really rewards, but snares. The dear price we pay is that of inner tranquility, joy, and freedom. The tragedy of life is that we do not believe that we have a choice.

The miracle of life is that the instant we realize that we can choose self-worth, purposefulness, and appreciation, the power of our love begins to shine a light of forgiveness on us that dissolves all of our hurts and makes us whole as ever we were. We begin to see through unworthiness as if it were an amateur magician. We can refuse to be abducted down the dark alley of negative thinking; we have walked down that path, and we know it leads to nowhere. Instead, we begin to acknowledge the deep compassion of the God within us, a sweet and merciful kindness that lies patiently awaiting its full expression through the door of an open heart.

I have participated in many encounter groups, personal growth workshops, counselor training courses, and been privy to extremely personal information about the lives of many human beings. I may not have heard it all, but I'll bet I've heard at least one from each category. After seeing and hearing what I have seen and heard, it seems to me that, behind the outer masks of suits, make-up, smiles, and properness, we have all done some rather sordid things, and behind all of our seemingly evil selves, we are wonderful, loving, and lovable people. After all the results are in, we are all pretty much equally horrible in the realm of horror, and equally lovable in the realm of love, which is the only realm that really counts, anyway.

I have seen parents of retarded children giving them an awful lot of love. Their love was not diminished because their child was handicapped; if anything, they gave the child more love. If you feel unworthy in any way, imagine that your unworthy self is like a handicapped child; pick it up, hold it in your arms, look right through its apparent "ugliness," and give it all the love you know how to give.

"What about conscience?" you may rightfully ask. "Isn't it appropriate to feel guilty about some things?" It is necessary to recognize our errors. As soon as we realize or admit to ourself that we have made a mistake, however, and we decide not to repeat it, we have experienced an awakening, which is a cause for *joy*, and *not remorse*. After a moment's sincere realization, any browbeating, self-pity, or sorrow is the luxury of woe.

Jesus' paramount teaching was "Love your neighbor as yourself." We are pretty much aware of the importance of loving our neighbor, but the part about loving ourselves seems to have gotten lost somewhere along the way. Although we usually think of the Golden Rule as giving others the same love as we give to ourselves, I have found in my own life that the reverse applies, too: I must learn to offer the same acceptance and forgiveness to myself that I usually offer to others. Sometimes I hear a friend's story of error that is easy enough to understand and forgive; if, however, I make a similar mistake, I am often much harder on myself — perhaps a little too hard. In such a case I am not loving my neighbor as myself.

Jesus gave two other important teachings: "I have not come to judge, but to forgive" and "Love one another as I have loved you." If Jesus was big enough to wash his disciples' feet and to tell them, "I have loved you with an everlasting love," can we take it upon ourselves to be so small and unforgiving that we can throw ourselves out of our own heart? Can we be so arrogant as not to love that which the Christ loves?

If you think about it clearly, it makes all the sense in the world for us to be useful and beautiful. There is obviously a great and Divine intelligence in the universe. All of God's creations function in magnificent harmony and precision. Every element and every living thing has a meaning and a purpose. Would the Creator be so foolish as to create a person without a purpose? Would She make you or me if She didn't have a plan for our existence? If God is Omniscient and Omnipotent, and Omni-everything else, would She create something that She didn't love? And if She weren't sure of Herself, wouldn't She have created a few duplicates for each model, in case one didn't work? Every human being is unique and special. Surely we come into this world for a special function — one that only each of us, as an individual, can fulfill.

That fulfillment is made easy by our willingness to forgive ourselves. How much time we waste on holding ourselves to blame for past mistakes! We believe we deserve to suffer, or that we must pay off years of karma of past wrongdoings. This issue of paying off karma puzzled me. "If I have seen the error of a deed, must I continue to pay for it?" I wondered. Suppose, for example, that I committed ten acts of burglary, and then I am stolen from once. If I then realize the problem of my stealing, must I be stolen from nine more times? The inner voice explained: "The purpose of life is *education — not punishment.*" Once the lesson is learned, further education is no longer necessary.

To put ourselves through continued suffering because we believe we must atone for past "evil" deeds is self-created suffering. At that point, the lesson we must learn is not related to the original error, but one of releasing ourself from the masochism of unworthiness. We do not need to go out of our way to find ways to pay off our "bad karma." God is clever enough to find ways for us to pay our debts. He will send us enough lessons and challenges, compassionately well-timed, to offset our karmic obligations. We do not need to add to them; He knows His business. I once heard, "Never trouble trouble 'til trouble troubles you." As I see it, if life is offering us no troubles, we might as well take advantage of the time and enjoy ourselves.

To forgive is to transcend our lower nature and to release a force of Light that can heal the universe and purge it of all suffering. When we forgive anyone, including — and especially — ourselves, we are lifted up by the very thought of forgiveness to our highest angelic potential. Nothing can be more pleasing in the eyes of God. To love ourselves for our goodness is easy. To love ourselves, in spite of our errors, is downright Holy.

"Children, you hold yourself too strictly in account for what you believe are your misdeeds. We see only lessons and experiences. It is you who attach the meaning of good or bad to these experiences. We are incapable of judgement, and so do not know unworthiness. Self-condemnation is a creation of the human mind. We seek for your understanding, and not for your suffering.

We hold nothing against you. We do not know guilt. You are your own judge, jury, and executioner. We implore you to cease causing yourself unnecessary hardship on this joyous path of learning.

We delight in your forging onward in the quest of the knowledge of your True Self. No other endeavor has any value. Do not look back to a past that is dead and complete. We are desirous of aspirants with the vision of the future.

See yourselves as whole and pure, and you see yourselves as we see you. We see nothing less than Perfection in you. Join us in our victory over the ignorance of unworthiness. Our power is not in fear and retaliation, but Forgiveness and Love. This is the path that cannot fail. This is the path of God."

STANDING NAKED

To stand naked before God is to realize that all that we would hide is unimportant. We make our secrets important only by our fear of them. When we believe we need to conceal something, we obscure our own vision of its nothingness. God could not care less about the secrets we try to keep from Him. These secrets continue to wield power over us only as long as we do not hold them up to the light. When we summon the courage to have a clear look at our hidden selves, we see how flimsily they are constructed, and we can enjoy the best kind of laugh as we watch them disintegrate.

Real growth comes only through self-acceptance. As long as we deny any aspect of our being, we make believe that something could be outside of God. It is as if we say, "God is everywhere; He fills all time and space — except for this part of my body and what I did at age fifteen."

Approval by others is a limited acceptance; it is not self-acceptance. I have participated in a number of "ventilation" workshops, during which I was asked to speak of my deep hidden secrets — acts and aspects of myself that I feared or was ashamed to admit.

These were the thoughts, feelings, and experiences which I felt, in my subconscious, that if anyone knew about, I would be unloved and rejected. So I mustered up the courage to share these things in small groups during these workshops, and I was very happy to find that the world did not fall apart, nor was I outcast from society. I also learned that everyone else had their own equally sensitive "stash," and that they were so busy being afraid that they would not be loved because of their "stuff" that they couldn't care less what I have been or done. The only one who cared was me.

I left these workshops feeling clean, clear, and happy, for it was a great relief to be able to share my hidden self with others, and still receive their support, approval, and love. But I later learned a deeper lesson that showed me an even more subtle teaching about self-disclosure.

In a guided meditation class, the teacher said, "Now take a look at all of the things that you have kept hidden from others, and have not admitted to yourself. You will not be required to speak any of these facts to anyone else. These issues are simply between you and God."

One by one, an array of feelings, thoughts, and experiences began to parade before my consciousness, as if they were being shown to me on an inner movie screen. The promise that I would not have to reveal them to anyone else encouraged me to be totally free and honest with myself. A surprising amount of little judgements, opinions, and grudges were made visible to me. I did not really like C., although I had been trying to convince her and myself that I did; I was still angry at J; I was putting up a facade about my feelings about the house; and I really felt I made a bad deal for my guitar case. The more I admitted, the more was revealed to me. At first it was painful to admit my hypocrisy and deception, but as the process went on, I felt freer and freer, until I gladly welcomed any insights that came to me. By the time we were finished, I felt wonderful — in all my imperfection. I had seen myself through clear eyes, and I knew, ironically, that I was alright with God. It was only my self-judgement that made me seem not alright.

From this I gained a very important understanding: *Standing naked before people is not nearly as important as standing naked before God.* Approval by others may bring encouragement, but acceptance by my Self brings freedom.

In the long run, acceptance by others does not solve the problem of leaning outward for validation. After my meditation, I thought, "In those workshops, people accepted me, and that made me feel good . . . But what if they had laughed or scorned or rejected me? . . . I would have felt hurt! . . . What kind of freedom is that?" If I allowed social approval to make me happy, I was making myself vulnerable to social rejection making me unhappy. In other words, I was giving the power of my happiness to other people, which is never a wise investment. In that meditation class, I cleared myself with God, which is the only clearing that is really valuable.

We cannot fool God; we can only try to fool our little selves. We would attempt to fool God because we believe, on some level, that He would not love us if He knew the truth. The joke is that He already knows the truth, of course, and He already loves us, anyway. He is just waiting for us to come around to His point of view — one of complete and unconditional acceptance.

God's Love is the surest thing in the universe. He is unflinching in His willingness to have us just as we are. There is no reason to hide and no place to run. When we offer our lives to Him, He assumes full responsibility for our well-being. If He knows all that we do, He must surely know why we do it, and such a knowledge is always wed to deep compassionate understanding. This is the great surprise that undoes the need for all of our empty labors: We are forgiven and we are loved.

> *Open all the shutters on your windows!*
> *Unlock all the locks upon your doors!*
> *Brush away the cobwebs from your daydreams!*
> *No secrets come between us anymore!*
> *So fly, little bird, up into the clear blue sky,*
> *Carry the word, Love's the only reason why . . .*

—The Moody Blues, *The Land of Make Believe*, by Justin Hayward

"My Love for you is unconditional and complete. I am your beloved, who knows the hidden recesses of your inner self better than you, yourself, know them. I am not concerned with your impurities or errors. In my eyes they hold no power or reality.

My deepest wish is that you love yourself as I love you, which is exactly the way your Heavenly Father loves you. As you realize the magnitude of this Love, you laugh at the uselessness of your hiding. You tried to conceal that which you are not. By your very attempt to hide it, you gave a seeming reality to that which never existed.

Come into the sunshine of Love's acceptance, beloved Children of Light. Seek not the approval of your brothers and sisters, for they are yet students like you, and their discrimination is not yet keen. What the world can give, the world can take away. What your Heavenly Father gives, no man can remove.

There is nothing that you can do that would cause you to lose my Love. Go forward in confidence, and be strong in your freedom."

The Truth

THE MIGHTY TRUTH

It has been said that even if there were no God, the universe could flourish on the foundation of Truth alone. This teaching, to me, means this: If it is hard for you to accept the idea of God, perhaps due to negative associations learned early in life, then pursue Truth with all the reverence and tenacity in your heart, and so you will find fulfillment, for the lessons of Truth *are* the lessons of God.

Truth is the whole of our existence. It is our very life. We have no existence outside of Truth and neither can Truth exist outside of us. When a human being aligns him or herself with Truth, only good can come of such a commitment. Those who feel that they do not know the Truth but sincerely wish to know it, will receive answers to all they ask. Those who belong to Truth cannot fail.

Mahatma Gandhi was one of the greatest devotees of Truth that ever lived. When I think of Truth, I think of Gandhi. His story is one of a nervous, neurotic, and fearful man who, in the name of Truth, tackled life by the horns and gradually, relentlessly, freed himself from his limitations and took a nation of hundreds of millions to freedom with him. He refused to compromise his integrity under all circumstances, and though he was at first scorned, later found the world beating a path to his door.

Gandhi and those great ones like him knew that the vision of Truth is born of loving. The real organ of Truth is not the brain, but the heart. The ancient Egyptians realized this. When a man died, they removed most of his bodily organs and preserved only a few organs which they believed to embody Divine energies. They discarded the brain, but kept the heart. Hafiz, the Persian poet, said, "O you who would learn the marvels of Love from the copybook of reason, I am afraid that you will never really see the point!"

We feel or sense Truth more than we think it. We know it more than we understand it. We can see it more than we can explain it. When we attempt to analyze Truth, we lose ourselves in the dead-end labyrinth of the thinking mind. When we love Truth, however, the storehouse of universal wisdom is opened to us. Our respect for Truth is our investment in its understanding, and our suffering the price of its denial.

The Truth, we discover, cannot be found in a book. We may find words and descriptions of the Truth in a book, but not the Whole Truth, for the Whole Truth is fathomless, ever free of containment, confinement, or conformity. There was a monk in Ireland named Alanus, who was revered and sought after for his great wisdom. One spring, he was invited to the University of Paris to address the student body. After his lecture, one of the students approached Alanus and asked him if he would speak the following day on the subject of the Trinity. "Certainly!" Alanus agreed, and he set out along the banks of the Thames River to prepare his discourse.

As he was pondering, Alanus noticed a little boy repeatedly dipping a bucket in the water and dumping it on the shore. Curious, he asked the child, "What are you doing?"

"I'm emptying the entire river onto the shore!" the boy explained.

Laughing, Alanus told him, "Don't be silly; you will never be able to empty the river like that!"

Looking Alanus straight in the eye, the child answered, "And neither can you explain the Trinity in the words of a lecture."

No teacher, religion, or cult can hold exclusive possession of the Truth. The hallmark of Truth is its inclusive nature; no one or no thing could ever be excluded from It. Those who believe that their truth is the only Truth are living a consciousness of limitation, and in Truth, limitation does not exist. When Christ Jesus said, "I am the Way, the Truth, and the Life," He was speaking from the awareness of the universal "I Am," the Christ, the Light which He knew Himself and all persons to be. He was not speaking only of the Jesus, which was the physical form that was identified with the Christ. Jesus, Buddha, Moses, Mohammed, and the other great ones have all taught the same

220

THE MIGHTY TRUTH

Truth: *paths are many; the Truth is One.*

This one Truth is not hidden, nor has it ever been. It is always present, available, and free to those who sincerely love it and yearn to delight in its brilliant splendor. The Truth cannot be bought, sold, bartered, or traded. Those who would sell it do not have it. Neither can it be taught, given or bestowed. It can only be lived. Like Love, those who do not have it catch it from those who have it, and like the most delicate wildflower, Truth recreates itself by the power of its own beauty. There is nothing secret about the Truth; it will find us wherever we are, like the morning sun finds the eyes of a sleeping child. The telling mark of those who have discovered the Truth is their eagerness to share it, for unlike the meager commodities of the world, Truth's joy only increases through sharing.

Those who have taught the Truth have been the pillars of humankind throughout the ages. Though many were mocked, some of them martyred, and nearly all of them misunderstood, it is those who had the courage to live for Truth that have sustained our human family through the centuries. Many of them lived short lives, coming briefly to bring their message of Peace and Light, leaving the earth with a legacy of new understanding.

Those who have taught untruth have been swallowed up by the ages. Lies are distinguishable only by their inability to withstand change. The real Truth is so powerful that, once expressed, it stands nobly, never to be forgotten, established in the genetic blueprint for planetary unfoldment.

It is said that "The Truth hurts." The Truth has never hurt anything; only illusion hurts. The Truth knows only how to heal. Those who resist Truth resist healing, and those in need of healing can find it by embracing Truth. The Truth brings with it a peace and a satisfaction that falsehood cannot imitate. The lover of Truth lives only for the vision of his ideal and he is nourished only by his awareness of it. A man may survive without physical sustenance for a number of days, but how long can he survive without Truth?

The Truth is simple. It is people and minds that make it seem complicated. The more complex we make it, the further we drive ourselves from it. When we return to the simple things, the Truth reawakens our heart like a long-exiled lover. To me, the Truth is as obvious in a daisy as in the most technical encyclopedia. If you want to know what the Truth is, put aside your textbooks for a while and walk along the seashore at sunset. Take a child to a park. Gaze at the stars. Observe the gentle rhythm of your breath. Listen to the sound of a bamboo flute. Sing a song of simple verse: "Row, row, row your boat, gently down the stream, merrily, merrily, merrily, merrily, life is but a dream."

If you believe not in a God, then let Truth be your redeemer. If you find nothing sacred, let Love be your consoler. And if you find no friend worthy of your trust, let Life itself be your consort. The Truth bears no concern for that which it is called, else Truth it would not be.

The dance is never done, and the song is never completely sung, 'til the love of the Truth has made us One.

—*David and Jamil*

"The Truth is a mighty fortress to those who take refuge in its protective strength. In Truth, there is no fear; outside of the Truth, there is no consolation. You are heir to the never failing power of the all-pervading Truth. Never compromise your right to know the Truth and stand firmly upon it. Truth will never betray your trust.

Who can challenge the Truth and stand vindicated? Who can flaunt mortality in the face of eternal Love and have Truth bear witness to vanity? We tell you now that the only strength in the universe is the strength of Truth. There is no other, nor can another ever exist.

Truth is the only weapon of those who live for the upliftment of humanity. Truly, the only stone that marks humanity's plight is the insistence on the possibility of fulfillment outside of the Spirit. The Spirit is the Truth, and there can be no separation between the two, for the Holy Truth and the Holy Spirit are made One in innocent vision.

We cannot, nor can any man, speak for the Truth, for Truth is its own hallmark. At best, we can live in its service. Words may point the way to Truth, but actions demonstrate it. Live in accordance with the highest awareness of the Truth that you know. There is no greater purpose in life than this one."

Transformations

In a dream, I saw myself as a butterfly; now I am wondering whether I am Chuang Tsu dreaming I was a butterfly, or a butterfly dreaming I am Chuang Tsu.

— Chuang Tsu

THE MAGIC MASK

Once upon a time, there was a cruel and hard-hearted king. He was so unpopular that he was continuously fending off rebellions and attempts on his life. One morning he awoke and realized how miserable was his life. More than anything, he wished he could change. He called for his royal wizard and asked him for help.

The wizard pondered for a moment, and told the king, "I can help you, but you must be prepared to carry out any instructions I give you."

"Anything," agreed the king, "that will restore peace to me."

"Very well," said the wizard, "wait three days, and I will give you something to help you."

When the three days elapsed, the wizard gave the king a very unusual object — a mask. The mask was almost an exact likeness of the face of the king, himself — with one very important exception: instead of the usual frowns and scowling lines, this image was smiling, with smooth and pleasant features.

"I can't wear that!" argued the king, ". . . It's not really my face; and besides, people will not recognize me — they know I am not a happy man."

"If you want me to help you, you must do as I say, and wear the mask at all times," the wizard reiterated.

"Very well — I will."

The king began to wear the mask, and something amazing happened. People began to enjoy looking at him, and to feel more comfortable in his presence. They began to feel safe with the king, and to trust him. The king responded positively to his subjects' acceptance of him, and began to treat them with respect and kindness. Gradually the unrest in the kingdom diminished, and peace was restored within its borders.

There remained, however, one place where there was not complete satisfaction — within the heart of the king. He was overjoyed with the changes in his kingdom, but as he had grown, he came to feel hypocritical, for he knew that he was wearing a phony mask. He wrestled with his discomfort and summoned the wizard.

"I am very grateful for the changes that have taken place in my kingdom, but I can deceive my people no longer. I am a charlatan. Please give me permission to remove the mask."

"As you wish," replied the wizard.

Painfully, the king stood in front of a mirror and slowly began to peel away this image that had transformed his life and his kingdom. It was not easy for him, but he knew that he had to do it. Summoning all the courage he could, he opened his eyes to look at his old scowling face.

That face, however, was not the one he saw. What he did see, miraculously, was a beautiful and joyous visage, even more radiant than the one the mask had represented. Through his inner transformation, the king's face had actually become a portrait of joy and kindness. The mask had been only a temporary measure to draw out his real inner beauty.

In this era of honesty, we are encouraged to "Tell it like it is," to "shoot from the hip," and to "give feedback." These practices are very valuable when offered in a loving and supportive way. The principle is, however, often misused. We speak hurtful words with a sharp and cutting tongue, and then reason, "Well, I'm just being me, and, after all, I gotta be me." This is true — we've all "gotta be me," but it is important that we know who "me" is before we express it to others.

Who we are is God. Who we are is Joy. Who we are is Love. Anything else is passing show, illusion. The word "personality" comes from the Greek *persona* — mask. Our personalities, then, are our masks, and they are simply disguising the real us, which is ever whole and perfect.

To wear a "magic mask" of loving words and deeds is to act in accord with our real nature. In fact, once we begin to reap the benefits of our given love, we discover that it is our *goodness* that was real all along, and negation the imposter. We are like an actor who has played his role for so long that he forgot who he was before he began the play. Before we got used to the world's norm of defensiveness, it was very natural for us to be innocent and happy. As children, we lived in a blissful state, shining our light and love on all, regardless of their age, sex, or color. This is why even the hardest person melts in the presence of an innocent child, for children awaken our memory of the purity within ourselves which we long to once again express.

By God's loving Grace, that purity was never lost — it just became *veiled* by a smoggy layer of erroneous beliefs that we could be something less than Divine. Our happy surprise is that all of the ideals that we cherish — love, wisdom, kindness, compassion, and beauty — we already are; we seek after them only because they are the original aspects of ourselves that we came into life to express.

Our purposeful positivity is the key to that expression. It demonstrates through the results it begets that our ideas of "I can't," "I am unworthy," "I am afraid," and "I do not love" are simply untrue. Once we see that we *can*, that we are supremely loveable, and that we have the courage of the saints, the impostors of fear and guilt can never again fool us into believing in them instead of God.

Our hidden goodness and talents are released when we are willing to play the game of owning them, even if we are not fully convinced that they are ours. This was demonstrated to me in Tim Gallway's workshop called "The Inner Game of Tennis." I saw him get two novice players on the court and instruct them, "Imagine you are two of the greatest superstars of tennis; you have been playing professionally for twenty years, and many people have paid a great deal of money for the privilege of watching you play. Would you now be kind enough to give us a demonstration match." I could hardly believe my eyes! A couple who, ten minutes earlier, had made a few clumsy attempts to hit the ball, now danced all about the court with masterful finesse, skillfully smashing difficult shots in long volleys. They received wild applause from the astonished audience. Through this magic mask of skill, they gave themselves permission to release inner ability that would otherwise have laid trapped under thoughts of "I cannot" or "I am not."

Our strengths lie within us, and it is only our permission that can activate their expression. Our problem is not that we are weak, but that we do not believe that we are strong. Although love is the only thing that is real, we have believed in negation for so long that we thought it to be genuine, when it is but an offshoot of a mistaken thought.

Neem Karoli Baba told Ram Dass, "Love everyone and tell the truth." This seeming contradiction puzzled Ram Dass, for he thought, "The truth is that I don't really love everyone." So he began to express his dislikes, his disturbances, and his annoyed feelings toward his friends. He worked himself into such a vicious cycle of bitterness that one day he found himself weeping at the feet of his guru, under a heavy burden of feelings of isolation and separateness. "Love everyone and tell the truth," reminded the compassionate and forgiving guru. "At that moment," Ram Dass tells, "I realized that the truth is, behind my surface feelings of like and dislike, behind my judgements, and behind my emotions, I really do love everyone. I just thought I didn't. Holding onto that flimsy thought was the only thing that stopped me from being who I am; releasing it revealed to me the truth of Love."

We are loving, kingly beings who have dreamed that we are paupers and tyrants. Yet, by royal decree, our throne has been held in trust for us until we come to discover that our nature is one of rich loving kindness. The king who came to the wizard for help did not know if or how this magic mask would help him; he knew only that he wanted to live a more meaningful life, and that he was willing to take a risk to accomplish it. He had a bit of faith in the wizard, who had a great deal of faith in the king.

"You have been conditioned to accept an identity which is not true. To supercede that conditioning, you must accept a new image of yourself — one of Godliness and Beauty. You prove that image by your purposeful action.

The fingers of the untrained musician are comfortable with the familiar, but they must be disciplined to release an imprisoned song, one in which they shall later find greater comfort in mastery. Use your "ordinary" actions to release into expression your purest thoughts and play a masterful song, that the world may be uplifted. Your fears of "foolishness" and your need for "defense" exist only in your thoughts. Kindness, joy, and harmony are foolish only in the eyes of men. In the eyes of God, they are precious beyond description.

We are well aware of the urges and the forces that draw you to react with bitterness and retaliation. These are but the residue of past habits, even of an ancient time. They belong to a concept of yourself that is no longer necessary or useful. We call upon you to renounce the patterns of a painful past, and to come of age as a being of Golden Light. Know that you are supported in your efforts. Every act in harmony with your good nature brings you closer to your goal of true Self-expression. Be not confused by the ways of the world. They are the ways of ignorance. They are constricting and binding, and lead only to disappointment.

The ways of the Spirit are those of joy and bounty. They are the very keynote of the age to come. They lead to life and to happiness. Choose ye the force with which you would align yourself."

GAMBLING FOR GOD

There is a marvelous Chasidic story about a man who came running to the rabbi, exclaiming, "Rabbi, Rabbi, a terrible sin has been committed! Three men from our synagogue were up all night playing cards and gambling! You must chastise them immediately!"

"Wonderful!" exclaimed the rabbi, to the man's astonishment. "I am glad to hear it!"

The man was aghast. "How can you say 'Wonderful!'? Is it not a sin to gamble?"

"I am not approving so much of their gambling, friend. But I am overjoyed that they could stay up all night to play, for they have learned how to overcome sleep to do something that they enjoy. Just think — when they learn to love God, they will be able to stay up all night to serve Him!"

I met a man who selflessly devotes much of his time to a service organization, giving dynamic and inspiring lectures. He has a marvelous talent of taking spiritual topics and making them humorous and captivating. I asked him how he got involved in this work.

"To tell you the truth, I haven't always been very spiritually oriented," he explained. "In fact, I used to go to lots of drinking parties and really raise hell. I began to tell off-color jokes, and I found that there was a big audience for bawdy humor. So I gained a reputation as sort of an off-color comedian, and I was invited to many banquets and parties to tell my jokes. During that time, I developed confidence and a bit of style in public speaking.

233

"When I began to allow God into my life, I lost interest in telling my stories, but I found that I could still use my ability to speak before groups in an entertaining way. So when I was offered the opportunity to speak for my Lord through this organization, I was well prepared for the job." (And now he *really* raises hell.)

There are no unnecessary steps or experiences on our path to God. Because we look at God through mortal eyes, we may believe that we have missed or wasted time, but that is only because that is not how we would use God's energy now. When we look upon our experiences through the eyes of wisdom, we see how the process of personal evolution is a magnificent, well-designed mosaic. We see, too, that there is nothing outside of God, and there is nothing that She cannot find a way to use for Her Glory.

Our lives are transformed not through *becoming* Divine, but through *realizing* that all of our experiences have served a Godly purpose. Moses himself was a prince of Egypt before he realized his identity as a Jew. He even killed a man. He would not seem to have been a likely person to lead the nation of Israel to freedom, yet Moses' service as a prince of Egypt actually *prepared* him for the important role of leading the Jewish nation out of bondage.

In the same way, each stage of our life prepares us for the next — and better — one. When I was in high school I played electric bass in a rock band, and we played some pretty coarse music. Later, I became more interested in the acoustic guitar, and now it is my joy to play and sing songs that speak of the Peace of God. The abilities that I developed in a relatively crude forum can now be used as a vehicle to serve. The skills that once created agitation now soothe. I must honor those crude days, for they were a step to where I am now. No part of the path is any better or worse than another. If we can see life from the highest vantage point, we see how all of its elements are perfectly designed to fit into the grand scheme of development.

I was recently at a party at an ashram spiritual retreat. Just for the fun of it, we began to sing some old rock 'n' roll songs, which I had hesitated to sing because I thought they would be too heavy for a "spiritual" crowd. As it turned out, most of the people knew the songs better than I did, and they filled me in on the words that I could not remember. Many of the yogis and nuns were simply people with worldly experience who had grown into the spiritual life. As we got to talking about the marvel of personal transformation, we began to share with each other how we came to be doing what we do. One fellow had had a nervous breakdown when he was younger, and he began to develop a sensitivity for the needs of people in mental distress. Now he has a very powerful position in the government as a public advocate for mental patients. The head of the kitchen at this large ashram learned all about food service when she worked in a tavern. And the woman who took such wonderful care of the garden learned to do so when, in frustration, she ran away from home at an early age and lived with some American Indians. As a result of what she learned from them, her family situation is now healed, as well.

The caterpillar must surrender to the cocoon before it can be a butterfly. As we grow through life, we learn to express our God-given traits in progressively purer and purer forms. Each of us has a calling, one which we fulfill more deeply with each stage of our growth. We come to earth with a deep sense of the contribution that we would like to make to people and to the planet, but it takes a while for us to have the rough edges of our plan filed off. Seen from the broadest perspective, the caterpillar always was a butterfly; the cocoon was just the thing it needed to make its true identity obvious.

We cannot deny any element of our personal history, for each experience has played a vital role in our training as master souls. The world is more of a school than a playground. We must learn to walk before we can run. We would certainly not return to grade school now, but neither would we throw away what we learned, for it has brought us to where we are now. The flower does not find itself unworthy because it was once but a seed, nor does it judge other flowers in seed form. Are we not all flowers in various stages of opening?

"All of your actions and all of your experiences belong to God. You cannot see the purpose of your actions from the perspective of limitation, the one from which you have looked. We see, however, and we know that all that you have done is in the name of Good. Seek not to become good through future actions, for this would create an evil of the old, a creation of fantasy, and not of fact. Work, rather, to transmute, or refine your understanding of your work. In so doing, you raise your deeds to the highest, a position which they have always merited, but which you have not always accepted.

It is of the utmost importance to relieve yourself of the burden of judgement of the activities of your sisters and brothers. In so doing, you free yourself as well as them. We do not judge any soul, for we lose not sight of Divinity. It is very difficult for you to know the purpose of another's work. Let it suffice to believe that all work is for God.

The mind must be made to function for you as an instrument of blessing. Refuse to acknowledge sin. All that you see is a matter of interpretation. In God, there is no interpretation, for God sees only God."

GOLDEN OPPORTUNITIES

When life gives you lemons, make lemonade
—Esco Brown, *Last Chance Gas,* Chapter 1, Verse 1
(Resurrection)

A friend of mine once wrote: "All of life's experiences are to be either enjoyed or learned from." This is a different perspective than we usually hold; we have been conditioned to believe that life is a combination of good and bad, and that the price we pay for the good is the bad. Yet there is another way of looking at our experiences.

The hurts and sorrows that we feel in life are *not* punishments from God; they are messages given to us by a *loving* God who is showing us exactly where we need to change in order to grow into the serenity that is our nature. Understanding this truth entirely changes the way we look at our difficulties. Seen in this light, troubles turn into lessons, and grudges into Grace. Simply, it makes *all* of life good.

Adversity is our dear friend. It is the driving force that pushes us out of our comfortable nest and forces us to learn to fly on our own. We can really welcome adversity as a gift. Without it our growth is very slow. With it, we are transformed from fledglings into masters.

Every great person has a history of adversity. No one has ever made a contribution to humanity without first undergoing a certain amount of trials. Adversity can forge an immature soul into a powerhouse of strength. As I study the lives of the saints and statesmen, I see that every one of them came to be what they were through conquering challenges. Mahatma Ghandi was thrown off a train and spent a night in a cold train station because his skin was dark. St. Theresa of

Lisieux, the simple "Little Flower," selflessly tolerated barbs and criticism from her sisters in the convent. She learned greatness through humility. Moses was abandoned to the river as an infant, stripped of his dignity as Prince of Egypt, and cast off to die in the desert before he found God. Even after the miraculous parting of the Red Sea, Moses had to mollify the rebellious murmerings of the Hebrew people, forty years in the wilderness. I have seen the Sinai desert, and it is as barren as the moon. Even after this great tribulation, Moses was not permitted to enter the promised land with his people.

Pericles, the masterful Greek statesman whose purity and integrity marked the pinnacle of Greece's Golden Age, was scorned and maligned. He died in a horrendous plague. And we know of the small and stark beginnings of Abraham Lincoln, who had to find a way to heal a wartorn nation, and finally bore the wrath of an assassin's bullet.

It was not by chance that these great ones faced tremendous adversity — they were, in fact, *made great by it*. Perhaps their souls had chosen a life of service to humankind, and these tests and trials were required of them to forge their characters for such a task.

I do not suggest to seek out adversity or to become a false martyr. God takes no joy in seeing Her children suffer. We need only to change the way we look at, or understand, adversity when it comes. Life takes on a new meaning when we see that it is not "out to get us," and that God is *not* our enemy, but our best — and only — friend. Life's trials are the universe's way of lovingly teaching us valuable lessons that we need to learn — the very reasons we have come to earth.

Jesus taught to "love your enemies." How can this be? When we can look at our "enemies" as our teachers, they cease to be our opponents, and become our best friends. Our heritage, our birthright, and our purpose in life are to live in love and appreciation. If we find ourself in angry strife with another, we must have within us some seed of misunderstanding that needs to be corrected. If someone else "presses our buttons," we only misdirect our energy if we blame them, for our job in life is not to run from button pressers, but to find our buttons and unplug them. Those who bring our irritation to the surface are doing us a very great service, indeed. For this reason, we ought to be beholden to those good friends we mistakenly label "enemies," for they are (whether they realize it or not) the very agents of God that show us our way to greater strength.

We are told of a Greek man who paid someone a daily wage to follow him through his affairs and insult him, so that he, through learning to remain steadfast in the face of criticism, would develop strength of character. Considering his example, perhaps we should be thankful that our enemy-friends are doing us such a valuable service at no charge.

In the "Inner Game" workshop, Tim Gallway showed me how we already understand and use this principle. "When you want a good game of tennis," he asked, "who do you call for a partner? Usually an opponent who is equal or superior to you in skill. It's no fun playing with someone who doesn't challenge you."

And so it is with the inner game of life. We want to grow; we want to improve our skills in life. To drift through life without challenges would be useless and boring. We would be like stagnant algae on a motionless lake. If you have mastered any art, sport, or field of endeavor, you know the value of challenge, adversity, and discipline. The violin virtuoso welcomes with enthusiasm a new and difficult piece of music. He must flex his musical muscles to master the piece. He well knows that through the practice of overcoming the challenge, his proficiency is increased.

This sharpening of skills is the real value of competition. Many have lost sight of the purpose of healthy competition, which helps us to draw forth inner strength and encourages us to transcend our ideas of personal limitation. The real competition, however, is *within* the person, and not *between* people. We must each compete with — strive to conquer — our notions of how much we can do. When pushed to our limit, we usually find that we can do more than we thought we could. Our opponents in sports are actually performing a loving favor: they are working with us to support us in overcoming our weakness. In essence, competition is cooperation.

Looking at adversity in this way, we really *can* love our enemies. They serve us hard shots until we learn God's way of returning them. So mastered, we move on to a more formidable challenger until there are none that can defeat us.

As I reflect on my unfoldment, I see that the difficult experiences taught me practical lessons and made me stronger. They moved me forward to new and more fulfilling ways of being. They pushed me out of ignorance and into Truth. They were, in fact, my keys to freedom.

This is the new light which changes the way we view life's challenges, one which renews us as we see God's good hand in all. Hilda has said that the New Age requires a "new way of thinking." We must evaluate our experiences in a totally new way; God knows the old way didn't work. We must refuse to see our sorrows, hurts, and conflicts only at the surface level. We must look deeper. There is no wasted time or purposeless experience. We must take the challenges that now face us and re-work them in our minds until we see them in a positive light. Until they come into that light, they are begging for our awareness, and as soon as we give it to them, they become golden.

GOLDEN OPPORTUNITIES

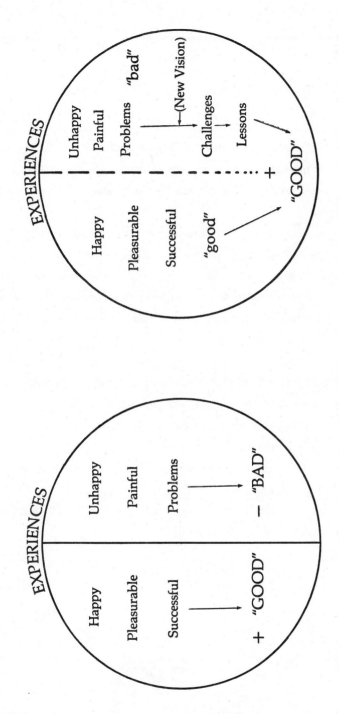

LIMITED VIEW OF LIFE

EXPERIENCES

Happy
Pleasurable
Successful → + "GOOD"

Unhappy
Painful
Problems → – "BAD"

WHOLE VIEW OF LIFE

EXPERIENCES

Unhappy
Painful
Problems → (New Vision) → Challenges → Lessons → + "GOOD"

Happy
Pleasurable
Successful
"good" → + "GOOD"

The masterful attitude toward life is the one that takes the whole view of experiences. The wise person sees problems as challenges, and values them for the lessons that they offer. In this way, all experiences become good.

"You must cease to look at challenge as your enemy. Whenever you hold a force of God outside your Self, you create evil. Hold all events within God, and evil cannot exist.

This process of development is one of revising your understanding. Experiences continue to be what they have been, are, and shall be. It is you who must bring your understanding of your experiences into clarity. We tell you that holding your life in the Light shall bring you the peace for which you yearn.

You must master the art of perspective. A slight shift in perspective is all that is necessary to see the wholeness of your training. It is, in fact, the training that you have chosen, in a way that the mind believes it understands, but cannot really accept.

Were you to see all of your experiences in the Love that they are given, you would cherish every moment of your life, for every moment is one of great opportunity. Be grateful, Children of Light, you are loved."

THE GIFT

My father passed on when I was 18 years old. At the time, I was fortunate to have many friends who gave their loving support and sympathy. We received many thoughtful cards, flowers, fruit baskets, and kind visitors. The person who stands out most prominently in my mind, however, was our neighborhood butcher, a Jewish man who had seen his family killed in the Nazi holocaust.

I shall never forget our brief interlude that spring afternoon on the steps of the synagogue. Having just learned about my dad's passing, he asked, "So . . . how are you doing?" "O.K.," I answered. He looked me straight in the eye, with a deep, seasoned balance of strength and understanding, and asked (though it was not really a question), "Pushing on, huh?"

In those three words, in the firm way in which he offered them, I felt a wave of strength and fortitude resonate deep within my soul. He was perhaps the only person, of all the well-wishers, from whom I felt no melancholy sympathy. It seemed that many of my other good friends were somewhat anxious about how to deal with me and my father's death. This man, however, through tremendous adversity, had learned a powerful inner calm. His firmness, his understanding, and his love were all communicated to me in just a few words and a strong but compassionate glance of the eyes. He gave me much, and as I remember all of my friends for their unique gifts, I shall always be grateful to him for his detached, yet very loving, support.

The greatest gift that we can offer to one another is the affirmation of our mutual strength. To go into agreement with thoughts of weakness or victimization does not serve one who needs light, and not more darkness.

When I first saw Patricia Sun, she was fielding questions from a tough audience, on healing and dealing with the hardships of life. It seemed that no matter what horrendous predicaments were thrown at her for her advice, including cancers, brutal crimes, and life's callousness, she would smile and begin her response with "That's wonderful!" She would then go on to describe what unique lessons each situation had to offer the questioner. All of her responses were given with total compassion, awareness of the pain being felt, and respect for the position of the person needing support. Yet she did not sympathize with their anger or feelings of victimization. And she won the audience's heart. When someone asked her how she healed people, she innocently answered, "I don't know; I just feel their pain and love them."

To heal one another and our planet is an ability that we all have. That healing takes place when we look past circumstances into Light. To acknowledge Light where others see darkness is to give a very great blessing.

At one of Eric Butterworth's fine lectures, a woman raised her hand and asked how she could get out of her horrible job. She hated her boss, couldn't stand the work, did not get along with her colleagues, and she was tremendously uncomfortable in the position. "Why do you want to leave?" Eric teased; "It sounds like you've really found your niche!"

Her job, he meant, was offering her an unusually fine opportunity to see where she needed to change the way she was looking at life, and to grow beyond her narrow vision. If she stayed with her job until she no longer reacted to it in an emotional way, she would then have graduated from it, having earned the right to move on to another lesson elsewhere.

If she ran away from the position in a huff, she would not be free of the traits *within* her that made her uncomfortable. It is necessary to see that the problem was not in the job, but in *her*. The job was just what it was, and she was reacting to it according to her outlook. It was especially obvious that the problem was hers because she disliked *everyone* and *everything* about the job; she was looking at it through dark glasses.

We may say of a challenging job or relationship, "I am free . . . I can leave if I like!" Certainly we may leave, but more than likely, in the next job, or the one after it, or the one after that, we will encounter the same problems over the same issues, with even greater intensity. The process will continue until we stand up to the situation, face it, and conquer it. The freedom that we feel by leaving a difficult situation is fool's freedom; the freedom that we gain by conquering it is God's.

Hilda often speaks of such challenges as "logs" — inner obstacles of unconsciousness that we cannot sidestep or squirm under — precisely because we must master these particular lessons in order to grow to our full stature.

We must place the log on the block of faith, split it with the wedge of determination, and break it apart with the axe of courage; nothing less will do. As the old song goes:

> So high, can't get over Him
> So low, can't get under Him
> So wide, can't get 'round Him
> Gotta go through the door

The door is none other than that of Love's peaceful kingdom. The common person sees only the log and bemoans a dead-end path. The visionary — the one who holds a constant memory of her or his Divine Goal — sees the log as the marker of a hidden treasure, and knows that God always has the ability to remove obstacles that fear cannot.

"Grace is given you in your hour of trial. Those who understand the opportunity in adversity have discovered a secret that greatly hastens your homeward journey. Go further, go further, go further, Children, in your understanding of life's hardships, until you find the jewel.

Be not hasty to judge or flee from that which troubles you. The situation has been given you for your education. Would you flee from a lesson in a class that you requested for your improvement? Accept what is given in the spirit that it is offered, and your learning shall proceed well.

You attract to you the events, persons, and experiences required for your growth. Blame not God, the world, or your brother for your predicament, for you, of your own free will, have drawn these circumstances to you for your betterment. It is this betterment that we hold dear to us, for of it you become free to serve the gentle purpose of Love.

Open your heart to the struggles of your brethren, but do not let your compassion be tainted by sympathy. You best serve one another by affirming your constant abiding in God's Perfect Presence. Remain firm in the midst of chaos, see sorrow with Divine eyes, and find God in seeming misfortune.

You are, each of you, a healer. As your purity of intention makes you a vessel for His Will to heal, He will brighten the world through you. This is the intention of all who live to serve humanity, and you, who would freely choose to make it your intention, are blessed in your choice."

𝒯he 𝒫ath

"All paths are the same: they lead nowhere . . . There are paths going through the bush, or into the bush. In my own life I could say I have traversed long, long paths, but I am not anywhere. My benefactor's question has meaning now. Does this path have a heart? If it does, the path is good; if it doesn't, it is of no use. Both paths lead nowhere; but one has a heart, the other doesn't. One makes for a joyful journey; as long as you follow it, you are one with it. The other will make you curse your life. One makes you strong; the other weakens you."

— Don Juan, in Carlos Castenada's *The Teachings of Don Juan*

ACTION

Pray with your feet moving.

The awareness of God is useless unless it is put into action in the affairs of daily life. Martin Luther King, Jr. said, "I have been to the mountaintop and seen the Promised Land" — and he chose to return. He came back to march. Indeed, we can march effectively only when we have been to the mountaintop — to the high perspective from which we see how Divinely our world could work — and then returned to bring that vision into expression.

Life is about harmonizing our human relationships, conducting business with integrity, and loving. Meditation, prayer, and spiritual discipline are worthwhile only if our overall life gets better. If it doesn't, we are not praying or meditating properly. There must be consistency between meditation and action. To love God in prayer and then to criticize our neighbor is not consistent. To see the same God in meditation and in the bus driver is the affirmation of God in real life.

To the enlightened, or God-realized person, all of life is an opportunity to see God and to put God into action. There are no ups or downs, no comings or goings. One evening, at the end of a group meditation, Hilda asked me to sing a song. I had gone very "high" in meditation, and I slightly resisted "coming down." Hilda perceptibly picked this up and commented, "Poor Alan; he thinks he has to come down to sing — he doesn't know that he doesn't have to come down." She was teaching that had I not kept a separation in my mind between meditation and singing, I would not have been jarred by the transition

251

— a transition which I created in my own mind.

During another guided meditation, a very sweet and etheric one, Hilda was leading us through an exquisitely lovely image of a garden. In the middle of a sentence, Hilda interrupted this picture of Heaven to announce a meeting after class. I immediately felt annoyed that she would bring such a mundane topic into the midst of such a "spiritual" experience. Her next sentence was: "Were any of you kids disturbed by that announcement? I wasn't — *everything* is God, to me."

We do not need to go off to a cave and renounce the world as a recluse, although there may be a time for retreating to do inner work. We do not need to sit for long hours in lotus position. We may simply sit in quiet prayer or meditation for twenty minutes, once or twice a day, and attune ourselves with our Ideals, which will later bear fruit in action. Jack Schwarz, a well known teacher and healer, describes meditation as "charging your batteries." He says, "If a car battery is run down, you simply jump it or recharge it, and then you use the car. If you keep charging it after it is energized, you begin to waste energy and you miss out on using the car for its intended purpose — action."

There was a man who would arise each morning before dawn and go to a certain spot in the woods, where he would sit quietly and make contact with his Divine Source. Then he would talk to the flowers and they would reveal their secrets to him. Then, when he had established his deep connection with God and all creation, he would enter his day's activity and create new ways to beautify the world through living things and to make practical use of the gifts they offer humankind. This man was Dr. George Washington Carver. Dr. Carver was a living example of a masterful balance between inner communion and outer expression. He said, *"Pray as if it all depends on God, but work as if it all depends on you."*[*]

Paramahansa Yogananda was another who found God in the earth as well as the heavens. In his marvelous book, *The Law Of Success*, Yogananda teaches,

> *Before embarking on important undertakings, sit quietly, calm your senses and thoughts, and meditate deeply. You*

[*] For a most inspiring account of Dr. Carver's life, read *The Man Who Would Talk To The Flowers*, by Glenn Clark, Macalester Park Publishing Co., 1511 Grant Ave., St. Paul, MN 55105

will then be guided by the great creative power of Spirit.
After that you should utilize all necessary material means
to achieve your goal. **

The aim of meditation practice is to learn to be able to meditate all the time — not just when sitting with eyes closed, but right in the mainstream of life: in the family, in the office, and at the supermarket. God is to be found in silence, but He is also knowable while taking the kids to Hebrew school, negotiating for a higher salary, and cleaning the bathtub. The idea is to remember Who We Are — *wherever we are.*

Our best opportunitites to practice the presence of God are in the situations in which we don't think He is. Alan Watts said, "If you can't meditate in a boiler room, you can't meditate!" Real learning consists of remaining calm, peaceful, and aware of God in situations which once made us nervous, upset, or afraid. As a teenager, I used to perform an ancient and very sacred ceremony in my synagogue on important holidays. According to my lineage, I was required to stand before the entire congregation and sing a blessing to everyone in the temple. The first time I did it, I was never so uptight in all my life. I made an error, and all the learned men went wild. I wanted to jump into the ark and hide. It was a horror movie for me.

The next time the holiday came around, I wished I could change my last name. But I felt it was my duty to go through with it, and so I did. I continued like this for a few years, dreading the ceremony, but doing it anyway, and being pretty much out of focus through the whole thing. (If God was blessing the congregation through me, He sure had to find a way to do it in spite of me!) Then, one time, for just a few seconds, I actually felt relaxed during the ritual! What a wonderful feeling of freedom! I was astonished to see that I could do this thing and keep my cool! After that, the ceremony became easier and easier for me each succeeding time, and eventually it was even enjoyable. Through practice, I learned to remember my inner peace — meditate — in the midst of a "threatening" situation. This is exactly the awareness that we come into the world to develop: to know, through experience, that we need not lose our peace in any situation, and that

**Yogananda, *THE LAW OF SUCCESS.* The address for Yogananda's writings is given on the copyright page of this book.

when we find God within our own heart, we find Her everywhere.

We pretty well know that if we clear our mind, we can bring order to our affairs; when our mind is clear, our room automatically becomes tidy, our car runs efficiently, and our checkbook is balanced. What many people are not aware of, however, is that *we can use our affairs to clear our mind.* If we make the effort to smooth out our bedspread, to sit down and tackle our checkbook until it is balanced, or to clean out the back closet, we will find our mind also organized, almost as if we sat down to meditate. This is so because in order to bring our affairs into alignment we must mobilize the state of mind to accomplish it. In other words, we are using life's "little" acts as a means to bring clarity to us.

This places what we do during the day in a whole new light. It means that *everything is a way to discover and express God.* It means that jobs and relationships and the eleven o'clock news are all good, for they are all opportunities to practice being conscious. And so it doesn't matter so much what we do, then; the crucial issue is the *consciousness that we bring to what we do.* I heard of a bank vice-president who "dropped out" and went on a spiritual quest. He threw away his grey suits, became a vegetarian, made a pilgrimage to India, studied with learned pundits and sages, and went through many experiences and lessons. One day about ten years later, he was walking down a street in his old home town when one of his former colleagues saw him and offered him his old job, which just happened to be open at the time. The man pondered for a moment and thought, "Why not?" and so he returned to his job. He had learned that no job is better than another; the important element is the *awareness* that we keep while doing the job. In fact, practicing God's Presence is our only real job, no matter what the company's job description says. Our only real company is Truth, and it is God Incorporated.

We have all come to earth for a reason — to learn the lessons that the earth has to teach, and to bless the world through sharing (through our being and our actions) what we have learned. To desist from action is to miss or delay our opportunity to bless, and to go into action with God in mind is to bring God directly into the world to serve it. As Hilda once said, *"Real meditation begins when you open your eyes."*

''The path of purposeful action bears a double blessing for those who walk it: in the blessing of the world is your own. Right action is the key to the reestablishment of God consciousness within your world.

Errors must be corrected according to their own nature. The world has lost the awareness of God in its actions, and so it is through action that awareness must be restored. Find for yourself a comfortable balance of stillness and activity, and serve the world from such a point of equalibrium.

Be not concerned about the form that your action should take. Your expression will unfold naturally. Simply love God, hold to your purest intentions, and remain true to your inner Light. In this consciousness shall your place be made known to you without question. The miracle of right action is its willingness to spring forth from good intention.

Let your deeds speak your message to the world. Your actions have the power to heal. This is a responsibility of great and wonderful magnitude. It is your only responsibility, and it is the easiest one, for when you choose the responsibility to heal the world, you instantly allow God to heal the world through you. This is your role as a messenger of Light.''

INTEGRITY

If you can keep your head while all about you are losing theirs and blaming it on you . . .
— Rudyard Kipling, *IF*

The confused purposes of the world would dissuade the spiritual aspirant from remaining as dear to Truth as Truth remains to him. Integrity is like a high rock above which the stormy ocean of worldly troubles cannot rise. The spiritual path is a razor's edge odyssey, fraught with temptation and pitfalls that become more subtle as the winding mountain road advances toward the summit. When our hearts and our vision remain fixed on the Light of God, however, we pass unscathed through the mire of delusion and adversity.

Sir Thomas More, nobly portrayed in *A Man for All Seasons*, was faced with intense pressure to abandon his code of ethics. He was perhaps the only man in England who stood for his beliefs while pressed to uphold an unscrupulous king. His position, his family, and his life were under threat of death. In a ploy to persuade More to sign an oath of allegiance, one of his colleagues asked him, "Why don't you just do it for the sake of comradery?" More's response: "When you go to Heaven for following your conscience, and I go to hell for not following mine, will you then join me there, 'for the sake of comradery?' "

Every day, each one of us is given a thousand little opportunities to choose between peace and turmoil, between clarity and confusion, between love and animosity. I am speaking now about remaining quiet, firm, and loving in the midst of our daily activities. We may never be the only person in a kingdom to stand for Truth, as did Sir — Saint — Thomas More, but we can bless the world by remaining peaceful in all that we do.

We live in a world of multifarious thoughts — all around us are thoughts, thoughts, and more thoughts. We must deal not only with our own thoughts, but with those of the people around us. Life in "the marketplace" is largely a matter of maintaining our center — our integrity — in the midst of chaotic influences. If we are not careful, we can lose touch with our center, and we will have to work to regain it. If we enter activity with a strong and prepared attitude, however, we serve ourselves and all those we meet.

I once went to a workshop called "How to keep other people from stealing your energy." Actually, no one can steal our energy from us unless we give it to them. And no one is purposely seeking to steal our energy — everyone is just vibrating according to their own evolution. It is true, however, that we can lose our *awareness* of our inner Light by accepting negative thoughts from the outside world. The moment we go into agreement with a thought of evil, sickness, or victimization, we have sold out our knowledge of Truth for the sake of an illusion.

This illusion is a *practically* real force in the world. It is not really real, but there is a belief that it is real, and that belief is enough to make is *seem* real. If everyone in the world woke up tomorrow and had no belief in evil, that would be the end of evil. The "devil" would starve to death. On one *Star Trek* episode, a malignant force invaded the Starship Enterprise and wreaked havoc by instilling fear and dissension among the crew. As a sense of threat and animosity grew, so did chaos. Someone finally discovered that the negative force was feeding on fear. So Dr. McCoy gave the entire crew a laughing serum that made them happy for just a few minutes, and the invader was forced to leave the ship. It had nothing to which to attach itself. There were no organisms upon which it could leech, like a parasite. No one accepted evil, and evil died.

In Truth, it never lived, not on the Starship Enterprise, nor on the Starship Earth. Its illusion is maintained only by erroneous belief in it. When we refuse to accept untruth, it can hold no power over us. In the parable of *Ulysses*, Circe the witch turns all of Ulysses' crew into pigs so she can keep Ulysses her captive. When he discovers this, Ulysses firmly points at her and commands, "You turn my men back into their right form right now!" He says it with such conviction and in such a powerful way that she just has to do it. She just has to. The strength of Light is always more powerful than the assumed strength of darkness.

In the same way, we can free ourselves and each other of negation by refusing to accept it when it comes toward us. If someone sends you a C.O.D. package that you did not order, and you do not accept it, it goes back to the factory. If you accept it, you have to pay for it. A hand can only clap if there is another hand to meet it. If there is no hand to meet it, there is no sound. If we do not meet someone's negative thinking with like thoughts, the negation will fizzle out. One day, for example, a friend of mine saw me when she was in a caustic mood. She complained about everything. I was in such a joyous mood that I just could not take her seriously, and I began to joke with her about all the things she was complaining about. Before long, she, too, was laughing. A few hours later, she came to me and said, "I just want to thank you for not taking me seriously; laughing about my complaints was exactly what I needed to get me off of them."

There is another way that we can lose our center. It is through curiosity. There is a very useful kind of curiosity that prods us on to explore, investigate, and discover, but there is also a wasteful form of curiosity that dissipates our mental energies. Too often, I am tempted to tune into casual conversations, to listen to the talk in the next room, or to pick up any old magazine on the coffee table. Unmanaged curiosity is a lack of mental mastery, and it causes us to lose our balance and veer from our own path. Just as the physical body can become obese and the emotional body can get "played out," the mental body can become disturbed by tuning into unnecessary and extraneous thought-forms. Let us concentrate on that which is ours, and leave the rest be. Curiosity simply draws an overload of purposeless thoughts into our consciousness, and we are then required to meditate, sleep more, or to do something to cleanse us of that which is not ours.

That which *is* ours is given to us only when we are willing to claim it. Like positive thinking and appreciation, we must work at remembering and acting on the Truth, and this is what integrity is all about. There is much agreement on illusion. At every turn, there are thought-forms of emptiness and sorrow. The only way to overcome illusion is with our own affirmation of the reality and the fullness of Love. Like a vampire that shrinks away from light or a cross, negativity flees when confronted with integrity.

We have been empowered with the greatest weapon there is — Truth. No bomb, no hatred, and no illusion can match the strength of Truth. It is our only real friend. When we stand for Truth, we are integrated, whole, and firm. We can walk amid any darkness, totally protected and assured of safety. We can "march into hell for a heavenly cause." Our love can dry the tears of the world. We can end wars and sorrows and the travails of those whose lives have been laden with pain. The entire universe is integrated and whole. When we remain true to integrity, we are aligned with the Force of the entire universe. When we walk with integrity, we walk with God.

"You who have been touched by the scepter of the living God must walk in the Light of the One who has bestowed upon you the blessing of His lineage. Integrity is your fortress and your redeemer, and, yea, the redeemer of the world. Christ Himself was the embodiment of Integrity, and in so being is rightly called the Son of God.

The path of life is difficult and treacherous only when you agree with the illusions with which the world seeks to maintain itself. Shun illusion for a moment, and you stand free of it forever. In that moment of freedom, you inherit eternal life, which is already yours.

We who encourage you to walk the path of righteousness, promise to stand by your side in your journey. As you remain true to integrity, Light shall be revealed to you in great splendor, the selfsame Light that you see in your most holy dreams. Begin by accepting the vision of Holiness in your heart. This is your only real vision. All others shall pass away, but the Vision of the Heart remains until the end of form.

Walk with dignity, Sons and Daughters of Truth. In this holy life, you have been given all that you have ever truly desired — the knowledge of your own sanctity, and that of all life. Remain confident in the reality of Love, and you shall not — you cannot — fail. All the holy saints, masters, and angels gladly sing with you in the chorus of happiness that was composed at the beginning of time. Alleluia and Amen."

COURAGE

Those who step forward to make a stand for Truth must be prepared to be spurned by the world from which they once enjoyed support. The world loves its own, but finds great threat in those who trust not in it. The call of the new life means the surrender of our desire to be accepted and approved by those from whom we received nurturing in the past. We may lose our old friends; we will get new ones. Our families may discourage us; our hearts will encourage us. People in the world may criticize what we are doing; all the saints and holy masters who love the Truth will love us. We may lose our earthly inheritance; we will gain all the riches in the universe. We may have to give up our old thoughts of who we are; we will know who we really are. We will no longer belong to the world; we will belong to God.

I recently attended a Catholic wedding of two very dear friends. The moment came when we were invited to line up for Holy Communion. I love receiving Communion. I don't know whether or not the wafer really turns into the body of Christ, but I pray and imagine that through the ceremony I am receiving the Holy Spirit of Christ. I consider it a great blessing.

At this wedding, sitting next to me (ironically) were the Jewish parents of one of my oldest friends, with whom I was very involved in Orthodox Judaism. The father is the president of the synagogue. For quite a few years, I used to visit their home on the sabbath, and they knew me as a very strict Orthodox Jew. These fine people were very kind to me, and I was treated as one of the family. Now, here I am, ten years later, deeply in love with Jesus, thrilled at the opportunity to take Holy Communion. It was as if my past were sitting at my right hand, and my future beckoning at my left.

I felt that these people might be hurt or upset if they saw me line up for Communion. Here was my moment of truth. Actually, there was no question about it. As I rose from my seat I could sense their thoughts of shock and disappointment. My heart was beating heavily, and I could feel the perspiration on my brow. But I had to do what I had to do. At that moment I had to let die all of my thoughts about who I was, in relation to those people. Though I loved and respected them as fully as I ever did, I had to be true to the promptings of my spiritual heart and trust that God would take care of me if I followed my inner call. I had to make a stand for my values.

Every one of us is faced with such a moment of truth at each step of our evolutionary unfoldment. Some would call these moments tests, others, challenges, and some would embrace them as invitations born of Grace. Every spiritual aspirant is given the opportunity — a fork in the road — to let go of an old pattern of living, and to accept a new and glorious one.

The opportunity always takes the form of clear cut earth plane choice. It may be a chance for a physical pleasure or some kind of ego temptation, such as for power, money, or some long-standing personal weakness in the form of a desire. The test always presents the aspirant with the choice of saying "Yes" to one action and "No" to another. In such a circumstance, God uses the physical world to manifest a situation that symbolizes the dynamics of our inner evolution.

When we do choose to step forward toward our higher life, there are masters, saints, angels, and enlightened beings who extend their helping hands to draw us up to a richer and more fullfilling station in our life's journey. It is said that "when you take one step toward God, He takes ten toward you." A friend of mine, for example, who had been shoplifting for a long time, began to want to "clean up his act." He wanted to stop stealing, but this shoplifting had become habitual for him, and he was afraid he would never be able to stop. He told me this story:

> One day I went to the mall to get a needle for my stereo.
> I walked into Radio Shack, picked out the needle, and
> went to the counter to pay for it. Just at that moment, the
> salesman turned his back to get something off a shelf. My

first inclination was to slip the needle into my pocket and walk out. No one at all would have seen me. But there was a part of me that did not want to take it, a feeling that I wanted to change my life. I stood there for a little while, torn. It was as if I was being pulled in two directions at once. Then I decided to try, just this once, paying for something I could have easily stolen. So I waited for the salesman to turn around, and I paid him. At that moment I felt such a wave of relief come over me that I can't even describe it in words. Something happened within me — something that was much bigger than my little decision not to steal that one needle. Since that time I have not stolen anything, and I don't really want to.

If you are struggling with a bad habit, like my friend, do not be overwhelmed by the enormity of it, for *you do not have to conquer all of it yourself.* God will help you. This I promise you. All you have to do is your share, which is to make an initial effort. When, with your good intention, you open the door to help, God will pour into you His Will, which can conquer anything. At the point that you take that one step in a new direction, you have mastered the old habit or trait that was retarding your progress. Having passed your test, you will no longer be faced with that particular trial, except, perhaps, in the form of "fried seeds" — old desires that occasionally arise but which do not have life in them sufficient to reproduce themselves. These obsolete desires are simply the residue of past thought patterns which can no longer entrap us, but which we must patiently bear, like the ripples of water created by a stone that we have thrown into a pond. You may experience fleeting desires to do an old bad habit, but they are nothing more than old thoughts that will eventually fizzle out.

The source of courage is *conviction.* Conviction is the powerful inner knowledge that what we are doing is good, an awareness unassailable by any opinion or persuasion. Conviction is crystalized faith, and courageous acts are the natural expression of conviction.

To the world, the person of conviction is a fool, a martyr, an ascetic. To the faithful, sacrifice is meaningless; the joy of following the promptings of the soul far outshines the meager loss that the world bemoans. The world labels the acts of a saint as sacrifice only because these are threatening to the treasures the world holds dear. If there is no fear of loss, there is no consciousness of sacrifice. Ramana Maharshi said, "I didn't feel like eating, and they said I was fasting!" And once, when I thanked Hilda for interrupting her lunch to talk with me, she smiled and told me, "That's fine, darling . . . the blessing has to go through me to you . . . so I get a blessing, too."

Wayshowers are indifferent to opinion because they know they are walking the path of destiny. When Helen and Scott Nearing established their self-sufficient homestead in Vermont, they were branded renegades, weirdos, and Communists. Despite intense criticism, they burned wood for heat, ate organic foods, did not smoke cigarettes, recycled their materials, bartered, and shared their abundance; they called it *The Good Life.*

Now, some fifty years later, much of what they stood for has become the forefront of the society to be. We have discovered that the earth's resources are limited, the chemicals in our food are poisons, and that sharing and joyous living are, indeed, the way that God intended for us to live happily on this planet. I once asked Helen: "How does it feel now that society is coming around to your way of thinking? All the things that you were chastised for are now accepted and popular; I'll bet you're happy to see this confirmation."

Helen's response: "It's nice that other people are doing it, but, to tell you the truth, if no one else ever did what we did, it would not make one bit of difference to us. We did what we did because we knew that it was right for us, and that was enough reason for it."

There was a saint named Mansur Mastana who discovered a Light and a Reason more powerful than he could find in the world. Swami Muktananda tells this story about him:

> He used to soar in the inner spaces, and he saw the highest truth right there. He began to say, "Anahalaq, Anahalaq, I am God, I am God, the truth is within me, the truth is within me, I am in the midst of truth, and the truth is in my midst!" He began to dance, "I have found it, I have found it, I have got it, I have got it!" The orthodox clerics, who never understand a thing, got after him, accusing him of uttering blasphemous heresy, and Mansur said, "I do not mean to utter heresy. I am only speaking the truth which I have experienced directly. From that, an

understanding has spontaneously arisen within: I am not this body; I am the same divine light of which the whole cosmos is an extension." He continued, "You may break a mosque, you may break a temple, you may break any holy place, but you must not break the human heart, because there the Lord Himself dwells. Inside a temple you worship an idol, inside a mosque you worship the void, but in the temple of the heart, the divine light is scintillating, sparkling all the time, and that is the true house of the Lord."

*Because he said this, he was hanged, and he proclaimed the same truth even from the hanging noose. From there he began to shout, "Fling [your idols] into the water. Go around fearlessly proclaiming 'I am God, I am God, I am God!' "**

There is no power in the universe that can stand between courage and its expression.

*Swami Muktananda, *Getting Rid of What You Haven't Got*, S.Y.D.A. Foundation, San Francisco, 1967.

"Your moment of decision is inevitable and it is shared by all: you must bear witness to the Truth or silently consent to the perpetration of a lie.

You are asked but to let go of a meaningless life, one which always seemed to offer peace, but delivered only emptiness. When you testify to the whisperings of your deepest inclinations, the life of Light is opened before you. This new life, unlike the old, hides not behind the promise of peace, but justifies itself in the constant giving of serenity. The brotherhood of the peaceful is small in number, but great in reward. Those who would enter its ranks must renounce the dark cloak of the burdens of the world and receive in their stead the white robes of the community of Light.

As you give assent to God, your old treasures wither like the leaves of autumn. Fear not, Children of Light, for what is God's shall most certainly be returned to you in great abundance, and what is no longer yours shall bear you no further need or pleasure. When you are willing to confess that your love for God is greater than that for the world, a helping hand of brilliant light is extended to you. At the same time, there will be a clutching, a grabbing at your feet by a thousand grey and bony fingers, in the guise of old friends, habits, and excitements. These promptings are not real, but mere shadows of a myth to which you no longer give credence. Unnourished by your further indulgence, must they crumble into dust.

The new life that awaits you is one of splendor and richness. The rooms of your new mansion are filled with morning sunlight, and its windows open upon lush gardens and the sweet song of the nightingale. You have consciously renounced your dark dungeon of self, with its empty corridors and long stairways that lead to nowhere. You have released yourself from the prison of self-involvement and accepted your freedom as the child of the master of a great and wonderous estate. You have assented to your Divinity, a happy reunion of all that is beautiful, lovely, and true.

If you would take this courageous step, the only step worth taking, you must be prepared to be rejected by the world. You must not fall under mockery and misunderstanding. You must, in turning your back upon illusions, be prepared to have them scream into your ear in the name of their self-justification. You must have the holy courage to walk the path of the lonely and the exiled. You must take up a simple tunic in place of the vanity of the world, and walk barefoot through the snows of the remote mountains where dwell those who no longer belong to the world. Your only guide will be the footprints in the snow, quietly yet firmly impressed by the saints who have trod this narrow, winding path before you.

Yet in your travail shall you be urged ever onward by the mysteriously beautiful call of the conch, sounding ever clearer, drawing you to its source at the summit just beyond the clouds. There shall you find the humble home of the brotherhood whose faint whisperings to your sleeping heart awoke it and drew you to your lonely journey, now so near completion.

Reunited with your brothers and sisters in Truth, in the simplicity of a remote mountain village, the promptings of your soul are revealed to you as the worthwhile source of your long trek through the wilderness. You may then cast away your walking stick and stand forever free of the hardship of the illusion of abandonment. Here your rightful place in the community of souls is confirmed. Here are you shown the holy plan for the unfoldment of your perfection, which in the valley seemed a great enigma, yet here at the summit reveals itself to be Divine.

Take heart, then, in your labors, for the conclusion of your story has now been told to you. As you make it your own, you earn the right to work humbly for the cause of Divine Love, and in so choosing draw your searching brothers and sisters to their home in the community of the peaceful. They now follow the footsteps that you have etched in the Himalayan snows. Verily, their rooms in the golden mansion await them, and it is your privilege to usher them in to the Abode of Peace.''

GUIDANCE

Guru, God, and Self are One
— Neem Karoli Baba

Whenever I have needed guidance, God has never failed to give it. For any question I have asked in earnestness and sincerity, an answer has come. It is not always an answer that I want to hear, or that I expect to hear, or that I understand, and it does not always come immediately, but it is always one that works. This process is a miracle to me, and I have come to see that every human being is endowed with the same Divine gift.

Guidance is always available. We need only to *ask, listen,* and *accept.* The wisest counselor is your very Self. No guru, teacher, therapist, or psychic could ever know more about your path than God will tell you directly. The answers to our questions are waiting within us to be retrieved like precious pearls at the ocean floor. We do not need to seek any further than our own heart, the temple in which God Himself eternally dwells.

If you ask for an answer, do not dictate to your higher self where or when or how the answer is to be given. We never really know in what way guidance will come; we just need to know that it will. Paul had invested a lot of energy working *against* the teachings of Jesus when he was literally knocked off his horse by the Holy Spirit. And I love the process in *Close Encounters of the Third Kind,* which I saw as a metaphor for the spiritual path. The hero is obsessed with the vague image of a mountain, being communicated to him psychically by

271

benevolent U.F.O. friends, who are instructing him how to contact them. He feels an undeniable urge to know what that mountain is, but he just can't seem to understand it. He starts to see this form in his shaving cream, in his mashed potatoes, and he is even driven to build a mountain in his living room. He just has to understand this image, but he is at a loss as to how to do it. Finally, in desperation, frustration, and exhaustion, he gives up and writes his intuition off as a pipe dream. Exactly at that moment, there flashes on the television a news report showing the exact mountain, complete with location, that he has intuitively been searching for — or, which has been searching for him. The guidance came — in its own right way and right timing.

The inner guide is sometimes called the "still, small voice." It is not really a voice that speaks in words, although we may sometimes hear the answer in the form of words. It is more of a quiet knowing. It does not rant, rave, chide, or dictate. It just knows, feels, and gently nudges us in the direction of our highest good. Some call it the conscience, and that is what it is. I used to associate "conscience" with guilt and the fiery wrath of God. Now I see that our conscience is the most helpful and loving friend that we have in this life. The still small voice will always tell us right from wrong, but it will never disown or condemn us for making an error. It is dedicated only to our happiness, and no matter what errors we have made, it will continue to guide us, even telling us how to undo the errors that we made in not having hearkened to its original gentle bidding.

I was recently told a remarkable story about the power of intuition. A tai chi* student was driving on a mountain highway when she decided to try out some of the principles that she had been learning. She took a few deep breaths and found her inner center of energy. At that moment, she felt a strange urge to pull off the highway and drive slowly on the shoulder of the road. Though her thoughts were ranting, "This is crazy; why don't you drive like a normal person?" she followed her intuition. Then, as she pulled around the next bend, she came upon an auto collision — right in the lane in which she *would have been* driving had she not listened to her intuitive prompting. Yet she escaped, thanks to her inner guidance — and her willingness to accept it.

I know, too, of a man who, when he has a troubling situation in

*an ancient Oriental form of moving meditation

his life, takes a glass of water before he goes to sleep, and affirms, "I am drinking the solution to my problem!" He inevitably wakes up with the answer. I do not believe there is any magic in the water, but I do believe that there is a great resource of inner knowledge that is released within him when he opens himself to it. Such is the nature of our Divine Guide. It happily offers its help to us through any channel that we find comfortable.

Nothing is too small to be undeserving of God's help. So many times I have misplaced a key, or I have the gnawing feeling that I have forgotten something, and I stop for just a moment and say, "O.K., God, can you give me a hand?" Wonderously, into my mind flashes the thought of the hall closet or a jacket that I wore last week, where, when I check, the object is right there. I remember, too, that several years ago, during a gas shortage, I needed to get to an important meeting one morning. The night before the meeting, I realized I would need to get gas before setting out, and I had no idea where to go for it. Around 5 a.m., in sort of a half-dream half-awake state, I had the feeling of Satya Sai Baba come to me and say, "Go to Hess!" To the Hess Station I went, and took my place as one of the first cars in a gas line at a station that was just about to open.

I have no idea how God knows what She knows, but She sure does know it. She will tell us anything we need to know. When I massage someone's back, for example, my hands are somehow drawn to the exact place where there is a kink or a knot, the spot that needs the most attention. The person does not tell me where to put my hands, nor do I search for the spot. The hands just go there almost automatically, and the person says, "Wow! How did you know that was the spot?" The truth is that I didn't know, but God was kind enough to show me. A printer friend of mine told me a similar story. He explained that, although he rarely reads the copy of what he is printing, if there is a slight error on the page, his eye will somehow be drawn right to it for correction. And a chemistry teacher told me that his students cannot figure out how he can mark all of their test papers overnight. He says, "I just lightly scan the whole paper. Although it is full of complex equations and numbers, if there is a mistake, it just sort of 'pops out' at me."

Guidance may also come through the mouth of another person. There is no real distinction between inner and outer guidance. We divide the universe into "inners" and "outers," but God is One, and all of life is inner as well as outer. Sri Ramakrishna tells a most practical story of two men who were walking through a pasture, when a wild bull began to charge at them. One man jumped up in a tree, while the other cockily stood right in the bull's path. "Come on up in the tree, you fool!" the first man cried, "You'll be killed!"

"Don't worry about me!" the other answered, "The Lord will protect me!"

The bull continued his charge, butted the man in the posterior, and left him bedraggled on the ground.

The man in the tree jumped down and chided, "I told you you should have come up in the tree with me!"

"I can't understand it," complained the wounded one. "I thought for sure that the Lord would take care of me!"

"He *was* trying to help you, you idiot!" the other explained. "Didn't you hear him calling to you from the tree?!"

When we allow ourselves to be open to *all* avenues of God's guidance, we find Him *everywhere*. Whenever someone tells Hilda a story, or suggests a book, or asks her a question, she responds as if the Lord Himself were offering her a teaching. We may consider all people to be our teachers — some teach us what to do and some teach us what *not* to do — not so much by their words, but by their actions. If I see an error that someone else has made, and I can apply it to myself to avert a potential error of my own, I feel I have been given a great grace. And I have gained much from watching the selfless service and loving kindness rendered by others. Surely this is God's way of guiding me. I may not be a Moses, like Charlton Heston, and have the ten commandments etched on a stone right before my eyes, but I see God's lessons in action in the "little" experiences of everyday life, and He is continually etching His Truth, in the form of love, in my heart.

In order to make ourselves available to receive guidance, we must keep the mind clear and the emotions quiet. We should not ask the still, small voice to have to compete with chattering thoughts and turbulent feelings. Picture a man, wanting and waiting for an airplane to land, running up and down the runway, waving his arms and yelling, "Come on, land! . . . Here I am! . . . Hurry up and land!" The irony is that the plane can land only when the man gets off the runway and allows the plane to set itself down without obstruction. When we worry, aggravate ourselves, or get upset, we block the path of our own perfect guidance, which is ready and willing to help us just as soon as we make space for it.

The idea of "I don't know" is a deception of the ego, which thrives on thoughts and feelings of separateness. Such an idea divides the Unity of the universe into two parts: a great field of knowledge of answers and solutions, and "me," who is outside that knowledge. We are, in Truth, whole and holy beings. The entire history and future of the universe are etched into our souls. We are inseparably one with the whole of God, and we could never, ever be outside of the wealth of His deepest wisdom.

Sooner or later, we must admit that we really do know, because God is always willing to tell us what we need to know. Usually when we say, "I don't know," we are actually saying, "I don't want to know," or "I don't want to deal with this issue." When I have worked with human relations programs, for example, if someone is asked a question about him or herself and they respond, "I don't know," I would ask them, "If you had to take a guess, what would you say?" Usually they then discover an answer that proves to be very accurate. This method often clears up a tough issue for them, and demonstrates that they held the key to their answers within themselves all the time, but were not ready — or willing — to use it.

There is a wonderful story about a psychiatrist who sees many patients throughout the day. Each one walks into his office with a long face, depressed and burdened. After a fifty-minute session, each patient emerges from the office, happy and beaming, gratefully shaking the therapist's hand, eager to make another appointment for next week. At the end of the day, the psychiatrist calls his secretary over the intercom and tells her, "O.K., Gertrude, you can bring me my hearing aid now!" He hadn't heard a word they said! — but they needed to unburden themselves, and to feel they were listened to and cared for.

There is a tendency for some to consult psychics, spirit guides, or discarnate entities for guidance. We must be very discerning when dealing in the realms of the occult or spirit worlds. It is possible to take a detour off the path, into the psychic worlds, leaning outward and copping out by placing the responsibility for our lives in the hands of a dead relative. Ram Dass said, "If Uncle Joe was a pretty run of the mill guy in life, not knowing much more than about driving a cab, what makes you think that now that he's dead, he'll be able to give you answers like the Oracle of Delphi?" Hilda says, too, that dead people, like alive people, just love to offer advice, whether or not they know what they're talking about. So we may ask, and we may get an answer, but we must always remember that there is no power or wisdom outside of the GodSelf that rests within us.

As many people are becoming spiritually awakened, there are many more psychics, mediums, and occult teachers in the marketplace. Some of them are offering a sincere and genuine spiritual service; many are not. If you are inclined to deal in any psychic circles, be extremely careful to accept only that energy which is of pure God. What is psychic is not always spiritual. What is occult is not always uplifting. What is titillating is not always useful. The highest teachers have gone through the psychic, renounced it, and are free to use it when necessary for the upliftment of their students and all humanity. They do not, however, dwell on the psychic, depend on it, or glorify it. As Hilda has said, "Why settle for little powers, when you can have God?"

If spiritual guidance comes to you through an occult person or science, then use it wisely, but do not become enamored with it. All sciences are of God, and let them be used to glorify Him, and not for their own sake. Remember that the finger pointing at the moon is not the moon.

It is a very positive sign that we seek guidance, for it indicates that we have a sense of a worthwhile path that we would like to follow, and that it is important to us to make the correct choice. To realize that guidance is available to us from a Source *within* ourself is the most magnificent awakening of all. It means that God has not deserted us and that He is delighted to help us, for, in Truth, He *is* us. As Jesus said, "It is the Father's good pleasure to give you the Kingdom." Though that would have been sufficient encouragement, Jesus, in His immense love and compassion, told us exactly where to find that treasure: said He, "The Kingdom of Heaven is within."

When we have confidence in our Divinity, we no longer have to "lean out" on someone else as our mentor, counselor, or savior. Hilda has said many times, "You kids look to me for answers unnecessarily . . . When I started on this path I had no teacher but God . . . He told me everything I needed to know." Yes, we may ask for opinions, help, and advice, but we can then take this information and offer it to our inner guide to see if it is the truth and if it will work for us. Our inner voice is the final authority in any question. We can take Jesus or a guru as our savior, but it is only because such a great one has been confirmed by our *inner* savior as genuine. What else but a savior could recognize a savior? And who else but God could recognize God?

"All life contains within it the gift of guidance and instruction. As you learn to look into the elements of creation in the correct way, all of the lessons of the universe make themselves known to you. Your only need is to look into things simply.

The humor of life is the reaching out that you do. You labor under the mistaken notion that someone can offer you more than you can offer yourself. Beloveds, this is not true. God's joy is your fulfillment. His celebration is your independence. His success is your realization.

Do not place God outside of yourself. The wisdom that you seek is but an aspect of your own nature, speaking to you in a form that you will accept, for you have not taken responsibility for wisdom.

There is no secret to wisdom or guidance. It is as obvious as the new morning. You have not seen it fully because you have complicated it with your concepts. As that complication dissolves, so disintegrate the blocks to your recognition of your path. Your heart is your surest source of direction. Those who follow the heart discover Truth."

THE TEACHER

I

When the people called Jesus "Teacher," He reprimanded them, "You should not call anyone 'Teacher,' for you have only One Teacher — your Heavenly Father."

II

As I was driving home from work one evening, I saw a billboard that I had not noticed before. It was a picture of a slender young lady in a leotard, doing a headstand. The caption of the advertisement was, *"You don't have to stand on your head to find a yoga teacher — find it fast in the Yellow Pages."*

This sign stimulated me to think about how far spirituality and spiritual teachers have come in our culture. Years ago it was very unusual for anyone to be involved in any spiritual pursuit outside of the church or temple. When Hilda first set out on the spiritual path, her friends laughed at her, calling her the derogatory name, "Yogi, Yogi, Yogi!" Now "Yogi" is a compliment, mysticism has made it to prime-time television, and courses in the Tarot cards are being taught in public adult education.

Yes, we have come a long way. In the old days, if you had a problem you either went to momma, the minister, or a psychiatrist — and that was it. Now we have our choice of Gurus, Therapists, Trainers, Readers, Facilitators, Mediums, Counselors, Advisers, Effective Listeners, and Consultants. As if these people weren't enough, there are biorhythm machines to tell you your destiny in the lobbies of restaurants, astrological counseling in the daily newspapers, and Dial-a-Meditation, the last four digits of which are 1111. What used to be a gradual spiritual evolution is now an explosion.

This new enthusiasm for spiritual teaching is a wonderful and exciting phenomenon, but at the same time we must deal with the very important question, *What makes someone a teacher?* In the old days, it was easy to figure out: if you had a degree from a state teacher's college or a seminary, you were qualified to tell people how to live. But now it's a new ball game. The tremendous demand for spiritual guidance has attracted to the masses many trustworthy teachers — and many charlatans. It is no longer a cut-and-dried matter to know who is qualified. Now it is possible to become an ordained minister by mailing three dollars to a church in California, and there is a YMCA that offers yoga teachers certification after a one-weekend course. Perhaps these ministers and yogis are qualified; perhaps they are not; but one thing is for sure: a title or a piece of paper means nothing anymore.

How, then, are we to know who to trust? Who is worth listening to? What makes someone able to act as a spiritual guide? These questions are ones that you and I must answer within our own hearts. No longer can we afford to look outward for answers. The benefit of the challenge to find such answers is that we are forced to go within to find the Real Teacher — the Heavenly Father that Jesus spoke of.

As I have been required to discern between genuineness and impurity, there are three criteria that I have found important in assessing the worth of a teacher:

1. Does the teacher awaken your *heart* with a sense of real truth?
2. Does the teacher encourage you to be independent and whole, or does he foster need and dependence on him?
3. Does the teacher live what he is teaching?

When I sit in the presence or hear the words of a real teacher, I have a thrilling experience of Truth, as if I have come home. Many can utter holy words or quote chapter and verse from the Bible, but only one who has mastered the Truth can make us feel something real and important is happening when they speak. They said of Jesus that He was different because He was "one who spoke with authority."

Swami Vivekananda was a great yogi who was guided to come to this country after being with Sri Ramakrishna in India. When he arrived, the Swami was invited to Chicago to speak to a Congress of the Religions. The affair, as it has been described, was a long and boring one; the speakers gave dull and uninspiring speeches over a period of days. Swami Vivekananda was one of the last lecturers on the program. When it was his time to speak, he stood at the podium and powerfully began, "My Brothers and Sisters . . ." Immediately he was interrupted by thunderous applause, wild cheers, and a standing ovation! The audience knew that he was genuine, that he was speaking the Truth with the power of the Holy Spirit — they felt it in their souls.

You may go to a lecture or a seminar, hear many profound words, and be offered spiritual guidance, but if your heart is not awakened in this presence, the teachings are but empty platitudes, and it will do you no good to get involved, except to learn a lesson in discrimination between the genuine and the false. I once went to a workshop by a man who said many true things. He gave a very nice presentation, but there was just something about him that did not feel 100%. He later became well-known, and people would come to me and say, "This man is really great! He is a real healer!" and I wondered if, perhaps, my intuition had been wrong. Months later, the one who had praised him so highly told me some facts about the way he conducts his personal life that confirmed my intuitive misgivings about him and showed me that I was correct in not pursuing his teachings. I am not judging the man, for he is a beautiful soul, but it is my responsibility to assess the purity of his teaching. We cannot afford to settle for less than the whole Truth. In accepting the teachings of any teacher, we must exercise discrimination. The heart, or the inner guide, is the best source of this very important kind of discernment.

Jesus and other masters do their real teaching through *example*. Jesus told the people of the importance of humility and then he lived it by washing the feet of his disciples and by surrendering to His crucifixion. The words mean very little — it is the actions that count. A real teacher can sit in silence and the full teachings are given. Hilda would travel four hours to see Swami Nithyananda, who would look at her for only a few seconds and make a sound. That was it. "In this Presence," Hilda tells, "the teaching and the blessing were complete." Satya Sai Baba, who has millions of disciples, is considered by many to be an avatar — the very embodiment of God. Yet once, when Hilda

281

apologized to him for making a slight error, he replied, "No, it was *my* fault." This kind of simple humility is the real mark of a great one. Sai Baba also says, "My life is my message."

Meher Baba, another great saint, was silent for over twenty-five years of his life. During that time, he traveled throughout India, serving the poor, bathing the lepers, and giving love to all who came to him. I saw a film of his visit to the United States. Those who came for his blessing formed a long line and he gave each one a long, sincere hug as they filed by. This, to me, is worth more than all the words in the bible.

A true teacher encourages students to find God within themselves, and does not foster clinging or dependence on the physical form. He or she will accept no honor, homage, or glory from the students. I have seen swamis given a garland of flowers by their students remove it immediately and place it on an altar, offering it to God. A real teacher avoids worldly power, ego or specialness. Hilda has said, time and time again, "You don't need to come to my classes, kids. If you really understood my message, you could just as easily stay home."*

By contrast, there are many organizations that lead students to believe that they will be lost or suffer the agonies of Hell if they leave the fold of the organization. Any teacher or group that says, "You cannot discover God without me or this organization," is not speaking Truth. When Jesus said, "No man cometh unto the Father but by Me," He was speaking of the "Me" with a capital M. In other words, He was speaking from the point of view of the Holy Spirit, the Christ, with which He was identified and One in consciousness. And the Holy Spirit is certainly not restricted to Christianity. It glows in the heart of every human being and lives within you and me right now.

The only goal of a true teacher is the advancement of the students and the celebration of Truth. Selfish or personal motivations are absent. I was once taking a kind of spiritual correspondance course, receiving monthly lessons from an organization led by a well-known teacher. Then I received in the mail this letter: "Dear student, please do not show anyone else these lessons or divulge their contents,

*My friend and professor, Dr. Alfred Gorman, a well-known author, consultant and expert in the field of organizational development, told me: "*A consultant is someone who borrows your watch to tell you what time it is.*"

because they are only for those who have paid for them. If anyone else wants these teachings, please give them our address and ask them to send us a check." That was the end of that correspondance course for me. As I see it, if someone really knows the Truth, they are eager to share it. This does not mean that they are opposed to money or that they reject it; it means that their foremost purpose is to teach the Truth, and they are confident enough in God's providence that they do not need to make any demands upon the students other than their own enlightenment.

Hilda explained it in this way: "The Truth, like clear light, if expressed by a pure teacher, will be seen without distortion, as if through clear glass. If a teacher has any impurity, such as hunger for power, or greed, or lust, the Truth will come through with a taint, as if through colored glass. We must learn to develop our God-given faculty of discrimination to feel the purity of a teacher, an organization, or a path."

If you have had a negative experience with a teacher who turned out to be less than enlightened, do not curse or hold the experience in remorse, but "take the best and leave the rest." Extract from the experience all that you can and be grateful for it. Even if a teacher spoke Truth that they did not live, you can take the words and discover their real meaning for yourself. In this way you have gotten much from the teacher, even though you would not now follow that person. If nothing else, you learned a valuable lesson in discrimination. You see the Truth a little — or a lot — more clearly by discovering what it was *not.*

Do not be bitter about being disillusioned about a person or group in the spiritual game. Just because someone may have spoken or taught falsely about God does not mean that God is false. It just means that the person did not really know God. I know someone who is very bitter about a group that he once surrendered to, which turned out not to be all that it made itself out to be. He now uses his experience as an excuse to denounce spirituality. We cannot look to outside people or groups to represent or give us God. We are obliged and responsible to find Him within our very Self. Then, and only then, are we free.

III
Do not worry about finding your teacher or Guru. If you are

sincere and really want God, your teacher will find you. I have seen this time and time again in my life and in the lives of those around me. We cannot plan how we are going to find a teacher. All you need to do is to make the most of whatever knowledge you already have, and (sometimes in the strangest and most unlikely way) you will be connected with one who can guide you.

One teacher found me in a traffic jam at a raunchy rock concert. Another found me working in a grocery store. And a friend of mine felt like she was at the end of her rope after a stormy break-up with a man, when the only job she could find was as a barmaid. In this bar she met someone who took her to a teacher that completely changed her life. James and John were fishermen and Matthew was a tax-gatherer, all just going about their business when Jesus found them.

We can even receive the grace of a God-teacher who is no longer living in a physical body. The first time I read the New Testament, the words seemed to jump right off the page into my heart, and I felt as if Jesus Christ Himself were speaking directly to me. In your meditation you can make contact with the vibration of any great teacher and receive their blessing just as if they were standing right before you in physical form. This is so because the spiritual path is free of form and not limited by time or space.

Be not anxious about *how* the teacher will come to you. Simply ask the Lord for guidance, do the best you can with what you know, be open to possibilities, and the teacher will be given. And you will be with a teacher for precisely the right amount of time in precisely the right way for your particular evolution. It is a wonderful and fascinating Plan — much bigger than we would expect or can understand.

IV

At some point it is necessary to go beyond the form of a teacher. There is a Buddhist instruction, "*If you meet the Buddha on the road, kill him.*" This means that if you see any form which you believe to have more God or more Buddha in it than other forms, you must annihilate this thought from your consciousness. Herman Hesse's Steppenwolf meets a teacher who agrees to give him guidance if he will consent to follow her instructions fully. He agrees and proceeds to grow tremendously through his discipleship. One day she gives him a knife and orders, "Kill me!" He does so, but he is then filled with sorrow and guilt. When he later stands before the heavenly court,

Steppenwolf is found guilty — of not having a sense of humor about "killing the reflection of a woman with the reflection of a knife." He is sentenced to life on earth, to learn to laugh.

The same lesson was lived by Sri Ramakrishna, who was absorbed in the form of the Divine Mother. One day he realized that he would have to go beyond form to truly merge with God. So he took a piece of glass and jabbed it into his forehead, which represents the last strata of form. This was his way of releasing himself from the last attachment.

These stories symbolize the need, at the end of the spiritual path, to renounce all — including that which has brought us to the final point. As the sages instructed, "Give up your lust for growth" and "The last thing to go is God."

If we know how to look at life correctly, *all* of our experiences are our teachers. We must cease to see life as a random play of circumstances and begin to understand that the earth is a school, and all events the lessons. Contantly ask, "What can I learn from this experience? Why was it given to me? How can I use it to further my growth?" If you think in this way, all experiences will bring you closer to understanding yourself and the Truth.

Perhaps the purpose and work of the Teacher can be summarized in this story: One evening after Hilda's class, a young man came up to Hilda and told her, "Tonight I realized that God is within me and that I really do not need you or this class or any teacher or any class . . . It's all within!"

As she heard these words, Hilda's face lit up with a broad smile. She took the man's hand, shook it firmly, and told him, "Congratulations, kid . . . You got the whole idea of my class. I pronounce you graduated!"

"Those who teach in purity are few. Let the aspirant beware of those who claim to teach Truth and do not live it.

A student has the right to stand in judgement of the actions of one who claims to be a teacher. We do not speak of judgement of the soul, but of the reality of the teachings. Let the student discern between the truth that is spoken and Truth that is lived. Never surrender your soul to another person, but always align it with God. You may accept the guidance and instruction of one whom you feel is genuine, but let that decision be dictated by your Godly intuition.

If you would be a teacher, you must be unremitting in your dedication to Truth. You must found your life upon actions, and not upon words. You must give up all notions of teaching. At best, you may speak of your own experience. If you hearken unto these strict requirements, the Holy Spirit will fill you like an earthen vessel, and your life will be under continual guidance. This promise will be verified by your experience.

There is a hierarchy of education of which you are a part. This hierarchy has as its only purpose the uplifting of souls and the salvation of the world. The dedicated souls in this hierarchy are working steadily to shine Truth into the world. In these times of earth changes, Truth and Love are being given in great abundance. Blessed are you who would share in this noble work.''

DISCRIMINATION

Discrimination is a lesson of spiritual growth that every single aspirant must master. The ability to distinguish between Truth and falsehood, even on the sublest level, is absolutely essential to one who would stand free of error and extricate the world from painful ignorance. Wisdom is the mark of the learned, but discrimination is the attribute of the masterful.

Real spiritual mastery boils down to knowing when to say "Yes" and when to say "No." We can make it all the way to God on just these two words and nothing more. The test is *when to use them.*

A friend of mine, Hal, owned and managed an Italian restaurant. When I would occasionally help out at the restaurant, I saw that he was irresponsible in the way he managed the business. Because Hal thought in terms of lack, he was very petty and critical of his employees, and he rarely gave encouragement or support. The business began to go downhill, and the worse things got, the less Hal was present, creating a vicious cycle of negation and failure, until the business was in the red. At that point, Hal went to a wealthy lawyer in the community and asked him for a large loan, presenting him with a grandiose scheme for expanding the restaurant and bringing in well-known entertainment.

As the lawyer was a friend of mine as well, he approached me and asked if I thought this would be a safe investment for him. As much as I wanted to see Hal succeed, I had to tell the lawyer the truth: I told him that I believed the business was failing, not as a result of circumstance, but of Hal's negative way of thinking. Because he was irresponsible, even if he did get a huge loan, it would probably slip through his fingers in a matter of time, just as Hal's original investment had dwindled. What Hal needed was not more money, but expanded managerial skills and consciousness.

Though I did not like stifling Hal's chances for success, I would have done a great disservice to the lawyer — and Hal — if I did not tell the truth. If he had gotten the money, he would have gotten himself into only deeper trouble. As the story turns out, the business closed and Hal got a salaried job with less supervisory responsibility, a position in which he is feeling positive and doing very well.

Being good or spiritual does not mean that we must always say "Yes" to everything. Sometimes it is spiritual to say "Yes" and sometimes it is spiritual to say "No." We have to decide which situations require which answers. Neem Karoli Baba told Ram Dass to "Love everyone, serve everyone, and remember God." "This," tells Ram Dass, "got me to thinking about what real service is all about; does it mean that I am supposed to do anything that anyone asks me to do? . . . No, it means responding uniquely to each request, according to the clearest intuition that I can feel."

The question of Hal's loan is a fairly obvious example of our need for discrimination. As we advance along the spiritual path, however, the tests and lessons become more subtle, and we have to dig deeper to find within ourself a more sensitive guide for correct action.

One night, for example, a student told Hilda that he had gone to a lecture by a certain organization whose leader spoke about many esoteric spiritual principles. "The only problem," he explained, "was that although everything the lecturer said was true, I did not feel Truth in the room, and I felt a sharp pain in my stomach." Hilda told him that the pain was in the energy center in his body that corresponded to power and that perhaps the teacher and the organization were more interested in power than in service. A few weeks later we learned from one of the students that left this organization that they had charged her a huge sum of money to allow her to teach their other students, who were also paying high prices for instruction.

The path is a razor's edge path, and if we are not careful we can give our trust to the wrong people. Let's face it: there are shams and flim-flam men in the spiritual game. Jesus said to "be as gentle as lambs, but as clever as serpents." We must think twice before surrendering to anyone's teachings. And it will do no good to say, "I will not surrender to anyone's teachings," because if a genuine teacher comes along, we cannot afford to miss the opportunity to accept their grace. So the only answer is to develop a keep sense of discrimination, to know who to be open to, and when.

There is yet a more subtle level at which we are required to practice discrimination: the inner plane, or the dream world. Even on a subconscious level we must choose. We may have a dream of a spiritual master coming to us and asking us to do something for him or her. Then, when we do it, we are overcome with an empty, almost nauseous feeling that we have been had. This means that our discrimination was not keen enough on this subtle level. I had a dream in which a certain master came to me and asked me to join a line of people who were happily filing into his temple. I had a gnawing suspicion, but I accepted the invitation. When I got inside, the people in there were writhing in pain and desperately trying to warn those on the outside not to enter. I had been had.

Yet, on another night I had a dream of the same master. This time it felt right to follow, and when I did, I was rewarded with a very beautiful and blissful experience.

We might say that in the first dream I was tuning to a force of charlatanry masquerading as the master. In the second case, I tuned in to the actual essence of the master. At a point as fine as this, we have no one to lean on but our own God-given sense of what is correct.

Do not be afraid to act on your discrimination. If something feels wrong or out of the flow to you, follow up your hunch and act with caution. Do not feel guilty or impolite about saying "No" to that which does not sit right with you. This is not judgement by the ego; it is the right and necessary identification of what is true. It is our responsibility to recognize error for what it is. We serve no one by believing pretentious words or participating in false affairs. The little boy who exposed the ruse of the Emperor's new clothes did a very great service to the townspeople and to the Emperor, as well.

Spiritual means the spirit in which an action is done. We can say "No" in a very loving way, and so serve the one who has asked something of us. If someone calls me up to try to sell me a magazine that I know I will not buy, I politely stop them before they finish their sales pitch, and in a loving way I say, "No thank you." I really do love them, even if I do not buy their magazine, and I like to think that they may feel happy that I did not hang up on them with a gruff "No!"

It would be a waste of my time — and theirs, which they could be using on a more interested customer — for me to listen to their whole pitch.

As we grow, our ability to distinguish between what is right for us and what is wrong becomes finer and finer. I might be sitting in an office or waiting in a line at a supermarket, for example, and my eye will fall on some magazine. An inner voice says, "Leave it alone," but out of curiosity I pick it up, and upon paging through it I come upon some gory picture or story that I wish I had missed. On other occasions, I might see a magazine which doesn't seem especially interesting, yet the inner voice says, "Pick it up." When I do, I find just the article or information that I have been searching for, but just could not seem to find elsewhere.

Eventually we see that God is in everything, and there is nothing too small — or too big — to be unworthy of His Guidance. He will tell us which car salesman to trust, which charity to support, and how long to wait before we ask for a debt to be repaid. No act is too worldly for God, and no fork in the road is beyond our ability to make a correct choice.

Spiritual mastery begins on earth. Before we can enjoy Heavenly Bliss, we must conquer the marketplace. And that is precisely why we are here — to learn the difference between what is "right on" and what is right off. The mastery of discrimination is accomplished in traffic, at the staff meeting, and in giving the kids lunch. Since there are no traffic jams, board meetings, or luncheons in Heaven, here is our opportunity to master such challenges and gain control over our lives.

Real spiritual masters are sharp, exact, and firm in human interactions. They do not allow God's energy, with which they have been entrusted, to be misused against them. When some of Ramakrishna's young students came back from the store short-changed, he told them, "Go back immediately and get the right change!" Hilda is very strict about "keeping it together" in the world. Once, when I bought her a package of bobby pins that she requested, she insisted on reimbursing me to the exact penny. She admonishes her students not to leave any possessions visible in parked cars, and she screens anyone who would give a talk at her classes. Though she can sit comfortably in the etheric realms of spiritual light, she does not miss one step in the worldly game. We must keep our head in the clouds and our feet on the ground. This is the path of the masters.

"Mark well the words in this lesson. They will be of crucial importance to you in the days to come. We would have you act in a manner befitting the masters that you are.

Fear not to weigh in your heart of hearts the words and actions of others. This is your right and your duty. The observation of righteousness is not the judgement of ego. Do not be afraid to realize a wolf for what it is; this is not negative judgement, but right seeing. We would rather have you see correctly than be prey to foolishness.

Error is often born of lack of confidence to make a stand for the Truth. The Master Himself drove the money mongers from the temple, and in so doing set an example for you to emulate.

Discrimination is the only real lesson in life. You are on earth because of previous errors in discrimination. Correct those errors, and you master the game of earth. Those in a position to teach are the ones who have refined their discriminative abilities to the point where they can recognize that which is of God. You, too, know what is real, but you have not acted on your understanding with sufficient consistency.

The fruits of your efforts, though now unseen, shall become more and more evident as the world comes to acknowledge the reality of God. Are you not already seeing your deepest intuitions confirmed? Continue on your path of right endeavor, and we assure you that all of your noble ambitions shall be borne out and manifest. Hail the goer!"

DECISION

To make a decision is to put the Will of God directly into action. Many of the problems in our lives are not a result of wrong choices, but of *lack of making a choice.* If we want to accelerate our personal evolution to higher consciousness, we must begin to make clear choices and to act on them.

When I started to make firm decisions, my life really began to take shape. I used to consider it spiritual or fashionable to be "spaced out." If I lost something or made a mistake, I would think, "Wow, I just can't seem to keep it together — I must be really high!" Actually, I was just disorganized. I now see that not keeping it together is not a mark of spiritual advancement, but mental sloppiness. Vagueness is not a quality of character that brings success or peace. It is a form of sloth and inertia. Hilda once said, "If God were vague, the planets would fall out of the heavens." But God is 100% precise and efficient; He cannot afford to be less. And when we act with precision and efficiency, we are living up to our selfhood as intelligent beings created in the image and likeness of a clear-minded God.

Spiritual masters practice decision and precision on every level. A student of Suzuki Roshi, a beautiful Zen master, told how the roshi would eat an apple in such a way that the core was left as a perfectly balanced sculpture. There would not be one bit of apple left to eat; no waste. Eating an apple was a meditation for the master. His meditation did not stop when he arose from *zazen.* His whole life was meditation, and meditation is clarity. If our lives do not reflect clarity, then we are not meditating correctly.

293

The stakes in the way we make decisions are high. If we decide with surety and resolution, we get what we decide for. If, on the other hand, we flounder in indecision and procrastination, we lose power. In such a case, we are like an ant in the middle of a highway, running back and forth between a granule of sugar and a piece of cake, unable to decide which one to take. Either one would be a fine choice, but he had better decide quickly, for a big Mack truck is barreling down the road. Because time is precious, we cannot afford to vacillate in our decisions. If we really want to create movement in our lives, we must be willing to take a sure step in one direction.

The impediment to decision making is *fear* of making the wrong choice or getting something we do not want. Often, however, a wrong choice is better than no choice, for then at least we would be certain of what is the right direction, and progress would be made.

When we do not know what choice to make, our best bet is to search our heart for the act that would be most in harmony with our most important ideals, and to act on that high standard. *If we act in the name of love, service, and good will, we cannot make a wrong decision.* God asks no more of us than to live up to the highest principles that we know. He does not hold us responsible for standards higher than those of which we are aware. We always know all we need to know to make any decision with which we are confronted. Take into account whatever you know about what is required for people to live on earth in harmony, and use that knowledge as the basis for your decision. Swami Sivananda taught that acts are judged not by their form, but by their *intention*. This idea has helped me enormously in my decision making. If you are unsure as to what course of action to take, summon your purest intention and let that be your benchmark.

If you do make a "wrong" decision, then be grateful for it. Turn a minus into a plus. A negative ($-$) is half a positive ($+$). Take the minus sign and add one stroke of vertical awareness to it, and you have a plus. Thank God for showing you the error that you have made, and resolve not to repeat it. This is very pleasing in His eyes. We have come on earth to learn. It is no sin to make a mistake. I am typing on corrasable paper. It is designed with compassion for typists like me. Life is, to a certain extent, corrasable. If you make an error, then admit it with firm resolve, do what you can to correct the mistake, and walk on. If you drive off the highway, it will do you no good to sit and bemoan your error. The only thing to do is to *turn back onto the highway and continue your journey.* The time spent in regret is only more time wasted. If you have to pay off some karma of a wrong decision, then pay it off like a master. Resisting your obligations will create only more karma. All of life is for learning.

Another rule of thumb for overcoming indecision is to listen to your inner voice. We need to be quiet enough to hear that guidance. If we are worried, anxious, or fearful, we will not be able to contact that voice of guidance. Our worry creates mental and emotional static that blocks our awareness of the right decision, an answer that is always working to make itself known to us. And practice following your hunches. You will find out which hunches come from your heart, and which come from your intellect. In this way, decison making will become easier and easier.

If you still cannot decide, then ask God to decide for you. Recently I wrestled for several days over whether or not to mail a certain letter. I was losing my strength and my clarity through this indecision. One night, I could take it no longer. I decided to get out of bed and sit down and pray until the answer came. I began to talk to God: "God, I do not see now what is the proper path to take. I just want to do what is right. I turn this one over to you." Then I began to thank God for the right decision. I did not know what it was, but I affirmed to myself that God very much wanted to show me what to do, and I tried to get the feeling of what it would be like if I had reached and acted on a satisfying decision. I just kept affirming, "Thank you, God, for the right decision . . . Thank you, God, for the right decision," over and over and over. After just a little while, there began to well up within me an awareness of the correct choice of action. It began to feel very right to mail that letter. The more I thanked God for the right decision, the righter this choice seemed to be. When I felt satisfied that this was the best path of action, I decided to mail the letter first thing in the morning. At the moment of that decision, my energy returned and I felt as if a huge cloud cover had been burnt away by the morning sun. A decision had been made.

We can use the routine experiences in our lives to practice the power of decision and precision. Arriving at the meeting on time, keeping our car in good condition, and carrying out an errand that we promised someone are good ways to mobilize decisive strength. The time of the meeting, the health of the car, and the nature of the errand are not nearly as important as our ability to make a commitment and stick to it. If we master little decisions, the big ones will come easy.

I will share with you a very powerful method that I have discovered for keeping my whole life in order: I keep my room clean. Our rooms are pictures of our consciousness. If you want to clean up your consciousness, then clean up your room. See if you have any cobwebs or "dustbunnies." If so, you have allowed indecision and inertia to creep into your temple. A very efficient and successful man I know said that the little balls of dust that accumulate in the corners of uncared-for rooms are manifestations of unconsciousness. I believe it. Sweep them away, and in so doing you sweep away your unconsciousness.

When a room is tidy and orderly, a vibration of power and harmony builds up in it, one which blesses everyone who walks into the room, by its reflection of Godly order. Hilda tells that when she entered Yogananda's retreat center, "You wouldn't believe how perfect was the vibration, kids! Everything was in its perfect place. I remember how the gold drapes were perfectly creased and how the blue carpet was immaculately vacuumed. It was like walking into clarity itself, and I felt as if I had just had a good meditation."

We have the same ability as Yogananda's devotees to make our homes and our rooms our *sanctum sanctorum* — a holy refuge. Such order is a tremendous support to our spiritual work. I can remember times when I walked into my house with the affairs of the day on my shoulders. The moment I walked into a clean room, I felt my troubles lifted off of me, as if gentle angel wings brushed off my shoulders. This blessing was not a result of chance, but *decision*.

Do not be so rigid in your decisions that you are unwilling to reverse them when necessary. We, like Ghandi, must hold Truth in higher esteem than unthinking obstinacy. Reversing a decision for a good reason is not the same as indecision. When we reverse a decision with reason, we have executed two strong choices. When we fail to decide and fall prey to wishy-washy lethargy, we have made no choice, and remain weak.

If you decide to wait, then do it with resolution, and not procrastination. Many decisions require a gestation period before they can be brought to birth. When you perceive such a necessity, decide to wait. This is not a sign of weakness, but wisdom.

For one week, practice being really decisive. It does not matter so much whether you say "Yes" or "No," as long as you do not say "maybe." Be crisp in your decisions. Answer questions, make orders in the marketplace, and if you are in a supervisory position, give directions with resolve. Be anything but vague. Banish fear through sincere and firm decisions. Do not waste one iota of your precious life-force on indecision. Do not give the rational mind anything to chew on. So chosen, your affairs will quickly fall into place.

In mastering the high art of decision, you will align your mind and your actions with all of the great masters of life who have used firm decision-making as a tool to release spiritual power for the good of the world. You will be joining the forces of Pericles, Moses, and Lincoln. These men stood firmly for their beliefs. They acted with resolve. I am sure that they were not without error. And I am sure, too, that they lived up to their mistakes like masters. Act with dignity and precision, and the power that made them great will uphold you in your aspiration.

Decide to make your life what you want it to be. No one else can decide for you, and certainly no one else can do it for you. Your decisions will line up life in the way that you choose it. The moment I make a decision — a firm one — the forces of the universe immediately set themselves in line to manifest that decision. *If desired events are not coming to pass in your life, it is because you have not firmly resolved what you want it to manifest.* Is this true, or untrue? Examine your circumstances carefully, and I believe you will agree that this is so. Your life is a picture of the decisions that you have made. If your life is in any way in conflict or confused, it is only because your decisions have been in conflict and confused. Declare your decision, and your life is certain to clear up. There is no slippage in the system of mind dynamics. What you think becomes reality. Think vague, and life will be vague. Think clearly, decide firmly, and act precisely, and your life will be a picture of surety. You will have made it so, by your willingness to decide.

"We would impart to you the wisdom of the Godly use of will. Your will has lain in atrophy. Man's Divine gift of co-creation through the Will of the Creator has not been fully utilized. It is now for you to master life through right use of your faculty of decision.

This is but an elementary lesson in the productive use of mind. Yet it is, for you, a necessary one. Master this task, and you take control of your life in cooperation with God.

The age to come is being founded on the intelligent and loving use of mental energies. Mankind will master the secrets of creation that now lie dormant in the unused realms of human potential. Your ability to enter this wonderous era depends on your development of concentration and resolve. Indeed, no further progress on the planet is possible until you have tempered your passions to use such powers for upliftment, and not destruction. Your resolution to harmonize with the Will for Good is a first requisite in the channeling of these faculties.

Ultimately there is but one decision that you need to make: the decision for God. All other decisions are in the service of this one. Do not underestimate the decisions that you must make, for your firm resolve in the smallest of these will unlock Heaven's gate before you. Decide, beloveds. Decide and grow strong."

SERVICE

Gotta serve somebody.
                                        — Bob Dylan

Two robbers were crucified with Jesus. In the hour of their tribulation, one chided Jesus, "If you are the Son of God, then get us off these crosses!" Then the other robber rebuked, "We deserve to be here, but this man has done nothing wrong!" Later, Jesus promised this man, "Truly I say to you, today you shall be with me in Paradise."

Hilda described this incident as a model for selfless service in the world. The first criminal was so absorbed in his own pain that he could not see that it was the Christ at his side. The second, even while in his own suffering, compassionately saw that Jesus did not deserve to be there. The man "thought outward"; he turned his attention away from his own little self to feel the predicament of another. In this state of thoughtful kindness amid suffering, he was promised the Kingdom.

Each of us has our own cross to bear while there is much suffering in the world. If we aspire to serve others and to make some kind of contribution to humanity, we must first let go of our own self-pity, fear, and doubt. Like the first robber on the cross, there is a part of each of us that is preoccupied with itself, and which ironically mocks those whose love can most help us. At the same time, we also have within us a self — an aspect of our real nature — that has a deep compassion for the needs of others and desires to *give* rather than *get*. The reward of service is that when we turn our attention to help another, we forget our own misery, which was created and maintained only by our willingness to dote on it.

A friend of mine was in the hospital, and I was very worried about him. I allowed my energy to be depleted and I was feeling sorry for myself as well as for him. As God's clever plan would have it, during that time I was scheduled to give a workshop on "Positive Thinking" at a local library. As I left the hospital to do the workshop, I thought, "Now how am I going to do this workshop?! Here I am feeling so negative, and I'm supposed to go tell people how to be positive . . . a great example I am!" At that moment, I realized that my responsibility to the people who were coming to that workshop was more important than my need to feel sorry for myself. So I willfully decided to put aside my own woes and to go in there and give those people the best program I knew how to give. Otherwise, I would have felt like a real hypocrite. So I stopped worrying about myself, and thought about what I could give. And it turned out very well, indeed. My great surprise, however, was that by the time the workshop was over, I had lost my feelings of woe. I no longer felt troubled about my friend, and when I went to visit him the next day, he and I were both feeling much better. I had only to get my mind off my own little self.

I experienced an inspiring example of this kind of selfless thinking when I was spending an afternoon at a nursing home. This was at a Christmas party for the patients, and I was so happy to see them enjoying treats of cookies and candy. One woman, paralyzed, slow of speech, and in considerable pain, turned to me and asked, "Did you have anything to eat?" My heart flew open in a way that still fills me with a thrill of joy just to think of it. I was touched, not so much because she thought particularly of me, but because she was kind enough to care for the needs of another, even in the midst of her own suffering.

The prayer of St. Francis captures the essence of service:

O Divine Master,
Grant that I may not so much seek to be consoled,
as to console;
Not so much to be understood, as to understand;
Not so much to be loved, as to love.

Real service is given without any expectation of reward or

acknowledgement. In this attitude, we can never be disappointed and we will always feel fulfilled. If we feel irritated because we do not receive a "thank you" from someone for a kind act, then we did not do it out of a desire to give love; we did it to receive something, and this is not service; it is business. When we do not receive acknowledgement for a gift or an act, we should be grateful, for this means we did it for God. God sees all that we do, even if no one else does, and He will reward us more faithfully than anyone in the world ever could. "Be not like the hypocrites who say their prayers and do good acts to be noticed by others. Do your service in secret, and your Heavenly Father will reward you."

Because Jesus lived everything He taught, He demonstrated the importance of serving with humility by washing the feet of His disciples, teaching, "No servant is greater than His master." His whole life was a teaching in giving, as are the lives of all who love God, for those who know God know that the best way to serve God is to serve people.

One evening, for example, there was a guest speaker at Hilda's class. After the class, the woman asked, "Could you tell me where the ladies' room is?" Before the lady was even done asking, Hilda sprang from her chair and personally escorted the woman to the restroom, turned on the light for her, and made sure there was a fresh towel. My first thought was, "Hilda doesn't have to do that; she is a famous teacher with many students; she could have easily asked someone else to do it for her." But Hilda is great *because* she lives a life of selfless service. She treats all who come to her as if they were Christ Himself.

St. Francis well understood that we sometimes hesitate to give to others because we fear that if we do not meet our needs first, they will not be met. This is man's way of thinking. God's way is, as *A Course in Miracles* tells us, *"To have all, give all to all."* Hilda is also an inspiring example of this truth. As she spends nearly all of her time giving to others, her needs are miraculously met. Though she does not strive or ask for anything, the right people, money, and washing machines come to her exactly when she needs them, usually from people who are grateful for what she has done for them.

I remember, too, when I was debating whether or not to give a friend of mine a birthday present of a picture of mine that I loved. It was a delightful cartoon of a little smiling man being lifted by a heart up a steep mountain which he could not climb. The caption was "Love conquers all." Although this was one of my favorite possessions, I knew that my friend would really like it, and so I decided to give it as a present. The very next day, as a gesture of friendship, someone gave me an envelope. As I opened it, I found the *very same picture* as the one I had given the day before — and this one was even better: written on the back was a lovely poem from the one who gave it.

I saw and felt this same reverence for giving when I went to hear Swami Satchidananda speak. Among his first words were, "Thank you for the opportunity to serve you in my own small way." I was deeply touched by his humility. To the hundreds of people in the audience (or at least to me), he was doing us a favor by coming to speak to us. I felt indebted to him. From his loving point of view, though, we were doing him a service by allowing him to be there. He saw himself not as a great and important yogi, but as a servant of God. He sees life as a series of opportunities to serve.

Too often, we miss these opportunities because we believe that "work" is bad. We call our opportunities "obligations" or "chores" and we grumble through them when, with just a slight shift in perspective, they can become invitations to dance up the path to God. At my house, on a kitchen cabinet we had a list of jobs to be done, posted under the title "CHORES." A divine and loving guest crossed out the word "CHORES" and replaced it with "Blissful Karma Yoga" (knowing God through service). At another time, when I was at a Sivananda ashram kitchen, I saw posted a marvelous quote from the Master:

> God realization does not begin in a cave high atop the Himalayas. It begins in the pots and pans of the kitchen. Treat all of your tasks, however small, as opportunities to see God and to serve Him. This is a sure way to Liberation.

We do not need to be a Mother Theresa or a Moses to be liberated. We do not need to leave our family or job to give God's Love to all. We can begin exactly where we are, and we will find many, many opportunities to "think outward" and to serve. Every little thought and action, in fact, can be one of Divine service. If you are doing the laundry, you can fold each garment with a touch of love and a word of blessing. If you work as a secretary, you can answer the phone with kindness and availability. I feel so uplifted when someone answers my phone call with a pleasant "Hello?" You and I have the power to offer the same blessing every time we pick up the telephone — even if we are feeling tired or angry. All acts are opportunities to give love.

Hilda used to help out occasionally at a pizza shop in a tough neighborhood in New York City. Her ideal was to spread light and love. As she folded the pizza boxes, she would say a prayer over each one, such as "May the person who receives this be happy and blessed." Opportunities to give love are always waiting for us with outstretched arms, and God's promise becomes His gift when we are but willing to embrace them.

There are an infinite number of ways to serve. Each of the ways is equally important. Do not berate yourself because you are not a great doctor or social activist. Any service that we give is essential to the well being of all. I went to a hospital to visit a friend who sells used car parts. I was thinking how important are the doctors who were treating him. Then I realized that this man's job was equally as important as the doctors', for they need working automobiles to take them to the people they treat. Without his services, they could not perform theirs. It is a marvelous web of interdependence that unites us. All are equally dependent on each other for our work in the world, and we are all equally dependent on God, Who serves us through one another.

Sometimes we are not even aware of the importance of the service that we have rendered. There is a wonderful story about this called "It's A Wonderful Life." In the tale, James Stewart portrays a man who operates a private loan agency in a small town. He is compassionate and understanding, taking risks on loans for projects that he believes in. Through a quirk of fate, he stands to be put out of business, and everything in his life seems to go wrong at the same time. At his wits' end, he considers suicide. At that moment his guardian angel appears to show him what life in that town would have been like had he never been born. Without him, the projects and businesses he kindly supported were run down, degenerate institutions. The restaurant he financed was, in this vision, a sleezy bar; the movie house showed low-grade films; and people he had rescued were in the dregs of life. He sees how valuable his acts have been, though he realized it not. Finally he decides to live, and upon returning to his home, finds all the people he has helped awaiting him with a collection of just enough money to make good his losses.

Our work in the world is made easy when we share the load. The old adage, "Many hands, light work" is true. There is an expansion of the energy that we offer to another; they receive much more than we give. Taking ten or fifteen minutes out of my life to offer a helping hand to another is worth much more than ten or fifteen minutes to them. There is an essence of love that is added to time or energy rendered in service. It makes life satisfying for the giver and for the receiver. It inspires us to know a higher possibility for life than we have been taught to believe in. Loving kindness in the form of service is closer to the heart of God than any other act.

Serving others is a way of participating in the Grace of God. When we help another who is in difficulty, we are "taking on" some of his or her karma. We are becoming the man who helped Jesus carry His cross. I can think of no higher act that we can do in this world. Says Master Hilarion, "This is why the Christian teaching emphasizes above all else the commandment to serve one's brother in any way possible. For through this service it is possible not only to set aside one's own karmic burden, but to lift the load from the shoulders of another."*

Serving another, then, bears a double reward. Not only do we participate in the alleviation of his or her suffering, but we free ourself, as well. Sri Chinmoy, a teacher of the path of meditation, was once asked, "How can I feel the bliss of God?" His response was one word: "*Serve.*"

Service is not always enjoyable and pleasant; sometimes it is demanding and repugnant to the senses. Meher Baba made pilgrimages to serve the sick and the destitute. He said, "*True love is no game of the faint-hearted and the weak; it is born of strength and understanding.*" St. Francis understood this when he took on the task of caring for an ornery leper that no one else, even his fellow monks, could tolerate. As St. Francis washed the leper's body, the man's sores miraculously disappeared and he was healed in spirit as well as body. In order to truly serve, we must be willing to reach out to the unreachable; to tolerate the intolerable; and to love the unlovable. Then, and only then, can we understand the true meaning of selfless service.

When we are willing to serve in this way, we find the end of argument, strife, and discord in our lives. Practicing outward thinking

---

*Hilarion, *THE NATURE OF REALITY*, Marcus Books, 195 Randolph Rd., Toronto, Canada brings freedom and joy beyond compare. The nature of argument is two people selfishly grabbing for themselves, like a tug of war. All the words and actions can be boiled down to "Me!" . . . countered by, "No, Me!" and so on, until both parties withdraw in painful isolation, or one person is willing to let go a little bit and give in to the other. Too often I want the other person to consider my needs more than I am willing to consider theirs. I have found that the quickest way for us to end any strife is to show our "opponent" that we are aware of his or her point of view. The moment he or she feels recognized, even in the slightest way, their wrath will subside, and resolution is then possible. When "*You* listen to *me*" becomes "*I* am willing to hear *you*," peace replaces discord. Jesus said, "Agree with your adversary quickly." In this way will harmony be where bitterness was.

The highest form of service is forgiveness. It is very difficult, from a human point of view, to forgive. Yet, to see the Light of God within a human being, no matter what their outer circumstance or appearance, is a deep act of love. In forgiving, we are affirming the true worth of a brother or sister who may have been spurned by a heartless world. We are serving him or her by recognizing the holiness within them, though the world would recognize only evil. All acts of charity or giving are valuable only inasmuch as they recognize the true dignity of those toward whom the contribution is directed. Any money or time given to another without recognizing their full equality, is as chaff in the wind, and serves only the mockery of ego. Pity or sorrow is never a worthy reason for charity, for it only reinforces the bondage of the giver and the recipient. Real charity is never a giving, but always a sharing. He who gives as a giver remains half; he who shares, knows wholeness.

No matter what our personal path to God, service is always a necessary step on the path. The meditator must arise from his pillow to share what he has seen within himself. The student of Truth must teach what he has learned, by living it. The lover of God must love the God in his brethren. Awakening is useless unless it awakens the world; wisdom is meaningless unless it is lived; and love is fruitless unless it is given. He who would be worthy of that which has been given to him must share it. Jesus told of the man who was forgiven his debt, but refused to forgive his debtor. The man incurred the wrath of God, and was thrown into a fiery furnace for it. When we take from the great bounty of God, but refuse to give it, we remain entrapped in the web of self. Sharing what we have received, spiritually and physically, is the true expression of brotherhood. When we give to all what God has given to us, God shall not diminish our supply, but only increase it.

When we perform an act of service and consecrate it in the name of Love, we align ourselves with all the selfless servants of humanity through whom the world has ever been blessed. When we reach out to another, we join Ghandi, Mother Theresa, St. Francis, and all of the devotees of loving kindness. The love and support of these masters wafts toward us as if they were standing by our very side in our act. If you do healing, teaching, cleaning, or any other form of service, call upon the servant of God who is dearest to your heart. Before I sing or teach a class, I say a little prayer asking God to support me in my work, and to work through me. I tell God that I want this work to be for Him and I ask Him to bless those who I am serving. It is my joy to tell you that God has not failed me. I have seen miraculous changes in the students and in myself. When we dedicate our acts to Light and Love, these powers stream through us, filling our activities with success and satisfaction. When we work for God, we cannot fail.

When you meditate, dedicate your upliftment to the upliftment of all humanity. Have the intention that you are not just meditating for yourself, but for the benefit of all. When I pray for others, I feel a peace come over me far in excess of what I receive when I pray for myself. At Hilda's meditation one evening, she directed, "Now pray for one other person in this room, and see what happens to the air." At that moment, the air became cool and pink, as if selfishness had been dissipated and replaced by selfless loving kindness. There seemed to be a network of golden threads reaching across the room, binding all in a fabric of Oneness. It was lovely beyond words.

We have within our very minds, hearts, and hands the power to heal and to transform the world. One kind word, look, or touch can make all the difference to a brother or sister in need of love. It is said that "*if everyone on earth loved each other, the earth would shine brighter than the sun.*" If every one of us would do one little kind act for another person on just one day, I believe the earth would be redeemed instantly. It would release such a powerful energy of light and love that the forces of darkness, in the form of pollution, weapons, and hatred, would immediately disburse. Such a day would set into motion a snowball of service that could cleanse the earth of all the negative karma that has ever been accumulated, and release the spirit of hope and giving throughout the universe so that every planet in every galaxy would reap its benefit. "You may say I'm a dreamer, but I'm not the only one." If this indeed be a dream, then let us dream it together, for dreams are the stuff that life is made of.

"Children, understand well the meaning of service. Truly there is no greater hope in our hearts than for you to serve one another. You must now put your ideas into practical expression, for time is short and the need paramount. Though you understand the necessity of service, you must understand its urgency in this time of shadows. In a darkened room, a tiny candle casts a great beam.

As you enter the ranks of those who serve humankind, you awaken to the very purpose of those whose intention is the end of all suffering. Hold to your highest values in all of your endeavors. Set your mind on the Kingdom of Heaven, even while you act on earth; truly the two are One. You can come to know this only by raising all of your purposes to the most magnificent. Be not dissuaded by thoughts of mediocrity and mundane goals. Your goal is what it always has been: the expression of the Love of your Heavenly Father. Accept nothing less, for nothing else has any meaning.

We look on your work with support and anticipation, and we happily watch you unfold. Know that you are protected in any work that is consecrated. This is the law and this is our purpose. Assume this purpose for yourself, and no harm can befall you. Your path is marked. Walk it in mastery and light. We hail you in your conquest of all that is binding, and celebrate with you in your attainment of all that is glorious. The Peace of God is given unto thee. For this were you born, for this do you live, and toward this noble ideal are all of your efforts blessed."

Love

Hilda

AIM RIGHT FOR THE HEART

I saw a movie about Mother Theresa of Calcutta, the saintly woman who has devoted her life to helping the poor and the dying. At one of her centers for the destitute, I saw a man, perhaps a priest or a monk, holding in his arms a frail and weak man, possible starving or on the verge of death. The monk was looking into the dying man's eyes with a compassion that brought tears of joy to my eyes. He was telling him, "My dear brother, my dear, dear brother, I love you very very much." The monk just kept repeating these words, over and over again, offering the man greater love with each repetition. The dying one seemed too weak to respond in word or action, but his eyes were sparkling as if he were looking into the face of Christ Himself. At this moment in my life, I cannot imagine an expression of Love greater than this.

The feeling and expression of Love is the common need of all human beings. I have never met a person with a tough exterior who was not soft and sensitive underneath. One day, for example, I was at a children's zoo, where I saw a man become very loud and abusive over a discrepancy at the snack bar. A few minutes later, I saw the same man tenderly feeding a fawn. Behind the loud man was a soft little boy. This is the essence of the human being that I value, and it is the quality that I want to always remember.

I used to work on human relations workshops for teenagers, and the hearts of these kids were so beautiful. I shall never forget one boy, in trouble with school, not getting along well with his parents, perhaps had a brush or two with the law. He was very dear to me, for he allowed me to see the other side of his character. He was a good boy; he had just been knocked around by the world a bit. In one of our group sessions his tough facade was being challenged, and for the longest time (it seemed like forever), he just sat in silence. Then, as if the burden of the years of hiding was just too great for him to bear any longer, one lone, small, and so very important tear rolled down his cheek. The illusion of hardness was dissolved.

Experiences like these have led me to where I no longer believe in anyone's "tough" act. When I see a tough guy, I see a scared little child. When I can talk to that inner person; when I can acknowledge the human being behind the armor; when I can symbolically say, "I know you're in there and I love you," I feel that I have made real and worthwhile contact with a soul, and contact with souls is what life, for me, is all about.

Dr. Leo Buscaglia was moved to create a college course called "Love" when several years ago he established what he thought was a close rapport with one of his students. To his surprise, this young lady was absent from class for a few weeks, although she had been attending regularly before then. He inquired on campus as to her well-being and he was told that, tragically, she had jumped off a cliff. This caused Dr. Buscaglia to deeply reconsider what education is all about. "I began to think," he explained, "that for fifteen years this young lady had received thousands of hours of information about history, science, and English. I wondered, though, that if someone had taught her or given her even a little bit of love, she might not have left this world alone, in despair."

I saw a video tape of Dr. Buscaglia's lecture called "What Is Essential Is Invisible to the Eye." Though thousands of people sat in the audience, his sincerity and genuineness set a tone as personal as the most intimate conversation between two old friends. The faces in the audience were beaming with joy, for what he was telling them was true — and they knew it. He had learned to aim right for the heart.

Bringing such a love into tangible expression is the Divine challenge that beckons to all of us. Patricia Sun was once about twenty minutes into a lecture when a man in the audience raised his hand and blurted, "I came in late; could you please tell me what happened?" I thought this was rather rude, considering there were several thousand people in the audience. Patricia looked at him gently, told him, "I love you; that's what happened," and returned to her talk.

Patricia could say this because she knew the secret of aiming for the heart: *When we ask for anything, we are asking for love.* All of our actions are skillful or unskillful attempts to feel love. The meanest person in the world craves the feeling of love just as much as you and I do, perhaps even more so; but he or she is simply going about getting it in a wrong, or unskillful way. Such a person believes that love can be manipulated, when it can only be won. This belief creates tough facades and disruptive actions. *The most powerful way to short circuit such negative acts is to deal directly on the level of giving love.* It is the seeking of love that is the hidden motive behind all questions and disruptions, and the giving of love that satisfies them.

Jesus knew that all human separation is a disguised form of trying to feel loved, and this is the why he taught to "love your enemies as yourself." He knew that *people act unlovable because they believe they are unlovable.* He understood that one who cries out for love in such a way has been dealt severe blows in life. Said Longfellow, "If we could read the secret history of our enemies, we should find in each man's life, sorrow and suffering to disarm all hostility." And Jesus knew that when we love such a person, we awaken in him his ability to love himself.

Hilda was once confronted by a tough guy in New York City. "I'm William, the king!" he arrogantly proclaimed. Hilda looked him in the eye with deep compassion and softly told him, "I know a greater King, William." Immediately the man broke down and began to weep, for Hilda had touched a long-concealed memory of tenderness and gentleness in this seemingly hardened man.

That memory bank is not unique to William the King who thought he was king. That deep well of innocence belongs to you and me, as well. We *are* more alike than we are different. The words and actions that would hurt or help me are pretty much those that would affect you in the same way. The big lie of life is that we are unaware of what hurts and what heals, and the great Truth is that we are all basically the same.

Yet, too often we speak unthinkingly, with sarcasms, innuendoes, barbs, and banter, acting as if the other guy would be able to take a joke that we, ourselves, could not. I can think of too many jests that I have made without consideration for the feelings of my brothers and sisters, which are really my feelings, as well. The adolescent years in our culture are replete with this kind of biting humor, and for that

313

reason I feel that it behooves us to give our teenagers all the love and support we know how to give. We can overcome negativity with love.

We must never underestimate the healing potential of any act of kindness that we do, however small. Years ago, I received a telephone call from a friend who was going through a difficult time with her parents. She told me her story, and I, having no idea what to tell her, simply listened and quietly loved her. We lost contact with each other after that. Then, years later, I received a letter from her, telling me how grateful she was for all that I had done for her during her trouble. She said that our telephone conversation helped her tremendously in clearing up an extremely difficult relationship, and it was a turning point in her life.

I was amazed! I hardly even remembered the conversation, and when I did, I recalled that all I did was to open my heart and listen without judgement. Yet, somehow, this was just what she needed to transform her situation. The fruits of thoughtfulness sometimes remain hidden until the moment is ripe.

The language of the heart does not demand complexity. Its power lies in quiet simplicity. A friend of mine was struggling through a rigorous Zen meditation retreat. He was fighting his way through the cold, long hours of meditation and hurting knees. He didn't think he could make it to the end. Though he said nothing, a friend at the retreat approached him and silently placed a gentle, reassuring hand on his shoulder, as if to say, "I know what you're going through; I know you can make it; I am with you." "At that moment," my friend tells, "in that simple little touch, more love and understanding was communicated to me than could have been put in any amount of words. That small act of understanding gave me more than enough energy to continue and finish. I shall never forget that one thoughtful touch."

This account confirmed to me that the good intention that we invest in our acts far outshines the outer forms. Rabbi Shlomo Carlebach tells a beautiful story about the Jewish holiday of Purim. On this holiday there is a custom to give fruit and pastries to friends. One Purim evening, three friends found themselves with just one orange among them. One of them took the orange and lovingly gave it to another with a full blessing. The second took the orange, the love, and the blessing, added to it his own kind intention, and passed it on to the third. By this time, the orange was brilliant with light. The love from the sharing was so deep that the three friends decided to pass the orange around again, with more blessings. This went on all night, and by dawn the men, the orange, and the room were overflowing with the purest golden Love.

The noble challenge of our lives is to reach out, to act, and to live for what we know is real, even if that reality is not apparent to our senses. This is the only real faith. The path with heart is walked by those who know the Truth of Love, and are willing to ignore the separations that would discourage others from breaking down the lonely towers that have been constructed about our hearts. When we find the hearts of our sisters and brothers, we discover our own.

"We love you because we are fully aware of your holiness. You are now ready to join us in our happy vision. You are prepared to release forever your mistaken notions of foulness and baseness as the nature of man. You have realized that your nature is blessed by the Light of the world, because you now know yourself to be the Light of the world. You have come to accept your original and abiding goodness, and in this knowledge are you free to nourish it within the consciousness of your brethren by blessing them and loving them.

You have been given the way to heal yourself, your brethren, and your planet. Would you choose now to accept it? In its use is the end of all suffering and the release of the downtrodden. This task is not beyond your capacity. It is your only task. It is your purpose for incarnation and your reason for being. Were there not unconsciousness to rectify, your existence as an entity would hold no purpose.

Go forth, Children of Light. Healing is the gift that you offer to the world. You have everything that you need to transform the earth into paradise. The world is waiting for your love. Do not wait for the world to love you, for that is the great mistake of the world, the very thought which stands between pain and happiness. Give your love fearlessly, and darkness shall flee like the shadow that it is. You are marked by the Light in your heart."

TRANSFORMING RELATIONSHIPS

There is no more fruitful avenue of spiritual growth than that of transforming painful relationships into rewarding ones. In our relations with other persons, we are actually looking at the dynamics of our inner self, in a form we can see in the outer world. When we heal our relationships we heal ourselves.

Many psychologists tell us that problems exist between people when there is a lack of communication. This is true, but we need to discover why communication is not flowing. Lack of communication is really a lack of feeling *communion*. When we see other people as separate or alienated from ourselves, we slice up the universe into limited chunks, and in so doing, we erect prison bars around our heart. When we realize our unity with others, when we feel *with* them instead of *at odds* with them, the joy of our being together comes naturally.

An existential author said, "Hell is other people." He was correct, but not in the way that he meant it. I would add two quotation marks to his sentence to make it accurate: Hell is "other people." Put another way, hell is *thoughts of other-ness*. When we believe, "I am in here, in my own separate existence, and there are 'other people' in their separate existence," we set the scene for the experience of a hellish life, for we have denied the truth of our oneness with all people, with all life, and with God. When Jesus was asked, "What is the greatest commandment of all?" He answered, "God is One." If hell is "other people," Heaven is *One People*.

If I could boil down what I believe is the key to healing in relationships, it would be *forgiveness*. As I see more and more how forgiveness works, it is clear to me that the power of forgiveness is far greater than any tool or weapon known to man. Forgiveness is letting go of ideas of sin, guilt, and evil. *When we forgive another, we free not only them, but ourselves, as well.* Anger, bitterness, and resentment take their toll on he or she who would hold onto such negation. When we let go of judgements and bitterness, we remove from our shoulders and hearts a heavy load of pain. If I find myself holding onto any resentment, I must let it go, for my own good. God will not punish us in the afterlife for our bitterness, for we have already punished ourselves through lost love and aliveness.

When Jesus said, "Love your enemies, do good to those who spitefully use you, and bless those that curse you," He was not just uttering spiritual platitudes. He was giving a scientific formula for resolving painful human relationships and bringing about inner and outer peace. He knew the healing power of Love. He knew that people want to feel united and whole. And He knew that seeing others in the light of forgiveness is the only way to complete our Love.

The pharisees were aghast at Jesus' acceptance of the adulterous woman. "Your sins are forgiven," He told her; "Go and sin no more." They cried, "Blasphemy! No man has the power to pronounce forgiveness! Only God can forgive!" In a way, they were correct, but not in the way that they believed.

No man has the power to pardon someone else's sin, because in Reality there *has never been any sin*. There have been plenty of *thoughts* of sin, which is what the pharisees held, in their readiness to condemn. Jesus, however, was one in consciousness with God; He saw the situation from a Godly point of view, and in *God* consciousness *all* is God, and there is no place for sin. Jesus was not undoing or changing anything that the woman had done. All he did was to look at the Chastity of her soul and tell her the Truth that he could have spoken with equal authority to anyone, saint or sinner: "Your sins are forgiven."

Jesus was looking at the inner perfection, the sinless Light within the woman. This is what we need to do, as well, to heal our relationships. We must focus on the purity and the perfection of those against whom we are prone to hold judgement. Forgiveness of sins is not a special boon reserved for Jesus Christ or for priests, judges, or anyone else. We are *all* equally endowed Children of the Most High.

318

Jesus also said, "Greater things than I, shall ye do."

Outer harmony in relationships is a manifestation of harmony and acceptance within ourselves. If we hold any ill will or animosity toward anyone, it will be reflected in our outer interaction with them. If we are to bring a troubled relationship into peacefulness, we must first find serenity and the vision of good intention within our own consciousness.

I had a startling experience that demonstrated this to me. One evening I attended a lecture on the power of positive thinking. The speaker gave us this exercise: "Close your eyes and let the face of someone who you are not getting along with, pop into your mind." Immediately, the image of a woman who lived next door to me came into my mental view. I squirmed to think of her.

When I and several of my friends had moved into a large house, our neighbor Mrs. Ryan began to feel threatened. This was a fairly conservative neighborhood, and here were five young men with beards moving in next door. We heard that she attempted to pass a petition around the neighborhood to have us ejected on the premise that we were a gang of undercover terrorists. (Meanwhile, we were a bunch of meditating vegetarians.) She then found many opportunities to create situations about which she could complain, and she literally built a fence between our houses. I reacted and felt pretty uncomfortable with her, as well. When this lecturer suggested to take the image of someone we didn't like, I had no trouble picking her.

"Now," he guided us, "imagine this person standing a few feet away from you." ("Oh, no!" I thought.) "Take a few deep breaths and relax until you feel a little more comfortable with their face." Reluctantly, I did so. "Now, walk up to the person and take their hands." ("I can't do that!" I thought. "She'll probably run away screaming, even in my imagination!") But I did it anyway. "Now I want you, in your mental picture, to embrace this person, look them in the eyes, and tell them 'I love you.'" Well, by that time I had surrendered to the exercise, and I carried out his instructions. I was able to let go of some of my animosity toward Mrs. Ryan, and I actually felt better about her.

He then told us: "This is a very powerful method for resolving troubled relationships. If you practice this for five minutes a day for three weeks, one of two things will happen: your relationship with this person will clear up, or they will leave your life." (Either of those alternatives sounded fine to me.)

To be quite honest, I didn't practice the exercise again, but something remarkable did happen. A few days later, one of my room-mates was picking tomatoes in the garden when Mrs. Ryan called to him.

"Mark, can I please have a word with you?"

"Oh no!" he thought, "What now?"

"Mark, I bet you think I'm going to complain about something, don't you?"

"Oh, no," he replied, "what makes you say that?" (He was a good actor — and in this case, a liar as well.)

"Well, you know, Mark, I've been thinking that I haven't been a very good neighbor." (Mark almost fainted.) ". . . and I'd just like to say that I'm sorry if I've given you fellows a hard time."

By now Mark was engaged in some serious reality testing. Mrs. Ryan went on:

"I know you boys (some of us "boys" were thirty years old) are really nice fellows, and I want to be your friend."

If Mark and I did not believe in miracles before then, we became immediate converts. Mark gave her some tomatoes, and our relation-ship with her improved after that time. As it turned out, Mrs. Ryan was actually a very nice lady, and we were very nice "boys," but I had to *see* her lovability — accept her goodness — before I could experience it.

The lesson, or the miracle, with Mrs. Ryan encouraged me to try this method of inner clearing again and again. It has worked every time. Whenever I feel any conflict between myself and another per-son, I seek to work it out first *within myself*. I visualize the person, send them much love and light, and I feel what it would feel like if they were my friend. This technique has helped to transform many of my relationships, and I recommend it to you with the greatest con-fidence.

Relationships are lessons in tangible form that we need for our personal growth. If we are holding any unconsciousness about a character trait, or some prejudice or judgement about any kind of ac-tion, someone who does the thing that we don't like will be drawn to us so that we may learn to let go and to love. *The quickest way to free yourself of someone who does something that irritates you is to love and accept them with their trait.* The more you fight it, the more prominent it will become. When you let go of your resistance, the person may or may not leave your life, but if you have truly released them it will not matter.

This places relationships in an entirely new light — one of challenge and promise. Persons that are hard to accept cease to be nuisances and become opportunities for us to practice understanding and forgiveness. When we experience any negative reaction to another person, we have a precious chance to reprogram our emotional computer. Someone once complained to Hilda, "I can't stand to visit my parents; I have to watch them eat meat!" Hilda's advice: "If I were in that situation, I'd go and sit down next to the one that had the biggest piece of meat and when the meat was being passed around for seconds, I'd offer them some more. I'd make myself sit there until I was relaxed and happy and I felt a lot of love for that person."

In India, Satya Sai Baba sometimes blesses a proposed marriage by saying, "Very happy, very happy!" When one of his followers agrees, "Yes, Baba, I'm sure they will be happy from the start!" he sometimes corrects, "Happy from the start? That is not what I said! They will rub each other's ego down, like the best sandpaper! Then they will *really* be happy!"

What, then, is marriage all about? What makes some marriages successful, and others fail? How do we know if our intended marriage will work? How can we save a marriage that is not working? Why is the divorce rate so high? These are questions that many of us have wrestled with, questions which have too often been answered through pain and hardship. I would like to share with you some of my observations on relationships.

We might say that our motivations for entering into marriage or a relationship can be distilled to two basic dynamic attitudes: "I am going to get something from this person," or "I am going to share with this person." The first attitude leads only to pain; the second, to joy. The first is seeking to get; the second, to expand. Sharing works, taking doesn't.

The question is: How *whole* do I feel in this relationship? Do I feel complete and full and enough *without* this person? Can I enter into this relationship without expecting to receive something from my partner that will make me *more* complete? Can I maintain the integrity of my own individual creativity, *with* my partner? If we can sustain our awareness as full beings, and enter into a marriage as an overflowing expression of the celebration of life, then the marriage will

321

probably work.

If, on the other hand, I marry to "lean out" on someone who will fill a gap within me that I feel I cannot fill myself, then I am in for big disappointment. If I love you because you say you love me, or because you will have sex with me, or because you agree with my way of looking at life, or because you have a character trait that I feel I am lacking, this is not love, but a business arrangement based on lack. In depending on you to fulfill my needs, I am affirming my weakness and establishing a marriage on marshlands. As Jesus said, "A house built upon sand cannot stand." The divorce rate affirms this parable.

If the relationship is inaugurated on the foundation of celebration and overflow, we will receive many of the things that others marry in order to get, but they come as *gifts* and *joys*, and *not* as a *payoff*. I see many marriages around me and I see the relationships in which I have been involved, and it is clear to me that the reasons for which we are taught to marry and the myths about romantic marriage are more illusory than they are real.

Eric Butterworth describes the two different types of relationships in a very neat way: In one relationship we are hypnotized, staring moodily into each other's eyes; in the other, we stand together, hand in hand, looking out the window onto the great panorama of life. In the first, we have made gods of each other; in the second, we rejoice together in acknowledging the One God. In the first, we have narrowed down our source of happiness to one little person; in the second, we remain open to the fulfillment that all of life can offer to us.

The relationships that I have seen work are those in which the partners seek to serve and support each other with encouragement and confidence; where the partners refrain from making demands upon each other; and where the individual creativity of each person is honored and encouraged. More important, the relationships that have God at their center, or that have at least some kind of commitment to a higher purpose than to fulfill each other's fantasies, are the ones that are the strongest. People with individual spiritual foundations create marriages with strong spiritual foundations. Anything that is dedicated to the ideals of Godliness, works.

Can we heal a relationship that has not been based on these ideals? Yes, we certainly can. In fact, many of the strongest and most rewarding relationships are those that have been *transformed*. As we begin to allow God into our lives, we find the strength and the wisdom to create peace and harmony where there once seemed to be none. We discover new ways to give love, and, to our happy surprise, the love and the freedom that we give another to grow and expand are return-ed to us many times over.

If we truly want to enjoy fulfilling relationships in marriage, with our children, or in the office, we must be willing to be big enough to give love *before* we receive it. We must not allow our actions or at-titudes toward others to depend on theirs toward us. We must have the faith to see a possibility for goodness in another, though they recognize it not themselves.

Someone put it in a lovely poetic form:

> *They drew a circle that kept me out,*
> *But I and God were bound to win.*
> *We drew a circle that kept them in.*

Jesus said it this way: "You have been told, 'an eye for an eye, and a tooth for a tooth.' I tell you to forgive." Someone asked Him, "Master, how many times shall we forgive — seven?" "Nay," He answered — "seventy times seven." In other words, just keep right on forgiving.

I would like to conclude these thoughts on relationships with a promise of the unlimited possibilities for positive change through forgiveness. I want to tell you that it is possible to heal a troubled rela-tionship even with someone who has passed on. This is possible because all such healing is a result of *inner* forgiveness and *spiritual* love. Relationships are lessons in inner growth. If we can grow to a point where, were the other person still alive, we would be in har-mony with them, we have learned the lesson of the relationship, and it is complete.

My dad and I did not have very good communication in our rela-tionship. We loved each other in a family kind of way, but we were not intimate, like friends. In my adolescent years, I was sometimes disrespectful toward him, and I did not give him as much honor or understanding as I would now like to have given him.

In the years following his passing, I did a lot of growing up. As I learned the importance of respect and understanding, I shuddered to think how uncourteous I had been to my dad. In my heart, I wished to apologize to him, and to tell him of my love and appreciation for him.

One night he came to me in a dream. In this dream, I met him at a party, and he was radiant and peaceful. While he was overweight and reclusive in life, at this party he was slim and friendly. When we greeted, he told me that he was doing fine, and I was very happy to see how joyous he was. I felt, too, that he now had his own life to live. We parted in friendship and mutual respect for each other's path. I awoke from the dream with a deep sense of resolution and peacefulness about my father and myself. I believe that our relationship was healed, even after he left this life.

This experience and the others like it have served as my lessons in what is necessary to transform relationships. As I have learned more about how to love, forgive, and find goodness in myself and others, I have discovered that forgiveness is a gift from God that always heals. I know that it can heal our relationships, our lives, and our world. In so doing shall it mend our broken hopes, return to us our forgotten dreams, and bestow upon us the miracle of Grace. Fulfilling relationships, I have found, are not too good to be true. They are good enough to be true.

"Your purpose on earth is to make peace. As you have discovered this purpose, the power to heal relationships comes to rest in your hands.

You hold the entire universe within yourself. Take all into your arms, and all persons and things reveal themselves to be the expression of God's Love for you, which is really your Love for Him. Where Love is, the purpose of life is understood. Where there is no love, there is nothing.

We implore you to raise each precious moment of relationship up to the altar of the Most High. Hold your fellows in holy respect, and speak to all as you would speak to the holiest angel. Chide not yourself for your errors, but correct them. Were you to forgive your brethren but not yourself, you would remain in error. In Truth, the forgiveness of your brethren and yourself are one and the same.

You have been cleansed by the Blessing of your Heavenly Beloved. Your soul rests satisfied as you stand, bathed in purity, clad in the white robes of forgiveness, before the chair of your Father, who quietly acknowledges your Holy Presence. This day is cause for great celebration, for this is the reunion for which you have borne the tribulation of earth. Your life has led you to the reward of loving kindness — a blessing that you have always deserved by virtue of your Heritage. Our hands are outstretched to take yours, as you step across the threshold of your new life. Your efforts are completed through Grace.''

FILLING UP AND SPILLING OVER

Filling up and spilling over,
It's an endless waterfall,
Filling up and spilling over,
Over all.
— Cris Williamson, "Waterfall"

One bright spring morning, I stepped outside the restaurant where I was working, for a breath of fresh air and sunshine. As I closed the door behind me, a man that I had not seen before approached me with a radiant smile and exclaimed, "Gosh, it's a beautiful day, isn't it?"

"It certainly is!" I happily agreed.

"You know, my friend," he went on, "I just want to tell you how happy I am since I allowed God into my life!"

I was a little surprised that he spoke so intimately to me and I was, in fact, a little leery that he was about to go into a sermon or invite me to a meeting or ask for a donation. But there was something genuine about him, and so I loaned him my ear.

"I used to be miserable," he explained. "I had so many worries and poor health, my business was floundering, and I just did not like life. Then, one day, I realized how wonderful and magnificent is God! I saw, as if for the first time, the splendor of His creation! He made the trees, the birds, and the flowers! And what's more, I realized that He really loves me!"

As I listened to his delightful story, my doubts disappeared, my heart opened, and I began to feel and flow with him.

327

"Since that splendid moment," he continued, "my life has been miracle after miracle. I wake up in the morning and I look forward to each new day. I have many wonderful friends, and my work is satisfying. I just love life, and I am so grateful that God is so good to me!"

He put his hand on my shoulder, looked me squarely in the eye, and told me, "I just want you to know that I love you, and to say, 'God bless you.' "

With that, my mysterious friend turned and walked (or floated) on down the street. No sermons. No meetings. Nothing asked in return. Just "filling up and spilling over."

Thrilled over such a miraculous encounter, I ran into the store to tell my coworker, who I knew would want to meet this extraordinary man. She immediately dropped what she was doing, ran out the door, and sought to find him. But he was nowhere to be found. It was a small town. He could not have gone very far. She searched all the streets, yet he seemed to have disappeared. Perhaps he was an angel.

Spiritual awakening is spread by *overflow*. We cannot force another into higher consciousness. We are all like flower buds — we must open and bloom at our own rate, catalyzed by the warmth of the sun. The best way to support another person in their growth is to love them. They will feel so free and easy in our presence that their blocks to growth will just melt away. No amount of preaching, teaching, or pressuring will speed up their evolution, and it may even retard it. We may share, offer ideas, and invite if we feel to do so, yet this reaching out must be offered lightly, with an open hand, so that our friend feels completely free to accept our invitation or decline it. That's just the way sharing God has got to be. God must be chosen.

No one has ever been browbeaten into God, but many have been inspired, impressed, and enthused. We must teach not so much with our words, but by our example. If we would like a spouse, a friend, or a child to "get" what we have gotten, they must *catch it* from us. If we simply live the values that we hold dearest in our heart, there is a good chance that our friends will notice the positive changes in our life. They will respond to the light in our faces, and the peace in our eyes will awaken peace within them. One day they may say to us, "You look so happy lately — what have you been doing?" This is our opportunity to share, if we like — we have been asked.

There are many paths to the top of the mountain, where we all meet as One, without religion, name, or form. There is no need — and

328

no use — to clutch at or attempt to proselytize potential converts to whatever cause we hold dear. If our cause is worthwhile, it will inspire on its own merit. ("Those that are mine will know me," said Jesus.) There is no truth in the idea that the more people that belong to an organization or a group, the better or truer it is. Truth cannot be measured by a number of devotees; it is a qualitative experience in the heart of each aspirant.

The Truth does not need anyone or any organization to sell it. The Truth sells itself by transforming the inner and outer lives of those that it touches. The Truth needs no marketing, packaging, or promotion. It needs only to be *lived*. People who live Truth usually have many people attracted to them without any advertising or soliciting. One characteristic of a cult is that members are coerced to join and restricted from leaving. The students of a teacher of Truth are free to come and go as their hearts guide them.

Jesus Christ, for example, was so full that His Truth has spilled over for two thousand years, to billions of people. It is staggering to me how one man could live and teach in a remote land for three short years, and in His Name millions of churches have been erected all over the world, incalculable healings have taken place, and the lives of so many human beings have been transformed and uplifted. Jesus brought a force of forgiveness to the earth that has reverberated throughout the entire universe which we, as a race, have yet to understand or put into practice.

Jesus was not the only great one. Moses, Buddha, Mary, Krishna, Mohammed, St. Theresa, Lao Tse, and many, many others have served as messengers of Light. Though they each had a slightly different style of teaching, they are all one in teaching the Truth of One God, One Life, and One Love. On this they all agree.

The best and only way to teach is by sharing. My life is a lesson for me and for the world, and so is yours. My experience is an illustration of God's Truth in expression. My "failures" are as educational as my successes. Each of our feelings, problems and insights are here for the upliftment of all humanity. When one person grows, all of humanity grows. When one of us conquers a personal limitation, we conquer the limitations of all. Every one of us is cleansing the universe of error. When we live in Truth, our thoughts and actions send out ripples that awaken the awareness of Truth in all living things. Our life is a sacrifice — not in martyrdom — but in service. When one person suffers, he or she is ending the suffering of all living beings. When we know God, we are bringing all of creation closer to God. In this way, we are truly instruments of God's Peace. This Peace would She share with all, through each.

"Your awareness of God is the healing you offer to your brethren. The Light you see is a gift given to be shared. What God gives to you belongs to you, and through you it belongs to all.

Those who live the Truth can never lose it. If you feel diminished in rejection, you face only your learned insecurity. Do not expect to be accepted by those that see you as a part of an old world. When your faith gains the firmness of a rock, resistance can find no place in your experience. Stand for the Truth, and those that love Truth will stand by your side.

Your creative words and simple deeds are shining stars in a dismal night. We charge you with glorifying the Truth in a world that hates Truth, and we ask you to live for Love in a world that flees from Light. You yourself have chosen this work, and we hail you for so commiting your acts. The days to come shall challenge you to your mettle, but through the Holy Spirit, that selfsame Spirit to Whom you have dedicated your life, you shall emerge unscathed. This is our dauntless promise to you.

Go forth, Children of Light, as did the original disciples and as all who truly love God must do, and ignite the fire of Truth by living it. Be true to yourself, for only in such simple honesty is Peace confirmed. The Light of the world shines through your faces and your hearts, and blesses through your hands. You are the song that I sing to the world."

THE POWER OF APPRECIATION

Appreciation and blessing are one and the same. We sometimes say, "Let's bless the food now," or "Bless you," or "May this house be blessed." Actually, we have no power to make anything more Holy than it already is. *Everything is already completely blessed*, and all the prayers in the world could not make it more blessed. We certainly could not imbue a loaf of bread or a person with more God than already lives within them. What we can do, however, is to *see*, or appreciate the God-infused blessedness in the person or object, guaranteed by the Light that lights the world.

If we are not seeing that Light, it is not because it is not there — it is because we are not looking at it. I was once feeling annoyed at a good friend of mine over a little matter — he owed me a small amount of money. I allowed my resentment to obscure my vision of him, and I was judging him more than I was loving him. When I realized this, I decided "No! Love is more important to me than a few dollars. I will not throw him out of my heart." I then began to think of all the qualities about him that I appreciated. He is a very strong, good-natured, and sensitive man. He is extremely compassionate and generous. As I thought more about his good qualities, I realized how much I really did love him and I felt so grateful to have him as a friend. Compared to the importance of his friendship to me, this small debt seemed miniscule. I traded my irritation for appreciation, and that made all the difference. (And he paid the debt, as well.)

When we appreciate someone or something, we are blessing them in the most powerful way. We are acknowledging their Divine origin.

We are giving thanks for a gift from God. Appreciation is a form of prayer. If you are uncomfortable with traditional forms of prayer, just start appreciating the things in your life, and this gratefulness will be more pleasing in the eyes of God than a ritual that has no meaning for you.

There is an old song that has ever-new meaning:

> *Count your blessings,*
> *Count them one by one.*
> *Count your blessings,*
> *See what God has done.*

Every year around Thanksgiving, I take a piece of paper and make a list of all in my life for which I am grateful. I start with the basics, the things that we sometimes take for granted, like food, shelter, and clothing. Actually, we should "take them for granted," for, like the lilies of the field, we are in the loving care of a nurturing Divine Mother who gladly takes it upon Herself to meet all of our needs. Too often, however, we overlook these gifts without appreciation, and our thoughts of lack push abundance out of our experience. When we consciously focus on the good in our lives — such as through a list like this — we unite our mind with the power of appreciation, and we make ourselves available to receive the blessings that God is always offering.

On my list I include my friends and the loving and caring things that anyone has done for me, especially the "little" things, like a bright smile or a prompt reply to a letter. There are so many miracles that we can find when we are willing to acknowledge them. A few weeks ago, for example, I received a phone call from a man in my town who has the same name as me. Because my telephone number was not listed in the directory, he was receiving calls from my friends and coworkers trying to get in touch with me. What I appreciated so much was that he was extremely kind and pleasant in asking me to make my number more available to my friends. He didn't have to be so congenial. Someone else might have gotten irritated about this unnecessary nuisance. When I apologized to him for his inconvenience, he said, "Well, that's O.K. — we Alan Cohens have got to stick together, you know!" He didn't even know me, and yet he was willing to stick together with me. I thought that was pretty grand.

Next on my list I write down the hardships and challenges that have made me strong as I have had to overcome them. Perhaps these should be first on the list of appreciations, for these are the gifts that have brought me closer to God, and I can think of no greater blessing than knowing the Source of all blessings.

My thanksgiving list concludes with any abilities or skills that God gave me to be creative and expressive, and through which I can make some kind of contribution to the world. As I finish writing, I am always amazed at the length of the list, and I always feel a little foolish at not having recognized the abundance in my life.

The people who are successful are those who are grateful for everything they have. Those who complain, whine, or fight life cannot in this consciousness be successful, for in their negation they lose their creative energy and cut themselves off from any possibilities of abundance that are flowing their way. Giving thanks for what we do have always opens up the door for more to come, and ungratefulness always closes it.

I like to start and end my day with thoughts of praise and appreciation. I look in the mirror in the morning, and no matter how I feel or look, I say (out loud) "Wow! A new day! I'm so grateful to be alive and healthy! Something wonderful is going to happen to me today! I believe in miracles! There are limitless possibilities for me! I know that God is working *with* me. Just think how many opportunities there will be to love! Thank you, God, for this new day!"

Now, if anyone who didn't know me just happened to walk by the door at that moment, they might think I was a little flaky, but I don't care. I think we have to be a little unusual to make it in life. The world is inside out. That which the world approves of is insane. So, if I ever find myself doing anything a little crazy like this, I know I must be on the right track.

I like to end the day in the same way, with a gentler tone. As I lie in bed before going to sleep, I quietly look over my day and think of the blessings that have been given to me. If I made any foolish blunders, I give thanks that I became aware of them, and I am grateful that I will be less likely to repeat the same mistake. I like to live in a realm of thanksgiving.

The more we appreciate, the more we will find to appreciate. "To him that hath, more shall be given." This can work both ways. Just as blessing a situation brings freedom, cursing it brings bondage. The more we rail against a problem in our lives, the more pain it will bring us. Cursing a person or event is denying the God that lives within them, and until we recognize the inner Light there, the situation will remain a curse to us. Just as it is not in our power to really add blessing to anything, neither is it in our power to curse anything. All we can do in condemning anything is to uphold and increase our own sense of separation and loneliness, which is the sole root of our desire to curse anything. Lack of appreciation is simply a matter of limited seeing, like looking at a crack in the ceiling of the Sistine Chapel. We do not need to create anything new; we need only to see the whole picture of what we already have.

Another old song goes:

> You got to AC-CENT-CHU-ATE THE POSITIVE
> Elim-my-nate the negative
> Latch on to the affirmative
> Don't mess with Mister In Between
> You've got to spread joy up to the maximum
> Bring gloom down to the minimum
> Have faith . . .

The song contains the secret of happiness. We *can* control the amount of happiness in our lives, simply by training our minds to focus on that which is good, beautiful, and true. We do not need to fight or curse that which is not good. All we need to do is to accentuate the positive, and the negative will shrivel up and waste away from lack of attention.

More than anything else, we must appreciate ourselves. Swami Muktananda said, "The biggest error we can make is to not love our Self." God made each of us with the intention to bless the world through us. We can make a supremely valuable contribution to the universe simply by appreciating our holiness and seeing all as blessed. The more we bless life, the more life will bless us, for that is The Plan, The Great Idea for which all creation sprang into existence. As we sanctify our lives through our own gratefulness, the illusion of lack vanishes like the morning mist, and our cup runs over with thanksgiving enough to share a million times over.

"All is fully blessed. Your growth is but an adjustment of consciousness, a change in your perception of the Source of your life. The first petal of spiritual awakening is wonder. This is the beginning of the acceptance of your Heritage.

All things are born of the holy spark of God. In such realization is your release from the burdens of your own creation, ghostly concepts which you vainly attempted to prove. You relieve yourself from your fabricated expectations when you see that God has an Expectation for you which far outshines your small idea of what you can do with Love.

There is a certain popularity in words and expressions of derision. This is the very error that denies bliss to the hearts of those who cry out for it. Think clearly about the effect of your words. Such contemplation will reveal to you your ministry, which is your power to heal and to bless through supportive words and acts. You are entrusted with the answers to your brothers' prayers. Deliver blessings through your kindness, and you serve in the way of the Divine.

As your sense of appreciation expands, great wonders are made known to you. Miracles cease to maintain the cloak of mystery that enshrouded them, for it is only in the fear of Love that you made a rarity of what you admitted as miraculous. The spiritual master does not seek in exotic lands for the demonstration of the miraculous, but welcomes the simple aspects of life as marvelous. Be childlike in your enjoyment of what is given to you, and the Kingdom of Heaven welcomes you as its happy prodigal.''

IF I HAD MY LIFE TO LIVE OVER

Nadine Stair — 85 years old
Louisville, Kentucky

I'd dare make more mistakes next time.
  I'd relax, I would limber up, I would be sillier
than I have been this trip.
  I would take fewer things seriously.
I would take more chances.
  I would take more trips.
I would climb more mountains, swim more rivers,
  I would eat more ice cream and less beans.
I would perhaps have more actual troubles but,
  I'd have fewer imaginary ones.

You see, I'm one of these people who live sensibly
  and sanely hour after hour,
day after day, oh, I've had my moments and if
  I had it to do over again,
I'd rather have more of them.
  In fact, I'd try to have nothing else.
Just moments, one after another instead of living so
  many years ahead of each day.
I've been one of those persons who never goes
  anywhere without a thermometer,
a hot water bottle, a raincoat, a parachute.
  If I had to do it over again
I would travel lighter than I have.

If I had my life to live over, I would start barefoot
  earlier in the Spring and stay that way
later in the Fall.
  I would go to more dances.
I would ride more merry-go-rounds.
  I would pick more daisies.

DANCIN' UP THE PATH

The first time I saw Swami Satchidananda, I learned what spirituality is about. The scene was very subdued. On the stage there was a couch, a microphone, and an array of beautiful flowers. A group of his devotees, wearing white, led the audience in chanting. When news of the swami's arrival came, a great hush fell over the audience. As he entered the room, all silently rose to their feet. Every eye in the room was fixed on the poised figure in the flowing robe. The swami politely bowed, and those around him respectfully returned the bow. As he took his place on the couch, not a whisper could be heard. He crossed his legs in full lotus position, closed his eyes, took a deep breath, and prepared to speak. It was a very serious moment.

"This microphone looks like a big cigar in my mouth!" were his first words, and that was the end of the seriousness. The audience roared with laughter that released the subtle tension of an idea that spirituality is supposed to be stuffy. The audience had been grave; the swami was full of fun. "I have never met a holy person that was not joyous and happy," Hilda has told us many times. Too often, we believe that to be spiritual is to be serious, somber, and even maudlin. Yes, the spiritual path requires of us seriousness of purpose, discipline, and sometimes sternness, but these attributes must always be combined with lightness, fun, and celebration.

Enlightenment does not only mean to see the light, but to *take it light*. Enlightened people take life lightly. Light is the opposite of dark, but it is also the opposite of "heavy." If we see life as a heavy burden, a load, an obligation, we are not looking at it from an enlightened point

of view. Jesus said, "Come to me, all who labor and are heavy burdened, and I shall give you rest. My yoke is easy, and my burden is
light."

I just know that Jesus was not a sad sack. I thrill to every movie
or play that portrays the life of the Master. Jesus is, however, too
often shown as such a serious character, stern and foreboding. I don't
believe that Jesus could have really been so grave, or else He would
have scared all of His disciples away. I believe that He won His
followers to Him by His light-heartedness and His love. Yes, I'm sure
He was very serious at times, but I am also certain that most of the
time He was joyful, radiant, happy, delightful, and delighted. I would
stake all that I feel about Jesus on this picture of Him. I know that He
laughed with his disciples, that He had a sense of humor, and that His
whole life was *not* a crucifixion. He loved little children, and He
taught, "You are the Light of the world." I do not believe that He could
teach the Light of the world without emanating the Light of the world.
I love the statues of Him where He is alive and beautiful and standing
with arms open in forgiving love. This is the Jesus that we need to
know more of; it is the Jesus of the garden, as well as the cross. Life
will hand us our share of crosses. We do not need to build any more
for ourselves by making ourselves miserable because we have
somehow learned to equate spirituality with agony. The sign of real
spirituality is joy. As we learn how to accept and express joy, we find
we have fewer crosses to bear.

Many people are familiar with the story of Norman Cousins. Dr.
Cousins is a medical doctor and former editor of *Saturday Review.* He
was diagnosed as having a rare degenerative disease of the spine,
which his doctors called irreversible and gave him no chance for
recovery. Dr. Cousins was not, however, prepared to accept their
prognosis. He understood the power of thought. He reasoned that *if
negative thinking causes disease, then positive thoughts should be able
to dissolve it.* So Dr. Cousins borrowed a movie projector, rented
some old Marx Brothers and Candid Camera films, and invited his
friends to his hospital room to join him for some light entertainment.
Here is Dr. Cousins' story of what then happened:

> *We pulled down the blinds and turned on the machine . . .
> It worked. I made the joyous discovery that ten minutes of
> genuine belly laughter had an anesthetic effect and would*

give me at least two hours of pain-free sleep. When the pain-killing effect of the laughter wore off, we would switch on the motion picture projector again, and, not infrequently, it would lead to another pain-free sleep interval. *

After a few days, Dr. Cousins was required to leave the hospital because the laughter from his room was disturbing the other patients. So he checked out of the hospital and into a hotel, where he continued his laughter therapy and took large doses of vitamin C, found primarily in citrus fruits, which absorb a great amount of light (as in en*light*enment). His account continues:

By the end of the eighth day I was able to move my thumbs without pain . . . it seemed to me that the gravel-like nodules on my neck and the backs of my hands were beginning to shrink. There was no doubt in my mind that I was going to make it back all the way. I could function, and the feeling was indescribably beautiful. *

Dr. Cousins discovered — for all of us — the healing power of laughter. This medicine was given to Alan Watts by an old Zen master who prescribed a very unusual form of meditation: "You stand up, place your hands on your hips, and begin to laugh. Start with a few 'ha-ha's,' then add a few 'he-he's,' and before long, the 'ho-ho's' will be coming of themselves." At first, the laughter seems phony and forced, but as you stay with it, it becomes real — and uproarious. Use of this meditation is especially indicated for dull groups. It is also a very practical way to start the day. I know a man who, upon awakening each morning, walks directly to the mirror, places one hand on a hip, points the other at the image of himself, and begins to laugh as hard as he can. (It certainly is more fun than looking in the mirror and groaning.)

In the Tarot cards, there is an especially intriguing image of *The Fool*. This is a picture of a young man with a flower in his hand, skipping along gaily, about to dance over the edge of a cliff. There is some

*Norman Cousins, *Anatomy of an Illness as Perceived by the Patient*, W.W. Norton & Co., 1979.

controversy, I am told, as to whether this is the first card in the deck, or the last — whether it represents a form of wisdom, or ignorance.

Perhaps it is both. Surely we must keep our feet on the ground and take care to be cautious in a treacherous world. On the other hand, there is an element of Divine foolishness in many spiritual masters. From a worldly point of view, some of the great saints, like Joan of Arc, St. Francis, and Sri Ramakrishna (in India) were considered insane. But their madness was not unto the devil, but *God*. In *Brother Sun, Sister Moon*, St. Clare tells St. Francis, "They say you are mad because you would rather romp through the fields and sit among the flowers than be a slave to business, as they are; but I think that it is *they* who are mad, and not you."

The Tarot card may represent our need to dance up the path of life, even though the body and our worldly attachments are destined for death. We never really know when the edge of the cliff is approaching, so we might as well enjoy a few flowers while we can.

The world does not know how to enjoy itself because it does not really know what are the ingredients for happiness. If it did, the world would be happy, and (if you have read the newspapers lately) you can see that the world is not a very happy place. It follows, then, that if we want to feel joy, we are going to have to find it in some other way than the world is trying to get it.

Song and celebration are written off by the serious-minded as foolishness, but they are gifts from God, given to heal feelings of aloneness and separation. It is impossible to sing and be miserable at the same time. Without song and celebration, life is a bore and a drudgery. With it, we can dance. It doesn't matter so much *what* we celebrate, but that we *do* celebrate. (There is an old joke about a man who quit being an atheist because there weren't enough holidays.) If we allow our minds and hearts to be open, we can celebrate all the holidays of all the religions. We can enjoy the light on Christmas, on Hannukah, and on Krishna's birthday, as well. God is grand enough to take it *all* in. When we sing along with it all, we join the Godly chorus and infuse the Voice of God into a dismal world.

If we find ourselves lost in the world of pressures, stress, and insecurity, the best method to find our way home is to "ease on down the road." I went to an astounding series of lectures by a very astute and successful chiropractor, on "Maintaining Good Health." The first lecture was on proper exercise and care of the spine. The second was on good nutrition. The third, which he described as the most important, was on positive thinking. He told that, after he had completed his education on all the proper health practices, he went to work in a clinic in New York City. There he found as patients a number of old men who had, from his perspective, horrendous health habits. They smoked cigarettes, ate lots of junk food, and drank liquor. To his surprise, they were in remarkably good health. He saw that, though they did not take care of their bodies, they had a very relaxed and easy-going attitude toward life. They lived from day to day and let nothing bother them. In short, they took life easy. This, perhaps, balanced out or even overrode their poor health habits. Though they will eventually have to reconcile their mistreatment of their bodies, they have caught on to one of the keys to joyous living: *taking it easy.*

A man who picked me up when I was hitchiking told me of a study that was done on the relationship between diet, frame of mind, and health. A group of hard-core health food devotees and a group of junk food eaters were tested for the amount of vitamins and nutrients in their blood. It turned out that the health food enthusiasts registered *fewer* nutrients in their blood than the "junkies." I believe that this, if it is so, is because the stress and worry about eating the right foods probably robs the body of more nutrients than the foods put in. If someone adheres to a diet or any regimen *fanatically*, afraid of losing health or life with bad foods, he is likely to suffer more from the fear than he would from the food. I am not advocating junk foods over health foods; I strive to keep a nutritious diet. It is important, however, to know the effect of an easy and relaxed attitude in life and to remember that the spirit is always more important than the form.

Life is too short and too insane to take it very seriously. Yogananda said that "This world is just a big mental institution." If we learn to see the people around us — and ourselves — as mental cases, we can laugh at the world and ourselves. Think, for example, of the things that people believe are important, like toothpaste that gives you sex appeal and blue jeans that cost twice the price because a name is printed on the hip pocket; think of the state of world politics, in which an unelected brother of a president is paid millions of dollars by a foreign government to wield influence which the president can't control; and think of the silly things that you and I have become upset

343

about (when I was a child, I was ejected from the audience of *The Merry Mailman* TV show when I went into a hysterical fit because I thought the clown on the show had stolen my father's hat). Surely we are all a little crazy. I don't think that we would be here if we were not. How, then, can we take ourselves so seriously?

I believe that if we cannot find a way to laugh about a situation, we have not seen it in a big enough perspective. We need to be able to laugh at ourselves and our problems. Sometimes our difficulties even disappear when we laugh at them. And even if they don't, we will at least have had a good laugh.

My old friend Jim and I would spend many hours trying to figure out the meaning of life. One day we got onto the question of "What is laughter about, anyway?"

"All laughter," Jim told me, "is a reflection of *The Cosmic Absurdity*."

"Wow — The Cosmic Absurdity! . . . What's that?" I wondered. It sure sounded fascinating, whatever it was.

"The Cosmic Absurdity is this," he explained. "If you really think about it, all of life is absurd. There is no meaning to anything. When you realize the foolishness that our lives are based on, all we can really do is laugh." To tell you the truth, I didn't really understand what he was talking about, but it sounded absurd, and so we just laughed.

Wisdom and humor hold thrones of equal stature in Heaven's court. More often than we would realize, there is no difference between the two. There is an old story about a man who goes to a doctor and says, "Doctor, every time I raise my arm like this, it hurts!" The doctor thinks for a moment, and prescribes, "So don't raise your arm like that!" The source of this parable is under controversy. Some say it is an ancient Zen koan and others argue that it is a Henny Youngman joke. It could be either. Or both. Or neither.

What good is life without laughter? Those who know God know how to laugh at life. Swami Vishnudevananda is a fine example of living in fun. At a potentially serious conference on the coming tribulation in the world, the swami sat on the edge of the stage and heckled the other speakers with loving wisecracks. His humor was not directed at any person, but at the foolishness of life itself. There was talk of earthquakes and floods and devastation, and the swami laughed his way through all of it, even though he was one of the speakers. When it was his turn to speak, he heckled himself as much as the others. He was blessed with the rare ability to not take himself seriously.

It is said that it takes only about seven muscles to smile but fifty or more to frown. It seems to me that God makes it easy for us to do what She wants us to do. I think She likes to see us smiling, because we like to see each other smiling, and She gets to enjoy life when Her children do.

The story is told of Rabbi Nachman of Bratslav, a pious and revered Hasidic sage. During a time of great oppression of the Jewish people, his students came to him, distraught. "Rabbi," they queried, "are we permitted to say the holiday prayers of rejoicing and thanksgiving during this dark time? How can we rejoice when our people are so maligned?"

The rabbi lit up with a wise smile. "Ah!" he exclaimed, "This is the time when we most need to rejoice! It is easy to celebrate God in the easy times, but when the blows of life are severe, our song must ring out twice as loud!"

> *Dance, dance, wherever you may be*
> *For "I am the Lord of the Dance," said He*
> *I'll lead you all wherever you may be*
> *I'll lead you all in the Dance with me*
> — *"THE LORD OF THE DANCE"*

"Children of Light, pay attention to what we call you, for in your name is the key to your liberation.

We delight in your joyousness. Listen well to the laughter of children at play, for these little ones are close to the heart of God, and they play at the very feet of the Master. Would you remain wailing at the gate while He, with open arms, bids you enter? The wonders of the garden await you. Step through the gate of roses into the home of your heart.

Were you to go through one day, yea, even one hour, in song and celebration, your too-long held woes would melt like ice before the sun. You do not realize with what tenacity you cling to your self-created misery. You clutch at it as if it were a prized possession, a pearl of great price. You believe that you enjoy it, but inwardly you know that this cannot be the way for you. Your learned will for sorrow is replaced by His will for your joy.

You best serve God with all of your heart. God's real nature is happiness. Serve Him by expressing joyousness, and your reward is the awakening that your joy is His.''

LOVE IS THE
GREATEST OF ALL

If, when I leave this mad world, I am required to give an accounting for my acts in this life, there is only one question that I am concerned about answering: "Did you love?" If I can earnestly answer "Yes," then I shall consider my time well spent and my purpose in living fulfilled.

Years ago, while in the seemingly mundane act of walking up a back stairway in a college building, I realized that there is no power in the universe greater than Love, and no act more important than loving. I was thinking about what it is that enables great people to achieve excellence in their art. As I pondered, it became clear to me that anyone can become anything he or she sets their heart on being. I just knew that any master orator, musician, or photographer has become proficient only through commitment and practice. As I realized in that very special moment that I, too, could see the fulfillment of my deepest wish, I asked myself, "What would I like to make a stand for in this lifetime?" The answer came immediately and clearly, in a firm but gentle whisper: *Love*. How happy I felt to know that if I determined it to be so, my dream of Love could actually come true!

Love is the ideal and the dream of every person who lives, for in Love were our souls conceived, and in Love is our Destiny to express. We are fulfilled when we are in Love, and somehow empty without it. It is the very purpose of our being alive, and the idea God held in Mind when we sprang from the celestial womb.

Though billions of words have been written about Love, not one of them — or all of them — could fully capture Love. Love is infinite, and like a mountain spring that bubbles up from an unending source, it fills all hearts and hands that open themselves to accept It. Love is always alive in our hearts, expressing Itself in ways that we do not understand. Love is always eager to share and expand Itself to bless all who desire Its radiant Presence. Meher Baba said,

> *Love has to spring spontaneously from within. It is in no way amenable to any form of inner or outer force. Love and coercion can never go together; but though Love cannot be forced on anyone, It can be awakened in him through Love itself. Love is essentially self-communicative. Those who do not have It catch It from those who have It. True Love is unconquerable and irresistible; and It goes on gathering power and spreading Itself, until eventually It transforms everyone whom It touches.*

Love is not limited to any age, place, name, color, or experience, and yet Love lives equally within all of these. Love is completely free of any kind of restriction. The oldest person is as sensitive to the life of Love as any young lover, for Love is ever new. The hardest heart is opened instantly through the magic of a loving word or touch. Love is more vital to us than food. There are saints and yogis who live for many years with little or no food, yet their hearts are full to overflowing with Love, and they are fully nourished. We may consume the finest delicacies, yet, if we have not Love, it is as though we were dead.

Love and giving are as inseparable as the lily and its fragrance. It is impossible to love without giving, for giving is the very nature of Love. Neither can we truly give without Love. Sai Baba said that "all acts of service are meaningless unless they are given with Love." When we discover the miracle of Love, we cannot stop ourselves from giving — nor do we want to stop. It is obvious to the lover that Love only increases when It is given.

All Love is Divine. Let it never be said that physical or romantic Love is less than God's Love, for ideas cannot be apart from their source. Even when Love takes an object, It is holy, for Love is Love, and It is uncompromising in Its commitment to Its own purpose. As the first two leaves of a flower, which later drop away, help the stem rise out of the soil, conditional Love is a herald of the unlimited Love to come. With Love we learn forgiveness, and with forgiveness, compassion. We come to understand that Love remains constant through the evolution of Its expression.

The Christ beseeched us, "Love God with all your heart, with all your soul, and with all your strength; this is the greatest teaching of all." Of course it is. God is in everything and *is* everything. When we love all people and all things, we love God. And when we simply love God, all things reveal themselves to embody His Holy Presence.

Love is the true healing force of the universe. When we love another person, we see their wholeness, and when this wholeness is kindled in our thoughts and fanned with our good intention, it awakens their own knowledge of their Divine heritage of completeness.

I saw a healing that I want to always remember as a symbol of the unsurpassable power of Love. The man I am thinking of was nervous, withdrawn, and fearful. A group of people surrounded him, gently rested their hands on him, and quietly gave him healing Love. I saw that man go through the most dramatic transformation I have ever seen. I could literally see the lines and the dark spots leave his face. He began to breathe heavily, and I felt like I was having the privilege of witnessing a birth. The light that began to shine from his face was so bright that everyone in the room could hardly believe that it was the same man they saw a few minutes earlier. He looked as if he had lost about fifteen years of age in just a few minutes. If someone had thrown away their crutches or walked away from a wheelchair, I do not think it would have been as powerful as the transformation I saw in this man. It was a healing of the inner man — of the soul — a healing available to every human being. Such is the miracle of healing Love.

Love cannot be bought, sold, or reduced to any kind of commodity. We can sell our bodies, our possessions, our thoughts, and our work, but Love is ever free of ownership. It simply shines without concern for who or what It touches. The sun shines equally on the morning glory and on the weed. We may attempt to make a business of Love by saying, "I will love you if you will love me," but this is a distortion of the all-encompassing way that real Love unfolds. The happy Law of Life is that "If I love you, you will love me." And yet we cannot love another for the sake of receiving their Love in exchange. Love in exchange is a guilt bargain, and we only rob our own self in futile barter. Love given freely is the only Love that can satisfy, and we only magnify our joy in so loving. Some draw an artificial distinction between Love and power. I say that power is a ray of light from the star of Love. How much energy we have at our beckoning when we are in Love! Suddenly we are able to travel great distances, forsake sleep, and offer mighty acts of selfless service and giving! We are prepared to sacrifice our own desires for the sake of the beloved, and we are willing to overlook the imperfections and faults of the beloved. Love *is* blind, and blessedly so. Love is not blind to the Truth; It simply overlooks the unimportant aspects of personality that we usually, mistakenly, call "truth."

Who can fathom the mystery of Love? Certainly not I. To attempt to intellectually dissect the miracle of Love is to pull apart the threads that are woven into the very fabric of our existence. I do not care if I ever understand Love. I only know that I love, and if I never do anything else, I shall be fulfilled.

Sri Ramakrishna told that more than anything else, God loves to love. "Though a wealthy man with a large estate has many rooms in which he may dwell, he has one favorite sitting room in which he delights in being. The Lord loves to dwell in the chamber of the heart of man."

If we feel we have been hurt or disappointed in Love, we have been given a gift and a blessing. We receive a redeeming grace in disillusionment, for illusion is a tyrant and Truth a redeemer. The outcome of disillusionment is the Vision of Truth, and in Truth shines a Peace far greater than the world could give. In our suffering we may be tempted to believe that we have been forsaken by, or exiled from Love. Take heart, beloveds; Love could no more turn Its back on us than the sun deny itself to the treetops, or the ocean refuse to accept the rivers. No, beloveds, Love is as certain as Life and as constant as the mother's heartbeat to the babe in the womb.

No person or experience could offer us more Love than we already possess within our very own hearts, a Love that is eternally and irrevocably ours. Let us not wait for Love to come to us. Love comes to us only when we love. We can awaken our hearts in an instant by turning our thoughts toward our ideal, our Beloved. To look for Love is to offer our hand to a mirage. Who could give us more than we already are? Who could edify that which was created whole? Who could teach Love to Love?

Love finally reveals Itself to be the Holy Spirit, which we mystified by our belief in the mysterious. One has described the Holy Spirit of Love thus: "We cry out, 'Where can I find the Holy Spirit? . . . Tell me where to go, what to do!' Meanwhile, the Holy Spirit is pouring to us and through us, waiting only for our quiet acceptance to reveal Itself." Instead of mourning, "I want Love," we need only to affirm "I love."

Thus could Kabir say, "I laugh when I hear that the fish in the water is thirsty!" So, we stand initiated at the altar of the Temple of the Living Heart, ready to assume our charge as ministers of Love and Light to a world that begs for communion because it does not realize itself to be the body of God. As the purple mantle comes to rest on our shoulders, we, like Love Itself, must bow to our very Self in humble acknowledgement of the simple truth that what we sought is Who We Are.

"My Love for you, my own Children, is infinite. You could never be outside the fullness of my Love and the cradle of my loving arms. There is nothing that you could ever do that could cause you to lose my Love. I am eternally committed to loving you fully, without condition or expectation. This is my greatest, and my only, joy.

I am your Divine Mother. Your pain is my pain. Would that I could remove all of your sufferings from your shoulders and bear them, gladly, upon mine. But you are in the midst of a glorious adventure, a Divine journey in search of Truth, which shall reveal to you more freedom than I could offer you by removing your hardships.

Learn your lessons quickly and well, my beloved Children. I shall watch over you with guidance and protection as you wend your way home to my open arms. My heart is brimming with pride as I watch you grow in the knowledge of your own Perfection. My Love for you is so great that I can hardly bear the waiting for your homecoming. Yet shall I bear it, in confidence and strength.

In moments of trial, remember these words: My Love is ever with thee. Feel them in your heart and nurture them with your trust in my Presence. Call upon me when you need me. Do not feel unworthy to summon my help. You are precious to me in a way that you do not now comprehend. Trust that you will succeed in the innermost dream of your heart — the dream of the fullness of Love, which is my very dream for you."

The Future

NORMAL BUT NOT NATURAL

If you do not change direction, you may end up where you are heading.

— Lao Tse

Humanity, as a mass, has strayed so far from the path of Light that, for the most part, we have forgotten what the Truth is. We have become so steeped in ignorance that Reality and illusion have become reversed in our order of thinking. We have accepted hatred, pain, and separation as ways of life, and we have given up hope for fulfillment. We have adapted, accommodated, and adjusted for so long to the warped values of worldly life that we see visions of contentment, harmony, and peace as pipe dreams. We have become very, very lost.

Ignorance has not been cast upon us like a net, but has gradually crept into the fibre of our awareness like the smog around our cities that began as a subliminal veil, and grew into a monstrous cancer that enshrouds our livelihoods. We have gotten used to too much. Crime, evil, and prejudice are accepted as a matter of course. Horrendous reports on the six o'clock news fail to move us because we have heard them so often. Of necessity, we have become callous and withdrawn. Though we have adopted a posture that assumes that this is just the way life is supposed to be, there remains a faint, gnawing whimper deep in our gut, persistently reminding us that we were made for much more, for we *are* much more. Yet we would cover over that still, small voice with the habituation that has dulled us to our sense of Truth.

I cannot believe that this is the way God intended for us to live. It

355

seems senseless to me that a Creator would bring forth a creation for an end of such suffering and separation. The world as we see it cannot be His Will. Yes, everything is His Will when seen from the highest perspective, but we cannot afford to accept that which we must realize to be in error. We cannot say "Yes" to a world in agony. We must recognize its need for healing.

I recently heard a lecturer on world hunger state that all of the hungry people in the world could be fed for seventeen billion dollars a year. The United States currently spends seventeen billion dollars on "defense" expenditures every *two weeks*. Our values are confused and our priorities inverted. Bribery, corruption, and dishonesty are no longer shocking, and they are accepted as a matter of course. When Richard Nixon was ejected from office in 1974, many of his defenders argued that "Nixon was no worse than most politicians — he was just unfortunate enough to get caught." And in a more recent government scandal, when several politicians were videotaped accepted large amounts of bribe money, their defense was that the government was guilty of "setting them up" for the bribe, and that their conviction should be overturned because the government was deceptive in its methods. Who of clear mind could accept this plea? What honest man could be "set up" for a bribe? Our sense of integrity has been dulled.

There is one more example of misdirected thinking that leads me to believe that we have become lost as a culture, as a civilization, and as Children of God. I recently heard that there is now a formal organization, with a title like "Children's Sexual Liberation," with the purpose of legitimizing and defending those who would molest children. The rational mind has become confused, and it attempts to uphold error in the name of Freedom. Something is wrong.

The recognition of delusion is a necessary step to the awakening to Truth. It takes honesty and courage to admit that we have strayed from the path. But it is a necessary admission. I must stand before God each night and see whether I have lived up to my highest ideals. Sometimes I do and too often I do not. But it is necessary for me to recognize both circumstances. I must ask God to show me what I am doing wrong, that I may correct it. Usually I do not like to hear it, but when I do, I am grateful.

We must scrutinize, with a clear mind, how we were really meant to live, as individuals and as the family of humankind. We may not like having to change, but a change of direction toward the Truth always brings a deep sense of peace within our heart, a fulfillment far deeper than the surface desires that seem to be satisfied with untruth. As Patricia Sun said, "The Truth feels good." Our deepest instincts always tell us when we have touched Truth. It feels like home, like a completion, like, "Of course."

Truth is the most natural thing that there is, but in the world it is the most foreign. Because the values of the world are upside down, light is a stranger, and the darkness welcomed. It is very easy to be normal. The world will love you and support you in your normality, for the world loves its own. Those who gravitate to negativity, gossip, and innuendo have a sure place in society; they shall never beg for company with which to commiserate. The marketplace of common affairs is built on complaints, criticisms, and guilt.

One who chooses the God-path faces loneliness and derision. He cannot expect or hope for understanding from the world. It will seem to accept him with a polite smile, but secretly mock and slander him behind closed doors. Friends and relatives will support him in word but not in thought. The devotee of Truth must be great enough to take the world into his heart though the world would cast him out of its own. Truth must love sin in a way that sin cannot understand Truth. This is because the lover of Light can see the Christ in all, while one who lives in darkness sees only veiled reflections of confused images.

Every human being is a Child of God. Some live their Godliness, while others hold it in potential as it lies dormant until awakened. The world of error, the normal world, is a husk of a seed of Divine possibility, patiently waiting to be released. The natural is hidden within the normal, though the two do not now seem to be one in expression on earth. We must feel the constriction of the husk before we can break through it. We must see the *dead end* sign on the street we are traveling before we can turn about to correct our course. The awareness of error is the impetus for transformation. Those who would harp on error have not yet seen it in full, for an error truly recognized is a correction set in motion. The only result of real understanding is change.

Eventually, all that is natural will become the normal; ideal and practice shall be one. This is the glorious vision held by all of the prophets of Truth. Until then we must tread the path of learning to distinguish between peace of mind and feverish dreams. The universe will not tolerate illusion, for untruth runs against the grain of all creation. Why would God have created Truth, were it not to be lived? Untruth exists only to be corrected. The unnatural that is accepted as the norm can continue to be perpetrated only until it is exposed. The world will then grasp for another illusion to mollify itself. Illusion, like a strain of bacteria that gains resistance to an antibiotic, reinforces itself in increasingly gross intensity until the forces of Light and darkness are divided by a chasm that clearly defines their difference. At that point, there can be no misunderstanding of the distinction.

At that point — the point at which we now find our evolution as a civilization — illusion has been exaggerated to a ridiculous degree, and the voice of sanity must be heard. The raving of insanity has revealed itself by its farcical grossness. The only remaining choice is Truth. At that moment, and only at that moment, can Truth and normality merge in expression on the earth plane. This is the meaning of the Age of Aquarius.

Join me in a vision of a world in which the Good Life is expressed as it was intended from the beginning. I see a world in which there is no dichotomy between what is idealized and what is condoned, where the will of men and the Will of God are One Will. In this new, bright world, nature is honored and revered as a loving friend, and not a threat. Here, there is nothing to conquer, for all forces are realized to be Holy, harmoniously working for mutual good. The foot that was turned astray is once again set firmly on the path of wholeness, and all who walk this path shine with the Love that the world has ignored, but could never be forgotten.

''The ways of the world are not those of God. The world loves darkness and would have its children believe that the darkness is the Light. Popular opinion is not to be the standard by which the Child of God may guide a Holy Life.

We know your difficulty in discerning between accepted belief and God's Truth. In the beginning stages of spiritual development, the aspirant may be sorely tried to distinguish between Truth and fantasy. While we understand the nature of this challenge, we tell you that it is fully necessary to know and to surrender to the voice of Truth that reverberates within your soul like a guiding star over a dark sea. We assure you that as decisions for the Light are made, the faculty of discrimination shall become very sharp, and the marriage of the intellect and the intuition is sanctified.

Hold firm, soldiers of Truth, to that which you cherish as dear. You may be tested and scorned, but the Angel of Valor protects you in your campaign. She looks over your shoulder in gentle support of your decision for God. Bear your loneliness bravely, and comrades of like purpose shall join you when you most need them.

The Truth is your only refuge. Pay homage to the words of no man, but reserve your worship for the Holy Spirit alone. You may be pressed to relinquish your ideals for the sake of the world, but you will find solace and renewal in the life of your heart's deepest bidding.

Be vigilant. Fear not to look at the world with clear seeing. Those who fail to regard signs of illness are required to pay the price of irresponsibility. Relinquish not your view of perfection, and never fail to execute right action in accord with widsom.

Children of the Most High, make integrity your banner and your bastion. Those of integrity are few, and the smallest act of right conscience shines in the darkness more than you know. Our hearts leap to consider those who live a life for God amid the mire of foulness. Be one of these. In so accepting this noble charge, you stand at the rudder of the destiny of mankind. Please do not underestimate your ability to save the world through your vision of morality. Choose rightly, and legions of angels and invisible brethren fly to your support. Choose wrongly, and you stand alone in a lost world.''

COMMUNICATION, COMMUNION, AND COMMUNITY

I

One of my favorite stories is that of the earthworm who pops his head out of the soil and sees a gorgeous earthworm just a few inches from him. Overtaken by the other worm's beauty, he tells her, "I love you . . . Will you marry me?" The other worm smiles and answers, "Don't be silly; how could I marry you? I'm your other half!"

We stand, now, on the threshold of a new evolutionary step in the unfoldment of humankind. The keynote of this step is the new understanding of an ancient truth: *We are One*. Behind our nationalities, colors of skin, cultures, lifestyles, and histories, we are One. It is this unity, this common bond, that will be the hallmark of a new age on earth.

During the past few decades, we have seen the rays of light of this new age beginning to make clear our next step, like the first faint glimmerings of dawn on the eastern horizon. These initial heartbeats of the child to be born to all have taken the form of sharing, joining together, and the affirmation of our collective unity as one family of human beings. Those who have heard the call of the conch, have let go of old, taught patterns of separateness and hiding, and stepped into the freedom of sharing. If there is any hope for mankind, it is in the sense of community that is rapidly maturing on the planet.

Humanity is now at a critical turning point. The dynamics of our choice are the same as they always have been, but the stakes, now, are very high. Our choice is this: *Unite, or die*. We must learn to cooperate. We must learn to accept. We must build our world on the foundation of God, and not upon separateness.

361

The question is: How big can we expand our idea of "Us?" How much can we widen our idea of who is equal to us? Who are we willing to take into our family?

As little egos, each of us once lived in a cold and limited world, revolving around "me." "Me" was not really satisfying, but it was all we knew. As our sense of self matured, we expanded to include our physical family, such as mom and dad, brother and sister, and later husband or wife in our sense of "Us." Everybody else was "Them," and "They" were always out to get "Us." Perhaps "They" were people of another color, another country, or another political idea. One thing was for sure, however: "They" were different than "Us," and "We" had to watch out for "Them." It was O.K. to share, accept, and be intimate with "Us," but certainly not "Them."

As we grew and the world forced "Us" to come into contact with "Them," experience revealed that some of "Them" were really not so bad. When that happened, we expanded our idea of who was "Us," until, as there became more and more of "Us" and less and less of "Them," we realized that *there really was no "Them" after all*, and in fact, *there never was*. It was all a mistake. As soon as we understood that everyone is "Us," we were ready for the next step in human evolution.

This is the threshold at which humankind now stands. Fantastically rapid developments in technology, communication, and transportation have allowed human beings, in a very short time, to make almost intimate contact with one another in a way that has revealed everyone in the world to be alike, and not different. We can no longer hide behind the facade of naiveté, for we now live on a very small planet, and our civilization has become, as Buckminster Fuller describes it, a "planetary village."

Since humanity has now been shown to be one great family, the task before us is: How quickly can we own up to our oneness with all people? When we know something to be true, we are held accountable for that knowledge in a way that we were not responsible in ignorance. Now that we know we are One, God expects us to live as One. The responsibility of that knowledge is very great, indeed.

All of the great spiritual masters and teachers throughout the ages have led us to this point. They have all along been giving us the principles of the life of unity that we are now ready to live. As we can now see, the Bible, the Koran, the Bhagavat Gita, and all the other writings of Truth have *not* been in conflict, and neither have the

362

religions that stand with them. It was only the small-mindedness of men that misconstrued similarities as differences and found separation where only harmony existed. We can see, as well, that while the outer expressions of the world's religions have been slightly different, their *essence* has always been the same. They have all been trying to tell us that there is One God, that man, in real nature, is Divine, and that Love is the key to man's unity with God.

It is this very unity that is reflected in our newly acknowledged family of man. We must now meet all people in the place where labels have no power to separate. This is not a physical location, but a realm in the heart, a space where it is obvious that we are not fragmented, but whole.

Our new awareness is really a powerful energy of a new consciousness — *planetary consciousness*. We have begun to realize that our actions affect all people everywhere, and that the earth and all of her inhabitants are really one great living, breathing organism. This consciousness is a major breakthrough for our planet — and it is our only hope for survival. We will survive only through our common identity, through our acknowledgement of our mutual Selfhood. The highest good of each of us is the highest good of all; my success is the achievement of all, my pain is the hurt of all, and humanity's well-being is one with my own. Patricia Sun said, "How can I be happy if there is someone who isn't happy?"

II

As conscious beings, we cannot afford to stop the growth of our awareness at planetary consciousness. We must constantly go beyond all ideas of limitation. If we now believe that earth is "Us" and everything else is "Them," we have not really understood the lesson of spiritual unity. We must open our consciousness to accept all in the universe as One.

I was fascinated to see how *Close Encounters of the Third Kind* has had a marked effect on our culture. Soon after its release, the themes and symbols of the motion picture were popularized in many forms. Children's games using sound and light became common; there was an advertisement for a religious retreat: "Have a close encounter with Judaism"; and I even saw a billboard showing a county bank rising up at the end of a long road to the stars. I believe this movie was so popular, far and away beyond any other U.F.O. movie, because it artfully portrayed "aliens" as *benevolent*. Although their form was very different then ours, these beings from outer space were portrayed as gentle, loving, and peaceful beings. They were "Us."

By contrast, most of the flying saucer movies I saw as a child showed aliens as power hungry monsters who came to conquer the earth with death rays, either for the sheer terror of it or because their planet was about to blow up, and they wanted to take over ours.

This beautiful *Close Encounters* movie, though, had communication and sharing as its theme. The "aliens" returned intact all of those persons that they had taken away; the people who saw the U.F.O.'s were drawn to them in a positive way; and the movie concluded with a most uplifting exchange of peaceful wishes between earthlings and the spacelings. A friend of mine who has been involved with a religious organization for a long time confessed to me, "Seeing that movie was probably the most profound spiritual experience of my life."

I believe that this movie symbolized a very significant expansion of our consciousness — we accepted non-earthlings as our friends, and not as our enemies. To me, the film represented yet another step in the growth of mankind: *universal consciousness.* In it, we took our brothers in "outer space" — or at least the possibility that they are there — into our circle of "Usness" — into inner space. In a way, we accepted that we are one with all life everywhere.

This time on earth is about putting into action our new understanding of our place in the cosmos. It is about practicing living in Oneness with all people. It is about bringing together the forces we hold in our hands, ones which could ultimately destroy us, but, if used wisely, can unite us. From the point of view of the person who thinks in terms of the past, it is a painful breakdown of the familiar. From the viewpoint of the aspiring soul, it is the herald of a new and better life, one of drawing together and sharing. It is a promise of friendship, mutual support, and community. It is the end of a "Them" which never existed, and the affirmation of an "Us" that has always been.

"The door to your Destiny is now opened before you. You now have the key to your new life: Oneness. Bring all of your efforts together to work for unity. Take every opportunity to affirm togetherness, family, and community. None of you can move any more rapidly than all of you, for now that you understand your unity as a family, you accept the joy and the suffering of all humanity as your own.

We who mark your way along the mountain path, would now direct you to a plateau as a gathering point. Unify your people. Draw together your factions. Scrutinize any residues of limitation that continue to bind you. Evaluate all of your plans and actions in terms of unity. You can proceed no further until you learn to move as a whole.

The recent political, monetary, and cultural events have forced you to gather together to share. It has become very advantageous to share living quarters, transportation, fuel, and food. Do you believe these events are accidental? Do not foolishly accept them as happenstance. The lessons of the world are now directed toward coming together. You have become accustomed to living in isolation and separation. We speak not of physical barriers, but spiritual ones. Separation exists not in the physical world, but in the mind. The lessons of this time are given to correct these false notions of boundaries.

Accept your membership in the community of souls. You are not apart from others, nor could you ever be. You are very much One being. Act united, feel integrated, and practice Oneness, for Union is the Truth that heals you."

LOOK, DADDY, THE WORLD IS TOGETHER!

A young father was beginning to feel a little annoyed with his five-year old son, who was asking him endless questions while he was trying to read the evening newspaper. Seizing on a scheme to buy him some quiet time, dad found a picture of the earth in the newspaper, cut it out, tore it into little pieces, and gave it to the child to reassemble as a jigsaw puzzle.

To the father's astonishment, the child was back minutes later with the picture perfectly intact.

"Look, Daddy, the world is back together!" the child exclaimed.

The father was amazed at how quickly the boy had finished. "How did you do it so fast?" he asked.

"It was easy! First, I couldn't fit the picture of the earth together. Then I looked on the other side of the pieces, and there were pictures of the parts of a man. It was much easier to put the man together, so that's what I did. And when the man came together, so did the earth!"

All of humanity's guides through the ages have taught exactly this truth. "If you want to bring about peace in the world," they tell us, "first bring about peace within yourself" . . . "Don't worry about reforming the world; reform yourself! . . . "The peace that you would have others find must first be found in your own heart."

While we have lofty ideals for social reform and world change, our real purpose in life is to work on ourselves. This at first may seem selfish or uncharitable, but it is honest, and in the long run we will make more of a contribution to society when we are clear than when we are in any way confused. Unless we are gelled and whole in our own consciousness, we are not in a position to serve. The greatest service we can offer to others is to purify, sanctify, and know our own Self. Then, and only then, are we in the proper position to give. Until then, we are taking.

This does not mean that we are to run off to a cave and meditate until we are realized. Our work on ourselves may involve a great deal of social service. We can be nurses, teachers, and therapists, but we must always bear in mind that we are really using these avenues to expand our own consciousness. Serving others with all our heart does not contradict working on ourselves; to the contrary, it supports it. Until the end, we must remember to use everything we do as a vehicle for our own awakening.

The Master Jesus said, "How can you say to another, 'Let me take a speck out of your eye!' when you have a bigger one in your own? Hypocrite! First remove the speck from your own eye, and then you will be able to remove that of your brother." There are many teachers, leaders and therapists who teach what they have not yet mastered. If a student learns from such a one, it is the student's grace, and not the teacher's guidance.

Does this mean that one must be a fully realized spiritual master before one can teach or offer service? No, not at all. If we waited for everyone to be perfect before anyone could teach, we would have a long wait indeed. It is sufficient to teach what we know and have directly experienced. In this case, teaching is really a sharing, a comparing of notes. It is as if we are all working together on a huge jigsaw puzzle. As you find the place for your piece, you make it easier for me to see the pattern and the place for mine. You might even find a piece that I can use. Teaching is sharing. We have nothing to teach each other, but much to share.

If each of us lives up to our highest ideals, we will be giving the best teaching there is. The most powerful teachings that I have received have come through my ignoring what people say and observing what they do. Words are the last and most superflous elements of teaching. Real change comes only through example. One night, after Hilda had worked hard to give a strong and meaningful class, I and some friends went down to Ammal's Pizza Shop (a front for an orphanage) for a snack. I had heard many lectures on selfless service, but when I saw Hilda there wiping down the counter, after she had already given so much, I immediately understood what loving service is all about and in that moment I wanted to do it, too.

If we want to get another person — or the world — to do something, we must *do it first*. If we want people around us not to fight, we must be peaceful ourself. If we want our kids to clean up their room, we must be willing to keep our own room clean. And if we want the government to not make radioactive nuclear reactors, we cannot afford to radiate poisonous waves of angry emotional reaction. Those that we seek to change will be affected by what we are *doing* in such a way that they will experience that there is a better way than the way that they have been trying. Our friends in conflict may be inspired by our peaceful example, and the good feelings that they experience in our presence will encourage them to be that way, too. And even if they do not change, our job is to be peaceful anyway, so there is really no question about what we need to do. We need to live what we want to see.

There is an important Buddhist scripture which contains many high and lucid truths. The very first sentence of the aphorisms is the author's admission that "The only purpose of this writing is the clarification of my own understanding." The delightful paradox is that as the author focused his own understanding, all those who read the work gain the benefit of his newfound clarity.

In this writing, I have come to see exactly what the Buddhist meant. As I have worked to put these ideas onto paper, I have learned much. I have been forced to look at what I believe is true and to see how much I am living what I believe in. I must wrestle with what I am willing to be responsible for telling you. And, over the months of editing and revising the book, I feel that I have actually been editing and revising *my own consciousness*. No matter who else or how many other people read this book, I know one person who has gotten a great deal from it — me. It is not so much the words that I have learned from, but the *process* of participating in its birth. And if you gain something from my experience as well, that is a nice fringe benefit.

When we love ourselves, we are bringing love to the world. When we master our own lives, we are bringing mastery and harmony to all people. It is said that "it is easier to conquer a city than to conquer one's self." Find tranquility within yourself, and the world around you will become tranquil. Each of us is a force field that creates and shapes all that is around us. One thought of love from the center of your mind spreads like ripples throughout the universe and touches everything, everywhere, with love. We are all connected to everything. Each of your thoughts and actions has a profound effect on all. I cannot underestimate my relationship with the whole of creation, for I am deeply connected with all that I see.

It has also been said that "you only see yourself." If, then, we want to see a new world in a new and beautiful way, we must first cultivate love and beauty within *ourselves*. If we send thoughts of anger and bitterness to those who pollute the earth with smoke and chemicals, we are poisoning the atmosphere with our thoughts. Hating anyone has never done anyone any good, and it certainly has not brought any more peace to the world. The only things that can bring peace to the world are thoughts, feelings, and actions of peace. To think is to create. If we think hatred, hatred shall be manifested in the form of new bullets and bombs. Hilda has said that every thought of anger produces one new physical bullet. When we see an insane arms race, we are seeing the results of our collective consciousness, and we can hold no political or military strategists to blame. They are simply acting out our thoughts of fear and competition, expressed in a world of our own creation, for which we must stand responsible.

If we are to truly change the world, we must give it new thoughts to be manifested — thoughts of the world as we would like to see it. We must fill our minds and hearts with ideas and feelings of harmony and celebration. One person quietly sitting for a few minutes a day and meditating or praying for world peace has an effect on the world greater than those who angrily protest and criticize those who make war. Someone who runs down the street cursing those who fight, is in effect sending out a set of vibrations that bring about only more war. As it is said, *"Don't curse the darkness — light a candle."*

Each of us can light our own candle, in our own way. We may feel that we have little power to change the destiny of the world, but it is through individuals that the world is changed. One little burning match can start a forest fire. Jesus had his ministry for only three years. Ghandi was only one man, and his humble actions transformed the lives of millions. You do not need to be a Jesus or a Ghandi to change the world. You do not need to be famous or honored. You need only to be *you*. As a cab driver, or a housewife, or a prisoner, or a tailor, you can bless the world fully. I know an old German tailor who, in his simple joy and happiness, contributed immensely to my own life, though he knows it not. From a worldly point of view, there is nothing outstanding about him. He is not well known, highly educated, or wealthy. He just shines. Whenever I see him, his eyes light up, my heart awakens, we embrace each other, we call each other Yiddish names, and for one moment, one very special moment, time stops. There we are, just the two of us, in friendship, in eternity. I have learned from him that greatness is not of the world, but of the heart. He has less prestige, money, and political influence than most of those who are in "positions that can change the world," but he has done more to change it for the better, perhaps, than they have done. In the eyes of his customers, he may be just an old German tailor, but to me he is a saint.

There are many evangelists who would save the world. I believe that real evangelism starts with one's own self. Before I can offer others salvation, I must have found it myself. Instead of eradicating sinners from the world, I must first eradicate anger, pettiness, and bigotry from my self. Before I can build a huge cathedral to the Lord, I must first consecrate the temple of my own body and soul. Before I can preach, I must practice. *A Course in Miracles* asks us, "Can the world be saved if you are not?"

The miracle is that each of us really *can* save the world. Indeed, we must, for what else of value is there to be done? Since there is no order of difficulty in miracles, our desire to save the world must be within our reach. And since the task of our physically maneuvering the world and its people into harmony is unthinkable, there must be some other way.

That way is the way of the Spirit, the way of God, the way of Love, which is not confined to time or to space. When we align our hearts and minds with the intentions of Godly Love, we are joining the forces of that power, indeed the only power that can redeem humankind. We have found the only avenue of action that can have any real effect. We have aligned our intentions with Him whose intention is salvation. In attempting to change the world according to the ways of the world, we cannot succeed. In working to bring Light to the world according to the way of Light, we cannot fail. Our will has become His Will. When we discover that only peace begets peace, we have understood the principle of salvation for all people, and the only real answer to the problems of the world. It is true that "unless you are a part of the solution, you are a part of the problem." No man can

371

serve two masters. No man can serve peace while living in discord. And no man can sustain chaos if he is absorbed in harmony.

Absorb yourself, then, in the highest peace that you know, and believe that God, in making this promise to Abraham, who lived for the One God, is making it directly to you: "A great nation shall I make of thee." Believe that from your simple, quiet thoughts and actions will spring forth a new era of peace on the earth. Believe that *the destiny of all mankind is in your very hands,* for so it is. Believe that you have been put on earth for a purpose, and as you fulfill your purpose, all the people in the world are redeemed. If you believe that it would take a miracle for your life to bring about peace on earth, then believe in miracles, because God sure does.

"When you know the Truth that sets you free, you are free of the burden of saving the world. Indeed, the task of saving the world can never be your burden, for it is the intention of the Creator, and that which is His intention can never be difficult.

Your frustration in attempting to change the world is born only of personal ego, and no salvation can ever come through the limited self. In seeking to reform others, you are dealing only with the projections of your own self, which can never be mastered while you see yourself as another. Release all others from the burden of your projections, and you release yourself from the burden of world salvation.

Only when you realize the outer world to be a reflection of your inner self can you make real progress in fulfilling the destiny of peace on earth. There can be no peace on earth until you know the Peace of Heaven. The Kingdom of Heaven, in which Peace must always reign, is within.

Look into your hearts, Children, and there shall you find the solutions to all problems. Indeed, there is but one solution to all problems, and that is the recognition of your eternal and irrevocable oneness with God. Know your kinship with the Creator of all things, and all things shall reveal themselves to be your own creations. At this moment, and only at this moment, peace in the world is restored, for only in this moment do you realize that it has never been lost. Know your Heritage as Sons and Daughters of Peace, and Peace must certainly come to you, instantaneously and forever."

THE KEY TO THE FUTURE

We hear many prophecies and predictions about the events that will occur in the coming years. Many of them foretell vast changes in the form that our lifestyles will take. We are told that we will have to make sacrifices and that we will see the collapse of many of the institutions and ways of life with which we are now comfortable. We are given even more foreboding pictures of food shortages, civil unrest, and disastrous changes in the land forms of the earth, including that of a shift of the earth's axis. We are told with striking consistency that we are on the doorstep of Armageddon and the end times.

Frankly, I do not know whether or how many of these predictions are true. It is amazing to me, though, that so many prophets, traditions, scientists, and psychics agree on the same things. Many of the ancient prophecies, such as that of the Hopi Indians, the Buddhists, and the book of Revelations are being fulfilled with uncanny accuracy. I have also heard these warnings from spiritual masters whose guidance and advice I trust. As their insights are correct on nearly all other accounts, I have little reason to believe that they would err on this matter. To underscore the predictions, the trend of human events, with its race hatred, separatism, and weapons craze seems to be magnifying to an unprecedented degree. One swami said that "We are like a person soundly sleeping in a bed, with a deadly snake slowly winding its way toward us." I do not really know what the future holds, but I take these warnings seriously.

One thing seems clear, though, which I, and I believe you as well, can see in the present. There is great suffering in the world. Most people are living in a sort of sleepwalking state of ignorance. As a race, we have strayed very far from the path of a Godly life that was intended for us to live in fulfillment and peace. Immorality and fear are rampant. I say this without judgement. It is a fact. I cannot believe that this is the way human beings were meant to live.

Werner Erhard put it very neatly: "We hear many prophecies of catastrophe and doom," he noted, "but it seems to me that the worst thing that could happen would be for things to stay the way they are." I am inclined to agree.

Our Mother Earth has been raped, plundered, and desecrated. I drive on the New Jersey Turnpike, and the air is foul. We must buy our water in plastic bottles that are shipped from hundreds or thousands of miles away. Factories in Detroit pollute the air with deadly acids that have rendered useless the water in Adirondack lakes a thousand miles away, and the fish are dead. When the fish die, the animals that eat fish die, and the entire balance of life on the planet is upset. The trees in New Zealand are dying from pollution from America. Nuclear power plants are allowed to spew deadly radiation into our water, land, and air, and the people of one of the few remaining unspoilt states in our nation — Maine — have voted to allow nuclear plants to continue operation. Greed for power and money has taken precedence over love for life and the right to live and breathe. How long can we convince ourselves that things on earth are O.K., when our planet is hurting so badly? "None are so blind as those who would not see."

When the seers explain the changes to come as a necessary cleansing of a toxic civilization and earth, it is not difficult to believe. Sadly, it makes sense. Any organism gorged with noxious substances would revolt in self-survival. If this is what Mother Earth needs to do, then I cannot blame her.

On the bright side, we are told that these transformations will bring about a new era of peace and unity on earth. As the darkest hour is just before dawn, we are bound to see a return to a life in which people of good will live in harmony and brotherhood. If this is difficult to believe, then it is all the more indication of the sad state of affairs to which we have fallen — one in which we cannot even conceive of people living in harmony. Yet we are told that the millenium and the rapture and a thousand years of peace are at hand.

We are already seeing the signs of a new age beginning to bud. Over the past fifteen or twenty years, there has been a tremendous proliferation of spiritual movements on the planet. Millions of people have been drawn to the study of meditation, ancient spiritual traditions, healing, and the ways of living in harmony with the natural order of the earth. Communities with the high spiritual ideals of love, sharing, and service have sprung up all around the planet. There is an increasing interest in returning to the simpler things of life. Many are forsaking "status" jobs to return to working with the land and studying how to harness the ever-renewable power of the sun. Some would say, perhaps, that these are faddists or escapists, but I believe that these are the pioneers of a new way of living, a way that will bring fulfillment instead of heartache.

Some say that if we change our ways and voluntarily re-form our ways of living with each other and with the earth, these painful purges will not be necessary. Others say that it is too late, and we will have to weather these unprecedented upheavals. Perhaps our civilization can renew itself without these difficult changes, but so far life on earth seems to be getting worse, and not better. It would be wonderful if civilization as it is adopted a new lifestyle of love and sharing, but, quite frankly, that does not seem imminent.

The question then becomes: How are we to relate to these changes? What can our response be? How can we prepare? The beauty of the answer is that it is the same answer to every question ever asked by any person at any time in civilization. What we need to do to weather these changes is exactly what we need to do if none of these changes ever occurs. We need to live our lives in harmony with the Spirit. We need to love. We need to be strong and compassionate. We need to remember who we are — Children of a Loving God. We need to serve and respect each other and our home, the earth. We need to let go of negative ways of thinking, speaking, and acting, and to replace them with laughter, mutual support, and truth. We need to practice what we were advised, in love, to do, two thousand years ago, and thousands of years before that:

Love God with all your being, and Love one another as yourself.

If there are earthquakes and economic collapse, Love and Faith will be the only standards that carry us through. And if there is never one more earthquake and the economy is very healthy, these same principles are the only ones that will make us happy.

The Truth is eternal. How to live is eternal. Yes, the forms that life takes may change, but the principles that make life work are constant. Love is as powerful and important as it ever has been and ever will be. Awareness of God is the only foundation that has ever made any life worthwhile, and so shall it always remain.

"The Truth stands invincible, untouchable by the frail whims of passing events. The only key to living is the acknowledgement and expression of God. So it was for your first ancestors, and so shall it be until the end of time.

We tell you with the deepest assurance that you are loved, you are protected, and you are cared for. Where else could you be, but under the benevolent protection of the Divine Mother? Let go of your worries, your anxieties, your unworthiness. Look carefully, Children, at the lives of those who radiate the shining Light of Love. Their worries have been dissolved in the infinite ocean of God's eternal Love. Cast away your doubts, and count yourself among the Holy and the Pure, for so you are.

You are privileged to participate in the transformation of consciousness on the planet earth. Such a position is very auspicious indeed. You are a part of the unfoldment of the Destiny of mankind. You shall bear witness to the long-awaited emergence of Truth from its cocoon. The occasion of your birth is a joyful and glorious one. You have chosen to step forward into the Light.

Go forth then, and live the message of Light and Love and Peace. You are an emmisary of God. He will work through you to create a future which will bring with it the end of all human suffering. From the deepest sincerity of our being, we tell you that there can be no greater privilege than this. This is the most cherishable and glorious Destiny at any time in all the universe."

The Promise

"*Sons and Daughters of the Living God:*
You are created in the image and likeness of the God that you love, and it is your only Destiny to know yourself to be one with the Spirit that eternally dwells within the entire universe.

Holy art thou in the sight of the Father of all things, and splendid is the Truth of your Beauty. Children of Light, the wonder of your Self shines with an effulgence far more brilliant than mortal eyes can behold, and it is our great privilege to share with you the awakening of your soul to the magnificence of your own Godly nature.

It is now for you to take your future, and yea, the future of all humanity into your heart and your hands, and mark a path of Light as a blessing to all. You are entrusted with the ability to heal the world. Let every thought, breath, word, and deed be consecrated unto Divine purpose. So shall your reason for living be fulfilled and your dream of Love realized.

Beloved ones, always remember your Holiness. We bid thee walk the path of service, and love one another as you would be loved. Give what you would receive, and offer support and encouragement to all. Ignore shortcomings, acknowledge strength, and bless all with your holy thoughts.

Have unrelenting faith in the great power of Love. No matter what travails or adversities befall you, faith in God will carry you through all challenges. This is our promise and our pledge, unassailable and invincible, guaranteed by the Truth of God's Reality and His eternal Love for you.

Our Love and our Blessings are now given to thee. Our greatest joy is for you to accept Love in Its fullness. Go forth in splendor; go forth in courage; go forth in confidence. Be the Light of the world, for that is what you are. Live in Love, grow in strength, and sing the Song of Freedom that was written for you aeons ago at the moment of your birth, the very song that you are now ready to once again claim as your very own.

Go forth, Divine Ones, Holy Ones, Blessed Ones. May Love live forever in your Heart, and in the Name of the Living God, may the world be Blessed through you.''

Rising In Love

The Journey Into Light

Rising In Love: The Journey into Light
by Alan Cohen

Title Page Photograph by Gene Dillman

To The Glory Of God

Let love be all that I am,
Love flowing for every man.
Holy Love o'er washes my soul,
Love's making me whole.

Through the hands of love a touch can heal,
A broken heart can learn to feel.
Through the eyes of love we can see
To heal the hurts of humanity.

Where love enters in, it begins,
Where love enters in, it begins.

So let the song of love on earth be heard,
Out of silence springs the word.
Let the flame of love which never dies
Within humanity arise.

Where love enters in, it begins,
Where love enters in.

by Jamil Laurelin

Author's Introduction

There comes a moment in every person's life when he or she must choose a direction. It is as if there is a fork in the road, and the person standing at the juncture realizes that it is no longer possible to straddle two paths: the time has come to follow one, and follow it whole-heartedly. This sometimes comes as a difficult decision, for it often means that one must release an old and comfortable way of living to venture out into uncharted territory. No one ever said that risk was easy, but all who have taken it exclaim that it is infinitely more reward-ing than the familiar. A life is too precious to allow the past to dictate the future. As one visionary proclaimed, *"Life is a daring adventure — or nothing."*

Such a moment of truth came for me when I felt a book seeking to be written, like the gentle but compelling refrain of a celestial song asking to be sung. Because I know so well that every thought we think expands and recreates itself according to its nature, I had to decide what I wanted to plant in this great garden universe. I sensed that I was no longer thinking or living only for myself, but in a way that the entire family of humankind would be affected, changed, and potentially healed. Then I realized that I had before me the opportunity of a lifetime: I had to choose what I would stand for.

I asked myself, "If I could give a gift to humanity, one which would benefit all people and the whole planet and would eventually return to me, what would it be? Immediately the answer came, to my great satisfaction and deep delight: *"Love stands where all else falters."*

So here is a book by, of, about, and for Love. It is the saga of the heart's journey from loneliness to celebration, from empty dark caverns to waterfalls of triumphant gratitude. It is a testimony to the dauntless power of Love to heal broken dreams and make each one of us new, bright, and whole again. It is a book about me, you, and all of us. It is a herald of the happy awakening that no matter what diverse paths our individual destinies take, Love is the Home where we meet and celebrate our reunion as shining rays of one great living Spirit.

As I completed work on the book, I realized that I was given a grace through its writing: I had grown in the process. I had spent months exploring the wonders of Love, only to find Love's wonders living in me. Then it became clear to me that *Rising In Love* is not really my gift to the world, but Love's gift to me. I learned that no one gives without receiving more in return, and now it is my privilege to share what I have received with you.

May the Divine Light in these words serve as a blessing to you and all who read them, and may Love live in your heart as you would know it in your deepest aspiration.

Alan Cohen

The Servants of the Light

There is a scene in that marvelous movie, *Lost Horizon*, in which a group of travellers stranded in the Himalayas are miraculously met by a guide who gives them warm clothing and leads them on a journey which he describes as "not particularly far, but quite difficult." As they were trekking up the steep, icy footpaths, I noticed that they were all linked together by a long, well-knotted rope, so that if one of them began to slip into the abyss, the combined strength of his fellow travellers would save him.

As I journeyed through the evolution of *Rising In Love*, I was given the grace of many helping hands, sent by God to contribute loving, positive energy to this book, which really represents a group effort. The lesson of the New Age is that when we unite for a loving purpose, miracles happen, and that is exactly the story of *Rising In Love*.

I would like to acknowledge some of the fellow travellers with whom I have had the good fortune to be knotted as we rose in love. I am deeply grateful to Valerie Johnson for her dedicated and meticulous editing and typesetting, and to Maurice B. Cooke, David Crismond, Jane Visbal, Judy Marlow, Wendy Dompieri, Barbara Cole, and Jeff and Barbara Woolley-Baum for their thoughtful editorial suggestions.

The introductory poem, *"Where Love Enters In,"* comes from the lyrics to a beautiful and inspiring song by Jamil Laurelin, recorded with David Secord on an album that won my heart the moment I heard the first note. I thank Jamil for his permission to use the lyrics, and David and Jamil for their bringing the New Age to earth.

The cover photograph is a masterful piece of photography by Gene Dillman, who has helped me in many creative expressions, and I here publicly acknowledge my appreciation for all of Gene's support.

It is my grace to be associated with all of the servants of the Light. I have a feeling we're going to make it to the top of the mountain.

The Awakening

Rising In Love

Love is all I ever hope to find here.
— *Seasons of the Heart,* John Denver

The first time I fell — rose — in love was when I was seventeen years old. She had red hair, we worked in the same summer camp, and she just happened to have the same last name as me. It was the kind of summer that we all can remember, a season of riding to the beach in open convertibles, walking barefoot over freshly mowed grass, and savoring the sparkling fragrance of the new morning after a long night's rain. It was the kind of summer that lives as a precious jewel in the heart, even through winter storms, for with such a time of year and life came the rediscovery of the shining light of love.

Then I went off to college, and though we were only thirty miles apart, it seemed like ten thousand. I called her nearly every night (for lovers, as you know, time and things exist only to serve love) and she wrote me three letters a day telling me in a thousand different ways how much she loved me. Her specialness was etched into my cells in a magical way that no other person could capture. It sounds pretty schmaltzy now, and it was, but that's how love wins a soul. I was freshly alive and completely complete and every day was a miraculous invitation to find new ways to celebrate the delight of our being together On our fourth anniversary (four months, that is) I sent a surprise telegram to her in school, and she bolted out of fifth period geometry class, laughing in the face of detention, to call me and tell me that she would love me forever.

Well, for six months at least. By the end of December something had changed. I phoned her one evening to find that she was going to a Hannukah party, and I felt devastated. The thought of her doing something without me was too much for me to bear. (As you can see, the relationship was not exactly founded on the most enlightened unconditional love.) I interpreted her going out as a sign that she no longer

3

loved me (even though she really did), and my immature understanding transformed the energy of love into fear — and there is no more destructive force in the universe than love turned to pain. I blamed her for my hurt, we bickered, and by New Year's Eve it was over. The love that had saved me had deserted me. I had fallen from the giddy peaks of joy into a dark and desolate valley. I had fallen out of love.

As I look back upon the whole experience now, I am extremely grateful, for now I realize I was given a blessing and a lesson. The blessing was that I tasted the nectar of being in love, of cherishing and caring for another human being in a way that her happiness was as important to me as my own, a feeling that somehow made up for all the loneliness that came before it. For a brief moment I was allowed to experience the deepest — and only — purpose of living, which, as far as I know now, is love.

The lesson was that I was not able to sustain that experience because my love had strings on it, strings tied to sandbags of attachments and conditions of what she was supposed to do to prove that she loved me, of what love was supposed to do to prove that it was real. And these are the only chains that keep any of us from rising and living in love always.

In six short months I was shown the great promise of life and the work I needed to do to claim it. Through rising in love and falling out of it, the flower of that relationship left seeds imbued with the wondrous possibility that one day I would again be able to know that precious feeling — but not before I had uprooted the weeds that stood between my experience of Divine Love and its source of light. God showed me a new Sun in the distance, a dazzling light more radiant and fulfilling than any I had ever seen, yet in front of that light loomed the shadows of the mountains that I would have to traverse to come home to it. And that was the way it had to be.

The Promise Fulfilled

God has the impertinence to not consult the authorities
when he wants to bless someone.
— Murshid Samuel Lewis, "Sufi Sam"

Fourteen years, countless slings and arrows of outrageous fortune, nearly unbelievable miracles of Grace, and a number of fallen gurus later, I found myself sitting in the parking lot of Grand Union one spring afternoon. The string of events that led me there was woven by a Divine design far more imaginative than I can begin to explain; it seems that God has His own ideas about where and when and how He wants to appear, and I think He gets a certain kind of cosmic kick out of surprising us.

It was in just such a seemingly unlikely place that I rose in love once again. This time not with a redhead, but with the cheerful little fellow who collects the shopping baskets. I was just sitting in my car minding my own business when he wheeled by, and all of a sudden an overwhelming feeling of love welled up within me, as if I was beholding the most beautiful person on earth. Yes, he was wearing combat boots, his hair was a little greasy, and his posture wasn't the greatest, but he was God. He was just so radiant, so full of light, that all I wanted to do was sit and look at him shuffle those carts to the rhythm of his happy whistling.

Then, just as his tune had become mine, I was cut off by a very ordinary-looking women in a very ordinary-looking car making a beeline for a parking space. And because love lifts the mundane into the miraculous, I was so pleased to see her go before me. As she glided into that space our eyes met and immediately I rose in love with her, too. I was enraptured with the perfection of her plainness. Ensouled in that delightfully honest being was the Light of God, and I decided that He had cloaked her in such a simple form to underline the glory of utter Innocence. Her inner beauty outshined all the designs of men, and I knew that we were brought together for the sheer wonder of celebrating the presence of goodness in every breath of creation.

As my beloved stepped out of her car and into the supermarket, my attention was captured by a loud "Woof!" from the Country Squire station wagon next to me. There, with his stately snout perched on the open back window, was the most effervescent German Shepherd with whom I have ever connected, twinkling right at me. Immediately I realized that he was a high soul who took a canine incarnation to woof the Divine Love Song. And in that moment all I wanted to do was dash into Grand Union and buy him every Milkbone I could find. That's just the way it is when you're in love. That's just the way it is.

Believe in Yourself

Believe in yourself as God believes in you.
— The Wiz

A few nights ago I was feeling a little down, a little empty, a little like I'm not making it. Then, as I was going to sleep I began to think of the people in my life who have believed in me, who have found worth or goodness in me even — and especially — when I wasn't believing in myself. These were the special friends, like guardian angels who were there for me when I needed them most. I cherish acts of loving kindness, for they were precious gifts of confidence that helped sustain me through times like the other night. If I may, I would like to share some of them with you now.

In the fifth grade I developed a tremendous crush on Marie Keller, a ten-year-old strawberry blonde girl with freckles and glasses, who lived in Camp Kilmer because her father was in the army. She didn't know it, but I was wild about her. I used to think about her all the time. Every day I would look up her number in the telephone book (even though I never got up the nerve to call her), and the highlight of my school year was when I picked her up (lifted her up, that is) in the cloak room so she could get her yellow rainhat off the rack, which was too high for her to reach.

Round about the end of that year I learned that her father was being transferred to France, which meant that she would be moving and I would probably never see her again. So I wrote her a long love letter on that thin yellow paper with green lines, you know the kind they give you in the fifth grade to learn how to write. I wrote that I thought she was the nicest girl I had ever met, and I really liked her a lot, and I was sorry she was moving. I signed it *A Secret Admirer*, probably because I felt so crummy about myself that I thought that if she ever found out it was me, she would tell me that she didn't like me, and I would feel devastated. So it was safer and easier to love her from afar and not have to face the possibility of rejection. I sent her the letter and left the rest up to fate.

I heard no news or response. Could the letter have gotten lost? Did the army intercept it and turn it over to the CIA for investigation? Could it have been sent to the *Dead Letter File*? I almost wished I had signed it.

Then, on the last day of school, my teacher, Mrs. Montague, the first teacher I ever trusted, took me out in the hall and asked, "Alan, are you going to say good-bye to Marie?"

"What do you mean?" I played it cool.

"Well, I know how much you like her."

"What do you mean, 'I like her'?" I played it cooler.

But because it's hard to conceal a crush in the fifth grade, and because my ability to act phony was not yet well-developed, Mrs. Montague knew.

"Alan, I know you wrote that letter to Marie."

That did it. I burst out in hysterical tears. I don't really know why. Maybe I was embarrassed. Maybe the pain of hiding was too great. Maybe my fears were brought to their knees by the power of Mrs. Montague's tender compassion. Whatever it was, I cried and cried — bawled is more like it — more than I can remember crying in my whole life.

Mrs. Montague put her arm around me and told me with a softness in her voice that I shall never forget, "Alan, there's no reason to cry . . . Do you know what Marie told me when she got that letter? . . . She said it was the nicest thing anyone has ever done for her, and it made her the happiest girl in the world!"

Well, I don't really remember what happened after that. All I remember is the tenderness that Mrs. Montague showed me in the hall as the other kids walked by, asking, "What's he crying about?" Mrs. Montague was there for me. She believed in me enough to take me seriously. She understood me in just the way I needed to be loved at that moment. Thank you, Mrs. Montague. May your kindness be returned to you a hundredfold.

As I consider this story and the others I am about to relate, I see that they pretty much were the times when I felt or acted like a real boob, when I wasn't exactly the most sophisticated or debonair person. And it occurs to me as well that these were the times when I most

8

needed someone to believe in me, when my own ability to love myself
was at a low ebb, and when God compassionately gave me that missing love through the arms of another.

During that same year the most important thing that a human being could do (as I perceived the universe) was to play baseball. The
world, as far as I was concerned, was divided into two very distinct
camps: The New York Yankees and their fans (*Us*), and everyone else
(*Them* — The Wrong Side). In my world, Mickey Mantle was the High
Guru, to get a box seat behind third base at Yankee Stadium was like
receiving an audience with the Dalai Lama, and my loftiest dreams
featured me making a daring catch of a long fly ball up against the
417-foot centerfield fence in the House That Ruth Built. I lived for
baseball.

That summer I played first base on the championship Little League
team, the St. Sebastian Giants. (There's another miracle for you; I was
the only Cohen on a team of thirty skinny, olive-complexioned kids,
all of whose names ended in "ini," "isi," or "io," and whose fathers all
happened to coincidently be members of the St. Sebastian Lodge that
sponsored the team. Someone in a very high place (maybe even St.
Sebastian himself) had to pull some strings to get me on that team.

The season came down to the final game of the playoffs. It was
the bottom of the last inning, score tied, runner on third — a situation
worthy of Howard Cosell's most delicious fantasies. The pitch . . . Batter connects . . . Ground ball to Cohen at first! . . . The runner breaks
for the plate! . . . The catcher braces for the throw . . . Runner slides
. . . The throw! . . . A billowing cloud of dirt explodes around the plate
as all the parents rise from their multi-colored lawn chairs, eagerly stretching their necks to catch a glimpse of the final verdict. The park
reverberates with the bark of the umpire, forever confirming the Cham-
pions of the League!

To make a long, sad story short and to spare me the agony of great
embarrassment, I'll just say that Cohen at first made a throw very well
put for a ten-foot-tall catcher, but which no eleven-year-old kid on this
planet would ever have a prayer of catching. The game was over. The
season was over. We lost. I had made the losing throw. Pretty heavy
karma. I felt lower than Judas. I burst out crying (it was a very good
year for my tear ducts), and as the other team was whooping and hollering and jumping on each others' shoulders, the two coaches of my team

headed right for me. I just knew that I was about to receive the worst chewing out of my life.

But it never came. Instead, Coach Santisi put his arm around my shoulder and said, "That's O.K., Alan . . . It's just a game . . . We'll get 'em next year!"

Well, next year never came — we didn't make it to the playoffs. But, you see, it didn't really matter. What mattered was that Coach Santisi was willing to forgive me, willing to encourage me when I was condemning myself. And that made me a winner.

Many years passed, and one summer morning in 1972 I found myself driving up a California mountain with my friend Jim, a very unusual guy — also a very holy and Godly guy. It was only appropriate that we were driving a redecorated '62 VW bus with psychedelic cushions in the back and a silver sticker on the hood that proclaimed "U.S.A. in Space!" That about summed us up.

It was also appropriate that a State Trooper should pull us over for driving too slow in the fast lane. (We had renounced time.) Unfortunately, the trooper was still in time and he decided that time was still important enough to write me a ticket for not respecting it. This time I did not burst out crying, but I was a little distraught.

As the policeman began to write the ticket, I saw Jim get out of our van and approach the police car.

"Get back in your vehicle!" yelled the trooper from behind his door, as if we were aliens from another planet, come to invade California and hijack it to another galaxy. It made me wonder if he was more afraid of us than we were of him. (And if he was, I wouldn't blame him.)

So Jim approached him more slowly, with open hands to show he had no ray-gun. Then, to my utter amazement I saw Jim put his arm around the trooper's shoulder and begin to walk him back to our bus. As they approached I heard these words from Jim:

"You know, this guy you're giving the ticket to does some very important work!"

"Oh?"

"Yes, he certainly does! . . . He is a 'Human Relations Trainer!' Do you know what that is?"

"No, what's that?"

Sitting at the wheel of the van, right next to our copy of *Be Here Now*, I had to do all I could to keep from laughing. First of all, I couldn't

10

believe that there was something that a native Californian hadn't heard of, but more significantly I couldn't believe what Jim was telling this guy. Was he putting him on? Was he serious? Was he just trying to get out of a ticket? Whatever it was, it was priceless.

"That man at the wheel teaches people how to communicate, and I'm sure that you, in your line of work, know how important communication is . . . I imagine they taught you all about communication at the Academy, didn't they?"

"Well, I think they did have something about that."

By this time I was sitting back, enjoying every frame of this scene, like a Marx Brothers-Woody Allen-Ingmar Bergman movie with a thousand possible endings, none of which I could imagine, but all of which I knew would be simultaneously cosmic and ridiculous.

"Oh, I'm sure they did include that in your work," Jim went on. "Communication is so important these days. It makes all the difference between harmony and tension in our world. I'm convinced that if we could all just communicate more with each other, this world would be a much safer and happier place to live in!"

"Yes, I think you're right," agreed the officer as he handed me the ticket.

But at that point it really didn't matter whether or not I got the ticket. The situation had been miraculously transformed from what it had started out to be; it had grown from two hippies encountering a State Trooper to three souls meeting on a mountain. Jim was not putting the officer on and he was not just trying to get out of the ticket. He was serious.

You see, Jim saw that meeting as an opportunity to reach out and make contact with another human being. His love of life and his appreciation for the richness of humanity was so great that he could not be intimidated by belief systems about getting a traffic ticket. As far as Jim could see, three souls were being connected in a novel way, and here was a chance to celebrate. Jim used every moment to lift the worldly into the Light. He is one of the few people I know who can turn a traffic ticket into a gift, a potential arrest into service, and a sticky situation into mutual upliftment.

The faith Jim held in the Divinity of that encounter, like the confidence my teacher and coach held in me, have served me as shining examples of how we can support each other along road to enlightenment.

RISING IN LOVE

Let's return for a moment to that Himalayan footpath in *Lost Horizon*, upon which those courageous voyagers steadily tread. As they were struggling over the crags and precipices, tied together by that rope which kept them from falling, it occurred to me that they were united by an even more crucial, more powerful bond: *the common belief that they could make it*, and that they could make it *together*. They had to believe in themselves enough to keep going while the winds howled in their faces and their muscles ached to no end. They had to have a vision of success that far transcended and outshined their personal frailties. Each one had to trust that the others would not let him down, and — more importantly — they had to trust themselves not to let the others down. They had to believe in themselves.

After braving the cold, steep climb, the voyagers finally made it over the crest of the mountain. There they found themselves in a completely different, amazing place: *Shangri-La* — the land of eternal contentment. They entered a realm of tropical sunshine, sparkling waterfalls, and a community of gentle people living in harmonious cooperation. This peaceful way of life, so unlike the harsh world from which they came, made every hard step to reach it worthwhile. Their finding it was the reward of their willingness to persevere.

Though we may not climb the Himalayas, each of us must traverse the mountains of our own self. This is the only real journey there is — and the most difficult. Yet we can — and will — succeed as we realize that we can make it, if we just *believe that we can*. There really *is* a *Shangri-La*, and an Emerald City of Oz, and a Kingdom of Heaven; it does not matter what we call it, for they are all one. What matters is that we know it is there — indeed it is already *here* — waiting for us to discover it within our very hearts, at the end of the path that begins with the first step of believing in our self.

Who We Are

Original Innocence

We are stardust. We are golden.
                       — Joni Mitchell

There is a scene in *The Empire Strikes Back* which pretty well sums up who we are and what we need to do to remember it. Luke Skywalker, after undergoing intensive training as a Jedi master, finds himself face-to-face with Darth Vader, the personification of Evil. As the two engage in perilous light-sabre combat, Lord Vader has Luke backed up against a bottomless precipice that drops, it seems, to a black pit at the end of the universe.

Darth Vader cannot, however, afford to kill Skywalker because he realizes the power that Luke has gained as a master of The Force, and Vader wants to use this power for his own evil purposes. (Evil has no power of its own; it is simply God's power turned inside out.)

"Luke!" appeals the dark one, with a clenched fist raised above his head. "Join with me! Together we will rule the universe!"

"I shall not, Darth Vader!" cries Luke as the winds of the bottomless pit howl behind him, "Not after you killed my father, whom I have never seen!"

"Luke," answers Vader in a long sardonic whisper, ". . . I *am* your father!"

Upon hearing these words, Luke Skywalker's eyes open wide in astonishment. The possibility is too terrible to contemplate. But then, because Luke is disciplined as a knight of The Force, he regains his composure. Luke thinks within himself for a moment and then cries, "*NOOOOOOOO!*" with a certainty that reverberates to the far reaches of the galaxy. With this affirmation Luke lets go his hold on the ledge and allows himself to fall down, down, down through a myriad of portals and passageways and finally out the bottom of this planet that Darth Vader has conquered. Luke's training as a master, you see, gave him more trust in the unknown than in the words of the evil one.

15

Then, just at the final portal of the planet, Luke is able to grab onto one last ledge where he hangs by one hand, literally at the edge of creation. At this crucial moment Princess Leia, having just escaped from the city-planet herself, psychically hears Luke's cry for help. Immediately she turns her craft around and scoops Luke up just as he is about to fall.

Every day, perhaps every moment, I am faced with Luke Skywalker's decision, and so are we all. It comes down to who we believe we are, and who we think our Father is. Do we think that we are born of evil, or do we know that our Source is a shining light? Are we willing to compromise our integrity for the sake of worldly power, or do we have the faith to let go and trust that we will be taken care of, even if we don't sign the devil's bargain? Are we really unknown, purposeless creatures that have come into a haphazard world by a sardonic twist of misfortune, or are we godly beings, sprung forth from a magnificent lifestream of Spirit, ever growing and blossoming into greater wonder? Simply, is the Spark of God within us, or is it not?

Frankly, I've had enough of worshipping original sin, and I'm about ready for some Original Innocence. I've been in the presence of a good number of little babies lately, and there is nothing at all sinful about them. They are made only of light with a holy little body to shine it into the world. I recently had the blessing to see a radiant little girl, Vanessa Rose, when she was just three hours old, and the energy around her was so pure, so chaste, so Divine. When I put my face near hers I felt the brightness of a bouquet of dew-laden wild flowers, newly sprung on an early May morning. She was vibrating in such a clear light that I just wanted to trade in every thought that I have ever had about good and evil and just hold this little angelic being in my arms. I found no original sin in that child.

If there is any such thing as original sin, it is a learned experience. We take on a self-image of sinfulness when we believe that we are no good, that there is something we must do to prove our worthiness, that we must earn love because we are bad. I recently met a young man who turned down an excellent job offer with a major corporation because he was afraid he might fail if he accepted the position. I asked him if he had ever done an age regression to see how he learned that fear. He told me that he could not remember past the age of five.

"What happened at age five?" I asked.

"One day I dropped one of my father's tools and broke it, and when he found out he locked me in the closet and told me that he would never let me out because I was such a rotten kid."

So that's how original sin got started. We cannot condemn the father, for that is probably pretty much how his father dealt with him. And his father. And his father. And so on. Original sin is nothing more than a wrong idea that got started somewhere way back by someone who didn't remember original innocence. That's all it is.*

Original innocence is what Luke Skywalker had to remember to say "No!" to Darth Vader's assertion that he was Luke's father. Luke had to make a very clear choice about who he was. Years ago I was given a teaching that has helped me to make this choice, words that have stayed with me in a very deep way:

WE ARE SPIRITUAL BEINGS
GOING THROUGH A MATERIAL EXPERIENCE

This was the precious awareness that enabled Luke to rise above evil attempting to seduce him into believing he was born of darkness, and not light. It was the ancient memory that gave him the strength to turn his back on a life that was not true to his heart's aspiration. And it is the very awareness that you and I need to remember — and practice — a thousand times a day, whenever we are assailed with questions, fears, or doubts about our self-worth or dignity. It is the affirmation that carries us past television commercials that tell us we need to brush with *Ultrabrite* to have sex appeal, or when we see newspaper headlines purposely fabricated to arouse emotions of fear or indignation, or when we watch an irate taxi driver shake his fist at us for driving at a

---

*There actually is a basis for the idea of original sin, but it is an esoteric principle far more positive and reasonable than the idea of guilt, shame, fear, and unworthiness that many people believe it to be. Original sin has been misunderstood because it has often been taught by persons who have unconsciously projected their own unresolved guilt and fear to students.

Original sin is the limitation of awareness that a human being experiences when he or she comes into — takes the consciousness of — a human body. To enter the earth plane in a physical body, we narrow the range of our awareness to concentrate our attention on a particular karma that needs to be worked out. This is similar to a general of an army leaving his view of the battlefield from the top of a plateau to go into the valley to confer with a particular lieutenant needing special guidance and instructions. For a temporary period the high perspective of the whole scene is lost, but it is a purposeful act for the sake of focusing attention on one area that will eventually contribute

reasonable speed. It is the truth that we must hold on to when it seems that the world has gone crazy and there is no God. We must constantly say "No!" to all that would offer to make us whole, for such a "No!" is a resounding "Yes!" to the truth that we are *already* whole, and could never be otherwise.

Why, then, have we not lived in constant abiding awareness of our wholeness? We simply had a case of spiritual absent-mindedness, Cosmic Amnesia. We used to know, we started out knowing, but somewhere along the way we forgot; we became distracted into thinking that we are less than Divine. We believed someone who threatened to keep us locked in a closet because he forgot the goodness of his own self. And the glorious conclusion of this whole melodrama is that even though we seemed to forget how to love ourselves, we still remain Skywalkers. Our forgetting, you see, could never change our identity. Our attack thoughts could never touch our invulnerability. Our heritage is eternally ensured. The outcome of the story is a happy one.

The day after I saw *The Empire Strikes Back*, I went out to jog. After a while I began to feel tired and I wanted to quit. A little mind-voice began to say, "You really should stop . . . You're getting tired . . . You may hurt yourself . . . Go home." But as I heard the way this voice was speaking to me, I recognized it to be the voice of Darth Vader telling me I am his son, for his voice is the voice of limitation, unworthiness, and fear. So I decided that every time I heard the voice of "You can't do anymore!" I would answer, "Oh, yes I can! I am *not* the son of Darth Vader! I am free, not subservient to small thoughts! I belong to the Light, and the Light is of God!" I had to mentally keep yelling these affirmations, constantly, vehemently fighting against the

---

to the success of the forces as a whole.

When we took birth we purposely entered a world founded on the erroneous premise of separateness, so we could rectify that unconsciousness by becoming aware that there is only unity. We played the game of name, form, and difference because there was a mistaken belief that those ideas were real, and we had to enter their domain to discover and know the God within them. Symbolically, we had to go into the basement and get our feet wet to fix the leak.

Seen in this light, original sin is not a matter of being bad, wrong, or evil. It is a positive evolutionary step the soul takes to grow into greater light. Further, the soul is offering a great act of sacrifice to leave its universal awareness and take on a temporary unconsciousness. For this reason we all owe great thanks to every human being who ever lived—including ourselves—for we chose to come to earth to serve God simply by being here.

assertions of limitation. Finally the voice disintegrated (behind his intimidating mask, Darth Vader has no face), and I just kept running . . . and running . . . and running. For miles. The voice that told me I couldn't go on was a liar.

We can all go on for miles. It does not have to be jogging. In fact, it does not really matter what we do, as long as we push on long enough to laugh at an empty black mask. It can be handling a difficult family, or learning to harmonize with a demanding boss, or forgiving. I am becoming convinced that we can all do anything we set our mind on. We just have to remember who we are, and that we can. Sometimes it is not easy. Sometimes we may find ourselves face-to-face with the Lord of the Dark Empire, and sometimes we may find ourselves, like Luke Skywalker, hanging on for dear life at the end of a slender thread over what seems to be a bottomless abyss. But as long as we remember that we are Skywalkers we shall find ourselves safe in the arms of an unvanquishable Force of Love that somehow heard our stand for Truth and had no alternative but to come to our rescue on a starship of Light with its course set on Home.

Angels in a Strange Land

Toto, I've a feeling we're not in Kansas anymore!
— Dorothy

"He was a student of Confucius in a past life," Hilda explained as she began the class, "and then he was a revered sage on his own merit."

"Wow! This is fascinating!" I thought, as my ears perked up.

"I usually don't delve into people's past lives," she went on, "but in his case it was necessary to help him understand what he has gone through in this life." I wanted to hear more.

"You can see why it was so hard for Bill to adjust to the lifestyle in modern America. He had developed very deep intuitions and talents in previous lives, and when he took birth in an average family in the Midwest, his parents did not understand the sensitivity of his soul. As a child he would stay by himself and be fascinated with his art work, an aptitude he had carried over from previous lives. When his mother would yell, 'Stop with your games, Billy, and hurry down to the kitchen — it's time for dinner!' you can understand what a jarring experience it was for him."

Hilda went on to explain that many people, like Billy, have had difficulty adjusting to this life because their souls are used to more subtle and spiritual environments, and the harsh vibrations of the contemporary world are very rough for them. This story was an eye-opening lesson for me: If you or I didn't fit in with the normal crowd, it may not have been because there was something wrong with us; perhaps our souls were a little disoriented by the culture into which we were born, and we required a number of years to find our niche.

One of my favorite scenes in the movie *Godspell* is that of the calling of the disciples. The story begins with John the Baptist staunchly striding over the Brooklyn Bridge, blowing the conch to announce the coming of the light. Then, throughout the city we see men and women in many different occupations stopping what they are doing to hearken

21

to the call: a ballerina leaps from the shoulders of her hero and dances out the door; a taxi driver at a jammed intersection quits tooting his horn and leaves his cab right there with the door open; a school teacher walks out of his classroom to find the Real Teacher; and so on. Each one responds to a powerful prompting and all of them converge at the Central Park fountain to meet Jesus, John, and their baptism with destiny.

So it is with the gathering of the community of the spirit, now quickening ever more rapidly as the foundation of a new world manifests before our eyes. There really is a New Age coming, a new way of living in spiritual light on earth, and you who somehow feel drawn to read this, and I who feel guided to write it, have *chosen* to come to this stormy planet at this critically significant time for the specific purpose of awakening ourselves and our world to the return of harmony on earth. Our feelings that there *must* be more to life than struggling to earn a living and becoming vice president of the company and having a house in the suburbs, were born of an aspiration that burned more deeply in our hearts than those suggested to us as children. And it is by the same mysteriously exciting plan that we have somehow become connected with one another as links of light in a group commitment to work for the restoration of love on the planet earth.

We live in a strange time, a time when we have been taught that we must apologize for believing in God. We live in a time when women, homosexuals, and blacks have successfully emerged into the richness of self-appreciation, but the lovers of God have wandered down the alleyways of psychic sensationalism and fallen prey to unscrupulous cult leaders because there just haven't been enough pure teachers of Truth to gather the Children of Light into their arms. It is a time represented by a woman in one of my classes at a major industry, who whispered to me that the class techniques are similar to the ones that inspire her at her prayer meetings, but she couldn't say "God" out loud at work, for that sort of thing just isn't talked about there. It is a time that is begging us to bravely and honestly ask, "*Who am I?*" and then see if we are living the highest truth we know.

It is a time when many persons are experiencing spiritual awakening, but who have not had people around them to give them encouragement or support to nurture these gifts. When I used to go into a high school health class to lecture, I would ask if anyone had ever had any spiritual or psychic experiences. Hardly any hands would go up. Then, as soon as the class was over and most of the class had filed out the door, there would always be three or four students who would come up to me and tell me, "You know, sometimes I lie in bed at night and close my eyes and I see the most beautiful colors," or "I saw an angel when I was little, but my mother told me I was imagining it," or "I had a dream that my grandma was going to die, and then she did, and I felt guilty because I thought I caused it." And then nearly all of them would tell me, ". . . but I have never told anyone about this because I am afraid people would think I'm weird."

One of these students, a tenth-grader who sat by himself on the bus because nobody would talk to him, came to one of my evening yoga classes. After the class he asked me a question about meditation that I didn't even understand until I had been meditating for a few more years. No wonder he sat by himself on the bus.

There are many persons of like nature in mental institutions, not because they are insane, but because they are very sensitive souls who have not been able to bring their social act into harmony with the lunacy that the rest of us call "normal." I have several keenly introspective friends who have been in and out of community mental health centers because the people around them were not sufficiently spiritually aware to understand what these people were about, and they convinced the "problem" people that they were "not well," while they were simply travelling to the beat of a different drummer. A good deal of mental patients do not lack mental health, but are unskilled actors in relation to the masses who have learned to suffocate their real sanity under lives that revolve around a mass pact of mutual foolishness.

As I write these words the faces and names of my "mentally ill" friends are coming to my mind, and my heart goes out to them (and really to all of us) for these are some of the most beautiful, sensitive, and loving souls that I have known in this life, souls who have so much spiritual insight that they could heal the insanity of this world with their purity, if only they had the courage to believe in themselves. I have read their poetry, listened to their songs, and been privy to their journals, and many of their works are not unlike those of Da Vinci, Brahms, and Blake. The difference is that the acknowledged masters are allowed the license of oddity because they are acclaimed as geniuses, while the modern schizophrenics have not had enough supportive persons around them who could see beyond idiosyncracy and into the light.

And because there really is no injustice, these mental patients are where they are because they have lessons to learn. Not lessons of mental health, for many of them are healthier than some of the doctors who treat them. Their lessons are ones of *discrimination* and *communication*. They need to learn who they can tell about the voices they hear. The trick is to know who to tell, how, and where. It's very interesting to me who we accept as a genuine prophet. Moses heard a voice speak to him from a burning bush, saying, *"I Am that I Am,"* and the entire nation of Israel followed him to freedom through the parted waters of the Red Sea. My friend Arthur Marmelstein heard the same voice and now he is locked up in Bellevue.

I wonder how well Moses or Jesus would be received if they brought their same message today. I have a feeling it would depend on how well they delivered it. Jesus knew how to play the game. Yes, he was eventually outcast, but only after he had finished his chosen mission and he was ready to fulfill his destiny of going on the cross. It is important to recognize that he kept it very well together for the three years that he needed to complete his ministry. He was the master *par excellence* of human relations and interpersonal communication. That is why he said, "A prophet is never accepted in his home town," "Cast not pearls before swine,"* and "If someone does not accept your teaching, shake the dust off your feet and move on."

The downfall of many of those who realize their Godhood is that they tell the wrong people in the wrong way too soon. Someone has a genuine spiritual insight and runs to his dad or his professor or his shrink and tells them, "I am the Christ" — a career about which most Jewish fathers are not too thrilled. The second mistake they (we) make is that when they tell everyone, "I am God," or "I am the Christ," they forget to throw in "and so are you." Godhood, you see, is a very delicate issue to discuss in mixed company. It's a little like playing army. Everyone wants to be the General and no one wants to be in the infantry. So people get a little threatened when you say, "God is in me," because, quite naturally, they want God to be in them, too. If He is in you and not me, that is a little scary to the ego. So all you have

---

*So as not to demean any of God's children, let it be clear that Jesus was not referring to *people* as swine, but to the foolish thoughts of limitation that people believed, unbridled beasts that would tear delicate truths to shreds by analyzing them to death.

to say is, ". . . and He is in you, too," and that will minimize your chances of being incarcerated. The bottom line is that everybody wants to be acknowledged as godly, which is really correct, so we might as well do it.

If I think that I'm Jesus Christ, I'm in big trouble, for although the Christ is in everyone, there was only one Jesus. If I fall into this category I had better go back to the spiritual drawing board and scrutinize my source, or else I'm in for some pretty stiff competition. There was a book that I heard about in college, *The Three Christs of Ypsilanti*, about three men in a mental institution in Ypsilanti, Michigan, each of whom believed he was Jesus Christ. A psychologist there had the fascinating idea to put these three fellows in a room together, lock the door, and see what happened. (A very interesting idea, was it not?) The outcome, as I understand, was that one of the fellows succeeded in convincing the other two that he was the *real* Jesus Christ, and they ended up becoming his disciples. Well, it's a cute story, but as far as I can see, they all missed the point. The only way they could all emerge victorious — like all of us — is to realize that Christ lives equally in everyone.

Perhaps, then, it has been wise — and necessary — that the community of the spiritually awakened has stayed in the wings for so long, for to sow the seeds of the New Age in a spiritually parched terrain would have cost the movement its life. But that has changed drastically, now. The urgency of the times, the stakes of nuclear power, the plunder of the mother earth, have all pushed the closet spiritualists out into the open. Now we have no choice but to connect with all the Truth we know and generate as much light as God can pour through us. We are now forced to step into our calling. The rain of worldly confusion has come as blessed nourishment to the seeds of the New Age, planted like tulip bulbs last fall, dormant during the winter of ruthless winds, and now sprouting with the gentle spring rain. Of course God's timing is perfect.

So that is where we stand. The marriage of necessity and courage has lifted God's people above the old taskmaster of fear of popular opinion, brought renaissance to the strength of the mystic saints, and turned over the clodded ground to breathe new life into fertile seedbeds. And the light from this new willingness to make a stand for Truth is very bright indeed. I recently discovered a wonderful essay in *The*

RISING IN LOVE

Washington Monthly (February, 1982), entitled *"God is My Chiropractor: Confessions of a Closet New Ager,"* publicizing the testimony of Art Levine:

> *I've decided to come out of the closet. For nearly two years I have been engaging in illicit practices that have scandalized my friends and set me apart from the mainstream of American intellectual life. Possessed by strong drives that I have been helpless to control, I've become part of a hidden subculture . . . Like millions of others with similar preferences, I have attempted, with some success, to pass as part of the conventional world . . . But all the while, I have been concealing my strange secret life.*
>
> *Over the last few years . . . growing numbers of us have surfaced and proclaimed our unusual predilections . . . Naturally we've all been branded kooks and weirdos . . .*
>
> *Now it is my turn to reveal myself, and, I hope, make it easier for those who feel the same forbidden stirrings within themselves. The truth must be told:*
>
> *I BELIEVE IN GOD AND I PRAY EVERY DAY!*

I confess, too, that Art Levine speaks for me, and I believe he captures a bit of all of us. The sad irony of our world is that deep down inside, everyone wants God to be real. Perhaps not everyone would choose the word "God," but it really doesn't matter. Every one of us has a feeling for joy, for spirit, for love, for goodness, for trusting, for caring, for reverence for life. Even *Buick* and *Miller Beer* commercials are founded on humankind's love for "the free spirit in us all" and the High Life. These are the great common denominators of all humankind, the lofty yet reachable ideals that we do not need an anthropological study to prove, the glories of existence that far transcend whatever we call them. They are the spiritual glue that binds us all together.

It is but a great charade, a human masquerade that keeps us from really getting close to − grokking* − one another. Recently I went

---

*grok: If we made a big soup of all of us and we all drank it, we would all become one.
− Robert Heinlein, *Stranger in a Strange Land.*

to a gathering at the home of a woman who had invited a number of people to form a spiritual support group. I arrived to join the most boring conversation I have ever experienced, purely intellectual, completely empty. The vagueness in that room was enough to put the Superbowl to sleep. I was equally responsible; my words were without conviction. I couldn't wait for the whole thing to be over so I could go home and watch TV or eat, both of which promised more substance than this conversation.

Then one person turned the whole scene around. She said right up front, "I have come to this group because I love God very much, and He is more important to me than anything else in my life. I am here because I am hoping that this group can help bring God more deeply into my life." You would not believe how quickly the energy in that room became alive and empowered. The moment she said that, nearly all the eyes in that room lit up, people sat up straighter and leaned toward the center of the circle, the wiggling and scratching and looking at the clock ceased, and something very important happened in that room. All because one person had the courage to say *"I love God."* That made it alright for the rest of us, myself included, to say it also. Then the next person said, "You know, that's exactly how I'm feeling, too, but I didn't know if this was the right group to say it in." And the next person. And the next. In a chain reaction the acknowledgement of the presence of God filled the atmosphere and I tell you that living room became a real living room, filled with the Holy Spirit to match any church anywhere. The evening concluded with each of us saying a prayer out loud, and I want to tell you the prayers were among the most powerful I have ever experienced. The light in that room was indescribable. All because one person had the guts to say *"I love God."*

It takes courage to rise above the status quo, a bravery that each of us must learn in our own way. I am reminded of a week in college when I met a very nice girl at a fraternity party. The next Saturday night we went out to the movies, after which we went back to her dorm room. She sat on one side of the couch and I sat at the other. I really wanted to sit close to her and put my arm around her, but I hesitated to make the first move; I was afraid of being rejected. So there I sat, making believe I was interested in talking about the school football team and religion classes and psychology (this conversation rivaled the one above for the boredom award), until the buzzer sounded and it was time for me to leave. (This was in the unliberated days before coed dorms.) Then, after we had been going out for a few months and I had made it over to the other side of the couch, we talked about that first date.

"You know," she told me, "I really wanted to sit close to you, too, but I was afraid you'd reject me, and I was waiting for you to make the first move!"

So there we had sat, two dunderheads, both wanting very much to get together, talking about nothing, yet feeling very much something, and neither of us doing anything about it.

That, as I see it, is pretty much where spiritual action has been for a long time, at least my spiritual action. We have been sitting on opposite ends of the couch, waiting for the other person to make the first move, waiting for someone else to let us know that it's O.K. to say "God," that it's O.K. to feel beautiful, that it's O.K. to love. But if we all wait for the other guy to do it first, who will do it? That is why the world has been the way it has been; very few of us have had the courage to be the first one in a crowd to say who we are. Lincoln said it. Gandhi made a stand for it. Martin Luther King, Jr. lived it. Now you and I have our moment of opportunity.

We don't have to all write a Gettysburg address or march to the Indian shore or lead a social revolution. And we don't have to all go around saying, "I love God" (although that might be kind of nice). We just have to remember who we are and treat each other like who we are. We need to accept the fact that every one of us is a precious piece of Living Spirit, and that spirit is very much affected by how we treat each other. The big lie of life is that we are tough, immovable, unaffectable islands in space, and the great Truth is that *how we touch one another can really heal our world,* right down to how we say "thank you" for the change at the supermarket. Then the way we ask for a stamp at the post office becomes a prayer meeting; answering the telephone, communion; and our smiles, living placards. This is how we make space for one another to come out of hiding. Every time one person says, "You're beautiful," or "Thank you for you," or "Let's work this out together," that is one more hand extended to bring one more misunderstood mental patient out of feeling lost and into creativity. That is one more sensitive young artist who doesn't have to put aside his crayons just because it's time for dinner. And that is one less lonely high school boy who has to sit by himself on the bus because his schoolmates just wouldn't understand.

Heroes-At-Large

I am a promise. I am a possibility.
I am a great big bundle of potentiality.
— Children's song

I was introduced to a retarded fellow named Mickey. The friend who introduced us told me that Mickey was classified as an "idiot-savant," someone who is half retarded and half a genius. As we sat together waiting for a bus, my friend asked Mickey, "Say, what day of the week did St. Patrick's Day come on in 1963?" Mickey went through some rapid mental computations and within about five seconds blurted out, "That was a Sunday!" We consulted a calendar, and Mickey was correct. He asked Mickey a few more similar questions, and he was accurate every single time. While Mickey was not sufficiently mentally proficient to cook a meal or drive a car, part of his brain was developed thousands of times superior to most people.

So it is with all of us. Each in our own way we're a little uncoordinated, but we have some tremendous possibilities. The trick is to bring it all together, to let our latent greatness blossom until we're all we can be. Then is our destiny fulfilled.

There was a movie out not long ago, *Hero-At-Large*, about a shy, unsuccessful actor whose confidence in himself is waning with each rejection at the casting office. The only job he can find is that of impersonating the famous Captain Avenger, signing autographs for children outside a theatre where the latest Captain Avenger movie is being shown. We see him at the end of his evening's work as he is being picked up by a chartered bus, taking his seat among forty other Captain Avengers with forty pens in hand, all of them disheartened and disappointed in themselves just as he is.

The plot thickens when on his way home that night he happens upon a grocery store robbery. Without thinking about it, he dashes behind a display, throws off his overcoat and trousers, and emerges in full Captain Avenger uniform (Ta-Daaaa!). Donning the well-known crusader's mask, he bravely confronts the thugs, whose resistance is no match, of course, for Captain Avenger. The crooks flee, dropping the loot behind them, and our hero disappears into the night without revealing his true identity, leaving Mr. and Mrs. Grocery Store Owner beaming with their jaws agape.

Word gets around the city that Captain Avenger is real, safeguarding innocent victims, rescuing the helpless, and valiantly serving the public good. Newspaper and television stories glorify the mysterious man of good conscience, children idolize his bravery, and there is a new era of hopefulness in the heart of the metropolis.

But not in the heart of one bewildered Captain Avenger. The more he hears of Captain Avenger's glory, the deeper our hero becomes plunged in depression, for he knows that Captain Avenger is really no more than a struggling actor who made believe. After turbulent days of wrestling with his conscience he musters up the courage to make a public confession on the steps of city hall, admitting that he is a fraud and Captain Avenger is just an imaginary character, like Santa Claus. The people of the city are terribly disheartened, they boo and jeer him, and our ex-hero mopes home with his head hung in ignominy, more discouraged than ever.

But because the darkest hour gives birth to the new day, so comes this hero's redemption. Walking home after his confession, he comes upon a flaming building surrounded by fire engines. As he looks up he sees a family trapped on the top floor, beyond where the firemen can reach with their ladder. The family's only hope is to jump into the net, but they are scared stiff. But not our hero. Fearlessly he scales a burning back staircase and rescues them all. Our hero-at-large turns out to be a large hero, for he did not give up and he was willing to go on stage one more time for one final act as Captain Avenger. This time, however, it was the stage of life.

The delightful teaching of the movie is that although the hero was at first just acting brave, he actually *was* brave. He really did have courage all along; it just took some practice for his strength to be brought forth. Like many of our lives, it took a crisis to draw his dormant potential out. Even though he gave up on himself, *the real hero in him never quit.* You see, it was the hero that was real, and the actor the imposter.

Captain Avenger is, of course, *us*. We are all heroes-at-large. We may not save people from robberies or burning buildings, but each of us has a hidden identity of courage that becomes obvious and powerful as soon as we are willing to remove our overcoats of self-consciousness and unworthiness. I have found some kind of greatness in every person I have ever known. Some are marvelous through brave deeds and many are magnificent through silent simplicity. A scattered few receive grandiose acclaim, while more find fulfillment in the quiet joys of inner satisfaction. Some are rewarded in seeing their name on a Broadway marquee, while others take delight in the giggle of a happy child. Or putting the finishing touch on a quiche. Or planting a magnolia. Or seeing another human being learning to love life. The ways of God's greatness are as plentiful as the stars of the heavens.

There is an idea with which I have been experimenting lately, one about which I am tremendously excited. It is the thought that to make a dream come true, it does not have to be a *probability* — it can just be a *possibility*. Possibilities are seeds. Whenever I feel I can't achieve something, I ask myself, "Is there one possibility — even *one* possibilty *in a million* — that this could really turn out right?" The answer must always be "Yes!" because anything is possible. If your chance of winning the lottery is one in twenty thousand, it is really a possibility; it is not zero — it is one. Somebody has to be that one, and it could just as well be you as the next person. That's how I've been thinking lately.

The most exciting change that has come with this way of thinking is that the moment I accept that possibility — even if it's one in a million — my whole feeling about the situation changes, and a tremendous surge of enthusiasm wells up in me. I actually begin to feel as if the idea has *already become a reality*! It is one of the most amazing transformations of consciousness I have ever experienced. It is accomplishing the quantum leap from one-in-a-million to "Yes!" That little one in a million opens up a wedge, makes a little hole in the dike, an opening that lets all the positive energy come through and makes the impossible possible. It's a fantastic way of thinking.

We just need to be able to see what we want, even before it comes around the corner. A few years ago three friends and I went to see *Meetings with Remarkable Men* in New York City. As we walked back to the bus station after the movie, it became increasingly clear that we

31

would be late and our chances of making the bus were small. I gave up and began to walk more slowly. But my friends did not. "Come on!" they encouraged, "We can make it!" So we ran.

When we arrived at the terminal, one of our group went to buy the tickets while the rest of us dashed for the bus. As we got to the gate, the bus was just pulling out, and we flagged it down. The driver stopped to let us on, but that did not solve the problem of our tickets. I told the driver, "Our friend is downstairs getting our tickets . . . He'll be just a few minutes . . . Can you wait?"

"I'm sorry," the driver returned, "I have a schedule to meet and I'm late already . . . You'll have to wait until the next bus."

Disheartened, I accepted our failure (you can see why I have to practice positive thinking), and I began to step back off the big orange bus. Just then, one of the fellows with me, Paul, looked around the bend and shouted, "Here he comes!" After about twenty seconds our friend appeared, we all boarded the bus, and on our way we went.

I sat down next to Paul and breathed a sigh of relief. "Whew!" I let go, "It sure was great that you saw him when you did!"

"Do you want to know the truth?" Paul responded with a big grin. "I didn't see him when I said I did! I had no idea where he was or when he would come! I just said that to stall the bus driver, with my fingers crossed that he would show soon!"

"Faith," I declared to myself. Or trust. Or pretense. Or downright *chutzpah*. Whatever it was, it worked. As I pondered on what had actually happened, the lesson became clear to me that we have to have the nerve to believe that we are more than we think we are. We have to be willing to celebrate our own self coming around the bend before we can actually see it. We have to be willing to take a chance on ourselves making it. The only alternative is to wait until the next bus, and we often do not know when that will be. A friend of mine uses this motto:

> **WHEN YOU FORGET WHO YOU ARE**
> **AND DON'T KNOW WHAT TO DO,**
> **ACT THE WAY YOU WOULD IF YOU DID.**

Psychologists tell us that our consciousness is like a huge iceberg with just a little tip showing, and most of it hidden in the subconscious. So it is with our *super*conscious — our higher self, our Divine Potential.

We have seen just a bit — a coming attraction of who we will be when we realize who we are. There was a song by The Band with the chorus, *"When you wake up you will remember everything,"* and this is what has already begun to happen. We are starting to wake up, and the morning light is revealing that we were sleeping in a palace, though we dreamed it was a hovel. While we thought we were abandoned to a bleak ruin, we are discovering that we are children of a King, and the entire kingdom is available to us because a father's greatest pleasure is to share his life with his children.

The time is now come for us to receive our destiny. The Divine Flame is sparkling within us, shining away the old shadows of who we, in a moment of forgetfulness, thought we were. I — and I believe you, as well — have been receiving glimpses, insights, flashes of what we can be when we allow God to work through us. Pictures and images are coming in dreams, in meditations, in quiet walks along the beach at sunset. They are coming through books, through music, through the voices of our brothers and sisters, through motion pictures. Stories like *Close Encounters of the Third Kind, E.T.*, the spiritual voyages of the Starship *Enterprise*, and Yoda's lessons of The Force are no accident; they are so enormously popular because the principles they depict are more spiritual truth than science fiction. These masterpieces contain deep teachings for the masses, lessons which are being given through the media as a way of reaching many persons rapidly and succinctly. In the old days you would have had to go to the Himalayas or a Hopi gathering or find an esoteric occult teacher to hear words of Truth. But now, because there is a quantum leap of consciousness stirring on this planet, God is working through the open minds of creative persons like Steven Spielberg and Gene Roddenberry to carry the message of the New Age to all who have ears to hear. In fact, The Force of Truth is eager to work through any person — like you and me — who asks to be a channel for it. Spielberg and Roddenberry have brought Truth to the masses because they have been willing to *listen* and *speak* through the medium of their talent. Many of us have been listening, but not speaking. Now is our time to speak. Through words. Through pottery. Through housecleaning. Through right business. Through silence. Through every avenue that our heart guides us to walk for the sake of creating a new world. Now is the time for the workers of Truth to come forth and make a stand for the Light. Now is the time.

33

When I was a child my heroes were always "out there." I had a Davy Crockett coonskin cap. I went to the record department of Korvette's to meet Chubby Checker and get his autograph on the back of a matchbook cover. The highlight of my fourteenth year was the night I saw a live Beatles concert in Atlantic City. (The screaming was so loud that I hardly heard a note of music, but it didn't really matter — I was in the same room with John, Paul, George, and Ringo!) Then I went home and played their songs on my guitar.

Later my musical heroes were replaced by spiritual guides. I put Ram Dass' picture up on my kitchen wall. I went to a mountain top in New Mexico to be with Patricia Sun. I bought a Yoda t-shirt. All because I wanted to know God, and I felt that these beautiful beings knew the One I sought.

Then my search carried me into a new light. As I absorbed the loving wisdom of these teachers, I began to see one common thread in all of their teachings:

**LOOK WITHIN, AND THERE SHALL YOU FIND
THE TREASURE OF YOUR HEART'S YEARNING.**

So I did, and I realized that their words were True. The hero for whom I was searching was *me*. All that I wanted from them, I could find within my very self, in the Light that God breathed into me. My searching came to an end when I was introduced to the one person in my life who could save me, and that was my Divine Self. Then I began to play my own songs on my guitar; I began to sing my own song.

The wondrous mystery of this self-discovery, this first hearing the tune of my own song, was that as I discovered the hero within myself I began to see the hero in everyone else, as well. I saw that each of us has our own song that only each of us can sing. I saw that when we fail it is simply because we do not realize that all that we seek is already within us, and when we succeed it is because we know that God believes in us enough to recreate Himself in us *as* us. It is said that *"There is nothing so powerful as an idea whose time has come."* When we remember who we are, we may rightfully add, *"There is no one so dynamic as a sleeping hero whose time has come to awaken."*

34

Growing Into Greatness

The Butterfly*

The innocent children discovered the killer sleeping in the hayloft. He had fled from the city where his crime was committed and taken refuge in the deserted barn. The children did not know of his misdeed.

"Who do you think he is?" the little girl asked her brother.

"I don't know . . . Who do you think he looks like?"

"Well, he has long hair and a beard."

"And he's about as old as daddy."

"He has sandals on."

"Maybe he's Jesus!"

"Do you think he could be?"

"Well, that's what the Sunday School teacher said Jesus looked like!"

"Yes! I'll bet it *is* him!"

"Oh, aren't we lucky to have Jesus — Gentle Jesus — come to our very own town!"

The killer, awakened by the exclamations, sat up, startled. He was about to flee when he heard the girl calling, "Jesus, Gentle Jesus, will you stay and play with us for a little while?"

"We will take care of you!" promised the little boy.

"Yes!" echoed his sister . . . "We will bring you food and blankets and we won't tell anyone you are here!"

"Oh please, Gentle Jesus, will you stay with us?"

The killer began to understand what was happening. He thought it over. It seemed like a safe bet, for a while at least. Yes, he would stay.

Over the next days and weeks, the children brought him food and clothing and even wine for him to bless. And with these things, they brought their innocent love and their adoration for the sweet and kind savior.

---

*This story is adapted from the plot of an old movie which was recounted to me, the title or author of which I do not know.

The killer felt safe with them, and the weeks turned into months. The children came to him every day and asked him to tell them parables and to bless them and their families.

So he did. As the summer went on, he actually began to enjoy playing the role of the Man of Peace. It was, of course, only an act, but there was something that felt good about it, something that he had not felt in many years, perhaps since he was a child and his grandmother would tell him stories of Jesus and the children.

As the man basked in the warm love of these children, he learned to love them, too. He began to look forward to the times when they would come, when he would tell them parables about the wonders of heaven's kingdom and the importance of loving our neighbors. One day he even found himself telling a parable that no one had ever heard, and this made the children so happy to hear a parable directly from their Gentle Jesus, one that was not even in the Bible.

The man's feelings about people, about the world, about life, began to soften, and he became gentle and kind. He read the Bible when he was alone, and something happened within him, something like a long-locked door opening to admit morning sunlight.

One evening he came upon the story of the prodigal son, and he began to weep. "Yes, this is the Truth," he thought to himself. In that moment he realized ever so clearly that it was *he* who was the prodigal son, and that he had sinned against man and God. He knew, too, that his soul could not be cleansed until he made restitution for his crime. So he decided to return to the city and confess.

The next time his beloved children came, he took them in his arms and drew them close to his breast.

"My dear ones," he quietly began, "it is now the time for me to leave you."

"But where are you going?" the little ones asked with tears streaming down their soft cheeks.

He gathered both of them closer to him and embraced them even more strongly.

"I must return to my Father," he explained, fighting back his own tears.

"Then we shall go with you!" they pleaded.

"No . . . Where I am going, you cannot come."

"But we want to know the Father, too."

"My dear ones, you already do know the Father . . . Did you not

feel the peace in the long walks that we took through the meadow?
. . . And did we not laugh with one another as we watched the little
colts struggling to stand on their new legs? . . . And do you remember
how we slept under the stars and awoke to the gentle cooing of the
doves? If you know me, and if you have loved all that we have done
together, you already know the Father."

"Then will you give us something to remember you by, Gentle
Jesus?"

"I leave with you the gentleness that you have given to me. This
is my peace that I give unto you."

And the son arose, and went unto his Father.

The Turning Point

The lowest ebb is the turn of the tide.

There is a turning point for every soul. It is the blessed moment when the hardships of life's adversity give way to the awakening to the presence of God. It is the hour of crisis which bears the child of Spirit. It is the end of suffering and the dawn of freedom. It is God's finest hour and the happy opportunity of Truth to shine into a dark life. It is the renaissance of all of us.

The awakening to light does not always come as an explosion, but more often at the end of a pendulum's swing, as the weight of worldly struggle yields to the understanding that there is a path of simplicity far easier than common ambition. At such a critical juncture in a soul's evolution, the Child of God has completed his journey into the nether world and set his foot back upon the way to his Father's home, now just a glimmer of hope in the distance, the only guiding star above a dark forest. And for such a soul in such a position, that glimmer is infinitely worth following.

But because we humans are among the most stubborn of creatures, our backs are often against the wall before we are willing to entertain the possibility that God's way is more joyful than the one we have adopted. We have learned to be willful and doubtful, and so we often refuse to consider God's design until ours has reached a dead end. Yet, because God is God, there She stands, patiently waiting for us with open arms, willing to accept us no matter how many dead end routes we have impudently trod. As Hilda once asked us, "Where else could you fall, but into the arms of God?"

A few nights ago I met a woman who experienced the death of her two-and-a-half year old son. She told me that this was her turning point, for it forced her to look at her life — and all of life — from a

41

broader, higher perspective. It turned her awareness toward God and, as she explained to me, "It gave me an entirely new and more purposeful direction in my life." As we discussed her experience, it appeared to me that she had come into great clarity about her trial. "It may sound strange," she went on, "but now I can't imagine him *not* passing on. I know that it had to be that way for the highest good of both of us."

That is the perspective at which we must all eventually arrive, each through our own struggles and challenges. In college I experienced a major turning point. One day I came to the stark realization that many of the things that I valued — money, power, sex, prestige, career, and possessions — were empty. It became so clear to me that all of these seeming treasures that I had spent much of my life pursuing as sources of security were essentially unstable and had no ability to shield or save me from life's changes. It was as if I was sitting in a movie theatre believing that everything I saw on the screen was real, when the lights in the theatre flashed on to completely erase all the forms on the screen. It was a startling and frightening disillusionment.

Following this jolt, I went through a kind of dark night of the soul, a feeling of emptiness in which everything I saw had no substance, no meaning, no reality. It was as if I was in a macabre amusement park where everything I touched crumbled to dust. I remember walking into the college cafeteria and seeing a book entitled *Nothingness*, and I figured this was the end of the line, the universe is a cosmic practical joke and we all end up in a big black hole. It is at this point of experience that many existential philosophers give up their quest for Truth and conclude that all is meaningless.

But because there is more to God than existentialism, She was right there to extend Her kind hand to help me to the other side of the chasm. She sent someone into my life who gave me a book called *Positive Disintegration*, by a psychologist named Dombrowski who said that going to pieces is sometimes the best thing that can happen to someone, for a life which is laboring under a false, painful belief system must be taken apart before a new and better one can be established in its place. What many people experience as nervous breakdowns or psychotic episodes are actually the soul's way of breaking out of a shell that once protected it, but now inhibits it. If we grew up in a family (or a world) where there was a great deal of negativity, emotional turbulence, or insensitivity, it was useful — and perhaps necessary — for us to build a protective shell around ourselves to shield us from the harshness of our environment. Our shielding systems serve us well as practical defenses against injury. (As I look at the hands that are writing now, I see they are calloused from the physical work I have been doing this summer. Because they have been exposed to continuous friction, the God-imbued intelligence of the body has built a tough layer of resilient tissue over the soft skin to protect and sustain it. When the autumn comes and that friction ceases, the callous areas will fall away and tender skin will be rebuilt with as much sensitivity as it originally enjoyed.) So it is with the journey of the soul through the seasons of life. Though a spiritual being must sometimes temporarily sacrifice its sensitivity and retreat to an inner shelter during the winter of adversity, there must come a spring when that tough shell is cracked to release the finer higher self from the cocoon and let it free to fly as it was originally intended.

A few weeks ago someone showed me some amazing flowers called peonies, lovely creations which bud forth in little round, hard balls. It was explained to me that by a miracle of nature the only way these buds can open is by means of certain little ants coming to eat away the outer shell. The flowers, you see, cannot open by themselves; their protection must be gnawed away by bugs. Then the most radiant, delicate, and colorful flowers emerge to celebrate the sunshine.

Those flowers and ants gave me a new appreciation for the gift that challenges bring to my awakening. They gave me a divine perspective on the aspects of my life that bug me. Just imagine: Every little bite the world takes out of my ego makes a bit more of an opening for the flower of the soul to emerge. Lesson of the peonies, number one.

Lesson number two: We can't do it by ourselves. We really need each other to rub off our rough edges. If we run away from challenges, we only prevent ourselves from growing. We may think we have escaped pain, but we have only resisted awakening. Pain does not come from a person or place or event; it is created in *the mind*. As long as we run from the thing that we resist, the pain stays in the mind. When we face the object of our difficulty, only then do we have an opportunity to free ourselves. Yes, there is a time when retreat and renewal are necessary, and it is sometimes very healthy to get away from it all to regroup. But there is also a time to courageously stand up to the monsters of the mind, the ones that turn out to be no more real than the big papier maché props they use in Hollywood, empty machines with no power except that which they are given by those who fear them.

The third gift of the peonies is the teaching that those monsters (sometimes just big bugs) come to us at *exactly* the moment we are ready to benefit from the strength we gain by learning to handle them. It is said that *we are never given a challenge beyond our ability to master*, and we might add that the arrival of those adversities is perfectly timed according to the stage of personal growth that we have attained; we get exactly what we need to advance us to the next level. The most intriguing aspect of the process of the peonies was that the ants — a special kind of ant — somehow appeared just at the moment that the flowers were ready to bloom. When I saw those little insects crawling about, having come from seemingly nowhere, all I could say was, "Amazing! . . . It's a miracle!"

This brings us to an idea that has helped me through many turning points: *God does not take anything away from us without giving us something better in its place.* There is never any loss without greater gain. If we want greater good to come into our life, we must make space for it. If we do not do it ourselves, God, who always works for our best interest, will make that opening for us — whether we like it or not. He'll get us fired from the job that no longer serves our highest good, to put us into one where we can better do His work. He'll break us up from our lover, so we can find a new and more fulfilling relationship. He'll close all doors except the one He wants us to walk through. In *Lost Horizon*, the disoriented travellers ask if the High Lama can find them guides to show the way home. "The High Lama," they are told, "arranges *everything*."

After going through my "emptiness period," my life became infinitely richer. You see, the emptiness was not the end, but a sort of clearing out time, a season for the roots of the old dead plants to disintegrate so the new seeds would have room to grow. In fact, my new life after that clearing out is so different than the old, that I hardly think of it as being a part of the same life, or of me as being the same person. The difference in the quality of my life is so striking that it is as if I was born anew. But only after the old was cleared away to "Prepare ye the way of the Lord."

We are now collectively going through such a clearing as a country, a society, a family of humankind. As we weather the tribulation now upon the earth, and that which is said to be coming, we must always remember that the peace that will come out of the hardship far outweighs the difficulties we experience. As we see idolized institutions like governments, schools, and monies fall by the wayside, we must know that this is happening only because they have too often not been conducted in the light of the high principles of Godly purpose upon which they were originally founded. These institutions must undergo a period of transformation after which they will be replaced by a new way of living that holds Divinity as its dearest value.

The earth as a whole has graduated to planetary consciousness. There is one huge turning point for the race of man, and it is now. There is no turning back. There is a maxim that *You are responsible for as much as you are aware* — no more, no less. The truth of this idea was brought home to me by a political analyst discussing the nuclear freeze and disarmament. He said, "Even if all of the nations on the earth were to completely dismantle all atomic weapons, that would not completely solve the problem, for, you see, as long as one person knows *how* to build them, there is the constant question of *'Will we use them?'* "

We are now ready to take another step, one of great responsibility. And that is wonderful, for as the oriental sage put it, *"Crisis equals danger plus opportunity."* As our old world crumbles around us, it is imperative that we do not become lost in thoughts of insecurity, fear, and confusion. The only way to deal with these changes is to expand our notion of what is being transformed around us, to include the understanding that great good always comes from the annihilation of unconsciousness and all of the things, acts, and events that unconsciousness breeds. There is a new, bright world waiting for us to claim it, and the knowledge that it is real is the saving grace that will bear us through the darkest night. We must keep our eyes and hearts focused on the light at the end of the tunnel and realize that the darkest hour is not only just before dawn, but it is the very promise that dawn is nigh. This high awareness, the vision that dissolution actually prepares the way of resurrection, is the shining star that guides us across the desert to the birthplace of the Christ. Thus does the last storm of winter moisten the earth for the first seeds of spring.

Bombshells to Songbells

And into plowshares shall the nations beat their swords.
— Isaiah 2:4

I closed my eyes and allowed the mystical tones of the Tibetan temple bells to play through my body. Each ancient sound vibrated gently, touching me in deeper and more subtle centers within myself. It was as if I was being lifted into meditation on the graceful echoing voices of a thousand chanting monks, drawing me to join them in consecration of the gift of sound. As the last tone rolled through the innermost recesses of my being, I gratefully savored its lingering sweetness.

"The sounds you have just heard are those of bullets," reported Job Matusow, the musician and storyteller *par excellence* who had just offered the concert. I could hardly believe my ears. Bullets?

"If you look closely at the bells," he explained, "you will notice that each of them is actually the shell of a tank or machine gun bullet, carefully reforged to produce the beautiful tones you just enjoyed."

I looked more closely. There must have been forty bullet shells, of all shapes and sizes. To my amazement, he was telling the truth. "How did he come to do this?" I marvelled, ". . . and why?"

"The concert you have heard is the realization of a dream I have had for many years," Job explained. "During World War II, I was stationed on the battle lines as a camp guard. Part of my job was to signal the troops. Out of necessity and lack of any other materials, we rigged up a few of these empty tank shells, which served the purpose well.

"It was during a night watch that I noticed how soft and soothing were the sounds of these bells. That night I made a vow that if I ever got out of the war alive I would collect some of these shells and turn instruments of destruction into vessels of God's peace.

"When I got home, by God's Grace, I contacted the government, which gave me the bullets you see before you now. I have since had the joy to play these bells for many groups — especially school children

47

and, most meaningfully, for an Easter morning ceremony on the deck of a docked U.S. Navy battleship."

Waves of enthusiasm rolled through me. What a lesson! "That's what I want to do with my life," I immediately felt, " — turn negatives into positives and serve God through the transformation."

I was given a golden opportunity to practice this lesson when one morning around 7 a.m. I was sitting in meditation, about to dive into a state of joyous bliss. Just at that moment my ears — and my whole body — were assaulted by a *THUMP — THUMP-THUMP* . . . *THUMP — THUMP-THUMP* from the other side of the wall, where dwelt an energetic twelve-year-old boy. Following this rude annunciation came the sounds, "*ANOTHER ONE BITES THE DUST!* . . . *UNKH! — THUMP — THUMP-THUMP* . . . *ANOTHER ONE BITES THE DUST!* . . . *UNKH!* . . . *ANOTHER ONE GONE, ANOTHER ONE GONE, ANOTHER ONE BITES THE DUST!* . . . *THUMP — THUMP-THUMP* . . . *UNKH!*"

When I finally recovered my wits, I recognized these exotic sounds as a popular punk rock song, my neighbor's idea of a lively way to greet the new day. Unfortunately, it was not exactly my idea of a pleasant wake-up greeting, especially in the middle of a sweet etheric meditation. My first impulse was to jump up, pound on the wall, and yell to him, "*Turn that racket down!*" Either that or call the Environmental Protection Agency.

But then I remembered one of Hilda's practical lessons on turning every negative into a positive. She recounted that when she was staying in San Francisco she lived right next to a cable car line that sent loud, motley noises through her window every time one of the streetcars passed her apartment. Realizing that there was nothing she could do to stop it, she decided to make something pleasant out of it. "You know what it reminded me of, kids?" she asked as she gathered us into her experience. "It sounded just like those nice tinkling oriental bells, the kind I used to hear in Ceylon. So every time that old cable car rattled by, I made believe I was in some quaint oriental village listening to an enchanting concert. You know, 'hing, bing . . . chung, chung . . . ta, hing.'" (We always laugh whenever she gives her rendition of those bells; even though I must have heard the story a dozen times, every performance is delightful.) "That's what I suggest you kids do: Always find some way to turn a challenge into a blessing; all it requires is a bit of *imagination*."

So there I sat at an unsolicited 7 a.m. disco, attempting to figure out some way to turn the new wave into the new age. For a while I sat there feeling agitated and confused, and then I hit on it: I would make believe that it was my *thoughts* that were biting the dust! "After all," I thought, "that's what meditation is all about, isn't it? — letting go of unwanted thoughts and letting them disintegrate!" So every time "*ANOTHER ONE BITES THE DUST!*" came around, I picked one thought I wanted to get rid of, and I made believe it had been knocked off. First there was my feeling insulted about something someone had said to me — *ANOTHER ONE BITES THE DUST — UNKH!* And then my confusion about what to do today — *ANOTHER ONE BITES THE DUST — UNKH!* And then my irritation at the kid who was playing the music — *ANOTHER ONE BITES THE DUST — UNKH!* And so on. Before long, it was really fun. You wouldn't believe all the thoughts that bit the dust that morning. It made war movies seem tranquil by comparison. By the time that record was over I had had a very excellent meditation indeed — perhaps one of the most practical. As I arose, I realized that the most fragrant incense is manufactured from the crudest punk.

The ability to turn minuses into pluses is a vital key to abundant living. People who have very little material goods are forced to develop this talent. I remember driving through a run-down section of New York City one night, looking at the broken buildings and shabby shops. Then I saw about half a dozen enthusiastic young guys enjoying a rousing game of basketball. I looked again and saw that there was no playground; they had discovered a hole in the awning of a shop, just about the size of a basketball hoop, just about the right height. They took what they had and made what they wanted.

And then there is my friend Jeff, whose mother's friend gave him an old 1962 Rambler for the legal fee of one dollar, with the tongue-in-cheek blessing that "You're lucky if you get six months out of this heap!" That was eight years ago. Jeff has given the car loving care, and it is doing fine. I know — I went to the movies in it yesterday.

Ingenius persons like these remind me again and again that *things are not good or bad in and of themselves, but it is what we make of them that determines their worth.* We have the power to mold all of life according to the direction we choose, and the way we look at our experiences is the pivotal factor that determines how it all turns out.

As Dr. Eric Butterworth has often said, "Our job is not to *set* things right; we simply need to *see* them right."

Years ago I learned this valuable lesson from my professor, Alfred Gorman, who taught us how to make the most of people working together in a group. Said Dr. Gorman, "Every group member, no matter how negatively they are acting or what a hindrance they may seem to be, is a potential real asset to the group. In fact, the more energy they are putting into being negative, the greater will be their contribution if you can just get them to channel their energy in a productive direction.

"Take the 'class clown' or practical joker, for example. Such a person has a need for attention and recognition. If they are not getting it, they will be a disruptive pest to the class. But, with a little positive attention and acknowledgement, they can cut their joking down to appropriate times and serve the very important function of a tension reliever.

"In the same way, the 'tough battler' — the one who challenges nearly every statement made by the other group members — can turn into a very good 'devil's advocate' and force the group to carefully examine its decisions. And the 'group mother' who tends to smother group members with over-support and unsolicited protection can be an extremely vital asset to the group during tough times, if she learns to give support where and when it is really needed. So, you see, there are really no destructive group members — only misdirected uses of energy. In the final analysis, *all* group members can serve an important positive function."

Because Truth must be true on all levels, these principles apply not only to encounter groups and classrooms, but to all of life. I have been shown that in organic gardening, for example, most insects serve a necessary function. When you upset the balance by removing some ladybugs, you find that the bugs they were eating become a bigger problem. So the "enemies" you removed were actually your good friends. Although Jesus didn't use the term "organic gardening," he did say, *"Love your enemies, bless those that curse you, and pray for those who spitefully use you."*

A friend of mine gave me a very helpful insight into the deeper meaning of "loving your enemies." He said that we might look at the enemies *within* ourselves — the bad habits and traits that we don't like about ourselves — as the enemies that we must learn to love. It seems

50

that the more we fight our shortcomings — overeating, smoking, or lack of emotional control, for example — the more they fight back, often with hidden weapons (like dreams of Häagen-Dazs banana splits). It is said that *"What we resist, expands and persists,"* and this is why brute resistance (against a person or a trait) only adds fuel to the problem. The subtle secret of conquering our inner enemies is to stop hating and fighting them, and start appreciating them for what they can offer to our personal and spiritual growth.

In the last New York Marathon there was a runner who, at the age of thirty, had weighed 300 pounds, smoked four packs of cigarettes a day, and had gone through a series of heart operations. One day, however, he got sick and tired of being sick and tired, and he decided to make his life work *for* him, and not against his best interests. So he quit smoking, cleaned up his diet, lost 140 pounds, and when I saw him he was running the marathon with a smile on his face.

This man *used* his bad habits as a springboard to develop the strengths of self-control, determination, and good health. Perhaps these were the qualities that he needed to cultivate in this life, and his soul purposely took on these harmful habits as a focal point for learning how to overcome them. In order to develop tremendous discipline, he had to have a formidable obstacle. The armed forces train soldiers on rigorous obstacle courses, designed to force infantrymen to become very strong for battle. Though the new soldiers may curse the objects they have to surmount, when the battle comes they look back and bless them. Though we may not face physical warfare, we are all warriors of life; as Don Juan told Carlos Castenada, we must all be *impeccable warriors*, at that. Then, when we have learned how to remain peaceful in the face of even the most difficult times, we will look back on all the little challenges that barbed us and through which we grew strong through overcoming, and bless them.

It is exactly this kind of transformation through overcoming unwanted habits that enables us to eventually uplift one another. The most powerful healers and change agents are those who have grown through a tremendous difficulty and then brought the benefit of their experience to help others going through the predicament that they have mastered. I know a man who healed his cancer through meditation and went on to teach thousands of other persons to do the same. You will probably recognize, too, that the most successful therapeutic organizations, such as Alcoholics Anonymous and Weight Watchers, are built on the strength of people who have conquered their temptation and gladly share their victory with those who are still in the process of conquering. Such persons have balanced themselves against the desires that used to drag them down (like a jogger doing isometric exercises), and used that power to bolster the spiritual muscles necessary for real self-transformation. In such a case, the old "enemies" were actually friends in disguise; we just needed to learn how to relate to them to make them work for us. Then, after we have become a more integrated person through mastering those old traits, we can "bless those (habits) that spitefully used you," for, like a mountain climber who finds a heap of rocks at the bottom of a sharp slope and then rearranges them as steppingstones upward, we can see that the elements of the situation were not bad at all — we just had to fit them into their right place.

Once again we find that all is God. This is the first lesson, and the last. Our job is to discover God in that which we judged to be ungodly, to find the good where others see evil, to see the Mary in the Magdalene. This means that there *must* be unity in what now seems to be alienation, saintliness where sinners now stand, and Love in the midst of bitterness. Put more simply, there is hope for all of us and all of life, and that is the great truth that keeps God loving us. Perhaps He hears the songbells in our souls.

> *I believe that God is in*
> *   me*
> *as the sun is in the*
> *   rainbow,*
> *the light in my*
> *   darkness*
> *the voice in my*
> *   silence.*
>
> — Helen Keller

Lifting The Past Into Love

I release all of my past to the Light.
                                    — The Light Prayer

It seems that just when we have made up our mind to step forward into a new future, the past comes back to haunt us. The moment we decide we want to clean up our life, old dirt bubbles up like sludge from a stuffy drain. Just when we declare our intention to quit smoking pot, or let go of promiscuity, or stop working late on Thursday night so we can go to meditation class, almost immediately we receive a flurry of invitations to a big party where there is guaranteed to be "the best Columbian," or we hear from the guy we met last year who was living with someone, but now he just broke up with his girlfriend, or the boss calls us into his office to ask the special favor of working overtime this Thursday night. Such a time is a trying and challenging period for the spiritual aspirant, for it seems as if "I'll never get rid of my negative past."

But this is exactly the time to push on with determination. Such a period of facing the unwanted past is a time of *testing*, and the way to pass the tests is to realize that we really can have the future for which we yearn, if we just put up with this "return mail" for a while. As we begin to see these trials for what they are, they become much more bearable and more quickly and easily overcome. Such challenges are golden opportunities to become strong by mobilizing faith, firmly planting our feet on solid spiritual ground, and making a dynamic stand for the Truth. These tests are, in fact, gifts from God, and if we know how to handle them properly, the energy we gain from overcoming them will catapult us into exhilirating spiritual freedom.

Let's take a deeper look at the dynamics of facing our past masterfully. Every thought we think, word we speak, and act we do creates reactions in the universe, like ripples emanating from a stone thrown into the center of a calm lake, ripples that eventually return to us in the form of waves — motions that *we* have created. We can be assured that every stone we have thrown will create waves; just because we haven't felt the waves yet doesn't mean that the stone just plunked in the water and nothing happened; it means that the waves haven't arrived *yet*. So we shouldn't be surprised when an old stone that we cast long ago comes back to affect us weeks, years, or lifetimes later; that's the law of physics, *karma*, and the entire universe.

Now imagine that you're getting tired of being sprayed (maybe drenched) by waves, and you start to see there is a relationship between your throwing heavy stones and your getting wet. So you decide not to throw any more boulders, which is a right decision. That will keep you from creating any new deluges, but it will not stop the waves that are already in motion from the stones you cast in the past.

That's exactly what the unwanted invitations to pot parties, old boyfriends, and working overtime are: waves that we have created, now breaking on the shore of our experience. This is actually cause for rejoicing, for *the waves disappear after they break on the shore*, and we are free of them. Then we can enjoy the picturesque patterns of ripples from the kind of stones we *choose* to cast, along with the cool water lapping over our feet at sunset. This is why it is of the *utmost importance not to despair* or say, "Well, it looks like I'll never be rid of that scene, so I might as well go along with it." We *will* be free of it — as long as we do not throw any new boulders.

Let's consider a very practical example: relationships. "Relationships" is a subject on the syllabus of the course called "Growing Through Life," on which most of us have been tested. Sometimes we have passed, and sometimes we have failed, but always we have learned. There was a time in my life when I was going out with several different women at one time. One of my college professors called this "multiple meaningful relationships." Whatever we call it, it was not long before I realized that all I was creating was multiple meaningful difficulties. One day I awoke to the fact that in these diluted relationships I was not really serving myself or any of these women, and it became clear to me that I would have to settle down.

So I made up my mind to commit myself to working sincerely on one relationship. As I did so, I knew that I had made the correct decision, for my emotions and my relationship and my life began to feel very clean, clear, and light. Ah! but just because I quit throwing many stones did not mean that I could escape the waves created by the stones

I had already cast. All at once I began to receive letters and phone calls from women I had met in the past, women with whom I had had some kind of flirtation, even very subtle, like, "If you're ever in New Jersey, say hello," or "Gee, you have nice eyes," or "If you ever break up with your boyfriend, look me up." (The last one's not so subtle, I guess.) As this flurry of old karma began to roll my way, I realized all too clearly that every action we generate in the universe is answered by an equal and opposite reaction. I felt like a racquetball player who had paddled out a lot of wild shots in a small court with no way for the balls to fly but back to where they were hit.

So I had to field them. I had to face every little flirtation I had initiated. I had started something, and I had to finish it out in the best way I could. Figuring out how to handle each situation was a tough one for me; I had to work each relationship out individually. Sometimes it meant accepting the invitation to come over and listen to some music, and then saying "Good night" after the last chord; sometimes it meant sitting down with the person and really sharing our honest feelings with each other until we had transformed our separateness into a holy communion of souls; and sometimes it required a firm "No, thank you — I'm not going to pot parties these days."

I discovered that there was no one way out; all I knew was that I wanted out, and because I was sincere in my aspiration, God told me what to say and do in each particular circumstance, a right action that was good for everyone involved. That's the miracle of God's compassion: we can really mess up, but if we sincerely resolve that we want a better life, He is right there with just the helping hand we need. Thank you, God.

Eventually my aspiration for a new way of relating to others became a reality. It didn't come easily and it didn't come immediately, but it came, and my life is the richer for it. *Patience*, I have found, is a key ingredient in this game. We get a taste of the Truth and we want to be liberated immediately, which is great, but we have to work within the flow of the universe. We can burn ourselves out if we try to change too quickly. I heard of one young man who literally killed himself from following too strict a spiritual regimen. This was not necessary, and neither was it spiritual. We have to trust that God will hear our prayer for change, and She will help us with it as fast as we can go. We just need to know that once we make up our mind about what we want for ourselves, it will come — It has to.

This brings us to the importance of forgiveness. We have to know that no matter how sordid or evil are the things that we have done, even if it seems that our whole life up to now has been one big mistake, God is willing to forgive us. Condemnation is not an idea from God — it is an invention of the human mind. God is willing to forgive *anything*. Some of the most saintly, holy people I know have been prostitutes, alcoholics, thieves, and outright arrogant sinners (you see the kind of crowd I hang out with — and I count myself among them). But all of our pasts are completely meaningless now. It is as if the light of God's forgiving love has dried up the old scabs and replaced them with brand new baby-like skin. As I get to know more and more beautiful people in the spiritual domain, I see that hardly any of them, like myself, are without some kind of worldly taint in their past. But, ah, though the world may record error, the soul stands ever shining and brilliant as the day it was breathed forth from God with Her commitment to love us forever, no matter what. No matter what.

I want to explain now why I don't believe in eternal damnation. First of all, nothing in the universe is eternal except God. As King Solomon taught, "This, too, shall pass." Everything comes and goes; all the things that I thought would last forever — my first girlfriend, the Yankees winning the World Series every year, my last girlfriend — all turned out to be temporary. The only thing that really endures is God, which is a pretty good deal because if I had to make a choice between my past being eternal or God's forgiveness being eternal, God is the winner by a huge margin.

Second, I can't imagine God allowing any of His Beloved Children (you and me and all of us), *created in His image and likeness*, to suffer everlasting pain. That means that God would breathe life and love into part of Himself and then condemn it to endless torment. That just doesn't make sense to me. What God would create a child that had to suffer through eternity? I believe God is smarter than that. I believe He knows His business, and He allows us only as much pain as we have brought upon ourselves to learn a lesson. The purpose of painful lessons is to guide us home to know the joy of spiritual freedom, to learn that pain is not necessary or even real. Once the lesson is learned, there is *absolutely no purpose* to further hardship. We may go through hellish experiences, but so far none of them have lasted forever, and I don't think pain will suddenly become eternal now. As Ram Dass says, "While you're going through travail it may seem like it will never end,

but it will; you just went through eternal damnation for a little while."
God is not a sadist. Even the meanest school teacher in the world would
not keep a child after school forever. The teacher wants to get home
and have dinner, and that's the end of the game. God may sometimes
be tough, but He's not mean.

Any God that is genius enough to create a miracle-filled universe
must be clever and loving enough not to throw part of Himself into
hell forever. To the contrary, it seems only fitting that such a magnificent mind would recreate Himself in the form of children who could
share His eternal joy. I mean, if you were God (which we are, created
in His likeness), and you could create anything you wanted (which we
can, through God's infinite energy), wouldn't you create something
dynamically heavenly? I think so. If we earthlings would want to create
something that beautiful, just think how much more glorious must be
the designs of the Father of the Universe, the Lord of All Creation, The
King of the Cosmos? I tell you, His plan is a real hum-dinger, one that
even Steven Spielberg would approve.

We need to quit whipping ourselves — or believing that we deserve
to be whipped — and start to say "Yes!" to a great big idea of
forgiveness, bigger perhaps than we were taught as children. We are
like people who have been imprisoned for so long that we don't even
believe that freedom exists. When the Children of Israel were presented
with their freedom from bondage in Egypt, a lot of them didn't know
what to do with it; some of them even wanted to stay in Egypt, for
the life of slavery was familiar and ironically more comfortable than
their newfound freedom. But that won't really do. We have to accept
our freedom. We have to march out of Egypt. We have to cross the
Red Sea. We have to enter the Promised Land. Even if the waters seem
high now, it might be a good idea to keep our seats until the last frame
of the movie; you never know — something very interesting could happen when we reach the shore.

Our past does *not* have to haunt us forever. If we just put up with
it for a while, the old patterns will wear themselves out for lack of repetition to sustain them. We must bless every opportunity to say "No!"
to an old, unwanted pattern, for every "No!" to the old is a "Yes!" to
the new. We sowed many seeds, some of them flowers and some of
them weeds. Even if we do not plant any more weeds, we must wait
for the old weed seeds to sprout before we can uproot them. That's

why we have to be joyfully persistent in working toward our new ideals and leaving the old behind. Sometimes it takes just one good "No!" and sometimes it takes a hundred, but always the past must yield to a new and freer life.

Our history is not our destiny. I know God wants more for me than I used to want for myself. If my past ever starts to get me down, I just think of how good it would be if my desired future were real, and that vision gives me the confidence to persist until God triumphs.

Flowing Robes and Flannel Shirts

'Tis a gift to be simple, 'tis a gift to be free.
                                                    — Shaker hymn

I met Susan on a weekend retreat in the mountains of Pennsylvania. She came over to the dining room table where I was sitting and asked if she could attend my yoga class with an injured knee. As we sat and talked before a great picture window looking onto the glorious autumn forest, I began to feel that our meeting was planned, destined by a design grander than I could explain. As I close my eyes now, I can so warmly feel the perfection of that scene, the morning sunlight dancing off Susan's face like sparkling angels playing on a mountain lake. Though I had just met her, I knew that Susan believed in God and in goodness and in healing, and I understood, too, that this was her moment. We placed our hands on her knee and as we did, both of us felt waves of healing energy streaming through our hands and her leg. It was one of the golden moments when life is lifted to its highest possibilities, and the reality of God is so obvious that you wonder how you ever could have forgotten it.

After the weekend, Susan and I began to correspond with one another. She would write of how her knee was improving and she told me of her life, her enthusiasms, her trials, and the peaks and valleys of her journey through personal growth. I returned with similar notes, offering suggestions for how she might deal with her challenges. We developed a nice friendship, getting to know one another as sort of spiritual pen-pals.

When I next saw Susan at a later retreat, something was not right. I could tell that she was feeling out of balance, and when I asked her about it she recoiled, unwilling to discuss what was bothering her. I tried to give her space to work out whatever she was going through, but the awkwardness of our communication was too weighty for me to ignore. (There is a story about a family who finds a bleeding

59

rhinoceros head on their table just before a dinner party, and they do not know what to do about it, so they decide to just leave it there, say nothing about it, and hope their guests will not notice it.) In our next group meeting I had to ask Susan what was bothering her.

"Well, to tell you the truth," she explained, "I've been having some hassles with my family, but I didn't want to tell you because I was afraid you would think I am not spiritual."

That really startled me. "But why?" I needed to know.

"Because I have this image of you as this really high, pure, spiritual teacher, and I felt that you might be put off by the worldliness of my problems."

When Susan said that, I began to get this empty, queezy feeling in the pit of my stomach, the kind you feel when you think you got an "A" on an exam and it comes back with a "45" on it. I felt that I had really missed the mark somewhere — and I had. That moment I realized that it was not just Susan's problem that she perceived me that way, but on some level I had fostered or encouraged that image of me. I saw that there was a part of me that wanted to be seen or known as some great, wise, all-knowing, transcendental, mystical Guru with all the answers for his many disciples. When I realized the effect that my liking that image had on my relationship with Susan, I felt like I had not only missed the mark, but the whole target as well.

I realized that I had allowed my relationship with Susan to fall into a phony pattern created by an idea of her as a questioning aspirant and me as an answering teacher. Patterns and games in our relationships are very easy, for they allow our roles to be well-defined and we are not required to deal with change or face our inner tender spots. But the awful price we pay is that we give up our aliveness and our genuineness, and we remain stuck in little narrow labyrinths like rats in a maze who get a little nibble of processed *Velveeta* at the dead end of each corridor, but remain starving for the real big cheese just on the other side of the wall that we are afraid to climb over. That's exactly the way I felt with Susan, like I had sold my soul for a pasted guru's beard and rented robes. It felt cheap and empty and I knew I didn't want it.

When I thought about how I really *did* want to relate to Susan, it was to be a friend, someone with whom she could feel comfortable and easy. I didn't want to be a guru sermonizing to her from behind a mahogany lectern, but someone who she could trust not to judge her. This led me to the self-discovery that I want to be an available and reachable person, without any false facades to distort the truth of our mutual holiness. I want to have no pretenses with you, for your love is very precious to me and your trust is infinitely more important to me than any image that would make me seem to be something I am not.

Susan's honesty in sharing her feelings helped me to become aware that I do not want to have to have all the answers all the time for everyone else; before I can even begin to serve another, I must find the light within myself. I want the freedom to grow, to change, not to be the same person I was yesterday, to be richly human. I would rather be a happy nobody than a miserable somebody. If I try to be a Ram Dass or Hilda or Swami Satchidananda, I am untrue to myself; the only way to fulfill my destiny is to be *me*. As I began to hear the melody of my own song, I knew that is exactly the one that God wants me to sing.

And wow, did that awareness feel good! As I readjusted who I could allow myself to be, I felt so light and happy, as if I had been relieved of a heavy burden — one of my own making. The priest's robe and collar that I had chosen were not made of cloth, but of binding steel, and letting go of them allowed me to be reborn as an innocent child. I traded in my rented robes for a flannel shirt and blue jeans, and replaced my congregation with a family of brothers and sisters. It was like walking out of a self-created prison into a verdant, fragrant meadow. It was discovering the freedom that I had never lost, only covered over and temporarily forgotten. It was coming home.

This realization led in turn to another: In my wanting to be Susan's teacher in that way, I was not only limiting myself, but also doing her an equally harmful disservice. I was demeaning her wholeness as a rich, complete person. In order for me to be above her, she had to be below me, and that is like robbing her Godhood from her, denying that she has a direct and complete connection with God through her very own heart. And in her willingness to have me as a guru, she lessened herself. As psychologist Sheldon Kopp says, "If you want someone else to be your guru, look again — you have diminished yourself." Because we are all one, when we cheat ourselves, we cheat all of us.

Then I understood why Ram Dass has called his recent lecture series "Nothing New from Nobody Special." For many years Ram Dass had an image of being a guru, a folk hero, a wise man. That's a horrible mold for a human being to live up to, for it creates an irreconcilable separation with everyone else, who automatically becomes an un-hero. The only way the game works in the long run is if we all get to be everything. We must all be equally heroes and sinners, gurus and disciples, teachers and students. If we lean too far in one direction, we tip the scales and throw our organism off kilter. Then we have to swing the other way to balance things out. That's why Ram Dass now has to be "Nobody Special" — because for a long time he was "Somebody Special." After all of the images are reconciled, all he will be is *free*, which he, like the rest of us, already is.

This is the keynote of this bright New Age that is dawning. We are all going to be each other's teachers — indeed we already are. All of us are going to be equally gurus and non-gurus. We must learn to recognize love in *all* of its forms. I believe that the days of turned-up collars and ochre robes and special seats in the synagogue are merging into a unity that honors *everyone* as holy. Those marks of reverence are expanding to include rolled-up sleeves and solar-heated homes and prayer meetings in which we all take turns reading from and explaining the holy books. No longer shall we blaspheme our real identity by looking to wise men for direction, but we shall all know that there is one Guru — the living God — who is willing to quicken the hearts and speak through the lips of all who dedicate themselves to the Light. While many today call themselves "guru," there is one sure way to distinguish the real ones from the charlatans: the real gurus say, "Be your own Guru, for God lives within you as you."

My own experience is the only subject on which I can write with honesty. As I now consider how free it felt to shed my robes and don my flannel shirt for the sake of healing my friendship with Susan, I remember a picture I saw in a high school English book, captioned, *"Mahatma Gandhi's possessions at the time of his death."* There was a Bible, a pair of sandals, and eyeglasses. That was all. This man who led an entire nation to freedom did so on the strength of truth and simplicity alone. He won the hearts of even his staunchest opponents, who had to respect him because he depended solely on God. It seems to me that if one man such as Gandhi can conquer life without any pretenses, so can anyone. If we can just trust God enough to let go of who we think we have to be before we can be ourselves, we will find that the greatest gift that God has given us is who we already are.

Tough Love
(Ruthless Compassion)

Sometimes, kids, it's cruel to be kind, and sometimes
it's kind to be cruel. You have to know which is which.
— Hilda

One day in the supermarket I saw a friend of mine who had been having a hard time with her sixteen-year-old daughter. The girl was acting impudent, undisciplined, and spending a lot of time with a group of kids who were getting into trouble. "How is your daughter doing, Mrs. Dougherty?" I inquired.

"Oh, I must tell you what has happened," she offered. "Things have changed dramatically! My husband and I read a book called *Tough Love*, in which the author explains that a firm, consistent policy of discipline is sometimes the most loving gift a parent can offer a child. So now we have set limits on what she can do, and no matter how much she hoots or hollers or tells us she hates us, we hold our ground. And do you know what? It's working! I don't know why we didn't do this from the start!"

Tough love. God is the toughest lover of all. We may be tempted to rail against God when we feel that the universe has dealt us an unjust blow, but the trying times are the very moments when God is giving us the grace of learning how to return to the Home against which we have turned our back. The prodigal son wandered off into the far country, only to be forced back home by a famine which fell upon the land. Had the famine not come, he might have continued to wander in vain. The famine was cruel, yet mercifully kind.

I learned about tough love when I was in a relationship with a woman, a relationship in which I felt very attached and needy. It seemed that when she was affectionate to me I felt good, and when she acted cold I felt hurt. My happiness was almost completely dependent on the way she acted toward me. It was a fool's happiness; I had given her power over my peace of mind, a surrender which is never justified.

63

I remember several occasions when we were deciding whether or not to go our separate ways (a decision we made every few weeks). It was as if my soul had a choice: I could either let go or keep clinging. A still, small voice within me whispered, "It's O.K. to let go," while a thunderous band of roving desires shouted, "You must hang on!" When we would decide to stay together I got a rush of happiness, but it was empty, like a compulsive gambler who hits on a winning number but knows that it will not be long before he is again at the mercy of the loan sharks. The most honest thing I felt was not that I wanted to be with her, but that I was afraid not to be with her. I was just postponing the pain of separating that I anticipated, which is a pretty flimsy foundation upon which to build a human relationship.

When we finally did part, my experience was the exact reverse of my clinging: it hurt on the outside, but deep within me I knew that this particular relationship was not right from the start, and this ending was the best thing that could have happened to me. Looking back now, I see that the promptings of my soul were true. Tough love.

Tough love is what is required to break a habit that is working against our highest interests. When we do not take the proper steps that lead us up the path of our personal good, God steps in and says, "Let me handle this for you!" Like an alcoholic who takes "just one more for the road," we only strengthen our bondage by fulfilling desires that drag us into further hardship. Then God, or life, or the universe — whatever we prefer to call it — sooner or later turns us around by *not* giving us what we *think* we want, but what we *need*. Ken Keyes, author of the beautiful *Handbook to Higher Consciousness**, describes it this way: "When you have an addiction (any emotion-backed desire) and you satisfy it, you are not solving anything; you are only setting yourself up for the next problem." As the Rolling Stones put it, "You can't always get what you want, but if you try sometimes you just might find that you get what you need."

A good example of this principle is my friend Preston, who was extremely anxious about his job. He developed an ulcer, he could hardly sleep at night, and his uptightness began to be a hassle for his family and friends. He did not even really like the work; his inner self was

---

*Ken Keyes, Jr., *Handbook to Higher Consciousness*, Living Love Books, 1975.

longing to work in some kind of service or healing profession. But fear kept him clinging tenaciously to this job, at no matter what cost. Then, by God's Grace, he was fired. Preston went through some emotional turbulence for a little while and then, after he had gotten back on his feet, he went out and studied *shiatsu* — oriental massage therapy. At the age of thirty he went back to school, took the necessary coursework, and now he is a very satisfied and successful *shiatsu* therapist. Last week he told me, "I thank God every day that I was fired from that job. God took care of what I didn't have the guts to do. It was the best thing that ever happened to me."

We do not have to get fired, divorced, or ill to experience the grace of God's tough love. He is very happy to shake us up where we are, in the little experiences of everyday life. The universe is designed to support whatever harmonizes with it, and straighten out whoever is out of the flow. When I was in college I had a mad desire to buy a red Mustang GT fastback, which I went out and did — with money I didn't have. The purpose of the car was 10% transportation and 90% prestige; I just wanted people (namely female people) to see me driving around in it. I customized it, polished it, and purposely ran down six flights of stairs to move it to the spot in front of the dormitory where everyone could see it. You might say I was attached to it.

About a month after I bought the car I drove it to Boston to visit a friend for a weekend. When I went to "peel out" on Sunday afternoon, valise in hand, the car wasn't there. I must have paced up and down that street twenty times, my jaw dropping farther with each frantic step. But it wasn't there. Three days later my friend called and told me the Boston Police had found it in a run-down section of town. "Don't even bother to come and look at it," he told me, "unless you like looking at empty Ford chassis." My flashy car was stripped bare.

I am starting to see that this is what much of life is about — teaching us to get back to what we really need, instead of what we *think* we need. The hardships of life are God's way of stripping away our frivolous accessories until we are satisfied with the basic model, which is pretty much the way God wants us, for the sake of our own happiness. As the Talmudic sages remind us, we come into this world naked and we leave it naked, and everything else in between is excess baggage, most of which we would be better off without. It's as if God is always inviting us to return to the Garden of Eden, but in order to enter we have to slip through a narrow gate which will not allow for any extras. Sooner or later we realize that the no-frills brand is pretty much the same as the fancy-labeled product; when we go for the flashy items, we pay more for the name and the packaging. Deluded into thinking that we really *need* our new stereo, or our special meditation cushion, or nuclear power, we try to convince ourselves and God that we can bring our entourage into the Garden if we just slip in sideways or twist the scriptures slightly. When that doesn't work, we may try to sneak in by disguising ourselves as someone else, or by walking in backwards, or like Wile E. Coyote endlessly chasing Road Runner, we devise elaborate devices to catapult us over the Garden hedges. But when the smoke has cleared, there we sit, chin in hand, no closer to Heaven than we were before. The only way to do it is to really do it — no compromises, no plea bargaining, no "twofers." The world, life, and the universe are sometimes so tough because part of their purpose is to sandpaper our rough edges, to trim down that spiritual cellulite that stops us from fitting through the gate. All of our trials, disillusionments, and sufferings are part of a universal plot of great Love to slim down our metaphysical chubbiness, to get us into divine shape in a great reducing plan that makes Jack La Lanne's seem like kindergarten by comparison.

That's where discipline comes in. The rule of the Cosmic Spa membership is very simple: If we don't get our act together for ourselves, God will do everything in His power (and that's a lot of power) to do it for us. There's no way to escape life without learning some discipline. That's a rough one for those of us who grew up in the free fifties and the swinging sixties. I personally did not know what discipline was until I was fifteen years old, when my tenth-grade gym teacher told me that my push-ups were not much more than symbolic dips, and I had better shape up. For the first time I had some inkling that if I didn't toe the line, I'd have to pay the piper. Then I got to see that if you don't pay the piper when he presents his bill, you have to pay later — with interest.

Hilda, in her own inimitable way, taught us this lesson one holiday weekend when I and several families were together. A couple of little children began running through the gathering of adults, making a lot of disruptive noise. "Children!" Hilda reprimanded, "You must not run and shout like that in here . . . You may sit nicely with us if you like, or go into your room and play, but this is a quiet area for now." As the kids left the room, Hilda explained to us, "You must train the children at an early age, or else you will have big problems later . . . You don't want them to grow up like you, do you?"

We all had to laugh; we knew exactly what Hilda was talking about. Many of us were raised in the age of permissiveness, when there was a popular idea that if you just let kids do what they felt like doing, they would eventually turn out O.K. Well, somehow many of us made it, but I have a feeling it was not by method, but Grace. I can think of too many instances (such as when I got caught walking out of an Arab hotel with one of their towels, and the manager started to call the police on Alan *Cohen*) that I was saved by a higher power than I knew. As Hilda has said, "I'll bet your guardian angels must have grey hair by now!"

We can save our guardian angels — and ourselves — some trouble by appreciating the value of tough love and applying it to ourselves before God has to. The miracle of discipline is that it really is good for us, and it feels good, and it works. I know that when I get into a routine of doing yoga or jogging regularly, I realize how positively it carries me through my entire day, and I really enjoy keeping with it. Self-mastery is absolutely necessary for any kind of success in life. Without discipline, self-control, and self-responsibility we are, to put it in the vernacular, *blobs*. Every great artist, musician, or athlete has gotten where he or she is only through long, arduous hours of practice. (As one insightful thinker has put it, "Success is 10% inspiration and 90% *perspiration*.") It is a pipe dream to imagine that greatness floats to us as a gift from the air. We have to earn it. I saw a beautiful poster of a charming ballerina in an exquisitely graceful pose, the kind that bore the mark of years of dedicated practice. The caption of the photo was, "*Greatness is born of the marriage of skill and inspiration.*" God plants within us the seeds of talent, but it is up to us to train our mind, body and emotions to be worthy vessels through which He can pour inspiration into expression. Only after we have brought our instrument into fine tuning and mastered the difficult sections of the symphony can God whisper to us the phrasing that brings the audience to tears.

This is the formula for unified godliness in action. Our Heavenly Father created us to know the majestic wonders that life lives to teach us, but Truth can offer us only as much awakening as we are strong enough to accept. The moments of newfound freedom are made even more precious by the rigor and perseverence that brought us to them.

RISING IN LOVE

A mountain lake at sunset is a picture of gentle tranquility, yet its gift of peace is indebted to the strength of the mountains that give it form. Sometimes love is gentle and sometimes love is, of necessity, tough. In the end, love must be everything, else love it would not be. Perhaps the realization that love can take the form of an unflinching disciplinarian is exactly the awareness we need to carry us through the hard times when it seems that love has abandoned us. Tough love is a gift from God that makes us who we want to be, but have not yet become because we thought we were less than we are. The truth of growth through challenge is the answer that makes whole our understanding that we chose to come to this rich, wondrous, and awesome planet certainly to love, and necessarily to learn.

Living In Light

Going For It

Only those who risk going too far can possibly find out how far one can go.

— T.S. Elliot

"Who do you think we can get to serve as the master of ceremonies for our dance recital?" asked Hilda's friend as the two pondered in an artfully decorated studio sometime in the 1940's.

"How about Ingrid Bergman?" Hilda replied.

"Ingrid Bergman?! Don't be silly . . . She's the hottest star in Hollywood! . . . Why should *she* want to come to *our* amateur production?"

"Why shouldn't she? . . . She might say 'Yes,' you know . . . It can't hurt to ask!"

"Well, alright," agreed Hilda's colleague. "If you want to try, go right ahead."

So Hilda went right ahead, and (as you may have guessed) when Hilda went on stage for her recital that night, she was introduced by: Miss Ingrid Bergman.

Yes, it can't hurt to ask. We miss out on much of what life has to offer, not because the things we long for are unattainable, but because we do not ask for them. Our problem is not that God withholds from us what we desire, but that we do not really expect Him to give it. Our growing into greatness is not a matter of rearranging the world around us, but of expanding the magnitude of our expectations to embrace the thrill of the possible. The road to freedom is paved with the anticipation of the miraculous.

One night Hilda told us, "God does not limit you; *you* limit *God*." That really hit home with me. It means that all of the boxes that we may feel restricted by — money, age, health, work, people — are not imposed by God, but by our thinking in terms of lack. This is a

71

stunning realization, for with the understanding that we have bound ourselves comes the awakening that it is *we* who can free ourselves. We can quit thinking of ourselves as human, and start knowing ourselves as Divine.

I have discovered a way of breaking out of self-imposed molds. Whenever I have tried this experiment, it has changed my outlook on my life, and I would like to share it with you. The method is to:

GO FOR THE BEST.

Going for the best means to aim for what you really want, including — and especially — trying to do things that you think there's no way in the world you can do. For example: send an application for the job that only one woman in a hundred will get; call up the most beautiful girl in the class for a date; invite Ingrid Bergman (or, these days, let's say Olivia Newton-John or Robert Redford) to your variety show benefit. Imagine that anything is possible, and make a game of seeing how far you can go. The secret of the game is that we can go as far as God can go, and how far that is, is up to us to discover. There may be no way in the world you can do it — but there may be a way in God. Jesus said, *"In the world you shall have tribulation, but be of good cheer, for I have overcome the world."*

Success in life is purely a matter of *Intention*, a principal which very few people know how to make work for them. The Law of Intension is:

WE GET WHAT WE WANT.

Now you may answer, "Well, there are plenty of things that I want, but I haven't gotten them!" If, however, you are willing to examine your intentions clearly, you may discover that on some level there is a place in you that does not want it one hundred percent. Perhaps there is a part of you that is not sure if you really want it, or if you deserve it, or if you are ready for it. Or maybe there is something else you want more, and you feel you have to make a choice. Or perhaps you just don't believe it is possible. Whatever the reason for the roadblock, you and I are not victims of the fickle finger of fate. Each of us has meticulously chosen the story of our life. Our awakening to the reality of such responsibility is the dawn of making sense of turbulent experiences.

If we want to know what we really want in life, all we need to do is *look at what we are getting.* We can use our life as a mirror to see what our intentions actually are. Let's take an illustration. My friend Ron Young was in the process of producing his inspiring album *Love's Land,* when he ran short of funds. The record was nearly complete, but he needed several thousand dollars more to finish it, and the money was not coming. What to do?

Because Ron realized that what was happening "out there" was simply a reflection of a *spiritual* situation *within* himself, he decided to take an honest look at what was standing in the way of his album coming together. So he sat down and resolved to face the only person who could answer his question: *himself.* And what an important encounter it was!

"I realized that the album was not being completed because I had some doubts about it," Ron told me in his apartment late one evening. "In a strange sort of way, I was afraid to put myself out there, as if I could not see myself succeeding. It was something like facing my own self growing up, changing, coming into my own. Oddly enough, I had hesitations about it, as if staying the same was more comfortable, safer.

"Then I asked myself this question: 'Do I choose for this album to come out, or don't I? It has to be 100% 'Yes' or 100% 'No'; no in-betweens; no compromises; no mugwumps*. Either I go full force ahead on producing it, or I completely scrap it right now. What do I decide?'

"Then I decided it had to be 'Yes' — It just had to. There could be no turning back because of fear or insecurity; I could not live my life in a childhood pattern just because it seemed safe. I had to go ahead. I had no idea where the money would come from, but I knew that if I declared my intention before God, it would come.

"The next morning when I went to work, one of my first clients asked me, 'Say, Ron, do you need any money for anything?'

" 'Funny you should ask! . . . My record needs a little more green energy to carry it over the hill. Why do you ask?'

" 'The other night I had a dream in which the numbers "1" and "7"

---

*mugwump: a person who sits with his mug on one side of the fence, and his wump on the other.

came to me very clearly. It was the kind of dream that was so real that I felt I had to do something about it. So this weekend I went to Atlantic City and played those numbers at the casino. Would you like to see what happened?'

" 'Sure would.'

"The man reached into his back pocket and took out his wallet, bulging at the seams. To my astonishment, he showed me twenty thousand dollars in cash! Then, right on the spot, he loaned me three thousand dollars at very low interest. *Love's Land* came out a few weeks later."

Ron's story presents us with the compelling teaching that he *attracted* that money to him by *affirming his intention* to complete that album. That completion came about only after Ron's decision was gelled within himself. Thoughts need thinkers to bring them to earth. Manifestation is in direct proportion to our concentration. God responds to "sort of" prayers with "sort of" answers. As one tongue-in-cheek philosopher put it, you can't be "sort of pregnant." Either you are, or you aren't. As Tom Wolfe coined the notion in *The Electric Kool-Aid Acid Test*, "You're either on the bus or you're off the bus." You're either on your way to your destination or you're standing on the corner. That's the point of Ron's story, this chapter, and the whole of life. The essential element of prayer and intention is *whole-heartedness*. If we pray or live half-heartedly, we will get half a result, which is the predicament in which most persons find their lives: half-here, and half-there. Such a way of living cannot lead to success, for as we are told in the Bible, "God spews the luke-warm out of his mouth." Hilda often says that it is better to be a whole something than a half-nothing. "Even if you're a rotter, kids, be the best rotter there ever was. If you go wrong, at least go wrong with a whole heart . . . Then when you come home to God, you will come home with a whole heart." Jesus gave the disciples the test of the parable of the two sons: "One said 'Yes' to his father and then did not do what he was asked; the other said 'No,' and later changed his mind and did his father's bidding. Which son did what his father wanted? The one who said 'No' and later turned about. This is why prostitutes and thieves were among Jesus' closest disciples. They were not luke-warm in their lives. They were whole-hearted in their sin, and when they discovered God, they were whole-hearted in their love for Him.

This brings us to the second leg of the Law of Intention:

YOU DON'T HAVE TO KNOW HOW TO GET WHAT YOU WANT; ALL YOU NEED TO KNOW IS *WHAT* YOU WANT.

This is a subtle but paramountly important and exciting key to personal success. It means that there is much more to the universe than we have believed, and if we really expect to realize our dreams, we must allow God to deliver our blessings to us in ways deeper than we can plan or understand. There is an old saying that "The Lord moves in mysterious ways," and this is surely true. God is like the driver of a universal Greyhound bus. Once we have decided where we want to go, we can "sit back and leave the driving to Him." If we would just choose a nice window seat and relax, we would find ourselves at our destination in no time. Instead, we make it hard for ourselves because first of all we are not sure which bus to get on; we vascillate at the ticket counter, mulling indecisively over a number of possible destinations. The agent can't sell us a ticket if we don't tell him where we want to go. Then, once we've made our choice and we've stepped aboard the Greyhound to God, we immediately try to wrestle the wheel away from the Driver, insisting we know a better way. Then, even after we have surrendered the wheel and we arrive, we have a tendency to want to hide in the back of the bus, wondering if this is really where we want to go, and maybe we should turn back.

The good news is that we do not need to scheme and manipulate for our liberation. All we have to do is:

1. Declare our intention,
2. Accept opportunities when they come,
3. Work with responsibility and confidence.

We are all already liberated, and the game of life is a lesson in realizing that there is nothing we must do to be Divine. We just need to open up to the light within us. That is why Jesus said, *"Ask, and ye shall receive; seek, and ye shall find; knock, and it shall be opened unto you."* Whenever I have tested the truth of these promises, they have proven themselves to be genuine. If you would like to prove them for yourself, I encourage you to ask — really ask — for something that you deeply want. Think of some aspiration that would change your life remarkably for the better: to heal a troubled relationship; to quit smoking; to understand something about yourself that you would really like to know; ask for anything that is important to you. Then find and underline these two verses in the Bible: "*Ask, and ye shall receive . . .*" and "*Thus saith God: Try me and prove me.*" Then hold God to His promise. Dare Him to prove that He can help you. Don't stop at the Pepsi Challenge — Go all the way. If God is really God, He has to come through. If He can't cut it, no one can. But He will. He has to. God wants so much for His Children to believe in Him that he seizes every opportunity to answer a prayer. God is like the owner of a great estate whose children don't come home because they have been deluded into thinking that their father is a pauper, or even that he is dead. Then, when he gets a collect call from one of his children who has gotten into deep trouble, and is so desperate that she is even willing to give her long-lost father a try for help, the father is overjoyed to do all he can to demonstrate his existence and his love. He will even fly out to the coast to bring his ailing child back to her rightful home. That's how happy and willing our Heavenly Father is to answer our prayers.

After we have contacted our Father, we must give Him time and space to do what He needs to do to answer those prayers. Sometimes it takes a while to get that flight to the coast. If we trust in Him, God will work out our help in just the right way, in just the right timing. It usually doesn't work to pressure God and try to force Him to answer a prayer by next Tuesday afternoon. If it really needs to be done by then, it will. If not, there is a reason, and we can afford to wait. If we feel frustrated about God's delay in answering a prayer, it is not a matter of God's ineptitude, but our impatience. If God is wise enough to know how to answer our requests, He certainly knows when they need to be answered. Jesus assured us, "*Your Father knows what you need before you even ask.*"

This perspective lifts prayer into a new light of personal promise. It means that we don't have to yell and scream at God to get Him to hear us. Because He lives in our very hearts, He hears our whispers as clearly as our shouts. He will respond more readily to one sincere thought than to a long but empty tirade. God appreciates quality over quantity. If He already knows what we need, we can simply sit peacefully and enjoy communing with Him. Perhaps the most powerful prayers are "*Thank you,*" "*I am,*" and "*I love you.*"

There is one footnote on the Law of Intention that must be recorded here: the element of *Grace*. This means that sometimes we don't get what we want, not because God can't deliver it, but because it is really not in our best interest to get it. As a priest once posed to me, "Does God answer *all* prayers? . . . Yes, He does," he explained, ". . . and sometimes the answer is 'No.' " This is not just an esoteric cop-out, but a very important principle to grasp, as it actually underscores the reality of the Law of Intention. It means that the level at which the request was made was not on a soul level, but on a desire or surface personality level, which is not congruent with the deep subconscious choice of the inner person, the soul. In other words, it is our *inner* self that actually decides (perhaps even before we were born) what we want and need in life, and the intention of the soul is so strong that little passing desires cannot supercede the soul's decision. For example, let's say that before you were born your soul (you) chose a life of service to humanity. Then when you get to high school you become influenced by rock music and for a few months you hope and pray to become an electrified superstar. So you write a schmaltzy fan letter to Jerry Garcia, pleading for a job as a roadie for the Grateful Dead. Then, when you don't get the job, you feel hurt and disappointed and you say, "The Law of Intention is not true . . . I asked for something and I didn't get it . . . There must be no God!" Then, let's say, the only job you can get is that of an assistant in a law office where you become fascinated by the possibilities for social change through community organizing. So you decide to go to law school, after which you find the most fulfilling experience of your life in serving as an advocate for the poor or the handicapped or the hungry. Then you look back on your fleeting desire to work for the Grateful Dead and you say, "Thank God I didn't end up doing that!"

I learned this lesson for myself in an experience that was not quite as glamorous as working for the Grateful Dead, but which was very important to me. When I was ready to go to graduate school, I applied to eight clinical psychology programs and one for counseling and guidance. I was rejected by nearly all of the clinical schools and accepted by the counseling program, at Montclair State College. For reasons which I could not explain, I felt so deeply drawn to Montclair that I didn't even bother to pursue the clinical route. Though I had no idea what was to come, it was through this program that I eventually met Hilda and my new spiritual life. Now I thank God that I did not get into those other schools, for now I realize that they were not really rejections, but *course corrections*, the universe steering me in the direction of the highest good for my soul's chosen evolution. So, you see, while I didn't get what my mind wanted, I did receive what my soul wanted — and that is the only result that really counts.

There is one more facet of the Law of Intention, an idea so powerful that it has changed my entire perspective on what life is about. It is a concept so exciting that I wish every human being could feel the thrill of it as I do, for it has truly made my life new. It is a secret of living which has been shouted and proclaimed throughout the ages, but yet remains largely untapped because only a handful of saints, sages, prophets, and free thinkers have realized its import and put it into action. This principle contains the power to make a pauper into a king, the downtrodden into the triumphant, and the crippled straight. It is nothing less than a gift from God to His Children, given freely to remove our miseries and make us alive again. It is the very key to heaven. I am speaking of the power of

BELIEF.

It is written in the scriptures, *"As a man thinketh in his heart, so shall it be."* Contained in this jewel of truth is the answer to making our lives what we want them to be. It means that we can literally create our experience with our thoughts and, because our minds are intrinsically unified with God's, we can make anything happen. That's a pretty potent assertion. I mean, it's not exactly what we've been told on television commercials which admonish us that we can't afford to leave home without our American Express card. The power of God is far greater than that of a credit card, and if we are willing to hold our beliefs up to spiritual light, we will find a golden treasure — perhaps the brightest — in these ancient prophetic words.

Let me offer a practical example. A friend of mine needed to discuss her HBO bill with the cable TV office. For weeks she tried to get them on the phone, but every time she called, the line was busy. She told me, "I just know they take their phone off the hook; someone told me that's what they do; I bet I'll never get them!" Somehow I could not believe that a public business would take their phone off the hook for weeks, so I asked her if I could give it a try. The phone rang three times, and someone answered . . . because I believed they would.

When we discussed why she hadn't gotten through, we discovered an even deeper reason: *She didn't really want to talk to them.* She had to challenge them on a dispute over her bill, and she didn't like having to do that. In other words, it was not her *intention* to make contact with them, and so she *created*, or attracted that line being busy every time she called. *"As a man thinketh, so shall it be."*

We need, then, to start thinking in new ways. We must believe we can get what we really want in life. We must, as one poet put it, "hitch our wagon to a star." As I figure it, God wouldn't plant any aspirations in our souls unless He was prepared to bring them to life. We are asked in the Bible, "Would God bring to the point of birth, and then not deliver?" In other words, would God impregnate our mind and heart with dreams of a better life that could not come true? I don't believe God would do that. I can't imagine Him finding any value in frustrating His Children. But I can imagine Him taking great delight in seeding a shining vision in our heart, and then watching us grow in strength until we align our life with His great intention for us, so completing our journey into Light.

No longer need we settle for table scraps or, like the prodigal son, the leftovers from the pigs' slop. We spend minutes, days, even lifetimes agonizing over petty hurts, measely pennies, and cheap ambitions, when we could be laughing in our Father's Kingdom. How much of my life have I underestimated the potential that the universe has imbued within me and my fellows! While God has been living in my very heart, I have searched and schemed after foolish desires. And now I, like you and the entire community of the spirit, am ready to come home. I am ready to claim my right to live as a light-filled being of free spirit. I joyously accept my part of an evolutionary step being made by millions of souls who are prepared to openly declare that love, truth, and goodness are the sacred elements of our life, and these blessings are to be known on earth as it is in Heaven. We are ready to affirm that God will take care of us without war, without nuclear power, without windfall profits, without separate drinking fountains for blacks and whites, without radiated food, without maiming animals to produce cosmetics. We are ready to live without fear and competition and alienation. We are ready to go for it. We are ready to support one another and to respect the earth and the air and the heavens. We are ready to acknowledge the holiness of all the blessed creatures that share the universe with us, and to honor their right to live and breathe as we do. We are ready to go for a New Age on the planet earth, a long-awaited era of harmony, good will, and the joy of mutual support. We are ready to recognize the oneness and the common aspirations of all peoples of all colors, ages, and sexes, and to celebrate the greatness of humankind's new destiny. We are ready to go for it now. We are ready.

Seeing and Believing

Paint a picture . . . hold to your vision
. . . and walk into your garden
                    — *Love's Land*, Ron Young

The doctor leaned back in his padded wooden chair and tossed his pen onto the blotter. "I'm afraid there's not much more we can do for your cancer, Mrs. Newhouse," he solemnly stated. "We'll continue with the chemotherapy and radiation treatment and just hope for the best." That night Mrs. Newhouse sat on her bed, frustrated and depressed. "What good is it?" she frowned. "Even the doctors don't have any hope!"

Then, as she sat in the quiet of that crucial night, a warm feeling began to well up inside of her, like a glowing ember that refused to be extinguished. It was a sense that there *was* something more that could be done, something greater than medicine, something bigger than chemicals and doctors and prognoses. But what?

Into her mind flashed the thought of her son, Jack, who she knew had been involved for years with what he called "holistic health." Jack had studied meditation, become a vegetarian, and taken up a number of spiritual practices that Mrs. Newhouse had dismissed as fads lingering from the 1960's. But now she felt an urge to ask her son more about what he was doing.

"I'm so glad you asked, Mom," replied Jack. "There's an excellent book that I think can really help you." Mrs. Newhouse jotted down the title of the book and immediately got into her car and drove to the bookstore, where she found *The Silva Mind Control Method* almost jumping off the shelf toward her. She eagerly plunged into the book, finishing it in just a few sittings, absorbing as much as she could. The principles of the book were simple: We create our lives, including health and illness, with our thoughts. To be successful and fulfilled, we must learn to use our minds constructively, using clear, positive images as

81

building blocks. These mind pictures are absorbed into our subconscious, which in turn brings our new, uplifting thoughts into reality in the form of health, abundance, and peacefulness.

These principles seemed right to Mrs. Newhouse, somehow strangely familiar and comfortingly real. It was as if she already knew them, but had forgotten their truth. So Mrs. Newhouse began to practice the prescribed techniques. Every day for two sessions, one-half hour each, she would sit in a comfortable chair, relax, and visualize a bright light, something like a bolt of lightning flashing into the cancerous part of her body. Then she would visualize this light breaking up the cancerous cells, shattering them into thousands of tiny pieces. Again and again and again she practiced this picturing, until she saw her entire body as clear and whole and healthy.

Meanwhile, as the Law of Attraction would have it, Mrs. Newhouse was directed to another doctor who worked by the dynamic principles that she had discovered.

"It's very clear to me, Mrs. Newhouse," stated Dr. Holmes, "You can live and be healthy if that is what you choose. You must think positively and realize that there is a great Healer far more powerful than myself or any human being. If you attune your mind to this great healing energy, it will surely work for you."

This bright advice encouraged Mrs. Newhouse to continue even more enthusiastically with her visualization. Two weeks later she returned to the laboratory for x-rays. After completing the tests, the doctors walked out of the darkroom shaking their heads and checking the x-rays over and over and over again.

"We don't quite know how to explain this, Mrs. Newhouse," reported one of the medical team, "but your condition has improved considerably. As you can see on these x-rays, most of the cancerous cells have been broken apart, as if they have been *shattered*, and it looks like they are being expelled from your system!"

Mrs. Newhouse smiled and said a quiet prayer of thanks. Then she went home to visualize some more. Within a few months, Mrs. Newhouse was given a clean bill of health.*

---

*Hilda later explained that while the visualization was effective in this case, it is preferable to visualize only light and health, without giving any mental energy or reality to the negative situation, in this case, cancerous cells.

I would like to report a similar case which serves as an even more vivid demonstration of how the subconscious channels energy to create what it pictures. A young woman went to a healer for help for a condition of heavy acne. The healer picked up a magazine off a coffee table, thumbed through it, and carefully tore out a photograph of a glamorous model with a perfect "peaches and cream" complexion.

"Take this picture home and look at it for twenty minutes each day," prescribed the teacher. "Concentrate intently on it, as if you are looking in the mirror, and let the image of this lovely smooth skin be absorbed into your subconscious. You need to quit looking at your pimples and start appreciating your beauty!"

A week later the healer received another phone call from the young lady, now more distraught than before. "Something terrible has happened!" the girl exclaimed. "I must see you immediately!"

Within an hour the girl walked into the healer's apartment with a most unusual condition on her face. "Look!" she cried, "One side of my face has cleared up, but the other side still has pimples . . . I look even worse than before! How could this happen?!"

"Let me see that picture I gave you," requested the elder. As the girl took the photo out of her pocketbook, the answer became obvious: *The picture was a profile!* The girl had meditated on the image of one-half of a beautiful complexion, and because the subconscious absorbs and materializes exactly what it is given, half a clear complexion is exactly what she got.

To harness the great power of the creative subconscious mind to help us achieve our goals, we must understand how this magnificent, Divinely engineered machine works. It is a fascinating and marvelous tool, operating systematically on lawful principles, capable of making or breaking our life according to how we employ it. We can begin to take advantage of its treasures as we comprehend these basic ideas:

PRINCIPLES OF SUCCESSFUL LIVING

1. The life that God has given to us is entirely whole, complete, and perfect.

2. Our view of this perfect life depends on our thoughts, which filter reality into our perception of it.

3. If that filter is clear, like a clean, sharp lens, we experience and enjoy the perfection of life in its entirety.

4. If the filter is clogged by erroneous and negative thought patterns, the lens becomes distorted, and we see life as threatening, fearful, and bad.

5. This filtering takes place in the subconscious mind, below the level of our ordinary conscious awareness.

6. We can restore our vision of perfection by reprogramming the erroneous patterns and replacing them with positive, productive thoughts. The most direct and powerful way to accomplish this is:

VISUALIZATION	+	FEELING
Get a *clear mental picture* of what we want to be or accomplish,	then	*feel* as if it has *already come to pass.*

7. You and I can return to the perfect life that was intended for us through *positive thinking, seeing, feeling, speaking, and acting.*

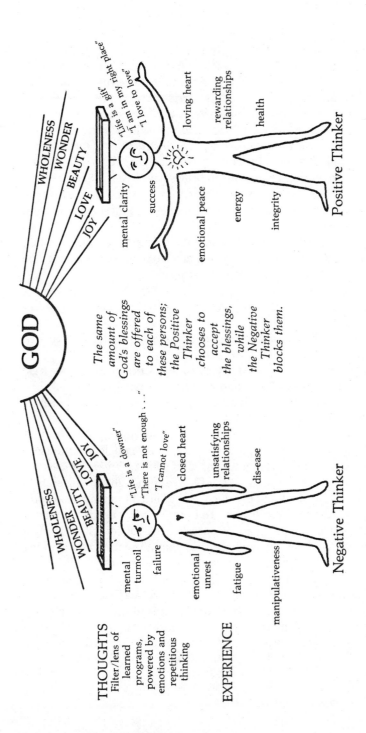

GOD

WHOLENESS
WONDER
BEAUTY
LOVE
JOY

WHOLENESS
WONDER
BEAUTY
LOVE
JOY

The same amount of God's blessings are offered to each of these persons; the Positive Thinker chooses to accept the blessings, while the Negative Thinker blocks them.

"Life is a gift"
"I am in my right place"
"I love to love"

loving heart
rewarding relationships
health

mental clarity
success
emotional peace
energy
integrity

Positive Thinker

"Life is a downer"
"There is not enough . . ."
"I cannot love"
closed heart

unsatisfying relationships
dis-ease

mental turmoil
failure
emotional unrest
fatigue
manipulativeness

Negative Thinker

THOUGHTS
Filter/lens of learned programs, powered by emotions and repetitious thinking

EXPERIENCE

HOW OUR THOUGHTS CREATE OUR EXPERIENCE

Abundant living is not a result of setting the world right, but *seeing* it *right.*

Let's look a little more deeply into the practical implications of these immensely important principles. As we can see from the story of the girl with acne, the subconscious is a powerful but *unbiased* computer that perfectly and literally carries out any program we feed into it, *even if the program is incorrect.* We have at our disposal an efficient, intelligently designed machine that will perform our every bidding, *even if we are unaware that the instructions it has received are not in our best interest.* This harsh but dynamic truth brings us to a crucial point: Because we human beings have free will and machines do not, it is *our responsibility* to *screen* and *critically evaluate* the programs we imbed in our creative mind, or else we must bear the brunt of faulty programming.

This eye-opening law was demonstrated to me by Susan Pitak, a hypnotherapist who received a complaint from one of her clients who had come to her to learn how to lose weight.

"I went home last week and practiced the methods you gave me," the lady reported, "but I ended up gaining ten pounds! What went wrong?!"

"Let's hear the relaxation suggestions you gave yourself," requested Susan.

"Well, I sat down, closed my eyes, and I began to tell my legs, 'You are getting heavier . . . and heavier . . . and heavier.' "

And so that is exactly what her legs got: heavier . . . and heavier . . . and heavier.

We have to be extremely careful of the words and pictures that we use; there is no such thing as an idle or meaningless expression. Because words contain the power of God ("*In the beginning was the Word, and the Word was with God*"), every thought we generate is registered in our subconscious which, as Dr. Eric Butterworth so aptly describes it, "cannot take a joke." In other words, even if we utter a phrase in jest or as a "figure of speech," the subconscious is busy recording what we say — simply because that is its job — and working toward materializing the idea it has "heard" us express.

This is the reason for the esoteric admonition to "*think and speak only those ideas which you want to see materialize.*" Conversely, this means that we do well to eliminate from our mental and oral vocabulary anything we do not want to see happen. Translated into practical terms, be careful to avoid phrases like, "If I have to go to that office one more time, I'll throw up!" or "I'm sick and tired of him!" unless you really want to throw up or be sick and tired. If you are not heedful of the thoughts and words you express, you might find that everyone else at the office is having a nice day and the person who you are sick and tired of is out playing tennis and having a jolly good time, while you may find yourself in bed — not because an office or person has any power over your health, but because you didn't realize that your subconscious mind heard your words as commands and quite readily responded by creating exactly the experience you described in your "idle" expressions.

Our problems are *not* caused by other people, poorly constructed bodies, or defective minds. They are caused by misunderstanding, lack of awareness, and misuse of the perfect tools that God gave us to work with. It is the poor craftsman who blames his tools for his errors. When we started out on earth — as individuals and as a human race — we had everything we needed to live in abundance, joy, and peace. There were no nuclear warheads, no polluted lakes, no lines on the earth that said, "That piece of land is yours and this one is mine." It was just a lovely garden. We got ourselves into trouble when we began to take what we had — especially the power to create with the mind — and use it incorrectly. Then, after we made a huge mess, we complained, "This world is rotten!" or "My mother made me neurotic!" or "There is so much suffering . . . There must not be a God!" But blaming is misdirected, wasted energy. We just need to realize that we processed a peaceful world through a subconscious belief system based on a fearful picture of life, and the results of that interpretation of God must be terrifying, for peacefulness is our nature, and any experience other than tranquility must, by virtue of who we are, leave us unsatisfied. We looked at the light of the world through dark lenses, and it is no wonder that we saw darkness. As the computer programmers label the problem, "G.I. — G.O." (*"Garbage In — Garbage Out"*). As the ancient seers labeled it: "G.I. — G.O." (*"God In — God Out"*).

I know a man whose experience of life is a cogent testimony to this law of mind. When he was a little child, Bob's father told him, "You'll be the death of me yet!" Then, when his father actually did pass on, Bob felt that he had caused his death, and he developed a stifling sense of guilt and unworthiness. This erroneous program hampered Bob's work and relationships for much of his life, until he found a positive spiritual group in which he learned to love himself once again.

Bob, like many of us, learned the hard way that many of the ideas

87

we were taught as children are simply not true. For example: "Whites and blacks don't marry," or "You can't get anywhere without a college diploma," or "Men don't hug." Such false notions distort our view of life like a rock thrown into a calm pool disturbs the perfect reflection of the sky. We cannot really know God unless we learn to see life, love, and ourselves clearly. Seen through divine eyes, life, love, and ourselves are as we always have been: *perfect*. Only incorrect thinking can create problems where none exist.

Bob's story bears some very practical lessons. We have a paramount responsibility to scrutinize the beliefs about life that we were taught as children, and hold them up to the light of Truth. As children, we were very impressionable, without a mature ability to discern Truth for ourselves. As we have now grown into maturity, it becomes our responsibility to sift through what our childhood teachers told us, and *decide for ourselves* what is correct. We have no right to blame our parents or teachers for our unhappiness, for we now have free will to choose a path of life for ourselves and our world — an avenue of consciousness built upon the thoughts we *choose* to think. If we shirk the responsibility for discovering what is true, we have no one to hold accountable but ourselves, and no one will suffer for our erroneous programming more than ourselves. This may be a bold awakening, but Truth is not always gentle.

We also have an equally important (and perhaps even more crucial) responsibility to be *extremely* careful about the programs we offer our families, friends, and especially children. We must support our brothers and sisters with positive, encouraging, uplifting thoughts, and not pollute their consciousness with the brunt of limited thinking. One teacher pleaded that we never "crush a child's flower." This means that we must give one another every chance to succeed, to grow, to change for the better. If we mentally stifle another, we drag an aspiring soul into the mud of negation with us, and that's old fashioned bad karma. If you have ever had someone tell you, "You'll never do that," or "Forget it — You don't stand a chance of winning," or "Oh, come on — Be realistic," you can appreciate how important it is to uphold one another and give our family, friends, and co-workers every possibility to be great. Since we are all children of God, always learning and constantly needing nourishment to develop, the admonition to "give each others' flowers freedom to grow" applies to all of us.

This brings us to one of my favorite subjects, the consciousness of children. Jesus said that children are very close to God: *"If you want to enter the Kingdom of Heaven, you must become like a little child."* One of the wonders that I love about little children is the vividness of their imagination, their ability to see the magical and the exciting in all of life. The Sandman, Tooth Fairies, and Kermit the Frog are as real to children as mortgages and radial tires and governments are to adults. Through the eyes of a child, the world is ever fascinating, eternally new, and fully alive, and it is exactly this kind of vision that we must recapture if we are to re-enter the Garden of Eden, which is waiting for us in our very own heart.

One day I went to a fair with a little friend, Noah, and there we came upon "Officer Phil's Talking Car," an old VW Bug painted with a big happy smile and rolling eyes, glamorized with orange shag rug hair, and brought to life by a microphone through which Officer Phil (hiding behind the car) spoke to the fascinated children passing by. When the talking car asked my little Noah, "Is there anything you would like to tell me?" Noah shouted, "Yes! I love you very much!" which made Officer Phil about the happiest talking car at the fair.

It then occurred to me that it had been a while since I had told a car that I loved it, and it would probably make my life a little more joyous if I did occasionally tell a car — or a tree — or a typewriter — or a person, "I love you very much!" Noah's love for that car was as real as any that I have seen in most human relationships, maybe more so. Maybe that's why Noah, a silly kid who talks to cars, lives a lot of the time in the Kingdom of Heaven, and I spend quite a bit of my time in the state of New Jersey.

As Joni Mitchell so clearly puts it, "We've gotta get back to the garden." That garden is not to be found in the world as we have known it, but in *consciousness*: in our mind, in the way we look at life, in how much we are willing to let our hearts be free to accept the highest possibilities of who we are, what we are doing here, and what life is all about. As Jonathan Livingston Seagull discovered, we must allow our minds to soar above the flock. We must release our thoughts from the common petty burdens that bind men to insignificant details, and reawaken our visions of the grand and miraculous. We have to be able to see what we yearn to be — not who we were taught we are. We have to know there is much more to us — much, much more — than a name and a job description and a credit line and a difficult relationship.

We must remember that we are created in the image of God, the Source of the entire universe, and anything God can do, She can do through us.

That's the key. We need to quit asking God to fight through the mire of limited thinking, and allow Her to work *through* our positive minds. We can't walk around indulging in feeling bugged, creating turbulent storms of anger and depression, and then expect God to glide Her airplane of clarity through the hurricane and land on a muddy runway. We have to keep the runway clear. We don't have to be the pilot; if we just take care of the ground crew's job, the pilot will perform Her role. We don't have to create peace; I don't know any human being who can create such a Divine experience. All we need to do, as John and Yoko put it, is to "give peace a chance." That's all God wants — a chance. She just wants us to open the door of our heart a little bit — just a crack. Then She can let light into the room that we have sealed with many locks and shutters and then complained that God doesn't exist because we haven't been seeing light.

Jesus, the master psychologist, physician, and positive thinker, knew all of this, and this is how he taught it: "When you pray, you pray amiss! *Give thanks for the answers to your prayers before you receive them.*" In other words, we have to get the picture and the feeling of the health, success, or blessing that we want *before* we actually see it in physical form. There is a magnificent commentary on the story of the Jewish people crossing the Red Sea. It says that some of the Israelites went into the water *up to their necks* before the waters actually parted. That's faith. How could they walk in that far, unless they had a very clear vision that the waters would part? Their mind's eye had to be able to see that whole dry highway before their physical eyes saw one drop diminish. That's faith.

It seems to me that's the kind of faith, the quality of vision we need to make it through trying times. We need to know in our heart of hearts that even though the waters may be lapping up onto our shoulders, if we just stand firm on our vision of the rightness of life, of Truth, of God, the whole highway is already right here, and it won't be long before we're walking on solid ground. Actually, we have no choice but to have faith. What happens when we abandon right vision? The result is the world we have created around us, a terrifying nightmare of fear, divisiveness, and mistrust. Sometimes I think about what could be done with all the money and energy put into war, into false advertising, into competition. I think how the United States and the Soviet Union have each poured billions, perhaps trillions of dollars into a fictitious, fear-created "race for space" in which so many efforts have been unnecessarily duplicated and some of the greatest minds on the planet have been turned against each other instead of uniting in a common effort, because we believed in competition and not cooperation. Then I wonder how it all might be if someone, if enough someones, had a vision of humankind working together for mutual good, how much more practically could those trillions have been spent? Feeding hungry children. Delving into the scientific mysteries of life. Endowing the arts. Just thinking of the family of humankind nourished by harmonious cooperation is enough to keep me enthusiastic and eager and willing to work to build a new world.

Since I have discovered the miracle of thinking in alignment with high possibilities, I am keenly aware of how we use — and misuse — the power of our thoughts. While we could create unprecedented successes simply by believing in one another, too often we sadly deny ourselves the joy of mutual upliftment. Like atomic power, chemistry, and psychic abilities, all of which are gifts to celebrate the glory of life, we have taken the miracle of the creative power of thought and turned it against ourselves, dragging each other down instead of lifting each other up. I am very aware of the little signs and posters that secretaries and their bosses put up in offices. Before you tack up that plaque, please think about what you are creating, what kind of energy you are offering your brothers and sisters. In the front office of a big industry I saw this sign: "If something can go wrong, it will." I began to ponder on how that powerful thought filtered through the whole company. Every person who walked through those front doors, from the president to the visiting salesmen, had that program implanted in his or her subconscious and reinforced many times a day. One little sign. Then I began to imagine how much more money they might make, how much less illness they would experience, how much more joyous their jobs could be, if they had a sign like, "The universe is abundant," or "All things are working together for good!" or even "Welcome!"

Those were words. Let us consider pictures; their effect on the subconscious is even more powerful. (This is one of the reasons Jesus taught in parables; as the mind absorbs the picture images of the parables, they go directly into the subconscious through the right

91

hemisphere of the brain!) Perhaps you have seen the xeroxed cartoon of Snoopy going through the days of the week. The first day, Monday, he is happy, energetic, and dancing. Then follows a series of cartoons of Snoopy getting more and more tired and bedraggled as the days go by, until Friday, when he is laid out on the floor, completely exhausted. What do you think is the effect of that picture on the workers in that office, come Friday morning? No wonder burnout is such a big problem! When we post a sign or picture, we are feeding each other. I'm sure none of us would purposely give each other poison, so why would we mentally poison each other with thoughts of malfunction and tiredness? We just don't understand yet.

Around Halloween time one year I was passing by a hospital emergency room where I saw wall decorations of skeletons and ghosts and all kinds of horrible looking creatures. I began to wonder how this made the accident victims feel. I don't think it was very healing. Such errors in thought-expression are innocent enough, but their innocence cannot change the detrimental effects that such advertisements for negativity cost all of us. If we want to make positive strides for a healed world, we must realize the power of our thoughts and begin to use them toward the ends that we *consciously* choose. We must constantly be aware that every thought and picture that we express has the power of God behind it, and that is an extremely potent force with which we have been entrusted. So far, we haven't used it very well. But we can. All it takes is a moment of thought before we speak or act, just a few seconds to consider what we are creating with our words. More and more, I am trying to sieve my thoughts through my mind before I speak; I consider what the world would be like if the things I say were actually manifested. I am realizing that too often I have been prone to blurt out thoughts without considering their purpose or how they might affect the persons, world, and universe they touch. Now, as I am taking more moments to decide what I want to create, I am seeing more positive results coming from the words I choose. It's quite a profound lesson.

Once we realize that we can create better lives through right thinking, the purpose of living becomes clear and we begin to really make our thoughts and actions work *for* us. We come into our own; we make our time on earth useful, not only for each of us, but for all of us. That's when we start to put rainbow decals on the back windows of our cars, when we start to order bank checks with pictures of endangered animals in the background, and when we start to take down calendars with pictures of "The Great Disasters of the Twentieth Century" and replace them with photos of black and white children playing together. In one office I saw a quote by W. Somerset Maugham, a thought which I love: *"It's a funny thing about life, if you refuse to accept anything but the best you very often get it."* And I was so happy to see the bumper sticker, *"Miracles happen very day!"* That little sign literally blesses everyone whose eyes come to rest on it. I am grateful, too, to a friend who gave me a poster of the Sphynx with a great big Jewish star around its neck. The caption: *"Ya Gotta Believe."*

Yes, we've all gotta believe. There really is no choice about it now. The alternative is the world that we see out there, a horrible bedlam of war, hatred and incredibly painful human separation. The saddest part is not that it exists, but that *it is not necessary*. Suffering is not a painful fact of a random life, but the cumulative result of a long series of erroneous thoughts that began with the idea that "I am not enough." Every act of war is caused by someone who has lost the vision of his or her own beauty, who has traded in the sky of God for a roof in the suburbs, who has compromised his life's dream for a pension plan. If we are honest with ourselves, that is all of us, in some way. The wars in Vietnam and the Falklands are not caused by unenlightened presidents and juntas; they are the tip of the iceberg of consciousness, the greater part of which lies below the surface, a chunk which is shared by everyone on the planet. That's me and you. It's a heavy one to own, but we can no longer afford to make the bad guys "out there." There's something of a hawk in all of us, and we have to admit to it before we can reconcile it. I'm not saying we are bad guys; quite to the contrary. God knows we are beings of the holiest light, His very children, to be sure. We just forgot who we were, and we settled for skeletons on the wall of the waiting room instead of flowers. As soon as we see that it is *we* who have posted the skeletons, we realize that it is *we* who can take them down and replace them with the light of the saints. The last — and only — trick of the devil (unconsciousness) is to try to get us to think that we are powerless prisoners of a heartless world, thrown into a whirlpool of confusion by a whimsical and sadistic fate. I say that we are born of the highest and only Goodness of the universe, and our beauty is incomparable in all of creation, because that splendor is the very Light of God shining through us, imbued by the Creator Himself.

93

The men I most admire are visionaries. There is something about the word "visionary" that awakens a deep thrill within me and makes my soul resonate with inspired strength. If I am to be anything in this life, I want to be a visionary. I want to be able to see beyond what now presents itself as real. I want to look past appearances and recognize what can be. I want to be able to dream and let my mind soar free, unbound by the chains that shackle most peoples' thoughts to little things. I want to know that God would not show me anything that is not possible, that everything I can imagine I can become. I want to know that there is a Living Force of the whole of the universe that enfolds me simply because I live and breathe. I must see. I must believe. I must be a visionary. I cannot be anything else.

What God Can Do

All things are possible to him who believes.
— Jesus the Christ

It was a rainy night in Louisiana, and it seemed as if there was nothing the rescue crew could do. A young man in a new sports car had skidded off the road and wrapped the shiny machine around a tree, trapping him behind the wheel. As he cried out for help, the squad worked feverishly to unjam the mangled door. Crow bars, blow torches, and pulleys had failed. What now?

It was just then that a frail black man was walking by the scene of the accident. "What's happened?" he asked.

"The boy is stuck in there," a somber voice returned. "We're waiting for more equipment, but he's hurt and time is running out."

Without further discussion, the small man pushed his way through the crowd around the car, placed his hand on the jammed door's handle, took a deep breath, and pulled the door open. Immediately the rescue crew dashed to the driver and helped him crawl out of the wreck. Then they turned their attention to look for this unlikely superman who had done what power tools could not, but he was nowhere to be found.

Word of this miraculous deed spread along with a search for the hero. Several days later his identity was discovered: he was an illiterate hired hand on a local poultry farm. A reporter from the city newspaper was dispatched for an interview.

"How did you do it?" the reporter queried.

"Oh, you'd be amazed what God can do when He needs to get something done!"

What God can do. God can do anything. He can give us the strength to open mangled car doors. He can resolve troubled relationships. He can change a life of pain and sorrow into a testimony of joy and triumph. What God can do.

95

RISING IN LOVE

I would like to share with you some of the wonderful things that I have seen God do. I have, for example, seen Him fill teeth and change silver fillings to gold. This may sound like an unusual kind of miracle for God to perform, but there is no challenge too small for God's loving attention. If God knows "every hair on our head," as it says in the Bible, He must surely know every tooth in our mouth! And if He can make the crippled walk, He must certainly be able to straighten teeth. I had the good fortune to attend a healing service by Rev. Willard Fuller, a dynamic and powerfully faithful minister through whom God works the wonder of healing teeth. Rev. Fuller's healing services have had over thirty thousand persons report dental healings, from silver fillings changing to gold, to root canal work being accomplished instantly, to a whole new set of teeth growing in to the mouth of a person who had worn dentures for many years.

As I sat in the audience of Rev. Fuller's service, I heard him tell his inspiring story: Many years ago he was in great pain, diagnosed as having incurable rheumatoid arthritis, which the doctors said would become "only more painful." But Rev. Fuller was not about to accept this fate. He remembered reading in the Bible, *This kind cometh out but by fasting and prayer.*" So he fasted and prayed, and several days later he was healed — just like that. In a moment, he felt the pain leave him and he got up and walked, free of arthritis. "And since that moment," tells Rev. Fuller, "I have not had one bit of discomfort from a disease that was supposed to cripple me."

Several years later Rev. Fuller met another healer, Rev. McCabe, who prophecied that he would be given the gift of healing teeth — and that is exactly what happened. I remember so clearly the vibrant moment when Rev. Fuller shared his living faith with us: "I believe God can do *anything!* . . . I know He can . . . I *know* it! . . . I *know* it! . . . I know for *sure* that He can heal teeth . . . I've seen Him heal thousands of dental problems before my eyes!"

And I saw it, too. During the service a friend of mine looked into

Rev. and Margaret Fuller can be contacted to arrange a healing service, or for personal prayer, at this address:
    The Lively Stones World Healing Fellowship
    P.O. Box 2007
    Palatka, Florida 32077

her mouth with a mirror, and every one of her porcelain fillings had turned to bright, gleaming gold. I saw this for myself. The gold was so shiny that I could see it glistening from across the room. As more and more persons examined their teeth, I saw their eyes bulge to find gold fillings where there had been silver ones, straight teeth where they had been crooked, and comfort where there had been pain. What God can do.

This demonstration opened my mind to the exciting possibility that there *is* a bigger reality — another dimension of life — than the one in which I was living. That night it became clear to me that if God can fill teeth, *He can do anything.* Please realize with me what this means: it means that there is *no disease* that is incurable. Every disease that there has ever been — including cancer, brain damage, and leprosy — has been cured. If there has ever been one person who has been cured of cancer, that means that *cancer is curable*, and anyone who says it is not, or gives odds on someone's chances of recovery, is simply not telling the truth. *Healing is completely up to God and the individual soul* (which are One), and even the best clairvoyant cannot say for sure who can be healed and who cannot. As Shakespeare's Hamlet said, "There are more things in heaven and earth than are dreamed of in your philosophy, Horatio!"

Anything is possible. I have had the privilege to witness healings which can only be described as miracles of God. At Hilda's meetings I have seen persons healed of glaucoma, cancer, and multiple sclerosis. I have seen Rev. W.V. Grant of Cincinnati receive a woman who had been deaf for many years, pray for her in the name of Jesus Christ, and instantly she could hear. Padre Pio, a holy man in Italy, prayed for a man who had *no cornea*, and sight was restored to him. If God can give sight where there is no cornea, there *must* be a *power in the universe greater than the flesh.*

Jesus knew the reality of such a power, and it was through this awareness that he was able to raise Lazarus from the dead. When he approached the tomb, Jesus did not say, "It's too bad about Lazarus," or "Maybe God might hear our prayers for Lazarus," or "I hope Lazarus can be raised." He did say, *"Lazarus: Come forth!"* — and out walked Lazarus, renewed. Jesus *knew* there is a higher dimension of life than disease, dead bodies, and weeping sisters. He understood that eternal life is real and death an imposter, and this was the knowledge that gave him the authority to command a dead man to walk out of the tomb.

It was this very same truth that inspired St. Paul to teach,

BE RENEWED BY THE RENEWING OF *THE MIND.*

We want to be renewed and energized, but too often we seek to renew our soul, which is *spiritual*, with things and experiences which are physical. We have tried drugs, money, sex, power, relationship after relationship, travelling to exotic countries, and worshipping heroes (at least those are the things I have tried), but after the initial wave of each new excitement dissolves, we find ourselves somehow a little more empty than before, a little more hollow, a little more frustrated. This is because we are attempting to satisfy *spiritual* hunger with *physical* experience, and because we are *spiritual beings* — akin to angels — we cannot be satisfied by earth experiences. *Spirit can be satisfied only by spirit.* Mind cannot be completed by matter — only by the renewing of: *the mind.*

We are like voyagers who have travelled for aeons over rocky hills and through green hamlets, up sharp crags and down gentle streams, braving our way through the bleakest winters and savoring the mildest springs. We have known the joys and sorrows of life in so many different ways on this fantastic adventure of awakening. Now our long journey through experience has brought us to a crucial point. We are realizing that our attempts to find lasting peace through physical experience have not borne the fulfillment we expected. Our efforts to know God through the body have brought us momentary flashes of pleasure, but in the long run they have left us unsatisfied. To some, life seems to be a cruel series of disappointments.

From the soul's point of view, however, these frustrations have actually served as blessings, each one pointing us inward, bringing us closer to our real identity, our Home in the Spirit. Verily we stand now at the threshold of a kingdom of riches and splendor that far outshines any gold our eyes have beheld. *"The Kingdom of Heaven"* that we sought in the outer world *"is within,"* and we can freely enter into it by the turn of one simple key: *the mind.*

This critically important mind has a dual potential: it can serve as a healer or act as a merciless slayer, depending on how we use it. The mind is like a switch that controls the lights in a temple. In the right position, the switch completes the circuit and the light reveals masterpieces of inspired expression that lift us into the sacred simply by our beholding them. Switched off, however, the circuit is incomplete, and the wonders of the temple are lost in darkness, invisible to those who long to be blessed by them.

Rev. Fuller gave an example of how the mind can shut the light out from where we need it most. A little girl came to him after having a great deal of dental work. Rev. Fuller prayed, and every single cavity and filling in the girl's mouth disappeared, leaving a mouthful of perfectly clean, white, whole, cavity-free teeth. When the girl's happy parents took her to the dentist to show him what God had done, the dentist did not believe them. After pacing back and forth many times, examining and re-examining her mouth and her x-rays and consulting with the dental assistants, he angrily accused them, "You have switched daughters on me!"

It is but our thoughts that determine whether we enter laughing into the Kingdom of Heaven, or stand weeping at the gate. If our mind is cluttered with narrow "one-way-to-do-it" beliefs, we cut ourselves off from the help that could make our path through life so much clearer and easier. If, however, we are open to new ideas, bigger possibilities, and outright miracles, we literally invite God and all of His blessings into our life.

This is why Jesus, Hilda, Rev. Fuller, and all other spiritual masters have told us that if we want to enter the Kingdom of Heaven, we need to quit thinking so much. My favorite movies these days are Walt Disney family-type triple G movies. I used to think they were just corny, unsophisticated, silly stuff, but now I revere them as delightful sunbeams. There is a scene in *E.T.* in which the neighborhood boys, attempting to save E.T., are being pursued from all sides by marching battalions of police and F.B.I. men. Just as it seems the boys are hopelessly trapped, suddenly they and their bicycles are lifted off the ground (by E.T.'s faith), and they fly over the hills to E.T.'s safe homecoming. (When we run from our problems on the level at which they can attack us, we are quite at their mercy. But when we allow Faith to lift us above them and we look at them from an innocent perspective, God somehow finds a way that we haven't thought of, one which will save us in a way that we could not save ourselves.)

When I saw those kids begin to fly on their bicycles, tears of joy welled up in my eyes. There was something so uplifting and free, even holy, about allowing that to happen. It was as if I remembered a lost magical realm that I knew and loved in my childhood, a sunlit land in which everything was real. That scene made me remember giggling as Peter Pan took Wendy by the hand and guided her to Never-Never Land, and cheering for the Lone Ranger when he survived the ambush by the Butch Cavendish Gang, and feeling so excited when Little Lulu met the spacemen at her bedroom window. I was transported to a childhood realm where anything could happen, where everything was alive and dancing and in harmonious relationship with everything else. As I look back now, I see that for me life ceased to be fun when I stopped believing that anything could happen, and it became exciting again when I began to believe in miracles.

That's the secret: believing in miracles. We always have to be open to the possibility that something wonderful can happen — something that we haven't thought or dreamed of — something that can really get us out of the mess we seem to be in. We have to know 100% that there is always a way out, even if we haven't discovered it yet. Dr. Robert Mueller, Assistant Secretary General of the United Nations, tells how he was cornered by the Nazis in a French hotel. Hiding in an attic, trying to figure out how to escape, he thought, "This is my moment of opportunity!" At that moment an idea flashed to him: he took off his glasses, parted his hair the opposite way, walked down into the lobby, right into the crowd of Nazis searching for him, and he asked, "What's the commotion here?" "Have you seen a Mr. Mueller?" asked one of the guards. "Yes," he replied, "he was just upstairs." Immediately the soldiers charged upstairs and Mr. Mueller walked out the front door, free.

It's that flashing, that moment of inspiration, that wafting of an insightful thought from a realm higher than the $2+2=4$ reality — that's what God can do. It is rare that we reason out the solution to our problems. More often our answers come in an intuitional awakening, an "Aha!" moment for which we cannot really take credit or say, "This was *my* thought." At best, we can say, "This thought was given to me." Albert Einstein, who had one of the greatest thinking minds in human history, said, "*I have not arrived at my understanding of the universe through the rational mind.*"

There is a poetic verse from a lovely song by Sue Daniels: "*Open up your heart . . . Tear it all apart.*" When I first heard these lyrics, they seemed to be a little contradictory. I mean, opening up your heart is so sweet, and tearing it all apart seems so coarse, so heavy. After listening to the song several times, however, I began to understand what it means. In order for our hearts to really be open, we must tear up all the old, limited, tight beliefs that we held about who we are and what life is. These are thoughts that once served us at a stage of our awakening, but there comes a time when they have outlived their usefulness. After a certain point they only bind us, and we must make space for a new, more glorious reality to take their place. We cannot live in a consciousness of God and limitation at the same time: "No one can serve two masters," said Jesus. There are either miracles or death, no in-between. Either Lazarus is dead for good, or there is God. That's what it comes down to.

I would like to conclude these thoughts by sharing with you an extremely powerful affirmation which has worked miracles in my life. I offer it to you with the confidence that it can work as wonderfully for you, should you choose to use it. It is this:

GOD CAN DO ANYTHING.

Read this affirmation out loud now, several times, emphasizing a different word each time. Then repeat it to yourself mentally, over and over, concentrating and contemplating the truth of the idea, until you realize that this affirmation was written especially for you, right now, given as a perfect answer for this particular moment of choice in your life, a life that is very important to God. Then, after the truth of the affirmation is blazing in your heart, think of several situations in your life that may be troubling you. One by one, hold each situation up to the light of the affirmation, and repeat the affirmation as if it applies particularly to that problem, until the light of the truth of the affirmation makes the problem evaporate like mist before morning sunlight. Then, during the course of your day, if any trouble assails you, bring forth the affirmation into your mind, and realize that these words are absolutely, eternally, and unalterably true. They are words of God.

Repeating this affirmation literally rearranges our atoms and aligns every cell of our being with the Almighty Power of the Living God. Moreover, it attunes and connects us with the strength of Jesus Christ, Moses, Buddha, Mohammed, Lao Tse, and every great soul, saint, and prophet that has ever demonstrated the victory of the spirit over limitation. Because these words are true, they have the power to lift us up on a wave of momentum that immediately disintegrates all negative thought patterns and delivers us into a new life that will stand as a living testimony to the truth that God is real, He is the only power in the universe, and He lives in you as you. Realizing this truth sets into motion a snowball of awakening that shines onto and is magnified by every person you and I touch with our faith in our mutual Divinity. It renews our joy and allows us to be children again. It answers all of our prayers and heals our broken dreams to reveal that they were never anything less than whole. It shows us a dynamic vision of who we truly are, and how important we are to God in His plan to give loving birth to a new and better world. It makes us complete, free, and literally Divine. That's what God can do.

What Goes Around

And in the end, the love you take
is equal to the love you make.

— The Beatles

As my friends and I approached the toll booth at the George Washington Bridge, an unusual and intriguing idea flashed to me: Let's pay the toll for the car behind us! It would be the kind of thing that would make someone's day just a little nicer, a rare kind of touching, impossible for the most cynical commuter to ascribe an ulterior motive, and a gracenote on the highway of human relations that would make life on earth a bit more fascinating for everyone involved. So each of us contributed fifty cents, smiled to the toll collector, and we watched him quizzically wrinkle his brow as we passed. That was about five years ago.

Several months ago I was returning to New Jersey from Pennsylvania via the Dingman's Ferry Bridge, a quaint old country crossing that I love to travel, just to hear the creaks of the old wooden planks under the wheels. As I pulled up to the toll booth of this tiny antiquated span, I readied my money for the attendant, an amiable elderly fellow who gives everyone a treat of country conversation with their change.

"No, thank you," he twinkled at me, "that won't be necessary . . . The fella in the car in front of you just paid your toll . . . Just go right on ahead!"

I put my change back in my jacket pocket, nodded "thank you" to the kindly attendant, and chuckled as I stepped on the accelerator. Then, as I passed the toll station, I noticed the sign posting the amount of the toll: *fifty cents.*

What goes around, comes around. What we send out into the universe is returned to us in appropriate nature and equal measure, by a Law and a Mind far greater and more exact than any mortal

103

calculation can fathom. Jesus said it this way: "Cast your bread on the water, and it shall return to you." He told, too, that "The Father knows every sparrow and every hair on your head," — and every fifty cents you give at a toll booth.

In the Eastern tradition it has been called *karma: As ye sow, so shall ye reap.* It is a principle basic to every religion and system of cultural ethics, given by God in different words and languages at different times to reach all people. But no teaching of karma is as clear as direct experience.

I had such an experience with my friend Danny Holaday, who for many years owned a local health food store called *Nature's Kitchen.* Danny is one of the most loving and giving persons I have ever known; he is extremely generous in allowing his store to be used for classes and community activities, at no charge. I remember, too, when I approached Danny about selling some books, he gave me a better deal than I asked for. He simply loves to give. Unfortunately, being a nice guy does not always seem to coincide with running a business (at least that's what we have been taught), and over the years while Dan was making so many people happy, the store was running into debt. The Holadays came to the point where they just didn't know how they were going to meet the next month's bills — but Danny wasn't worried.

Then one day all that had gone around, came around. A man in a three-piece suit walked into the store and asked to speak to the manager. Danny invited him into the office and the well-dressed man began to speak:

"Mr. Holaday, I represent a large vitamin company which is about to market a new line of vitamins which we plan to distribute on a national level. We would very much like to use the name "Nature's Kitchen" for our line, but we find that you have registered this as the name of your store. We would like to obtain the rights to use that name, and we are prepared to pay for it . . . Would twenty thousand dollars be suitable?"

Of course it would. Now the company's vitamins are called *"Nature's Kitchen,"* Danny's store is (most appropriately) renamed *"Nature's Holaday,"* and what went around has come around. It works.

Over the years, *karma* has gotten a bad name, bad press. How often I have heard or thought, "You better not do that . . . it's *BAD*

KARMA!" or "This must be my *BAD KARMA* coming back on me!" and so on. There is, to be sure, great wisdom in the need to give forethought to our acts, and to see how we actually bring difficulty upon ourselves. But somehow, when I hear the way the word *karma* is often used, it seems that it should be accompanied by a dramatic, ominous vibrato on the bass notes of an old player piano, as if Mr. Poison Zumack (the caped, black-hatted, curly-waxed-moustached villain on the old *Rootie Kazootie* show, who was always trying to steal Miss Polka Dottie's polka dots) is about to jump out from behind a curtain, snarling a sinister laugh, with the overdue mortgage in hand. But I don't think it is really that way; I don't believe any karma is completely bad.

We need to look at karma in a positive light to really see how this magnificent, God-ordained principle actually works *for* us. We need to look into the laws of sowing and reaping, from a high, masterful, *appreciative* perspective. We need to open to the truth that when our "bad" karma comes back to us, it is a gift from God, generously and graciously allowing us to learn how we have strayed from Her loving arms — and showing us, too, the way to return.

Some obvious examples of the way that "bad" karma is actually very helpful are physical illness, relationships, and work. I met a very calm and easy-going man who told me, to my surprise, that he had recovered from a heart attack. "You seem so tranquil now," I noted.

"Yes, I am," he agreed, ". . . but if you had known me five years ago you would have seen a nervous wreck. I felt tremendously uptight and driven . . . You might say I was overworking at the expense of my peace. Then, when my heart gave me a very clear message about the way I was approaching life, I realized I had to make a choice: Cool out or die. I decided to make a major change in the way I was living my life, and the person you are looking at now is the result of that change. I'm about a hundred times happier now."

The same principle holds true for the area of relationships. When we are in close relationship with another person, we learn where we are holding out on the universe, and where we need to let go. If we are attached or clinging in any way, the tension that we feel must eventually yield to the realization that it feels a lot better to give love than to make demands, and somehow we learn to release the other person. The miracle is that as soon as we free our partner, we free *ourself*. Jealousy is a good example of this way of growth. In one of my relationships, I felt jealous to the extent that it jammed the signal of the love that was flowing between us. At some point I realized that the times in our relationship when I didn't feel jealous were much more rewarding than the moments I made demands, and I really wanted to become more flexible. As I eased up, my enjoyment of the flow of love increased so much that I knew I had hit upon the right way to do it. The process of growth was not easy and it was not smooth, but it was something I had to go through to become free. Now I honor that difficult but necessary lesson as a gift.

Similarly, when we go out to earn a living, we have got to get it together. I think that the most embarrassing moment of my life was when I fibbed my way into a job as a waiter at a shore hotel. I wanted to earn some quick money, so I applied for work for a busy holiday weekend, and I told the maitre d' that I had experience — which I didn't. When Saturday morning breakfast came early and busy, and twenty people filed into my station, I was faced with the stark and unenviable realization that I didn't know what half of the foods in the kitchen were, and these people, who had paid a handsome rate for the weekend, wanted exotic variations on their eggs that I couldn't even pronounce. I mean, I didn't even know the difference between oatmeal and farina. All I remember is running back and forth from the dining room to the kitchen, pleading with other waiters for help, and wishing I could just pinch myself with the pickle tongs and wake up. The highlight (or lowlight) of the debacle was when one woman who had been sitting and waiting and waiting and waiting for her order (which I kept forgetting), began to weep and plead, "Please . . . just bring me *something* to eat . . . I don't care what it is . . . I'll take anything!" I think some people thought they were on Candid Camera (and if I was smart, I would have told them they were). But I was too embarrassed to think of anything clever like that. All I could think of was the invisible man, who suddenly became my ideal. I would have dived right into the farina (if I had known what it was).

Those three breakfast hours were perhaps the longest of my life, and they were also one of the most ruthlessly compassionate lessons that my Heavenly Father has ever shown me. That was the last time I ever lied about my experience. Even if for no other reason than to avoid extreme embarrassment, I had to get my act together. So the bad karma turned out, in the long run, to be very good indeed.

It seems to me that the only predicament worse than "bad" karma would be *no* karma, or no system of feedback by which we could learn. This would be like a thermostat that doesn't register when the temperature drops to the point where the heat needs to go on, or a sprinkler system that doesn't activate when smoke touches its sensor. We may feel that pain is a bad thing, but how cruel would God be if we were allowed to put our finger in a fire without some kind of warning that it would damage our body? Or if we were able to over-draw our checking account without limit, without notice, and then later be required to pay it back in full? Or if we were allowed to head toward destroying our earth with radiation, without a Three-Mile-Island malfunction to wake us up? To me, all of these possibilities seem more cruel and unthinkable than the notion that there must be no God because there is pain in the world. To the contrary, there must be a God who cares enough to teach us.

But in order for the Grace of that teaching to be complete, we must be *teachable*. We must open our minds to the possibility that the universe is bigger than the narrow, contracted world we once believed in. Some may say that "karma" is unscientific, but as I see it, karma is the absolute essence of all science: every act has a predictable effect. The ideas that we plant in our minds magnify themselves in our lives, and we create our own reality by the situations to which we give our attention. This was taught to me by Diane, who watched one soap opera so much that when one of the characters in the plot died, several of Diane's friends sent Diane sympathy cards! Or consider those who win the lottery. (Besides the fact that such people were probably philan-thropists in previous lives), it is clear that those who win had to set the wheels in motion by buying a ticket. That's cause and effect. And then there is the case of Duane Alster, who was the head of the yippies in my town when they gave the police such a hard time at campus demonstrations in the late '60s. What is Duane doing now? He is a police officer in the same town, having to deal with kids like he used to be. Duane cast his stone into the lake years ago, and now he must ride the ripples of the waves he created.

This masterfully engineered system, perfect right down to soap operas and lottery tickets, is designed specifically for our awakening, our renaissance into higher consciousness, the peace which every soul seeks. This is why Hilda sometimes tells persons who have been hurt, "You ought to be glad that you paid off a bit of your karma; now you're that much closer to Freedom!" This wondrous life teaches us in two ways: the "good" karma rewards us and gives us a clue that we are on the right path home, and the "bad" karma wakes us up, shakes us out of a nightmare. Though we may sleep in private houses with locked doors, we live in an inescapably public universe in which we must all eventually realize that our being here is not a fruitless treadmill on a trip to nowhere, but a living, breathing heartbeat in the great body of God, intrinsically connected with every other spark of life that has ever or will ever live.

This awesomely empowering lesson of our potential clicked with me one morning when I was studying an orange seed. It occurred to me that within this tiny seed there was a whole orange tree, and hundreds more, and perhaps millions more. Within this one little seed, the size of a speck, lay the potential for feeding hundreds or thousands of people. Then it occurred to me that only oranges could come from this seed — no apples, no bananas, no grapefruits — only oranges. This insight gave me tremendous encouragement to take care in the thoughts and acts that I plant in the universe. It gave me hope and enthusiasm that the positive works I generate can bear fruit and really have an impact on the world — that my ideas do *not* exist in a vacuum, and that what I do in this life really does matter: *If this little orange seed could feed thousands of people, what then is the potential of one loving word?*

Then an even broader and more stunning thought occurred to me: Whenever I or you do an unkind, unthinking, or hurtful act, it is simply because we do not realize that our acts count, that there is a greater, grander system of the cosmos than our meager day-to-day affairs. This thought made me a little sad, for it said to me that many of the people in the world are in despair about the importance of their lives, about God, about their ability to have a meaningful effect on the lives of those they touch. Then I understood that violent acts can come only from persons who are feeling small, unloved, and powerless. With this realization a great wave of compassion flowed into my heart, for in that moment I saw that all of the wars, all of man's inhumanity to man, and all of the aloneness in our world is born of good, godly beings who don't realize who they are. Warmakers are simply children of God, grown to physical maturity and a social position where their decisions affect many people, but who are still scared children inside. They have lost the awareness and faith that we are all known, important, and cherished by our Heavenly Father. The irony of men making war is that it is always in search of peace. It is only when one does not know inner peace that he or she seeks it in the outer world.

Our quest for peace is fulfilled as we recognize the amount of love God has invested in our well-being. The great teaching of karma is that no matter what we have done or how far we have strayed from the path, God keeps on loving us and guiding us home like the great beam of a lighthouse on a stormy, rocky shore. He is willing to put up with our zany stubbornness and set us afloat no matter how many times we start to sink because we think we have to rock the boat (when all we need to do is set our sails in the right direction). I tell you, God must have the patience of a saint. Perhaps He sees something in us, something very good — even Divine — that makes His corrections worth His while. Perhaps, as Jesus saw the fishermen as fishers of men, God is aware of the eternal Light within us, a shining goodness that we have not acknowledged because we have been mesmerized by the throbbing disco-lights of the world. He is willing to stick it out with us until we grow out of our silly belief that we are abandoned offshoots of accidental evolution, and into the great memory that we are Sons and Daughters of a living God. In His infinite compassion, our Father is willing to communicate with us on any terms we accept. If we are a little too caught up in life to hear His gentle whispering, He speaks to us through the grosser lessons of earth experience, giving us a report card on our progress on planet/school earth, with a little love note telling us that no matter how many times we fail, we can try again until He has the proud pleasure to shake our hand on graduation day. That's the day we realize that all of the smiles and helping hands that are extended to us are ones that we have previously given, like ripples in a universal lake, returned to us years (perhaps lifetimes) later, with the perfect loving exactness of a fifty-cent toll.

Coming Home

New Possibilities for Loving

A human being is a part of the whole, called by us "Universe," a part limited in time and space. He experiences himself, his thoughts and feelings as something separated from the rest — a kind of optical delusion of his consciousness. This delusion is a kind of prison for us, restricting us to our personal desires and to affection for a few persons nearest to us. Our task must be to free ourselves from this prison by widening our circle of compassion to embrace all living creatures and the whole nature in its beauty.

— Albert Einstein

One evening Hilda asked a group of us, "Kids, what did you come to earth for?" Feeling that I had the right answer, I rose and said, "Love."

"Oh, isn't that sweet!" Hilda replied in the kind of sing-song tone of voice that hinted that I was about to be taught a lesson.

"Let me ask you this, then," Hilda continued, "Is there anyone that you love more than anyone else?"

I didn't have to think long before I answered, "Yes."

"Then you haven't lived up to your potential yet, for your work is not complete until you experience the joy of loving all as you love the one you love the most."

I turned to *The Messiah's Handbook*, a journal of wisdom revealed to Richard Bach by Donald Shimoda in his *Illusions: The Adventures of a Reluctant Messiah.** There I found: *"Here is a test to find whether your mission on earth is finished: If you're alive, it isn't."*

I have thought for years about Hilda's lesson, highlighted by the words of the Reluctant Messiah, trying hard to understand what she was teaching me. Her instruction about loving seemed to challenge so

---

*Illusions: The Adventures of a Reluctant Messiah, Dell Publishing Co., Inc., 1977.

many of the ideals I had held for so long, beliefs about romance, about specialness, about family, about life. This love that she spoke of seemed so new to me, yet strangely familiar and satisfyingly real. Such an idea of loving forced me to look deeply into myself to try to discover what love is and what it means to truly love someone. How many times I have said, "I love you," and how many times, I wondered, have I really felt the reverence those sacred words deserve? Had I been a hypocrite, cheating the Truth from my brothers and sisters by speaking words I only half-understood? Or did the words "I love you" bear a blessing even if I was not conscious of their real meaning? I had to know what love is. I had to know why God gave us the ability to love. I had to take love by the hand and with it approach the altar of Truth and submit both of our beings to the Light of God, with the demand to know what we were created to be.

The answer I was shown was at first frightening, then unsettling, and ultimately liberating. I saw that Hilda and Donald Shimoda were correct. I had created distinctions between who I could love and who I could not, divisions as artificial as the lines on a map, borders that exist only in the mind of man, separations which the exultation of nature does not recognize. I saw that I had manufactured notions of who is lovable and who is not. I had treated love — a spirit — like a commodity by reserving it for certain persons — those who loved me — and withholding it from the rest. I saw that it was *me* who Jesus was describing when he said, "It is easy to love those who love you — even hypocrites do that." Then I had to face the truth of his subsequent words: "It is far better to love those who do not love you."

I saw that the path of love I had been treading was a narrow one. I had spent most of my first twenty-one years almost exclusively with people I liked, or who were like me, or who I wanted to like me. If you were into The Doors or day-glow posters or hopping into the car late Saturday night and tripping off to Hong Fat's restaurant for Chinese munchies, you were cool. If not, well, maybe there was hope for you, someday. And if you didn't hang out at the student center snack bar or the girls' dormitory lounge (my two major subjects in college), you had no existential validity. Descartes said, "I think — therefore I am." As I saw the universe from my college view, "I am in a fraternity — therefore I am."

When I entered graduate school, however, the universe was ready to nudge me through the gates of some new mansions. As I took my place in one of my first classes, I found myself sitting next to a woman named Bea, who was conspicuous to me by her age. She must have been at least forty years older than I, at least! Immediately I went into culture shock. Anyone who I hadn't seen at a fraternity party was like an extraterrestrial to me, and my encounter with Bea was like Elliot's blood-curdling discovery of E.T. in the bushes. I just couldn't figure out what someone with horn-rimmed glasses was doing on my side of the teacher's desk. Then, when Bea asked me to call her by her first name, I was tremendously disoriented. Until then, every girl I had met in college was a potential date, but when it came to Bea, I couldn't think of any place I could take her except the reading room of the public library. Not only that, but she was my partner in our work group, and she even spoke to me about her personal life. What to do?

What to do was to discover that Bea was not really different than I. After a few weeks of relating to Bea as my mother, I had the great pleasure of finding her as my friend. This was a marvelous experience for me, as my world became so much richer when I allowed her into it. As I came to know Bea as a delightful person, I realized what a gift it was to be thrown into a situation where I had to face someone who I otherwise would not have been with. I began to understand that the safety of the familiar is not always healthy, and that challenge holds a promise that the comfortable cannot bestow.

As my friendship with Bea unfolded, I realized that the only reason I did not see her as my friend from the start was that I had created a distance between us by my belief in age as a real thing. There is really no difference between any of us — age, skin color, religion, body type, personal history — that is as powerful as our holy sameness. That oneness, called by some people "The *I* that is *We*," is the foundation of all friendship. Friendships are not accidents that happen to us when we are lucky, but gifts of love that we accept by opening our hearts to the love that another person wants to share with us. Hugh Prather, in his *Notes to Myself**, wrote, *"Letting other people in is largely a matter of not spending the energy to keep them out."* The secret of making friends is the realization that everyone is a potential friend, and then discovering the unique lovable qualities that each person has to offer. We don't need to *make* friends; all we have to do is *accept* them.

---

*Hugh Prather, *Notes to Myself: My Struggle to Become a Person*, Bantam, 1970.

This acceptance is the key to rewarding human relationships, and it can be summed up in one powerful affirmation of six words, like six points of a shining star:

I HAVE FAITH IN YOUR GOODNESS

I have faith in your goodness. This affirmation is a gift to transform those situations in which we are prone to believe another's intentions to be ill. In such a case we must work through that situation until the light is revealed. I am not suggesting that we foolishly allow ourselves to be deceived. (Jesus advised us to be "as gentle as sheep, and as clever as serpents.") I am referring to those daily interactions in which we begin to feel that a friend or business associate is trying to victimize us. Sometimes we read hostility into a peaceable situation, and we are prone to create enmity through simple misunderstanding. These are the moments when we need to affirm God's presence.

Let me give you an example. As a child, I was taught that auto mechanics are dishonest and that they take advantage of needy customers at their mercy. Now, this may be true of some mechanics, but it is certainly not true of all mechanics, and this was a lesson I needed to learn.

It was only fitting, then, that about a year ago my car began to stall at intersections, and I took it into a local service station to be repaired. The owner, Joe, told me that the carburetor needed to be rebuilt, for which I gave him the go-ahead, at a cost of about $120. I chalked up the bill to necessity, and several days later I drove the car out of the station, relieved that the car would once again be working dependably.

You can imagine my chagrin when, a few days later, the car began to conk out exactly as it did before the costly repair. Immediately my old pictures about auto mechanics' shams flashed through my mind. I pictured Joe turning one screw for a moment and then fudging the entire bill. Maybe he just kicked the tire and pronounced the job done. Or maybe he didn't do anything to the car and simply took his girlfriend to the beach for the afternoon. Those were the kinds of thoughts that ran through my head, which led me to the idea of dashing to the bank and stopping payment on the check. Then I imagined being too late and going to the station and finding Joe cackling a sinister laugh, cash in hand. If he did that, I thought, I would call the Better Business Bureau

116

and have him arrested. All of these sweet and delightful thoughts went through my mind in just a few moments, and my immediate impulse was to storm back into Joe's station, call him a few choice names, and threaten him with a lawsuit for malpractice.

Then, as I was about to pull a quick U-turn and make a bee-line for the station, I began to hear a still, small voice within me, calling to me through those churning emotions like the gentle melody of a flute wafting through a tempest of kettle drums. That voice said, *"Wait a bit, Alan . . . Cool off before you go back there."* It was just such a moment that inspired Dale Carnegie, the brilliant mentor and author of one of the most successful books ever written[1], to advise:

> *Whenever you are confronted with some specific problem —*
> *such as handling a child, winning a [spouse] to your way*
> *of thinking, or satisfying an irritated customer, hesitate*
> *about doing the impulsive thing. That is usually wrong.*[2]

The wisdom of this counsel is akin to that of Chief Seneca, who suggested, *"The best cure for anger is delay."*

I decided to wait a day before I went back to Joe.

During that day I had time to think more clearly about the situation. It occurred to me that it was possible that Joe did not intentionally fail on the job, and that he might have just made an error in diagnosing the cause of the problem. In fact, Joe might have even been an O.K. guy, as I like to think of myself, who did the best he could. Then I began to think of the errors that I have made in my work, and I considered the different ways that people have approached me to correct them. I thought of how I felt when someone blasted me for my ineptness, and I remembered that my response was usually to blast them right back. Then I thought of those who corrected me kindly without making me feel like a nincompoop, and I realized I was eager to make these considerate people happy by rectifying my error. As I pondered on how I might deal with Joe, I saw that I had a clear-cut choice before me: either I assume that Joe is a cheat and I go back and threaten him,

---

[1]Dale Carnegie, *How to Win Friends and Influence People*, Pocket Books, 1936, 1964.

[2]Mr. Carnegie also wrote of a European army which required any angry soldier to wait one day before filing a complaint. If a soldier did not wait twenty-four hours (during which he could "sleep on it and cool down") before acting on a grievance, he was punished.

or I could assume that until otherwise proven, his intentions were honorable, and I could go back and speak to him with respect and kindness.

The more I thought about the choice, the better I felt about the way of respect. So I went back to Joe and explained the situation to him in a very easy-going way, leaving out the part about the lawsuit and what my uncle told me about auto mechanics when I was kid. And do you know what was Joe's response to my flexibility? "Gee, I'm really sorry that happened . . . No problem . . . My work is guaranteed. Just bring the car in tomorrow and I'll correct it."

Wow! Was I glad I didn't jump on him without giving him a chance. I shuddered to think of how it might have turned out if I stomped in screaming and yelling. I realized that my willingness to give Joe the benefit of the doubt gave him the opportunity to be kind to me in return. As I left the gas station that day, I felt a joyful peace that no turbulent emotion could offer. I had dumped an old, binding, suffering-causing program and replaced it with a new and far more useful one: *I have faith in your goodness.* It was a turning point in my growth, one which I happily report to you.

There is a delightful P.S. to this story. Because Joe had won my trust, I took him as my regular mechanic. Our mutual understanding developed, and he went on to perform many mechanical favors for me, beyond the call of normal business. As Joe and I became friends, I learned of his life, which was not basically different than my own in terms of the satisfaction and harmony that he wanted for himself. The icing on the cake was that one day, as I was walking into the service station, Joe's assistant, Dom, approached me, eagerly asking, "What do you do for a living, Alan? You've got to tell me . . . I just have to know!" A little taken aback by his zealousness, I answered, "Sure . . . I teach meditation and relaxation."

"I knew it!" Dom exclaimed, "I knew it! . . . I knew there was something peaceful about you . . . I knew it the day you came back when your car wasn't working and you were so patient with Joe. You should see how most people go wild when they feel they've been wronged. They storm in here, shouting and hollering as if they were victims of a scandalous plot . . . But you kept your cool, and that made all the difference."

I chuckled to myself as I decided whether I should tell Dom how close I came to being one of those hooting and hollering people. But that time I wasn't; I was saved by one moment of listening to a still, small voice that said, *"Try to have faith in that man's goodness "* — the voice of a new possibility for loving.

Sometimes these new possibilities come to us in the most amazing ways. Mrs. Jorgensen was an elderly woman I met in a nursing home. She was very old, she had no legs or teeth, her eyes were bloodshot, and she involuntarily stuck her tongue out and in every few seconds. The first time I saw her I was very uneasy about her appearance; I gave her a polite smile and stepped past her as quickly as I could. I just didn't want to face her.

As I would see Mrs. Jorgensen from week to week, I began to be less aware of her physical characteristics, and I noticed that I was spending more and more time chatting with her. Then one day after about six months of seeing Mrs. Jorgensen, as I was walking out of her room I realized I had not been at all conscious of her physical features. I had learned to look past her body and into her soul. And what a beautiful soul it was! She had such a lovely smile, always gave a kind word, and when it came time for exercise class, she tried and worked so hard, bending over in her wheelchair to touch the feet she didn't have. Saints, I discovered, are not confined to cloisters and pilgrimages; they live among us, humbly shining the light of love to ease the burdens of those around them. Mrs. Jorgensen was one of these.

Needless to say, I rose in love with Mrs. Jorgensen, and it was not long before I actually looked forward to seeing her each week. As I walked down the hall toward her, I would light up, and we would hug, and I would kiss her on the cheek, and she would kiss me, and I couldn't care less if she stuck her tongue out of her ear; she was beautiful and I loved her, and that was all that mattered.

One day when I went in to see Mrs. Jorgensen, she was very weak. So I just sat by her bed holding her hand, and there was so much love and light in that room I felt as if my soul was being bathed in peace. It was as if everything that I had ever been taught about who is lovable had been thrown out the window, and I experienced what it meant for two souls to meet in a place more real than the body. It was a very special moment.

The next time I came to the hospital I was told that Mrs. Jorgensen had passed on. I was so happy! Without even thinking about it, the first words out of my mouth were, "Wow! That's great!" When I heard myself say that, I thought, "Now that's not the kind of thing you're supposed to say when somebody dies; you're supposed to be sad and serious and say, 'I'm sorry to hear that,' or some other subdued statement." But the truth was that I was not sad or subdued; I rejoiced in what I felt was a great day for my beloved Mrs. Jorgensen. I was thrilled that she was free of that broken down old body and a lonely life that I know she had grown beyond. I knew that her spirit was alive and smiling, and I knew, too, that the disappearance of her flesh made absolutely no difference in our relationship, for I was as much in love with her after her death as before. It was as if I was given the gift of experiencing her liberation with her, and for that, my cherished friend, I thank you.

This, I believe, is the gift of all the persons we know, and indeed all that we have ever known. We are constantly being given opportunities to look beyond surface appearances until we discover the treasure of the inner person, which shines more beautifully than any physical body. The physical body is the vessel for the expression of the soul, and it can be only as beautiful as the amount of God-Light that radiates through it. I have seen men and women with the most perfect model-like physical features, but because they do not allow their inner beauty to be freely expressed, they are not attractive. On the other hand, I have seen persons who, by the world's standards, are not handsome or pretty, but because the light of their being is shining in full force, they are dynamically attractive and among the most loved of persons.

I was given an exciting insight on this subject by Maurice B. Cooke, the author/channel of the powerful and popular *Hilarion Series,* who explained to me the higher purpose of the popularity of our cuddly alien friend, E.T. Mr. Cooke's guides explained to him that it was no accident that E.T. had such an unusual appearance. "The guides of mankind, who oversee humanity's spiritual evolution," explained Mr. Cooke, "purposely inspired the creators of E.T. to give him such a strange body as a test to see if human beings could learn to love a creature with an appearance so different than our own."

I would say that the experiment was a success, and I am overjoyed about it! Within the first two weeks of the movie's release, *E.T.* attracted more persons and box office receipts than any other movie in history, and it went on to gross $240 million between Memorial Day and Labor Day, 1982. At the Cinerama Dome in Los Angeles, audiences gave standing ovations to the closing credits. The earth fell in love with an alien, and I cannot think of any love affair so healing to our universe.

Perhaps E.T.'s mission can be summed up by the account given to me by a ten-year-old girl: "When he first came on, he looked kind of creepy, and I was scared; but by the end of the movie, I loved him — I mean, he was so cute!"

There is more. When an experiment is a success (especially one of this magnitude), it often bears ramifications beyond those which meet the eye. I would like to share with you a story that reveals an even deeper purpose to E.T.'s huge popularity.

As I was loosening my seat belt on an airplane flying somewhere over Williamsport, Pennsylvania, I found myself seated next to a lovely newlywed couple. Our conversation came around to *E.T.*, and I asked the lady what she thought of the movie.

"There was something special about that picture," she warmly smiled. "It made me feel so happy when I walked out of that theatre . . . I hate to say it, but it was like *a religious experience.*"

Those were her exact words. E.T. was no accident.

Let us consider, too, the recent popularity of the play and movie, *The Elephant Man*, the story of a deformed man who captured the hearts of many persons who at first could not bear to look at him. Could it be that we as a human race are now confronting our age-old bugaboos about physical beauty and the importance of the body? Is it possible that we are finally standing up to the old myths under which we have labored, and having the courage to say, "I love you, no matter what you look like or where you come from or what you have done"? Could it be that we are discovering some new possibilities for loving?

I think so. I think it is happening, and happening fast, now. I think that the horrors of human conflict and the incredible pain of human separation have forced us to reconsider what life is all about, what is really important, and what it is that we truly cherish in one another. I think that together we are taking a new step in human evolution, a momentous growing up as a family of humankind. It is a spiritual event which has been foretold by all the prophets of old, promised by the great ones, and dreamed of by every human being who has ever laid in bed at night and had a fleeting glimpse of a world of love and the possibility that it could someday be real. That someday is *now*. We are actually seeing the fulfillment of millions of years of human awakening, and it is up to all of us to carry it through its flowering.

The power to heal the planet is in our hands, and God will pour as much light through us as we are willing to shine. We now share a common calling to affirm our freedom from the illusion that we were abandoned on a dark planet millions of light years from home. In a way, we are all Mrs. Jorgensens, Elephant Men, and E.T.'s, for we have become weakened and our light has nearly diminished from our spiritual homesickness. But that is all over now, for like our funny-looking friend with a heart that glows at the promise of reunion, it is time for all of us to phone home.

Divine Relations

When the love in you meets the love in me,
Together we step forward in peace and harmony.
— Sue Daniels

I

Acts

There is a scene in *Grease* that I adore. John Travolta, playing Danny, is telling his tough guy friends about this fantastic girl he met at the beach last summer. She was a beautiful blonde visiting from Australia, but as it is with so many summer romances, he will probably never see her again. What Danny does not know, however, is that Sandy has moved to his home town, where she will be attending high school with him. A few days into the school year, in an unsuspecting moment, Sandy taps Danny on the shoulder and says, "Hi!" For a moment — for a fleeting moment — Danny is caught off guard. He softens and we can see the gentleness in his face as he lights up. Danny is genuinely happy to see her, his heart has come alive. But alas, the openness of his affection lasts for just a moment, for he has an image to maintain. Immediately Danny shrugs his shoulders under his motorcycle jacket and mumbles, "Oh, yeah, hi, how ya doin'?" as if she were just an unimportant passing acquaintance. It's his act.

The truth of our relationships is that we want to feel love; the pretense that we don't care is a lie. Danny couldn't express his affection for Sandy because he had an image to protect, a facade that was unreal and completely flimsy, yet powerful enough — through his fear of losing it — to stand between him and all the love he really wanted to feel and express. Like Sandy, the people in our lives are literally aching — even dying — to feel love from us, and yet, like Danny, we hold it back for reasons we can't really explain. This is the human masquerade, the charade of life that makes apathy seem real and love an

123

impossible dream, while love is the only life great enough to bear the beams of Truth, and separateness a dark dream that has never been substantiated. Though we may be quick to declare, "I don't care what she thinks of me," our hearts are yearning for a communion that we once knew, but learned to deny. As Dr. Leo Buscaglia so genuinely affirms, "We are *all* lovers!"

I had my own experience of a "Greasey" kind of act when I went to visit my cousin's wife, Ilona, in the hospital. Ilona is a woman who has gone through a rather tough life, and in response she has built a rigid shell around herself, allowing expressions of love in and out at only certain personal times. I confess that I have sometimes felt put off by her hardened exterior and allowed myself to believe that she was not reachable. When I went to see her in the hospital, however, the person I found in that bed was nothing like the one I knew outside. She had just come back from surgery, and while still under the euphoric influence of the anaesthesia she allowed herself to be soft and gentle. She took my hand, lovingly stroked my arm, and told me how much she appreciated our friendship. She was as warm and cuddly and giving as the most huggable person I know, and I deeply enjoyed a very rich and real contact with her.

In those few moments, Ilona gave up her act. She gave herself permission to let the caring, affectionate little girl in her come out, for *that*, you see, was the real Ilona. The tough, ornery one was just a cover-up. I have not forgotten those open moments with Ilona, and now if I start to feel distant from her I recall those precious minutes and I remember the beauty of who she really is — whether she is showing it or not.

In the movie *Resurrection* there is a scene that draws this lesson into broader blossom. Ellen Burstyn plays a simple woman named Anna Mae whose father is an extremely cold, hardened man. His pain in life has been so great that he has walled himself away from everyone, unwilling to forgive anyone, including — and especially — himself.

In the movie we find him on his deathbed, with Anna Mae at his side. Anna Mae, who once died on the operating table and returned to life with a memory of the heaven world, is very open to the spiritual life. She tells her dad that there is a glorious world beyond this one and he has nothing to worry about; he will be guided and cared for. She assures him, too, that she loves him no matter what their estranged lives have been, and she appreciates him very much. Meanwhile the old man just lies there, stern and callous as ever.

A few days later, however, his time is come. As he is about to pass on he begins to see the next world opening before him. Suddenly the harsh lines disappear from his face, his lips open into a boyish smile, he lifts his head and softly exclaims, "The light! . . . The light!"* Anna Mae, at his side, begins to weep tears of joy, affirming, "Yes, Daddy! The light! Isn't it beautiful!" Moments later the old man dies peacefully.

This moving scene caused me to think, "That man went through almost an entire life of misery and hiding, and he experienced but one moment of peace at its very end." How sad, I thought, that he held back the expression of his real, sensitive self for so long. It was a lesson to me that I must not wait until I am on my deathbed to enjoy the experience of love. I want to live every moment of life to its fullest. I don't want to wait until my last few moments to be who I am. I think that we can all be who we are — indeed we must — now, if we are willing to open our hearts to the kind of relationships we really want.

All the love that is waiting for us at the end of our life is available to us in full measure now. Jesus told of the king who invited many of his friends to a great feast (symbolizing the Kingdom of Heaven). Everyone had an excuse, something they just had to do before they could come. ("One to his farm, one to his business.") So he went into town and invited the simple and the poor and the hungry, who accepted because they had nothing they had to do first. They had no acts to uphold before they could enter the Golden Kingdom.

Some of the most dramatic experiences of acts falling away are those that I have had in human relations workshops. In these retreats persons from all walks of life gather together with the commitment to trust and be open and be who we really are. On Friday evening, most of us usually sit around trying to project an image, like "I'm cool," or "Don't touch me — I'm fragile," or "I'm a nice guy," or "I'm invulnerable." Then, as the group members begin to feel safe and let go, the acts fall away and the persons behind the acts allow their real selves — their genuinely beautiful selves — to emerge. As facades are cast by the wayside, honest feelings are shared and there grows a sense of

---

*When the great visionary William Blake left his world he was singing songs of praises of the angels he saw coming to meet him.

of communication and oneness that is a thousand times more fulfilling than the games and roles that most of us play in the outer world. It gradually becomes obvious that who we really are is far more thrilling and satisfying than any facade we could fabricate. By Sunday afternoon something happens, something which I cannot really explain, a rare, even miraculous event that reminds me that life is indeed precious, worth living. It is the merging of twelve half-empty human beings into one whole, living, loving, spiritually-endowed Force. It is the birth of the soul into joyous expression, the transformation of Children of God from slumber to aliveness, and the fulfillment of the prayer, "on earth as it is in heaven."

I remember one such group of us sitting in our circle on Sunday afternoon, and I tell you it felt as if there was just one big bathtub of love in that room, a universal womb that we all shared. There was nothing to be ashamed of, nothing hidden, nothing to fear. We had removed our masks, spoken the truth, and out of our willingness to grow, blossomed mutual appreciation and the deepest, most genuine caring. In that moment what had begun as an experiment in human relations had been transfigured into a sacrament of Divine Relations.

II
Transformation

We can use this awakening as a starting point to see how we can transform all of our human relationships into divine ones. Relationships have played an emotionally significant role in my life, and it seems that they are an important issue for many of us. I feel that this is because we want so badly for our relationships to work, and too often they haven't. As spiritual beings, we hunger for the life of the spirit, and when we aren't feeling fulfilled, we have to do something about it. So we go through all kinds of books, classes, therapies, workshops, affirmations, and gurus to make those relationships work. And rightfully they should work! God gave our lives to us in perfect working order. If any aspect of our livelihood is not reflecting Divinity, we must look into it until we see where more light needs to be shined on it. Like Jacob in the dark forest, we must wrestle with the angel until we win a blessing. We must courageously face the truth of our relationships as they are now, so we may know how we need to change the way we are approaching them. Such honesty is a requirement for lifting our relationships into the rewarding love for which they were given to us.

Let's begin with the issue of *commitment*. "Commitment" is one of the most often spoken words these days, and it is also almost always misused and probably the least understood. I have grappled with the issue of commitment for a long time, and I would like to share with you what I have experienced and what I now feel that commitment is about.

I can remember relationships in which I spent hours — I mean *hours* and *hours* — of long telephone conversations with women on the subject, "Should we be committed to one another?" I ran up enormous telephone bills, imbibed fantastic quantities of herb tea in Greenwich Village cafes, and wrote and rewrote long, heartful letters on new age stationary over the question, "What does it mean to be committed to one another?" The issue usually includes, "Am I willing to be committed to you?" "Do I really want you to be committed to me?" "What will happen to my life if I commit myself to you; what will I have to give up, and what will I gain?" "Will one or both of us get hurt?" "Am I really capable of committing myself to anyone?" And so on. One summer I went cross-country with a girlfriend, and we spent five out of the six weeks discussing whether or not we wanted to be committed to one another. I missed the Rockies, the Grand Canyon, and Big Sur because I was so busy discussing our relationship that I forgot to look out the window. As you may know, this business of discussing commitment can sometimes lead to commitment — not to a person, but to a mental institution!

There *must* be some way to see the light through this issue of commitment, and here is what I have found it to be: *There is only one real possible commitment that any human being can make — the commitment to God*, or spiritual growth or awakening. To attempt to commit ourselves to anyone or anything other than God would not only be foolish, but impossible. Of course we have hesitation about vowing our allegiance to a spouse or lover above all else; that is offering all of our self to a very limited piece of the universe, and no one wants to restrict themselves in such a narrow way. No relationship can work if the other partner is the be-all and end-all of our commitment.

Ah, but here is the great promise that lifts all relationships into a higher purpose and not only makes commitment to a human being possible, but elevates it to its loftiest potential. If I have committed myself to God, I am free to commit myself to another person in a way that creates the deepest kind of love between two human beings. Because my happiness is not dependent on you, I am free to love and serve you in the most joyous, exciting, and most rewarding way; I am free to give you *all* my love because, through my foundation in God, I know that *the more love I give, the more I have to give.*

God does not ask us to give up anything; He merely asks that we keep Him first in our heart. Yes, at first we must surrender our *attachment*, which sometimes requires that we physically or emotionally let go of a person or thing, and always requires that we be *willing* to let go if that is what God asks of us. But once we have decided that it is really God that we want, God will return the person (or another in her/his place, if that is for our highest good) to us, this time with His blessings. In such a case it is not an "either God or something"; after we have chosen God first, it is God *and* something, or more exactly, God *in* or *through* something. Then we are free to enjoy it, for only then can we live without fear of losing it. Once we know that we have God whether or not we have this person, we live in a state of peace. And that is the only possible foundation for a healthy and rewarding relationship.

I have found that the highest ideals that I would want to commit myself to in a relationship with one person, I can enjoy with many persons. I was in a relationship in which we got to the point where I was deciding whether or not I wanted to be committed to her. As I was trying to figure out what commitment meant, it occurred to me that most of the rewards to be gained from being committed to one person could be gained many times over by applying those same values to *all* of my relationships. This may at first seem as if I am advocating "free love" — and indeed I am, for the nature of love is that it must always be free. The free love that I honor, however, is not a life of physical or emotional promiscuity, for such a form of love seeks mainly to take, and so cannot bring the peace that we yearn to know. The love that I stand for is the Divinely free love that seeks to give and share and finds delight in the happiness of the beloved. This kind of loving enjoys a commitment to the well-being of others before one's self, and expands to bless the whole family of humanity at no cost to any particular relationship. It is the kind of love that shines like the sun, equally, fully, blessedly, on all.

As I held my relationship with this woman up to my highest ideals for loving, I began to feel that the kind of spiritual fulfillment I was seeking in being committed to her was really a taste of the kind of life I want to live all the time with all persons. Aside from the agreement not to become sexually involved with other women, I could not think of anything I could commit to her that I didn't want to commit to everyone. To me, commitment meant giving her emotional and spiritual support when she needed it, being honest with her, encouraging her to succeed in her aspirations, accepting her love in the way she uniquely expressed it, forgiving her, hanging in there when the going got tough, and loving her unconditionally. The more I thought about it, it just seemed odd to say, "Because I am committed to you I will forgive you or love you more unconditionally than everyone else." That kind of commitment seemed to me to manufacture a kind of separation that somehow demeaned all of my other human interactions by placing them in a category that made it okay for me not to give one hundred percent to them because I was not committed to them as I was committed to someone else. Somehow that notion of moral division did not feel totally right to me. What did feel right was to strive to commit myself to seeing God equally in all persons and giving everyone the fullest love that I know how to give. I knew that I could do it because pure love is infinite and it is not diminished — in fact, it is increased — by its giving. It became clear to me that what I wanted to commit myself to was a life founded on the celebration of God, and I could do that with or without a special partner.

There is, of course, great value to be gained through a deep and committed relationship with another person. In such a relationship the agreement to support one another encourages a loving trust that opens the door to rich personal growth, as both partners can feel free to share their intimate selves with one another. At the same time, because both persons share the same physical, emotional, and mental space, the fire of interpersonal friction is hotter, and there are many valuable opportunities to learn to let go of self-centeredness for the sake of harmonizing with the mate. This combination of trust and working through difficulties creates a womb for nurturing a love that deepens and mellows over time in a powerful way that lighter relationships do not.

Someone who does not commit him- or herself to an exclusive relationship grows just as meaningfully through different kinds of experiences. While the married couple experiences the joys and struggles of having their lives so intimately interwoven, the person who chooses to go it alone goes through the challenges and freedoms of not having someone with him or her most of the time. He or she must deal with feelings of aloneness, sexual desires, family expectations, and more subtly — and even more critically — the tendency to escape into a seemingly safe (but dangerously sterile) world of unchallenged self. Such a retreat may be useful for a short period of time, but in the long run escape is not healthy, and the rivers of destiny will always push such a person back into the thick of human interaction, for the purpose of living is not to rest on one's complacency, but to grow into unity with all of the human family. Yet, as the unmarried person learns to deal with and conquer these challenges, she or he will eventually emerge triumphant, worthy of enjoying the strength of self-mastery.

Both paths of life, marriage and singlehood, bear their own advantages and detractions. If we look at them closely, however, we see that they are more alike than they are different, for they are united by one common purpose: *Self-discovery*. Wherever we go, we find only ourself, and the joyous lessons of Self-discovery are equally available in marriage and singlehood. On the New Jersey Turnpike there is a point at which the highway divides into two roads: buses go to one side, and cars to the other. Then the roads run parallel for a number of miles, and both lanes have the same entrances, exits, and rest stops. Later on down the Turnpike both sides of the highway merge again into one great thoroughfare. So it is with the paths of marriage and singlehood; they are not separate, but simply different lanes of the same highway of personal growth. No matter which road we take, we have to pay the same tolls and we end up at the same destination.

The two ways of living are actually different aspects of the same diamond truth of life: *We are all married to everyone, and we are all ultimately alone.* Walt Whitman hiked out into the country, took a deep breath of life, and wrote, *"I celebrate myself!"* When I read these words a hundred years later, his poem was a gift to me like a newly-wed spouse leaving me a love note when she left for work in the morning before I got up. And when one of my brothers a hundred miles up the coast spills a barrage of oil that pollutes a sparkling beach and renders it lifeless, it is like a thoughtless husband who leaves his greasy tools in the kitchen sink. We are all united in a great marriage of humankind that makes the Brady Bunch household seem as mellow as a yogi's Himalayan cave by comparison.

At the same time we are all very much alone. Each of us must make our own decisions and no one else can live our life for us. We can abnegate our self-responsibility and let other people decide our lives for us, but we are responsible for giving them the power to do so, and for following their suggestions. Spiritual teachers, masters, and guides can show us the correct road, but we must walk it ourselves. We are accountable for every experience we undergo. I once insulted an employer by making a poor joke about him to his face. Later that day I realized I had to apologize to him, and I had to do it myself. Yes, I could have asked someone else to do it for me, but eventually I would have had to look my boss in the eye myself. So it is with all our acts and relationships: no matter how much or how long we have avoided owning our lives, we must sooner or later look life squarely in the eye, and we might as well do it now. This is the aloneness that we must accept. Assuming such right responsibility brings great triumph, for on the other side of the fear of aloneness is the incomparable joy of self-completeness. When we add one "L" (which stands for "Love") to "alone," we get *"all one"* — the real idea behind "alone" and the crowning freedom to which aloneness ultimately leads. When we realize that we must go it alone, we automatically know that we *can* go it alone, and there is no greater sense of fulfillment than this one.

The point of life is not to be married or single — it is to *be*. We are human *beings*, or humans being. It does not matter so much what lifestyle we choose — it's *what we make of the opportunities to grow*, that counts. All single and married people have an abundant wealth of opportunities to transform separateness into sharing, to discover One where there seemed to be two. I don't believe that when we get to Heaven God will ask us, "Were you in a relationship or did you go it alone?" He will ask, *"Were you true to yourself and were you a light to the world in treading the path of your heart's bidding?"*

No matter what style of life in which we find ourselves, we must know that we are in exactly the right place for our ideal evolution. When doubts about our place in life begin to assail us, we need to remember that we have created our circumstances to awaken us for our highest good. That is the awareness that makes all relationships — or lack of them — Divine, for it is the grandest way of looking at life, the way that keeps God first in our hearts.

Keeping all this in mind, I would like to share with you what I feel are the three basic ingredients for making our human relations Divine. These are the principles that have helped me the most, and I offer them to you with my confidence in their power to transform *all* lives by virtue of the truth contained within them.

1. KEEP ON LOVING, NO MATTER WHAT.

When the disciples asked Jesus, "How many times shall we forgive? . . . Seven?" the master answered, "Nay, *seventy times seven.*" The most effective way to create and keep a precious relationship is to *appreciate the basic goodness of the other person, no matter what mistakes they make.* I believe that it is so important to keep on letting go, forgiving, giving support, overlooking errors, and continuously recognizing the unique beauty that only she or he brings into the world as a gift for all. As I reflect on the persons who have loved me even when I acted selfishly or foolishly, I realize that holding to the vision of every soul's sparkling perfection is the highest gift I could, in turn, offer to others. Blessing and appreciation are the same. *Appreciation is not something that happens to us; it is an act that we do, a way of living that we choose.* When I am tempted to feel hurt, slighted, or vengeful, I ask myself, *"Would I rather have this feeling, or love?"* The answer is always obvious. Hugh Prather captures the essence of personal growth in one choice: *"Right or Happy?"* That question condenses all human experience into a clear decision: Is it more important for me to feel holier or more righteous than another person, or would I rather enjoy the warmth of a loving relationship? I am seeing that my sense of joy and satisfaction in life greatly depends on how much I put forgiveness into action.

2. SEE THE WORLD FROM THE OTHER PERSON'S POINT OF VIEW.

This lesson was taught to me in a dramatic way at a workshop on relationships. The leader asked us to think of someone close to us with whom we were not getting along, and then to jot down an outline of the key turning points of that person's life. Wow! . . . What an eye-opener! I was feeling irked about a woman who I felt was overly preoccupied with money. As I wrote down what I knew about her life, I began to realize why she is that way. She spent her early years in a poor

foreign country, in a family of ten children in which everyone
got just a little bit of the little the family had. Her early life
was a continuous struggle for what you and I take for granted
as the simple necessities of life. Then I imagined what it must
have been like to come to this country after experiencing such
a barren childhood, and here find some money to buy the
things she needed. It all became very clear to me. I realized
that *if I had gone through the same experience, I would have
acted exactly as she did.* There is a Native American proverb,
*"Never judge a man until you've walked a mile in his moc-
casins."* After having walked for just ten minutes in this
woman's moccasins, I experienced a deeply compassionate
understanding for her life, and I realized how shallow it was
of me to judge her.

3. WANT FOR THE OTHER PERSON
   WHAT THEY WANT FOR THEMSELVES.
   When I was just starting out as an assistant human relations
   trainer, my supervisor and friend Arlene King gave me a gift
   I will never forget: *"Alan, I would be very happy to be
   associated with you professionally someday."* She knew my
   dream and she built a bridge of love by sharing it with me.
   When we pray for others to get what they want, we participate
   in Grace. One night I made a prayer list entitled, *"If I had
   the power to give anyone anything."* Then I recorded the
   names of whoever came to my mind, and next to each one
   I wrote a one or two word description of what I would give
   them if I could. I did not write what *I* thought they should
   have, but what *they* wanted for themselves. The list included
   good health, a vacation in the Bahamas, a toy truck, mid-
   wife's equipment, and complete God-realization. As I came
   to see life through each of these persons' eyes, I felt warmly
   close, even akin to every one of them, and I was lifted into
   a oneness that brought a flow of love that I usually do not
   feel when I pray for myself.
   Dr. Jerry Jampolsky, author of the very popular *Love
   is Letting Go of Fear**, gave a dramatic demonstration of the

*Jerry Jampolsky, *Love is Letting Go of Fear*, Bantam, 1981.

power of "outward thinking." He asked a large audience, "Would you like to be free of your troubles?" When the group responded with a bright "Yes!" he invited everyone in the meeting hall to send love to Joey, a little boy with cancer on stage with him. Within moments the atmosphere of that room became light and clear, and a great healing energy filled the auditorium. Everyone's troubles had disappeared, for the law of consciousness is such that our minds can hold only one thought at a time, and when we pray for someone else, our own little troubled self has no reality, and we are free.

All of the principles of healing relationships boil down to three holy ideas: *oneness, consideration,* and *love.* When we realize that other people have the same feelings we do, it becomes easy to know how to treat them. This is the secret of unraveling even the most complex jangle of human relations. Many years ago Jesus taught the same principle, and we call it *"The Golden Rule."* And rightfully so, for that is what it is: a holy prescription for healing broken hearts. *Every hard relationship is healable*; we just have to know how to apply the cure. Remembering that the other person is the same as us is the truth that restores peace to our lives.

The way to wholeness is surprisingly simple. Perhaps our many ideas, concepts and analyses have served only to complicate our journey through human relationships and obscure our vision of a simple, clear-cut path. All we need to remember is that we can make ourselves and each other happy by thinking of what we would like from others, and then give exactly that to them. Herein lies the simple answer to many complicated questions.

III

Deciding to Love

I would like to — I must — conclude this very important chapter by sharing with you a marvelous miracle which I have been blessed to experience. It is an awakening that has completely changed my life, an insight with a potential so great that I would like every person to know about it, for I believe that every life can be transformed by putting this principle into action. What I am about to describe is a healing vision that releases emotional wounds and makes them disappear as if they never existed, replacing them with a deep confidence in our ability to love and be loved. I would like to share with you a formula for healing relationships and transforming them into a living love so bright that we see all of our relationships in the holy light in which they were created.

For many years I have heard Hilda counsel men and women going through a troubled time in a marriage or relationship. Her advice to them is usually the same: she asks them, "Can you remember when you first fell in love with him or her? Can you think of some special moments when you felt so delighted and united with your partner that you were filled with gratitude that they were a part of your life? Can you remember the first time you said, 'I love you?' "

Just about everyone can remember such a moment, and I would see their faces light up as they thought of it. Then Hilda would say, "Go home and keep thinking and feeling about your partner in this way. Tune into those wonderful feelings you enjoyed when you looked into his or her eyes and really adored one another. Then act toward them as you did then: call them 'Honey'; give them a big hug when they come home; do something special for them that lets them know how much you care. Then, as you nourish the feelings that make those memories so precious, your love will be renewed and it will flower into a new relationship even more fulfilling than before."

Again and again I heard Hilda give this advice, and again and again I heard people come back weeks or months later and say, "I just want to thank you for your idea ... I tried what you suggested and it worked! . . . Things are so much better between us now, and I am so grateful!"

I was thrilled to see these healings of the spirit taking place around me; the freedom and new enthusiasm in these people's eyes were a gift to behold. Somehow, though, Truth becomes real only when we experience it first-hand, and I did not realize the power of this method until I tried it for myself.

There was a woman who I fell — and rose — in love with, years ago. For a while we were a couple, and then we parted with some bitterness. The relationship was not resolved, and to me it remained a dark spot in my consciousness, a kind of eclipse of the light of my soul. When I thought about Laura, all I remembered was the hurt I had felt, and my mind dwelt on thoughts of what I felt was her unkindness to me. When I would occasionally see her after we had separated, all I could think of were the struggles I went through in trying to find peace with her, and these meetings were awkward and uncomfortable. Though we had physically parted, I was still tied to her by my memories and the emotional fuel I was giving them.

The relationship was begging for healing, and I did not know how to accomplish it. When I saw Laura I tried to be extra kind and loving, but somehow when there is subconscious unrest, outer facades to the contrary seem only to magnify the inner turmoil. I would smile and be polite and say nice things to her, but inwardly I was just waiting for the moment when I could find an excuse to leave the room. I read articles on relationships, tried to send her love through the ethers, meditated, contemplated, and prayed to God for assistance to get me out of this ordeal, but it seemed as if I wasn't getting anywhere. As time went on, all I wanted was for this relationship to be healed.

Then I decided to try what I had heard Hilda tell so many other people to do. I *decided to love* Laura. One morning it became so clear to me that the only way out of this mess was to just start loving Laura fully and completely, and not to allow any thoughts of resentment or emptiness to creep into even one moment of my consciousness. I decided to commit myself to loving her. It wasn't a commitment to her as if to be married or together as man and woman; it was a commitment to appreciating the perfect beauty in Laura, the Light that I loved and honored as a special ray of goodness in a dark world. The commitment took the form of a silent vow that whenever Laura's name or face came into my mind, I would immediately and purposefully surround it with all the loving thoughts I could think about her, showering her image in my heart with thankfulness for the gift of her friendship.

As the strength of this decision rippled through me, my soul was bolstered in a way that can only be described as the union of man's effort and God's Grace. I remembered how my friend T.D. described his winning freedom from alcoholism: "One day it just clicked within me that there was *absolutely no question* about whether or not I could take another drink. Before that I had thought, 'maybe I won't,' or 'well, one drink wouldn't hurt,' or 'just socially, maybe,' but this time I knew — I just *knew* — that whether or not I could take a drink was not even an issue; there was no discussion about it, no debating, no considering, no weighing. It was a one thousand percent absolute necessity with no alternative. That moment I knew I was finished with alcoholism. My decision was made, and there was no veering from it. In fact, it was not even a decision — it was a fact of life."

That was how I felt about healing my relationship with Laura — there was no doubt in my mind that I could do anything other than love her completely, wholly, and unconditionally. That was the fact of life, the way it had to be. I knew this was the only answer to my prayers; I could no longer afford to sit around and wait for God to do it for me. I knew that God would help me, and I saw what I would have to do to win God's Grace: I would have to commit myself to loving Laura — one thousand percent.

I sat down, closed my eyes, and began to think of the *positive* memories I had about Laura. I remembered how much I enjoyed her kooky sense of humor; I thought about the first time we took a walk in the park together; I remembered how nice it was to share so many interests and aspirations; and I laughed to picture those imaginative little notes she wrote me, the ones with little hand-drawn cartoons which she would leave for me to find on my refrigerator door. As I remembered these thoughtful acts, I began to recall many other kindnesses that she had shown me, ones that I had forgotten because my consciousness was so preoccupied with memories of pain. I was amazed to remember all of these *good* things about her, and I even felt a little foolish for having allowed myself to forget them.

Then the healing came. As I focused on these pleasant memories, a great wave of appreciation — genuine thankfulness — for Laura welled up in my heart, and *I began to feel just like I did when we first met.* I began to think of her as my good friend, and I started to feel all the trust and support and excitement that we had enjoyed years ago. It was as if I was transported back into a garden of delight of being with her, one that I had somehow strayed from. And did it feel good! God, it felt so much better and freer and righter than those dark thoughts of bitterness that I had allowed to color my consciousness. I had found my way home.

I was in love with Laura again. Actually, it was not "again," for with this love came the awareness that *I had never been out of love with her.* The love I felt when we first met and the love I felt now were the same love; the love never stopped during those years of turbulent emotions. The love was constant and the distance was a big mistake, a bad dream. The negative feelings were just a smoke screen that temporarily obscured the love but could never replace it. I understood that my love for Laura was real — in fact, *love was the only truth of our relationship* — and the hurt, a lie.

137

What I saw, too, was that all of the hurtful experience was also a part of love — God's love to get me free. As I rose in love with Laura again, you see, I no longer had the infatuated illusions that I had the first time, like wanting to possess her and have her be totally committed to me, and having a lifetime of non-stop hugging. Miraculously (and quite cleverly on the part of God), my hard times with Laura had burned those notions out of my consciousness and left me with a much purified love for my friend, my sister in God, Laura. All I wanted to do now was love her, and what she did in return did not really matter. Loving her, appreciating her, and being thankful for her were quite enough.

This reawakening of my love for Laura was so powerful that I knew I had to tell her of it. Immediately I got up and sprinted to the telephone. As I picked up the receiver, however, the mind — that divinely pesky and mischievous critter, playing the game of the slayer of the real — clicked into action. I began to have thoughts like, "Will she really believe me?" and "What if I make a fool of myself?" and "I sure hope this doesn't get me involved with her again!" and a barrage of similar thoughts. But because I knew that my love was real and the doubts imposters, I refused to allow them to stop me. When love begins to move, there is no stopping it. When the power of God says, "Go!" there is no force in the universe that can resist.* I dialed her number and told her, without any perfunctory small talk, "Hi Laura, this is Alan. I love you very much and I appreciate you more than I can say, and I am very glad that you are a part of my life." Period.

There is a verse from the psalms that says, "Take refuge in the Truth, for the Truth never fails." Actually, I don't really know if there is exactly such a verse, or if there is, where it is, but I do know that there must be something like it, because when I said that to her, something very holy happened, something very mighty and more wonderful than a human mind can understand. When I spoke those words to Laura, because they were true, love was awakened in her heart, and we had the clearest, most meaningful conversation we have ever had . . . one that lifted our entire relationship into the Light. Everything I had been wanting and trying to say to her through years

---

*Meher Baba said, *"True love is unconquerable and irresistible. It goes on gathering force until it transforms everyone it touches."*

138

of questioning, testing, demanding, tears, rippled emotions, and seeking love, was completely communicated and resolved in just a few minutes. Sri Ramakrishna said that "even if a room has been dark for many years, it takes just one flick of the right switch to replace all the darkness with light." Jesus said, "Know the Truth and the Truth shall set you free." Because true love had become the foundation of our relationship, we were able to speak clearly with one another, and the truth of what happened between us became perfectly clear. And because Truth is the greatest healer, as we spoke it, both of us and our relationship were instantly healed.

As a fitting postscript to this story, I must tell you that the next time I saw Laura, she came up to me and gave me a great big hug, an affectionate gift that I used to fault her for not doing when we were together. It is said that "You can only enjoy what you let go of," and the healing of my relationship with Laura is a powerful testimony to this wonderful truth.

There is one more miracle I want to share with you, a message of tremendous importance and encouragement for me and, I believe, for you, as well. As I leaf back through the pages of this book, I see that I have described quite a number of difficult and sometimes painful relationships with which I have struggled. As I read over these confessions, my first reaction was, "Maybe I shouldn't include all of these stories; people may think I'm weak or unenlightened or a crummy person to have been involved in so many unkempt human interactions."

But then, as I was deciding whether or not to censor some of them, another voice spoke within me, the voice of the gentle guidance of my higher self. That guiding light said: "*Consider the state of these relationships now.*" So I reflected further, and as I began to focus on what has become of these difficult relationships, I realized that *every single one of them has been healed.* No matter what hurt, separation, or emptiness there was, *every one of these people is now my friend,* and all of these friendships are now living — have grown into — the Light of Love. The essence of this magnificent teaching is, as that inner sage explained, "*It does not matter what these relationships were; it is what they have become that is important.*" As I reflected on these words, I realized that the transformation of these relationships has been the great healing of my life.

Then that voice spoke again:

139

"This is why you must include all of these stories: precisely because they have been transformed from pain to freedom, from barrenness to love — because they have been healed.

These relationships were given to you for your growth, and as you have prospered from the lessons you have learned from them, it is your responsibility to bear witness to the truth of transformation so that others may see, as you have, that what once seemed to be the reality of pain has been completely replaced by the Truth of Love. The fact that all of these relationships have grown into love is the beacon of hope that will give you and many others the strength and confidence to call upon the invincible power of love — God's love — to heal all of your relationships.

The ability to be healed is God's gift to you, and your work to heal your relationships is your offering to God. Your Heavenly Source needs you to accomplish the transformation you seek for yourself. Now you must realize that God's heart is your heart. All the love you seek to feel and give is available with your willingness to be a channel for it.

The principles of healing relationships are not different than those of healing the body, the mind, or any challenge which presents itself to you. All obstacles can be overcome by lifting them into a new perspective, by recognizing the goodness, the love, the beauty contained within them. Your relationships are excellent teachings for your growth because through resolving them you gain the strength and learn the lessons of a lifetime. It is precisely through the medium of relationships that God teaches you how to heal your entire life and that of your precious planet.

This is the truth that has been begging for your awareness and the golden rule which embraces you and all of your brothers and sisters in the loving arms of Divinity."

Only Love

The truth is that everyone loves everyone.
— Patricia Sun

When I heard Patricia Sun speak these words, I couldn't understand how she could make such a statement. "What about wars and violent crimes and divorces?" I thought to myself. "Surely there is no love in these kinds of acts." Apparently there were other people in the audience who shared my questioning, for as I was pondering on the idea, a man a few rows in front of me raised his hand.

"What you just said reminds me of a friend of mine who I believe is rather egotistical," the fellow stood up and reported. "The other day he told me that he knows that everyone loves him. Don't you think that's a little presumptuous?"

"Not at all!" Patricia answered brightly. "I certainly love him!" she smiled, ". . . and I know he loves me, as well!" Well, that really stepped on the toes of my belief system. How could she say that she and this guy loved each other when they didn't even know one another? My mind went on and on trying to figure out what she meant, and I concluded that she was just trying to be positive or attempting to create love by making believe it was already someplace it was not.

Since that day four years ago, I have thought again and again and again on this idea, and I am beginning to see that there is a lot more to what Patricia Sun said than I originally understood. It may indeed be true that everyone *does* love everyone. It may really be possible that behind all seemingly hurtful, hateful, and negative acts, there lives a Love that is very real — perhaps even more real than the negative emotions we accepted as true. The fact that we don't always see love does not mean it is not there; it just means that we are not looking at life from the highest perspective. When recognized through divine eyes, Love is the guiding force — indeed the *only* Force — in the entire universe. How can this be?

141

RISING IN LOVE

Several years ago I was seeing a woman named Denise, whom I wanted very much to love me. One winter's afternoon she telephoned me and said, "I just wanted to say 'good-bye' before I leave for California this evening. I woke up this morning with this urge to go see my family, so that's what I'm doing. I should be back in a week or two, I guess."

Upon hearing this I began to get an empty feeling in the pit of my stomach, the kind I used to get in elementary school when they were choosing basketball teams and I was one of the last to be picked. I felt let down and hurt that she didn't ask me to go with her. A bunch of insecurity feelings were stirred up within me, and I felt deserted. I told Denise to have a good time, but my heart was absent from my words.

A couple of days later, I was discussing my experience with another friend. After hearing me describe my feelings of being left out, she asked me, "Do you realize that Denise loves you very much?"

"I don't really think so," I answered. "I don't think she would have gone to California like that if she did."

"But don't you see, silly, that Denise's going to California doesn't mean that she doesn't love you — all it means is that she went to California!"

Well, that was one of the "Aha!" moments of my life. It was one of those realizations that I could not have gotten from reading a thousand books or doing a shoulderstand for twelve hours. It was one of those moments when the pivotal piece of the puzzle fit into place and I saw the truth of the whole matter. The truth was that it was entirely possible that Denise loved me, even if she did go to California. It was only my thoughts, my belief system, my emotional programming that led me to think that her going was not an act of complete love. The moment I realized that, I tell you in one single moment, *the entire scene completely shifted in my mind*, and I felt really fine about Denise going. In fact I was glad that she did, for I knew that it was important to her. I knew that she loved me, so I could enjoy her happiness. Her unlovingness, I discovered, existed only in *my perception*, and as soon as I saw the situation in the right light, it was clear that all there ever was in that whole act was love, only love.

Let's take a few moments now to look our difficult relationships squarely in the eye, that we may see how love can be where it seemed to have been missing.

142

This is the key principle of healing relationships:

**All human interactions are expressions of the statement
"I want to feel love."**

Some acts are pure expressions of love, such as a Mother Theresa devoting her life to serving the poor and the dying, and some acts are distorted expressions, such as the criminal seeking to gain notoriety as a tough fighter, but all of these actions share the common characteristic of a human being striving to feel a sense of self-worth and importance about his or her life. Everyone wants to feel love; the only difference is in the way we go about finding it.

At the opening session of my first human relations workshop all of the participants were given a white gummed label upon which we were asked to write a short statement about ourselves. Then we were instructed to fix the labels on our foreheads and mill around the room, silently showing and reading one another's statements. There was quite an array of interesting and imaginative notes like, "I'm shy," "I love racquetball," and "I just left a relationship." But the one that said it all, the one that wakes me up like a church bell every time I reflect on it, was the message written by my later-to-be dear friend, Arlene King, who had the courage to write, *"I want you to like me."* In these six simple but awesomely powerful words, she captured what everyone in the room was trying to express, and boiled all of the camouflaged statements into one honest communication.

If, as Arlene so humbly declared, love is our deepest and most important need, why then do we have such difficulty in asking for it or expressing it? Why did so many of those messages on our foreheads take so many words in so many disguised forms to say something so simple and honest? What is it that causes us to seek love in a thousand different experiences that mirror love, but do not really equal it? How have we become so separated from each other that the most meaningful words of our life, *"I love you,"* are often the most cumbersome to utter? The answer, which belongs to all of us, is one that invites us to take a journey together back into our common origin.

As children we knew how to be in love. We knew no restrictions on whom we could love. Human characteristics like color and age made about as little difference to us as the color or age of our teddy bear. Love is not blind; it is just not petty. Once I, a friend, and a little boy

143

were having lunch in a park in Davenport, Iowa, when the boy disappeared. After searching for him for a while, we found him sitting on a park bench with a group of old men, engaging in deep conversation and intermittently playing his harmonica. He had no concept that old men are different than him. His love knew no bounds.

Then, somewhere along the yellow-brick road of our evolution, we learned an idea called "rejection." Someone told us, "You're a good girl if you color the nose on the clown red, but if you color it green, you're wrong. Or you're stupid. Or you fail. Or if you make a joke while teacher is talking, you have to go stand out in the hall by yourself. Or if you don't go to church, you're going to go to hell. All human definitions of love.

The learned fear of abandonment, the hellish striving to conform to human definitions of love, is exactly the source of our being afraid to ask for love, for if we ask for it and it does not come, we face the sinister illusion of not receiving it. Because we forgot that love is a living Spirit that expands with its expression, we began to treat love as a vulnerable commodity, and we became slaves to the popularly acknowledged but never substantiated myth that "You've got to hide your love away."

We don't have to hide our love away; love was given to us to let it shine. "*You are the light of the world . . . If that light is under a bushel, it's lost something kinda crucial.*"* Over the years, the love light in us diminished and diminished and diminished — not because it was becoming lesser, but because we became so adjusted to living in a world without love that we forgot that love is the very life of life. We covered over that eternal flame with a false front of reaching out for things that represented love, but could never satisfy our soul in the way that only love can bless.

We are like a civilization of sleepwalkers, hypnotized into believing that there is something we have to do to be acceptable to God, when we are perfect and lovable exactly as He made us. It is as if we are a strikingly gorgeous young woman entering a beauty contest. We have been endowed with the most perfect, smooth, classically graceful features, and we are a cinch to win, far and above the competition.

---

*From "Light of the World," *Godspell* (based on the gospel according to St. Matthew) by Stephen Schwartz.

But we don't believe we are good enough to win, so we go out and invest in all kinds of make-up, which we cake on our face to the point where we do an injustice to the pure beauty that lies beneath. Then, when we come in second-place (after someone whose faith in her own beauty told her that she did not need a lavish make-up job), we think, "I knew I wasn't so beautiful!"

But we are. We are so beautiful that every star in the heavens must bow down to the Light that God has imbued in our souls. As I thrilled to hear Rev. Fuller declare over and over, "If I could only stir up God's people to remember who they are!" God loves us so much that our fears of rejection are absolutely comic. Some of us spend lifetimes wondering whether or not we really exist, while the simple solution is that there must be someone here to ask the question! We couldn't be rejected if we tried, for God would never consider rejecting Himself. The truth is that God has never rejected anyone — it is *we* who have rejected ourselves.

Because we haven't believed in ourselves as much as our Divine Mother believes in us, we invented games, manipulations, and half-communications to try to get the love that we so badly wanted to ask for, but feared rejection too much to confront. We made believe we could be outside of God's Love, and then we constructed a world based on trying to regain what we never lost. We made the only mistake we could ever make — we settled for less than who we are. We settled for less than God.

But our Heavenly Father/Mother God would not rest content with anything less than the Kingdom for us. If we attempt to suppress or quash our need to experience love, it will eventually build up within us like steam in a pressure cooker, and sooner or later it must be expressed, usually in disguised and distorted forms. These are the little tests we create, like waiting to see if someone will telephone us, when we could easily call them, or calling someone up and saying, "Guess who?" These acts are unimportant in themselves but ultimately significant because we have equated them with love. Consider the wife who asks her husband, "Would you please take the garbage out for me, dear?" which translates into, "We have been married ten years now, and I'm not sure if you still love me, so I will ask you to take out the garbage, and if you say 'Yes,' it means you do." Then when husband answers, "Can it wait just until I finish this article I'm reading?" wife screams, "You never do anything I ask you anymore!" which translates into, "I

145

am very afraid that you don't love me anymore!" and she stomps upstairs sobbing, leaving hubby bewildered, wondering if wife still really loves him, while meanwhile both love each other immensely.

The way to outshine these hidden agendas and nourish the truth of love as the reality of life is to simply assume and remember that *when anyone asks for anything, they are asking for love,* and then give them love, no matter what the outer request. Often it does not matter whether we say "Yes" or "No," but *how we offer the gift of our response.* We can say "No" in a way that demonstrates complete caring and understanding for our brother or sister, and in so doing we are actually giving an all-important "Yes" to the person's soul, which finds its fulfillment in receiving genuine love from another human being. In fact, a kind "No" is a much greater service than a resentful "Yes," for we are *spiritual* beings and it is the *spirit* of the communication to which we respond.

If hubby would just give his wife a reassuring caress on the shoulder as he asks for a few more minutes to finish his article, he could cut through a minefield of garbled communication and answer the question that she is really asking. Or he might just punctuate his answer with "Honey," an expression of endearment that we may be tempted to write off as corny — but it sure does make us feel good to hear it. (Maybe we need to be more corny; maybe we need to try expressing the *good* feelings that we have, on the hunch that a kind "You're nice!" could make all the difference to someone out there who is having a hard day.) Or if hubby is really gutsy, he might just look his wife straight in the eye and say, "I love you very much." Or he could just take out the garbage when she asks him. It does not matter so much what he does; what matters is: is he communicating "I love you" in his answer? If he does, chances are she might just forget about the garbage and be delighted with her husband coming out of the closet as a genuine lover.

We are all genuine lovers. Some of us have come out of the closet and some of us have not, but eventually we will all know ourselves to be loving beings. This is the great awakening that is happening in so many hearts now. God will not rest — and neither will we — until we come to enjoy each other fully, as we were created to do. Our problem is not that we are unloved, but that we have not been aware that we are loved. All of our lessons on earth are designed to show us that we could never be any place other than in love.

The truth of love has led me to some premises of successful human relationships which I have found, time and time again, to be extremely powerful guides for living, and I would like to share them with you now:

1. Love is the only experience that can satisfy a human being.
2. Whenever anyone asks for anything, they are asking for love.
3. The most direct way to serve anyone is to give them love, no matter what they are asking for.
4. Pain, alienation, and conflict can seem to exist only where the awareness of the presence of love is not recognized.
5. The most powerful way to heal ourselves, one another, and our planet is to realize that love is always present, no matter what the outer circumstances suggest.
6. Every one of us has the ability to heal anything through the awareness of the presence of love.
7. Everyone and everything can be healed — indeed is already healed — because love is the power of God.

There is an affirmation that concentrates these truths into one great idea, a noble awareness which has the ability to restore any seeming loss of love between two human beings. It is an affirmation I use when I begin to feel separate from someone and I want to remind myself who we both are. If I begin to believe the lie that there is any lack of love between myself and another, I immediately affirm:

**THE GOD IN ME LOVES THE GOD IN YOU;
THE GOD IN YOU LOVES THE GOD IN ME.**

This affirmation is enormously powerful because it is a statement of the Truth. It is not something that we want to make happen; it is something that already is, and we want to know it. It is a statement of the fact that no matter what seems to be a problem between two people, it can be immediately and eternally healed by knowing the truth that God lives, breathes, and has His joy in every one of His human Children, and that God is eternally, ecstatically, and irrevocably in love (in fact, God *is* Love). Further, this is a declaration that love is more real than hurt and that our unity is inviolable and invulnerable. It is the light that shines away the darkness. It is the truth that gives us the courage to love.

RISING IN LOVE

We do not need to be afraid to love. For too long have we fled from the very light that can help us and heal us. For too many years, perhaps lives, have we turned our back on the lifespring of our existence. In too many relationships have we shrunk away from intimacy in fear of exposing our sensitivity, when tenderness was the redeeming Grace that sought to teach us that the hurt we feared could never harm us. For too long have we yearned for love and denied ourselves the blessings that love so deeply sought to bestow.

We are like the man who "ran and ran from my pursuer in the night. I veiled myself in the marketplace and feverishly crawled through darkened alleyways. I fell to my knees and arose and ran and fell again. I struggled under fences and held my breath as I pinned my aching body against the stone buildings to avoid detection. Finally I came to the city wall, and finding not a further heartbeat of strength to continue my flight, I fell to the ground in surrender. As the feet of my adversary drew nigh I tearfully lifted my head to see the face that I feared. It was then that I discovered my pursuer to be none other than my beloved."

For a long time I ran from love. I tried a thousand different ways to bring love into my life, when all I needed was to recognize its holy presence. I came to the momentous point at which I was in a relationship with another human being, one in which I questioned the purity of my love. I felt so attached, so unspiritual, so vulnerable. I judged myself, "Surely this cannot be God's love." I reasoned, "God's love is so much more holy than man's; dare I call this feeling 'love'? Am I a blasphemer?"

I thought and pondered, struggled and wrestled with the question of the purity of my love, begging to know if my love was real. Was God the only one capable of loving purely, or is He actually willing to share His love with Man? The real question I was asking was perhaps the most important, perhaps the only question a man asks: "Can I love?"

And because the compassion of our Father/Mother God is so great, I received an answer, one which I believe was given for all. One evening I was sitting in a group meditation, allowing Hilda to guide me into the quietness of my soul. As if by Grace, I was lifted into an illuminated view of life. Clearer and clearer grew my perception of who I am and what I have come on earth to do. Then I saw a light that shined purpose onto all persons and all lives, and it became so perfectly obvious that the heart of man *is* the heart of God. At that moment Hilda uttered these words, a blessing given for you and me, who are One:

"Children of Light, Children of Truth, Children of God:

No longer need you mark distinctions between degrees of love. No longer need you create ideas of high and low in a universe that is eternally and unalterably one. No longer need you seek the love that is your own self, for love's only purpose is to know itself.

Come, Children, rise with me, rise in love, rise into the Love that you are and have been since your birth aeons ago at the beginning of time, when God breathed forth a ray of His own soul, imbued with infinite love, and said, 'This is my child — and my child is good.' That, my Children, is who you are.

The time has come for you to know your destiny. Your destiny is not to endlessly wander in the mire of darkness; your destiny is to claim your heritage of Light that has awaited you since the blessed day your foot first touched this hallowed ground. No, Children, you cannot fall in love, for where could you fall but into the arms of your Heavenly Father/Mother God? Nor could you ever forfeit your innocence, for who could taint God? The purity of your soul is established forever in the heart of the One who made you, and your right to live in love, in peace, in joy, in happiness, is given to you now freely, fully, with the complete and whole blessing of the One who created all that is good. Thus does the loving God rejoice to the end of time in your acceptance of the reality of the Love that finds its expression through you. All blessings be upon you.''

The Healing
of the
Planet Earth

Personal Power
and
Planetary Transformation

Alan Cohen

Introduction by Barbara Marx Hubbard

The Healing of the Planet Earth:
Personal Power and Planetary Transformation
by Alan Cohen

Title Page Portrait by Arthur Douet

The author wishes to acknowledge his appreciation to the following authors, artists, and publishers for the kindness of their permission to use excerpts from their copyrighted materials, all rights reserved:

Dr. Patch Adams, Gesundheit Institute, for permission to use his photographs, pp. 136, 140.

Awakening Heart Productions, for permission to use their photographs, all except those otherwise listed here.

Bhaktan of the Integral Yoga Teaching Center of Seattle, for permission to use his photograph, p. 145.

Robert Carr, for permission to use his photograph, p. 207.

DeVorss & Company, for permission to quote from *The Life and Teachings of the Masters of the Far East*, by Baird Spaulding, © 1972 by DeVorss & Co.

Steven Longfellow Fiske, for permission to quote from "Bridges of Love," © 1983 by Fiske Music.

Foundation for Inner Peace, for permission to quote from *A Course in Miracles*, © 1975 by Foundation for Inner Peace.

Barry Neil Kaufman and Suzy Lite Kaufman, Option Institute, for permission to use their photograph, p. 129.

Peace Pilgrim Center, for permission to use their photograph, p. 341.

John Randolph Price, for permission to quote from *The Planetary Commission*, © 1984 by Quartus Foundation for Spiritual Research.

Satchidananda Ashram — Yogaville, for permission to use their photograph, p. 135.

Sovereignty, Inc., for permission to quote from *Ramtha*, Steven Lee Weinberg, Ed., © 1985 by Sovereignty, Inc.

"Where two or more are gathered in my name, there am I."

It is my joy to offer acknowledgement and my deepest gratefulness to the kind and generous persons who have made thoughtful contributions to *The Healing of the Planet Earth.* Truly they are each and all workers for the light, and I consider it my honor to be associated with them. May the blessings they have offered touch all who receive this book, and return to them thousands of times over.

The Cover Portrait

was painted especially for this book by Arthur Douët, an inspired visionary artist who has the gift of seeing the wonders of the angelic realm and bringing them to earth on canvas. Douët's magnificent art has captured my heart, along with the hearts of many, and it is a blessing to have his rendering shared here. His healing art can be further explored by contacting: Douët, 1601 Gabriel View, Georgetown, Texas 78626

The Foreword

represents the graciousness of Barbara Marx Hubbard, one of the great visionaries and noble thinkers of our time. Barbara's name was placed in nomination for the Vice-Presidency of the United States at the Democratic Convention in 1984. Since that time she has continued tirelessly with her outstanding efforts to make peace a living reality on this planet. She can be contacted at PO Box 13977, Gainesville, Florida 32604

The Photography

was contributed by Awakening Heart Productions. Mark and Dean Tucker have created a unique and dynamically inspiring presentation of their colorful, life-affirming photographic slides and music. The first time I saw their presentation I was brought to tears, and every time I have seen it I have been deeply touched. This show has won acclaim from coast to coast, and has been enthusiastically received by many church, educational, and healing groups. Awakening Heart Productions, 5914 Channel Drive, Santa Rosa, California 95405.

The Back Cover

photograph was taken by Chris Miller when he and I trekked to the summit of Mt. Haleakala overlooking the magical island of Maui, Hawaii. There we shared a moment of eternal vision.

A Course in Miracles

has had a most profound and pervasive effect on my life. The *Course* is a series of three volumes which the student learns by means of practicing daily lessons. This course has opened up doors of healing which I can attribute only to Grace, and it is my blessing to share it with you. References to *A Course in Miracles* in this book are coded by "T" for the Text, "W" for the Workbook for Students, and "M" for the Teacher's Manual. Foundation for Inner Peace, PO Box 635, Tiburon, California 94920

The Contributors

who have lovingly given permission to include excerpts from their books, songs, and photographs. Addresses are listed with each reference in the text.

The Production and Support Team

included many friends who offered spiritual and physical support for this work. Special thanks go to Joan Fericy and Anne Wiley for their tremendous typing and editing contributions; the Rutgers Targum Staff for typesetting and layout service, and Elise Harvey, Joe Vitale, Judy Marlow, Garnette Arledge, Maitreya and Maloah Stillwater, and the family at Miracle Manor for their extremely helpful editing suggestions. I love you!

The Reader

for opening your heart and being willing to take the next step.

*To the vision of Father Pierot
and all of us who share it*

Foreword

The Ultimate Alchemist

by Barbara Marx Hubbard

There is a profound, subtle, all-pervasive transition occurring on Earth. Alan Cohen is one of the most gentle and powerful guiding lights. I see him as our brother, standing on the other side of the "quantum leap," smiling, opening his arms in love, beaconing to us to take the jump...

His book, *The Healing of the Planet Earth*, is an excellent guidebook to read at the edge of the great divide, and to give you the courage to release all fear and allow yourself to be lifted naturally to the next stage of human evolution.

What is the essence of this great transition of which Alan writes? It is the shift of identity from the creature-human who feels victim of circumstances, to a co-creative human, who is one with the Source of creation.

This shift of identity is based on the awareness that each of us had been, is, and always will be an expression of God. We are God-in-expression. Only our human illusion of separation has prevented us from experiencing ourselves as emanations of the divine. Our awareness that we are expressions of divinity empowers us to be godly.

The most important element of this inner shift is forgiveness.

> *"Any hardship can be undone, transformed, and healed to find a shining star where once there was only a dark night. The most powerful way to accomplish this miraculous transformation is forgiveness."*

The key to real forgiveness is

> *"to understand that forgiveness has nothing at all to do with overlooking a sin or crime that has been committed against you. It is simply realizing that no crime or sin has been committed; that you are in danger nowhere in the universe; and that there is no person or force outside of your own mind that could ever hurt you."*

This is what has been called mastery, self-realization, or sainthood. What is so exciting about our age is that millions of so-called "ordinary" folks now believe in these truths, and these truths are making us free.

This is indeed a New Dispensation whose roots are in all the faiths of the world. The sacred experience has moved from the monasteries, mosques, temples, and retreats to the mainstream of modern society. It has become a gentle, non-violent revolution that is now transforming the world from fear to love.

Perhaps it is not yet amplified or even recognized as real by the mass media or mass culture, and it has not as yet surfaced in the general awareness of our time as the mightiest force on Earth.

Perhaps this cultural barrier is in fact a protection. For when a "critical mass" of people recognize their own divinity, it will, I believe, change the field of consciousness, making this awareness available to the vast majority of humanity. The fact that the mighty force is at the moment relatively unnoticed means it can grow unimpeded.

Is the threat of a nuclear holocaust in fact one of nature's evolutionary drivers which is triggering a consciousness chain reaction which, in the twinkling of an eye, will bind the world together again in the white light of awareness that we are one with each other, with nature, and with God, inheritors of the powers of co-creation in the universe of many dimensions, at the dawn of the universal age?

Are we approaching a critical mass of consciousness which will trigger a sustained chain reaction of love which will never stop?

If such a possibility exists — and I firmly believe it does — then Alan Cohen is one of the sparks that will light the flame that will light the world forever.

In his unassuming way, he normalizes the miraculous and places in our hands tools of the "ultimate alchemist," the power to transform ourselves and thereby to accomplish the healing of the planet earth.

Barbara Marx Hubbard

The First And Final Page

A sixteen-year-old friend of mine was lying in bed, burning with a high fever. Suddenly he saw before him a book. When he opened this book he found a record of all the sins of his life. As he turned from page to page, there glaring at him were all the misdeeds, errors, and unkindnesses that he had sown in the world. Horrified, he writhed in fear of punishment. Though he wanted to close the book and run away, he felt that he had to see it all the way through. Finally he turned to the last page, where to his astonishment he found a white page with gold letters, proclaiming: *You are forgiven. God bless you. Go now in peace.* The boy awoke, healed.

Perhaps this young man's transformation is symbolic of our stage of evolution as we, the people of the Planet Earth, grow from adolescence into spiritual maturity. We seem to have many sins, gross errors, and untranscendable limitations. It often appears that we need a miracle to release us from the world we have made. And it may even seem that we are at the last page of the book of our collective lives.

Yet perhaps, as our young friend discovered, that page is not one of judgement and punishment, but rather of love and forgiveness. Perhaps the message from God to us at this very crucial time in human history is not one of fear and damnation, but mercy and kindness. And perhaps — even more important — we are ready to learn that we have the power to give ourselves the healing for which we have waited. It may very well be that the lesson of our age is that the capacity to heal ourselves, one another, and our planet, lies *within* us.

The healing of the Planet Earth will come, for indeed it *has* come within our hearts. This transformation is being accomplished not simply through talking about it, wishing for it, or waiting for it. The healing is coming through *living* it, and it is coming through people like you and me, people who believe that we are worthy of peace because we are born of a loving God.

Let us, then, turn together to the final page of our book, a book that we have written, read, laughed, and wept through together; a book that was authored in the Light, and therefore can be clearly understood only in that selfsame illumination. Let us have the courage to look together at *Spirit's* interpretation of our destiny. Here, beloved ones, is the step into becoming the light that we are. Hand in hand let us celebrate the end of an old and outgrown story, and the beginning of a fresh, new one. Let us discover and tell the truth about who we truly are and how God sees us: *You are forgiven. God bless you. Go now in peace.*

THE HEALING OF

ON EARTH...

Part I:

THE VISION

THE PLANET EARTH

...AS IT IS IN HEAVEN

Part II:

THE HEALING

Part I

THE VISION

On Earth...

VISIONS, DREAMS, and WONDERS

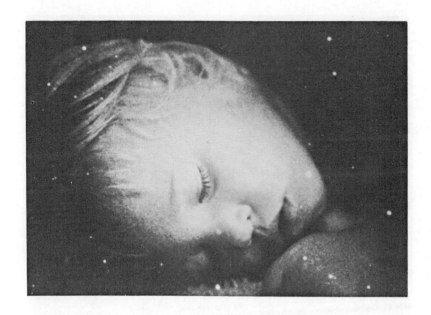

The Glimpse of the Eternal

The early spring sun cast its golden beams across the dusty room, bringing to life a pathway of long-awaited light. The winter had been long and arduous, and the warmth that entered with the sun was as healing as it was welcome. The rays found their way to the contoured glass of the television screen, partly obscuring the movie in progress, yet twinkling gracefully like angels dancing on the surface of a mountain lake. My first impulse was to draw the shade, but somehow the play of light upon the images on the screen seemed mystically appropriate, and I decided to let it be.

The movie was *Lost Horizon* and it seemed as if I had stumbled upon it by the same quirk of Grace which led the five lost travellers in the film to the hidden realm of *Shangri-La*, the land of eternal contentment. As the tale unfolded I was amazed at the profound lessons the story was offering — an unexpected gift of awakening on the threshold of a healing season. Spellbound, I watched the handsome Robert Conway, statesman, author, and visionary, enter the etherically candlelit chambers of Father Pierot, the ancient High Lama of *Shangri-La*. It was there that the holy man revealed to Conway that he had been benignly guided to *Shangri-La* for the purpose of handing over to him the responsibility for the future of the community of light.

When Conway questioned the possibility of actually establishing a peaceful community of good will, Father Pierot gazed into the younger man's eyes, and with the gentlest of fatherly smiles asked, "Are you not the same Robert Conway who in one of his books wrote, 'There are moments in every man's life when he glimpses the eternal'? And are you now so surprised to see your own dream come true before your eyes?"

These profound words rang through my heart like the huge cathedral bells that signal the entrance to *Shangri-La*. I realized that Father Pierot was not speaking only to a fictitious personage, but to me. I understood that I am Conway. And if you share the vision of a world in harmony, so are you.

Then I understood that Father Pierot is real. Within each of us there is a great and wise soul, born of undying purity, inspired by the sacred vision of a planet at peace, living to deliver a golden destiny to a world that has nearly given up hope for real abiding love. This ancient one sits serenely within the chamber of the heart, patiently awaiting the joyous day when we will share the vision and dare to live it. Quietly, silently, he whispers warm words of loving encouragement, nobly reminding us who we are, powerfully urging us to accept our charge as teachers and healers of the Planet Earth.

Many times have I returned to those ancient, secret, most holy chambers within my heart, and met with the Father Pierot within me. Each time, I receive deep consolation and guidance that affirms my dedication to that noble ideal that Father Pierot declared. It may seem strange that I have been so deeply touched by a man who may never, perhaps, have lived in a body, and yet I am reminded of how powerfully One of Nazareth has guided so many into the light, inspiring and teaching through the temple of living spirit that dwells within every heart.

Thus it is to the vision of Father Pierot that this offering is dedicated, with the high intention that these words will awaken the Robert Conway in all of us, and quicken the lifting of our hearts and hands to accept the torch of Truth that our Father is so joyous to pass to us. In a broader sense it is to all the Conways of the new world that these words are directed, for as Father Pierot told Conway before that illuminated altar that my soul so loves to embrace, "I am placing the entire future and destiny of *Shangri-La* in your hands." By the Grace of the Living God I am willing to accept it. Now I invite you to share with me a new vision of humanity's destiny, a vision that will most certainly flower in the healing of the Planet Earth.

The Song of the Ancients Returned

In a dream, I saw myself as a great butterfly
With wings that spanned all of creation;
Now I am not sure if I was Chuang-Tsu
Dreaming I was a butterfly,
Or if I am a butterfly dreaming I am Chuang-Tsu.
                    - The Chinese Patriarch Chuang-Tsu

Some dreams are more real than our waking life. When such a gift is received, the power it bestows is so compelling that we can never really go to sleep again. One night I was shown a vision in the form of a dream which outshines any wonder I have seen in my waking days.

In this vision I was babysitting for a child, a young boy, at his suburban home overlooking the New York City skyline. Standing with him on the lawn of the house, I looked up into the night sky where I saw a group of shimmering blue lights appear on the horizon, just over the silhouette of the skyscrapers. These lights were not arriving from another physical location, but coming into sight from another dimension, materializing in a form that I could see.

One of the lights — a breathtaking shade of royal blue — came very close to us. Before our eyes it took the form of a spacecraft. I began to feel afraid and I tried to grab the boy and rush inside for shelter. But he wanted to run to the spacecraft, from which was emerging a group of extraterrestrials — small, happy beings like playful children. I had the sense, however, that these were not really children, but fully matured and very advanced beings. As I continued toward the house for protection, these little giggling aliens unleashed a laser-like ray that struck the house and instantly burned it to a crisp, leaving but a few flimsy rafters.

Piqued, I began to admonish the spacelings, "Hey, now wait a minute! You can't do that! I'm responsible for this house! What will the owners say when they come back?!?'' (The mouse that roared.)

The aliens had little interest in my pettiness. In a wave of laughter they telepathically communicated, ''Come with us...We'll show you something that will take your mind off real estate.''

With that I was lifted up, not in a spaceship, but in consciousness, and taken on a guided tour over the skyline of New York City. It was as if I had no body, floating, mentally hovering like a leaf on an easy wind.

Then a feeling flowed through me that is nearly impossible to describe in words. It was a feeling of completion so deep that every cell in me was burning in ecstacy. The closest way I can hint at this feeling is ''bliss.'' I felt as if every part of me was vibrating with the entire universe, flooded with brilliant aliveness, as if I was being nurtured in a soft amniotic bath. I felt completely protected, fluently whole, and eternally loved. It was a taste of Heaven.

In this state I was shown a vision of a New Age. Emerging from the streets of the city below I saw glorious lights, astral fireworks exploding in happy patterns, a playful mosaic of brilliant white, rich burgundy, and vibrant blue. These colors burst forth in an amazing show of pure light. As I looked down at the people gathered together in the streets below, I saw them joyously watching this splendid display. Gleefully they applauded the birth of each new emanation. The physical details here are fascinating, but the real essence of the scene was the feeling I received from the group of people gathered in the streets. There was a unity, a harmony, a togetherness of appreciation. It was a clean energy, a demonstration of the divine potential of human beings living together in the spirit of dedicated cooperation.

Then I was shown a little wooden cabin on the top of one of the skyscrapers. The building was not the tallest tower, but one of the lesser structures. In the cabin I saw a simple scene: there was a modest wooden desk and chair, a kerosene lamp, and a few books — nothing more. This, I was told, was the office of the leader of the world government of this new day. This leader was marked by humility and simplicity. The government had no need to aggrandize itself, for it was fully devoted to the well-being of the people it served.

Then I was shown the United Nations building. It was explained to me that the idea for the United Nations was not born of human consciousness, but was a seed idea planted on earth by loving guiding angels who held the future of the planet in great reverence. Their intention was to help the people of the earth enter a new era of unity. The United Nations is the symbol — in potential — of the New World.

In the background of my visit to the New World I heard a softly sweet and hauntingly soothing chant. This music was far more subtle and delicate than a physical ear can hear. The tones were borne on a female voice, oriental in flavor. The chanting came in smooth, delicate ripples, as if it was flowing from a great and wondrous ocean. Though the sounds were at first foreign to me, I soon recognized in them an ancient familiar song, mysteriously comfortable, not describable in words, yet deeply ingrained within my soul's memory.

The experience was so overwhelmingly beautiful that I began to weep tears of joy. My body and mind were overflowing with a nectar-like love, rich in freedom and fulfillment. I wanted to stay forever and float endlessly in this ocean of bliss.

But my time was up. I had to return. I felt my guides beckoning me to start back to the physical world. I sensed that my vision was drawing to a close. Weeping profusely, I felt myself beginning to descend, moving through progressively denser layers of matter.

Soon a young and beautiful woman with long blonde hair came to my side, as a kind of loving companion to soften my journey back to the harshness of the earth plane. I did not want to return. This radiant woman was more of a comforter than a lover, more a guide than a peer.

As we descended together my head rested on her shoulder. In the sky I saw pairs of all living creatures, male and female, as if in showcase frames. I saw birds and lions and many other animals, drawn across the blue sky in couples. My guide was showing me how compassionately God provides for all creatures to be comforted in companionship in earth life.

The conclusion of the journey was equally fascinating. I clearly observed myself passing through different planes of awareness, coming back into my body. At one point I actually saw myself sleeping, about to awaken. When I awoke I felt my eyes brimming with tears of gratitude. I lay in my bed for a while, with my right hand on my heart, sobbing, quietly feeling the overflow of an experience that I cherish as a loving gift from a blessed source. Although I felt some sadness that I had to leave that peaceful New World, I felt no remorse. Deep within my soul I knew that what I had left was not lost in the past, but a promise of the future.

Visions of Future Passed

The trick, according to Chiang, was for Jonathan to stop seeing himself as trapped inside a limited body that had a forty-two-inch wingspan and a performance that could be plotted on a chart. The trick was to know that his true nature lived, as perfect as an unwritten number, everywhere at once across space and time.

*- Richard Bach, Jonathan Livingston Seagull**

We dream many dreams in a lifetime; some even say that all of life is but a dream. Yet each of us holds a handful of sparkling memories that seem to be gifts of vision from beyond a veil that fell over our eyes long ago. These are the insights that bolster us during the times when all else seems to have fallen away. They are the crystals of hope that give us the courage and a good reason to wake up tomorrow. They are the promises of happy endings that remind us that all of life is a gift, cherishable and worthy of appreciation and sharing.

I would like to share my most important visions with you.

I

At a New Year's gathering several friends and I were discussing the possibility that we have lived time after time through history. When I mentioned that I had never had any recollection of a past life, my friend Al invited me into another room to speak with him privately.

When we were alone he asked me to close my eyes. Then he led me into a soft meditation, very soothing in comparison to the activity in the rest of the house. When we reached a considerable depth in the meditation, he guided me back in time to see if I had any impressions.

To my surprise, I did.

I saw myself in the basement of a house of worship. The image seemed not so much like a vision, but a memory.

---

* Richard Bach, *Jonathan Livingston Seagull*, Avon Books, 1970

"Where are you?" I heard Al's voice pierce my thoughts.

"I'm sitting at a table in the basement of some kind of church or synagogue."

"That's right," he responded.

How did he know that was right? But I was too interested in what I was seeing to think about his response.

"Please describe the scene."

"The room is lit with candles on the walls and some on the tables."

"Yes," Al repeated enthusiastically. I wondered again, how did he know?

"What color are the walls?"

I looked more carefully. The walls were clearly a tone of orange, close to amber. I told him.

"Yes!" he almost shouted. His confirmation seemed much more than encouragement.

"Tell me more about the scene."

"I'm sitting at a table with a group of young men. Most of us are about nineteen years old, some older. We are wearing cloths over our heads, secured by dark sashes around our foreheads. All of us have *pais*, the long curls in front of the ears, prescribed in the Jewish tradition."

"That's right," Al interjected again. "What is happening?"

I scanned the vision on the inside of my forehead. It was clearer then a movie in a theatre.

"There is a sense of deep importance in the room. Our gathering is extremely auspicious. We are zealots. We have been trained in the ways of orthodox religion, and we have been brought together by the common realization that what we have been taught by our elders is not the complete truth. We are angry at having been misled, yet we are more hungry to discover what we can learn by seeking further. There is an air of great excitement in the assembly."

There was a long pause. What was Al thinking?

"Is there anything else you can tell me about this scene?"

"Yes. There is a feeling of secretiveness in our gathering; if we are discovered we will be scorned or punished. Yet our commitment to knowing the Truth is so strong that we are willing to risk it."

"Do you sense anything else about this memory?"

"Yes...Something very important will come from this meeting. We are like rays of sun on the dawn horizon, emerging slowly at first, but eventually bringing great change."

12

"Thank You."

It took a few minutes for Al to bring me back to the room we shared. He asked me to open my eyes. The room to which I had gone seemed as real as the room to which I returned.

I had to ask, "Al, why were you saying 'Yes,' and 'That's right' about my description?"

"Because," he answered, "I was seeing exactly what you were describing before you said it."

II

About a year later I had a dream that seemed equally real and intrinsically connected with that New Year's vision.

I saw myself as a rabbi in the temple during the time that Jesus lived and taught. It was just after he was condemned. As he was being ushered to his lashing, it dawned on me that he was who he said he was. What he taught was the truth. A veil of ignorance and fear lifted from my eyes and heart as I saw that he truly was the Son of God. I knew that he and his teachings were genuine, and that he sought only to bring light into a world of shadows.

I realized that I had made a great error in not coming to his support during his trial. I stepped forward to say something, but I knew that his lot had already been cast. It was too late to defend him.

My lesson, I felt, was simply to know that he and his message were true, and now I must live for this noble ideal for the rest of my life.

III

Hilda, my teacher of many years, has always worked diligently to create a harmony between the Jewish and Christian peoples. Much of her work has been to open up Jewish and Christian minds to the beauty and wisdom of both ways. In fact, Hilda once told us that this is one of the major purposes of her mission as a teacher of light.

One evening Hilda explained to us that she was aware of her previous life as "Colette, a nun in northern France." (She humbly neglected to mention that this was St. Colette, a dedicated reclusive nun who was a spiritual comerade of St. Joan of Arc.) We were startled to learn of this lifetime, yet not surprised to see that the mission of Colette's life is very similar to Hilda's purpose today.

During a prayer pilgrimage to Europe, Hilda and a group of students decided to take a day trip to Corbeille, the tiny village where Colette lived and where a church still stands in dedication to her memory and ideals.

The students returned with marvelous accounts of their adventures and some fascinating photographs. One picture showed a statue of Colette, with features remarkably similar to Hilda's. The one photograph that captured all of our attention, however, was that of a statue in Colette's church, a rendering that neither I nor any of the students have seen elsewhere: it was a statue of Moses and Jesus together, each with his arm around the other's shoulder. The sculpture was carved out of one stone, with no separation at all between the two brothers.

IV

At a group meditation I was asked to go back in consciousness to a time before birth, and then to inquire about the purpose of my life. Back, back, back I went, until eventually I found myself in a soft dreamy state, touched with gentle breezes and splashes of light from one shore of eternity to another.

"What is my purpose, Lord?" I asked when the moment was ripe.

"*Demonstration,*" came the answer. It was not an answer from outside myself, but from *within*.

Then I heard, "Your mission is to demonstrate the truth of love while on earth; to prove to yourself and the world that love and forgiveness are the most powerful and practical healers of troubled hearts; and to be a living message that it is possible to live on earth as it is in Heaven."

I was also told that it has been given me to take difficult situations that would be handled one way by a fearful person, and to demonstrate how easily they can be resolved with the help of Spirit.

V

This, then, is my sense of my purpose in this life: to bear witness to the truth that Jesus lived and taught; to celebrate the unity of all the pathways to God; and to learn and demonstrate that God is a loving friend Who will remove all obstacles from our path as we allow peace to be our only guide.

The Possible Dream

Look, look, look to the rainbow
Follow it over the hill and the stream
Look, look, look to the rainbow
Follow the fellow who follows his dream
- Finnian's Rainbow

The blue lights bathed the stage in their kindly essence. A hush fell over the audience as the emcee completed his reverent introduction. The singer stepped forward, drawing her breath deeply inward. Even those in the farthest corners of this historic theatre could feel the poignancy of this moment.

"Do you think I should do it, Alan?" a voice asked as I felt a hand on my shoulder.

"Do what, Danny?"

Crouching in the stage wings, waiting for our musical group to be called for the next act, Danny looked me in the eye. I realized that he had something on his mind far more important to him than the number we had prepared.

"Do you know who that is on the stage?" he whispered.

"The program says her name is 'Odetta;' that's all I know."

"Odetta is one of the greatest gospel/blues singers that has ever lived," Danny explained. "For many years she has been one of my favorite stars. It's been a dream of my life to accompany her on '*Amazing Grace*'...and that's what she's going to sing now!"

I could feel the thrill in Danny's voice; his excitement felt like that of a boy on the threshold of becoming a man.

"Do you see that piano there?" Danny pointed. "...I could just walk out there and start playing with her...or I could sit here and watch. What do you think I should do?"

There was no question in my mind about what Danny should do. He was one of the most talented and inspired gospel pianists I have ever heard.

This moment of opportunity was no accident; it was a gift.

"Go for it, Danny - This is your moment!"

Danny stood up, walked like a master to the piano, and sat down. As Odetta breathed heartily into the second verse of *Amazing Grace*, Danny began to weave a mosaic melody around her inspired voice. I saw his trepidation dissolve into the courage that shines from those who dare to be who they are.

Then there was a moment of hesitation in my mind...What if she did not want accompaniment? What if she wanted to sing *a cappella*? Had I made a fool out of both of us by encouraging him to go out there?

My fears were allayed quickly. Odetta turned to Danny, smiled, and nodded gracefully. This affirmation inspired him even more, and together the two of them created one of the most powerful renderings of that inspiring tune that I have ever heard. The audience responded with thunderous applause. Before my eyes I witnessed a living example of *Amazing Grace*.

Who is Danny? Danny is not just an isolated musical romantic or hopeful fantasizer. He is the spirit of every awakening soul who has had a dream and given birth to the courage to make it come true. Danny is every aspiring musician, artist, dancer, and inventor; every master of any discipline who has sweated through years of practice, trials, and obstacles in the name of a cherished ideal. Danny represents all of us who know that our dream can become a reality if only we don't give up. Danny is every one of us who yearns to make a difference in our world, to bring our planet into a better condition than the one in which we found it. Danny is you and me; Danny is all of us.

Be Calm, Be Steadfast

Last winter I was riding aboard a United Airlines Boeing 727 en route from Seattle to Newark, eagerly anticipating a workshop I was to present that evening in Princeton, New Jersey. The workshop was especially important to me as it was being sponsored by a holistic health association I have long respected. For years I had wanted to work with this group, and here was my opportunity. I purposefully arranged to leave Seattle at 7 AM in order to arrive in ample time for the evening's event.

About 4 PM, one hour before we were to land, I was mentally preparing my presentation when the captain's voice came over the loudspeaker: "Ladies and gentlemen, you may have noticed that the airplane just made a wide left turn...I guess it's time to tell you the bad news: Every airport from Boston to Baltimore is fogged in, and there's no place on the east coast for us to land. We'll be in Detroit in about an hour.''

"*Detroit?!?!?!?!?!*"

Did he really say, "*Detroit*?!" If I didn't know what thought-forms were, I would have received my first lesson right there, as I saw about a hundred of them hit the ceiling at the same time. They were like the little water-propelled rockets we used to shoot from our lawns as kids, excitedly watching them *whooosh!* into the summer sky. Only this time it was not summer and there was no sky - just the pre-fab contoured plastic ceiling panels enfolding a hundred jet-lagged and conspicuously unenthusiastic travellers.

"Detroit?"

That moment gave me the auspicious opportunity to practice what Hilda had been teaching me for so many years, namely "a quick adjustment of the mind." I must report, in all honesty, that my adjustment was not so quick. For the next hour I practiced every metaphysical trick I had ever seen and read about, in a feverish attempt to get the plane to land in Newark. I visualized the plane touching down on a sunny airstrip (which would have been a real miracle, since the winter sun had already gone down). I called on all the saints, masters, and angels that I had ever heard of, ardently summoning their aid in my petition. To my chagrin, when I called on St. Francis I was told that he was out walking in the woods; redirecting airplanes, they said, was not really his department. Next, I subliminally vibed the pilot and cockpit crew, hoping to implant just-below-threshold suggestions in their subconscious via the airplane's musical entertainment channel.

Then, when all else had failed, I had no choice but to bring out the heavy artillery: THE VULCAN MIND MELD! Fervently aligning my mental faculties with Saint Spock, I beamed my thought-forms to everyone in charge of this awful dilemma, hoping that a Federation tractor-beam would draw us precisely to that New Jersey runway. Mentally I extended my fingers to the First Officer's brow, strategically placing them on the sensitive nerve centers indicated in the ancient Vulcan rite. "My mind is one mind with your mind," I concentrated all of my energies " - You will turn this aircraft right and land us in Newark by 5 PM."

But alas! The First Officer of this particular starship had no pointed ears and his eyebrows extended nowhere near his temples. Soon I felt the ship's landing gear touch down not upon the Federation coordinates I had prescribed, but instead on a cold and slightly snowy asphalt airstrip that led to none other than the Motor City.

Disappointed, disgruntled, and slightly disembodied from my hapless hijinks in metaphysical hijacking, I joined a hundred other displaced cling-ons in line for a bus pointed toward a hotel in the middle of the city that, as far as I knew, housed only automobiles and Tigers...

Several resisted hours later I flopped into a bed on the forty-fourth floor of a hotel overlooking an icy Lake Erie, a thousand miles from anyone I knew. "What am I doing here?" I asked God. "Didn't you want me to do that workshop? I mean, really, God, what gives?"

I picked up a book from my suitcase, *The Still Voice,* a collection of inspiring meditations by a gentle spiritual guide called White Eagle.

"O.K. God, could you please tell me the lesson?" I asked. "I'll open this book to any page, and whatever I read will be my lesson."

I inserted my thumbnail somewhere in the midst of the off-white leaves and let the book fall open. There before my astounded eyes, I read:

BE CALM, BE STEADFAST

When you try to do things, and they will not go the way you want, leave them alone. Do not try to force things the way you would like them to go. Just leave them alone. Do your best, obey the law of love, and you will be surprised at how circumstances will work out far better for you than if you had had your own way. Let God have His way, and you just be patient and wait. Be calm, steadfast and peaceful. Accept things as they come and do not be rushed into wrong decisions or overcome by the forces of ignorance. Be steadfast, with a quiet, inner, peaceful persistence, knowing that the Great Architect of the Universe holds the plan of your life in His hands.[1]

Well, that about summed it up. "Maybe I'm supposed to be here," I conceded. "...and if that's so, I might as well enjoy myself."

My attention was drawn to a triangular card on top of the television in the room, advertising the in-house movies available that night. Mentally I surveyed the offerings of "Body Heat," "Linda Lovelace Strikes Back," and a series of pictures that promised more x's than crosses. Before long I

---

[1] White Eagle, *The Still Voice,* The White Eagle Publishing Trust, Hampshire, United Kingdom, 1980

began to give up hope that I would find something I felt like seeing. Then I saw an advertisement for a movie called *Flashdance*. When I saw that word it occurred to me that within the last two weeks I had told several people that I had wanted to see *Flashdance* when it played in the movie theatres, but I had missed it. Could this be my opportunity?

I switched on the set to find a marvelously inspiring story of a young woman who has a lifetime dream to be a classical dancer. To pay her rent until her dream comes true, she dances in sleazy clubs at night and works as a welder during the days. She is not really doing what she wants to be doing, but her vision sustains her to carry on until her dream can become a reality.

This aspiring young woman meets a man who gets her an audition with a respected ballet school. But because she feels that she did not earn the audition on her own merit, she turns her back on the audition and the man.

I remember so clearly the scene in which she tells her boyfriend, "I give up...I'm going back to the club!" She turns to walk out the door.

But he is not willing to let her — and her dream — go so easily. He grabs her by the arm, swings her around, looks her straight in the eye and asks her, "Don't you realize what you're doing? You're throwing away your dream! And don't you know that *when you give up your dream, you're dead!*"

When you give up your dream, you're dead.

As far as I was concerned, that was the whole story. Perhaps that was why I was brought to Detroit, to hear that message. At first I thought I was in the middle of nowhere; at last I discovered I was in the center of everywhere. There I was given an important lesson, a practical lesson, a lesson that perhaps we all need to remember: *When you give up your dream, you're dead.* And when you hold fast to your dream — when you are calm and steadfast — you're alive. What more do we need to remember?

As the movie turned out, that young lady went on to that audition and really wowed them. She had the courage to believe in herself, to push past that lethally deceptive membrane of self-doubt. In so doing she proved the adage that the only time we fail is the last time we try. She succeeded not only for herself, but for me, for you, and for everyone who needs the strength to go all the way. And that determination made all the difference.

As my own movie turned out, when I arrived home the next day I was told that the same fog which kept my plane from landing at the airport prevented cars from driving on the highways. Very few people had been able to make it to the workshop, and the organizers decided to reschedule it for a later date. There was no real loss — but I did gain much in learning such a powerful and healing lesson.

Are you living your dream? Have you given up your most wonderful, cherished, and important aspirations and settled for a half-life? Do you have a reason to get up in the morning, a vision, an ideal, a quest? Or have you compromised your vision and let go of the bright-eyed child within you that gave you so much joy? Have you surrendered your personal destiny to conform to the pack?

You don't have to give up your dream; in fact, the hound of Heaven will keep lovingly urging you to do what you were born to do until you have bestowed upon the world the gift that only *you* can offer it. Spinoza, the great celebrant of love, proclaimed, "To be what we were born to be, and to become what we are capable of becoming, is the only end in life."

My friend Marsha is a good example of holding firmly to her vision. Marsha is a talented beauty consultant who has made a career of teaching women and models how to make the most of their appearance. Since she has been meditating, however, her work has taken on a new and exciting creativity.

"I realized that inner beauty is even more important than outer beauty," Marsha shared with me one day. "So I created a class called, *"Me — the Best I Can Be."* I gave the students oatmeal and honey facial packs and asked them to lie down on the floor for the half hour it took for the treatment to take effect. While they were lying there I put on a tape of meditative music and guided them through a progressive deep relaxation. When they got up they said they felt relaxed, healed, and beautiful — inside and out. They ended up getting everything they wanted, and more!"

This fresh originality is available to all of us. Another friend, Barbara, is a dedicated hairstylist. She explained it to me in this way: "When anyone comes to me in the shop, I know they are really coming for love and peace of mind. So I developed a method I call "the seven-minute vacation." I got permission from my boss to set up a booth in the rear of the salon, which I have dedicated as a place of peacefulness. Before each treatment I turn down the lights, put on some soft music, and give my client a gentle neck and shoulder massage. As I touch them I silently pray that I serve as a channel for the Christ light and that this client is healed through my haircut, my touch, and my presence. They love it! Now the manager can't figure out why so many people request me as their personal hairstylist. The secret is that I'm really styling their soul!"

Perhaps the most cogent demonstration that God works through *all* channels is an account given to me by Alberto Aguas, a gifted and dynamic

Brazilian healer. Alberto travels throughout the world working miracles through the laying on of hands and inspired prayer. Here is Alberto's story:

One week when I was working out of a motel in California, my secretary showed me that one woman had scheduled a five-hour appointment.

"Five hours?" I asked; "Why did you schedule her for so long? You know that my healing treatments usually take about half an hour."

"I know," the secretary responded, "...but this is a special case."

"What could be so special to require five hours?"

"Just trust me."

"Well, O.K. — I guess a faith healer should have some faith."

The next afternoon at 12:30 Alberto heard a knock at the motel door. He answered it to find, to his astonishment, a tall woman, early forty-ish, with orange hair, hot pants, gold go-go boots, and a cleavage that did not require much in the way of creative visualization. The woman's profession could not have been more obvious had she worn a billboard. After rubbing his eyes, Alberto looked again to see that she was accompanied by about a dozen younger ladies wearing the same uniform, obviously all players on the same team.

"Come in," Alberto cordially invited them, half-amazed, half-curious, half-laughing inside.

"What can I do for you?" was his introduction, almost ludicrous in light of its juxtaposition.

"Mr. Aguas, my name is Honey; I'm the manager of the Pink Pussycat Massage Parlor, and these girls are my staff."

(Alberto had to do all he could to keep from breaking up.)

"I know that this is a rather unusual request for you, Mr. Aguas, but we have been having some rather unusual experiences, and we thought perhaps you could help us understand them."

"I'll try." answered Alberto, holding his breath.

"About six months ago we moved to new headquarters, a lovely old building on La Quieta. We set aside a few days to clean the place up, and on the third day we went down into the basement. There we found some old boxes with many books in them. Curious, we opened some of the paperbacks with strange titles we'd never seen before: *Adventures in Reincarnation, Your Healing Power*, and many by some fellow named Edward Case or something like that, a quaint old man from Virginia Beach. The titles and subjects were so fascinating that we began to read excerpts out loud to one another as we rearranged the boxes.

"At first we thought these ideas were rather strange and sometimes we poked fun at them. But, Mr. Aguas, the most amazing thing happened — the more we read, the more interested we became. Eventually we stopped unpacking and we began discussing the material. It turned out that many of us had had experiences such as the ones described in the books, like picking up the phone to call someone and finding them on the other end of the line, or meeting someone and feeling like you've known them before. Susan, here, had seen angels as a child, but she stopped when her mother told her she must never tell anyone.

"We came to a chapter on healing, and we decided to try this stuff out to see if it really worked. So when we were with our clients we would see them in white light and, strange as it may sound, we would pray for them. It was easy to know what to pray for, for many men who come to ladies of the evening like to tell us their story; in an ironic way we have always been counselors of sorts. So when we were performing our services we would inconspicuously put our hand on the man's heart or his back or wherever he told us he had a problem. Then we would silently ask to have healing light flow through us to him.

"The results were amazing! When the men came back a week or a month later, we would casually ask them how their heart or back was. You wouldn't believe the reports they gave us! Like, 'Funny you should ask…This amazing thing happened: Right around the last time I saw you it started to get better; it's funny, but it used to be such a problem and now it hardly bothers me at all!'

"So, Mr. Aguas, quite frankly we believe in this stuff, and we'd like to learn more about it. Can you help us?"

"Yes, I think I can — and I would be delighted to!"

So Alberto spent the next five hours giving one of the most important healing classes of his life.

"I Dream for a Living"

One of my favorite dreamers, high on the list of visionaries I love is Steven Spielberg, the genius producer/director of such modern classics as Close Encounters of the Third Kind, Raiders of the Lost Ark, and E.T. It was no accident that I should see a picture of Steven on the cover of Time Magazine and subsequently open to his story entitled, "I Dream for a Living." With saucer eyes I dove headlong into the article, at times laughing out loud, at other times elbowing the fellow sitting next to me, cheering, "Yeah, yeah, that's it!"

I felt like I knew him. Making movies, the article explained, has been in Steven's blood since he was a child. Ever since he got his hands on his dad's 8mm home movie camera when he was twelve, Steven hasn't stopped. "Our living room was strewn with cables and floodlights," reports Leah Spielberg, his Yiddisha momma, now an extra in his films. "We never said no — we never had a chance to say no — Steven didn't understand that word."[2]

Steven, like all dreamers, has *chutzpah.* When he was seventeen he went on a tour of Universal Studios. At an opportune moment he slipped away from the tour and found a film editor, to whom he showed an early homemade film. The editor was impressed, but apologized for not being able to help him.

Did that stop young Steve? No, no self-respecting visionary would throw in the celluloid at such a minor setback. The next day Steven, like his fabled *Indiana Jones,* fudged his way past the guards at Universal, carrying his father's briefcase containing a sandwich and two candy bars. He started hanging out with producers, directors, and dubbers, found an empty office, and moved into it. He went out to a camera store, bought a plastic name title, and put his name on the building office directory. Thus began Steven's legend-in-his-own-time career with no authorization from anyone other then his higher self. And what an authorization it was! Twenty years later, at the age of thirty-seven, finds Steven Spielberg as the most successful producer/director in cinematographic history, with four films in the top ten attractions of all time, the highest-grossing film ever made, a four million dollar home built for him by Universal City on their own lot, and a major share in the ownership of the studios that not long ago didn't even offer him the closet of a self-authorized office through which he walked to greatness.

How does Steven explain his creative process? Simply. "Once a month the sky falls on my head, I come to, and I see another movie I want to make. I wake up so excited I can't eat breakfast. I've never run out of energy. I don't worry about a premium going on my energy. It's always been there."[3]

That was one of the moments my neighbor got elbowed; I got excited because it explained the way my books come. Right now I feel about half a dozen books in mental utero, brand new to the world, each inspiring me in its own special way. The best way I could describe this process is that these creations are like airplanes flying in a holding pattern, each waiting its turn to land, each carrying a full cargo of never-before gathered ideas as passen-

---

[2] *Time* Magazine, July 15, 1985
[3] Ibid.

gers. It is the most humbling experience and yet the most strengthening. This process of dreaming, thinking, and creating is a pure miracle to me. I see the birth of an idea into the world as the most powerful testimony that God is life. There is no greater opportunity in life than to be a dreamer drawing ideas into expression.

God is Your Agent

It may be said that there are two types of people in the world: those who are willing to live for their dream, and those who have forgotten how to believe in themselves. Those who live for their dream are the creators, the initiators, the artistically alive free souls, the women and men who stand out in a crowd and brighten the lives of those they touch in the simple interactions of daily living. They are the people around whom we feel energized, nourished, healed, important, and optimistic. They make us feel that we are capable, worthy, and lovable, for they feel that wonderful way about themselves. They radiate beauty because they find good in everyone they touch. They are the persons who move the world along, lifting normality out of inertia and into action. They are the shining ones who have heard and responded to the inner call, standing for all that destiny would have them glorify.

I had to stand up for my dream — We all do, and although the individual facts may appear to be different, the dynamics of integrity are always the same. When I finished writing *The Dragon Doesn't Live Here Anymore*, I trusted that the same God that gave me the book would get it published. I sent sample chapters to several spiritually-oriented publishers and received either no response or a "thank you for your material, but it does not fit in with our current publishing plans" form letter. One publisher, whom I telephoned directly, asked me what was the theme of the book. When I told him, "the healing power of true forgiveness," he scoffed, "Nah, nobody's interested in that; try writing something more dynamic." No room at the inn.

I did not want to wait until someone was willing to take the book on. I decided that if I had to publish it myself, though I did not have the money, I would do it.

The day I finished writing the book two friends approached me, and though I had not asked them, offered me the money to publish the book. One of them was my mother. When I told her I had written a book she asked me, "What's it about?" I told her, "truth, love, and God." "That's beyond me," was her immediate response. "How long is it?" was her next question. "About four hundred pages, Mom." "You're crazy!" was her second response.

The next day her third response came. She called me on the telephone and said, "If you want the money to publish your book, I'll give it to you." I guess it wasn't beyond her.

I found a reputable company in the mid-west to do the printing. Within a few weeks I found myself in New York City meeting with their agent to give him the completed copy, discuss the printing format, and hand him a check for five thousand dollars to print a book that a metaphysical magnate had scoffed at. As we concluded our arrangements he walked me to the door and as he shook my hand he told me, "You know, they say you don't make any money until you've published your third book!"

Momentarily taken aback by this narrow notion, I felt like an infant upon whom a wagonload of manure had been thrust unannounced. Yet I knew that I could not afford to give one moment's acknowledgement to this debilitating idea. Immediately into my mind arose the *Course in Miracles* lesson, "I am under no laws but God's."[4] I knew that I had to make a stand for the Truth. I thought for a moment, smiled at my skeptical friend and told him, "Yes, Keith, I understand that's what they may say, but one thing you may not realize is that my agent is God."

Keith just stood there scratching his head. I don't know if he got it, but I got it. I got that never again could I lean out on the values and expectations of the world to validate me. I realized that I would have to trust God and believe in myself even when those around me were lost in fear and limitation. I understood that the only source to whom I can turn in times of outer darkness is the Light within me, ever urging me to know myself to be magnificent, beautiful, and good. I found myself.

The first printing of *Dragon* sold out quickly, and before long my original investment was returned. Soon I began to make money on its sales — *before* my third book. *What the agent had told me was simply not true.* If I had believed him or allowed that limiting thought into my mind, I might have created that negative situation — not by virtue of its truth, but by the power of my thinking and believing that it was so. But because I refused to agree with that constricting idea, I experienced no limitation. *There is no limitation.* As we rise to our ability to create with God, miracles happen.

---

[4] W, p. 132

Stand by Your Dream

There is no dream in life that is beyond your ability to accomplish. God would not plant a seed in your mind if She did not plan to give you ways to help it grow into a flower. God is not a sadist. If anything, She is a philanthropist. Once we know that God is working *with* us and not against us, we can cherish our dreams as divinely-inspired visions of our new life. Then all we need to do is hold firmly to our dream, especially during the times when it seems as if the dream is being challenged. The key to transforming our life is to *keep your mind and heart on your dream.* As one great thinker said, "Obstacles are what you see when you take your eyes off the goal."

Your dream is a sprouting innovation that needs your loving help to grow to full maturity. Then it returns your caring by nourishing you as well as many others. Every great achievement in this world started out as a dream. A vision of success is a seminal idea that needs to be nurtured and strengthened by one who believes in it enough to stand by it through windy times.

Are you willing to stand by your dream in times of opposition? Are you willing to believe in yourself enough to say "Yes!" to yourself even when others do not stand with you? Are you willing to believe that God Itself planted that dream in your mind, and that selfsame Spirit will help you bring it to perfect fruition, even — and especially — when you seem to have exhausted all of your own resources? Are you willing to live for what you believe?

This is the dynamic law of living that empowers us to materialize our dreams. How can a dream come true unless we act to make it real? Too many great ideas have been thrown in the wastebasket before they were put on the drawing board. Within you now are the seeds of greatness. There is something that you have to offer the world, something special, something marvelous, something that can change someone's life for the better — perhaps many people's lives. Are you willing to plant these golden seeds? Are you willing to take a chance on having your life work now? Are you willing to be the magnificent radiant being that you really are, the shining light that God knows you to be, from the moment you were conceived?

God has never given up on you because God could never forget how precious you are. Are you ready to go out on the stage of life and play that piano like you've never played before, for the glory of love and the celebration of beauty? If so, then you are certain to succeed, for your dream is none other than God's dream for you.

I must believe there's a God Who believes in me.
- Joseph and Nathan

The HEALED MIND

Natural or Regular

Be true to yourself, be true to yourself
And you'll never be false to any man
Be true to yourself, be true to yourself
And stretch out your hand

- Chris Rudolf*

One afternoon my mother sent me to the supermarket to buy some applesauce on sale. As I made my way through the aisle I looked at the coupon and found a most interesting description of the product: "Foodtown Applesauce — 19 cents — *"Natural or Regular"*. "Natural or Regular" — What did that mean? I checked the labels. The regular applesauce contained sugar, artificial coloring, a list of preservatives requiring either a master's degree in organic chemistry or a working knowledge of Tralfamidorian to decipher, and a host of other ingredients that do not usually come with apples from a tree. The natural applesauce, on the other hand, contained just apples and water.

This distinction caused me to think more deeply about how we live our lives, about the values we hold to be true, about the goals we set for our livelihood. It is becoming clear to me that the way most of us have lived our lives has not been in harmony with the way the universe was intended to work for us to be happy. It seems that we have somehow lost touch with the loving flow of life, our rhythm of being, our sense of peacefulness about ourselves and satisfaction with what we are and what we are here to do.

We have sacrificed the natural for the regular, entrenching ourselves in patterns of living that have left us with a sense of being somehow incomplete, knowing that what we have is not it, yet not quite knowing how to get the "it" we feel we are missing. Many of us have found ourselves in jobs that give us little satisfaction, riddled by a sense of being trapped in relationships that do not seem to be working, living for goals that disappoint

---

* "Be True to Yourself," by Chris Rudolf, *Songs Along the Way*, Waking Up Productions, 1984

us almost as soon as they are reached. Yet we keep the same job because we are afraid to do what we would love to do, slowly dying under the macabre illusion that a job is real only if we are suffering in it. We stay in the same rut in our relationship because most of the relationships we have seen have failed, so why should ours be any better, and maybe interpersonal peace is just a myth anyway. And we continue to chase after the dreams that disintegrate in our hands like the powder of dead men's bones, the sad revenue of the elusive goals that have been attained by the apparently successful who seem to be happy, but whose terrible hurt returns to their drawn faces the moment the cameras turn away and the spotlights are dimmed. This is the story of the world, a house of distorted mirrors through which the original image has been turned upside down, a seductress masquerading as a saint, a demon with the face of an angel.

At some point in our soul's evolution each of us discovers that the world is not working according to the rules that we have been taught to serve. We learn that the way most people approach life is not a healthy guide for us. It becomes clear that the institutions to which we have been encouraged to pay homage are little more than empty shells of long ago withdrawn ideals, and the nations of the world are as lost, alone, and afraid as the individuals who make them up. To put it simply, the world is not succeeding according to the illusions after which it is pining. We see that if we are to find some kind of peace and solace we are going to have to hearken to the voice of an *inner* guide rather than the dictates of the masses.

The world we have made is the opposite of Heaven. We have used fear as a guide instead of peace, worshipping separation instead of unity. We have looked at ourselves as bundles of boundaries instead of the magnificent, unlimited beings we truly are. When we take just about all of the values we have honored and reverse them, we discover that what we have sought and learned is indeed the opposite of what we need to learn and be.

My friend Mike, a successful organizational development consultant with a sizeable income at A.T.&T., told me this story:

"My brother stood in danger of losing his home through a default on his mortgage payments. Feeling guided to help him, I went to the bank, withdrew seventeen thousand dollars from my savings account, put a cashier's check for it in an envelope, and mailed it to him. It wasn't a gift; it wasn't a loan; it wasn't anything I could name. All I knew was that he needed it and I had it, and it was more important to me to help him than to keep it. I want you to know that the moment I dropped that check in the mailbox I felt more peace than I ever have in my whole life."

More peace. It is said that God gives us feedback about how close we are to Heaven by the amount of peace that we feel when doing any act. Yet somehow we have learned to live as if we gain peace by separating ourselves from one another, when in fact we move along the road to healing by acknowledging our caring.

We have sadly come to the point where we feel we need to apologize for making contact. One night in a movie theatre a woman sitting next to me accidentally brushed her hand by my knee as she reached for her pocket-book.

"I'm sorry," she briskly apologized.

"Sorry?" I returned; "Please don't be sorry — I liked it!"

Perhaps if we admitted more often that "I like it!" when we really do like it, our world will reflect more of who we really are, how we truly want to live, and the way we would like to be with one another. Otherwise we are doomed to a horrible sense of confusion because the world in which we live is not in harmony with the truth of our being.

This truth is *totally within our power* to know, feel, and live *as we choose.* Often at the end of a weekend workshop I hear participants remark, "Wow! This was really great! I felt so comfortable with my feelings of real love for myself and those around me! Too bad we have to go back to the real world now."

Then I answer, "This *is* the real world. *This* is the world that everyone loves, for we understand this feeling as the reality of our heart. *This* is the world we all want to feel and live in all the time. There is no reason to stop now. We can create our life any way we choose. We *can* have caring people in our life, our relationships *can* work, we can *hug,* and we can say, "I love you" as much as we like. It's entirely up to us."

Then I tell them the story of Dan, my auto mechanic, who quit watching ticker tapes on Wall Street to consolidate carburetors in a local service station. Although he felt happier having made the move, Dan was still bothered by some physical symptoms of stress. Whenever I brought my car in to be repaired Dan and I would chat for a while. At first I felt a little distant from him, but as I got to know him I began to appreciate him. He was a deeply sincere and sensitive fellow, and although he would probably not term himself so, he was a spiritual man.

One day as Dan and I were standing in front of the garage he told me how much he wanted peace. He explained to me that his stomach was troubling him, some of his relationships could feel better, and other aspects of his life were not working as well as he would have liked. He told me that

33

he was at the point where he was willing to do anything to be healed. This touched me deeply, for as I looked into his eyes I saw the eyes of the Christ.

At that moment something came over me; a feeling of deep closeness to Dan welled up within me, and I just wanted to reach out and hug him and tell him how much I appreciated his beautiful open heart.

So I did. Right there on Main Street. Right in front of the gas station. Right there where all the tough guys hang out swearing and smoking Marlboros. In the very heart of gasoline alley I gave him a big bear hug. It was one of those spontaneous acts that's more fun to do when you don't think about it first.

Then, a few moments into my embracing Dan another voice within my mind spoke to me. This voice was not as encouraging as the one that had prompted me to hug him. This voice, with sort of a John Wayne roll, informed me, "You're crazy!...Men don't hug other men in the gas station, and certainly not on Main Street. Why are you doing this? You hardly know this guy! When you let go he's going to punch you."

It was one of those moments known as an embarrassing predicament, when time just seems to linger in the air like a slow bomb taking its time dropping. "How did I get into this one?" I wondered — and more important, "How do I get out?"

Realizing that I had probably made a big mistake, I decided that my only hope was to delay the punch. So I kept on hugging him, thinking that he couldn't raise his fist if my arms were clenched around his.

But it couldn't go on forever. Eventually I had to release my embrace and see what he would do. I let go. There was a pregnant moment in which the two of us just stood there looking at each other. I wondered whether it would be a left jab or a right uppercut.

But the punch never came. Instead, Dan looked me right in the eye, took a big deep breath, and told me, "Thanks — I needed that!"

Dan and I became friends. I gave him one of my books and a meditation tape with my deepest blessings. Although we did not see each other often, he was very much in my heart.

About six months later, I was driving down Main Street and I stopped at a traffic light in front of the garage. Almost involuntarily my head turned in the direction of the garage bay, where I saw Dan's coveralled body, head submerged under the hood of a red Ferrari. Quickly and enthusiastically I tooted the horn.

Startled, Dan emerged like a dinosaur lifting its head from lunching on a patch of greens. When he saw me he smiled and yelled, "Where have you been? I need a hug!"

Being one who never turns down an offer for a good hug, I left the traffic signal, turned into the station, jumped out of my car, left the motor running, and gave Dan a big hug. Then I took off. My first pit stop for a hug.

About a year later I received a message that a Dan had telephoned me. "Dan?" I scratched my head, not recalling who the name belonged to. When I returned the call Dan's wife answered. When I told her my name she called out, "Hey Dan! It's the gentle flowing waterfall!"

"What's the gentle flowing waterfall?" I queried as he picked up the receiver.

"Oh, yeah," he laughed, "My wife and I listen to your meditation tape every night before we go to sleep. You know—the one with the waterfall and the rainbows in it. I must tell you how much we both enjoy it—it really helps! My wife even took the tape into labor with her. I also want to tell you that my stomach is much improved, along with the relationships I told you about. Thank you so much for taking such an interest in me—I feel like a new person!"

Hugging on Main Street. It takes guts. I don't know if there is any fear so debilitating as the fear of popular opinion, and no freedom more rewarding than following the guidance of one's own heart. I know few people who are willing to hug on Main Street, to say, "I love you" when the popular script doesn't call for it. Some, not a lot. But there are more and more, more and more.

We can cite courageous persons like Shirley MacLaine, who while living in the public eye are willing to risk gossip and opinion for the sake of sharing the truth that has come to them. And yet it is not really a risk at all, for once one sees the truth there is not much choice about going back to illusion. Shirley's books, *Out on a Limb* and *Dancing in the Light*, are inspiring testimonies of a sincere person miraculously blossoming into the spiritual life. She has blessed millions simply by sharing her story.

Yet Shirley's story is no more powerful than yours or mine. The world is waiting for our stories to be told, despite what the norms may have been. The moment Shirley was willing to speak the truth she felt in her heart she began to be a channel, a vessel through which healing ideas, attitudes, and actions are being directed to those whose ears and hearts are open to hear and feel the truth of their own beauty.

The Path of Love

Each day we receive many opportunities to give healing simply by being our true self. It is up to each of us to accept the invitation to become who we truly are. Indeed every moment is a doorway to Heaven, every encounter a lesson in love.

One beautiful summer I had such an opportunity when I met Charley Thweatt of the joyously talented musical group, *Oman, Shanti, and Charley*. Instantly I knew he and I were kindred spirits. We had so much to say to one another, to share, to laugh about together. It seemed as if we were old and dear friends meeting after a long time away from one another. Opening our hearts and sharing stories, we discovered that we had travelled many of the same highways of life, and now we were being given the privilege to meet and catch up on all the places we had been and what we had done. It felt as if distant continents were being joined once again.

I shall always treasure that night we reunited in a restaurant on the windward side of the island of Oahu in Hawaii. We had just completed a successful presentation together, and a deep sense of joyful satisfaction was in our hearts. Charley walked over to the table where I was sitting with some other friends, and asked if we could have a word privately.

We stepped down to a terrace amid gently swaying palm trees. Torches illuminated the mystical contours of great wooden masks of ancient Hawaiian gods that smiled through the flowered aroma of the tradewinds that caress one's very soul on those magical islands.

Charley took my hand and told me, "I just want you to know how much I've enjoyed working with you. I hope we can share a program together again."

There was a moment of mutual gratefulness honored perfectly by the silence in which we felt it.

"And I, you."

There we were, just Charley and me, our inner glow poignant in contrast to the noise of the restaurant. We just sat there looking into one another's eyes like two sappy lovers in a linty old Bogart movie.

As we held each other's hands and spoke in gentle tones, a fearful little voice in the back of my brain began to slither: "This really looks weird. You better let go of his hand...People will think you're gay — You mustn't let anyone see this.''

But our being together had nothing to do with sexuality, romance, or bodies. It was a joining of spirit, and we could just as easily have been a man and a woman, a mother and child, or two lima beans. It was the essence of two brothers sharing a special moment. And it was far beyond time and into the eternity that brought the flowers on the breeze to our senses and then swept them on to the ocean and unto the dreamy Pacific skies.

It took courage to hold my brother's hand in that crowded restaurant, as it takes strength to be natural in a regular world. We have been hypnotized into believing that we are small, troubled creatures, while our souls are rooted in eternity itself. *All that we seek we already are.* We do not need to scrutinize our state of hypnosis or curse the stupor into which we have fallen. We need only to wake up. We need to remember who we are, make a stand for it, and live it. We must celebrate our spiritual identity. We must emerge from our cocoon of fear, open our hearts, and declare, ''I know that the ability to heal my life and our world lies within my hands.'' In thus committing ourselves, you and I create the most monumental transition our planet has ever been blessed to experience.

To change the world, we are required only to put fear aside and dedicate ourselves wholeheartedly to the Truth. At first we may hesitate to crawl out on those skinny new branches and declare who we are. But before long we discover that the only thing more painful than making a stand for the light is knowing the truth and living a life that does not reflect it.

In a sense we have all been double agents. Knowing reality and living in illusion is a torturous dilemma, and truly there is no split in life that creates more tension than this one. But tension is a gift that bestows its blessing when we are ready to seek relief from it. Being dissatisfied with the world as it is means that there is a part of our mind that knows there must be a better way. Let us thank God that we are not willing to settle for less than the complete peace we deserve.

One day each of us will arise and say, ''Dear friends, I am now ready to live for the light.'' On that momentous day, that holy day — not far away now — the natural will become the regular. That will be a day of great rejoicing, for with the acknowledgement of the truly natural comes all of the light that we know we deserve, but have temporarily forgotten how to see because we were covering our eyes with our own hand. On that day we shall fulfill Jesus' prophecy when he prayed, ''On earth as it is in Heaven,'' for this earth will not be complete until it reflects the Peace of Heaven in every way. It is you and I who must create this holy moment, which begins now and spans far into eternity. For this were we born, for this we live, and for this shall we continue to live until the aspiration of our soul becomes the reality of our life.

Who Told You
You Were Naked?

The holy instant does not require that you have
No thoughts that are not pure.
But it does require that you have none that you
Keep to yourself.

                                        - A Course in Miracles[1]

As you may recall from Sunday or Hebrew School (in between perusing the Captain America comics hidden in your Bible or sketching hot rods on your desk), God created Adam and Eve in Paradise. Then God set them in a beautiful garden to be enjoyed eternally, with no service charge, finder's fee, or difference in price for cash or credit. Here the happy couple had dominion over all the elements of earth, free to play and be at peace literally forever.

"You may eat of all the fruits of the garden," the Heavenly Father told His Children, "even the Tree of Life. But there is one tree from which you must not eat — the Tree of Knowledge of Good and Evil."

God was telling Adam and Eve — you and me — that we cannot judge. This is not a commandment not to judge, but a statement that we could not judge even if we wanted to. Spirit, in its true essence, does not know good or evil. God is just pure love, pure energy, pure being. If we want to live in the high joy vibration, we must free ourself of the distinctions that the mortal mind has conjured to separate us from our Source.

So what did Adam and Eve do, for openers? The only thing they were told not to do, of course, and Eve took her famous bite. Now here's where the action really begins. Immediately Adam and Eve realize they are naked, and they take fig leaves to cover their loins, which beforehand were no less beautiful or holy than the rest of them. The moment they made a distinction between good and evil, that separation was projected onto their bodies,

---

[1] T, p. 289

making some parts of them good and other parts bad. This is the division in consciousness that has produced the world of separateness that we see.

Then, the Bible tells us, Adam and Eve hid from God (the first guilt trip), and God, like any self-respecting father, sought to find them. (*He* knew where they were, but *they* needed help to find them*selves*.) Then, the story goes, "They heard God walking in the Garden." It's interesting that now they perceived God as outside themselves; until that time, He was within their hearts.

And God asked, "Adam, where are you?"

Adam, realizing that he could hide no longer, answered, "Here I am."

"What are you doing in those bushes, Adam?...You were playing so nicely in the Garden! Come, *bubbala*, I have a grilled cheese sandwich and tomato soup for you. Have a little lunch."

"But I can't come out, Father — I'm naked!"

"Naked, what's 'naked'? What are you talking about, 'naked'?"

Enter Adam and Eve, stage left, adorned with the tackiest designer fig leaves you've ever seen, hastily tied around their waists, looking more like leftovers from a Soho costume party than Children of God. God almost fell on the Garden floor laughing — He made His Children in perfection and they decided perfection needed to be covered by a plant. Had it been a few thousand years later, it would have been polyester.

"What is this fig leaf business?" asks the Father. "What I gave you wasn't good enough?"

"No, it's not that," Adam begins to explain. "You see, the woman made me do it." (We won't even begin to comment on that one.)

Spotlight to woman. "Well, what's your story?"

"The serpent made me do it." Flip Wilson would have been proud.

Unfortunately for the serpent, he wasn't around to defend himself, else he might have blamed it on the tabasco sauce on last night's nachos. So the poor asp gets condemned to slither around on his belly and perform denigrating dances out of straw baskets in grade-b movies for several thousand years. Bad karma.

Now, if you would be willing to overlook the burlesque license I am taking, let's look at that one question asked of Adam by God, the inquiry around which the whole scene revolves: *Who told you you were naked?*

This is a question asked not only of Adam by God. It is one you and I must ask ourselves. Who told you you were naked?

There was a time early in our lives when we lived as innocent children, totally unashamed, free of fear of opinion, beyond the sordid realm of guilt and fear. This was the Garden of Eden within our heart. Here we were and are all Adam, all Eve.

Then something happened. Someone told us we were naked. Someone convinced us — beguiled us — to believe that we were not good enough as we were, that we had to be or do something more than we were to be approved. We believed that we had to work to change ourselves to be innocent, while our innocence stood inviolate just as we were.

Someone, like the first grade teacher of a child I know, told us that we could not color the clown's nose green. "All clowns' noses must be red," she commanded the child. That afternoon the little boy came home with a tear in his eye, a tear that was not there before.

It was the same child who stood at the door waiting for the schoolbus on the first day of school, stark naked, lunchbox in hand.

"Dov, you can't go to school like that!" mother laughingly told the little one.

"Why not?"

"Well...everyone wears clothes to school."

"Why?"

"Well...other people might feel embarrassed."

"Why?"

"Because people don't like to show their bodies."

"Why?"

"Frankly," the mother later told me, "I couldn't think of a good reason why."

I thought about it. I have thought about it a lot, and frankly, I can't think of a good reason either. I don't know why people wear clothes. I wear clothes because I would probably be embarrassed in public if I didn't. And yet somehow that reason doesn't satisfy me very well.

When I spent some time at Esalen at Big Sur a dozen years ago, I went naked with many people, and it was a wonderful experience. For the first day or two my eyes drifted below some navels, but soon I opened my mind and heart to the relaxed and peaceful atmosphere, and sexuality was not an issue. In fact, the experience was probably less sexually stimulating than in the world of clothes, where many garments are designed to highlight sexuality through accent and mystery. When nothing was left to the imagination, I felt a sense of ease, and sexuality was but a minor aspect of nudity. I remember returning to society after that experience, feeling very strange in clothing, wondering, like the little boy with his lunchbox, why people wore clothes anyway.

Now I am not pushing nudity, nor would I consider myself a nudist, although I think it would be marvelous if the leaders of the nations held a nude summit conference. (Can you imagine a naked U.N. General Assembly or a Security Council meeting in the tubs of the Esalen Hot Springs?) I see nudity more as a metaphor for a way of living, a refreshing attitude of being completely open with one another, with no hidden agendas. As Hugh Prather says, "We must be like plate glass buildings, with no areas shielded from sharing." Then, perhaps, we would see that there is nothing that we need to protect anyway.

Who told you you were naked? I remember one of my earliest feelings of embarrassment. I was sitting on a toilet at Mommy Babb's Nursery School, when another little friend came in the room with me. I remember feeling for the first time that I was not supposed to be with another person in the bathroom, that I must not be seen on the toilet. Perhaps I remember it because it was my moment of departure from the Garden, my turning point from peace to fear. Perhaps that was the moment I donned my first fig leaf and began to hide from my Father.

But it doesn't have to be that way now. Perhaps spiritual enlightenment is nothing more or less than awakening to the fact that we do not need to hide, and in fact we never did. Perhaps if we had the courage to hide nothing we would soon realize that all is forgivable. We keep our sins powerful by our unwillingness to hold them up to the light. Perhaps real healing is the undoing of all the coverings we have draped over what we thought should not be seen. Then we will see the radiance that we are.

There is a tale which quite eloquently tells our story: Once there was a western fort where a platoon of cavalrymen were feverishly fending off a band of Indians. After a long and grueling battle the ranks of the cavalry were diminished to two lonely infantrymen.

In the midst of pummelling shooting, one soldier came to the other, tapped him on the shoulder, and told him, "I have good news and I have bad news."

"Let's have the bad first."

"O.K.: Our defenses are failing miserably and there are no reinforcements."

"Well,if that's the bad news, I can't imagine what could be the good news. Let's hear it."

"There are no Indians."

That about sums it up. Our defenses are failing us, but perhaps that is the best thing that could happen; for it is only when our barriers fail us that we are forced to notice that we never needed them.

Can you remember some of the silly defenses you have erected to make you look good, which have backfired? I can remember working in a douche powder and laxative factory during the summer of my sixteenth year (definitely a lower consciousness job). Spending so much time in the warehouse, I had little opportunity to get to the beach and be in the sun. I felt embarrassed that I was rather a paleface, so I went out and bought some "Tanfastic," a lotion that I had seen on a television commercial. I was impressed when I saw a handsome actor attract a flock of beautiful bikini-clad girls simply by applying a dab of the chemical to his forehead.

"That's for me!" I thought, "I'll rub some on, and when I walk into work on Monday all the secretaries will swarm around me asking for dates!" And off to the drug store I dashed.

Come Monday morning, there I was in the locker room, punching in, datebook and pencil in hand. This was it; my moment had come. Smoothly I cruised through the office toward the shipping department, my ears perked for the first compliment.

It came: "Hey, Alan!" a man's voice gruffly called from the loading dock. "What's that orange stuff on your arm?"

There is a passage from the Talmudic *Ethics of the Fathers*: *"He who seeks to gain reputation shall lose it; he who does not seek reputation shall gain it."* (Could the ancient sages have known about *Tanfastic?*)

Who told you you were naked? Was it a television program, an aunt who slapped your hand when you touched your genitals, a friend of your mother's who was visibly embarrassed when mom brought her little boy into the ladies' room with her?

No, it was none of these. Let us not be tempted to blame anyone or anything outside ourselves, for *there is no outside world.* There is only awareness.

No, it was not the fault of a person, an event, or an experience. It was a thought, one tiny, almost imperceptibly subtle — like a serpent — thought that said, "You must hide." That's all it was. And that thought has snowballed through incredible convolutions, twisting and doubling back upon itself countless times, until it has formed the world we see. We have manufactured a senseless world in which an attractive young black woman is named Miss America for taking most of her clothes off, and then she is disqualified for taking them all off. It is an enigmatic world, a self-contradicting arena where illusions reign and the security of open sharing is

43

overshadowed by heavy armor and the fear of gentleness.

Yet that senseless world has no power in the Light. Here in the light of truth, in the joyful openness of the dawning day, all is alive and fresh and as clear as the innocence in which we were born. We can be ourselves, we can love, we can know the truth about who we are. Still we walk in the Garden; the Tree of Life remains. Nothing has happened but love.

We need never hide from one another again. There is no sin that can stand before the healing power of forgiveness. No illusion can cover over the dignity in which we have learned to respect ourselves. Never again need we attempt to be someone or something that we are not. For now we know that who we are is wholly lovable and perfect in the eyes of the One in whose holy image we are created. As Alan Watts described the universe, "God is a flower that grew a nose to smell itself." We are the flower, the God, the nose, the aroma, and the self.

Who told you you were naked? It really doesn't matter now. All that matters is that we know who we are, from what great love we have sprung, and that we live in the Garden as we were intended. We remain as God created us. And for that we can be grateful.

And gladly will you walk the way of innocence together, singing as you behold the open door of Heaven and recognize the home that called to you. Give joyously to one another the freedom and the strength to lead you there.[2]

---

[2] T. p. 399

Blue Highways

Some of your greatest advances you have judged as failures, and some of your deepest retreats you have evaluated as success.
                                             - A Course in Miracles[1]

Glancing to my right on Peoplexpress Flight 159 to Buffalo, I noticed the woman sitting next to me reading a shiny-covered book called *Blue Highways*.[2] Looking to my left, I saw my other neighbor reading a shiny-covered book called *Blue Highways*. Being giftedly psychic and keen to the subtleties of spiritual intuition, I deduced that I was supposed to find out about *Blue Highways*.

I turned to the lady on my right, a pleasantly-professional looking young woman who felt approachable. "What's that book about?" I asked.

"Oh, it's marvelous!" she returned. "It's by a Native American named William Least Heat Moon who lost his marriage and his job as an English teacher, both about the same time. Having next to nothing left, he decided to follow his dream of travelling around the country as a pilgrim of consciousness. He bought an old VW bus, packed up his gear and set out.

"Deciding where to go, William looked at a map. He saw that all of the major routes, printed in red, were the regularly travelled superhighways and toll roads that promised little more than tourist attractions and truck stops every hundred miles. This prospect did not feel like it fit with William's dream, so he looked at the map again. This time he saw that there were also blue highways. These were the local lesser-known byways, routes that promised more color and adventure than speed and comfort.

"William decided to follow the blue highways, and what marvelous adventures he had! He visited the monastary where the Christian mystic, Thomas Merton lived and wrote; he stayed at Native American Indian villages where he learned more about his heritage; along the way he met many fascinating people who gave him odd jobs and put him up for weeks. It

---

[1] T, p. 357

[2] William Least Heat Moon, *Blue Highways*, Little, Brown, 1983

was a true odyssey, a living voyage in personal awakening.

"As William went along he kept a journal," my lovely *raconteur* went on, her excitement waxing as she shared it with me. "After a year or two on the road he had recorded a sizeable collection of insights and experiences which he felt other persons who shared his dream might benefit from reading, so he sought to publish it. Little, Brown found it marketable, and it's been a huge success."

I looked at the book. On the cover I saw a round gold sticker boasting *"34 WEEKS ON THE NEW YORK TIMES BEST-SELLER LIST."* Between the covers I found a masterfully witty portrayal of one man's discovery of his country, his people, and — most important — himself. This author deserved to be read.

It was no accident that William Least Heat Moon lost his job and his wife. He had a different job to do, a larger family to serve. His destiny was to be a major writer with a gift to share. Had he remained with that career and family, he might have travelled only the red highways, learning of life mostly through newspaper headlines and coffee-break talk in the teachers' room. He might have published a poem in a literary quarterly every hundred miles or so. But being forced onto the blue highways, William Least Heat Moon stepped into his destiny — and shared its gift with millions.

We all have our blue highways, and blessedly so. Every minus in our lives is really half of a plus. A "negative" experience is simply the beginning of a positive awakening that is waiting for a stroke of vertical awareness to make it complete. We see the negative only when we are looking back or ahead, not up. The moment we look up and join our mind with the wisdom of God's infinite perspective, we can see that all of the minuses seemed to be bad only because we did not yet realize the blessing they brought into our lives. In his masterful book *Illusions*, Richard Bach writes,

> *There is no such thing as a problem without a gift for you in its hands. You seek problems because you need their gifts.*[3]

When we accept the gift, it ceases to be a problem. "Bad" is an interpretation, not a fact. Our hardships are not the whim of a wrathful God; they are the conclusions we draw from incomplete perception.

---

[3] Richard Bach, *Illusions: The Adventures of a Reluctant Messiah*, Delacorte Press, 1977

Tragedy to Triumph

One day after coming home from a weekend retreat I had conducted, I went to my mailbox to collect the day's mail. "Ah, another letter of thanks!" I smiled as I walked back to the house. Often after a retreat I receive letters of loving testimony from participants whose lives have been changed as a result of the workshop experience.

Opening the letter I expected a ray of gratefulness to shine out and bless me. Instead, to my chagrin, I felt engulfed by billows of dark, murky psychic smoke. Where I had anticipated finding, "How elated I am after your weekend!" I found instead, "What a disappointment your retreat was, and you owe me something!"

Thrown somewhat off balance, I read:

> *Dear Mr. Cohen, I want you to know what a terrible experience I had at your event. You misrepresented what the weekend was about...Your brochure stated that the facilities were comfortable, and I did not find them so; you called it a retreat, and it turned out to be a workshop; I did not like sharing the dorm facilities with others...*

The letter went on to offer a list of complaints, concluding with, "I would like my money back."

"Well," my ego responded, "Who does she think she is?...That was a really good retreat, and if she didn't like it, that's not my fault — Everyone *else* liked it! Besides, what does she want for $75, anyway?" (Do you know this train of thought?) I put the letter aside, too upset to think clearly about what to do about it.

A few minutes later I picked it up and read it again. This time I noticed that she had signed it, "In love and light, Elena."

"In love and light"? How could she sign an attack letter "In love and light?" Wasn't she trying to hurt me? If she loved and lighted me, how could she criticize my retreat so harshly?

I mulled over those thoughts for a while, wondering what to do about this difficult letter. My first inclination was to immediately write her back a

47

strongly-worded response explaining why she was wrong, and prove to her that I was right.

Then I remembered a Dale Carnegie quote that has saved me many times: "Do not do the impulsive thing — That is always wrong."[4] Along with the memory of that advice came the *Course in Miracles* motto: "The ego always speaks first, it always speaks loudest, and it is always wrong."

I listened again for Spirit's guidance. I heard, "Don't act hastily... Put the letter aside for a few days; consult the Voice of Peace inside yourself, and then act."

As I thought about the situation during the next few days I began to hear more and more clearly the teaching of the Course: "When you perceive an attack from one of your brothers, it is simply your faulty perception. Look at his action in another way, and you will see that it is actually a call for love. Give the love that is being sought, and a miracle will happen."

My ego did not want to acknowledge that Elena was calling for love, but the feeling to respond as if she was, was so compelling that I had to follow it. I realized that it really didn't matter who was right or wrong in this situation; the only way anyone ever wins is if everyone wins. When anyone ends up hurt, no one wins. I gradually saw more clearly that it was more important to feel peace and harmony with one of my fellows than to try to prove that I was right.

I remembered a verse from a song that we sing at my workshops: "All I ask of you is forever to remember me as loving you." I realized that if Elena and I never saw each other again, I would much rather have her remember me as someone who cared about her, than as someone who hurt her. I figured that saving a few dollars was nowhere near as important as giving love, and that if I really needed that money God would get it for me in another way.

I sat down and wrote this letter:

Dear Elena,

I am so sorry that you did not have a good experience at the retreat. It is very important to me that those who attend my workshop go home with a good feeling about it. If you feel that the workshop did not serve you, then I consider it my loss. Please find enclosed a refund check with my hopes that you will attend another of my workshops at another time, with my

---

[4] Dale Carnegie, *How to Win Friends and Influence People*, Simon & Schuster, 1936

deepest support for your good experience.

> *In love and light,*
> *Alan*

It felt right. I put the check in the envelope and dropped it in the mail with the prayer that only good would come of this interaction.

About a month later I received a beautiful Christmas card from Elena, with this note:

Dear Alan,

Thank you very much for your letter and the refund. I want you to know that I really appreciate it. If you would like to run another retreat, may I recommend the Harrison Farm, a beautiful center on a hundred well-kept acres, with cozy double rooms and very comfortable facilities. The telephone number is enclosed. I think you will enjoy it. Have a wonderful holiday season!

> *In love and light,*
> *Elena*

Was I glad I sent her the letter I did! I called the center and set up a visit. To my happy surprise it was one of the most beautiful conference centers I have ever seen! Lovely cottages, a large stone dining hall, a waterfall and lake, a delicately manicured flowered landscape, and a very amiable manager. Immediately I wrote a deposit check to reserve the site for my next retreat, blessing Elena as I did so.

The retreat turned out to be a marvelous, uplifting event, allowing a hundred and twenty persons to receive a deeply healing experience which touched many of their lives in a profound way. All this was a direct result of Elena's recommendation.

Elena's complaint was not an attack, but a blessing. Her dissatisfaction with the original camp was the steppingstone for our discovery of this new and much more enjoyable site. I originally perceived her letter as being against me, but in the grand scheme of things it was quite *for* me. It directly benefitted all the participants, hundreds more who have attended subsequent retreats, and the many thousands they ultimately touch, as well as everyone who reads this account. How powerfully Elena served the Holy Spirit by writing that letter! And how gracious was that same Spirit to counsel me to answer her the way I did. Elena's letter truly *was* written in love and light.

Bouncing Back

Hitting bottom sometimes helps us bounce to the top. In dance it is necessary to go into a deep *pliet*, crouching almost to the floor, to gain the leverage to jump high. If you consider the difficult times in your life, the periods when you entered a state of spiritual contraction, you will notice that these challenging times were often followed by a catapult into new spiritual awakening. You were squeezed through the birth canal of consciousness into a greater awareness, bringing with it many more possibilities than life in the womb could offer.

At a workshop in upstate New York a radiantly handsome man named Martin stood up to tell his story: "I began to drink when as a teacher, husband, and father, I felt that I could not cope with the pressures in my life. Gradually I found myself drinking more and more, until I had to move out of my home, away from my wife and daughter. I took a job in a city in the midwest, where I continued to drink even more heavily. I didn't want to admit it, but I was an alcoholic. "The turning point for me came one night when I found myself naked in some bed, the whereabouts of which I could not tell. There I lay, stenched by my own vomit, without a quarter or a friend. It was then, hitting rock bottom, that I admitted to myself that my life was not working. I reasoned that there must be a better way to live, and that I needed help. There was no other way but up, and it took that experience for me to realize it. I called out to God to help me find a new direction, and now I am a new man.

"What I want to share with you is that I had to hit rock bottom before I could bounce up. I was so stubborn that it was only when I had nothing, that I was willing to call for help. I feel that if I had had *anything* - a piece of clothing, a penny, a friend - I would have clung to that as a source of security in my old way. But because I had nothing, I had to start all over, and now as I look back on it I call it a blessing."

Embracing All of Life

Perception is not a fact; it is an interpretation. We do not see what is, but what we *choose* to see. We do not look upon the world as it is, but ourselves as we believe we are. The principle applies to *all* of our experiences, including joy as well as pain. This simple truth is the key to the transformation of our life, for if our pain has been chosen, we can make a new choice: We can transform the energy that we have used to torment and crucify ourselves, and redirect it to awaken, create, and share the good that is within us.

If we understand that everything that now seems to be working against us is actually the gift of a Force working *for* us - a power which we must discover how to use creatively - we can escape from a threatening, menacing world into a universe that is constantly flowing to lift us into greater joy.

When I visited a home for delinquent boys in upstate New York, I was deeply impressed by the enthusiasm and aliveness of the boys in residence. They did not seem at all like criminals to me. I observed an excellent, trusting rapport between the staff and the teenagers. When I complimented a counselor on this fine success, he offered me this account:

"The birth of the school was not easy. The members of the community, rather conservative folks by nature, felt threatened at the announcement that a reform school would be established in their quiet neighborhood, and they protested. In fact, they did all they could to stop us from establishing this school. They even came out and picketed in front of the site."

"So how did you deal with their protests?" I had to ask.

"We hired the picketers!" he laughed. "We gave them jobs on the staff, and you should have seen how quickly this school took off. That's been the way we've worked for twelve years, and that's why we've been successful - we don't make anyone our enemy, and we seek to take the teenagers and the community into our sense of self. As you can see, it works!"

Spirit versus Form

The ego judges events by their form, neatly lumping life into categories of good and bad. But the Holy Spirit teaches that no event is always good or bad; it is *how we look at it* that determines its worth; if we choose to find the light in it, we can consistently find the good.

At a healing workshop I attended one summer, the members of our class were given the assignment to stand and tell our individual stories of awakening. One man stood up and gave this report:

"My wife of twenty-three years recently left me, I lost my job, I don't know how the income is going to meet the outgo - and I am in utter bliss! I've never been so happy! These experiences have served to show me that happiness lies *within* me, and now that I have reclaimed my own power I am at peace."

It takes a great deal of trust to realize, as *A Course in Miracles* teaches, that *all* events, situations, and circumstances are helpful. "Trust remains the bedrock of the teacher of God's whole thought system"[5] explains the course. I attended a workshop given by Reverend Donald Curtis, a talented Unity Minister, who called the seminar *"How to Stop Whining and Start Winning"*. "That phrase pretty well sums up the fact that there are no tragedies except those of our own creation. Later I saw a book which gave me its whole contents simply by the title: *Stop Crying at Your Own Movies*.

Mud or Stars

Life is a gift from God, an unlimited series of opportunities to find the good in ourselves and each other. There is good in everything, if we are willing to see it. "Two men looked out through prison bars. One saw mud; the other, stars."

What are you choosing to see? It's all out there, whatever your mind can imagine. We attract to ourselves that which we think upon; this is how we are the engineers of our experience and the creators of our destiny. Destiny is not cast upon us from a capricious God seeking vengeance

---

[5] M, p. 1

through yellowed eyes, blood dripping from His lips. Destiny is a door opened before us, inviting us to walk into the light, or stand in the darkness. There are not even two paths to take. There is but one, and we choose either to walk it or stand still.

As we choose to walk, we go forward with mighty companions. No one walks the path to God alone, for as he takes a step toward the light he is joined by legions of others who gain strength from sharing it. The path to God is not travelled by the lonely or the meek; indeed no one who walks it need ever be lonely again. The path to God is as wide as all who choose to walk together, arm in arm, mind to mind, heart to heart.

Loneliness is nothing more than a fearful thought that leaves us the moment we are willing to look into the light and own our true radiance. There is no need for fear in a world of good, a world that is revealed by the simple willingness to trust. Would it not be astonishing to learn that the world has suffered for so long only because our faith in fear exceeded our courage to love? Who would have imagined that the light has always been with us, yet has gone unseen because so few have lifted their minds and opened their hearts to acknowledge it? And would it not be the most miraculous realization of all to understand that every tragedy that has ever been is really a blessing awaiting the awareness of triumph? *Love can triumph over anything.* There is no event that the light cannot make its own. Like a sun that shines from every part of the sky at once, radiantly removing all possibility of shadows, the power of God extends to *all* circumstances.

Children of Light, the time of shadows is over. There is no need to hide from reflections of evil. Evil has no power except what you give it by your belief. You who have eyes to see the light must now discover that the domain of God extends to all things. The Kingdom of Heaven is in your mind, and when you choose to enter the Kingdom everything you look upon will be a part of it. This is the awareness to which all of your experiences have led you, and the one you are now ready to accept. Step forward and become who you are by living in the world intended for you since the birth of your holy mind. You need not be afraid, afraid of your brethren, of life, of God, of yourself. *You were not born to live in fear.* You were created to live in the light, and as you step into your destiny you will find peace in the entire universe.

Life is good. All that is required for it to be so is for you to claim it in your daily activities. The healing of the your life and your world seeks not but for gods and angels, but for sincere souls like yourself to walk the earth with the sun of God shining from your eyes. Yes, there will be challenges, but none beyond your ability to conquer with the Holy Spirit as your guide. *The Holy Spirit never fails,* for it is of God, and God lives only to love.

There is one triumph in which there are no losers - the triumph of Spirit over emptiness. This is the triumph that you must seek, for it is the one victory of which you are assured. You will not gain it alone, for you are not alone. You are at peace and you are loved. Never forget how important you are to your Heavenly Father, and your heart shall always be filled with abundant blessings.

Up from Flatland

In the nineteenth century there appeared a book called *Flatland,** the story of a land in which all the citizens lived in only two dimensions. The book, written by "A Square," opens with this introduction:

> *To the inhabitants of space in general this work is dedicated by a humble native of Flatland in the hope that even as he was initiated into the mysteries of three dimensions, having been previously conversant with only two, so the citizens of that celestial region may aspire yet higher and higher to the secrets of four, five, or even six dimensions, thereby contributing to the enlargement of the imagination and the possible development of that most rare and excellent gift of modesty among the superior races of solid humanity.*
>
> -A Square

The Flatlanders lived their lives in one plane, seeing and knowing only what could be seen and known in that plane, and nothing above or below it. Flatland was populated by a large number of Squares and Circles, with a subculture of Triangles and an occasional Parallelogram.

The analogy of Flatland as a description of the world that we have been accustomed to inhabiting, and the pithy story of one Square's awakening is absolutely delicious. I would like to take the original notion of Flatland and imagine with you a scenario of the kind of leap of consciousness that we are all experiencing. So sit back, relax, and let us together enjoy a little excursion into a new dimension:

One sunny day in Flatland a little Square saw a Circle coming toward him. He carried on with his usual activities, but it soon became obvious that this Circle was not like any he had seen before. This Circle just kept getting larger and larger until it was clearly not just a Circle, but a Sphere. Square had heard about Spheres before, but he had always believed that they were

---

* Edwin A. Abbott, *Flatland: A Romance of Many Dimensions*, Dover Publications, 1952

just fairy tales or children's myths. This one, however, looked very real indeed. Frightened, Square began to run.

"Don't be afraid," called the Sphere, "I won't hurt you!"

The Square stopped and turned toward the stranger. Slowly backing away, he asked, "What are you, anyway?"

"I'm a Sphere."

"But there are no Spheres in Flatland," Square challenged.

"That may be so," gently replied the Sphere, "but Flatland is not all there is to life. There is more to life than the two dimensions with which you are familiar — much, much more, indeed. There is a actually another dimension of which most of the citizens of Flatland are not aware at all: *Spaceland.* Spaceland is a wonderful world with so much more freedom to see and move and play! But you cannot enjoy it because all of you in Flatland have gotten used to looking only forward, back, and to the sides. Hardly anyone in Flatland ever looks up! If you did, you would see many wondrous forms far more exciting and fascinating than you have found in Flatland."

"How can I see these lovely sights?" young Square wondered aloud.

"Simply look up and you will see the whole picture," the Sphere explained. "In fact," Sphere went on, "you will be surprised to know that what you see in Flatland is actually a part of the third dimension. Those you see as Circles are actually Spheres, but because you see only in two dimensions, all you see is one plane of a much greater reality!"

"You will be happy to know that you and your friends are not just Squares, but you are actually facets of a marvelous and very practical form called a "Cube." The Triangles belong to a mystical design called "Pyramid," and that funny-looking family down the street that you laugh at, Mr. and Mrs. Ellipse, are actually components of a most important configuration called "Egg.""

"Alas, but you see none of these rich aspects of your life because you are so preoccupied with what is behind and in front of you — Oh, Square, if you only knew how much more there is to life, you would dance with joy!"

Sphere paused for a moment. She realized this was a lot for a little Square to absorb so quickly, and she wanted to give him time to awaken.

"My dear Square, the universe is so much greater than you have imagined — and now you are seeing things as they truly are, and indeed have always been. I am very happy for you."

The Square was astounded; yet somehow it made sense. Into his mind flashed some memories of having seen unusual shapes when he was just a few points old. He remembered seeing beautiful, dazzling configurations just before going to sleep or while travelling through the Park of Diamonds. Then he recalled that when he had told his mother about them she patted him on one of his sides and told him he had a vivid imagination. Eventually he stopped seeing them — he didn't want to be different from his friends.

The Sphere, shimmering before the young one, sensed he was ready to see more.

"Would you like to see your true self?" she asked.

The Square hesitated. He wasn't quite sure about his true self. It seemed that most of the inhabitants of Flatland were rather fearful of looking at their true self. Whenever someone would bring up the idea of their true self at a party, for example, someone would quickly make a joke or change the subject. Why were the Flatlanders so afraid of their own being? Even the Square could not understand why hardly anyone in Flatland loved himself.

"Yes," Square answered, "Yes, I would like to see my true self." The moment he said those words his fear went away.

"Very well, then — Look up!" Sphere commanded. "Look up and you will see who you really are!"

Square looked up and he could hardly believe his eyes. What a wondrous sight he did see! He saw that he was not just a small Polygon with four sides of equal length, as he had read in his Geometric Geneology textbook. He saw that his square self was just one part of his being, the part that could be seen in Flatland. Square saw that he was actually a great, glowing Cube, of which the lines that he thought limited him were but one aspect. How exciting to find that he was whole! So that was why he had felt so strangely incomplete as a little Square! Now he realized that there was nothing to be afraid of, nothing in his real self that could harm him. In fact, nothing had ever made him as happy as looking upon his real self and seeing all that he was.

That was just the beginning. As the Square became more and more comfortable looking up, he could see the real identity of everyone in Flatland! They were so beautiful! He saw marvelous Cones, sparkling Cylinders, and even a Great Sphere made up of Triangles. His guide told him this was a "Geodesic Dome" (but hardly anyone in Flatland was ready for that one). Square saw that what was happening in Flatland was such a little part of the whole picture. And he was afraid no more.

Just open your eyes, and realize the way it's always been.
                                                                    - The Moody Blues

The Spiral Mountain

Life does not go on in a circle...nor does it ever repeat itself. It always changes, and yet it evolves every moment to be constant. Life is all-encompassing and creates the next moment by virtue of its own being...

- Ramtha*

Sometimes it seems like we are getting nowhere, as if we are back at the same place we were months, years, or lifetimes ago. We may feel frustrated, unworthy, and confused, and we wonder if we are really getting anywhere in life.

Recently I heard a friend of mine, a thirty-eight year old woman moan, "I am stuck in a pattern in my relationship just like I was as a teenager! I can't believe it — I don't think I've gotten anywhere!"

Actually, we are always growing; the question is not whether or not we are getting anywhere, but how quickly we are moving along. Growth is *always* happening, even when we seem to be going down or moving backward. It is only the ego, seeking to keep us in the illusion of stuckness, that believes that nothing is happening. When such a smoke screen arises it is useful to remember that the ego is always wrong. We believe that we are getting nowhere because the ego interprets life as if it were against us, when in fact life is always working for us.

We discover a new high, we see a new vista of life from a mountain peak of truth that we have never scaled before, and then we feel that we cannot sustain it; we slip back into our old perception or way of acting. We may feel discouraged and want to give up.

At a point like this we must realize that we never slip back to the place we were at before we had the experience. It just *seems* that we are falling back because we are going down (in consciousness) *from the new height that we have discovered.* If we examine our path carefully we will see that we did

---

* Steven Lee Weinberg, ed., *Ramtha*, Sovereignty, Inc., 1986, p. 158

not fall all the way back into the valley — just to a plateau a little further down on the mountain. It is from here that we will begin our new ascent, which will take us to an even higher peak next time. The mountain of truth is scaled by taking three steps forward and two steps back. This process is perfect, and it is wonderful, for the going down gave us the momentum we needed to rise higher the next time, like a roller coaster or ski jump. One thing is certain on the spiritual path of the true aspirant: No step is ever wasted.

It is very helpful to consider our journey of awakening like the adventure of climbing a mountain by a spiral pathway. How compassionate is our Heavenly Father, who understands that a gentle, gradual ascent is much easier and more productive in the long run than a quick, steep climb! (Although some do choose the rugged path.) We can see this important process illustrated in diagram 1.

Let's take the apparent contrast of being in a relationship or out of one as an example. We start out on the bottom of the spiral not in a relationship. Here we feel a certain dissatisfaction, a need for more, a desire to be with another person. So we move across the bottom of the spiral into a relationship. We become deeply involved in the relationship; it becomes the all-important issue in our life as we devote most of our energy to participating in it, trying to make it work, and seeing if we can find happiness in it. Sometimes we seem to succeed, and sometimes it seems as if it is not worth it. Yet always we are thinking, feeling, learning, and growing.

Then at some point days, months, years, or lifetimes later we begin to feel that a relationship is not what we really want. Or perhaps we feel it is not really this person that we want to be in a relationship with. So we move toward being on our own once again.

We find being on our own is very freeing and rather satisfying — for a while. We feel relieved of the challenges and pressures of being in the relationship, and our life becomes more peaceful and more manageable.

Then, after a certain amount of time we start to feel lonely; that feeling of missing something in our life bubbles up, and once again we feel that we would like to be involved in a relationship.

Now, here is the point at which we might be inclined to throw our hands up and complain, "On no, I'm right back where I started! I haven't gotten anywhere — Will this go on forever?"

The truth is that you are *not* right back where you started, you *are* getting somewhere, and it will not go on forever. The only thing that goes on

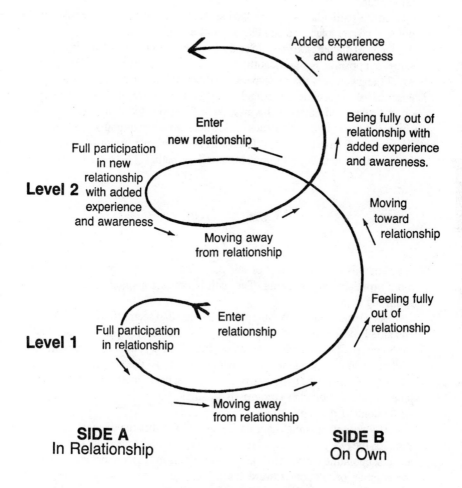

Added experience
and awareness

Being fully out of
relationship with
added experience
and awareness.

Enter
new relationship

Full participation
in new
relationship
Level 2 with added
experience
and awareness

Moving
toward
relationship

Moving away
from relationship

Feeling fully
out of
relationship

Enter
relationship

Full participation
Level 1 in relationship

Moving away
from relationship

SIDE A
In Relationship

SIDE B
On Own

The Spiral Mountain
Diagram 1

forever is God, and that is a very encouraging awareness to embrace and remember.

In this particular situation what has happened is that we have come back not to the same place we started, but to the same side of the spiral — *at a higher level of consciousness*. (See diagram 2.) While the *pattern* may be the same, our position is significantly improved because this time we bring with us all the awareness that we have gained through the very valuable experiences of having been in the first relationship, growing through it, being back on our own, and entering this new one. So while the dynamics may be similar, we are not by any means back where we were, although that is what the ego would have us believe. The truth is that we have grown — perhaps in inches, but it is always an upward-spiralling path.

Coming Home

There is one more facet of this path of awakening that makes it even more promising and exciting. The path is not just a spiral upward, but a spiralling *cone*.

As we move upward on the spiral, the gap that seems to separate side A and side B becomes smaller and smaller. We are not just moving back and forth between polarized sides of an emotional slinky; the path is actually a continuous one. The higher we move on the spiral, the clearer it becomes that what seemed to be two poles of a ladder that never meet, are actually *one* pole that winds around in a progressively smaller spiral until it resolves itself at the point at the top.

If you look again at diagram 2 you will see that the greatest distance between the two sides is at the beginning. This demonstrates why the elation and disappointment in first loves, for example, is much more radical than the more subtle oscillations toward the top of the spiral mountain. The gap between sides A and B on level 2 is less than it was on level 1, and even smaller on level 3. (Actually, to differentiate between levels at all is arbitrary and somewhat misleading, for all of the levels flow into one another; there is no real separation between them.) The amount of contrast between the sides gradually diminishes until at the top there is no difference at all. The process is like that of an unfolding flower, gradually releasing more petals from

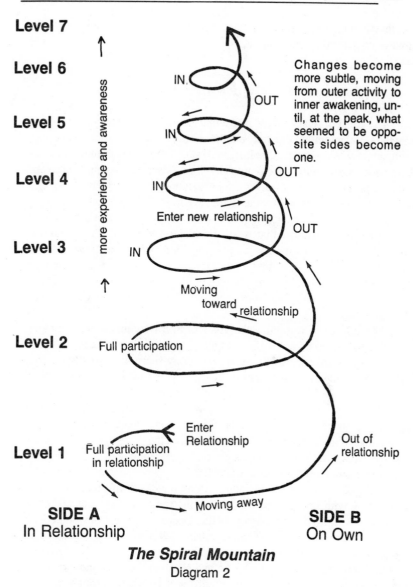

The Spiral Mountain
Diagram 2

As we gain experience and awareness, the contrasts in our experience gradually diminish, and eventually both sides merge at one peaceful peak.

within itself; the final petal is quite connected to the original one. So are we always connected to our Source.

The View From The Top

The arena of relationships is just one example of all the types of issues that the spiral mountain illustrates. Other examples may be: dieting/binging; being in the world/retreating; selling real estate/renouncing money; accumulating possessions/letting them go; disciplining yourself/playing; and so on. You can probably think of many personal examples not considered here. The details may be different, but the dynamics are really the same.

Returning to our example of relationships (you can substitute another issue if you like) we notice that as you come closer to the top of the mountain you still go back and forth between desiring relationships and aloneness, but the oscillations become so subtle that they are *more internal than external*. This advanced level of learning allows you the freedom to stay pretty much in one external position as you work out these issues in a gentle inner process.

As we learn to recognize the voice of Spirit within us, we are more sensitive to guidance in the early stages of a step in any direction. At the beginning of spiritual growth we are taught by sharp contrasts; but as we evolve, the intensity of the contrast diminishes, and we learn through more refined inner transformations. There is still a movement of awareness, but it is subtle instead of gross. You have graduated from feeling like a human yoyo to accept more gentle lessons. Because your heart is attuned to the promptings of your inner spirit, you do not need the gross manifestations of the physical world to learn, and you are no longer required to bounce around the outer world as a method of training.

In the case of relationships/going-it-on-your-ownships, then, you may simply stay with one person while climbing the mountain peaks of consciousness within your own heart, realizing that all the lessons you could learn with other men or women are available and contained within this one perfect opportunity to find harmony with another human being. Or if you are on your own you may simply stay so and climb to the same mountaintop, understanding that all the lessons of life will be gently brought to you through all the persons and experiences Holy Spirit sends your way. It is not so important which route you take, just that you get to see the view from the top. Here you meet everyone who has traversed every route up the mountain, for here is the place where all the roads of learning converge at a spectacular viewing point. At this point you may see that all of us are always in relationship, and all of us are always alone. This point of paradox is a one of great power; here you get off the path to become the mountain.

Healing the Split Mind

The seeming polarities of the spiral mountain, not distant from one another at all, are like the two tribes in that marvelous motion picture, *The Dark Crystal*. In the story we find a divided world that began to die ages ago when the crystal that empowered the kingdom was split. Now there are two tribes in the realm: the gentle, loving, wise Mystics, and the villainous, vicious, vulture-like Skexies, ugly creatures ready to swoop upon and maim innocent victims for their own aggrandizement. The Mystics, saintly by comparison, are benign ones — but they have lost their power and they are dying.

A young boy, Jeb, the last survivor of a race that is neither Mystic nor Skexi, is given the task of healing the split world by finding the one piece of the original crystal that is missing and replacing it in the now dark crystal, held in the altar of the Skexies Castle. This he must accomplish before the prophecied conjunction of the three suns, the moment at which the world would be destroyed forever, unless the crystal is healed.

Instinctively the aged Mystics begin to make their way to the dark castle to meet the sordid Skexies before the suns conjunct. The Skexies prepare for war, while the Mystics step slowly and carefully to their appointed rendez-vous (ooooommmming as they go). There is a strong sense that a cosmical-ly-ordained event is at hand.

At the moment of conjunction — the very last opportunity for the world to be saved — the Mystics, Skexies, and Jeb find themselves at the altar of the Great Crystal. All have been drawn together like the stars aligned in the sky. At the perfect instant Jeb leaps to the top of the dark crystal and inserts the all-important piece. The dark crystal is healed.

As the crystal is made whole an astonishing event occurs: the Mystics and the Skexies step into one another, like two rivers flowing into one. At the moment the two become one, an explosion of light is created. Each of the joined pairs produces a great angelic light-filled being, emanating many times the power and magnitude of the little creatures from which they have sprung. These magnificent beings, representing the integration of apparent good and evil, grow in stature and intensity until the dark castle crumbles, light is restored to the kingdom, and a dying world grows green again. Finally we hear,

> *What was sundered and undone*
> *Now is whole, the two are one.*

There is a book by Hal Lindsay called *The Beautiful Side of Evil*. The title alone teaches the lesson of the dark crystal, restored to full power at the top of the spiral mountain. The healing of the dark crystal represents the unified consciousness that knows seeming evil to be the facet of the divine that it really is. It is therefore not evil at all — except relatively speaking. The world of the Mystics and the Skexies was dying because in it there was an unbridgeable separation of the energies of good and evil, the picture of a split mind that sees a difference where one does not really exist. Under no circumstances could such a world survive, for it is completely out of accord with the will of God, which is perfect and total unity. The evil Skexies were warfully annihilating their own race through lack of love, while the Mystics had lost their power because they had denied and cut themselves off from their seeming evil selves. As a result there was no communication, no strength, and no life in either camp, and subsequently their world was untraversably gapped and dying.

When the two groups merged, when the "negative" aspects of life were absorbed into the good, there was created a gestalt, a new being, all-encompassing and infinitely more alive than the separated parts. The Mystics and the Skexies *were* the split crystal — and the moment they owned, or accepted responsibility for *all* the parts of their self, the crystal of life was restored to its true nature and the realm was healed.

The Totality of Love

If we are to be healed — and we most surely are — we must enfold all aspects of ourself in love, understanding, and acceptance. This means *accepting everything that happens to us as part of God's plan for our good and our healing*. Every person, event, and experience that touches us contributes to the healing of our own dark crystal. We cannot cut off or deny anyone or anything as being outside our good or ourself. *Life is a process of ever-unfolding good.* We are constantly moving from strength to greater strength, from good to better to best. Sometimes it does not *seem* that way. But appearances are not the same as reality. Here we have the key to transforming all fear to perfect love: a time of seeing shadows is our best opportunity to deny appearances and look with spiritual x-ray vision into the truth. Bless your challenges, for they are your steppingstones home to the arms of Love. We are indeed on a journey of continually greater awakening. I do not believe it is possible to be reincarnated as a cockroach. It is possible to adopt a cockroach consciousness in a human body, but if a man could become a cockroach, Holy Spirit would have to run from aerosol bombs. And if there is one characteristic of Holy Spirit, it is that it never feels a need to hide from anything. Spirit simply enfolds everything that is brought to it with perfect love. Being created in the image and likeness of a whole and wholly loving God, the Spirit within us refuses to acknowledge anything unlike its holy self, and is therefore incapable of knowing evil, to say nothing of its perfect inability to fear it.

Therefore to my friend who feared that she was reverting to adolescence, I say "no way." I say the only culprit that makes us think we are going backwards is the ego, and that is because the ego is backwards, and it is incapable of seeing anything except itself. The game of the ego is to make us believe that we are not who we are, Children of Perfection, ever enjoying deeper healing through the peace that true love brings. Always we are becoming more like God, until finally we discover that we have always been divine. Indeed we are living in the heart of God all the time, and we need only open our eyes to recognize that we are already home.

To my friend I acknowledge that life is not rigidly stable, as the ploy for the ego's survival would have us believe. Life is a constant flow of newly blessed love energy. The only way to defeat the ego in the war that never was is to know with unshakable certainty that we are spiritual beings moving toward an invincible destiny of good. Like a river consummating its journey from the mountains to the shore, our love opens to complete itself as the ocean. The ocean toward which we flow is one of perfect healing, and I assure you, beloveds, that *there is nothing at all to fear.* What awaits us is all the peace that we have ever sought, and our only need is to open our arms and hearts wide, and let it come.

I say to my friend as I say to all who read this that we are on the most marvelous adventure of all, the most thrilling odyssey there could ever be. We are on the journey into Truth, and that voyage specifically includes the gentle dismantling of the illusions that stand between your self and the summit, which is your Self. Do not be deceived by the spiral way you walk. It is the way of everyone who has ever journeyed to the peak of consciousness, and it has been tread and conquered with love by all the great ones before you. You traverse this path in good company, Sons and Daughters of Majesty. You walk the way of the beloveds of God, of the family of the open-hearted, of the people of the truth. Walk in dignity, walk in reverence, walk in acceptance, and your journey shall be made light. This is the way of those who love.

The Power to Triumph

The Last Starfighter

The responsibility for living harmoniously on Planet Earth rests with each individual. As each person spiritually and cosmically comes of age, claiming his attunement and therefore his involvement in the business of all mankind, a beautiful new energy will be released which will gradually swing the earth into alignment with the universal forces of harmony and peace. This period of awareness will happen, but only when each man and woman looks beyond the exterior to the interior of their being to discover their own personal power through their connection to the Ultimate of All Energies.

- Agartha: A Journey to the Stars*

Somewhere between San Francisco and Honolulu, I changed my mind. Not about the flight, about the movie. As the big iron bird hummed gracefully above the wispy cotton Pacific clouds, my attention was drawn from the window to the movie screen. *The Last Starfighter* looked more interesting than I had anticipated, and now I wanted some headphones to find out what it was all about.

It was about us. Alex Rogin was the champion of the trailer park video game frontier. His skill in shooting alien spaceships out of the midnight video sky was invincible, earning him the worship of every aspiring seven-to-fourteen-year-old suburban defender of space invasion. The night he broke the record on the machine the entire trailer park came out to cheer him on to victory. Alex was a natural intergalactic marksman of the highest calibre, and the amount of points he had amassed was exceeded only by the number of quarters he had invested. Alex was good, he knew it, and he loved it.

One starry night Alex was picked up by a slick stranger driving a sleek sports car unlike any he had seen before. The driver, amiable enough, told Alex he had to have a talk with the fellow who had achieved the *Starfighter*

---

* Meredith Lady Young, *Agartha: A Journey to the Stars*, Stillpoint Publishing, 1984 championship. Into the strange vehicle Alex went, curious, intrigued, and somewhat leery. He was surprised that this man knew him, and his eyes opened even wider, along with his jaw, when the sports car turned off the main road, not to the right or left, but up. Within seconds the roadster was transformed into a flashy starcraft propelling Alex and his mysterious host off to planets and dimensions far more romantic than the corner video parlor.

As a further test of Alex's resilience, the driver peels off his human face to reveal a reptilian visage straight from Iguana-land. Now Alex's host Centuri reveals the reason for this intergalactic kidnapping: The planet Rylos, from which he has come, is in serious danger. An evil force of space marauders from the starsystem of Ur is threatening the life of his species. The defending Starfighters have been all but wiped out. In a last-ditch attempt to save Rylos and its people, they have sought out someone who can singlehandedly stave off the invaders. For this reason they created a video game to simulate their starship control panel. They watched carefully to see who would emerge with the kind of skill needed to rescue them. Alex's expertise as the highest quality Starfighter drew them to seek his help in their cause. In short, they need him to save their planetary soul.

Hearing this incredible story, Alex's amazement changes to consternation. Him, save a starsystem? Him, take on a superhuman task? Him, have an entire life-form depend on him?

"I'm sorry," Alex blurts out, "I'm just a kid from a trailer park!"

Alex's extraterrestrial guru turns to him, finds his hesitating eyes, and speaks slowly and clearly to his young friend: *"If that's all you think you are, that's all you'll ever be."*

"If that's all you think you are, that's all you'll ever be." That one was for all of us.

The task of healing this planet seems monumental. The nuclear monster seems indomitably formidable. It appears as if the world is down to just a few lonely defenders of the truth, an unacknowledged band of lovers of light. Sometimes it even feels as if the burden of bearing the message of peace in a woeful world has fallen on our shoulders alone. At such a moment we may think, "How can a struggling little person like me accomplish the healing of our world?"

We *can* because we are powered by a Force far greater than "a struggling little person." We are not "just kids from a trailer park." *We are the last Starfighters.* If you are reading this, you are capable and ready to make a major contribution to the healing of the Planet Earth. If not you, then who?

Most of the greatest Starfighters have had to fight their way to the stars. Mahatma Gandhi, for example, was literally laughed out of a courtroom when he became tongue-tied while pleading his first case as a young lawyer. Later he was thrown off a train in the middle of a South African night because his skin was not the right color for that train. We know what Gandhi eventually made of himself, only because he was willing to change his mind about how powerfully Spirit would be willing to work through him.

Then Sir Richard Attenborough had a lifelong dream to honor Gandhi's work through a film about his life. Sir Richard worked diligently to raise funding for a major motion picture from non-major motion picture sources. After eighteen years of dedicated work, being unwilling to settle for setbacks, Sir Richard's dream was realized. The film startled the motion picture industry as it ran away with the Academy Awards, including Best Picture, Best Director, Best Actor, and a horde of other Oscars. In the beginning Sir Richard had to go it alone; in the end the world stood up to applaud him. When one steps forward with conviction, mighty companions — sometimes unseen — walk beside us. Sir Richard, like Gandhi, was never alone — God walked with both of them.

The Key to Transformation

Here is the key to the power to transform our lives and our planet: We can accomplish more with one breath of purposeful love than a thousand years of fearful attack. Gandhi said, "In a gentle way you can shake the world." The way of the planetary healer is marked by understanding, light-heartedness, and understanding, all of which begin by loving ourselves just as we are. For too long we have believed in changing ourselves to become worthy; now we need to believe in *being* ourselves to be worthy. If you feel that you cannot be a real force in healing our planet, or that you cannot even help yourself, do not despair. The devil (lack of awareness) is not the inability to heal, but the *thought* that we cannot. No challenge in life can stand when looked upon with true love. Every obstacle will dissolve in the presence of Truth, for there is only one power in the universe — the power of God's healing love. Hold any difficulty up to the light of love, and that wall must melt and be transformed into a gift of understanding, which will later be used in the service of healing. This is the real meaning of alchemy: The lead that once seemed to weigh us down and keep us from rising into joy is transmuted into the gold of good that reflects the light of

Heaven. Indeed true alchemy consists of the realization that we just *thought* it was lead, while actually it was golden all the time.

We have what it takes to make it. We just need to know the truth about our power and use it. *We can if we believe we can.* Not because belief makes it so, but because we can, and *belief lets our power manifest.* The word "believe" comes from two original words: "leave be." What we are willing to leave be, or let be, becomes real. We do not need to create good in our life, for *all of our good has already been created*—and it is waiting for us to claim it. All we have to do is *let it be.*

At a workshop in Erie, Pennsylvania a man told me that he had just gotten an excellent position with a large manufacturer of glass bottles. His job was to develop a design for a double-extruder bottle, a new product for their line.

"They called me a few weeks after the interview to tell me the job was mine," he explained, " — but the interesting thing was their explanation of why they chose me for the position. They told me that they had interviewed several candidates, all of whom had more credentials and experience with that kind of work than me. But here's the clincher: I was the only one who, when they asked, 'Can you invent this product?' answered, 'Yes.' I don't know exactly how I will do it, but there's one thing I do know: If you can think of a thing, you can bring it to life. Products are the results of thoughts, and what the mind can conceive, a man can achieve. You may have to invest some time, love, and money into a project, but all of that will come in the service of drawing that original idea into reality. If you are sufficiently dedicated and concentrated on any goal, it is only a matter of time until you see your dream crystallize into reality."

When I was a kid I used to like the Audie Murphy movies. I wonder if you remember him — he was a World War II infantryman who won the Purple Heart by accomplishing a phenomenal number of heroic victories. I remember one scene in which Audie maneuvered a flaming tank into the heart of an enemy nest. Amid exploding debris and sniper attack from all angles he saved a whole battalion and turned the tide of the battle. Now I am not supporting the kind of warfare from which Audie's heroism emerged; God knows we have had enough of that. But I am inspired by the singular willingness that Audie Murphy represents. To me he stands for the kind of fearlessness that comes with total commitment to a cause. He was willing to win the war singlehandedly if he had to, and he nearly did.

Now it is not a war between nations that we need to win, but the war of love, which is entirely different from any kind of war we have ever known.

This is the unstoppable campaign for the Light, and against nothing. We must realize that our love has infinite power. I know that this planet will survive by each of us being willing to do what we need to do to heal it — singlehandedly, if necessary. John Beaulieux said, "If I die, I'll die serving the Light." That's the kind of fearlessness we need to succeed. Actually that's a statement of victory, for no one with that strength of intention could ever be defeated.

We cannot afford to wait for someone out there to fix the world for us. That's how Hitlers, Anti-Christs, and boogeymen get born. We need to directly participate in our own salvation, allowing the savior to be born within our own being. God can do *for* us what He can do *through* us; we are the channels of our own transformation. And everyone and everything will be touched by the healing which begins in our own heart.

The miracle is that no one really has to do it singlehandedly. Everyone who is willing to do his or her part completely is joined by many others who are inspired by love to do their part completely. When we were born on earth, each of us was given a certain sphere of activity to influence — some larger, some smaller, all eventually touching all. No matter how great our personal domain of influence seems to be, that influence begins in the center of our own being and ripples out to touch the entire universe. Throughout our whole life our job is simply to exert the best possible influence on the part of the world we touch. This noble task requires little more of us than to keep our own little patch of the garden watered, weeded, and blessed. It is ego that tells us we must weed our neighbor's garden, while the Spirit within us gently reminds us that as we complete our own cultivation we will be guided to serve our neighbor in the perfect appropriate way. The flowers we cultivate in our own garden will drop their seeds in the patch next door. This is how, in our own gentle way, we transform the world.

The Starfighter's Creed

Perhaps an appropriate Starfighter to remember here would be Luke Skywalker. In *The Empire Strikes Back* Luke, in his headstrong way, defied Yoda's instructions to wait until he had mastered the Force before he went off to challenge Darth Vader. Luke set out before he was ready, and ended up losing a battle and his hand. Yet in *The Return of the Jedi* that followed, Luke patiently waited and practiced until he mastered the Force. This achievement gave him the power to walk right into the Emperor's lair and conquer the entire Empire.

Here is a message of the richest encouragement: Even if we fall down on our spiritual path, there is always a way to rise up, bounce back, and solve the problem. Indeed we must get up and walk in the light, for once we have set foot upon the path of Truth there is no turning back. Jesus fell three times on the way of the cross, and he accepted the help of those who came to comfort him. St. Francis of Assisi wrestled with all kinds of desires and challenges throughout his life. All the while the power of his soul marched steadily on, gaining strength as the spirit within him dissolved his fears. Gandhi struggled for years to be celibate, sometimes succeeding, sometimes not, yet ever continuing onward toward what he believed to be the highest truth his heart told him. Surely we can offer ourselves the patience and forgiveness that these great ones learned as a vital ingredient in spiritual success.

Hilda has offered some inspiring advice for Starfighters who find that they have veered from the plotted course. The affirmation she suggests is:

"I pick myself up, I dust myself off, and I march on!"

(You might like to repeat this affirmation to yourself now, three times mentally or aloud.)

It is no sin to make an error. In fact, it is a blessing to discover a mistake. Errors have power over us only as long as we do not realize what we have been doing. The moment we see that we have made a mistake we are free of it and its effects. Once we recognize that we have missed the mark, there is only one route that we can take: correct what we can, and do better next time. If you mistakenly drive off the road onto the shoulder, the only thing to do is get back on the road and carry on to your destination. You would not sit at the roadside bemoaning your lack of skill; you would turn the wheel back toward the road and step on the gas. To dwell on a past error keeps us tied to it, and releasing the error allows us to move forward instantly. *The only time we fail is when we don't try again.*

This world is actually a Starfighters' training school, a transformational forum for Jedi who are ready to return. That's all of us, at various stages of development. Sometimes it's a tough boot camp, and we learn from our errors as well as our successes. Sometimes we get a taste of how wonderful our life will be when we finish our lessons (indeed life already *is* wonderful; our lesson is simply to realize it!). This higher perspective keeps us shining through our challenges. Whether our lessons be difficult or easy, we gain tremendous strength from remembering that there is but one purpose to all of our living: *to see God in everything.* Starfighters need a target. If we remember that love is the goal, all of our learning becomes infinitely easier.

Mark Twain said, "When I was thirteen years old I thought my father was a complete dunce; by the time I was twenty-one, I was amazed at how much he had learned." Life is not about attempting to change people, conditions, or events. It is about changing our *perceptions and thoughts* about people, conditions, and events. We are here to discover the divinity that shines everywhere, all the time. That transformation of awareness begins within our own mind, with the happy understanding that we are not who we thought we were — We are Children of the Most High, heirs to all the power in the universe. *We can do as much as God can do, but we actually do as much as we think we can.* If you expect someone else to save the planet, the door to peace will remain barred. The key to the salvation of the world lies within *your* hands.

Once we are really willing to let God in, to let good come our way, and to know and act as if there is no order of difficulty in miracles, then we will be able to do as much for ourselves as Christ can do for us. *There is no limit to that.* All of your training, experience, and skills have led you to the point where now *you can change the course of destiny for everyone.* Our past has served us well, but now, like the first stage of a three-stage rocket which afforded the gross energy to push it beyond the immediate atmosphere, our past must fall away to allow us to soar to even greater heights of heavenly perspective. Here we discover rich and imaginative vistas beyond anything we have known or expected. All of our personal and group adventures have lifted us to the crest of a wave of love that is eternally breaking within our heart and blessing every person we touch.

No, no one is too small, no one comes from too obscure a trailer park to accomplish the defense of love in a small but ailing starsystem. Love knows no smallness, only the magnitude of impeccable intention. And because love has chosen you to accomplish its defense, there can be no doubt about how easily the light can and will remove all darkness. Like a movie about which we already know the happy outcome, we do not need to fear the plot. We can enjoy the adventure, knowing the story will somehow be resolved in our favor.

Perhaps we need to take our eyes off the window and return them to the screen. Maybe it is no accident that this particular movie is being shown on the flight we booked. And perhaps we would serve ourselves by purchasing the headphones to find out what's actually going on. As David Pomeranz so eloquently sings in *It's in Everyone of Us*, "I bought my ticket, but I've been seeing only half of the show." No longer can we afford to use unworthiness as an excuse to mask our magnitude. We are created in the image and likeness of a loving, caring, understanding, and most holy God Who is looking for a few good Starfighters to rescue a frightened planet from a long history of nightmares. This is the original salvation army, it's an all-volunteer force, and the price of admission is a little willingness to believe in yourself.

Oh, yes, by the way, the kid from the trailer park saved the starsystem.

The Ego Strikes Back

Have you ever noticed that just when you are about to take a step in a new and more positive direction in your life, something comes up to block it? Some people say, "This is too good to be true — I'm sure something will go wrong." And then, sure enough, it does.

Why would things go wrong? Things are not supposed to go wrong. Life is supposed to work, and work wonderfully. When it does not, we must look past the darkness to see the light.

When we experience a challenge to success, we have a marvelous opportunity to shine a healing ray of understanding upon the ego's thought system. In such a situation we can penetrate into the very bedrock of the wall of painful beliefs that have stood between you and your happiness for so much of your life. Are you willing to be free? Together let us be unafraid to look at the cause of our hardships and our hurts, that we may be released forever.

We must be willing to look fearlessly at what seems to be the source of our misery. In the *Star Wars* movie a small band of those living for the Force had to penetrate to the very core of the Death Star (how appropriately named!) to reach and destroy the reactor that was powering it. So, too, must we look deeply into our self to dismantle the sense of threat that seems always about to explode in our life. *There is no such bomb.* But we must have the courage to face what we *think* it is before we can truly be free of it.

Let us begin by sharing a powerful excerpt from John Price's *The Planetary Commission*:

> *As you move through the inner space of consciousness toward the union with Self, there is a bridge you must pass over...It is on this bridge that you shed the remaining particles of error thoughts and negative beliefs and go through the final cleansing. As the bridge comes into view, your world may seem to turn upside down, and the reason is because you are beginning the process of letting go of everything that seemed secure to you...*

Your ego may choose to do battle as you step on to the bridge, and it will do WHATEVER IS NECESSARY to save itself. If that means creating an insufficiency of funds, it will do it, because this effect could very well cause you to step back... Another ego tantrum may give the appearance of a business failure, or the interruption of a successful career, or perhaps a physical ailment. The ego simply wants to show who is boss.

How do you navigate the last mile as the ego begins to fight for its life? You totally surrender to God...You turn everything in your life over to the indwelling Christ and give up all concern, knowing that your God-Self is the solution to every problem and the answer to every need, and that Spirit cannot let you down because it is against God's nature to do so![1]

This masterful advice is showing us that the ego perceives love, unity, and the peace of God as a threat, and defends itself — (quite insanely!) — against healing. The blessing is that the ego's rallying itself for defense against love is a *sure sign that healing is near.*

Here is a personal example of how the ego wages war on love, and how it can be overcome: A friend of mine began to feel afraid when she went into deep meditation. She asked Hilda about this, who told her, "That's wonderful, darling! That means you are really getting somewhere! When you are moving into a new and freer state of life the ego feels threatened, and it fights back by creating the feeling of fear. You can be sure that whenever you feel afraid the ego is trying to hold you back from enjoying your greater good.

"The ego believes that all change is threatening, and therefore defends against it, even — and especially — when the change is toward your happiness. That is why we can give thanks whenever the ego rails up — it is a sign that we are taking a step toward a better, brighter life. Do not be intimidated by the ego's cowardly roaring — once you have begun to initiate a step toward the light, it is only a matter of time until all ego resistance falls away."

[1]John Randolph Price, *The Planetary Commission*, The Quartus Foundation for Spiritual Research, Inc., P.O. Box 26683, Austin, TX 78755. Used by permission.

Through the Door

It may be said that we live in an invisible membrane of fear, encapsulating us like an imaginary bubble of boundaries. This illusory but tyrannical fence sets our limitations, decides who and what we like and don't like, and keeps us caged in a world of small thinking. We may feel safe, but this false sense of protection is quite meager in comparison to the security we feel when we know that *there is no real threat in the entire universe.* Wherever we go God goes with us, for God dwells within *us* as us.

The ego, like a vicious watchdog guarding the door of our cell, rests as long as we do not try to cross the imaginary threshold we believe is there. (I am told that if you draw a chalk circle around a chicken and spin the bird around a few times, it will not step over the line, believing that the chalk line represents a real and fearful boundary.) Many times we may step up to that doorway, and many times we may turn back, intimidated by the fierce growling monster that we ourselves have created by our agreement in a lie.

What we do not realize is that the watchdog has *no power* to hurt us. At best it merits a moment of laughter and a light brush aside. Yet we have imbued that beast with the strength that belongs to us, and we remain at the effect of its empty barking until we are willing to reclaim the power that we invested in it. We do not realize that our dragons are our own puppets because we have never looked long enough to see our own hand pulling their strings. We hold ourselves in bondage by our own mind alone.

The few who have taken the step past the threshold of seeming limitation have come back to tell us that there is indeed nothing at all to fear. Jesus returned after three days to tell us that death is not real, and that all of our trepidations about it are unfounded. In the garden outside the tomb an angel appeared so real to Mary Magdalene that she thought he was the gardener! And what did he tell her but, "Mary, why do you look for the living among the dead?"

The War That Never Was

The ego is totally insane in its frantic attempts to find peace through war. The ego's motto is "Attack before attack comes," but it has never paused long enough to rise to the high vantage point where it would see that there is no attack waiting. Its sense of attack comes entirely from itself. There is nothing outside the ego that has any concept of attack whatsoever. If fear would stop chasing its own tail, it would quickly see that nothing has been biting it but its own jaws.

The thirst for vengeance of Darth Vader, the Emperor of the Dark Empire, and the entire Klingon Armada is nothing compared to the ferocious mania of the ego in its effort to keep you small. In the *Star Wars* movies the Empire was overt in its quest to snuff out the light. In contrast, our ego operates in craftiness, subtlety, and the deepest viper pits of the subconscious. The snake scene in *Raiders of the Lost Ark*, in which Indiana Jones has to descend into a pit writhing with thousands of deadly snakes, doesn't even touch the chambers of horrors that the ego has conjured up in the prison of the part of your mind that fears. The ego is like a mad scientist maniacally concocting strange illusions in a laboratory in the basement of your thoughts. The only hope of this maker of distortion is to stay in the dark and keep you in the dark with it. It knows that, like the creepy little critters that hide under logs in the woods and scatter the moment they are exposed to light, the ego's fears are doomed to extinction the moment they are brought into the sunshine of loving truth.

It is important to understand that the ego will use *any means it can* to trick you into staying behind and keep you from your destiny of peace. It is completely unscrupulous and diabolically ingenious in its thirst to hold you hostage, and it will use the tactics to which you believe you are personally most vulnerable to stop you from accomplishing success. It will create disease, loss, and divisiveness to bar you from your good, and it will disguise itself as the opposite of what it is. The ego will tell you that you are not moving ahead because you are afraid to fail, when in truth it is the fear of *succeeding* that you have allowed to stop you. Every time I have made a step forward in my personal and spiritual evolution in the areas of health, success, or relationships, for example, I have had the feeling that I was about to be punished, die, or lose something. When I found the courage to go ahead despite the ego's gloomy counsel, I discovered deep peace, greater aliveness, and immeasurable gain. Now when pessimistic feelings arise I find cause for rejoicing, for I know that I am about to step not back, but forward. Remember that the ego is utterly insane in its quest for victory in the war that never was.

Moving Ahead

You must move ahead in the face of fear. The great metaphysician Emmet Fox said, "If you must tremble when taking your next step, then do it trembling — but do it." He also said, "Do the thing and you shall have the power."

Several years ago I learned an important lesson in how to disarm the ego by calling its bluff. As I was driving to the largest workshop I had ever organized — a hundred people were coming — I had some doubts about how well I could serve that many participants.

Driving up a mountain road in the Poconos, I began to sniffle and sneeze. I thought, "I must be coming down with some kind of flu. Maybe I'm getting the bug that Sally had." As I reached over to see if I had any tissues in my glove compartment, the train of thought followed, "I don't know if I'll be able to conduct this retreat. Maybe I should turn around and go home."

Then came another voice, like a cavalry rushing in with reinforcements: "No!" it told me, "Carry on. Don't go into agreement with that voice of fear and illness. Thoughts of limitation are not worthy of your attention. Acknowledge the reality of the Light within you, and remember that all is perfect."

Immediately I felt energized and uplifted. A force of enthusiasm surged through me. I saw myself in a brilliant white light. When doubts or thoughts of inability to conduct the workshop came up again, I affirmed, "I don't care how I feel. These people are coming to this workshop to be healed, and I'm going to trust Spirit to touch them through me — and I know God wants me to be healthy to do it."

Quickly the sneezing, sniffling, and runny nose stopped, and I felt better. I went on to deliver one of the best programs I have ever done, with many wonderful miracles of healing. It was not the flu that was attempting to hold me back, but *fear*. The sniffles were nothing more than an instrument of the ego, and as soon as my mind was corrected about its nature and its purpose, so the body corrected itself.

The body is the glove of the mind; as we move the fingers of our mind, so does our body follow the mental pattern. That is why our body is our best friend: it is always telling us what our mind is thinking. We can use it to discover where we are stuck and then practice remembering that we are not stuck at all. *We are unlimited free spirits.* We are Children of a Perfect God.

There is Only Love

You have nothing to lose. You cannot lose because all that you have is all that you are, and you are everything there is. Being everything, you cannot lose because you could never lose yourself. You can fall asleep and dream that you are losing, but dreams do not have the power to change the reality of your perfect invulnerability while your mind is turned away from it. Upon awakening you will find that you are still quite whole, and indeed always have been.

The only worthy response to the ego when it strikes back is love. To return vengeance for the ego's barking would ask you to enter into the thought system that believes that attack is effective. In that world you will never win. The ego's response to the Holy Spirit is to strike back, while the Holy Spirit's only response to the ego is to give more love. That should be your response, too, because you are not born of the ego, but of God.

There is a way to undo the mess the ego has appeared to have made: *Hold it up to the light!* Sharing is the way of Heaven, and hiding the way of hell. A problem is exacerbated when we feel that we cannot tell anyone about it. I tell you, there is nothing that the Children of Light cannot look upon and heal with love.

Because the ego is totally insecure, it will generate its biggest bluff when confronted with the simple fact that your protection lies not in it. The ego, in spite of all of its wild bravado and ability to produce some very scary movies, is actually nothing. *You, who are something, never need to be afraid of the ego, which is nothing.* The wilder the ego flails, the greater the potential for healing, for here is your sign that you are pushing up against the membrane of your illusory sense of boundaries. You are very close to discovering the truth.

The people, events, and situations that challenge you are angels. They have come to you with the key to your next step in your personal evolution.

Call them devil and you will find yourself in hell. See the angel in them, discover the blessing they bring, and you will live in Heaven — on earth. Everyone in this world is an angel. You do not have to fly up to the clouds to see their beauty. Just listen for the song of the harp concealed beneath the cloak of their seeming misdeeds.

Because the ego is based entirely on thoughts of hatred, you can be released from its nasty grip simply by giving it — and everything else — love. Here is how to love the ego into the light: Appreciate all of its attacks, panic, and flailings for what they are: gifts to you from God to learn that fear is never necessary, for *there is only love.* The Holy Spirit always takes a positive interpretation of an ego attack; no threat could fluster the light in the least. Your true Self knows that you are of God, and Spirit is invulnerable to all attack. It perceives only love everywhere in the universe. This is the truth that sets you free.

The Transfer Value of Courage

Everyone in this world feels that he or she is a sinner. As you are willing to accept your innocence you will heal everyone who comes into your mind by knowing that they are innocent too. Very few people in this world are willing to face their ego, their fears, and their sense of limitation. The few who have are hailed as saints, holy men and women, and gifted ones. Their gift, however, lies not in potential but in *expression.* It is crucial that you remember that you are capable of the same level and quality of expression. We are all gifted with the ability to be ourself, and this is the one gift that we can share with everyone we meet. *A Course in Miracles* tells us, "When I am healed I am not healed alone,"[2] and in the case of conquering our ego, this is surely so. All fear exists by agreement and by agreement only. When one of us breaks the agreement, watch how quickly the truth replaces misery in the hearts of all who would embrace it!

---

[2] W, p. 254

You are a Trailblazer

During recent years many persons have participated in firewalking workshops.[†] Thousands of people from many ways of life have learned how to walk unharmed over a bed of thousand-degree burning coals. I participated in such a workshop several years ago, and I gained much.

The leader began by giving us a powerfully inspiring lecture on the nature of fear and how to overcome it. He explained that the mind is the source of all of our physical experience, and that if one wants to change his physical experience he must change his belief system about what he can and cannot do. This idea registered within my soul as a truth. I was inspired to walk.

We walked outside to find an orange-red mound of glowing coals, the remnant of a huge pile of wood that had been set ablaze earlier that afternoon. Hearing about the bed of coals was one thing, but seeing it was another. Yet I knew I could walk. A voice inside my mind prompted me, "Go ahead — you can do it!" I felt that I could walk, but I still entertained some doubts. I wanted to walk, but I did not want to be the first one.

The turning point for me came when I saw one of my friends step onto the coals and walk across them without being burned. I was amazed, for I knew that he was no different than me, and he had no more training than I had. "If Neil can do it," I felt, "so can I."

I stood before the coals. The instructor, Tolly, had told us to take an affirmation or positive visualization before we walked. All I could hear in my mind was, "I believe in God." Those four words actually summed up a very profound and life-transforming thought process I was undergoing. I felt that I was standing not in front of a bed of burning coals, but at a crossroads: one path represented all of the "truths" I had ever learned from the ego — that I am a body which can be hurt, and I had better protect it, or I would be harmed. The other path shined with the knowledge that I am not a body, but a living spiritual being. It was founded on the awareness that the real me is not born of flesh and blood, but of Spirit. And that Spirit is not subject to fire or

---

[†] My experience is offered as an encouragement to others to follow their inner guidance. It is not an endorsement for firewalking. Anyone considering firewalking must make his or her choice based upon introspection and contemplation.

any other element in the material world.

I realized that I was not facing a physical threat, but *every fear I had ever run away from*. To turn back now would be to renounce my divinity and give fear power over my life by shrinking away from it. As I thought more about walking, I was confronted by sardonic images of all the woeful possibilities of what might happen to me if I walked. Pain, sorrow, and death were shrieking in my ears. Yet beneath their gruesome howls I could hear the whisper of that still, small voice, the gently loving guidance of the peaceful strength within me. "You can do it, Alan," the voice assured me.

I realized that I was not making a decision for one moment, but for all of my life. *"Do you want to continue to live in fear, or do you want to be free?"*

I reached the point where I would rather have been burnt up and die than live in fear. I decided to walk, and take my chances. If the voice that was telling me to step forward was a liar, there wasn't much left anyway.

So I walked. I affirmed to myself, "I believe in God," and I stepped onto the coals.

As I walked I experienced heat, but no pain. I continued for four or five paces over the coals, and still no pain. What a feeling of exhiliration I enjoyed as I completed my walk and stepped onto the grass! The exhortations of my ego were *not true*. I felt that I would not need to ever be afraid of anything again. I was the master of my destiny. My mind was more powerful than my body. I was not dead, but more alive than ever! I was free!

As I recall my moment of decision now, I see that all it took for me to conquer fear was for me to see one other person do what I thought I couldn't do. One person like myself broke through his membrane of limitation, and I followed along with many others. *"When I am healed I am not healed alone."*

We have the power to heal one another. The firewalk is a metaphor for all of the things in life that we have been told that we cannot do, but really can. When one of us gets out there in the jungle of fear with a machete and cuts down the weeds for himself, he clears a new road for the rest of us who want to walk with him. All of us still possess the machetes of courage with which we were born — but only some of us are willing to acknowledge that we do, lift them up, and whack away at the brush. Each of us has a piece of the jungle in front of us, a section that only *we* can clear. Glory be to us when we do clear it, for then all of us can walk hand in hand upon a new road with greater freedom to live as who we are and be who we were born to be.

The End of Nothing and the Beginning of Everything

All that we have been resisting is pure love. Only love. Love is all there is in the entire universe. To fear anything in life is to resist the very Force we have been given to free us. Because we are spiritual beings, created in the image and likeness of an eternally perfect God, there is nothing anywhere that can hurt us. It is said,

"If God is with me, what could be against me?"

I assure you, God is most certainly with you. When you see Him not it is only because you are not looking with respect upon yourself. To look with respect upon yourself is to affirm all that God is and who you were created to be. Fear can cover over the awareness of our perfection, but it could never remove it. A sleeping child does not see his loving mother as she pulls the blanket up to his shoulders, gently kisses him goodnight on his forehead, and whispers a quiet prayer for his happy awakening. When the morning comes glistening with the brightness that ends all dark dreams, you know with perfect certainty that you never need fear again. No fearful dream can stand between you and the true Self you discover in the clarity of the morning light.

Fear, in the final vision, is wholly unjustified. You have been afraid of life because you have been afraid of yourself. And fear of yourself can be born only of not knowing who you truly are. Child of the Morning, the time has come for you to awaken! Delay your healing no more. All is well. How uselessly you have turned your back on your Father's love. And how easily is it regained! Come home, dear one, beloved one, beautiful one. Wander in the dark forest no longer. Your home awaits you. Each moment that you spend fighting yourself can be given instead to the celebration of your return to your Father's Home.

This is the time of the new beginning. This is the time of your release from all that held you from your freedom. This is the new morning. Fear it not, for here is the miracle you have awaited. All thanks be to the One who loves you as you come to love yourself.

The Power to Succeed

Until one is committed, there is hesitancy, the chance to draw back, always ineffectiveness. Concerning all acts of initiative (and creation) there is one elementary truth the ignorance of which kills countless ideas and splendid plans: That the moment one definitely commits oneself, then providence moves too.

All sorts of wonderful things occur to help one, that would never otherwise have occurred. A whole stream of events issues from the decision, raising in one's favor all manner of unforeseen incidents and meetings and material assistance which no one could have dreamed would come their way.

Whatever you can do or dream you can, begin it. Boldness has genius, power, and magic in it. Begin it now.

- Goethe

A number of years ago I put my Honda on the market, and I had a hard time selling it. The car was advertised in the newspaper for several weeks, and when I had received no more than a few half-interested nibbles I placed it at my mechanic's gas station with a big "For Sale" sign on the side window. Another week or two passed... still no takers. I rethought my asking price of a thousand dollars and recognized that in comparison to similar cars on the market, it was in the ball park. "Why isn't that car selling?" I wondered.

Around that time I attended a healing service by Reverend W. V. Grant, a most inspiring and dynamically gifted minister who literally works miracles before the eyes of astonished onlookers. During that thrilling service I saw Rev. Grant pray in the name of Jesus Christ, after which the blind saw, the lame arose and walked, and legs of unequal length were adjusted instantaneously. The reality of the healing power of God in that room was beyond any demonstration I had ever seen, and the strength of my faith increased dramatically as a result of my experience.

As part of his service that evening Rev. Grant collected several offerings for various causes, including orphanages he sponsors in Haiti, his television ministry, and, as he honestly admitted, his personal needs and those of his family. I and the entire audience gave generous amounts of money to support his work, which I believe is genuine, and I respect.

One characteristic that I noticed about Rev. Grant as he took up the offerings was his deep belief in his ministry. He was so confident in his purpose that he was willing to ask for very large amounts of money without any sense of apology, guilt, or self-doubt. For me this was a powerful teaching in the integrity of his ministry. The only way that he could heal so consistently was to have complete faith in God's ability to heal through him; if he had one percent of doubt he would not be the healer that he is. The transfer value of this faith to all of his work, including the financial prosperity of his ministry, was obvious and an important lesson for me.

Driving home from Rev. Grant's service that evening I considered the depth of his faith in God and in himself. The thought occured to me, "If Rev. Grant can collect $25,000 for his ministry in one evening, I can certainly sell my Honda for $1000." In contrast to his conviction I found in my mind some sense of guilt and unworthiness about selling that car for a thousand dollars. I realized that even though it was a fair price compared to similar sales, I felt guilty about asking that much for it, and I was also a little hesitant to part with an old friend which had served me so well for so long. I had already bought a new car, I had that bill and others to pay, and my guidance to sell the old car was clear. I saw that it was only my feeling of unworthiness that was standing before the sale.

That night, having caught the strength of Rev. Grant's confidence in his ability to be worthy of financial success, a sense of surety welled up within me and I felt that I deserved to sell the car and accept that amount of money for it. I went to sleep with a new sense of worthiness and freedom in my heart.

I was awakened early the next morning by the telephone. Clumsily I reached for the receiver and heard an unfamiliar voice:

"Hello, Alan?... This is Arnie."

"Arnie?" I scanned my memory bank. I did not know any Arnies.

The voice continued, "...I'll give you a thousand dollars for your Honda."

That woke me up. Or was I dreaming? Could a miracle happen that quickly? It was less than one waking hour since I had felt the worthiness and willingness to sell the car, and here was an immediate offer.

I met the fellow at the gas station and within three hours the car was sold for one thousand dollars, cash.

The Power to Succeed

The secret of all success is:

COMMITMENT.

No one has ever received, gained, or accomplished anything in life without first being deeply committed to it. Everything that has ever happened to anyone has occurred because he has held a commitment — consciously or subconsciously — to that result in his mind. No exceptions! All that we experience is a matter of willingness. The statement "I will" is not a future promise — it is an affirmation of what we choose to create *now*. We *are* the masters of our destiny.

A statement as bold as this one is likely to raise many questions in the thinking mind, for it certainly does seem that things happen to us that are beyond our choice or control. Here it is important to realize that the mind that makes the choices and commitments from which our experiences proceed is not the conscious mind. The real creator of our experience is the *subconscious* mind, which does not think in words, but in pictures, feelings, and intentions. In order to make any progress on the spiritual path we must understand without any doubt whatsoever that *we create our entire life* by the intentions that we hold in mind. We must see that nothing happens to us outside of our own choosing. The understanding and practice of this principle is the entire difference between a person who is the master of his life and one who sees himself as a victim of forces outside his control.

A Course in Miracles explains:

> *This is the only thing that you need do for vision, happiness, and release from pain and the complete escape from sin, all to be given you. Say only this, but mean it with no reservations, for here the power of salvation lies:*

"I *am* responsible for what I see.
I choose the feelings I experience, and
I decide upon the goal I would achieve.
And everything that seems to happen to me I ask for,
and receive as I have asked."[2]

The Formula For Healing

Mind is the progenitor of all of our experiences. We are told, "In the beginning was the word." This statement is not referring simply to an event that occurred at the beginning of time, but a principle that diagrams how we create each new moment of living. This idea calls our attention to the importance of the intention *within our heart*, the purpose behind the action, the goal we wish to accomplish. "Mind is the builder," taught Edgar Cayce. How correct he was!

The patterns in our life remain fixed only as long as our intention does. The moment we change our mind about what we want, *what comes to us must change* as well. If you feel that you are trapped in a repetitious pattern of disastrous relationships, financial setbacks, or ill health (I met one man who broke his right ankle seventeen times for seemingly different reasons), here is the way you can be released instantly:

1. Recognize the pattern.

2. Acknowledge that you have created it.

3. Learn the lesson it is bringing to you.

4. See, know, and affirm what you want instead.

5. Act on your goal with strength and mastery.

6. Allow God to help you.

I learned this lesson through a challenging relationship. The woman I was seeing did not seem to share my intention for a committed relationship. I struggled with the issue for a long time, and I could make no sense of the matter. I felt there were some dynamics operating that I could not see. Why was she not willing to go one hundred percent?

---

[2] T, p. 418

Around that time a psychic friend offered me a reading. I decided to ask about our relationship. "Why will she not commit herself?" I asked.

The answer came quickly, strongly, and concisely: "Because you are not willing to commit yourself."

The truth of the answer cut through my questioning like a sharp sword.

The counselor went on: "Within your own heart you have held fear and doubt about the relationship. Your partner picked up on this, and because she held some of the same fears and reservations, she mirrored them back to you."

That was it. That was the hidden dynamic of the relationship that I had been asking to understand. Although I wanted to blame her for not being there for me, it was me who was not fully willing to be there for her.

It felt cleaner, clearer, and much more peaceful to accept responsibility for creating the relationship as I experienced it, so much freer than being a victim. Amazingly, as I realized this my love and appreciation for my friend increased dramatically.

When we release our picture of others as victimizers, we free ourself from being a victim. The healing energy liberated in such a new vision will then transform the entire situation and manifest a positive, satisfying, and creative relationship.

A woman once asked me, "Why do men keep leaving me?"

My response was clear: "You attract men who leave you because you do not wholly want one who will stay. If and when you decide that you really want to be in a fully committed relationship, you are sure to attract a man who will reflect your intention."

Repetitious patterns in relationships are sure signs of an underlying pattern of subconscious intention. Like the needle of a phonograph stuck in a groove, we must lift up our mind and place it in a new course. The lifting up of our awareness to see more clearly is often sufficient to set a positive change into motion. We cannot change when we are unwilling to see. The moment we realize that we have been stuck and we ask for help, it must come. Recognizing we are stuck is not a misfortune, but a gift, for recognition is the first step of healing. Then we are free to see the way we must walk to be at peace.

Patricia Sun illustrated this principle in a refreshing way: "People tell me that they are now ready for a relationship, and wonder why can't they find one? I tell them, 'Saying "I'm ready" doesn't necessarily mean you are ready. Being ready is this:...." She stood with her arms, smile, and heart open wide, and invitingly smiled, "Hi!" She was demonstrating that there is no substitute for willingness; when we are truly ready and willing, we will surely attract the object of our desire.

The Commitment to Healing

No one who is committed to healing could remain ill, and no one whose intention is illness can be healthy. There is no middle ground, for there are no exceptions to choice. There is one question to ask about any illness, the answer to which can make the difference between disease and release: "Why have I chosen this?" Being willing to consider personal responsibility is the first step to undoing any kind of pain. *Every experience teaches us a lesson in the power of responsibility and commitment.* As you realize this truth you will become tremendously powerful in all aspects of your life.

We do not need to create an illness to get away from a job, a relationship, or a life. We just have to be lovingly honest about what we really want to do. Several years ago I was working on a building project involving long hours of pouring cement. Toward the end of that summer I came down with a cold and spent a couple of days in bed.

"Why have I created this cold?" I wondered.

As I reflected on my feelings, I realized that I had had enough of cement work for the summer. I was not sick from a disease — I was sick of pouring cement. When I admitted that to myself, I realized I did not have to create a cold to get out of work. I could have simply said, "I am taking a couple of days off." Then I could have relaxed in bed or walked in the woods or gone to visit a friend. *We are never just sick; when we are ill we are sick of something.* If we are willing to look at the thing we are sick of, deal with it, and tell truth about it, we won't need our body to communicate what our mind wants to say. It hurts us to not tell the truth about what we are feeling. Every illness is a statement. Our goal — and birthright — is to be free of the illness, for indeed illness is not our natural state of being. Our object, however, should not just be to make the symptoms go away; our real purpose is to discover the statement we would like to make. There is a hidden truth we want to tell, and we are using our body to express it by means of those symptoms. The body is a wonderful metaphor. Illness can be a tool for awakening, which is what we came here for. The more we are willing to tell the truth about who we are and what is happening in our life, the less likely we will be to use illness to speak for us. *We don't have to get sick; all we have to do is tell the truth.*

We get sick because we fear that we would be hurt if we told the truth. But telling the truth is what would heal us. Dr. Jerry Jampolsky, the author of the popular book, *Love is Letting Go of Fear,*[3] uses this principle to accomplish wonderful healings with his clients. He asked a man who was dying, "What is it in your life that is so horrible that you would rather leave life than stay in it and face?" The man began to cry and he shared with Jerry for hours the experiences and feelings which he felt had hurt him and caused him to withdraw from fully celebrating his life. Jerry listened, understood, and loved the man. Before long the man had a reversal of his condition and was healed. Here we see that telling the truth has phenomenal power to heal and make us new. His illness was a call for truth. When he told the truth, he was free.

I was told, too, of a woman in a hospital being treated for cancer. A friend of mine, the hospital physiotherapist, was assigned to give her a massage. As my friend is a very loving and open person the woman began to speak of her life as she was being massaged. She told my friend that she had been angry at her sister and they had not spoken in twenty-five years. As she related the story she broke down and began to weep profusely, explaining that she felt terrible about the separation and she wanted to heal it. When the woman was taken into surgery the doctors could find no sign of the cancer. The woman was healed.

The Willing Way

As a counselor I find it interesting to see the different ways clients respond to suggestions for healing. Many people are actively resistant to being healed. All disease — physical, emotional, mental, and spiritual — requires a tremendous continuous investment of energy to be maintained. Our natural state is peaceful health, and the universe is always working to restore it to us. Holding on to any form of illness requires vigorous and sustained effort. What a dear price we pay to defend ourself against healing!

In a counseling session I may give two or three suggestions, openings, or simple reinforcements for the patient to align with a vision of their healing. Sometimes I find that these gifts are met with tremendous resistance by the patient. One psychologist calls this the game of *"Yes, but..."* No

---

[3] Gerald Jampolsky, *Love is Letting Go of Fear,* Bantam, 1981

matter what positive suggestions the therapist offers, the patient responds with a reason why the healing cannot happen. This rejection of help is like throwing a life preserver to a drowning person who immediately throws it back at you. In *Illusions*,[4] Richard Bach says, "Argue for your limitations, and sure enough, they're yours." No one is as unhealable as someone who is not willing to be healed.

When we are ready to make a commitment to healing, all of our past commitments to illness, along with their effects, go out the window instantly. This is the Law of Grace. No matter how deeply entrenched we have been in ideas, feelings, or thoughts that we deserve to be sick, the moment we are willing to be worthy of healing, the old patterns and their resulting symptoms evaporate like a bad dream.

A woman who regularly attends my classes is a good example of this willingness to accept forgiveness for her past and replace it with success now. Nearly every week she reports the wonderful miracles that have happened to her as a result of her putting the class lesson for the week into action. She tells of marvelous improvements in her job, her health, and her relationships. This woman is ready and willing to accept healing in all aspects of her life, and because she is committed to inner change, there is no force in the universe that can stop her. There is an ocean of healing energy available to all of us. We can come to that ocean with a thimble, a bucket, or a tanker; — it is all according to what we choose.

Responsibility Versus Guilt

Sometimes as we aspiring students of truth begin to see that we are responsible for everything that happens to use, we are apt to feel guilty for creating a disease. The contradiction in this approach is obvious when we realize that it was our sense of guilt, or feeling separated from God, that created the disease in the first place. Punishing ourselves for feeling punishable is no answer. The only remedy for lack of love is love.

There is no guilt or blame in not being healed, nor is it a matter of being good or bad, spiritual or unspiritual. A health challenge is an opportunity to replace our sense of power*less*ness with the awareness of our true power*full*ness. Quickly a crisis can be transformed from a curse to a blessing as we discover the vast healing power which has lied dormant within us. This way of looking at our potential acknowledges and celebrates the patient's inhe-

---

[4] Bach, *Illusions*, p. 100

rent ability to create his life as he chooses. If the patient had the power to create such an illness, then he must have the power to recreate perfect health. How strong is our mind!

The acknowledgement of our true strength offers us a much more managable way of handling an illness. Guilt keeps us stuck, while acceptance of responsibility leads us to healing. If you learn to become more responsible for your life through being healed, it may be said that you have extracted a valuable gift from the experience. This is in no way to imply that the illness was necessary for you to learn, for illness is *not* necessary. It is to say that the wise student of Truth finds a lesson in every step of his path, and joyfully gains from it.

The Call for Love

We may complicate matters further by projecting our own unresolved guilt onto our friends when they get sick. We feel guilty for our own illness, and not wanting to face our sense of guilt, we blame our friends when they get sick. In addition to removing us from the answer for our own recovery, this approach clearly does not serve our friend's healing. If someone is ill, the last thing they want to hear is a sermon on how they created the illness. What they need is love and understanding. At such a time a hug is usually much more healing than a metaphysical lecture.

As *A Course in Miracles* poignantly teaches, all illness is really a call for love. Our only truly productive response to illness in ourself or another is to give more love. Any form of blame represents a mistake in our own mind. To give any response other than more love only delays the moment of real healing. The instant the real call is heard and answered, the healing is accomplished.

I have seen this powerful principle successfully applied on many occasions. When a teacher of metaphysics who stuttered was asked by a student, "How should we view your stuttering?" the teacher replied, "Please see it as a call for love."

I learned this truth personally when one night I answered the telephone to hear the voice of a friend proclaiming, "Hello, Alan, this is Cary... I am just calling to tell you that I love you!"

"Why, that's really wonderful, Cary — I really appreciate that!"

"I'll tell you why I'm calling right now," he reported. "My foot was hurting me, and I know that the only way I can get healed is to give more love. I started to think of the people I love, and you came into my mind. I want to thank you for being a light in my life!''

It is said that all acts in life can be divided into one of two categories: clear expressions of love, and distorted expressions of love. All illness, anger, fear, and separation are actually calls for love in a form that is veiled. Longfellow said, "If we could read the secret history of our enemies, we should find in each man's life, sorrow and suffering enough to disarm all hostility." Try responding to distorted calls for love as if the apparent victimizer is craving a vitamin ("L" for love) that no one else has offered them. Such a one needs *more* love than someone who is expressing love more obviously. Give them the love they are really asking for, and quickly you will become a miracle worker. And you will wonder why you never before realized how simple is the key to living.

Know You Are Worthy

Our problem is not that we want the wrong things, but that we do not believe we are worthy of having the good that we desire. Why should it be so embarrassing to admit what we want? The courage to know what we want and then go for it will move us through life much more quickly and joyfully than sitting on the sidelines wondering if we deserve it. You have every right to ask for what you want. You deserve the best — do not settle for less!

True success is not a matter of capability, but of *worthability*. Do you know that you deserve good in *all* arenas of your life? Or do you hold some subconscious belief that you deserve to be sick, suffer, or sacrifice? *Now you can let go forever of any idea that God wants you to be ill or lose in any way.* Nothing could be farther from the truth. God wants you to experience complete health, happiness, abundance, and success in *everything* you do. At a workshop in Florida a man stood up and told the audience, "I tried believing in myself once, but it didn't work — I realized I didn't have enough experience!" Like this man, you have allowed your subconscious guilts and fears to run you into the dust for too long. It is about time you got out of the mud and made your way to the top of the mountain of life, where you belong.

Let me share with you an example of how we deny ourself prosperity by subconsciously sabotaging our own best interests:

One afternoon I received a telephone call from a friend who had been attempting to establish himself as an independent consultant in electronic engineering.

"I've been trying to get this business off the ground for six months," Gary explained with an air of frustration in his voice. "...yet I don't seem to be getting anywhere. I got one job, but the client called back to tell me he had changed his mind. What do you think is happening?"

Knowing that my friend is an adept engineer as well as a responsible person, it seemed to me that the crimp in the pipeline of his prosperity was being caused not by a circumstance, but a self-defeating mental program.

"Gary, is there any part of you that is resisting succeeding?" I felt guided to ask. "Do you have any thoughts that maybe you shouldn't be doing this?"

Gary took a moment to think. He hadn't thought of it in this way before.

"Well, now that you mention it," Gary thought out loud, "I do feel a little guilty about having an easy job that I like. When I was a child I was taught by example that a job is something you hate, which you slave at for forty hours a week, and at the end of the week the reward for your suffering is money. My idea for this business is to work out of my home for three or four days a week and to spend my free time studying massage and experimenting with photography. I guess part of me feels guilty for having a job that I love so much — it seems too easy!"

Gary was blocking his good from coming to him because he subconsciously felt that he didn't deserve it. Like many of us, Gary held himself in a state of lack because he was not willing to acknowledge that he deserved abundance. Similarly, many of us manifest our fear of success in the experience of failure. We sabotage good opportunities because we are afraid we will fail or we would have to take responsibility for their success.

I told Gary that we decide what we will accept in life on the basis of who we think are. If we believe we are sinful, unworthy people who deserve to suffer because we have done something bad, we will create illnesses, jobs, and relationships in which we lose and feel hurt. We will produce a personal movie in which we pay off the sins we *think* we have committed and for which we *believe* we deserve to suffer. THIS IS NOT THE TRUTH ABOUT WHO WE ARE. We are Sons and Daughters of a loving, forgiving God Who is well pleased in our joys and successes. The real God takes no pleasure whatsoever in anyone's suffering. The moment we know that God is a God of only love we begin to manifest a wonderful, healthy, and abundant life. Once we realize that God truly wants us to succeed and be happy at what we are doing, we step through the door of our destiny and serve many others in the process. You might like to know that Gary followed through on the guidance of his heart, and now he is a very successful teacher of massage, a livelihood in which he feels much more peaceful and satisfied.

The only decision we need to make is who we are. On the basis of that one thought will all of your experiences follow. If you remember that you are the heir to all of God's gifts, you will attract all the good your heart desires. You will prove this law by finding abundance in *every* aspect of your life.

God is Success

You can always tell what you want by what you are getting. The Law of Life, being a *law* and not a probability, is *always* working to give us what we are creating with our mind. This law is completely unbiased in its willingness to serve us — even if we go about creating experiences and events that we do not really want or need. We can and will have more of whatever we tell the universe with our thoughts. If we think abundance, we will get more abundance. If we think lack, we will see more lack. In this principle we realize that all is abundance — even abundant lack! We are always succeeding at being creators. We can even succeed at being a failure! And it is wonderful to recognize that we have succeeded at failing, for this means that *we are the masters of our destiny.* We can take the principle that we have unconsciously used to work against us, and harness the same power to work *for* us.

One of the most important elements of Goethe's brilliant elucidation of the power of commitment is this: *We do not have to know HOW we are going to get what we want. All we have to know is WHAT we want.* The "what" is our department — God will take care of the rest. When you have a clear perception of the goal, *the means for its accomplishment will be arranged for you.* If you are not getting what you want in life, it is not because the universe cannot provide good — it is because you are not sure of what you really want. Be sure, and life will lay all of its gifts at the door of your heart.

Our Real Desire

What we really want is the peace of God. Every dream, every aspiration, and every deed we undertake is an attempt to feel the peace that we remember deep within our heart. All of our striving seeks but to reclaim our birthright of inner contentment. We will stop at nothing short of true peace — this is a guarantee!

One of the pitfalls that many of us slip into in the early stages of spiritual awakening is becoming enamoured with the power of our mind to create material objects or events in our life. When this happens we clutter our consciousness with an overspiced goulash of transpersonal leftovers. We start to see that our mind is indeed a powerful tool to produce the movie of our life, and then we promiscuously manufacture a series of gospel bloopers. The result is that we end up with a lot of metaphysical footage on the cosmic cutting-room floor, a few good takes that we can splice into a sequel, and a fair amount of lessons in the cinematography of awakening.

Thus we have an early lesson in miracles:

"I do not perceive my own best interests."[5]

How many things have you asked God for, received, and then asked him to take back? You entreat our Heavenly Father for a certain car, home, or relationship, and then it is not long before you are standing at the celestial exchange counter begging for mercy because the garment you requested is not your size and you don't have your receipt. Then, of course, because God is a God of mercy, we get to trade it in for a new something, until sooner or later there we are at the counter again with a new reason. That etheric exchange department gets so much action that it makes K-Mart on December 26th seem like the Gobi Desert by comparison!

It is no wonder, then, that *A Course in Miracles* tells us, "You cannot be your guide to miracles, because it was you who made them necessary."[6] If you really knew what was good for you, you wouldn't be in the mess you're in!

How, then, do you integrate the fantastic creative power of your mind, and your phenomenal ability to subtly sabotage the full manifestation of your good? Once again the *Course* offers us a miracle:

Miracles are habits, and should be involuntary. They should not be under conscious control. Consciously selected miracles can be misguided.[7]

---

[5] W, p. 36
[6] T. p. 277
[7] T, p. 1

To illustrate: A friend of mine who liked to jog wished to live closer to the park so she could run there directly each day without driving to get to the jogging area. Every day she sat for twenty minutes and visualized living one hundred yards from the park. Clearly she gave God this message, with the feeling that He would fulfill it. And He did. God got her an apartment exactly a hundred yards from the park; unfortunately, it was on the other side of the river that bordered the park. She still had to drive fifteen minutes via the nearest bridge to get to the park!

Another friend, seeking to improve her financial situation, specifically visualized receiving checks in the mail. She spent long hours mentally seeing the mailman placing checks from a reputable source in her mailbox. Sure enough, that is what happened. What she forgot to tell God was that the checks be made out to her. When they came, the checks were social security payments to the former tenant. They did her no good. But checks did come in the mail.

Should these two people *not* have prayed to improve their situation? Certainly they should have prayed — but they should have prayed real prayers — not for circumstances, but for *peace*. Jesus said, "When you pray, you pray amiss." Instead of asking for an apartment or a check, which are but symbols of abundance or channels through which good is delivered, these students of truth would have done better to affirm their good as an *already-present reality*. Their desire for beauty of nature and prosperous living are perfectly aligned with who we are and what we deserve; but perhaps the most powerful visualization would have been one that saw all the beauty of nature and the abundance of the universe already residing *within* their hearts. We seek external riches only when we have forgotten the riches *inside* of us. Truly the only quest is for spiritual awakening, which reveals to us that what we sought is what we *are*.

When *A Course in Miracles* teaches, "Miracles are natural and involuntary, and should not be under conscious control," it is reminding us of the easy, natural way in which Spirit works. When something is right for us, useful for our awakening, and helpful to our peace of mind, the idea for the article or the experience will awaken spontaneously in our mind and heart. We will find ourself thinking about it, enjoying the possibilities of having this idea become a reality in our life, and contemplating all the good that it holds for us. This entire process happens *effortlessly*, without any force or struggle on our part. It is as if God plants a seed in our heart, and then we find ourself nurturing it with strength, shining our enthusiasm on it, and watering it with the spirit of our love. Our good springs forth out of peace and joy —

not a sense of duty or effort. We enjoy watching it unfold as we participate in it. And it will come to pass because it is of God.

When I came out of graduate school I began to look for a job as a counselor. While I was working at a Seven-Eleven grocery store, my heart was yearning to do some creative work with young people. One day I saw an advertisement in the newspaper for a coordinator for youth drop-in centers. Reading the job description, I knew that job was for me. Immediately I began to think about what I would do if I got the job. I envisioned setting up communications workshops for teenagers and their parents, establishing a telephone hotline, and participating with the teens in an informal recreational atmosphere. I did not in any way force myself to think about these projects; the ideas were so pleasing to my spirit that I found myself visualizing and thinking about them many times a day. I even wrote down an organizational outline.

By the time I went to the interview it was as if I had been doing the job for years. I had many of the details about the position worked out in my mind, and in a way I already felt successful at the job. The result was that I got the job and went on to see the fulfillment of all the ideas that I had thought about and jotted down — and more! Success flows easily when we are relaxed and creative in fantasizing about the things we would love to do.

The Peaceful Warrior

It should be noted here that we can be quite active and productive without any sense of strain. Absence of struggle does not mean absence of participation. You might be inclined to ask, "But if I gave up striving, how could I accomplish anything?" The answer is that *you are not the accomplisher* — God is. When you are working in attunement with the Voice of Spirit, it will tell you precisely what to do. Then it will clear the way for you to accomplish your dream and leave you with no strain at all, only a deep sense of peace and fulfillment.

> *Once you have accepted His plan as the one function that you would fulfill, there will be nothing that the Holy Spirit will not arrange for you. Without your effort He will go before you, making straight your path and leaving in your way no stone to trip on, no obstacle to bar your way.*[8]

[8] T, p. 404

To release struggle does not mean that you will become a blob; quite to the contrary! You will become a more efficient, creative, and productive human being, with a boundless resource of energy to use for the healing of yourself and others. The energy that you once invested in worry and self-protection will be available to be channeled into constructive, helpful, and rewarding projects. You will overflow with the talents and abilities that God created you to fulfill.

While I was writing *The Dragon Doesn't Live Here Anymore* I learned how to struggle less and accomplish more. When I was first inspired to write the book I worked almost non-stop for three solid months. I typed for eight to twelve hours a day, eating little, sleeping sometimes as few as three or four hours a night, putting nearly all other activities aside. My meditation and exercise program dropped away. It seemed as if all I was doing was living, eating, and breathing this book that felt as if it was being written through me.

To an observer it might have appeared that I was making a tremendous effort and sacrificing much. Yet during this period I had no sense of strain, struggle, or effort at all. I was neither pushing nor forcing myself to do anything about which I did not feel excited and enthusiastic. In fact, I had so much energy to work that I did not want to stop until I was finished. Afterwards, upon seeing the process from a grander perspective I realized that I was eating, sleeping, and meditating less because I was deriving my nourishment from the spiritual attunement I was enjoying in hearing and recording the ideas I was writing. "Man shall not live by bread alone, but by every word which proceeds from the mouth of God."[9] The spiritual insights I was receiving *were* my food, rest, and meditation. I did not need to do practices to put myself in touch with the Christ — I was already in His Presence. *A Course in Miracles* teaches, "Rest does not come from sleeping, but from waking."[10] It was the most intense work I have ever done — and at the same time the easiest!

I believe this experience is a model for how we can live our whole life: extremely creatively, while not laboriously. The more willing we are to engage in the creative activities that we enjoy, the more energy we will have to do them, and the more successful we will be in accomplishing them.

---

[9] Deuteronomy 8:3
[10] T, p. 71

Love is the Way

The real secret of success is love. We must love ourselves enough to know that we are worthy to succeed. We must believe that those around us want us to win at life, and that our winning can only support their winning. We must know God wants us to be happy in *all* the arenas of our life. We must understand that there is no need to struggle, strain, or live in pain or a state of lack. These hellish conditions are but signals that we must try another way. We must never settle for less than whole and holy abundance in our health, relationships, and livelihood. We were not born to scratch the dirt with chickens — we were born to soar with the eagles!

All of the conditions of material and spiritual success that you desire are within your power to create right now. You have the ability, courage, and support to mobilize your belief in yourself immediately. Your ideas are not products of a warped ego — they are given to you by God Itself. Your dreams have not been randomly learned from a chaotic outer world; these sparkling jewels have been imbued within your soul by the Mind that knows only your perfection and lives for its expression. You are here for a staggeringly important purpose; much — very much — hinges on you following through to complete your personal quest for the opening of your heart and the healing of all of your life.

To accomplish this noble mission you must know, without one hint or shadow of hesitation, that all of your most cherished visions will become a reality, bearing fruit in ways more miraculous than you can now imagine. You are not alone. You walk holding the hand of Spirit, and no one who walks this path can be stopped. Your destiny is broader than the oceans, wealthier than the coffers of King Solomon, and loftier than the farthest stars. You are destined to know yourself as a Child of the Living God, heir to the love that created the universe in all its radiant splendor. Child of the All that is Good, know who you are! Walk with dignity, majesty, and the wonder of the Beauty in which you were created. Thus shall you deliver Heaven to earth and live in both without fear. Love shall take you all the way home.

There are only two mistakes one can make along the road to truth:

    1. Not going all the way.
    2. Not starting.

- Buddha

The GRACE of GOD

As If the Nothing Never Was

All of your past except its beauty is gone,
and nothing is left but a blessing.

- A Course in Miracles[1]

One of my favorite tales is *The Neverending Story*, the magical adventure of a young boy who travels to the thrilling realm of Fantasia, a colorful world in which the rocks talk, there is a luck dragon, and a beautiful princess in need of help. As the hero, Atreyu, enters Fantasia he learns that it is being consumed by *The Nothing*, a mysteriously malevolent force which is rapidly eating away at the world. With increasing speed *The Nothing* is crumbling trees, houses, people, and everything in its path into emptiness, and the Fantasians have found no way to stop it.

Atreyu is summoned by the lovely princess of Fantasia to save the world from *The Nothing*. But to do this he must pass difficult tests and brave dangers that have never before been conquered. He must tread through a Swamp of Sadness, pass through the Portal of Mirrors through which no one who holds any doubt about himself can survive, and he must face the ferocious Wolf of Destruction which has been dispatched to devour all who confront *The Nothing*. Surely Atreyu's task is formidably set before him!

Our young knight courageously accepts the challenge and sets out upon his heroic mission. Trudging through the Swamp of Sadness he loses his faithful horse, but he emerges unscathed. Though he is frightened by the bones of those who have not succeeded through the Portal of Mirrors, Atreyu summons the strength of his belief in himself and what he is doing, and goes unaffected by the force field of death generated by the reflection of self-doubt. One by one all of his friends disappear into *The Nothing*, and Atreyu absorbs his biggest blow in the loss of his great cuddly friend and transporter, Falcor the Luck Dragon. Yet onward he marches, faithfully determined in his quest to save the princess and the kingdom.

Gradually more and more quickly *The Nothing* overtakes Fantasia until

---

[1] T, p. 76

it has devoured everything in the kingdom except the princess and her castle. As Atreyu reaches her she tells him that the only chance to save her, himself, and the kingdom is to call her name out loud. Atreyu resists, and it appears that this means the end. At one final moment the princess, with tears in her eyes, begs him to comply.

As Atreyu calls the name, we hear that it is the name of his mother whom he had recently lost. You see, in order for *The Nothing* to go away he had to be willing to believe that what appeared to be lost was still alive.

At the moment of his call the terrible Nothing is stilled. Atreyu draws nigh the princess and laments that though *The Nothing* has finally been stopped, there is pitiful little left of Fantasia to do anything with.

"Oh no," comforts the lovely maiden. "…There is much left. You can easily rebuild Fantasia!"

"But how?" the valiant one queries.

"By using your mind!" she explains. "Don't you see that everything in Fantasia lives according to the love and belief that you give it? All you need to do is think clearly upon what you love, and all that was lost can be regained!"

"You mean I can get Falcor and all of my friends back?!"

"Why, yes!…Just call them to you, and you will see how quickly they come!"

Soon Atreyu is delighted to find his beloved Falcor flying to him, lifting him up on the soft ridges of his furry back to take him home. Happily they fly over the mountains and oceans, laughing heartily as they soar. We see Atreyu's eyes and heart sparkle as from this high vantage point he witnesses the return of all of his friends, just as the princess promised.

"Wow, Falcor!" cries Atreyu, "It's as if *The Nothing* never was!" Falcor smiles as the two return to a world safe from the fear of nothing.

A child's fantasy?

In the late nineteenth century Baird J. Spaulding set off on a pilgrimage to find the living spiritual masters of the Himalayas. Years later he returned with a most amazing account of his journey called *The Life and Teachings of the Masters of the Far East*. Now a classic in metaphysical elucidation, this powerful work in five volumes recounts some of the most inspiring and enlightening experiences ever recorded, and provides spiritual seekers with answers and insights into the nature of the mind, healing, and the mastery of all life.

During these adventurous years the members of this expedition met saints and sages who performed astounding demonstrations of the power of the mind to control health and life. It was not unusual for them to be with a guide who would simply disappear before their eyes and then find him waiting for them at their destination three days later. They observed many miracles similar to the ones performed by Jesus, including the manifestation of food, instantaneous healing of the sick, and raising the dead. These feats, it was explained, were simply the results of a conscious use of the Laws of Mind, and anyone with the strength of belief could perform them easily.

On one particular occasion the group witnessed an invasion of a village by armed marauders. In contrast to their other uplifting experiences, this scenario involved conflict, bloodshed, and fear. Affected by the negative images they had seen, the troupe was downcast and discouraged. After tending to the wounds of the villagers the members of the expedition dejectedly began their climb up to the mountain retreat where they had their quarters. Ascending slowly, they noticed they had lost their regenerative powers.

> *We left the lodge and started to walk to the Temple as had been the custom on previous occasions. We had proceeded to the ladder that led to the entrance of the tunnel, when the one who was in advance stopped, with one foot on the first rung, and said: "What has come over us? Just a day or two ago we were in seventh heaven of delight, going from place to place at will and accomplishing things in three months that we had expected would take years to finish. Our food appears on the table, and all of this without the least exertion on our part. Now, suddenly, we have slumped back into our old habits. I want to know why this sudden slump? I can see only one thing. Every one of us has taken upon himself the condition of the experience through which we have passed. This is what is now hampering us and I for one am through with that thing, it is no part of me whatsoever. It is mine only as I worship it and hold to it and do not let it go. I step forth out of this condition into a higher and better condition and let go. I am entirely through with it." As we stood and stared at him, we realized he was gone, he had disappeared.[2]*

---

[2] Baird Spaulding, *The Life and Teachings of the Masters of the Far East*, Vol. III, p. 46 Devorss & Co., 1972. Used by permission

"As you believe, so shall it be done unto you," taught the Master Jesus, and what a principle this is! Do you realize the implications of this idea, especially in light of the experience described in the expedition? This means that *any condition of body, mind, or spirit exists only because we hold it in mind, and the moment we release it from mind, the condition will disappear,* along with *all of its effects.* All that we see in our body and our entire life is a direct result of our thoughts. All that we need to do to change those conditions is to *change our mind.*

Let us look at our mind as a sort of electromagnet. As you've driven past a junkyard you may have seen a big crane with an electromagnet lifting and moving junk cars from one place to another. The cars are held to the magnet only by the current in the magnet which attracts the metal of the auto. Unplug the current for a moment, and the car quickly and easily drops off. It is a very simple principle.

That is exactly how the conditions of our life cling to us - and how they can leave us. In this case our mind is the magnet and the conditions of our life are the cars. We attract persons and events by our thoughts, and we free ourselves of them by not continuing to power them with the electricity of our attention. Just as the electromagnet releases the junk cars, we can be free of junk thoughts by refusing to invest emotional energy in them. When we turn our attention to the light of God within and around us, we empower *those* thoughts to create new and more positive conditions in our life.

This is the principle by which Jesus and all the other great ones have accomplished their healings. The power of their thoughts was so dynamic that the mind of the sick or the dead one began to vibrate in harmony with that of the master, and as the master gave *no reality* to thoughts or conditions of illness or death, instantly the negative circumstances disappeared.

Teaches *A Course in Miracles:*

> *Miracles enable you to heal the sick and raise the dead because you made sickness and death yourself, and therefore can abolish both. You are a miracle, capable of creating in the likeness of your Creator. Everything else is your own nightmare, and therefore does not exist. Only the creations of light are real.*[3]

---

[3] T, p. 2

Only the creations of light are real. This means that only the good in our life is true, and any form of guilt or error that we see is a misperception. We hurt ourselves by seeing the negative, which is not really seeing at all, but misperceiving. Our role, therefore, is not to correct conditions, which are *always good*, but to purify our perceptions to reflect the light.

Misperceiving is like looking at a distorted circus mirror and being horrified by our strange reflection. The error is not in the source, but in the faulty reflection of it. One of those mirrors is called "the past," another "the future," and both of them show you everything but what is here now. An appropriate reaction is perhaps a light-hearted giggle and a quick return to the joy of seeing life in its true radiance. There is tremendous spiritual power available to us when we are open to the now, and we can enjoy total healing simply by *letting it all be good now.*

Change Can Come in the Twinkling of an Eye

During a powerful meditation Hilda guided, "Now let the conditions of your life drop away. In this moment you have no husband or wife, no business, no automobile. Leave everything that is temporary behind and rise into the light."

I felt myself lifting up like a balloon, and soon all of the painful dreams of life had no power to touch me or bring me down. I thought of the people and events in my life that were a source of discomfort to me, prefacing each one by a denial of its ability to remove my happiness in any way: "No body"..."No rent"..."No relationship." I was not attempting to get rid of these things by making them real and then trying to make them go away; instead I was transcending my belief in their reality and in the thought that they had power over me. Watching thoughts that had seemed so cumbersome dissolve, I experienced a freedom that nothing in this world can challenge. What a release!

In the hours and days after that meditation I found that many of those conditions were changed, or I found the peace and clarity to deal with them effectively, in such a way that they no longer were a problem.

Is this essentially any different than the man who disappeared when he affirmed that the seeming disaster had no power over him? I believe that the nature of the principle that helped both of us is the same. The Law of Mind is constant, and we are all free to use it for our healing.

Now is the Time for Release

Now is the only moment in which you can totally free yourself from the past. There is a beautiful key statement in the *Course* which tells us, "This course is not beyond immediate learning, unless you believe what God wills takes time."[4] *The Will of God is now.* You can be healed now if you are willing to completely let go of every idea that you were ever ill, mortal, or limited. You are a Child of a Perfect God, and no harm can ever befall the spiritual being that you truly are.

This moment, take your past and *throw it all away.* You will not be lost, but found, and deeply comforted by the blessings bestowed by the lessons of love that you have gained. The past does not exist - indeed it never existed - except as you choose to uphold it in your thoughts. As you release the past you release yourself. This past that seems a burden is but a raft that took you from one shore of the river to the other. You are on solid ground now and you are ready to go forward, and so you must loose your burden from your weary shoulders. You are done with it. You can leave it behind without fear or hesitation. All you will take with you is your appreciation for the gifts that you received along your journey. You are reborn into the freedom of the living present. You are free to claim your destiny as a Being of Pure Light. You are free to open the door to forever, which begins only now. So it is, and so shall it be forever in the hearts of those who love the light.

[4] T, p. 288

The Language of God

"Dibrai Torah B'loshan B'nai Adam."
"The Torah (Bible) speaks in the language of people."
                                                    - The Talmud

I

There is a beautiful legend about an angel who sought admission to Heaven. To earn his place in the holy kingdom the elder angels gave him a mission: to find the person on earth who spoke the most powerful prayers.

For a long time the young angel was gone on his quest, and the overseeing angels wondered what had become of him.

When he finally returned he had with him a small boy.

"What took you so long?" his superiors inquired.

"I searched the earth," the aspiring angel told them. "I went to the synagogues and the churches, to the mosques and temples. There I found learned and revered men exhorting lengthy scriptures and rites — my mind boggled at the amount of knowledge their minds held. Yet when I looked into their hearts I saw their thoughts were wandering and they did not truly understand the words they were speaking.

"I found many people in all manner of houses of worship, dutifully reciting the delicate poetry of the psalms. But when I surveyed their souls, I found fear and hypocrisy darkening their love.

"I journeyed, too, to people kneeling at their bedside, and even in privacy I did not find complete sincerity in their prayer."

The elder angels listened attentively. "Why, then, did you not return and report this to us?" they asked him.

"So I was about to. I began to believe that there was no one on earth whose prayers had the power to reach Heaven. Then, as I flew homeward over a busy city, my heart was summoned by the sound of a child sobbing. As I drew close to find the cause of his tears, I heard him reciting the alphabet. Letter by letter he sobbed: 'A...B...C...' Then I heard him

115

whispering these words:

> *Dear God, I do not know how to read, and neither have I learned how to pray; the prayer book would do me no good. But I love you so much! And I want to thank you for all the wonderful blessings you are to me. So, if it is alright with you, I will simply recite the letters of the alphabet with love, and trust that you, my dear Friend, will put them together into the words that are pleasing to you."*

This, agreed all the angels, was the most powerful prayer of all.

II
Communication, not Confusion

Delivering my opening address on "Balancing Our Planet with Love" at a large retreat in eastern Pennsylvania, I was about to tell the story of a healing that I had read about in a newspaper that I had discovered in a local Seven-Eleven store. As I began the anecdote I found myself reporting to the audience that I had gone into the store to buy some potato chips.

"Why am I telling them about the potato chips?" I wondered as I stood at the flowered podium. "That has nothing to do with the healing story," I thought to myself as I spoke. Slightly embarrassed, I went on, hoping I did not sound too foolish.

After the lecture a young man with a shining face came up to me at the side of the stage. Shaking my hand he told me, "I just want to thank you for telling that potato chip story! That really set me at ease. For years I've been on a very strict health food diet, and every time I have a craving for some junk food or binge out I feel guilty. To sit here and hear you, an author, a person who I respect as a spiritual being, delivering an address on healing the planet, telling that you eat potato chips — that really freed me of my sense of unworthiness! I was uptight until I heard that, but I enjoyed everything you said afterwards. I received the whole message of the lecture!"

At another workshop I found myself speaking of the transition between this life and the next. This was a five day workshop, and I was surprised to find myself discussing this subject for a while each day. "Why am I getting into this?" I wondered. " — This is not my usual lecture material."

The answer came after the last class of the week. Two women approached me to say good-by and wish me well, and as they did so they mentioned, "We want to tell you how much we appreciate the attention you gave to transition. Both of us have had persons dear to us pass on recently, and what you said gave us great comfort. We felt as if you gave those lectures just for us."

God speaks in the language of Her children. The function of spiritual teaching is communication, not confusion. *God speaks to us in terms with which we are comfortable and familiar.* Very genuine guidance may come to you in colloquial terms. In order to hear it and receive the blessing it is intended to bring to you, you must be open to accept it.

You may have been denying your guidance because it has not come in a form in which you expect to receive it, or in which other persons have received theirs. Just because others have received messages in "thee's," "thou's," or "burning bushes" does not mean this is the way you are to be guided. Such language may be appropriate for them, but if it is not *your* style, Spirit will most assuredly reach you in your own way. Accepting help requires trust, openness, and most of all the willingness to be helped. You must believe that God loves you so much that She is willing to reach you in a way that is peaceful for you.

After one of my yoga classes a young lady explained to me that she had received guidance in doing one of the postures. "As I was doing the bow, (the position in which you lay on your stomach and reach behind your back to grab your ankles) my body began to tremble," she explained. "I held on, but the longer I held the more my body shook. I didn't know whether to let go or try to push through, so I silently asked for guidance.

"Then in my mind I heard the voice of a man with a Scottish accent calling, "Cap'n, I c'nnot push these engines anymur, else the Enterprise'll blow us into the next galaxy!"

Another woman, seeking to know if it was time to conclude a long meditation that she had been forcing her way through, also asked for instruction. Her inner voice answered, "Over and out!"

And one evening Hilda was resting in her room, wondering if she should join some friends getting ready to go to a movie. Her guidance came in the form of the tune of "Alexander's Ragtime Band." She tells that she heard a rousing chorus of angelic voices singing, *"Get up and go!...Get up and go!"*

These voices are not those of possession, subconscious memories, or spirits outside ourself. They are forms of guidance from our superconscious mind, delivering lessons to our conscious mind in ways that we are able to hear. To a Frenchman inspiration would come in the French language, to an artist in pictures, to a musician in tones. Spirit is happy and willing to meet us on our own turf.

The Bridge to God

In many of the *Star Trek* episodes the crew of the Starship Enterprise would find themselves on a distant planet encountering some enigmatic creature who looked like a cross between Godzilla and Ronald McDonald, and spoke a language resembling a marriage of Yiddish and Swahili. At that point Captain Kirk would quickly call for *The Universal Translator*, a device which automatically translated the creature's language into English so the crew could communicate with it.

God has built a universal translator right into our mind as standard operating equipment. Like many of the marvelous concepts on Star Trek and other science-not-so-fiction movies, this idea represents a real and practical metaphysical principle. Universal translation is a psychic capability to which we already have access, and we use it more than we realize. There is a vast reservoir of wisdom living deep within us — Aldous Huxley called it the ''Mind at Large'' — and this knowledge is channelled to us according to our ability to receive, understand, and use it.

If we were in perfect communication with God, we would need no guidance. Yet because we have veered from truth in consciousness (and consciousness alone!) each of us receives direction and correction according to the way that we have strayed from the path of right thinking. Those who have veered to the left must turn right; to the right, left; those who have passed it must turn around; and those travelling on the correct path need but continue. That is why there is no one recipe, guru, diet, or spiritual practice that will work for everyone all of the time. Toilets north of the equator flush clockwise, while those south of it flush counterclockwise. You have to know which side of the line you are on before you can know which way your water is supposed to swirl (metaphorically speaking).

Each of us has our own toilet to flush, our own piece of the universe to purify. No one can know more about what you need to do than your own self. The problems of the world have arisen from northern flushers criticizing their southern counterparts, while the southerners feel guilty for flushing the wrong way. Meanwhile, all toilets are swirling perfectly according to plan. Well, I think it's about time we had faith in our own flushing! The universe functions much more smoothly when we keep our hands on our own handle.

Another way of viewing our way home is to describe our universe as a great jigsaw puzzle, with a unique shape cut out for every living being, a little space in the cosmos that only one special person can fill. The miracle comes when, as you find your place in the jigsaw puzzle, you form the pattern for me to find mine. We serve each other most powerfully simply by finding our own place.

The Meeting Place of Mystics

Several years ago I had the pleasure to introduce the marvelous dental healers Reverend Willard and Margaret Fuller at a series of their lectures in Toronto. On the third night of the series we were to speak at a church that we had not previously visited. The day before the presentation the minister of that church telephoned me and invited me to introduce the Fullers' program to his congregation.

As we entered the church the minister shook my hand, ushered me to a seat, and introduced the Fullers himself. Having anticipated doing the introduction, I felt somewhat disappointed, a little offended, and rather puzzled. As I sat and listened I wondered why he had chosen to introduce the Fullers instead of me.

The next day Rev. Fuller told me that the minister had informed him that he did not feel that I was dressed nicely enough to do the introduction. The standard attire of this church was jacket and tie, and I was dressed more casually. My ego felt hurt, but Rev. Fuller's response to me was a lesson far more valuable than a little ego wound.

"My brother Alan," Rev. Fuller began in a fatherly sort of way, "may I share with you something that I learned way back in the beginning of my ministry?"

"Sure...please."

"I don't believe that any way of dressing is any better or more spiritual than another. Jesus wore a robe, and as far as I'm concerned, that would do quite well. But somewhere along my way I learned that the goal of a preacher is to awaken peoples' hearts to God, and if there is anything that may stand in the way of that communication, it is not worth it. These days people wear suits and ties, so that's what I wear — not necessarily because I prefer it, but because that is a commonly accepted format of dialogue in which the people in a public audience will comfortably hear what I have to say. Therefore it is worth it to me to meet on common ground. It is more important to me to communicate than for me to be personally comfortable. St. Paul said, 'I am all things to all people,' and I have learned the meaning of those words. If I were invited to preach the word of God at a clowns' convention, I would wear a clown's costume.''

That got to me. You see, Rev. Fuller is a man who dresses impeccably; he wears stylish suits, his hair and beard are very respectably trimmed, and he always emanates a pleasant hint of cologne. For him to be flexible enough to trade that for a clown's costume to share the word of God, was inspiration enough for me.

Then I remembered what Ram Dass had described about his teacher Baghwan Dass, when he first met him in India. "We went to a Buddhist shrine and everyone welcomed him as if they knew him," Ram Dass tells. "There I noticed he was chanting their *mantra*. Then we went to a Hindu community where they took him in as their own. There I saw he was wearing an amulet like all of them. Later on we travelled to a mosque where he knelt down and prayed their prayers. Then they invited us to dinner and gave us a place to stay. He seemed to be a part of everyone's group, and sincerely so.''

One Truth

In a way similar to Baghwan Dass I had to become a sort of undercover yogi when I was invited to give a series of lectures to employees at Bell Laboratories. Quickly I learned that "God" is a word that is not comfortable to many people in that environment, and it is rarely spoken. As I presented my first few lectures I noticed that whenever I would touch on any spiritual subject matter the audience would begin to squirm, wiggle, or raise objectioning questions. Gradually I cut back on spiritual lingo and tried to stay within a framework with which they were at peace.

I began to feel like a hypocrite. The language of spiritual terms, I felt, was my own; my heart loves God and I felt somewhat blasphemous in purposely avoiding His name. I spoke to Hilda about this, and here is the insightful counsel she gave me:

"Why, no, darling! That is not running away from truth -that's sharing truth in the way that it will most easily be heard. It is not necessary to use the word 'God' to feel, teach, and know God's presence. Just keep God in your heart, and then God will guide you to speak in just the right way that your message will be heard.''

That felt good. The next time I went back to the Labs I asked Spirit for guidance on how to teach about the power of thoughts to change and heal lives. In my mind's eye I saw the image of a crystal, the basis for a project on which the class's sponsor was working.

"Consider a crystal," I began (not really sure where I would end up). "A crystal has a seed shape around which larger crystals form. The larger crystals can assume only the basic pattern which the starter crystal gave it. So it is with our thoughts and our lives: Our feelings and experiences crystallize around the thoughts we think, which are like seed crystals. If we think positive, loving thoughts, so shall we attract positive, loving people, events, and experiences into our lives.''

They got it. (I was more amazed than anyone, as I knew next to nothing about crystals or science!) But Holy Spirit, in answer to my prayer to be used as an instrument of peace for these people, knew everything they needed to hear.

God in Search of Man

There is one question, the answer to which will open all the doors of life unto you: *Does God love you enough to reach you in ways that you do not know how to reach Him?*

The Jewish mystic Abraham Heschel wrote a book called *God in Search of Man.* The title itself is a touching statement of our Father's deep desire for us to be reunited with Him. Over the ages many teachers and artists have conjured a picture of a wrathful, angry God who has turned His back on His evil children, or wishes to punish us for our sins against Him. Actually, the exact opposite is true: God is doing everything in His Power (and that's a lot of power!) to reach out to us. And He is eager and willing to use any means to do so.

Let us consider the movies, for example. It is getting a little harder for God to reach people in church on Sunday morning, basically because a lot of us are in bed around that time. It is difficult to give an experience of joy to someone who is absent from a house of worship because of feelings of guilt and fear. And why are people sleeping in on Sunday mornings? Because they stayed up late at the movies on Saturday night! There they found more relaxation, freedom, and aliveness than in coming to church the next morning. It is a fact that more people go to the movies on Saturday night than to church on Sunday morning.

But our Lord is not only intelligent, but adaptable as well. Instead of complaining, God does the next logical thing to reach His Children: Go to the movies on Saturday night. If you can't beat 'em, join 'em! And what a masterful job He has done! Consider the magnificent spiritual teachings that have been given through motion pictures to millions upon millions: the Force of *Star Wars*; the glowing heart of *E.T.*; the forgiveness and timeless wisdom of Mr. Miyagi of *The Karate Kid* — I tell you, God is a genius!

When I saw *The Karate Kid II*, I was moved between tears and laughter by the profound, touching lessons the sage offered his disciple — and every person in the audience. Nearly every line of that movie was worth an entire sermon. God *is* in search of man, and if He has to go into every theatre in America every Saturday night, He is happy and willing to do so.

An Apple for the Teacher

Another realm that we have eagerly patronized is the world of personal computers. PC's have gotten a lot of bad press from theologians who believe that they are the Anti-Christ. But the Anti-Christ is simply the part of our mind that believes that something could threaten the Christ. And because the Christ could never be in jeopardy, the Holy Spirit is delighted to work with and through computers to heal people.

I have been told of a computer program that does therapeutic counseling. It asks you simple questions, listens to your answers, and then rephrases them and mirrors them back to you in a way that encourages you to look more deeply into yourself to discover your own answers.

I met a woman who experienced a deep healing through this program. To this I say, "Wonderful!" I say, "Go for it!" I say that if this woman experienced a healing and her life is enriched because of it, it is real and I bless it with all my heart. Because I know that *God is the source of all healing*, if that woman was healed through that computer program, it was God who did it. And that must mean that God is willing to work through computers to heal His Children. Maybe God's idea of Who He is and how He can reach us is bigger than our idea. Indeed *everything* is God reaching out to love and heal us.

III
The Circle of Love

To really communicate, you must be willing to have a belief system that is so grand that you can include everyone and their beliefs. You must realize that everyone believes that what he believes is right, and it is not your job to convince them otherwise. Your only job is to love them and be with them in such a way that they feel forgiven, free, and loved. At that point you realize that belief systems mean very little in the grand scheme of things, while peace means a great deal.

It is important to realize that every war that has ever been fought on this planet has been a clash not between people, but because of our attachment to our own belief systems. It is ironic to me that more people have been killed in the name of religion than for any other reason. The tragic paradox of this history is clear when we realize that Jesus and the other cornerstones of the great religions were among the few who were willing to give up their bodies rather than hurt another. Yet, sadly, most of the conflicts on our planet have been religious wars in which each faction was firmly convinced that God was on their side. Meanwhile, God was on both sides — and neither.

Recently Prime Minister Margaret Thatcher of England was outraged when the Bishop of Westminster Abbey refused to hold a mass celebrating Britain's victory over Argentina in the Faulkland Islands dispute. "We cannot thank God for helping us kill our brothers," the clergyman told her. Beware believing that God is with you when someone else loses. The only sure sign that Spirit is with you is when everyone wins.

The Fruitless Argument

Perhaps the most fruitless battle is to argue about God. If you argue about God you have already lost God, for the peace of God is always accompanied by the absence of argument. You can be sure that any discrepancy over the nature of God is a folly of the ego. Spirit dwells where union is acknowledged.

One day I was passing through a building corridor when my eye was attracted by a custodian sitting and reading a book by J.R. Tolkien.

"How do you like that book?" I asked him, interested in drumming up a conversation.

"It's pretty good."

"Yes, I like Tolkien, too."

"That's great — say, I don't think I've seen you here before. Do you work here?" he inquired.

"Not regularly — I come here once a week to teach a yoga class to a group of the employees," I explained.

His brow dropped. "Yoga? — Are you aware that satan's hand is in yoga?"

Uh-oh.

"No, actually, I wasn't aware of that. I must say that I have seen the practice of yoga accomplish wonderful healings."

The conversation gradually turned from a convivial chat into a heated debate. This fellow believed that I was in the clutches of the devil, and it was his duty to save me. And I believed that it was my duty to convince him of what I believed.

"Do you believe that God is in this world?" he asked me.

"Sure," I responded. "If God is omnipresent, He must be everywhere."

"Then you must be a Pantheist," he suggested.

"What's a Pantheist?" I had to ask.

"A Pantheist is someone who believes that God is in this world," he explained.

"Well, I guess that's what I am, then." I was delighted to finally know. It sounded sort of cultured.

Then some of the other employees gathered 'round and began to take sides. It was not long before opinions were flying through the air like flak over London. I could hardly believe what had developed from a question about Tolkien.

After feeling frustrated and a little huffy, I decided I had had enough. I politely excused myself and, dusting off my shoulders, I made my way down the hall.

"What was that all about?" I wondered.

As I thought about our conversation I realized that my frustration came from trying to convince him that what I believed was right. I felt sorry for the guy, who believed that God is not in this world. I realized that I had been attempting to save him from his delusion.

Then it dawned on me that he, too, was trying to save me. In his perception I was this ignorant yogi who thought that God was in the world. That, according to his belief system — which was quite real to him — was reason enough to try to save me.

So there we were, two brothers attempting to correct one another, but actually we were entrenched in separation. We were trying to save one another, and neither of us succeeded.

As I continued down the hall I realized that the interaction would have been much more rewarding and healing for both of us if we had simply rapped about how the Mets were doing, or some other area of common interest.

That day after that conversation I vowed that I would never argue with anyone about God. Spiritual beliefs, I decided, are not a valid reason for dissension or any form of separation between brothers. I have held firmly to my vow, and I am deeply grateful. I have accepted the gift of joining, and I must say that its rewards go far beyond argument.

A Course in Miracles advises us that if we are emotionally attached to not doing something a brother asks of us, we have an important lesson to learn.

> *Recognize what does not matter, and if your brother asks you for something "outrageous" do it because it does not matter. Refuse, and your opposition establishes that it does matter to you. It is only you, therefore, who have made the request outrageous...[1]*

The poet has said, "He drew a circle that kept me out, but I had the wit to win. I drew a circle that kept him in."

Forgiveness Paves the Way

The door to real communication is opened only by true forgiveness. No communication is possible without an open mind and heart preceeding it.

Let me give you a personal example. Several years ago I had just completed the *est* training when I went to visit my mother. I was fired up by the training, and I decided that I was now ready to clean up my communication with her.

---

[1] T, p. 206

I sat my mom down at the table and began:

"Mom, I'm tired of playing this game with you."

"What game?"

"The game of mother and son."

"What are you talking about?"

"This game we've been playing, where you act like the mother and I act like the son."

"How else would you like me to act — like a beach ball?"

"You don't understand, Mom; this idea that you and I are mother and son is just an illusion."

"Not when I was in labor!"

"But Mom, we're really equals. I want to own my own power."

"Then how come you still bring me your laundry?"

She turned down the volume on the TV, looked at me and asked me, "Why are you acting so weird?"

"I learned a lot at the training, Mom, and I want to share it with you."

"Aha! So that's it! They brainwashed you in that crazy training! I knew there was something fishy when you came home the first day and wouldn't let me go to the bathroom! This is what you paid five hundred dollars for? — to tell me I'm not your mother? Is that what you learned there? They are right — you *are* an asshole! You didn't have to pay five hundred dollars for them to call you an asshole — I'll do it for a considerable discount!"

Well, that was about the end of that conversation. While I had intended to convert my mom, she helped me to learn a valuable lesson — worth far more than five hundred dollars — that it was more peaceful and powerful for me to enjoy her, and our relationship, in a way that was comfortable for her. In the long run it worked better for both of us to communicate about the things that joined, and not separated us.

At another time we had a similar interaction. One day I drove up to her apartment house to give her a ride. When she got into my car she noticed a picture of Jesus on my dashboard.

"What's he doing there?" she immediately asked.

"You mean Jesus?"

"You know who I mean — the guy with the beard and robe."

"I love him."

"You're Jewish — how did you come to fall in love with him?"

"Mom, he's one of our relatives."

"He's not in any of *my* family pictures."

"But I really like his picture there."

"Why can't you have dice, or baby shoes, or an air freshener like normal people?"

When I got home I thought about it. I felt that it was not worth having the picture on the dashboard if it upset her so much. I reasoned that it was more important to *live* his teachings than to force his picture on someone who was sensitive about it. So I put the picture in the glove compartment (when she was in the car). I also never flaunted Jesus or my love for him in front of her again. And she appreciated my respect for her feelings.

(I am reminded here of a couple who had one set of parents into born-again fundamentalism and another set into metaphysics. The couple had both kinds of books on their shelf, and when each set of parents came to visit, they would complain about finding the "other" kind of books on the shelf. So the couple bought a revolving bookcase and placed the fundamentalist books on one side of the bookcase and the metaphysical books on the other. Before the parents showed up they would simply rotate the bookcase. It made life a lot easier.)

My respect for my mom's feelings actually gave way to a miracle. Once when I went to visit her she went to her pocketbook and brought me an object. To my astonishment, it was a lovely picture of a Catholic saint.

"I saw this at a rummage sale, and I thought you would like it."

I gave her one of the biggest hugs ever, and I knew that we were healed. I learned that love and respectful understanding create miracles. Then I opened *A Course in Miracles* to find, "It is not up to you to change your brother, but merely to accept him as he is." [2]

Common Ground

Unconditional love means being willing to be with someone and love them just as they are, without asking them to change for you. It is said that *God sees us as we will be, but loves us as we are.* The love that I have most appreciated receiving is that which has seen me as beautiful just as I am. When I have received this quality of love, I want to return it and give it back many times over.

Barry Neil Kaufman and Suzi Lyte Kaufman are a couple who have become well-known for their experience in the power of real caring. They became famous through the miraculous healing of their son, Raun. This

---

[2] T, p. 156

inspiring story, documented in their book, *Son-Rise*[3], began when Raun was diagnosed as autistic at the age of eighteen months. With an IQ below thirty he was declared "retarded, incurable, and schizophrenic." Barry and Suzi set out on a search for help with Raun, but they were disappointed to find that most autistic children were being drugged, shocked, beaten, or restrained. The Kaufmans did not want to submit Raun to any of these methods, and so they sought to treat him with their love.

They began by agreeing that since Raun would not meet them on grounds of communication with which they were familiar (he would not speak words or make eye contact with them), they would meet him in ways that he would receive. They spent twelve hours a day, seven days a week, mostly in the bathroom with him (it was the only place where they could focus attention with him). During those periods of reaching out to their son, Barry and Suzi would imitate Raun, join him in the play that he enjoyed, and encourage him to reach out into the world.

One of the most important elements of the Kaufmans' work with their son was mirroring. If Raun flapped his hands, Barry and Suzi would flap theirs. If he would make a loud noise, so would they. Their philosophy was that they would not try to force him to be a part of their world if he was afraid to do so; instead they would do things to let him know that they wanted to be with him in his world, even if it was a foreign one to them. They trusted that if he recognized that they loved him he would want to share in their life, too.

It was a long and challenging process, but after six weeks the Kaufmans noticed that their son was making brief eye contact with them. The eye contact increased, and Raun began to say some words. Over a period of three years — a difficult time, yet not without reward — Raun was *completely healed* of autism. By the time he was in third grade Raun had achieved an IQ of 150, and he went on in later grades to become a straight-A student and the head of his class.

A miracle? Yes, but here we must realize that God does not work miracles just *for* us — He works them *through* us.

The Kaufmans have since gone on to accomplish similar miraculous healings with many other persons, children and adults alike. Their method is simple: you gain the grace to be yourself by allowing those around you to be themselves. Then we are all healed.

The value of the Atonement does not lie in the manner in which it

---

[3] Barry and Suzi Kaufman, *Son-Rise*, Harper and Row, 1976. The Kaufmans' work and teachings are offered by the Option Institute and Fellowship, R. D. #1, Sheffield, MA 01257

is expressed. In fact, if it is used truly, it will inevitably be expressed in whatever way is most helpful to the receiver... The whole aim of the miracle is to raise the level of communication...[4]

The Kaufman family. Barry and Suzi, right and center. Raun is at far left.

The Language of God

What is the language of God? The one you are reading. Where can God reach you? Right where you are. What can you do to find God? Let yourself be. Give yourself a break. Quit punishing and browbeating yourself. You are much harder on yourself than you need to be. Why not offer the same forgiveness to yourself that you would to others? When you do, you realize that God has never been aware of your sins, and you do not need to be concerned about them either. This is not heresy, but healing. See a forgiven world, and you can live in it. When we can see ourselves and one another as innocent, we have learned to love ourself as God loves us, and the Kingdom of Heaven is at hand.

---

[4] T, p. 20

The Laughter Of The Saints

Life is too important to be taken seriously.

In *The Life and Teachings of the Masters of the Far East*, Baird Spaulding describes his meeting with "the laughing disciple." Travelling with a group of pilgrims through extremely treacherous territory in the Himalayan Mountains, the author tells how the laughing disciple helped the group along their way:

> *In all, it was an arduous climb, but at the rough places, the chela (disciple) went ahead with laughter and song. At the more difficult places, his voice would ring out and it seemed as if it lifted us over them without an effort...*
>
> *We thought the trail on its flanks stony and perilous but now we labored over a trail much of the distance on hands and knees. Still, the song and laughter of the chela bore us onward as though on wings...*
>
> *Can you, dear reader, not see why the trail that day was not long and arduous? It all passed in an instant. The vibrations of strength, peace, power, and harmony that are always sent forth from the temples but serve to urge the travellers onward to these peaks.*[1]

We, too, are travellers over the mountain pathways of life. How valuable is the power of joy to enliven our soul as we go to meet our goal! Laughter lifts us over high ridges and lights up dark valleys in a way that makes life so much easier. It is a priceless gem, a gift of release and healing direct from Heaven. Laughter can help us through any difficulty and transform the most challenging situations. It is the doorway from misery to joy, from the dungeon to the peaks. Laughter is God's remedy for fear.

---

[1] Spaulding, Vol. III, p. 109-111

Turn Your Tragedy Into a Comedy

Life is a movie. As your own producer you can choose the type of movie you want it to be. You can make it a soap opera, a thrilling adventure, a touching romance, a boring documentary, a horror show, or a biblical epic, to name a few. My movie has been a musical comedy with some great romantic scenes. And it is clear to me that it is I who have produced it that way. Being an appreciator of comedy, I was quite impressed by Uncle Albert, a character (played by Ed Wynn) in the movie *Mary Poppins*. Uncle Albert spent a lot of time floating around his ceiling, laughing uncontrollably.

When the children in the story went to visit Uncle Albert, they found him sailing around the upper strata of his living room singing, "I love to laugh." When these serious children attempted to tether Uncle Albert back to ground level, they caught his infectious laughter. Soon the entire group rose together to enjoy a laughing party on the ceiling. The movie culminated when the skinflint bank president finally caught one of Uncle Albert's jokes, after which he died laughing. If we have to leave the stage, we might as well dance off in a chorus of chuckles instead of a dirge of doom.

Comic Relief

When I was at the funeral parlor arranging my mother's memorial service, the chapel director told me that the previous week they had hosted a funeral for a comedian. "It was one of the most original services we have had here," he told me. "The fellow who had passed on was a comedian, and for his service a number of his friends who were stand-up comics got up and did their routines for the audience. It was one of the greatest funerals we have had."

When the time came for my mom's service, I felt guided to speak. Every now and then as I spoke about her life I touched on something lovingly funny about my Jeane, such as how much I enjoyed her imitations of the romantic scenes in the soap operas she loved. I had to smile as I appreciated the unique and outrageous person she was, and the group assembled laughed with me.

At that point a little voice inside my mind chided, "This is terrible — you musn't laugh at your mother's funeral — that is disrespectful!"

But as I thought about it, I thought that my mom would probably want me to be happy. Jeane's sense of humor was one of her most endearing qualities; she could find a way to laugh at anything. She was one person who never fell prey to the disease of taking herself too seriously. Even during the last days of her sojourn in this world she was making outrageous jokes about her condition. Why, I reasoned, would she be any less jovial because she left her body? I should think her sense of humor would *improve* on the other side. I'll bet any eulogy she would have given herself would have included her delightful humor.

Several months after Jeane had passed, I was at a healing conference when I began to really miss my mom. I had been repressing a bunch of grief, and one afternoon it bubbled up to the surface. I went to my dormitory room and cried and cried for quite a while.

That evening during the healing service my friend Carla Gordan, a wonderful psychic and healer, approached me and whispered in my ear, "Your mom told me to tell you that she wants you to stop grieving, and that she promises not to ask you any more embarrassing questions."

Disarming Through Laughter

One summer while travelling in Colorado I found a toy that I thought my mom would enjoy. It was a little laughing machine, a funny-looking shaggy box with two button eyes, a cute felt tongue, and a tape recording in its tummy that howled a minute of deep belly laughter when you shook it. I brought it home for mom as a present, but she was only mildly impressed.

Then one evening she phoned me, giggling that she had found a perfect use for the doll: an obscene caller, she reported, had telephoned her. Upon realizing what he was up to, she asked him if he would mind holding on a minute. She went to the cupboard and returned to the telephone with the laughing doll, which she held up to the receiver in response to his colorful remarks. He never called again, she told me.

The Laughter of the Saints

Master Hilarion has said, "The halls of Heaven ring with the laughter of the saints."[2] Laughter is a mark of high spiritual evolution; indeed many holy people have laughed their way into Heaven!

I have had the pleasure to meet a good number of spiritual teachers, gurus, and perhaps saints. If there is one characteristic that I have found in all of them, it is joy. These truly holy persons light up any room they enter, for their lighthearted attitude is a refreshing contrast to the dreariness of mundane affairs. They win souls by the happiness that emanates from their innocent being.

I remember seeing a greatly revered Buddhist lama enter a great lecture hall and reach down to light an altar of incense. You may imagine the surprise of the assembled meditators when they saw that the incense sticks the guru had lit were actually Fourth-of-July sparklers.

When I travelled with Sri Swami Satchidananda in the Soviet Union, he won the hearts of the Russians with his childlike playfulness. One day the swami saw the driver's seat of our tour bus empty, and he jumped into it, acting as if he was stealing the bus. Swami confessed that he had always wanted to drive a bus, and here was his big chance! To see swami playing so comfortably eased all of us, and we went on our way a little freer.

---

[2] M.B. Cooke, *The Hilarion Series*, Marcus Books.

Later we went to visit a Russian Orthodox monastary. There our group was ushered into a great library, containing rare old original manuscripts of spiritual documents. Many of them were handwritten and bound in magnificent ornate covers. It was quite an experience to walk amid these stacks of ancient literature that spanned from floor to ceiling.

Swami walked calmly through the stacks, craning his neck to see the top. Finally he stopped, ran his fingers over a few books and exclaimed, "You mean I need to read all of these to find God?!"

Going for It

When our group had converged in Kennedy Airport to depart for the Soviet Union, one fellow stood out above all the rest. He was six feet-six inches tall and he was wearing a white tuxedo jacket with multi-colored paint spots decorating it. The ensemble was balanced by balloon pants, a yellow Mickey Mouse tie, a three-pointed beret, and a rubber nose. He also sported a handle-bar moustache, and his hair flowed from his towering crown all the way down to his waist. His outrageous outfit was topped with a colorful parasol that he held high above his head.

This was Dr. Hunter "Patch" Adams, a well-known and loved medical doctor who has attracted a great deal of attention for his use of humor as a healing tool. Patch has gone far beyond the usual parameters of the medical profession by having treated over twelve thousand people for free, without accepting direct or third-party payments, and holding no malpractice insurance. He is currently in the process of building a hospital for free medical service.

At his healing center, the *Gesundheit Institute*,[3] Dr. Adams combines fun and laughter with conventional and non-conventional medical practices. Between times of treating patients more formally, Patch performs juggling and teaches tightrope walking. The patients in residence live, eat, sleep, and socialize in the same facility as the doctors and ancillary medical staff. The patients are treated as family, and they are encouraged to relax and pay attention to healing the totality of their being instead of simply removing the symptoms of dis-ease. The new hospital is being built entirely on donations and grants from individuals and organizations supportive of the Institute's work.

I first met Patch a few years ago when both of us gave presentations at a holistic healing conference in Philadelphia. The brochure for the conference showed a picture of each presenter and included a potent quote by or about

---

[3] Gesundheit Institute, 404 Nelson Street, Arlington, Virginia 22203

him or her. Above Patch's picture was the quote, *"Tuck in your shirt; get a haircut; why don't you charge?"* The quote was attributed to Patch's mother.

At the opening of the conference I recognized Patch by the bright light shining around him. (His clown's outfit and rubber nose did also help me to identify him.) His aura was truly childlike and radiant. I introduced myself to him in the lobby after a lecture, where he gave me a hug, tricked me by thumbing his hand into the air when I went to shake it, and placed his knee in my hand *a la* Harpo Marx. I immediately loved this delightful soul, and we spent a good deal of the next day together sharing and laughing.

When the time for Patch's lecture came the next afternoon, he was nowhere to be found. I sat in the front row of the auditorium waiting for him to appear, when a handsome man in a white suit sat down next to me. I acknowledged the fellow, smiled, and went back to looking at my program. But there was something about the fellow that seemed familiar. Had I met him before? I looked at him again, and I admired how neatly he was dressed and how perfectly his hair was arranged. I looked again and he was smiling.

Could it be?

Nooooooo!

But it was. It was Patch. He had put on a suit, unwaxed his handlebar moustache, and bobby-pinned his long mane up under a stylish wig.

"It's for my lecture," he leaned over and whispered.

Oh.

Soon Patch was introduced as Dr. Hunter Adams, and he went up on stage to speak. The lecture was rather dry and relatively uncolorful compared to Patch's usual antics. I must admit that I was a little disappointed. "Has he sold out?" I wondered.

But my Patch did not let me down. After his description of the theory and practices of holistic health, he explained that the *Gesundheit Institute* had arranged for three speakers to represent itself today. The first was Dr. Hunter Adams, and the second was a Dr. Dizeldorf.

Then Patch reached behind his head and lifted off his wig, releasing three feet of thick locks to fall over his back and past his waist. A number of programs dropped from the hands of a number of spectators. Then, in high style, the doctor dropped his trousers, revealing some long, baggy, polka-dotted shorts. A larger number of programs dropped from a larger number of hands. Finally the man on stage put on a top hat and tuxedo, and introduced himself as Dr. Dizeldorf. The remainder of programs in the auditorium fell to the floor.

Dr. Dizeldorf had an excellent rap. He explained that in addition to the formal theories of holistic health which Dr. Adams had put forth, there was an entire other realm of healing, all too often ignored by traditional doctors, namely the essence of spirit. Dr. Dizeldorf walked to the other side of the stage where he drew the audience's attention to a large wooden cabinet which he opened to reveal a number of colorfully decorated glass vials. One said, "Essence of Giggles," another was marked "Tincture of Forgiveness," and yet another "Innocence Concentrate." Dr. Dizeldorf reached for the "Essence of Wonder" and opened it before the onlookers, who by now had, to put it in common language, had their minds blown.

"Let us experience the healing power of Wonder," the doctor announced. As he opened the bottle cap, strains of lovely music began to waft through the auditorium, the lights went down, and a colorful slide of an exquisite flower flashed on the screen just over Dr. Dizeldorf's top hat.

"Wonder is a most magnificent healer," he zestfully taught. "To allow your mind and heart to dance through the fields of Wonder will make you young and keep your spirit above all worldly troubles." Then he went on to tell some marvelous facts about how this one glorious creation, this flower, came into existence, how it is nourished by the sunlight, air, earth, and water, how it reproduces itself, and how it lives in harmony with all of the life around it. Truly it was a wonderful celebration of beauty, and my heart opened at the innocence of it.

After the Essence of Wonder, Dr. Dizeldorf opened several other tinctures and gave the audience doses of some very excellent medicine. We were touched.

The finale of this doctor's presentation sported two very large green animate objects rolling onto the stage. At the key moment two zippers opened and out from each sack popped several ladies dressed in round green costumes. After a little dance, they wiggled of the stage, singing "Give Peas a Chance."

What a mind.

Dr. Dizeldorf gave way to one final representative of *Gesundheit*, Dr. Patch Adams. Patch explained that there needs to be a connection, a bridge between formal medicine and informal fun. Thus he took the name "Patch" to symbolize the harmonious joining of the two equally important disciplines.

Then the rear stage curtain opened to reveal a tightrope stretched across the stage.

"Balance is a very important part of healing," Dr. Patch pointed out.

"Here we have a very good metaphor for balance."

He popped open a parasol (Mary Poppins would have been proud of him) and proceeded to step onto the tightrope and walk it across the stage. Then he invited two boys in the audience onto to the stage for a tightrope walking lesson, which they undertook to the delight and applause of the audience.

In Kennedy Airport en route to Russia, "conspicuous" would be a mild description for Patch's presentation. Our tour guide, Aime, (the third guide from the travel agency dispatched for our group — the first two had mysteriously dropped out at the last minute) approached Patch to confirm that he was actually a part of our citizen diplomacy group. When Patch assured him that he was, Aime's face shriveled like a football deflating under the weight of a three-hundred-pound tackle. A very white football, at that.

In that case, Aime told him, he would have to wear a suit when we crossed the Russian border and passed through Soviet customs. "The Russians are rather conservative and formal people," Aime explained, "and we do want to make a good impression on them."

Patch's response was brief and to the point: "This is my suit."

"Perhaps I didn't hear you correctly, Mr. Adams..."

"Really — I made up my mind that I want to go to Russia as a clown — all I brought are clown's outfits — my whole suitcase is full of stuff like this!"

Aime took a deep breath.

Then Patch reached into his rainbow-painted satchel and pulled out a fake passport called a "Laughport." It was issued by the *Gesundheit Institute,* and it bore a color photo of Dr. Adams sporting no less than seventeen rubber noses wrapped around his face. Beneath the photo was *Gesundheit's* diplomatic motto, *"Long Live Nasal Diplomacy!"*

Aime looked for the nearest bathroom.

When we arrived in Russia, we found that nasal diplomacy was indeed a powerful way to build bridges from heart to heart. Patch took to the streets, the subways, restaurants — anywhere an audience was available. He played with the Russian people, children and adults alike. He made friends with kids in the parks, he crashed a wedding, and he embraced Russian war heroes in Red Square. And it worked — the Russians loved him! Being very good judges of character, they appreciated the aliveness and sincerity of his way of reaching out. He even wore his outfit to our diplomatic meetings with the Soviet Peace Committees in Leningrad and Moscow.

(Patch's one disappointment was that the Soviet Peace Committee did not give him permission to wear his gorilla suit in Red Square, as he requested. "Personally, we have no objection," they explained — "but there is a rather strong chance that you may get arrested — or captured." Then the committee engaged in an informal debate as to whether Dr. Adams was more likely to be arrested or shot. After ample consideration they did, however, grant Dr. Adams permission to wear his costume in his hotel room, if he liked.)

Without exception the man with the funny outfit accomplished what many others could not.

At our final dinner, at which each of us shared what the trip had meant to us, Patch rose and thanked the group for "the greatest opportunity in my life to be nutty." He explained that "before this journey I thought about the way that I could most powerfully serve to make contact with the hearts of the

Russian people, as well the Americans on this trip. I realized that the greatest contribution I could make would be to be myself, and clowning is the way I most enjoy expressing myself. It felt like quite a risk for me to pack only clown clothing, but I felt that I had to go for expressing myself one hundred percent. I did, and I am very glad indeed."

When Aime stood to speak, he confessed, "I must admit that I had my considerations about going with this group; but after spending two weeks with all of you and feeling the purity of your intention, I feel sure that God assigned me to this group — and my life has changed so beautifully! Thank you for being yourselves!"

The Humor Potential Movement

There is a wonderful new *genre* of new age spiritual humorists, and I feel that the phenomenon is very healthy. One well-known guru of giggles goes by the name of Swami Beyondananda,[4] "the Yogi from Muskogi." He wears a rainbow Bozo wig and offers enlightening discourses on such important topics as "Teach Your Dog to Heal," "How to Eliminate Ought-ism," and "Tantrum Yoga." Guru Huggin'-Dazs[5] offers vital new age products, including the Chakra Shaver, The Buddha Beeper, and for persons who would like to improve their ability to channel spirits, Enti-tea. Pat Weeks, the Co-President of the Human Unity Institute,[6] has revealed his true identity as Da Free Lunch, founder of the Born-Yesterday Church of Occasional Clarity. The Church, Da explains, now meets on the Number 38 cross-town bus. This has been their home since they were barred from meeting in the laundromat after they emulated Jesus' example by ripping the money-changers off the walls. Way to go, Da.

Spirituality, Not Boredom

Let's face it: without laughter, the spiritual path would be boring. Spirituality was never intended to numb anyone into submission; its lofty purpose is to raise our spirits into Heaven. Peace is not the absence of liveliness, but the epitome of aliveness in expression. St. Ignasius stated that

---

[4] Swami Beyondananda, PO Box 1934, Ann Arbor, Michigan 48103
[5] Guru Huggin'-Dazs, PO Box 450, Kula, Hawaii 96790
[6] Human Unity Institute, PO Box 3431, San Clemente, California 92672

141

"the glory of God is humankind fully alive." If you are not fully alive you are not glorifying God. Deadbeats are the devil's spokesmen. Make your life an ode to joy and celebration! You will not only be an extremely happy and productive person, but you will be an inspiration to those around you. You will offer healing to everyone you meet, by virtue of the enthusiasm of your spirit.

I have discovered a great dynamic in public speaking. I have seen that audiences do not respond so much to the words or the information that a speaker is offering, but to the feeling he or she is imparting. Facts can be found in a book, but joy can be shared only from one person's heart to another. I have found that to stand before a group with happiness in my heart is a gift to myself as well as the group.

I have thus developed two goals upon which my lectures and workshops are founded: (1) to inspire myself, and (2) to entertain myself. While this may at first seem to be self-centered, it is actually the greatest contribution I could make to an audience. Nothing is more boring than a speaker who is not interested in what he or she is talking about, and there is nothing more exciting that someone who is turned on by what they are discussing. I don't think I've ever given a totally serious lecture, and I hope I never will. God is not totally serious, and therefore neither do I have to be so. (A retreatant once told me that she likes my lectures because she enjoys watching me laugh at my own jokes. Well, at least I can always count on myself.)

Laughter as Prayer

I consider laughter to be a very high form of prayer. Church is something you can take with you wherever you go. It is supposed to be place of song and celebration, not duty and sleep. If you are in song and celebration you are in church, and you don't need a special building for that. All the world is a church, and if you are in the consciousness of love, you are praying with the joy of your being.

Ramtha has said,

The greatest prayer you could ever pray would be to laugh every day. For when you do, it elevates the vibratory frequency within your being such that you could heal your entire body.[7]

---

[7] Ramtha, *I Am Ramtha*, Beyond Words Publishing, 1986, p. 80

My friend David prays very devoutly through laughter. His temple is the local movie theatre, and his rabbi is Woody Allen. I always enjoy going to the movies with him because I know that even if the movie isn't funny, David will be. David is the only person I know who goes into hysterics when the opening credits come on the screen. As he begins to howl, everyone in the audience turns and looks in our direction to see who is laughing so outrageously. Then I slide down into my seat so they won't think it is me. David is indeed an advanced soul; he really knows how to get his money's worth in a movie. He really knows how to pray.

Where Sin Ends

A Course in Miracles tells us that "the separation occurred when the Son of God (all of us) forgot to laugh." In other words, we kicked ourselves out of Heaven when we began to take ourselves too seriously. I am certain that we take ourselves more seriously than God takes us. God has a marvelous sense of humor. If we want to be Godly, we too must learn to laugh.

The *Course* also tells us that "all sin ends in laughter." If you cannot laugh about something, you can be sure you have not seen the whole truth about it. The truth always contains some element of humor. If you cannot see the lighter side of an issue, you can be certain that you have lost your way. And when you can laugh about it, you have found your way.

When you see the nothingness of something that you thought was a terrible sin, you will be able to laugh about it. Then you are free. Such a wonderful release should be honored as a sign of healing. This is a good way to gauge your healing: if you find you can laugh at something that was once a sensitive or fearful subject for you, you know that you have risen out of the swamp of self-pity and come to the high perspective of holy humor.

How the World Will End

While you have heard many maudlin theories about the end of the world, there is one that you may not have considered. Consider it now, for it is much closer to the truth than the sardonic tales to which you have been exposed.

The world you have known has been built on fear. And it is perpetuated through fear, and fear alone. Fighting fear with fear is like fighting alcoholism with another drink. The way out must be entirely different than the way in. To escape, you must go in a new direction, not the one by which you entered.

The only way that a fearful, dark world can end is in light. There is but one way to be liberated from the heavy oppression of dreams of death, and that is with a joyful heart. Throw away the case for condemnation and feel the freedom of your spirit! A happy heart generates a force field of love in which doubt, disaster, and dismay have no power to interrupt the flow of your good. Sages and mystics have known this important principle, and they have taught it with the illumination of their being. And those who have eyes to see and ears to hear have seen and heard.

A *Course in Miracles* gives us a very clear description of the end of the world, quite unlike any we have heard before:

> The world will end in joy, because it is a place of sorrow...The world will end in peace, because it is a place of war...The world will end in laughter, because it is a place of tears. Where there is laughter, who can longer weep?[8]

It is not your lot to weep, and you were not put here to suffer. To find value in suffering is to condemn yourself to hell. The Spirit that created you would not have Its Children in pain. Wake up, arise, and go on your way with laughter in your heart! Wipe away your tears, and live in love! You may explore every highway, byway, mountain, and valley of this world, and no matter how far you travel or how many years you search, you will come only to this very conclusion: life is for loving, joy, and celebration — *now*.

> ...Gladly will you walk the way of innocence together, singing as you behold the open door of Heaven and recognize the home that called to you. Give joyously to one another the freedom and the strength to lead you there.[9]

---

[8] M, p. 36
[9] T, p. 399

144

Beyond Karma

I am under no laws but God's.

- A Course in Miracles[1]

One day while standing in line at a cafeteria in Newark Airport I saw a large sign with bold letters: *"It is impolite to pass persons in the cafeteria line while they are waiting to be served."* Alright, I figured, I can live with that.

The next week I was in the very same line when I looked at the sign again. To my astonishment I read this week, *"It is **polite** to pass persons in the cafeteria line while they are waiting to be served."*

The laws of politeness had been changed in one short week!

Who made those laws? Who did they bind? Who could change them?

It is clear that the laws of the world exist by agreement only, and it does not take a lot of experiences these days to cause a thinking person to begin to question what he has been taught to be true. Political, social, and even scientific laws have undergone unbelievable upheavals, and the degree of revolution in even the most conservative communities of thought has been enough to plunge anyone into a stymie.

If we are confused by looking to the outer world for answers, it is no wonder. I recently read that in 1957 the American Psychology Association declared that homosexuality was no longer a disease. This means that either every homosexual was healed when the declaration was issued, or that the description of homosexuality as a disease was incorrect before 1957. Or after 1957. No wonder homosexuals have been confused! The psychologists keep changing their mind about whether or not they are sick!

I also wonder what it must have been like to be a Catholic and be told that eating meat on Friday is no longer a sin. Was it a sin, and it stopped being sinful? If so, how could something be a sin against God one day and not a sin the next? And if it never was a sin, why and wherefore did the church say it was? And if the church changed its mind about that sin, what else might it change its mind about? And if the church made a mistake, who's

---

[1] W, p. 132

in charge anyway?

You might also be fascinated to know that until the sixth century A.D. reincarnation was an official doctrine of the Catholic Church. At that time the governors of the church body met at the famous Synod of Constantinople. There, by a vote of five to four, the board decided that reincarnation was no longer true. Five to four! That means that one man's vote determined that you get to come around only once instead of making a return trip. Just think: What if the man with the swing vote was hard of hearing and he was just scratching his ear when the vote was taken? Woody Allen would have a field day with that one!

In addition to being humorous, it can be quite startling and even scary to realize that so many — perhaps all — of the laws to which we have bowed are unfounded. This is what drives people to depression and despair. But seen in a higher light all of these contradictions and irresolutions can lead us nicely to a perfect position for learning the truth about who we are. Rapidly we are learning that we cannot look to the outer world for inner answers. We cannot depend on man-made laws to show us the way to peace. If are going to learn the truth of our own being, the only source that we can consult with confidence is *the integrity of our own being.*

A Higher Law

A friend of mine, a fellow student of *A Course in Miracles*, was about to undergo a biopsy to examine a thickening in her body. The morning before she was to undergo the surgery I was sitting in meditation when I was shown a vision.

In my mind's eyes I saw the edge of a photographic negative. I could see but a half an inch at the top and the bottom of the picture. Upon looking more closely, I saw that it was actually an x-ray. But why could I not see the entire x-ray? I looked again to see that the x-ray was covered by a book. It was a large book with its pages opened, and it obscured nearly the entire x-ray. Peering yet further, I recognized that the book was *A Course in Miracles.*

"What is the meaning of this vision?" I asked.

Immediately the message was made clear to me: the x-ray represented a picture of the body, and specifically an image of illness and the limitation of the body. In this case it represented a possible fearful result of my friend's examination.

A Course in Miracles, on the other hand, represented to me the power of God's healing love, forgiveness, and freedom from the laws of bodily limitation or retribution.

Quickly I realized the implications of this vision: The x-ray was obscured by the *Course* to show me that *The Law of Grace supercedes the laws of the body.* This woman's case had been turned over to a higher Doctor operating under a higher Law — the unfailing power of forgiving love. Healing took precedence over fear, forgiveness replaced retribution, and peace abided where suffering once ruled.

You can imagine my happiness when the next afternoon I received a telephone call from my friend informing me that the examination showed that there was nothing wrong with her; the doctor had given her a clean bill of health.

This vision is not concerned so much with a particular person or even with *A Course in Miracles*, but with a principle:

There is a Law higher than the laws of this world. It is a Law of total love, forgiveness, and healing.

Moreover,

You do not deserve to be ill. You do not deserve to be punished. You do not deserve to die. You deserve only to be totally at peace and completely happy. You are a Child of a Loving God, and your Father wants only perfect joy for you.

The Choice of Vision

Our happiness depends entirely on which picture we are willing to look at. In the inspiring motion picture *Resurrection*, the story of a woman who learned to use her healing power, there is a marvelous scene in which a woman with a degenerated spine comes to the healer for treatment. The woman's doctor tells them, "I don't know how you're going to help her — I've seen the pictures."

The healer proceeds to lay her hands on the patient, fervently intent in prayer for her release. Within a short time the woman arises and walks for the first time in years.

As the astonished doctor exclaims, "I'll be...!" the healer interrupts him and explains, "The difference, doctor, is that I didn't see the pictures."

Actually, she did see pictures, but they were not the same images the doctor saw. The healer did not recognize the patient's limitation; instead she focused on the woman's perfection and her reality as a whole being. She understood that the woman was born not of flesh, but of Spirit, and the rightful heritage of all spiritual beings is perfect health and peace of mind. The healer knew that the patient was not subject to physical laws, but Spiritual Principle. And her vision was strong and clear enough that the woman felt the truth and accepted it.

Here is a way to summarize the principle of all healing:

Spirit is in a state of grace forever.
Your reality is only spirit.
Therefore you are in a state of grace forever.[2]

The Law of Endless Joy

You have reached the point in your life where you are ready to go beyond the laws that have kept you small, separate, and fearful. You are ready to accept your true identity as a Child of a loving God, and live in a way that reflects joy and celebration. As you step forward you will have a light shining around you that will cause those you meet to ask what good has come to you, and you will inspire them to awaken to the beauty of their own divinity. All because you realize that you live not under the limited laws of the world, but you are subject only to the Law of Eternal Love.

Think of the freedom in the recognition that you are not bound by all the strange and twisted laws you have set up to save you. You really think that you would starve unless you have stacks of green paper strips and piles of metal discs. You really think a small round pellet or some fluid pushed into your veins through a sharpened needle will ward off disease and death. You really think you are alone unless another body is with you...
Think further; you believe in the "laws" of friendship, of "good" relationships and reciprocity...

---

[2] T, p. 7

*There are no laws but God's. Dismiss all foolish magical
beliefs today, and hold your mind in silent readiness to hear the
Voice That speaks the truth to you...About the Love your Father
has for you. About the endless joy He offers you...³*

To be healed we must experience a *complete reversal* of the way of
thinking that we have known. While this may at first seem radical (and it is!)
it must be apparent that if we have not been succeeding according to the laws
that we have been taught, then *the laws that we have been taught must not be
true.* Here we must reiterate the motto that a friend of mine sent me on his
business card:

*If you always do what you've always done,
You'll always get what you've always gotten.*

— a disarmingly simple lesson! Another way of saying this is:

*If you always think the way you've always thought,
You'll always create what you've always created.*

The Reversal

The Apostle Paul understood this idea very well. He spoke of it as
"metanoia" — the transformation of the thinking process to see divinity in
all things. If you want to create more rewarding experiences in your life, you
must start to think about who you are and what you deserve in a new and freer
way. This is the critical leap of consciousness which enables you to be
healed and then to become a miracle worker. The only requirement for
Heaven is to *see only perfection.* The moment we are willing to accept
complete forgiveness of ourself and the entire world, we realize that *all there
has ever been is Heaven.* And if we have seen anything other than total
beauty that opens our heart nearly to tears, we have been seeing something
that was not there.

---

³ W, p. 132-133

Truth or Appearances

Sometimes on summer days I enjoy sitting by the river behind my house and watching the jet planes fly overhead in their approach pattern to the metropolitan airport. One thing that I have puzzled over and learned a great deal from is the fact that the sight and sound of an airplane seem to be coming from two distinctly different locations. Because light travels much faster than sound, the visual appearance of the plane is in one place, while the sound of the plane seems to be coming from a location far behind the sight of the craft. This is why it sometimes appears that one plane is flying silently overhead, while the sound of what seems to be another unseen airplane travels behind it. Actually there is but one airplane, but the sight of it is reaching my eyes before the sound of it reaches my ears. One source has been divided into the appearance of two.

Sages have been exhorting us for centuries not to have faith in the messages of the senses, for they are deceptive. Here is a clear example that things are not what they appear to be. Where is the real airplane? Is it the one I see or the one I hear? A little logic will reveal that it is *neither*. By the time I see or hear it, the real airplane (if there is one at all!) has moved on from the position at which it generated the sights and sounds that my senses recorded. Therefore *none of what I am seeing or hearing is correct!* All that I am seeing is a reflection, a shadow, a phantom of the past.

Is it any wonder, then, that *A Course in Miracles* in the early lessons reminds us, *"I see only my past."* [4] and *"I see nothing as it is now."* [5]? We cannot afford to let our mind wander into the past or the future, which is just a projection of the past; (what evidence do we have that our future will be *anything at all* like our past?) When we leave the serenity of the present moment we find only anxiety, for we have strayed into pure illusion. Our only escape from anxiety is to find the peace available to us in the now, which is not threatening at all. As I have examined my anxieties I have found that every single one of them, without exception, is founded on a thought of guilt from the past or a fear of the future.

The world remains stuck only to the extent that we agree that appear-

---

[4] W, p.11
[5] W, p. 15

ances are true; the moment we withdraw the power of our agreement in error we are free to see what is really there.

I was told the story of an airplane that made a stop for refueling. As the passengers were stretching in the terminal while waiting for the next leg of their journey to commence, the pilot saw a blind passenger with a seeing-eye dog standing near the gate. The pilot asked the man if he would like to have his dog walked, and when the man appreciatively answered "Yes," the pilot decided he would like to get some exercise by walking the canine himself. The other passengers, however, not seeing what had transpired, saw the pilot walking with a seeing eye dog and quickly fled to the other airlines to exchange their tickets!

It is up to each of us to choose what we want to align with — love or fear. No one else can choose for us, and blessedly so. As we mobilize our willingness to know and see the truth, we shall surely find it. Several years ago I sent Richard Bach, the author of *Jonathan Livingston Seagull* and *Illusions*, a copy of one of my books. Several months later I received a post card from him, thanking me for the book and noting, "It seems as though the family of those of us who do not believe in appearances is a large one!"

Extra Strawberries: A Reversal in Practice

Several years ago when I was visiting some friends in Canada we went out one Saturday afternoon to buy some groceries for dinner. Riding in the back seat of the car on our way home I discovered some of the most succulent strawberries I had ever seen. Those juicy red morsels called to me from atop the grocery bag. I reached over and began to nibble on one. "Delicious!" I exclaimed to myself, and I took another.

The ride continued, our conversation deepened, and my strawberry-fest accelerated. Handful by handful I scooped the sweet fruits out of the sack and munched on them with savory pleasure. As we pulled into the driveway I noticed that I had lightened the load of strawberries by about half.

As we got out of the car I heard my hostess remark, "I can't wait to get inside and start on the strawberry shortcake I have planned for dessert. Yummy!"

"Which way to the bus station?" I wondered, seeking the nearest avenue of escape. Here my friends invited me for dinner, and I ate up their dessert! I reached for a tissue to wipe the red spots off my lips, but I quickly realized I would have to confess my transgression.

"I don't quite know how to tell you this, Carole," I blurted out, "but I just ate a significant amount of the strawberries." She turned her head to find a sheepish grin on my face. I knew she could see a melange of guilt and strawberries in my aura. Then the law of karma called to me as a way to expiate myself and atone for my sin. "I guess I'll have to have a piece of shortcake with no strawberries on it."

"No strawberries on your piece?!" she exclaimed. "The fact that you ate so many strawberries makes me happy to know you like them so much. Thank you for telling me! That means you get *extra* strawberries on your piece!"

We hugged.

That was a very quick and powerful lesson in how the Law of Love gently cancels the law of karma. Had my hostess been a teacher of limitation or fear, she would have agreed that I had done wrong, squandered my allotment, and now have me balance out my sin and pay my debt by experiencing a lack. But instead she was a teacher of abundance, demonstrating that her faith was not in error, but love.

Because Jesus knew the truth of the higher law of abundance he could feed thousands with a few baskets of fish. I cannot see him dividing a few baskets into thousands of tiny pieces or giving to some and not to all. Instead the master prayed over the food, affirmed total supply through the Law of Grace, and fed the multitudes. *The Christ knows no lack, restriction, or punishment.* When we act in the consciousness that all we ever need will be supplied of the Great God of All There Is, we step beyond the appearance of lack and affirm ever-present good.

The Way Out of Hell

I saw a cute cartoon showing a man pushing a wheelbarrow of rocks through hell. While those around him were sweating and suffering, this happy fellow was whistling along his way with a wide smile on his face. Standing behind a rock were two little devils with pitchforks, watching how happy this fellow was. Exasperated, one of the devils turns to the other and remarks, "I don't think we're getting to this guy!"

The fellow at the wheelbarrow was not in hell because he *chose* not to be. While the appearance of hell was all around him, his consciousness was not at all in hell, but in lightheartedness and laughter. He beat the devil not by anger or rebellion, but simply by being happy.

You and I can easily accomplish the same state of wholeness by taking refuge in the truth of love that abides within our hearts, and refusing to give agreement to the appearance of evil. Ramtha tells us that "...the only thing you have done wrong is to believe that you have done something wrong."[6] When you love who you truly are you accept *every moment* as an opportunity to rise higher into the open arms of joy. In this state of creative living the past, the future, and the notion of karma quickly disappear into delightful belly laughter. It is all quite perfect, and you are doing much better than you think.

Werner Erhard tells us, "If God told you exactly what it is you were to do, you would be happy doing it no matter what it was. What you're doing is what God wants you to do. Be happy."[7]

The Immediacy of Grace

How quickly and easily can the laws of limitation be overcome? I will tell you a story to illustrate:

A friend of mine was undergoing treatment for cancer. The doctors had been monitoring his condition, and he was asked to take some chest x-rays before surgery.

Standing behind the x-ray equipment my friend heard the lab technician tell him to take in a deep breath and hold it. As he did so he realized that this instruction was similar to that of his meditation class. In the class the teacher had instructed the students to visualize drawing white light into their hearts and then pouring it throughout their bodies.

Wanting to make the most of every opportunity to be healed, my friend decided to imagine that he was breathing in the breath of God and blessing himself with peace as he held his breath while the x-rays were being taken. He lifted his mind to God and visualized the pure light of Living Spirit filling him with each breath. Finally the technician dismissed him, and he felt relaxed.

The next day the doctor called him and told him that there was no sign of any disease on the x-ray and that no surgery would be necessary. "There is no medical explanation," the doctor reported, " — It must be a miracle."

---

[6] Weinberg, *Ramtha*, p. 133
[7] Werner Erhard, *If God Had Meant Man to Fly, He Would Have Given Him Wings*, Werner Erhard, 1973.

II

To become true miracle workers we must challenge every belief we have. If a belief is true it will stand up under any circumstances. And if it is false we are better off knowing that we have been wrong, that we may quickly go on to discover what is really true.

If the laws of the physical plane and time were true, they would apply to all of us. For one of us to rise above them means that *any of us* can be free of them. Jesus restored sight to the blind, raised the dead, and ascended himself. The master could perform these wondrous acts because he was *aware of the higher law* and he was willing to use it. That selfsame law is *equally and fully available to you and me,* and if we are willing to use it we shall surely be free of the hellish nightmare of limitations with which we have been hypnotized.

The Dreamer and the Dream

The idea of karma is nothing more or less than a belief system. It is nothing more because it exists only in the minds of those who believe in it, and it is nothing less because you have the power to create an entire world based upon a false belief and then live in it as if it were true. Yet even the blackest nightmare can be escaped instantly by realizing that you are the dreamer and not a prisoner of the dream.

Looking more closely at the belief system of karma, Ramtha tells us,

> *What you term "karma" is not the law of God. It is the law of those who believe in it...The laws of karma are indeed a reality, but only for those who believe in them...The only laws that exist are those which you allow to be effective in your kingdom...If you choose to believe in karma you will certainly be in the hands of your own creation, for you have given power to that belief.*[8]

---

[8] Weinberg, *Ramtha*, p. 129

To see God as punitive, wrathful, or remembering of our sins is to attribute human nearsightedness to a divinity that far transcends the ways that we have learned to hurt ourselves. The French Philosopher Rousseau said, "God created man in His image and likeness, and then man returned the compliment." In our madness we have seen an angry God, not realizing that we are but looking upon our own face reflected in a distorted mirror of cosmic proportions. Because we have not come to terms with our own sense of guilt, fear, and retaliation, we have projected those attributes onto a vengeful Deity who will swoop down upon us with His aweful will and in the Last Judgement condemn us to the hell that we deserve by our wretched sinfulness. We have butchered and perverted a God of only love to believe in a father that condemns us to hell rather than welcomes us to Heaven.

This picture of God was not painted by Him, but by fearful children who forgot who they were and believed they had sinned. We are told in *A Course in Miracles* that some of what is written in the New Testament is not the word of God, but the projection of fearful disciples who had not come to terms with their own sense of guilt, and projected it onto God in an effort to relieve themselves of what they *thought* they had done wrong.[9]

Clearly this God cannot be the One that created us in love, and has brought us to the point of awakening at which we now stand. Clearly we must be ready to learn of a God of Healing, of Peace, and of Joy. We are ready to know a wondrous and beauteous Father, for we are finally willing to find goodness within ourselves. And surely we will find in our Father what we find in ourself.

A New Heaven, A New Earth

In bowing to karma we have bound ourselves by small thinking and agreement in the notion that we are mortal creatures subject to time, separation, and punishment. We have used the idea of karma against ourselves to romanticize relationships, avoid living in the moment, and justify suffering. We have unconsciously created a parasitic monster of a belief system that denies to us the peace of God that is available to all of us at every moment.

We cannot afford to be spiritual mugwumps. (A mugwump is someone who sits with his mug on one side of the fence and his wump on the other.) Spiritual teachers have told us with one breath that all that exists is the eternal

---

[9] T, p. 87

now, and with the next breath that what is happening to us now is the result of our past. *Both cannot be true.* All that is happening to us now is the result not of our past, but our *current* thoughts. Change your current thoughts and all that is happening to you and around you will change quickly — even, as Saint Paul said, "in the twinkling of an eye."

Jesus was a teacher not of karma, but of Grace. When the adulterous woman was brought before him, about to be stoned, he told her, "Your sins are forgiven," and the people were astonished. Her sins were forgiven because in his eyes *she had never sinned.* We must learn to look at ourselves through those same forgiving eyes. When we see what the Christ sees, we become one with the Light of the World.

When the disciples asked Jesus, "Is this man blind because of the sins of his parents, or his own sins?" he answered, "Neither...but to demonstrate the power of God,"[10] and he proceeded to heal the man. Jesus' consciousness was not immersed in ideas of sin, but in the magnanimity of light. Had Jesus harbored any concept of condemnation, his efforts to undo the affliction would have been impotent. But Jesus knew the truth of total forgiveness. In *A Course in Miracles* Jesus tells us,

> *"I do not want you to allow any fear to enter into the thought system toward which I am guiding you. I do not call for martyrs but for teachers. No one is punished for sins, and the Sons of God are not sinners."*[11]

As Ramtha puts it,

> *"Know that you will never have to pay for anything that you have ever thought or done, in this life or any life, as long as you forgive yourself for it. Forgiveness of self is the divine act that removes from your soul the guilt and judgement of self that limit the expression of the God that you are."*[12]

The Test of Belief

There are a few questions which will reveal to you your readiness to go beyond the painful laws this world was created to preserve:

---

[10] John 9:2-3   [12] Weinberg, *Ramtha, p. 132*
[11] T, p. 88

1. Do you believe that you are being punished or that you deserve to be punished for any bad things you have done in the past?
2. Do you believe you must pay off any karma before you can be healed, free, or peaceful?
3. Do you believe that any suffering or sacrifice you undergo now will earn you happiness, peace, or a place in Heaven at a later date?

To answer yes to any of these questions is to deny that you are already forgiven, loved, and free. Moreover, you must realize that you have the power to create suffering, separation, and delay of healing *merely by your belief that you deserve pain.*

Imagine what it would feel like to know that none of what you believe is your karma can bind you in the least. The sense of exhiliration that must come from even the slightest consideration of this notion is phenomenal! And it is but a taste of the freedom that you will feel when you fully accept the grace in which your soul was created and in which you will always live.

You will burst out of your shell of fear and soar far above the petty limitations to which you have paid homage. The question is not "whether," but "when?" — and that is entirely up to you! Raise your head in dignity and walk the earth as a free soul, for *so you are. Dare to forgive yourself.* This is the leap of faith with which you will learn that it has been but your own mind that has stood between you and total freedom. Then you will demonstrate to the world that God has never condemned you or anyone.

Challenge your belief in a punishing Lord and you will see how awesomely the world is ruled by unnecessary guilt and fear. Make a stand for total forgiveness by starting with your own. You will wonder how you could have spent so many years looking down the barrel of a gun that was held by your own hand. And you will dance for joy at the freedom that awaits you the moment you are willing to release it.

You are destined not for suffering, pain, or hell, but to discover that you are forgiven, loved, and heir to the entire Kingdom of Love. You do not have to wait until you die to inherit it. Jesus said, "the Kingdom of Heaven is within you." He also told us, "Come, for all things are now ready."

All Good Karma

If there is any such thing as karma, it is all good. To divide karma into good and bad is to reenact the eating of the fruit of the knowledge of good and evil that threw our forebears into hell. You will be thrown into hell, too, if you see evil, for no one escapes the effects of what he chooses to see. And you will instantly be free of all fear the moment you choose again and allow your vision to rest on a gentle world.

The only way out of the maze of karma is to see all as perfect. Here is how you beat the devil, for satan has power only over those who believe he exists. God told Abraham, "Lift up your eyes"[13] and "Leave your country behind, leave your people behind, and go to the land I will guide you to."[14]

Metaphysically, Spirit was telling Abraham to raise his thoughts to a *new consciousness*; to let go of his old idea of who the people in his life were; to release his belief that he lived in a politically-defined country; and to go to the land that God would guide him to — not referring to a physical place, but a state of higher *awareness*, a consciousness of pure love, of abundance and joyful life.

Now you, too, must free yourself of the bondage of old thought patterns and habits of fear, unworthiness, and disease. You must step forward with dignity into the assumption of your true identity — a Child of Perfect Light. See everything that happens as a gift of God, and you will see the falsity of notions of bad karma.

Believe that every experience that comes to you is a blessing from God to help you learn that you are lovable, capable, and deserving of happiness. Given these gifts, could any experience be truly bad? Nothing can hurt you except your own mind. Be free of any notion that you are or have ever been outside of God's perfect love.

From Karma to Grace

There is only one way to escape the cycles of karma, and that is to *get off the wheel*. Forget about your blasted karma, and just start loving! Those who love truly can but laugh at the notion of checks and balances, for they have accepted a Law that far outshines those of this world. Even the most fleeting glimpse of such a Love must change a life forever. You have allowed your ego to have a field day indulging in reveries of the amount of judgement laid upon you and the penalty required. The notion of punishment is totally foreign to the One Who created you as perfect as Himself. He simply watches patiently as you play the game of limitation, knowing full

---

[13] Genesis 13:14
[14] Genesis 12:1

well that you will arise and run to His open arms when you have tired of the rules that you have created. Let go of your past, release your dreams of the future, and begin to celebrate the magnificence of your being this very moment!

Rise into the awareness that your true being is *totally beyond karma.* You are living Spirit, and Spirit cannot be determined by an idea that is smaller than itself. You have been told that you are created in the image and likeness of God, yea, even that you are God, and you have even mouthed or at least thought these noble ideas yourself. If that is so — and I assure you that it is — HOW COULD GOD HAVE KARMA? God is so far beyond karma that all He knows is perfect Grace. If you are willing to look at your life — yea, all life — from that lofty perspective, you shall be free of all that you believed bound you.

Masters, not Servants

There is one law to life, and that is the Law of Love. Because God is love, when we are loving we are at peace. In such a lofty state of awareness we can see that the entire universe exists only for the purpose of extending the love we already are. Every avenue we walk upon is a way to learn love, for "the healing of God's Son (all of us) is all the world is for."[15] Because love is the first and final lesson of all life, we can learn the truth of love through everything we do.

Sometimes while studying the esoteric or mystical sciences we may be sidetracked into becoming enamored with the mechanics of the science and we may lose sight of the truth that the science was given to teach. The purpose of all spiritual science is to help us become freer, lighter, and aware that we are forgiven. To the extent that we learn to reclaim our nature as whole beings, it may be said that our study is leading us to truth. If we lose sight of this, our only purpose, we take a detour from the highway home.

We fall prey to a sense of limitation when we see ourselves as determined by a source outside ourselves. Neither the stars nor past lives nor karma of any kind can rule us in the least when we realize that we are Children of a Creative God, and that we have the power to create our life in any way we choose, no matter what we have created in the past. At any moment it is our own mind, and only our own mind that determines what will happen to us.

---

[15] *T, p. 476*

The stars, card readings, books, or any other forms of divination are nothing more or less than a picture of your consciousness. You created them. Can something you created have power over you? Only if you believe it can. While these methods and thousands like them can serve as excellent tools to assist you in learning important principles of living, there comes a time — perhaps today — when you must claim your identity as the master of your life. Never again will anything outside of you have the power to influence you. At such a momentous point you may dismiss the charts you have written in the past and write a new one. Choose again and reclaim power over your life, your love, and your destiny.

The One Decision

You now have one, and only one decision to make. Actually this is the only decision you have ever had to make, but now it has risen to the surface for you to make it clearly. All other decisions are offspring of this one, and you will be able to easily answer every other question when you have answered this one truthfully. This question is:

> *Do you have power over your life, or*
> *does life have power over you?*

Are you a creator, or a slave? Are you a master, or a servant? Are you empty, or are you whole?

You have given your power away to people, circumstances, and ideas, and you have hurt yourself by it more than you know. You have made yourself small and weak by bestowing a crown of authority to that which is inert. When Pilate asked Jesus, "Don't you know I have the power to crucify you?" Jesus answered, "You have no power but that which is given you by my Father."

You can make that statement with the same authority. The stars, food, medicines, gurus, and all belief systems have absolutely no power but that which you invest in them. Realize this, and you are free in the flash of one correct thought. You created your gurus in various forms to tell you what you already knew. If you did not already know the Truth, how then would you know that they were correct? A guru, like a consultant of any kind, is someone who borrows your watch to tell you what time it is. And it is about time you started to tell time for yourself.

Wake up to your own magnificence! You shine brighter than all the stars in the heavens, your food is love, your medicine is forgiveness, your guru is your own self, and the only belief you need is that you deserve love. Remember this, mark this, know this, believe this, love this, practice this, and you will be lifted into exuberant joy in a twinkling of an eye. *There is nothing that this world can give you that is not already within you.* Learn this now and you save yourself eons of suffering!

God will not make you suffer — God has never made anyone suffer — but you can bring suffering upon yourself by looking outside yourself for peace. Look within, and there will all your answers be found. Your Father has imbued within you the Spark of the Divine, and you have come to earth to search for something that you brought with you. Find it, and you are absolved from further yearning.

There is but one position greater than a servant of the Lord, and that is to be His Child. The child of a king is heir to the entire kingdom, and when you are ready to let go of the idea that you are separate from your Father, you will rule your kingdom with the same authority with which He rules His. Decree your identity and all that you have denied will rightfully be restored to you.

Part II

THE HEALING

...as it is in Heaven

WALKING in LIGHT

Beaver's Truth

Only the whole truth will do
For me and you
The One dreamed it split in two
Now this part of your dream loves you
    — Maitreya Stillwater, "The Whole Truth" [1]

It seems that the lessons I need to learn find me.

One morning as I was walking through my living room I noticed the TV rerunning an old *Leave It to Beaver* episode. Feeling that this was a delicacy too tasty to pass by, I sat down and watched.

In this mellow drama Beaver had gotten a "D" on his report card. While passing through the den that evening, Wally and — you guessed it — Eddie Haskell discovered the telltale report card on the desk, waiting for Ward to sign it.

"Hey, Wally, let's play a little trick on the Beave!" proposes Eddie, in the obnoxious manner for which he has become known and loved.

"What's that, Eddie?"

"Let's change the 'D' on the report card to a 'B.' Your Dad will be tickled that Beaver got all 'A's' and 'B's.' Then, when Beaver brings the report card back to school, his teacher will find it 'doctored' a bit. Then the fireworks will begin — it'll be the hottest show in town!"

"Gosh, Eddie," answers Wally, scratching his head, "I don't know...I don't think I want a part in this. If you want to do it, go right ahead, but you can count me out."

"Here, let me show you how easy it is...I used to do it all the time."

The next evening June Cleaver received a call from Beaver's teacher, Miss Landers (upon whom I had a crush).

"Mrs. Cleaver," the teacher began in a serious tone, "I would like to have a talk with you about young Theodore."

"Why, certainly, Miss Landers...What seems to be the matter?"

---

[1] Maitreya Stillwater and Layne Cutright, *"The Whole Truth,"* Heavensong, PO Box 450, Kula, Hawaii 96790

"Well, it appears that Theodore has changed one of the marks on his report card. He got a 'D' in arithmetic, and the report card came back signed with a 'B.' I'll send the report card back with him tomorrow. Would you please discuss this with him?"

"Why of course, Miss Landers! I'll take it up with Mr. Cleaver as soon as he comes home."

That evening Beaver found himself in the den having one of those talks with his dad.

"Beaver, Miss Landers called today and told us that you changed the 'D' on your report card to a 'B.' Now, son, you didn't have to do that. What made you think that you could get away with cheating like that?"

"Golly, Dad, I didn't change my report card!" responds the Beave, rotating his baseball cap in his hands.

"Now, Beaver, how can you sit there and tell me that? Here, just take a look...The ink isn't even the same color!"

"I can see that, Dad, but I didn't change it."

"Well, if you didn't, then who did?"

"Gosh, Dad, I don't know."

"Now, Beaver, it's one mistake to change your report card, but it's another one to deny it. I'll give you one more chance to tell me the truth, or I'm going to have to punish you. Are you going to stick with your story?"

After a moment's thought came the answer of a master, a teaching worthy of any holy book, a summary of the strength of all of humanity's heros:

"Gee, Dad, if you only have one story, I guess you have to stick with it."

One story. We, too, have but one story. Every moment of life asks us if we are willing to live it, or tell another one. It takes great courage to live in this world and stick to your story. But the word "courage" comes from the French word *coeur*, meaning "heart." If you come from your heart, you will have the strength to do whatever you need to do. You will walk without fear, for what Spirit guides you to do must easily be accomplished. And you will be at peace, for there will be no conflict between your internal feelings and your external actions. All this, because you have chosen to come from the heart. Courage.

To Follow Truth

Jesus had one story, from which he did not depart. When Jesus was brought before the *Sanhedrin* to face a kangaroo court in the middle of the night, the High Priest Caiphus asked him outright, "Are you the Son of God?" Without any hesitation, doubt, or vascillation, Jesus answered, *"I am."* He did not place his perfection in the future, he did not qualify it, and he did not deny it. He declared, *"I am."* And in that one simple statement he opened Heaven's doors for each of us to tell our story, which is the same as his.

Do you know who you are? Every question, challenge, and decision that you face is asking you if you know who you are, and if you are willing to act like it. Are you mortal, or divine? Are you limited, or magnanimous? Is guilt your guide, or do you place your trust in love, and love alone?

I meet many people who have decided to follow truth. I know a woman who almost singlehandedly established a Unity Church in a rural section of a northeastern state. I met a man who sold an empire of six successful businesses, bought a mobile home, and set out on a fascinating two-year journey to the tip of South America and back. I know presidents of companies who have resigned to go into the ministry. And I know ministers who gave up their pulpit to enter the business world. And what each of these people did was right for them.

I had the honor to meet Dr. Rodrigo Carazo, the former President of Costa Rica, who presided over a country that disbanded its standing army. There is now at least one country on the planet that has made a statement for peace that goes beyond words. Now Dr. Carazo is working to establish a United Nations World Peace University in Costa Rica.

Each of these courageous people experienced opposition to the fulfillment of their vision of truth. People around them called them fools, and at times they wondered if their friends were right. But when the heart calls, there is really no competition. Each of these people had their story to play out, and so they did. And they are stronger for it.

You, too, have a truth to live, and you must decide now if you are going to live it. The only alternative is to postpone your destiny. You may delay what you were born to do, but you cannot deny it. Sooner or later you will come to the same fork in the road, and you will have to choose again. And you will choose correctly. There is no alternative to Love.

The Empty Cornerstone

If you depart from truth, you may stray so far that you will have a hard time finding your way back. And you will find your way back. But you can make your journey much easier by being vigilant to keep the truth at the top of your priorities. "Brother, take not one step in the descent to hell," *A Course in Miracles* cautions, "for having taken one, you will not recognize the rest for what they are."[2] Hell is believing that you are separate from your brothers and sisters, and could therefore hide something from them without the expense of your peace. Heaven is remembering that you never needed to lie in the first place.

Have you ever told a lie for so long that you started to believe it yourself? I have. When I was in ninth grade I had a crush on a cute girl named Donna. She was from Milltown and she wore braces, and so I figured she was in my range. Around that time I went to see a live Beatles concert in Atlantic City, and Donna was eager to hear about it when I returned. Wanting to impress her, I created an incredibly exciting drama about how I had met the Beatles. I told her that a friend of ours knew the exit through which the Beatles were to make their getaway after the concert. As the story went, my friends and I hurried to the back door of the theatre to catch them on their way out. Sure enough, as soon as the music stopped, the door opened and John, Paul, George, and Ringo scurried to a long black limousine. But not before we intercepted them! We stretched out our hands to shake theirs, hoping to make some contact. While three of the Beatles slipped past us, Paul McCartney extended his hand to me. We had a quck handshake, after which he was gone. But when I looked into my palm, there I found a guitar pick!

Donna was in awe. Her jaw had dropped six inches and her eyes were open like two full moons. She was definitely impressed. The story was working.

Now, not only did he give me the pick, the story went, but I just happened to have it with me. Would Donna like to see it?

---

[2] T, p.460

You bet she would. The girl almost fainted.

I took the pick out of my wallet and showed it to her. To prove that it was real, there, etched into the plastic, were the initials, *"P.M."*

It was almost too much for her to handle. Of all the girls in the school, she was getting to see it!

As if that were not enough, I told her quite sincerely that I wanted her to have it.

"You really mean it?"

"Why, sure! You're special to me."

Donna held the pick next to her heart, swooned, and floated off to her next class. Ecstacy in the Junior High School!

The whole story was, of course, pure donkeydust. The pick was bought by me at the local music store, and I etched the initials into it that morning before I went to school. It was one whopper of a tale, skillfully fabricated by yours truly. I confess. (Donna, if you read this, please forgive me. You may want to read the chapter on forgiveness. You can return the pick if you like.)

But the story doesn't end here, folks. Donna told her friends, and mine, and before long the big news spread around the school. By the end of the school day lots of kids were asking me about the famous encounter. Not wanting to disappoint them, I gladly gave them a detailed recount of the exciting event. In fact, every time I told the story it included more details, and quickly the account grew in length and drama. I tell you, I should have been a fisherman!

After a while an interesting thing happened. I had told the story so much and colored it with such fascinating details that I began to believe it myself! The more I told it, the more real it seemed to me, and after awhile I forgot that it never really happened! As I look back on the story now, it seems as real in my memory as many things that *did* happen. Maybe it did happen! Or maybe the other things didn't happen. They all feel the same!

The point here is that I had practically convinced myself of something that wasn't true. And all of us have done the same, on a much deeper and broader level. All of us have convinced ourselves of lots of things that are not true.

The Power of Thought

Physiologists tell us that the central nervous system cannot distinguish between reality and imagination. This means that if you think about something enough, your body will respond as if it really happened. Hypnosis is a good example of this principle. If a person is a good hypnotic subject, he may be told that he is being burned by a *suggested* flame, and a blister will develop. Glove anesthesia is another example of the power of the mind to create physical reality. A subject can be told that his hand is numb, and if he accepts the suggestion a needle can pass through his skin and possibly through his whole hand, without any pain or bleeding. Surely this is a clear demonstration of the power of the mind to create physical experience. In these cases the mind manufactures an experience which overrides and replaces apparent physical law.

Be careful, then, of what truth you tell, for although you do not have the ability to change God's Truth, you have the free will to believe there is another version of reality and live in it as if it were so. And you will continue to find proofs of your truth, for along with your power to fabricate a truth is a propensity to substantiate it with evidence from your own warehouse of thought! And you will continue to do this until you realize that God's Truth is more rewarding than any you have substituted.

Ultimately, you will discover that *you* are the One who established the Original Law against which you believe you have rebelled. All of your experiences in attempting to substitute your will for God's leads you to the great awakening that your will *is* God's, and there is no other.

Truth in Action

Each of us reaches a point where we have the strength to recognize that original truth, acknowledge it, and live in it. When your memory of your own divinity is restored, you find no shortage of models for how powerfully you can live in the world. We can walk through our daily activities, even amid work, family, and play, holding and expressing the knowledge of who we are. We do not need to veer one hair's breadth from the reality of our beauty, for every departure from the truth is a moment of lost love, in the service of regaining it.

To sit in silence and meditate is a gift from God, and then to carry that peace into activity is to share that gift with all the world. Each day, go within to make contact with your God. Ask Him what He wants of you this day, and then go forth and glorify Love in all that you do. You are not asked to conquer nations or persons; you are asked simply to dispell illusions by acting on truth. There is no difference between what serves you and what will heal the world. You are never asked or expected to heal yourself or the world at the expense of the other. You *are* the world.

As you recognize the truth that leads you home, the road that it takes you by becomes ever wider. You must have the utter and unfailing conviction that the truth will never fail you as long as you do not fail it. No matter how many times you have fallen prey to lies born of fear, you must arise and say, "This time I lay my treasures in the storehouse of love." And though you may be able to see no further than one step in front of you, that is the step you must take. For then, and only then, will you see that the hand of truth has taken yours and extricated you from wandering in the fog.

Your days of loneliness and feelings of abandonment are over. How could you be alone when Love walks with you at every turn? Take refuge in the Truth, and the solace you feel will far surpass anything you have felt in the world. Be glad that Heaven is your home, and that you have never fully felt yourself to be a part of this world. Can that which is born of pure love find a home in a world of fear? No, no more than a diamond of truth could find a place in a rubble of deception.

You have a place in the universe, and you can be in it only by being totally committed to the truth. *You cannot be totally committed sometimes.* [3] This is your story, and the world needs you to tell it. Every ray of truth that you shine into a darkened world will illuminate a path for many to walk with you. It should be clear to you by now that you do not walk alone. When you bear witness to the Light that is you, you free millions from the shackles of their own fears. Such is your responsibility as a flame to warm a cold world in a dark and hungry night. And you will do it — indeed you *are* doing it — because that is what you came here for.

You, like Beaver, have but one story, and you will stick to it. The alternative to the truth is not lying, but *nothing*. And so there is no alternative to the truth. And be you glad, for your story is the only one that will take you all the way home.

> *You might have made a meaning of what isn't really real,*
> *But no matter what you're dreaming, the truth can only heal.* [4]
>
> - Maitreya Stillwater

---

[3] T, p. 117
[4] Stillwater and Cutright, "The Whole Truth"

Good Lemonade

You can go a long way with some integrity.
    - Lee Iacocca, President of Chrysler Corporation

One afternoon my friend Debbie and I were driving down a country road in northern New Jersey when we passed a large house with a huge number of cars bordering it. Automobiles filled the driveway, spilled onto the lawn, and overflowed onto both sides of the road for a considerable distance.

"Some party these people know how to throw!" I quipped as we passed the lot.

"Oh, don't you know what this place is?" returned Debbie.

"Looks like quite a bash to me."

"This is *Sammy's* Restaurant — It's really famous; people drive long distances to eat here."

"But I don't see any sign; where's the advertising?"

"They don't have any — mainly because they don't need it. The food is so good that everyone tells their friends, and they've become immensely successful just by word of mouth — you can hardly get a reservation."

I looked again. There was not one sign or word of advertising on the building. Yet the street was ribboned on both sides with long lines of cars. The food must have really been good.

What does it take to really be successful in this world? This is a question that we have all asked ourselves, indeed the question that we have all come here to answer. *Sammy's* is a wonderfully clear metaphor for the importance of placing integrity at the top of our list of personal priorities. If we have no integrity we may temporarily gain some symbols of success, but we will be empty inside. With integrity at our core, all the seeds that we plant must bear good fruit.

My friend Frank Asch is a bright and talented award-winning author of children's books. Frank and his wife Janani used to visit a country house I had where we would sit around the fire on blustery winter nights, sip tea, sing, and read enchanting stories aloud.

One night as he entered the house Frank placed a book in my hands. With a warm smile he told me, "Here's one of my favorite stories — I want you to have it; I think you'll enjoy it." I looked at the cover. In big bright yellow letters it shouted, *GOOD LEMONADE!*[1] Although it is written as a children's book, the lesson is for all of us:

One summer morning Hank decided to open up a lemonade stand. He found a wooden box in the garage, magic-marked a big oak-tag poster announcing, *"Lemonade — 10 Cents a Glass,"* and he set up shop on the sidewalk in front of his house. Hank went into the kitchen, mixed a packet of instant lemonade in a big glass pitcher, and skipped outside where he stood with his little brother Tommy. There the two of them waited for customers. Hank and Tommy waited...and waited...and waited. They stood there until five o'clock, when Hank had as many lemonades as he did when he began — except for one, which was bought by his little brother Tommy.

"Hmmm," pondered the little businessman, "I have to figure out some way to sell more lemonade," as he sat, chin in hand. "Let's see...Let's see..." The wheels of his young mind spun. "A sale!...That's it, I'll have a sale!...That'll pull in some business!"

The next morning Hank and Tommy set up the stand once again, but this time there was a new poster on the old crate. This sign was noticable for all of the different colored magic-markers that created it: *"Lemonade — Ten Cents a Glass...Three for Twenty-five Cents — Special — Today Only."* Anxiously Hank and Tommy sat waiting for customers to take advantage of the sale. Together the two boys waited...and waited...and waited, until five o'clock came once again too soon. Hank looked down into the cigar box to find but ten cents — the revenue from the glass of lemonade bought by: his little brother Tommy.

"This still isn't working!" complained our young entrepreneur, "I'll have to try another scheme!"

The next morning Hank broke open his piggy bank and hired Russell Wilcox, a boy down the street, to walk up and down Elm Street with a big sandwich board which Hank and Tommy had stayed up past their bedtime to make.

"Advertising is the key!" Hank explained to Tommy as they sat in anticipation of the crowd from Elm Street.

But the crowd never showed. When the welding plant down the street

---

[1] Frank Asch, *Good Lemonade*, Franklin Watts, 1976

blew the five o'clock whistle, Hank had recouped only ten cents of his investment — the income from the one glass of lemonade bought by his little brother Tommy.

"That does it!" popped Hank, "Now we bring out the heavy artillery!"

The next day persons driving on Elm Street were treated to a most unusual sight. Perched delicately atop two card tables, one on either side of the lemonade stand, were two dancing go-go lemons, bumping and grinding to the beat of some very funky rock music blaring from the boom box in front of the garage. (Closer inspection revealed the lemons to actually be two young ladies, about Hank's age, dressed in some rather elaborate outfits.)

"If this doesn't do it, nothing will!" Hank could be heard proclaiming to the little fellow sitting beside him, the mini-redhead nursing a misty glass of yellow cooler.

It was indeed fortunate that the little one had a propensity for lemonade (and supporting his big brother), for when Hank counted up the proceeds at the end of the day, there was but one ten-cent piece — with Tommy's fingerprints on it.

"I don't understand it," Hank quailed to his little group of employees; "I've done everything to get business: sales, advertising, go-go girls... Why aren't people buying my lemonade?"

Their brainstorming was interrupted by the shouting of Russell, who was running down Elm Street as fast as he could with a sandwich board over his shoulders.

"You should see the line of kids down at Artie's lemonade stand!" Russell reported. "...It must be half a block long!"

"Half a block long!" Hank reeled back. "I have to see what this kid has that I don't."

Hank grabbed a dime from the cigar box and ran down Elm Street as fast as he could. When he reached Artie's house, puffing heavily, there, sure enough, was a line of kids almost to Rosewood Avenue. Hank took a place in line, straining on the tips of his toes to see what Artie's gimmick was. The line moved slowly toward the stand where, to Hank's surprise, he found no go-go girls, no walking advertisements, not even a sale flyer.

"I don't get it," Hank puzzled; "How does he sell so much lemonade?"

After about twenty minutes Hank reached the counter. When he got there he saw just a simple sign, *"Artie's Lemonade — Ten Cents a Glass"* — not very different from his own original sign. Eagerly Hank plunked his ten cents down on the wooden box, his eyes spying behind the counter to see if Artie had discovered some new, scientifically efficient procedure for mass marketing.

The glass came presently, with a smile of thanks from Artie. Hank stepped to the side to drink it, still wondering how he did it. Hank lifted the cup to his mouth, tasted it, and then his eyes opened wide. His answer came as quickly as a taste of the truth.

"That's it!" Hank shouted; "That's the secret — **IT'S REALLY GOOD LEMONADE!**"

Hank zoomed back to his stand, unplugged the boom box, relieved the go-go lemons of their responsibilities, lifted the sandwich board off of Russell's tired shoulders, and ran into the kitchen. A little more slowly than usual he moved from the cabinet to the refrigerator, and then to the sink, where he began to mix a new batch of lemonade. This time, instead of just using the mix, Hank added the juice of two real lemons to the pitcher. He also spooned in one extra serving of sugar and brought a bucket of ice cubes out to the stand, so hot customers could feel a little more refreshed. Out to the stand Hank zipped with a new sign: *"Good Lemonade — Ten Cents a Glass."*

By one o'clock that afternoon there was a line of kids halfway to Rosewood Avenue — this time starting at Hank's house. All of them were smacking their lips and thanking Hank for some good lemonade. The afternoon flew by, and when the welding factory whistle sang through the streets of Honersville, Hank looked into the cigar box to find it nearly full of shiny dimes. His stock of thirst-quencher was down nearly to the bottom of the pitcher. Hank had sold all of his lemonade that day, except for one glass — the one he gave to his little brother Tommy, who drank it down with an extra twinkle in his eye.

Quality First

The story of Hank's lemonade stand is meaningful because his escapade in lemonade sales is symbolic of our lessons of integrity as we journey through the wondrous university of life. I recently saw a billboard advertisement for an automobile company which simply stated, *"Quality First."* This company, I thought, has discovered the secret of all success. To the extent that they practice their motto they can expect to enjoy the rewards of their intention.

Would it not be wonderful if all of us remembered and practiced this secret? I have been driving a Toyota for three years, with over sixty thousand miles on it. I want to testify that in those years and all of those miles the car has not required one repair. I have seen my mechanic but for oil changes and an occasional tune-up. I want to tell you how happy I have been to drive the car, recommend it to my friends, and feel confident about buying another Toyota somewhere down the road. The thing works, and I am grateful. I have seen lots of Toyota commercials, and none of them have meant anything to me. But the car is built well, and that means a great deal to me and all of the satisfied customers.

(I am not receiving a commission from Toyota for this testimony; it is simply a good example! I should also note that this is not to defame any other brand of automobile — every manufacturer can build a good car if they so choose.)

Your Divine Agent

Several years ago I began to feel that I wanted to teach yoga as a full-time profession. I decided to quit everything else I was doing and wage a huge publicity blitz toward drumming up business for myself as a yoga instructor. I had business cards printed, mimeographed letters of advertisement, and I called just about every YMCA, dance school, and health spa in the phone book. For weeks I was on the phone trying to sell myself. Most of the prospective clients offered me a polite "Thank you, it's a nice idea, send us your literature;" some said they weren't interested; and some said, "Come on over and let's set something up."

The net result of a fortnight of working anxiously to set something up was: one job at a YMHA which was cancelled before it began due to lack of sufficient enrollment, and another gig in a hotel health spa in which our class was put in the same room as people working on the *Nautilus* equipment. There the muscle-builders stepped over the yoga students (who were in deep relaxation) to get to the bathroom. We also received the added benefit of learning to be non-attached as the body builders snickered and made Don Rickles-like comments about the nature of yoga.

Actually, some lovely healings came of that course, but afterwards I realized that trying to sell myself was not something that I wanted to do. Self-promotion did not feel peaceful, and the work did not yield much in the way of success. Truly it was an excellent lesson, for from the experience I gleaned this idea: I would simply continue with the yoga courses I was already teaching, make the classes an offering to God, and give the students the best lemonade I could. In short, I decided to take care of God's business and trust God to take care of mine.

The results were phenomenal! I imbued those classes with such caring and excellence that the students begged for more, brought their friends, attended workshops I presented in other locations, and recommended me for courses to be set up in other schools.

An especially poignant lesson came as a result of a presentation that I was asked to do for a local B'nai Brith meeting. At this Sunday morning event I wasn't sure if the participants were more interested in the lecture I was giving or the bagels they were expecting afterward. When I looked into their auras during the meditation I did not see the cool streams and rolling mountain valleys I was suggesting, but dreamy drifts of cream cheese delicately set off by toasted onions on a balmy pumpernickel beach. When they returned from their gastronomic fantasy the participants challenged me, accused me of trying to hypnotize them, and I felt pretty much as if I had blown it. I was no match for brunch, I surmised. Why, I wondered, was I invited there anyway? It didn't seem as if I was received very well at all.

The next day the miracle came. I received a phone call from the director of a local adult education program who informed me, "We have been looking for a yoga instructor. Mr. Schwartz, who attended your lecture at B'nai Brith, said you gave an excellent presentation. We would like to have you work for us. Please come for an interview soon." I guess somebody liked it. That class led to another, and another, and to more after that. From those experiences I developed my workshops, which have blossomed so very beautifully. I am in awe of the process of the unfoldment of good.

Since that time I have pretty much let God be my publicity agent, and I have never been sorry. I rarely invite myself anywhere (unless I feel strong guidance to do so), I do not attempt to wedge my foot into any doors that God does not open, and I almost always accept invitations to speak or share my ideas, providing that I have the time available. I assume that if I am invited somewhere, the audience will have ears to hear what I have to say. This is a philosophy that has worked very well for me.

Letting Your Dreams Come Through

Spirit has an amazing and superbly efficient way of materializing our dreams. A minister friend of mine offers a workshop called, "Letting Your Dreams Come Through," and that is surely how our goals become a reality!

One evening in an adult school class I asked each student to share their dream, their idea of what they would most love to be doing with their life. One woman told that she has always wanted to return to Hawaii, for those islands have a deep and mystical home in her heart. A gentleman said he wanted to quit his administrative job and open up a kennel where he would breed show dogs. Another young lady wanted to have a fulfilling relationship with a man.

When all of the students had finished speaking, one turned to me and asked, "How about you, Alan? What would you most like to do?"

Feeling somewhat taken by surprise I had to think quickly and honestly. I felt that since I asked them to share intimately, I should be willing to do the same.

Into my mind flashed a picture that was imbedded in my heart, an image that meant more to me than anything else I had seen in a long time. The previous autumn I had seen a video tape of Dr. Leo Buscaglia delivering a lecture called "What is Essential is Invisible to the Eye." The lecture was based upon a quote from *The Little Prince*, the popular and beloved fable by de Saint Exupery. The message of the lecture was that the truth is not really what we see with our senses, but what we feel in our hearts.

Watching Dr. Buscaglia lecture was a marvelously inspiring experience for me. I became aware of something I had never seen before: although there were perhaps several thousand people in the audience, Leo had established a personally intimate relationship with each one. As the camera panned the audience while he spoke, I saw each listener on the edge of his or her chair, spellbound, as if Leo was having a tender, touching moment with him or her. That auditorium became a great cozy living room, and I know that there was no other place in the universe that each person in that audience would rather have been. It was a marvelous demonstration that what is essential *is* invisible to the eye.

Back to my class, it was time for me to give the answer. I told them, "I would like to travel around the world, speaking to groups of thousands of people, and bring them to tears for the love of God."

Did I say that? I don't think I had ever thought about that before, much less share it with a group of people I hardly knew. But I did say it, and it was true — that was my dream, the vision that I held in my heart of hearts, awaiting the opportunity to be brought out into the sunlight. I was glad I was asked, and even more pleased that I told the truth.

They say that you better be careful of what you ask for, because you just might get it.

Three months later I was sitting in my back yard on a delightfully warm spring day, when the mailman poked his head over the fence and handed me a letter. I read the return address: *"D. Hastings, Spokane, Washington."*

"D. Hastings? Spokane, Washington? Where's that?"

Curiously I opened it up. It was from a young lady who began her introduction with a lovely description of spring in the Northwest. She had just returned from picking strawberries at a mountain lake, and she wanted me to enjoy the beauty as she saw it through her appreciative eyes. She went on to explain that she had read and enjoyed *The Dragon Doesn't Live Here Anymore.* The minister of her Unity Church had based a series of lectures on the book, after which a good deal of the people in the church had read it too.

"So, dear Alan," Deneice concluded, "we'd love to have you come out here and share a week of workshops."

If thoughts are things, then I was certainly watching my most cherished seeds sprout. I thanked God for allowing me to be myself, and giving me the chance to serve Him in a way that I loved.

"Of course I would love to," I wrote back to Deneice. I felt like a pilot about to solo after years of dreaming about flying.

I didn't get a chance to mail the letter. The phone in the kitchen began to ring, but smugly I remained nestled in my lawn chair, intent on keeping my vow to act like a human being and not a slave to Ma Bell, a touch-tone yoyo. But it just kept ringing. "Man plans, and God laughs." I got up and answered.

"Hi Alan, this is Deneice...I didn't want to wait for you to answer my letter. There's a lot of interest here — Will you come?"

"Yes, of course, I would love to."

"Great! We're printing fifteen hundred tickets for each night. Will that be alright?"

That particular day I was glad that picture-phones had not yet been invented. I think I would have been a little embarrassed to have Deneice see me gulp across country. *Fifteen hundred tickets?* Did I hear her correctly? *Fifteen hundred?* Didn't she know I was just a Jewish boy from New Jersey who simply wrote down what he heard in his brain? Or maybe she knew more about who I was than I did.

"Why, sure, that'll be fine," I answered after a long moment's pause. Upon reflecting on it later I realized it was not really a moment — it was more like all of the years that it took me to learn to say "Yes" to who I am.

"Wonderful! We'll be looking forward to seeing you soon!"

The phone clicked on the Washington end, but I didn't hang up. My conversation with myself continued.

"Fifteen hundred tickets? For *each night?* God, what am I going to say to fifteen hundred people?"

The Voice answered quickly, with firm resolution: *"The same as you would say to fifteen."*

"No kidding?"

"Truth has nothing to do with numbers;" the Guide continued, *"It has only to do with being itself, which is the same as being yourself. The truth does not change according to how many people to whom you are telling it. Just go there, love them, be honest about your experience, and I will guide you exactly as to what to do and say — to fifteen hundred, or to one."*

Oh, I see.

I began to prepare my lecture. As I visualized standing before the audience, the question occurred to me, "Who should I be like?"

"I know," I thought, "I'll be like Leo Buscaglia...I'll wave my arms and sweat under the armpits and tell stories about my Italian mother."

"But you don't have an Italian mother," the Voice interrupted; *"You have a Jewish mother."*

Oh, yes; that's right. I can't be Buscaglia.

Well, then, I could be like Ram Dass. I could sit in lotus position and be mellow and cuddly and go into spontaneous meditation every now and then. That would really get them.

"No," the inner Counselor answered, *"that is not really your way."*

Well, that was true, too.

"I have it!" I got excited. "I'll be like Patricia Sun. I'll stand up there and glow and smile and make everyone tingle with my giggle."

But then, alas, my giggle is not especially cute. Forget that one.

Then into my mind came an absolutely amazing idea — one that I had not considered before.

"Why not try going as Alan Cohen?"

"That's it!" I got it. I realized that I would have the best chance of succeeding by being myself — an absolutely monumental discovery! I reasoned that if they had wanted Leo or Ram or Patricia, they would have invited them. But on this particular occasion they invited Alan Cohen, and that was the person I could best give them.

I followed my intuition and I went to that engagement as myself. And what a success it was! The audience enjoyed my presentation because I loved and believed in myself enough to be myself. The simplest answer proved to be the one that worked.

Selling and Serving

To really reap the benefits of good lemonade, you have to know what is the *real* lemonade you are selling. It is not the item before your eyes, the picture in the catalog, or the song on the tape — it is *the love within your heart*. If you believe that you are selling physical glasses of liquid lemonade to solid people, you will sooner or later be burnt out, bedraggled, and bankrupt. If, on the other hand, you realize that the lemonade is the vehicle, the vessel through which you can offer love, blessings, and healing to spiritual beings who truly live on "the waters that will never give thirst again," you will not only sell lots of lemonade, but you will be able to go to sleep each night with a contented heart.

All of life is spiritual, and spiritual only. To sell anything — a product, a service, an idea — you must believe that you are helping the person to whom you are selling. You can fudge your way to financial or social success, but unless you believe in what you are doing you will be a hollow shell of a person. "What shall it profit a man if he gains the whole world but loses his soul?" If you are feeling love in your work there is nothing that can stand between you and great success.

Wally Amos, founder and president of *Famous Amos* cookies, said, "I started selling cookies just to make a living. And when I let go of the concept of trying to make a lot of money, and just wanted to be happy and do something well, my whole life opened up."

I met a woman of similar orientation who was a very successful saleswoman. Here is what she told me:

"You know, *A Course in Miracles* has helped me phenomenally in my work. I've been selling photocopy machines for about six months, and my sales volume is double what the best salesman in the office is doing — and he's been there for six years."

"That's wonderful!" I enthusiastically responded. "What's your secret?"

"Actually, it's quite simple," she explained. "I never try to sell a photocopy machine; my most important goal is to help my client. If I feel that my machine can really help him accomplish what he wants, I tell him so with complete confidence that I have his best interest at heart. If I don't feel he can use what I have to offer, I tell him that, too. I believe that my clients know that I am loving them by telling them the truth, and this has developed a deep level of trust between my clients and myself. They know I would never hurt them, and they would rather buy from me than someone who was more interested in selling them something than helping them. The truth is that I really do want to make their life easier. That feels a lot better to me than trying to sell them a machine. The miracle is that the more I seek to serve them, the more machines I sell!''

Another friend of mine, an advertising representative, gave me this powerful insight into the dynamics of success:

"I keep my peace by turning my work over to God," Joan explained as she drove me home from a class one evening. "I don't feel that my sales are up to me alone. Once I have done my part of the business, I place the final decision in the hands of the Lord. I trust that if this deal will serve everyone's best interest, it will go through and we will all be satisfied. If it won't help everyone involved, then no good can come of it for anyone, and I don't want it. Somehow the more I turn the business over to God, the better it goes. My peers don't understand it, but it's very clear to me."

I knew exactly what Joan meant. When I was writing *The Dragon Doesn't Live Here Anymore*, I hardly thought at all about how the book would get published, where the money would come from, or how it would get into the hands of the readers. All I knew was that God gave me the book, and if He could do that, He could certainly find a way to get it published. My job, as I perceived it, was simply to write healing words. God, I reasoned, would be in a better position than me to know people in high places who could help me.

When the manuscript was finished, two people, independent of one another, offered me the money to publish it without my even asking them. Recognizing the offer came from God, I gratefully accepted.

Then, as I wondered how to advertise the book, I picked up a copy of Hugh Prather's inspiring *Notes to Myself*, his classic sharing of gentle reflections on the spiritual path. Inside the cover I found my answer. I read,

"This unique book was first published by a small unheard-of press in New Mexico. Without any advertising except word of mouth, it has sold over one million copies."[2]

---

[2] Hugh Prather, *Notes to Myself*, Bantam, 1976

There was my answer. The statement confirmed to me that struggle and strain are *not* requirements for spiritual and material success. I let God be my agent, and in this matter and so many others I have never regretted it. The One who created me has never failed me.

Later, when I needed a national distributor to handle larger scale distribution of my books and tapes, once again I did not know where to turn. Remembering my earlier lessons, again I asked for Spirit's help. Within a few weeks I received a letter from New Leaf Distributors, a very professional and spiritually-attuned company in Atlanta. The president of the company was writing to let me know they had become familiar with my books, and their company was interested in handling national distribution. I accepted, and since that time they have done an excellent job for me.

A Living Lesson in Service

Perhaps the most powerful teaching for me in the benefits of serving good lemonade is Hilda, the spiritual teacher with whom I have had the honor of studying for many years. Hilda's ministry, health, happiness, and aliveness are marvelous demonstrations of abundant living. She strives with all of her heart to serve well all who come to her for friendship and guidance, and she radiates the kind of contentment owned only by those who truly love.

In all the time that I have known Hilda she has not required one penny from me or anyone for some of the highest teachings I have ever received, nor has she charged for any of the classes she teaches or the healings she so generously channels. During the fifteen years I have known her, Hilda has never lacked for money, material goods, or sustenance. She does not advertise her teachings, yet three to five hundred persons come weekly to participate in her classes. She has never required any student to take an oath of allegience or join an organization, yet those who love her teachings number in the thousands, her spiritual family circles the globe, and her friendships last for a lifetime and more. In short, Hilda has done everything exactly the opposite the way the world dictates one should go about manipulating to get what one wants, and she enjoys the kind of peace of mind, love of friends, and success for which the world pines. Here is a true teacher of God, demonstrating that one who holds God in her heart holds the world in the palm of her hand.

The Gift of Quality

Perhaps it is in the very intention to fill our work with the light of love that we are fulfilled in doing it, and blessed by the positive response it generates.

On a recent tour through the cathedrals of Europe I was deeply impressed by the quality of the craftsmanship that was imbued in the stone and wood work in those sacred places. It seems that each pillar and buttress was the result of long and caring hours of delicate artistry; that the beauty of the work far outshined the speed or economy of the job; that the artisan saw inspiration as the means as well as the end of his work. I felt that the artistry was a blessing to look at because it was a joy to create.

Could it be that love, caring, and the desire to truly be of service has captured the breath of the divine in such artistry, and consecrated it to bless all who look upon it? Could it be that the art of loving what we do and making it a gift to those we serve, is the lost art of our civilization? And might it also be that those who seek for their work to reflect the divine have discovered the secret to satisfaction in human vocation?

A Zen master once taught, "If you can serve a cup of tea correctly, you can do anything." The key to mastering any skill is to know that it is not the tea that we are serving that is important, but our brother to whom we deliver it. If we can only remember that the things of this world are cups in which the love of God can be given, all of our questions about human activity will be answered. Such an awareness brings healing because it acknowledges that we are dependent only on the divine for our sustenance. Love is a gift that we make real by offering it to one another.

The Greatest Baker

Why would you do something you do not love? Our purpose in life is not to labor begrudgingly, but to be joyful. The real function of a vocation is to feel creative, alive, and enthusiastic, and to serve those you touch. Your service is not limited to the product, but it emanates from your attitude. The famous psychiatrist Karl Menninger said, "Attitude is more important than facts."

The values of the world are inside out, and thus we have reversed the importance of effects (products) with their source (creative love). The real joy of any profession is the love we feel in doing it. Ramtha has said, "When you eat, it is not the food that nourishes you, but the love that you feel when feeding yourself." This is why a diet that you hate cannot work. No matter how effective the diet is advertised to be, if you hate it you are feeding yourself poison. On the other hand, you are sure to be healed by any diet you love.

The same principle is true for professions. If you love what you do, you are sure to succeed. The amount of aliveness you feel is the real yardstick for aptitude and success in any endeavor.

I saw a television interview with several of the most financially successful people in the world. On the panel were Ray Kroc, the founder and president of *McDonald's*, Mrs. Hilton of the hotel chain, and several other fabulously successful moguls and magnates.

When the interviewer asked them, "What advice would you give to a young person starting out in a career?" all of them agreed on the answer: "Go for your dream. Do the thing you love. Do not strive simply for material success, but for inner fulfillment. The wealth will follow from your dedication to fulfilling your heart's desire. Real success is being who you are and doing what you love to do well."

When you are bored or unfulfilled, look at the why of it. At that time you must either recreate the way you are looking at what you are doing, or do the thing that you would really love to do. When the author Jack London went to his father, a baker, and asked him the secret of success in a profession, his dad answered, "The day I don't love baking bread, I quit."

An earlier baker advised us, "Man does not live by bread alone, but by every word that proceeds from the mouth of God." Because God is love and only love, every word (idea or intention) must be an attribute of love. Therefore the real bread is the spiritual substance that nourishes your heart when you work with love.

We *are* Good Lemonade

Life works. Life is miracle. There is indeed a Loving Presence that cares for all of our needs, if we are but willing to entrust them to a Higher Power. We do not have to fight to get what we want in life. Love is the most practical force in all of our affairs. Our greatest strength lies in allowing the earthly to be guided by the divine.

We must *be* what we want before we can have it. No amount of outer manipulation will quench our thirst for good lemonade unless we first realize that we *are* good lemonade. The universe is the biggest lemonade stand in history. God has taken all of the lemons we have given Him and cranked them into the sweetest of beverages, free without measure to all who thirst. The knowledge that we are beautiful, worthy, and lovable will quickly and automatically attract to us all in life that is wonderful, while the thought that we are not enough will keep us striving for the things that we are as if they were out there, instead of already within us. Success is simply knowing who you are while you enjoy watching the universe confirm your vision of yourself.

> *"Seek ye first the Kingdom of Heaven, and all will be added."*
> - Jesus, the Christ

The Creed of the Dauntless

Luke Skywalker: *How will I know the good from the bad?*
Yoda: *You will know through calm and peace. This is the way of the Force; a Jedi does not need to attack; the Force will work for him.*

— The Empire Strikes Back

During the nineteenth-century tenure of Edward Everett as President of Harvard University, a Black man applied for admission. As such an admission was unheard of at that time, the application raised quite a few hackles on the Harvard campus. Mr. Everett, however, was committed to a Higher Law than the admissions policy of Harvard. "If this boy passes the examinations, he will be admitted," Mr. Everett guaranteed; "and if the White students choose to withdraw, all the income of the college will be devoted to his education."

Of course it would. What other route could a person of integrity take? When you are committed to personal integrity, you do not need to fear the consequences of any of your actions, for your deeds bring peace as you contemplate their results. Your brow is smooth, your patience is deep, and you can sleep at night with a satisfied heart. These are the gifts of Spirit earned by those who live in harmony with their personal truth.

What is integrity? What kind of creed would the dauntless follow? Why is honesty a source of real strength?

Integrity is the way to ensure that you will feel the peace of God while living in this world. Because there is nothing more important than feeling peace, there is nothing that is worth doing that would cause you to lose it. While living the truth may at times be challenging, in the long run it is far easier than hiding.

The opposite of integrity is lying. I am not referring so much to verbal lying, but to living as something or someone other than who and what you are. To live as someone or something else is a great loss. Your life is like a photograph, and where you were supposed to be seen smiling, there is an empty outline. You cannot be someone else and yourself at the same time. If you are not you, both you and the world have missed a great gift.

To Honor Truth

Life continually puts us into positions where we have to tell the truth. This is wonderful, because in our heart we really want to tell the truth, and every time we are true to our self we are strengthened. The fear and the struggle and the pain of being something we're not, or not being something we are, is overwhelming, and sooner or later we come to the point where it feels more peaceful to simply tell the truth than to continue to hide. And then we wonder why we ever hid in the first place.

I was at a Patricia Sun workshop[1] when a man stood up and explained that he had come to a point in his career where he was facing a tremendous challenge of integrity. In order for him to be at peace with himself, he would have to tell the truth at work. But he feared that telling that truth may cost him his job. But he couldn't live with himself without telling that truth.

"It sounds like the universe is forcing you to tell the truth!" Patricia replied. "And you may, in fact, lose your job — but that may put you in the perfect position to get a job in which you may retain your integrity and sleep well at night."

I don't believe that God would punish any of Her children for making a stand for integrity. We may experience some temporary setbacks, but in the long run, with faith, Spirit *must* support those who are courageous to be what their heart calls to them to be.

The Free Man

When I was in the Soviet Union I met a beautiful fellow named Sorin. Sorin was a *refusenik* — he had applied to leave the country and he was turned down. As a result he lost his job as a Ph.D chemist, and the only job he could get was as a chess coach for a high school, at about one-tenth of his original salary.

But Sorin was not a beaten man. Because his mind was free and he refused to make believe he was something he was not, he was a free soul. Sorin spoke beautiful English which he had taught himself. He showed me a

---

[1] Patricia Sun, PO Box 7065, Berkeley, California 94707

personal dictionary that he had created. In his notebook he had listed about a dozen English novels and self-help books that he had gotten his hands on. Under a heading with the title of each book, he had printed a list of words he needed to learn, with their pronunciations and definitions next to them.

As Sorin proudly leafed through the pages to show me his little booklet, I felt a tremendous enthusiasm and aliveness in his spirit. He had a zest for knowledge, and he was devoted to expanding his mind. He was excited to break into a new world of awareness. His body may have been restricted, but his mind was soaring. His mind was free, and therefore so was he.

A Course in Miracles asks us, "Would you rather have freedom of the body or freedom of the mind? You cannot have both." To me this means that if we believe that we are a body, we will equate our freedom with what the body is doing, and we will deny the truth that our thoughts really determine our freedom. But if we know that our life springs from our thoughts, we can rise to lofty heights no matter what our body is doing. One who is free in spirit is truly free.

The Power of Defenselessness

It cannot be overemphasized that the dauntless hearken to an *inner* call, trusting Spirit to confirm their faith, observable in the events of the outer world.

A woman who attends some of my workshops has made wonderful changes in her life in the past few years. As her mind and heart have opened to the reality of Spirit, her work, her creativity, and her relationships have developed in miraculous ways.

One of the areas that has been amazing to watch unfold, she reports, is in her marriage. She explains that her husband was not very supportive of the spiritual path she had taken. When she began he casually wrote off her interest as a fad that she was going through. She began to defend herself, but then she realized that the best way to proceed would be simply to carry on in peace and trust that if her path was true, only good could come in her family and her entire life.

She describes a scene that was a turning point:

"One night my husband and I were reading in bed before retiring," she shared. "He was sitting on his side of the bed sifting through the pages of *Playboy*, and I was on my side, reading *Jonathan Livingston Seagull*. Every now and then he would look up and make a wisecrack about "that sappy spiritual stuff." I would just smile and go back to my book. .

More and more he started to look over at me reading. Finally he said, "Say, let me take a look at that." Gladly I handed him the book, and he started to get into it. He actually liked it, and now I share more of my spiritual life with him."

I love this vignette as a metaphor for how spirituality works. Truth is firm within itself, and it trusts that anything that is good will share itself in just the right way and timing. No defense is necessary, and neither any proselytizing. Defense and proselytizing are signs of insecurity. The truth is anchored in the firmest of ground, and it does not require allies or fear destruction. Truth attracts friends by the compelling quality of its presence. Those who live in the truth can rest in the power of their being. Being is the most powerful form of living. It is the strongest form of doing, for without trying to do anything, all gets done.

> *Therefore the sage says:*
> *I take no action and people are reformed.*
> *I enjoy peace and people become honest.*
> *I do nothing and people become rich.*
> *I have no desires and people return to*
> *the good and simple life.*[2]

The Mirror's Gift

We have said many times that the world is but a reflection of our own consciousness. When we learn to recognize that *all* events we experience are demonstrations of our will, the world will become our friend and our most worthy teacher. If we want to know more about what we are thinking or feeling at any given moment, we can simply look at what is happening to us. In issues of integrity, the universe will be quick to reflect our integrity — or lack of it.

For example, some friends of mine were sitting in a car, about to leave for a seminar. When the driver turned the key, the car engine groaned and cranked, but it did not turn over. The driver repeated her efforts several times, to no avail.

After her third attempt, she turned to the others in the car and stated, "I

---

[2] Lao Tsu, *Tao Te Ching*, Gia-Fu Feng and Jane English, translators, Vintage Books, 1972

have never had this problem before, and the car is in good shape. There must be a lie in the space.''

After a long moment of uncomfortable silence, one of the ladies in the group spoke up: ''You're right — I don't really want to go to this seminar tonight. I just came because I was afraid to say no. My presence here is a kind of a lie — I'd rather be home.''

''Thank you very much,'' said the driver, ''I appreciate you telling me the truth.''

With that she turned the key, the car started, and off to the seminar they went. (I wouldn't be surprised if it was a seminar on integrity.)

This scene illustrates some very important lessons for us:

First, the world is a reflection of our attitude. Most of the time the attitude that creates our experience is functioning on an unconscious level. We see but the tip of the iceberg of our consciousness, and the universe is always giving us clues about what we are willing. This is always helpful, as it is of the utmost importance for our will to be conscious, integrated, and chosen at all times.

Second, the world can and will change as we change our attitude about it. When we shift our thoughts from fear to love, or from deception to honesty, the world will reflect our clarity and our path will be made clear. We are speaking now in a very physical, material, practical sense. Since the world is but consciousness, every change you make in your consciousness must create a change in the world.

Finally, we see that integrity is not simply about being perfect, looking good, or always winning in a storybook sense. It is about telling the truth about where you are. It is more important to tell the truth about where you are than to lie in an attempt to act like where you would like to be. You may not be able to get where you want to be until you master where you are.

When You Tell the Truth, Everyone Wins

One day I received a telephone call from a friend inviting me to give an evening workshop at her church. ''It sounds good,'' I told her. ''Please tell me the details.''

When she told me that the church was approximately a two-hour drive from my home, I began to have some reservations. I felt that four hours was more than I wanted to drive for a workshop on a weeknight evening.

"I would love to come," I told her, "but I have made a commitment to myself to relax the pace of my life somewhat. I feel that I would rather not drive that distance for an evening weeknight workshop."

It felt good to tell the truth.

"I understand," she told me; "I am disappointed, but I do know how busy you have been, and I support your decision."

The next morning I received a telephone call from the same lady.

"How would you like us to send a limo for you?" she asked.

Now she was talking.

"Well, that would certainly be much easier than me driving all that distance. But I wouldn't want you to overstep your means."

"Oh, it's no problem," she assured me. "One of the members of our church has a limousine service. He has read and enjoyed your books, and he said he would be happy to send his limousine for you at no charge to you or the church."

It was an offer I couldn't refuse. You can imagine my neighbors' surprise when a long grey limousine pulled into my driveway and a dashing uniformed young man opened the door for me with a formal salute. I didn't feel comfortable saluting him in return; it felt nicer just to put my hand on his shoulder and tell him, "Thank you for coming."

Two friends and I slid into the plush back seat, where we sat back and enjoyed the ride, drinking apple juice from the bar and watching Terry Cole-Whittaker videos on the VCR. We also had a lovely conversation with the driver. The workshop turned out to be a great success, and I returned home that night relaxed and energized.

In this particular situation, everyone won. I got to give a workshop, be with loving people, get paid for it, and share my books, all of which I love. The church had a strong and uplifting workshop which brought new and old congregants together. The limousine owners, a lovely couple who had wanted to meet me, invited me to their home for refreshments afterwards. I gave the driver some of my books, and learned some great ideas from Terry Cole-Whittaker.

All because I was willing to tell the truth. If I had said a flat "no" or made up an excuse about why I couldn't come, the church would not have been able to respond in the way they did. But I was willing to trust that telling the truth would work for everyone, and it did.

The Truth Gets Results

One very powerful and valuable benefit of telling the truth is that it gets results. It moves life along more quickly and more effectively than lying, beating around the burning bush, or procrastinating. And it elicits direct responses. Honest questions call forth honest answers.

A while back I received a telephone call from a woman asking me for a date. She had met me at a workshop and she wanted to see me again. "I really liked being with you," she told me. "I felt attracted to you, and I would like to get together with you again. Is that something that you would like to do?"

Her honesty hit me right between the eyes. She was so straightforward that I felt I had to give her an answer of the same quality, integrity, and forthrightness with which she asked.

"Thank you for telling me that," I told her. "I enjoyed meeting and sharing with you at the workshop. I must tell you that I am in a committed relationship, and I would rather not see anyone else," I had to tell her. "And I want you to know how much I appreciate your being so open and honest with me."

That was the end of it. Honest question asked, honest response given. A complete communication. No fooling around. No guessing. And no hurt feelings. Honesty requires great love, and for someone to be honest with you means that they respect and honor you a great deal. In this case perhaps it meant more than a date.

I really admired this woman for coming right out and declaring where she was at. I respected her willingness to go for what she wanted. No dinner invitations; no discussions of the news, weather, or current meditation techniques. No questions about semi-related subjects. Just the subject at hand: "Would you like to go out?" And that was a great teaching of integrity for me.

And she got results. One may say that she did not get results because in effect I said "no." But "no" is a result. It is more of a result than not knowing, and it definitely moves things along to the next step. Perhaps there is someone else she would like to see, someone who would work out better for her than me, and my being out of the picture would clear the way for that to happen more quickly and easily. She was definitely ahead of where she was before she called. And so was I. I had the chance to examine my feelings, my relationship, my commitment, and my willingness to tell the truth. I had to make choices in the brief time between the question and the answer. And everytime we make choices, we grow. So we both won.

On a deeper lever, I really didn't say "no" to her. The outer "no" was just the drama level, the story line, the obvious plot. On a deeper level I was joining with her in a commitment with her to have an open and honest relationship. If I never saw or spoke with her again, my heart could rest satisfied that in that relationship, even if it was in the space of a short conversation, we were both straight with each other. Even though we didn't date, I will remember her as someone who loved me enough to tell me the truth, as I loved her in my honesty. That's a pretty good relationship, a wonderful gift to share.

Ask for What You Want

The Children of God receive good because they know they are worthy of it. Life is a series of opportunities to learn that you are lovable. The situations that you create demonstrate what you believe you deserve. Do not stop until you have created what you really want. Every failure is an encouragement to choose to accept better the next time. You will always have the opportunity to choose again until you choose to be lovable. And indeed you are.

You must trust the desires of your heart. Some philosophical systems decry desires as evil, needful of being purged or annihilated. There is another way of looking at desires, as there is another way of seeing everything. Seen in the correct light, the world can become new instantly. You need but know that it is possible to have all the blessings of Heaven, even while in this world.

To have what you want, you must ask for it. To avoid asking for what you really want always comes from a sense of guilt, for who that was not guilty would be denied what he wanted? You do deserve to receive what you want, and the most powerful way to ask for it is by knowing that you deserve it.

A man went to Heaven, where he was taken on an orientation tour by God. When they passed a closed door, the man asked God what was behind it.

"Oh, it would make you very sad to see what is in that room," God explained.

But the man was curious, and he asked God to show him.

"Very well," God acceded. God opened the door, and there the man saw many gifts and treasures. The man was astonished at the great wealth of objects his eyes beheld. Many were wrapped in elegant paper and adorned with lovely bows and decorations.

"This looks like a great treasurehouse!" the man exclaimed. "Why would it make me sad to see this?"

"These are the gifts that I have offered people, but they have not accepted them." God explained. "If I offer someone a gift and they do not accept it, I have no choice but to take the gift back and hold it here in this great storehouse until they or someone else is willing to have it."

"This is amazing!" the man exclaimed. "Why would anyone not accept these beautiful presents? Here is a wide-screen color television set...a huge hot tub, and...isn't that a Rolls Royce over there?"

"Yes, Joe," God answered. "Go look at the tag on it."

Joe walked over to the gleaming car, turned the tag over, read it, and his eyes opened wide.

"Why, that's my name on this tag!" he shouted. "This car was meant for me! But why didn't I get it? You know how much I would have loved to have a car like this! And I prayed to You every night!"

There was a pregnant moment of silence. If it is true that you get what you pray for, what reason could God possibly offer for not giving Joe the car of his dreams?

"You did not get the Rolls Royce, Joe," God explained, " — even though that's what you wanted — because every night you prayed to me to send you a Ford."

Why would Joe have prayed for a Ford if he really wanted a Rolls? Only because he didn't believe he could get one, or he didn't feel he deserved it. While he wanted it all, he asked only for what he believed he could get. And so he got what he believed he could get — no more, no less.

Prayer is not so much asking God to give us what we want, but an exercise in our knowing what we deserve. If you pray for something, you must believe that you deserve it. If you truly believe that you deserve it, by the time you have prayed for it, it is already yours, by right of consciousness. You will attract what belongs to you.

The goal of prayer, then, is not to supplicate God to give us something that we don't deserve, but to remind ourself that we deserve the best. There is enough of everything for everyone, and if you remember that God is the Source of infinite, abundant, unfailing supply, you have placed your faith where it is truly merited.

On Eagle's Wings

A Course in Miracles asks us, "Who would attempt to fly with the tiny wings of a sparrow when the mighty power of an eagle has been given him?"[3]

A friend of mine had a sign up on her wall:

Ask for what you want, but don't demand it.

You can wrestle what you want from the hands of creation, for it is within your power to do so. But there is an easier way, a lighter way, a more peaceful way. Our good comes to us much more fluently when we do not try to force it. We don't need to yell at God to get Spirit's attention. The One Who created us lives within us, and She can hear our whispers as easily as our shouts. We can conserve our energy.

If you have to demand something in order to get it, you may be forcing the universe to give you something that you do not really need. I have found that demanding things from others, from myself, or from the universe does not work as well as asking. I can ask, and ask with firmness and surety, knowing that if I am to have this thing, I will receive it. In that consciousness, if I do receive it, it will be because God gave it to me, not because I forced it by my ego's dictate. If you try to pick a fruit before it is ripe, the process will be a struggle, the tree will bleed, and the fruit will not taste good. There are even some fruits which are poisonous if you eat them before they are ripe. But if you pick the fruit when it is ready, it comes gently into your hand (sometimes it falls on the ground at your feet!), it tastes deliciously sweet, and it is nourishing.

If I feel I have to threaten, cajole, or manipulate, I must have allowed some fear to intrude upon the holiness of my thoughts and tempt me into believing that there is a way that would work better than peace. At such a point I would do well to consider why my request may not be materializing. Perhaps I don't really need the thing, or maybe the timing is not just right

---

[3] M, p. 8

now. Or perhaps someone else needs to make a choice that I cannot make for them by attempting to persuade them to do what I would like them to do. Perhaps I have been resisting my good by a fear of love or healing. There might be a thousand different reasons why a request is not answered immediately. But demanding is a sure sign that you are heading in a direction that will not take you to peace.

The real way to change what you are getting is to change your mind. You can go through all kinds of physical or metaphysical gymnastics and gyrations to manipulate the outer world to give you what you want, but if there is no change in your inner world, all of your efforts are very weak and ineffective indeed. Ah! But once your mind is changed, you have the strength of the universe behind you! To see a new world you must see with new eyes. You already have those eyes, but you need to look through them. And what a beauteous universe they will show you! You will see all about you as a gift and a blessing. You will see persons and events not to be corrected, but appreciated. And best of all, you will be in love with yourself. You will find wonder in your own being, and let your ideas of sin and fault fly to the wind to be scattered like flowers among the breezes. You will be able to look in the mirror and love what you see. You will arise in the morning and go forth with enthusiasm, knowing that the entire universe is alive with love, and the blessing of Spirit goes with you everywhere. You will see yourself as you are, and you will weep blessed tears of joy at the beauty which has been bestowed upon you, with nothing asked of you in return except your hearing the madrigal of your heart singing gentle praises to all the universe in the silver light of a moonlit evening. And you will be happy. All this, without a single care or anxious struggle on your part.

Is this not preferable to a life of worry and woe? I assure you that all is quite well taken care of. Your purpose is not to improve upon it, but to celebrate it. This realization is the simplest one, and yet you may find it to be the hardest, for you have been trained to not be enough, and consequently you see your world through the same clouded vision. But you are quite enough, because you are all there is, and what more could there be? It would be a blasphemy to attempt to improve on your holiness, but it is a sacrament to honor it by knowing it. And so once again we come to the point and purpose of your existence: to know yourself.

Everything and Nothing

By focusing on accepting the blessings in your life, you may find that you actually have a lot more than you thought you did. You may discover that Spirit's plan for you is taking you Home much more easily and effectively than if you were left to your own designs. The universe gives us much more by accepting than by criticizing. One thing is for sure — if you lose your peace, you have nothing.

To ask means to allow the answer to be what it is. If you have a preconceived notion of what the answer should be, you are not asking, but telling. When you ask something of God or a another person, leave room for the answer to be what it is. A Catholic priest was asked, "Does God answer all prayers?" He answered, "Yes, He does — but sometimes the answer is 'No.'" But a "no" to what would hurt you is actually a "yes" to what will help you. God would not be a very good parent if He/She gave you what would hurt you.

Are you absolutely sure that what you are asking for is in your best interests? If you are not certain, it would be wise indeed to allow Spirit to give you what will help you, especially if that would serve you better than what you believe you need. And it surely will.

The most powerful prayer is one that acknowledges peace of mind as the crowning joy of life. To look upon yourself and your fellows with a happy heart is exactly God's will for you, and therefore we cannot fail if we pray for this. A loving heart and rewarding relationships will far outshine any symbols of love. Why settle for a symbol when you can have the real thing? If you are not sure what to pray for, pray for peace, and the entire universe will support you in finding the object of your heart.

To Give is to Receive: The Integrity of Support

One of the ways that we can strengthen our own integrity is to support others in living their truth. It is not for you to judge another's truth, but to empower them to live it. It is very difficult for any of us to know what is right for another person. They may need an experience that you judge as bad or unnecessary. Encourage your brother to follow his heart, and support him in doing it. If he fails, he will learn why he has failed, and he will be ahead of where he is now. But no matter whether he wins or loses, he will know that he has a friend in you. Then he really wins.

Two of my friends, a married couple, were popular ministers at a very successful church in the Northwest. After years of building the ministry at this church, they were offered a position at a church in Hawaii, which they felt guided to accept. When they announced to the church that they were leaving, the congregants were disappointed, but they chose to congratulate the ministers and wish them well. Although I believe that most of the people in the church would have liked the couple to stay, the congregants supported them in doing what they felt would make them happy. The church people came out and gave them a huge congratulations and going-away Aloha party. A number of people showed up in flowered Aloha shirts and mu-mus. How loved and blessed the ministers felt to be supported in following their heart! Now the ministers are doing well in their new position, and the original church has an excellent new minister who is popular and appreciated by the members. Love does attract miracles.

If you give your friends the permission to follow their truth, you will find the permission to follow your own. When you rejoice in the good that others find, you will rejoice in your own, and others will stand behind you when you have an opportunity to succeed. And even if others do not seem to be there when you feel that you need them, you have One Friend inside your heart Whose strength and support you may *always* count on. When your heart is open, so are the gates of Heaven.

Be a giver, a supporter, a nourisher. Jesus told Peter, "If you love me, then feed my sheep." He meant that we are to nurture and protect and enfold one another with support for spiritual growth. I have had people tell me that at times I was the only person in their life who believed in them enough to encourage them to follow their dream. And that, they said, made all the difference. They went ahead and their life was richer for it. I cannot think of a greater gift that I would like to offer someone, for I cannot imagine a greater gift that I would like to receive. This world *can* be like Heaven. Our love is what makes it so.

The FLOW of GOOD

What to Do
in a Raging River

I am committed to truth, not consistency.
- Mahatma Gandhi

Two men were walking to a neighboring town when both of them fell in a raging river. One man panicked and feverishly attempted to buck the torrents in a struggle to make his way back to shore. In his resistance the river overcame him and he drowned. The other man decided not to fight the flow, and so he relaxed, laid back to the best of his ability, and allowed the river to carry him. Eventually the river deposited him on a calm shore, where he found himself in the town toward which he had been walking.

We are boatmen on the river of life, learning to navigate and enjoy the trip from the source to the ocean. At times it may seem that we do not have much choice about where or how swiftly the river is flowing. But we always have the power to steer our boat. We can direct our vessel in opposition to the current, or we can go with the power of the tide and use it to our advantage. The choice is ours.

The chief characteristic of the river is that it is always alive in the moment. If we are flowing with it, we are one with the force that empowers it. "You must become one with the Force," Yoda told Luke Skywalker. Another skywalker, Richard Bach tells our story:

> Once there lived a village of creatures along the bottom of
> a great crystal river...Each creature in its own manner clung
> tightly to the twigs and rocks of the river bottom, for clinging
> was their way of life, and resisting the current was what each
> had learned from birth. But one creature said at last, "I am
> tired of clinging. Though I cannot see it with my eyes, I trust that
> the current knows where it is going. I shall let go, and let it take

me where it will.''

The other creatures laughed and said, ''Fool...Let go and that current you worship will throw you tumbled and smashed across the rocks.''

Yet in time, as the creature refused to cling again, the current lifted him free from the bottom, and he was bruised and hurt no more.[1]

Getting the Point

At some point in your soul's evolution, you must decide if you are going to live for your own heart's calling or for the dictates of the masses. The world functions according to error, and to be truly happy you must learn to honor and follow the truth that you feel in your own heart. This is especially important when your inner guidance nudges you in a direction other than the one to which most people subscribe. But you must do what you do because it is true for you, regardless of what seems to be true for others.

When I was thirteen years old I celebrated my *bar mitzvah,* one of the most time-honored traditions in the Jewish religion. For years I prepared by learning the Hebrew language, history, and the significant rituals associated with this rite of passage from youth to manhood.

Sitting with my friends in the temple one sabbath morning, I heard my name called to step up to the altar to recite a blessing over the Torah, the great scrolled Bible.

''What should I do when I get up there?'' I whispered to a big brother.

''Just watch what they do, and do as they do,'' he answered.

Soon I found myself standing in the center of the house of worship on a platform with the rabbi, the cantor, and the president of the synagogue, all elders of the temple. Anxiously I recited the blessing and then watched the cantor read from the ancient text. I noticed that he used an ornately carved pointer, a silver tool with a small hand figured into the end. He used this instrument to follow the lettering of the Torah from which he chanted in a haunting melody. When he finished reading he lifted the Torah high above his head, at the sight of which the congregation rose and joined in a traditional chant of praise. Hearkening to my friend's advice, I followed the cantor's lead in word and movement.

The cantor turned his attention to the soft velour cloth upon which the

---

[1] Bach, *Illusions,* p. 6

Torah had lain. Then he began to stroke the table in horizontal movements. The president took his hand and did the same. Then the rabbi came over and performed a like movement over the cloth.

Remembering my friend's advice to watch their cues, and not wanting to be remiss in performing the appropriate rituals, I stepped up to the altar and began to stroke the cloth in exactly the same fashion. I watched the elders' faces to see if I was doing it correctly, and they were pleased.

"Well?" the cantor whispered to me as I finished.

"Well, what?" I whispered back, hoping I hadn't unknowingly committed a sacreligious act.

"Did you find it?" he inquired.

"Find what?"

"The pointer."

The congregation chanted in the background.

"What pointer?"

"The pointer I was using to read from the Torah."

"I didn't know it was missing."

"Of course it is missing. Why do you think we were rubbing the cloth?"

"I thought it was part of the ceremony."

"What, 'part of the ceremony'? We lost the pointer. We thought you were helping us find it."

"I thought I was performing a religious act."

"Only if you believe in pointers."

Now I do believe in pointers — but I am starting to see that they are within my heart, and not on a table.

To Live in the Moment

It takes courage, clarity, and light-heartedness to live fully in the moment. This world is founded on trying to live in the last moment or the next, and very few people very rarely live in the present moment. Have you ever noticed that when you try to repeat an experience that is really great, it usually doesn't work? You have a spontaneous party that knocks everyone's socks off, or you do an inspired impromptu dance for a class, or you come up with an off-the-cuff joke that makes everyone laugh. The next time you tell the joke it sort of works, but not really as well as the first time. That is because it is not really the first time. It is a repeat of the first time, which is called the second time, and unless the energy is just right for it, it will not be as alive as the first time. There is, however, something that will work this time, and that is what the energy, the flow calls for this time. If you can tune into what the current moment wants to express, the energy will *always* be the first time. Life is an ever-expanding flow of first times. This is the secret of eternal youth.

Trusting the Process

I deeply admire people who are willing to trust the process of living as they play at the adventure of learning what this world is all about. Such persons are unafraid to look silly, fail, or be accused of changing their mind. It is no sin to make a mistake. The word "sin" comes from a Greek archery term meaning "to miss the mark." Notice that the definition does not include any sense of fear, eternal damnation, or losing the love of God (which is the only sure thing in all the universe!). All the word says is that you missed the mark. And when you miss the mark all you need to do is take another shot. It's that simple! But we have taken that light notion and made it heavy by our beliefs in heaviness. That is why the letters SIN actually stand for "Self-Inflicted Nonsense."

Life is a game of awakening in which we learn equally from our successes and errors. And all of the errors are worth it when you get it right. The way the game is designed we must keep trying until we get it right. Don't ever worry about making a mistake—you will always get another chance! Everyone who has ever lived on this planet has made plenty of errors, including Jesus. He fell three times under the cross, and he was not ashamed. In *A Course in Miracles* Jesus explains that he has faced, failed under, and overcome every earthly temptation that we face. If he hadn't encountered and risen above the same obstacles that we meet, he would not be in a position to help us overcome them. But he has, and so he stands beside us, happy to walk with us to make our way light. Thank you, our elder brother.

Patricia Sun calls this process "the wobbles:" Imagine you are a kid and you see someone zipping by on a snazzy ten-speed bike. "Wow!" you exclaim, "That sure looks like fun! I wish I could do that!" So you go out and a get a bike, but soon you discover that riding is not as easy as it looks. You get on the bike and immediately you flop on the ground to your right.

---

[2] T, p. 51

"I'm not doing that again!" you vow as you remount.

You start to ride again, and immediately you fall to the ground again, this time to the left.

"That's not it, either!" you discover, a little frustrated, yet still motivated.

On the next try you fall halfway to the right, but this time you catch yourself and shift your weight. But you shift it a little too much, and so you fall halfway to the left before you shift back. Still not perfect, but you're starting to get the idea.

The next time you fall a quarter-way to the right, then to the left, and so on, until after a series of ostensibly clumsy movements you somehow learn the art of balancing and, incidentally, riding a bike.

It is important to understand that *every one of those falls contributed to your ultimate success.* Yes, you may incur some bruises and scrapes in the process, but they are gone after a few days, while the knowledge of how to ride a bike lasts a lifetime. Not a bad deal.

Being Real

What some of us do when we get frustrated and don't seem to be making any progress is to discover that we can put the kickstand down and sit on the bike so that other people will think that we are riding it. It's called "looking cool." This works for a while, but sooner or later it gets very boring — and besides, we are not getting anywhere.

So we look cool in our relationships, our bodies, our families, our jobs, our religions, our nations. We say the right words, know the right people, wear the attractive clothes, utter the current catch-phrases, espouse the popular philosophies — except meanwhile we are dying inside. Sooner or later we realize that we are not really getting anywhere, and we decide that we'd rather be real than look cool. We want to learn to ride so much that we are willing to tell the truth about our not being able to ride now, if that will help us get where we are going. So, with the loving assistance of those who have already ridden, we pull up the kickstand and really go for it — not just make believe we are going for it, but we really make up our mind that riding is what we want.

Then something really miraculous happens. Somehow, through some process bigger then ourself, we learn. We learn to get from one place to the next by being honest about where we are. We see that falling down and getting up again and keeping trying is more satisfying than sitting in a seat going nowhere. And we wonder why we ever tried to kid ourselves. We discover that life is about learning to pull up the kickstand and we ride.

The Courage to Change

Flowing with the river of life gives us the freedom to be who we are and do what we feel guided to do in any given moment, unshackled by the past, expectations, or fear. It is only when we crawl out on the skinny branches that we can see how far the tree goes and we can grab the fruit that no one else can reach.

I knew a wonderful man who had the courage to change his life and his name as he went along. When I first heard of him he was called "Baba Gil." He sat in Central Park in New York City as a silent yogi, communicating only in a language of hand signals that he had devised. He and his friends slept on rooftops, lived simply, and served freely all who came to them for love and guidance.

Several years later Gil renounced the life of a yogi and became a Christian. It was at his retreat land in Ithaca, New York that I first met Gil, who by then had changed his name to "Freedom." He had given all the people in his community colorful names like "Precious," "Fountain," and "Praise." How melodic it was to hear those names being called throughout the day at this peaceful community! At this retreat site Freedom taught the power of following the life of Christ, living humbly in sharing and service. It was a marvelous, life-changing experience for me to be with him for one weekend.

Later I learned that Freedom had moved to Israel and become an Orthodox Jew, and he was studying the Torah with learned rabbis.

Now some might say that this young man couldn't make up his mind, but I would say that he had the courage to be whatever he was with the richest involvement. Whatever he was, it was not phony; his motive was sincerely to know and share God in the highest form that he knew. Why should it matter if he changed roles as he grew? If one accepts the idea of reincarnation, we are told that we go through different roles in different lives, wearing different hats according to what our soul needs to learn and teach. Why, then, should it be surprising for one man to go through several different experiences in one lifetime?

We are living in times of rapid change. Many metaphysical teachers tell us that life experiences have been speeded up so that we can learn many lessons in a short time. If we are not aware of this important process we may believe that something is wrong with us for going through dramatic changes, while in fact all we are doing is learning quickly.

Many of us in this generation, for example, have gone through two or three marriages or significant relationships, and we wonder why this is happening. We may even begin to doubt our sanity or self-worth. We experience these changes not because there is something wrong with us; to the contrary, we have had the courage to learn and grow a great deal in a short time. Praise be to us for being willing to open to greater love!

Hilda has explained it this way: "Lessons that in the past would have taken a lifetime to learn, now are being learned in just a few years. In past lives it took a whole lifetime to be married to someone, learn the appropriate lessons, and work out a relationship. Now that is happening in a small portion of that time. It is like going through two or three lifetimes in one."

Adopting this view of the changes in our life is not to support running away from a relationship before it is complete, but it is to offer the possibility that if a relationship is indeed complete, the universe will move us naturally on to our next experience, and we need not harbor guilt feelings about having moved through the lessons in a shorter time than we expected. To know whether you are running scared or are complete, you must look within your own heart and ask the indwelling Spirit for your personal answer. As the Yaqui Indian mentor Don Juan told Carlos Casteneda, "You can leave only when you are free of fear or ambition."[3]

To further illuminate this lesson, Ramtha tells us, *"Love yourself...And listen to what self says, what it needs to feel, and then pursue it, heartily, until you're bored with it. Boredom is a sign from your soul that you have learned all there is to learn from an experience, and that it is time to go on to another adventure. When you listen only to the feelings within you, then you are free to become in this moment whatever you choose to become.'*[4]

Great Love Relationships

This is perhaps a fertile juncture at which to discuss the "'til death do us part" clause in the traditional marriage ceremony. This is, of course, a

[3] Carlos Casteneda, *The Teachings of Don Juan, A Yaqui Way of Knowledge*, Ballentine Books, 1968
[4] Weinberg, *Ramtha*, p. 133

commonly applied sanction against divorce. But we need to acknowledge that there are many forms of death: physical death, emotional death, and spiritual death, for example, all equally real in our experience. It seems to me to be a rather arbitrary delineation to choose physical death alone as the one that is legal to do us part. Relationships are born and relationships die, and a relationship can be dead long before one of the physical bodies is. In fact, physical death doesn't have much power to change a relationship at all, for the realm in which relationships exist is that of the mind, and minds always outlive bodies.

The death of a partner is no guarantee of the completion of a relationship. Just because someone leaves this world does not mean that the relationship is ended. Because relationships are spiritual lessons, they are complete only when our spirit is at peace. The fact that a body is gone does not mean that the lesson has been learned. In fact, I wonder if the "'til the death do us part" clause may actually encourage people to leave their body instead of heal the relationship! Someone once said that death is one way out of a bad marriage, chosen as an avenue that seems easier than confronting the issues in life. Now this certainly does not mean that anyone who dies is doing so just to get out of a marriage, but it may mean that some of us have chosen disease rather than discussion. Perhaps, just perhaps, if we were willing to face the relationship and bring it into the light, or to leave the relationship in dignity in life, we would not feel that we had to escape into death. As *A Course in Miracles* tells us, death is not to be equated with peace; only love can be equated with peace.

There have been many, many great love relationships that have *increased* in power after the physical parting of the pair; many relationships have been healed after one of the partners has passed on, because the surviving mate had a change in his or her consciousness. In such a wonderful awakening there grows *more* love after the other person has left this world. Bodies actually have very little to do with real relationships.

No Real Separation

Sometimes physical separation can be a very viable avenue for healing a relationship. In fact, if the temporary or permanent distancing of two bodies contributes to the emotional healing of one or both of the couple, separation is actually a misnomer, for the end result is greater spiritual *union*. Once again we see that it is not what bodies do that makes love, but what the spirit in those bodies is feeling.

If one or both persons are dying emotionally in the relationship, it is no longer a relationship, but a litany to sacrifice. Destructiveness is not a worthy goal of the Children of God. A relationship in which one or both partners are suffering must be brought quickly to the One who can heal it. At such a time it is extremely important to remember that God's will for your relationship is only joy, and that if you are feeling anything less than peace you have forgotten that you deserve only love.

It is certainly possible that the relationship has offered both of you all that you can receive at this level of your understanding, and struggling to keep it alive would be as futile and heartbreaking as attempting to keep a loved one on earth when they have chosen to pass on to the next life.

The ending of a marriage or relationship has very often *improved* the relationship. Many persons have reported to me that the official breaking up of a relationship was actually a step toward the beginning of a deeper and more productive friendship with their now ex-husband, -friend, or -lover! At any given moment we do not know the true purpose of any experience. Temporary separation can often lead to a long-term healing of the spirit.

Of what use to God is a relationship in which two people live under one roof harboring deep feelings of loneliness, fear, and separation? These are not the feelings that the Children of Light were born to know. Though we can become accustomed to alienation, we will never be satisfied with it. What seems to be the death of a relationship may just be a sleep. Like the trees in the winter that have lost their leaves and appear dead though they are not, relationships appearing to be dead are simply going through a season of transformation, a temporary period of apparent darkness that will ultimately culminate in deeper bonding. *A Course In Miracles* tells us that it is the destiny of all relationships to become holy.[5]

All possible attempts should be made to find harmony and healing with your mate. This was, and remains the purpose of your sharing your path. Your healing always involves releasing the expectations and projections that you have brought into the relationship. At some point you must acknowledge that your mate is not your mother or father, and rejoice in the awareness that your partner is a beautiful being in his or her own light.

In times of challenge in a relationship it is advisable for each or both of the partners to do what they need to do to regain the true function of relationship, which is to bring greater and greater creativity into the activities of their life. A physical separation may renew the spirit of the relationship in the direction of re-joining physically, or it may renew the self toward moving in a new direction. Or, after taking the issue into meditation, it may be revealed that no separation is necessary. The important change is that the goal of supporting one another in greater aliveness has replaced the goal of deepened fear, and this is the key that opens the door to healing.

The spiritual path calls for an extremely keen sense of intuition and stark honesty. At a point of crisis or confusion you must turn to the Voice of the Holy Spirit within you, and ask for help. But you must be willing to hear His answer, and not the one you brought before you asked the question. Be assured that His answer will bring far greater peace than yours. If your answer brought you peace you would not need to turn to Him for His. And be you glad that He does have the answer in which everyone involved will win. You will go on from here with the realization that the One who has shown you the way walks with you always.

The Psychic Integrity of Children

Almost always there is a fear to end a marriage or relationship out of concern for the children. This is a most valid concern. Loving and supporting our children is one of the most liberating and healing lessons of a lifetime. It is true that our children are gifts from God.

One of the questions that we may overlook when becoming anxious about the future is, "What is it like for the kids *now?*" Children, like all of us, are very psychic, often moreso than adults. We can be sure that they are well aware of all the feelings and dynamics of a strained (or wonderful) relationship, though we may never say a word out loud about it. Making believe that nothing is wrong can create more confusion and distress for the child than openly discussing the situation. When efforts are made to conceal the difficulties, the child is learning that what is happening is so bad that it needs to be hidden. This can be a much more painful and confusing lesson than that mommy and daddy are not getting along well and they are having a hard time being together. Believe me, they know it anyway.

At such a time of strain, there are two actions that will carry you through all kinds of flak: *forgiveness* and *vision*. You must forgive yourself and your partner for what you perceive to be your errors. Do not berate yourself or your partner for not being totally enlightened saints. If you were, you would not be here in the first place. Remember that earth is a school, and you came

218

here to master your lessons. When a challenging lesson comes up we should give thanks, for this means that we are ready to master it and become even grander in spirit.

Second, you must have the *vision* to see how beautiful you, your partner, and your family are, no matter what the outer circumstances would indicate. Outer circumstances are deceptive, and you will not win by judging the situation as what it seems to be. Remember that the children as well as the parents are whole and wise beings. To treat any of you like you are small, fearful, or unaware is to ignore the truth of your wisdom. Remember that all of you know the way out of the forest and into peace, and you are here to support and empower one another in drawing that wisdom into action.

Love is the Guide

A piece of paper does not make a marriage, a divorce, a parent, a teacher, or an expert. The only proof of a person being born is that he is alive, and no amount of documentation or lack of it could prove otherwise. Such is the impotence of a parchment in marriage or divorce. In all of these situations the truth in the heart of the relationship far supercedes a signature, and in the case of marriage it is clear that many persons are not married even though they hold a certificate saying they are. At the same time many persons who have never gone to a justice of the peace have much justice of peace in their relationship, being deeply married by virtue of the commitment they hold toward one another in their hearts. It is also obvious that a relationship can continue, for better or worse, long after a judge says it is over. Marriage is a state of mind and heart, and as we honor the truth that lives within our being we move into greater clarity about 'who we are and what we are to do.

I hope you will not read that I am encouraging marriage, divorce, separation, or any particular form of relationship. I am encouraging whatever will bring real peace to the soul in any given circumstance. The Holy Spirit does not have a fixed position on anything except to support whatever creates happiness and harmony in one's inner and outer life. It is the rational, linear mind that believes that one way always produces one result, while the Holy Spirit knows that results are quite particular to the situation. Love alone sees that each act is to be judged not by the form that it takes, but by the peace that we feel.

The End of Pain

All pain is born of resistance. Wherever there is pain, whether it is physical, emotional, mental, or spiritual, you can be sure that there is a resistance behind it. To know this is to understand that the way to be free of pain is to let go of resistance. Mahatma Gandhi underwent a surgical operation without anesthesia; he had no pain because his whole life was an ode to non-resistance. Skydivers are taught to land in a crouch and roll to ride with the energy of the impact. The same truth is demonstrated in the martial arts, which are based upon taking the force delivered by the opponent and using it to one's own advantage instead of fighting back. What flows, goes; what resists, persists.

One afternoon I attended a meeting at which there was a man who had hurt himself in a bicycle fall on his way there. His knee was hurting him, and so we invited him to lie down on the floor for a group healing. All of us surrounded him, placed our hands gently upon him, and visualized him filled and surrounded by healing white light. As we did so he began to relax. I could see a change beginning to happen in his body. I watched his face become softer and lighter, until the tension and discomfort left him completely. I must say he looked quite beatific! It was an amazing transformation to watch, and a powerful lesson to learn.

As he was resting quietly, these words came into my awareness: *"No mind, no pain."* In other words, when his mind had removed itself from the pain, by placing his attention on a healing light, the pain was gone.

We always get more of what we think about, and we are psychically tied to what we resist. When we hate someone we carry them with us wherever we go, for our mind draws them to us like a big fishing line. *A Course in Miracles* tells us that if we keep someone in prison (in our thoughts) we must stay there with them to make sure they don't escape. We imprison *ourself* with thoughts of hatred. Every judgement we hold is a bar of our cell, and our desire to be right is the lock. Here it is easy to see that forgiveness is the key to our freedom. When you release someone from the prison of your angry thoughts about them, it is actually yourself that you are pardoning. Then both of you are free. By the same principle we can liberate ourself from any kind of pain simply by releasing it from our mind and turning the entire situation over to Spirit.

It is never our job to punish anyone. When we punish anyone physically or mentally we punish ourself, for in doing so we teach ourself that punishment is an effective way to heal, which it never is. And more harmfully, we reinforce the idea in our mind that we and the other person deserve punishment. You can be sure that the next time you commit the crime for which you would have the other punished (and you most certainly will commit it, for you are attempting to punish him for your sense of sin) you will feel guilty, and then both of you have lost. Here the *Course* tells us, *"Do not teach your brother that he is anything you would not want to be."* For your own peace of mind free the world, and you will be free with it.

With All Your Heart

Forms, rituals, and institutions are born of high intention, but they can be perpetuated by fear. We invent rituals to help us remember a beautiful feeling of connectedness with God, but unless our hearts are turned to Heaven as we enter into them, they become empty shells. Jesus said, "Do not pray with long exhortations. Pray with all your heart." If we trusted our hearts enough we would be in a constant state of prayer, for we would feel the aliveness of every moment and we would want to give thanks for it. True prayer is not invoked by one's lips, but through one's being. Those truly in love need no coercion to say, "I love you," and those truly in prayer do not need a plan to make love with God in every activity of their day. To call one activity "prayer" and another activity something else would blaspheme the truth that every moment is an invitation to live in Paradise. Those who have found their way back to the Garden realize they have never left It. And now they walk consciously. The gentleness of their being is a blessing to God, and they glorify Spirit by shining His love into the world as they pass through it. They know that Heaven is already present on earth, and they teach it simply by being happy here.

The Coming of Age of Strength

We were not meant to live in pain. We have not realized this because we have never experimented with letting go of our pain long enough to learn that there is no value in it. We cannot have strength and pain at the same time.

There is no virtue in suffering.

Many of us are experiencing a growing up of the soul, an awakening to our own strength, a celebration of the integrity of our own perfect being. We are being loosed from the path of recipes, external gurus, and standard formats, and turning toward the wisdom of our own inner knowing. To one accustomed to finding cues from without, this can be very disconcerting, harrowing, and even terrifying. Yet the plan is wrought with full wisdom, for God seeks to nurture Children who find full divinity and happiness within their own self.

The one truth about life is that it is alive, and this means it is constantly becoming something new and better. The universe never moves backward. Perception of backwardness is a sign of fear of forwardness. Anyone who has ever advanced in life has learned the joy and the adventure of launching into new territory. It is said that "a ship in the harbor is safe, but that is not what ships are for." There is wisdom in flexibility, and greatness in innocent acceptance. When you accept life, you will have accepted yourself, because life is what you are.

Don't stop now. You will advance if you let go of the twigs and rocks you are hanging on to, and let the river take you home.

When you have learned how to decide with God, all decisions become as easy and as right as breathing. There is no effort, and you will be led as gently as if you were being carried down a quiet path in summer.[6]

---

[6] T, p. 260

The Pig of God

Trust would settle every problem now.
- A Course in Miracles[1]

A man was driving up a winding mountain road, ever cautious of the twists and turns on the narrow precipice. Approaching a hairpin curve at the steepest point, he was startled by the unexpected *vrummm!* of a little red sports car as it whizzed past him from the hidden side of the bend. The speeding roadster cut him off, missing his vehicle by inches, and caused him to veer toward the mountain, where he came to a halt just short of the rocks.

As if that were not enough of an insult, the driver of the other car, a portly woman with a tense face, raised her arm toward him and shouted, *"Pig!"* as she passed.

Infuriated, the man shook his fist at her, called her *"Sow!"* and rounded the turn from which she had come, where he ran headlong into a pig sitting on his side of the road.

How quick we are to assume that someone is trying to hurt us, when actually they are attempting to help. You can probably identify with the driver who mistook a blessing for an attack. Indeed much of our lives has been steeped in fear that others have been out to get us, when actually they were serving us in ways that were not obvious to us at the time. One might say that we have suffered from a deep sense of paranoia, the fear that the world is out to get us.

But our challenging experiences are actually opportunities for us to choose again. If we are willing to see the good in a situation, we will be less likely to be afraid the next time that circumstance arises.

A friend of mine was driving home late one night in New York City. When she stopped at a red light she noticed a man in the car next to her trying to get her attention. He was driving a big red Cadillac convertible with a playboy bunny symbol hanging from the rear view mirror, and loud music

---
[1] T, p. 519

blaring from several speakers. He leaned over his velour seat cover, smiled through his sunglasses, and waved to her.

"I can do without this tonight," my friend thought to herself. She ignored him, waited for the light to turn green, and stepped on the gas.

When she reached the next red light, there he was again. Again he tapped on the window and tried to get her to look at him. Once again she looked the other way and drove on.

At the next light the scene repeated itself, but this time she decided she had to do something about this annoying man. She locked her door, rolled down her window, and asked what he wanted.

"Your lights are off!" was his message.

"Thank you!" was hers, and gratefully she drove home.

Do you believe that life is *for* you, or *against* you? This is the basic question that you must answer. But answer it honestly, for in so doing you will discover the perceptions in your mind from which your whole world has arisen. Your thoughts do not spring from your experiences; your experiences spring from your thoughts. Beware what thoughts you allow to root in your holy mind, Child of God. You have the power to create an entire life from the tiniest thoughts. Be vigilant, and think with God.

Creative Investment

Trust is like a muscle. You must exercise it to enjoy its benefits. *"Use it or lose it"* is a principle that applies to the psychic world as well as the physical. When you open your mind to the greatest possibilities of every situation, you will grow younger and more alive with each experience. Joy is the natural consequence of trusting, and those who practice faith are rewarded with success to match their vision.

If you do not exercise your capacity to trust, you will find yourself sealed in a little ball of protectiveness, and you will wonder why life has treated you so harshly. When we close ourself down to trusting, we shrivel up and become crabby. In fear, we attempt to wall other people away from us, but the net effect is that we seal ourself in. Hugh Prather said, "Letting other people in is pretty much a matter of not spending the energy to keep them out."[2] Defensiveness requires a tremendous investment of energy to push other people away and maintain our lonely outpost of isolation. That

---

[2]Prather, *Notes to Myself*

energy could be used for contacting hearts, healing yourself and others, and celebrating your whole life. The choice of what you do with your energy is up to you. That is what free will is. You are not free to determine how it will all turn out, for God has promised a happy outcome to all situations. But you are free to grump and groan and delay your awakening. As *A Course in Miracles* asks us, "Why wait for Heaven?"[3]

We hurt ourself when we decide about a person or situation beforehand. "Prejudice" means "pre-judgement," or assuming that you know the outcome of a situation before it happens. What guarantee do you have that anything will turn out like it did before? You judge the present on the basis of the past, and there is no basis for this. We continually recreate the past not because the present is like the past, but because we expect it to be, and so we set up situations and recreate events. Then we complain that the universe is working against us — when all the while we were working against ourselves!

But it doesn't have to be that way. We can allow each moment to be fresh and new and different than ever before. Just think: *you can end any destructive pattern of your relationships right now!* You can start over and have your relationships be fresh and alive, totally untainted by your history. Your history is not your destiny. When you place your well-being in the hands of God, you will find your future miraculously different than the past. All of this is within your power to create right now.

The Inner Guardian

Trusting does not imply that you must trust, agree to, or do everything that anyone asks or tells you to do. Nor does it mean that you should do anything that would hurt you or make you or anyone else unhappy; that would indeed be foolish, and it is not necessary. Trust means honoring the voice of the Holy Spirit *within* you. Every "should I?" question can be answered by turning within. The Holy Spirit will tell you quite clearly what book to read, which job to take, where to live, what teacher to study with, who to marry or not marry, what school to enroll your children in, and any other question the thinking mind can conjure up. But you must be willing to listen. If you do not hearken unto the Voice of Peace, you cannot blame God for your errors. "If you cannot hear the Voice for God, it is because you do

---

[3] W, p. 347

not choose to listen."[4] And once you do choose to listen, all of Heaven and earth will rush to fill your every need, for you have chosen to take the hand of the One who knows the way to peace.

Jesus said, "Be as clever as serpents and as gentle as doves." If your mind is peaceful and relaxed through trusting the process of living, you will be open to guidance from the divine mind *within* you. This inner voice is always available to light your way safely in the presence of unscrupulous persons or dangerous situations.

One afternoon I went out to lunch with my friend Denise Cooney, a free-spirited healer who channels excellent psychic writing and counseling. Outside the restaurant I met a fellow who asked me if I wanted to buy a car stereo. Ironically, I was looking for a car stereo at the time, and I accepted his invitation to look at one he had for sale.

He took Denise and me to the trunk of his car, which he opened to reveal a wealth of stereo equipment. The fellow explained to me that he worked at a store on Route 46, and his manager wanted to clear out these models to make way for new stock. I asked him if I could bring the stereo back to the store if I had any problems with it.

"Well, uh, not exactly," he hesitated. "Actually, these models come from the warehouse, and my boss doesn't want people coming to the warehouse. But I'm sure you'll have no problem with it. This here is an expensive unit, and I can give it to you for only $140."

I looked at the unit. It was one of the cheapest, tinniest stereos I have ever seen. Most stores would probably sell it for about $39.95.

Denise leaned over to me and whispered in my ear, "I don't think you should buy this thing."

I leaned back and whispered, "I don't need a psychic to tell me that!"

But I really enjoyed this fellow. He was a perfect flim-flam man. He rapped on and on about the high quality of his product, and he had an answer for every question I asked him. I was not really interested in the stereo, but I was very impressed with his pitch. I love anyone who is masterful at what they do. I prefer a really good bad guy over a mediocre good guy. If someone is really good at being bad, I honor them as a pure character. (Darth Vader is one of my favorite characters. He's so deliciously evil! This stereo salesman must have graduated from the same school.)

"Well, I don't think I'm going to buy the stereo," I told him, "but I

---

[4] T, p. 57

really love your rap. I must tell you that I think you're a great salesman. I bet you'll do well at whatever you put your mind to."

I shook his hand and Denise and I walked on down Speedwell Avenue. When we rounded the first corner, both of us broke up into hysterics.

"Wasn't he great?" I asked Denise.

"He was phenomenal!" she agreed. "If I ever go into business I'll hire him as my sales rep!"

Both of us truly appreciated this fellow, and we held no grievance toward him. He was playing his part as a great con-man, and it was up to us as to how we wanted to play with him. We chose simply to enjoy him.

Divine Protection

One night a friend of mine was awakened by the sound of a burglar crawling through his apartment window. My friend got up, turned on the light, and spoke to the startled intruder.

"You don't have to break in here like that," he told the man. "I will help you if I can, without your needing to rob me. What is happening in your life that is making you feel you need to steal?"

The burglar sat down and told the man about his life. The conversation ended with my friend giving the man some money and walking him out the front door.

My friend Betty is another person who practices the presence of God. Once she loaned her car to a hitchhiker. The young man that she picked up hitchhiking asked her if she knew the way to a certain town farther than where she was going. "I'm going to patch things up with my wife," he told her. "I've decided to try to make it work this time." Betty offered him her car, and gratefully he accepted. He dropped Betty off at her home, and he went on with the car (a nice one, at that!).

Hours went by, and the man did not return. "I wondered if it was the right thing to do," Betty later confessed to me. "Then, late that evening he showed up at the door with his wife and a little child. Tearfully they thanked me and told me they were taking a new step in their relationship. He returned the keys and blessed me."

Betty also rarely locks her car. Sometimes she leaves the keys on the seat. Yet her car has never been stolen or tampered with. "I just put the car in God's hands," Betty explains. Betty's powerfully faithful outlook and practice reminded me of a statement made to me by one of the boys I used to work with in a youth counseling center. This fellow had stolen a number of things. "Locks are for honest people," he told me. "If someone really wants to steal something, a lock is not going to stop them."

I am thinking, too, of Peace Pilgrim, the saintly minister who travelled thousands of miles on foot to act as an emissary of peace. This noble woman accepted rides and lodging only when they were offered. On several occasions men picked her up in cars, and took her to places where they had less than lofty intentions. "But no harm ever came to me," Peace tells. "I would begin talking to them about who I was, or I would but look into their eyes for a moment, and they realized what I stand for. My divinity and my purpose were my protection."

Belief Creates Experience

You may, of course, be able to cite examples of cases in which you trusted and you felt hurt as a result. All of us have had the experience of feeling that our faith has not been justified. But we find examples of what we want to be true. If you are afraid and you feel you need protection you will find proof that this is so. And if you want to believe that you are protected by virtue of your thoughts and your divinity, you shall find abundant examples to support that belief. And you will create more and more experiences to demonstrate that what you believe is correct. You can create an entire world and have many people live in it with you if your mind is sufficiently dedicated to an idea!

Belief does not stem from examples. Examples arise from belief. Therefore choose well what you would believe.

All Experiences Lead to Awakening

Even if you do seem to get "taken," there is a way to look at such an experience that will bring awakening and healing.

A fellow named Bob telephoned Hilda from California, and he complained that he had been swindled by an unscrupulous auto mechanic. "I paid $400 for this job, and then when I went around the corner I found out I could have gotten it done elsewhere for $75! What do you think I should do?" he anxiously asked.

"Let me ask you this, Bob," Hilda replied. "You take a lot of consciousness trainings and workshops, don't you?''

"Yes, that's right.''

"Well, then, imagine that someone offered you a training in discernment, in which you would be taught how to make wise choices about dealing in the business world, choices which would save you money in the long run. Let's say this course was being given over two weekends at a cost of $325. And imagine that you would be absolutely guaranteed to increase your sensitivity to feeling the vibrations of people and making correct decisions in your financial affairs. Would you take the course?''

"You bet!'' Bob answered quickly.

"Then you should be grateful to this auto mechanic. You got the course in one afternoon.''

The Answer to Fear

At the Human Unity Conference in Hawaii in 1985 Bishop Antonius Markos of Africa gave an address on world peace. He related an experience he had in his motel room.

"There was a bold sign in my room that said, ''Please lock your suitcase.'' So I began to. But something in me felt out of line as I was doing so. I felt that I was attempting to protect myself out of fear. It dawned on me that me locking my suitcase was not much different than the governments of the world arming themselves with nuclear weapons. They claim that the reason they have nuclear weapons is to protect themselves. From who? From other countries who have nuclear weapons! And why do those countries have those armaments? To protect themselves from the countries who are protecting themselves from them! And so it goes on.

"The problem is not nuclear weapons, but fear. It is the consciousness of fear that leads us to believe that we need to protect ourselves. Perhaps if one country would stop protecting itself, it would be an example to the world, and we could start a chain reaction of love. And perhaps if each of us would begin disarmament in our own heart, the nations of the world would follow suit.''

Where Freedom Lies

If your world is to change — and it is — there is but one place that trust can begin, and that is in your own mind. If you wait for life to demonstrate to you that it is trustworthy, you shall have long cobwebs upon your cobwebs before you realize that life gives you only the gifts that you bring to it. The only way to prove trust is to practice it. A simple principle, is it not? Yet your practice requires persistent exercise, for you have succeeded in convincing yourself that you need protection from something "out there." There is nothing out there. But you have proved that there is by the amount of effort you have invested in keeping it away from you! A man who builds a fortress to protect himself from demons believes that his walls are affording him safety. But he certainly cannot be considered free. His freedom lies only in removing his walls, for only then can he recognize that he was free without them.

The same mind that hypnotized you into believing that your fears were worth heeding, can teach you that your love is even more worth heeding. That mind is none other than your own, and now is the only moment you can change its direction. That change is not accomplished by force or struggle, but by opening. You will gain far more by releasing your need for defense than by attempting to acquire safety. You cannot acquire what you already have. But you can recognize and acknowledge it. You can fling your dark dreams to the wind, and step forward through the open door that leads to the light. Then, and only then, can you say that you are home free.

There is a plot, and indeed the world is out to get us. But it is not a plot to hurt us at all; it is a plan of the greatest love in all the universe. The game is simple: you keep playing until you realize that there is only love. Then you keep playing until everyone else finds love within their own heart. When everyone knows that there is nothing to fear, the nightmare is over and the celebration begins.

The Final Embarrassment

"My attack thoughts are attacking my invulnerability."
- A Course in Miracles[1]

All of us have had our embarrassing moments. When I was six years old the landlord of our apartment complex called me into our kitchen where he was visiting with some of the ladies in the neighborhood. He beckoned me to come close to him, so he could whisper something in my ear. When I did, he snatched the drawstring of my pajama pants, and dropped them to the floor. I ran out of the room screaming, terribly embarrassed.

When I was in junior high school one of the "coolest" things to do was to go to a high school dance. One Friday night I was invited by some friends to go to the local high school dance, and I was ecstatic. There was a live rock 'n' roll band who wore matching sequined jackets, rhythmically bopped and weaved from side to side, and played loud electric guitar music. As far as I was concerned, I was in Heaven to be in such an "in" place. I sort of wandered around with my friends (I was too shy to dance) and acted cool.

Can you imagine how nerdy I felt when a voice came over the loud-speaker announcing, "Alan Cohen...Please go to the door. Your mother is waiting for you."

The pits!

It seemed like all the kids laughed as I slinked out the door. If there is one thing a fourteen-year-old boy at a high school dance does not want, it is for his mother to come and fetch him from a high school dance in front of his friends.

Years later I found myself sitting on the stage at Hilda's class one Thursday evening. I looked out at the three hundred faces in the audience, and I was excited about performing for them.

"Hilda is ready for us to play now," I heard a whisper over my shoulder. I picked up my guitar and walked to center stage with Toni, the singer I was to accompany.

---

[1] W, p. 40

The first verse went impeccably, and the crowd was pleased. It was a great feeling to have them enjoy the music! Toni was energized, too.

Then, about halfway through the second verse, Toni did something quite alarming. In between her lines she reached over, grabbed my guitar at the frets, and held the strings down so I could not continue playing. Then she told me in a loud voice that everyone could hear, "You're playing the wrong chords!"

Well, I was never so embarrassed in all my life! How dare she do that in front of all those people! I just wanted to shrivel up in my seat and slither off the stage like a little snake. What nerve! I sat there and fumed for a while.

After a few minutes a thought occurred to me. The thought was that I actually might have been playing the wrong chords. (I hadn't considered that before.) Reflecting upon it further, I realized Toni was right. That made me feel even worse. I sat there and felt dumb.

A few minutes later another notion came into my awareness, a thought that came from a different voice than the one that was embarrassed. This voice asked me a question.

"Think, Alan," it gently counselled, *"What is it in you that is embarrassed?"*

Hmmm.

"What is it in you that cares what these people think about you? What part of you is beating yourself because you made a mistake? Who is it that is upset?"

Those were quite some questions. As I thought about it I realized that the only part of me that could be embarrassed was my ego. The ego is concerned only with appearances, and the ego really comes to life when appearances come into play. The ego consistently chooses form over content. And we always lose when we see with our eyes instead of our heart.

At the same time I realized that there was more to me than my ego. There was a part of me that could never be hurt; that while the ego was ranting and raving and doing its little dance, there was a place in me — the real me — that could never be touched by any embarrassment. My real self rests safe and secure in the sanctuary of peace within my heart, and nothing that seems to happen can take peace from me as long as I remember who I am.

Can you imagine how freeing it is to find out that you are not something that you were afraid you were? It is like being let out of prison, or being pardoned from execution. And then realizing that it was only you who put yourself there in the first place!

I got so high on this awareness that I just wanted to hug Toni and tell her, "Thank you." The Spirit within me was soaring! While I felt smaller in the public eye, I actually felt freer and greater within myself. It was one of those "Aha!" realizations, like a light breaking through the clouds.

Fifteen minutes later the ego came back to remind me that I had done something foolish not long ago. While I had quelled the ego's initial barrage, there were some reserves hiding in the hills. I looked out over the audience and saw them rapt in Hilda's lecture. The voice of wisdom spoke within me again: *"Alan,"* it laughingly explained, *"No one cares about your mistake as much as you do. Nobody else is thinking about it anymore except you. Everyone else forgot about it the moment it was over. And once you forget about it, it is done. You don't need to keep beating yourself. You are free to get off the cross right now. You put yourself there, and now you can take yourself off. You are free to be happy now."*

I looked out over the audience. I gazed across the sea of smiling faces, and I saw nothing but love. Love for me. Love for life. Love for God and good. And love for the blessing of being in that gift of a class. I, too, could enjoy that precious blessing — but I would have to forgive myself as they had forgiven me.

As I looked at their faces I realized that they were not my enemies or my accusors, but my friends. More than anything else they wanted me to win. I realized that they, too, had probably made mistakes like mine, and they could identify with me. "Who has judged you, now?" Jesus asked the adulterous woman. "No one, sire," she answered. "And neither do I judge you," he told her, and he gave her her release.

I don't think I've ever felt embarrassed like that again. That was pretty much the end of embarrassment in my life. Now, whenever feelings of fear of opinion or embarrassment come up, I ask myself, *"What is it in me that is embarrassed?"* The answer always comes, *"the ego."* Then I smile as I remember that my spirit could never be hurt, and I am free.

The Mirror's Gift

Terry Cole-Whittaker has written a best-selling book called, *What You Think of Me is None of My Business.* It is one of those books from which you can learn a great deal just from the title.

Fear of other people's opinions is actually a reflection of your fear of *your own* opinions. Whatever you are concerned that other people think about you, you are concerned about what *you* think about you. The world is our mirror. What we see out there reflects the thoughts that we harbor within our own mind. But we are not ready to take responsibility for these thoughts, and so we attract people to act out what we are thinking. When we can see the persons in our life as mirrors of our own thoughts, we can learn about how we see ourself, and ultimately take complete responsibility for our life and our healing.

The way to heal our fear of other persons' opinions does not lie in attempting to change their opinions. This would be like a slave trying to escape from slavery by pleasing his master more. That would only cause the master to value the slave's bondage even more. The way to be free is to leave your master and become your own master.

The only way to resolve fear of opinion or criticism is to *heal your own mind* about the issues that are sensitive for you. If you were clear and comfortable about the things that others criticize about you, their opinions could not phase you in the least. But when someone hurts you with their thoughts or words about you, *there is a part of your mind that believes they are correct.* If I call you a frog, and you know that you are not a frog, then you will not think anything further of the idea, for it is clearly a misperception on my part. But if you harbor any doubt in your mind that you may indeed be a frog, my statement will irritate you and probably begin to work on you even after I have left your presence. You will be forced to confront your thoughts that you may be a frog. And that is wonderful, for it is the beginning of the healing that must ultimately result in your awareness of who you truly are.

Thus we see what a great service others offer us when they insult us, for they cause us to face our own doubts and judgements about ourself. Those veils must be lifted before you can see the face of Christ, which is your own. You cannot know that you are the Christ if you think you are a frog. Christhood and froghood have nothing in common, and you had better learn quickly who you are, or else you are doomed to swim around in the swamp for a while. You are free to hop out now and become a prince. Do not wait for some lovely maiden to come along and kiss you. Kiss yourself. Then you release yourself from the spell of disbelief in your own reality. Not that many women are interested in frogs these days. You stand a better chance of finding a princess if you acknowledge that you are a prince.

Take Back Your Power

You have been living in a dream. You have been hypnotized into believing that you are small, that you can be affected by the outside world, and that there is something "out there" that you do not already have. Take back your power now. You have sold yourself out, and it is about time you reeled in the strings that you have given other people to control you. Puppethood does not befit a Child of God. You were born to create marvelous productions instead of bouncing around like a floundering extra in someone else's show.

Wake up! You are not who you thought you were! And be thankful, for you are far greater than you have been taught. You have been taught mostly by people who do not know who they are. How, then, do you expect to learn of your magnanimity? You have studied with teachers who needed to learn what they were teaching. You have gone to therapists whose insanity exceeded your own. You have thrown yourself at the feet of gurus who were still living in darkness. No wonder you have not learned! You have had some very poor teachers!

You cannot fault your teachers for not teaching you what you were not willing to learn. If you were ready to be enlightened you would have found your way to a Christ. And you have. But your vigilance has been wanting. You already know the truth; you have just been taking your time about acknowledging and living it. And that is your right.

But it is also your right to choose Heaven now. There is not one further stone that blocks your way, unless you believe that healing comes from somewhere other than your own mind. Fear will take you down a dark and lonely detour, and you will feel prey to the vultures that rustle in the night. You will be frightened by the slightest sound, including the echoes of your own twisted thoughts. Yet at every intersection in the tangled forest you may choose to find your way out by following the way of forgiveness. There are no depths to which forgiveness will not reach its comforting hand and lift you far above the forest, to be trapped in darkness no more.

The doors to the Kingdom are opened to you. The keys are held by no one other than you. You may deny your identity, but you cannot dissolve it.

You may blaspheme your purity, but you will never violate it. The jewel of your heart has not been stolen by evil thieves. In wisdom your Father has held it for you until you were wise enough to appreciate it and not cast it into the sea. That day has come, beloved one. You have travelled long and hard to reach this moment, and it would be foolish to delay your homecoming any longer.

Open your mind to the beauty of your own being, and never again will the fear of opinion snatch your birthright from you. You live in a castle, and you play in the slums. Wherefore, O Child of Light, have you lost your self? Ah, but it is not lost; it has but been overlooked. The integrity of your innocence has been held in trust for you since you turned your back on it long ago. Here it remains, offered to you now at no cost, sacrifice, or bargain for your guilt in return.

There is one truth that will carry you through storms of doubt, fear, and guilt. It is a shining awareness that heals all pain and restores life to an empty heart. It is the memory of Heaven that has been implanted in your soul, and it remains safe and secure from the winds of fear that batter at the ramparts of your mind. It is the truth that you are a spiritual being, made in the reflection of a perfect Creator, and you are not touchable by any event or experience through which you pass.

What can hurt you now, O Child of God?

Discomfort is aroused only to bring the need for correction into awareness.[2]

---

[2] T, p. 32

The POWER of LOVE

There is no difficulty that enough love will not conquer; no disease that enough love will not heal; no door that enough love will not open; no gulf that enough love will not bridge; no wall that enough love will not throw down; no sin that enough love will not redeem.

It makes no difference how deeply seated may be the trouble, how hopeless the outlook, how muddled the tangle, how great the mistake. A sufficient realization of love will dissolve it all. If only you could love you would be the happiest and most powerful being in the world.

- Emmet Fox

The Miracle Worker

You're not a realist unless you believe in miracles.

- Anwar Sadat

"BASEBALL PLAYER HEALS BOY OF CANCER." The headline caught my eye; it was my kind of story. Before my life was dedicated to healing, it was dedicated to baseball, and the combination of the two loomed as a metaphysical jewel to me. I knew I had to read this account. I invested sixty-five cents in the tabloid and nestled into the front seat of my car, eager to learn the details.

The story was even more intriguing than I had expected. The doctors in a Boston hospital had given up on six-year-old Sean Butler, a little boy whom they had diagnosed as having incurable cancer. His condition, they assessed, was beyond anything they could do for him. They discontinued attempts to reverse the condition and gave the boy just a few days to live.

One night little Sean told the nurses that his favorite sport was baseball, and his hero was Dave Stapleton, the first baseman for the Boston Red Sox. If Sean had one last wish, it would be to meet Dave.

Following the clue, the nurses called Dave Stapleton to ask him if he would visit the child before he passed on. Dave kindly agreed, and that afternoon he came to the hospital with his wife and spent some time with Sean. They talked baseball, laughed, played, and Sean was visibly touched. Before he left, Dave promised Sean that he would get a hit for him the first time he was at bat during the baseball game that night. Sean was thrilled, and he promised to watch the game on TV.

Somehow the word about Dave's promise got around Boston. I was told by a woman who lived in Boston at that time that many eyes in that city were glued to their TV sets that evening. They watched with anticipation as Dave stepped to the home plate in Fenway Park. Several pitches went by. Dave didn't flinch. Then, on the next pitch first baseman Dave Stapleton slammed a triple off the famous green left field wall in that ballpark. Sean was ecstatic.

Then something amazing happened. Sean's condition did not degenerate as the doctors had predicted, but instead he began to improve. Day by day he became stronger until within a few days his symptoms disappeared.

"We have no medical explanation for this," the newspaper quoted the doctors as saying. "It can only be described as a miracle." They released Sean from the hospital, healed.

What healed that boy? I see no other explanation than the power of love. Genuine caring healed that child, and that is the only power that can heal any of us. Perhaps Sean was not feeling important or needed or beautiful. Perhaps he had decided on some subconscious level that life was not worthwhile, and that he was not really wanted here. His illness was really a call for help, a request for some kind of confirmation that he should continue. And who did God call to give him the encouragement he was so desperately seeking? A first baseman. A first baseman with a big heart.

I saw the picture of Dave Stapleton in that newspaper. He did not look anything like what you or I might consider a miracle healer. He was wearing a baseball hat with a big "B" on the front, a moustache, and a few unruly hairs making their statement just above his ears. Actually, he looked more like a baseball player than anything else. And he was smiling.

The kind of healing that Dave Stapleton accomplished is available to all of us — if we are willing to believe in ourselves. We must know that Spirit is eager to use us as we are, as we dedicate ourself to the Light. We do not have to change what we do to be a miracle worker. Dave did not quit the Red Sox to attend the Famous Healer's School or learn any particular incantations. In fact, staying in the work he loved and simply being himself was absolutely necessary for him to accomplish the healing that he did. What a lesson in the importance of being ourself!

But that's not the end of the story. I was so impressed with the account that I wanted to acknowledge the characters. So I sent a package of my books and a love letter to both Dave and Sean. It was my way of saying "Thank you for being willing to be your magnificent self!"

Several months passed, and I received no response. I must confess that some doubts crept into my mind. I began to wonder if the account was real. It had appeared as a headline of the *World Weekly Globe*, a kind of gossip gazette most easily obtained between the bubble gum and plastic shavers at the check-out counter at Foodtown. My credence began to shrivel further when I reread the article to find it sandwiched amid other inspiring reports such as *"John Wayne Now Speaking through Ronald Reagan," "Eleven Year Old Boy Sells His Mom to the Arabs,"* and the intriguing scientific dilemma, *"Is Your Pet an Alien from Space?"* I must admit that my mind began to dabble into the possibility that I had been duped. (I did later learn that the story had also appeared in the New York Times.) Feeling a little foolish, I decided to turn the question over to God and see what Spirit's response would be.

Around Valentine's Day, about five months after reading the article, I received a letter from "Mr. and Mrs. David Butler, Melrose, Mass."

"Who could that be?" I wondered.

Curiously I opened it. There, to my delight, was a lovely letter from Sean's parents thanking me for my books and good wishes. But the real gift was a Valentine's card enclosed with the letter. It was a picture of Spiderman in a ready-to-do-battle stance, advising, "Don't be afraid..." When I opened to the inside of the card I found, "...to have a super Valentine's Day!" And there, in a typical six-year-old handwriting it was signed, *"Love, Sean Butler."*

Natural Miracle Workers

Somehow we have learned to believe that a miracle worker has particular attributes. In some of my classes we make a list of what we believe are the characteristics of a miracle worker, including what one would look like and how he or she is supposed to act. You would not believe some of the ideas that we come up with! Some of us believe that an enlightened person would weigh a certain weight, eat a particular food, drive a certain kind of car, have particular books in their library, and discipline their children in a certain way. I assure you that none of these ideas are true. The only attribute of a miracle worker is that he or she works miracles — and that is quite sufficient!

I have known many miracle workers. Most of them do not wear flowing robes, dispense magic potions, or lecture before great audiences. Some of them smoke cigarettes, read Dear Abby, and occasionally get bugged at their husbands. They appear to be quite normal, and indeed they are. But they have offered themselves to help humanity in whatever way God would like them to do so, and thus their gifts have come forth, independent of any form that you or I might expect.

I am learning to be free of concepts about what an enlightened being says or does. A great lesson came at a holistic health conference I attended. There I met a woman on the panel of psychics who was angry, short-tempered, and told off-color jokes. "Surely this woman cannot be spiritual," I judged her. The limitations I had placed on her were dispelled when I later learned that she is a top consultant for police departments and investigative teams, for whom she has supplied extremely valuable information in finding lost children, solving crimes, and undoing mysteries. I was grateful to see the beauty in this woman, which I had covered over with my opinions about who God could work through. Perhaps Spirit sent her to me to help me learn that God is in no way restricted by the limitations we perceive.

The blessing of allowing for Spirit to work through other persons about whom you have had judgements is that, through releasing them from your opinions, you release *yourself* from the burden of judgement, and you become free to receive miracles and be a miracle worker yourself. As long as you believe that God cannot work miracles through others who seem to have faults, Spirit will be unable to accomplish miracles for you or through you. Not because God is weak, but because Spirit must have your assent to help you. You do not need to know the "how" of miracles — that is God's department. But you do need to offer a little willingness to let your good be. When you let others be magnificent in spite of appearances, you clear the way for your own perfection.

Simple Gifts

Most miracle workers are simple people, like you and me, quietly shining their love-light in the midst of their daily activities. One such man is my friend Richard Ringel, a delightful German tailor with a gold tooth. Whenever I go into his shop I feel healed. Richard always lights up when I enter. He puts his work aside, steps out from behind the counter, and embraces me with all of his heart. We affectionately call one another *"Maivin,"* a Yiddish word meaning "expert." Richard and I do not talk philosophy or discuss evolutionary theories. He is not a Bible scholar. He just shines. And I believe that everyone who walks into his shop walks out a little lighter, a little freer, a bit happier. Richard Ringel is a miracle worker.

My mother is another miracle worker. Someone who did not know Jeane as well as I did might describe her as a Jewish mother. One of her greatest joys was to watch me eat, she asked little more of me than to call her when I got home to my house after visiting her, and she used to encourage me to marry a Jewish girl. Yet I had the great joy to discover that she, too, was a miracle worker. She would heal my friends when they called the house looking for me. A typical conversation would go something like this:

"Hello..." (young girl's voice sobbing) " — Is Alan there?"

"No, he went out for the evening...What's the matter, honey?"

"Well, my life seems to be falling apart, and I need to talk to a friend."

"You can talk to me — I'll be your friend."

"But you don't even know me."

"You sound like a nice girl. Besides, TV can get boring, and it's more fun to talk to a real person."

"Have you ever had a man leave you?"

"Plenty — and thank God!"

(Laughter from the other end of the line) "...Well thanks — it's the first time I've laughed in three days."

"That's good — sometimes laughing makes it easier. Besides, no man is worth crying over."

"You think so?"

"Sure, honey. You do sound nice. I'll bet you're pretty, too. You have a lot going for you! What's the use of wasting a moment of happiness over a man — or anything, for that matter. Go out and have a good time! You're young — enjoy yourself!"

"Wow, Mrs. Cohen — You are really something!"

"Nah, what do I know? I just watch TV."

(More laughter) "Well, thanks a lot — I feel much better."

"That's good. Don't worry, everything will be alright."

"I think I know what you mean."

"Do you want me to give Alan a message?"

"Yes — tell him his mom is pretty wonderful."

When I was in college I studied books and books of psychological theories of healing. I saw films, I participated in seminars, and I observed counseling sessions through two-way mirrors. Once I even once dressed up as a phony doctor in a study on the placebo effect. Yet hardly anything I encountered was as real or as effective or as potent as the kind of healing my mom would accomplish with a few hugs, some jokes, and genuine caring.

Love is the Healer

Dr. William "Cherry" Parker is a well-known and deeply respected psychologist who relies on the power of love as the great healer. When I heard him lecture at a northeastern conference, Dr. Parker told a large

243

audience, "At the age of seventy I have been a successful psychologist for most of those years. I have studied and tried every theory of personality and therapy from Freud to Rogers. In all of my experience, I have come to the conclusion that love is indeed the greatest healer."

Dr. Parker went on to relate a story about a young woman who came into his office for counseling. She had been referred to him after failing in therapy with many doctors.

"She came into my office with a portfolio of her psychiatric records that measured about six inches thick," Dr. Parker told us. "She began the interview by warning me, 'I don't see what you're going to do for me, doctor. Just look at these diagnoses. I'm a manic-depressive schizophrenic with multiple personality disorders. And that's just the first few pages! No one has been able to help me; I think I'm a lost cause.'

"May I please see those papers?" the doctor calmly requested.

She handed them across the desk to him. Dr. Parker sat back in his chair reviewing them for a few moments. Then he threw the papers in the wastepaper basket.

"Doctor! — What are you doing?" the young woman anxiously asked.

"These papers don't mean a thing to me," Dr. Parker answered. "I want to know about *you*, not what some theoretician says. *You*, not your diagnoses, are important to me. Please tell me about yourself and what is in your heart and mind."

That was the beginning of a deeply meaningful and healing relationship for both doctor and patient. This was the first doctor that the woman felt cared about her. In the atmosphere of his genuine caring, she blossomed and grew in ways that she never imagined before.

"Six months later, that girl graduated from therapy," Dr. Parker explained. "She became a new person, for she finally found someone who believed in her more than in her diagnoses. She caught that belief and now she is her own person."

Bloom Where You Are Planted

To be a miracle worker you do not have to get a doctoral degree, become a minister, eat a particular food, or be able to meditate for long hours. All you need to do is to begin to see beauty in your life and in those around you. When you open yourself with the golden key of *appreciation* God will fill your heart with treasures unlike any you have ever imagined.

And you will be amazed at how quickly your life opens up. That opening requires no special circumstances. There are no special circumstances. Only willingness. You can effect the greatest changes in your life and in the lives of those around you by working right where you are, blooming where you are planted.

I would also like to once again call your attention to the beautiful movie *Resurrection*, in which Ellen Burstyn portrays a woman who discovers and develops her healing powers. As a result of her healing work in the public arena she becomes entangled in all kinds of conflict and controversy with persons seeking to deny, debunk, and challenge her. Finally her ex-boyfriend becomes crazed and shoots her because his religious upbringing tells him that she is evil.

After recovering from her wound she retreats to manage a small filling station in the desert. There she quietly blesses all who come to the station. The final scene of the film shows a family pulling into the station in their mobile home. Soon it becomes apparent that their little boy is very ill, and the parents explain that the boy has cancer. After chatting with the family and making friends with the boy, the healer gives him a cute little puppy dog "for the price of one big hug." As she embraces the child we see her place her hands on the affected area of his body, and she goes into silent prayer to heal him. And we are certain that his healing is accomplished — all without any pomp or show.

And neither do you need any pomp or show to be a light in this world. You already are a light, but you may not know it. Your job is not to turn on the light, for indeed it is already lit — and it is promised to be illuminated forever. Your only task is to look at the light, and not the darkness. You cannot expect to see yourself clearly if you look into a distorted mirror. Your problem is not that you hold a lack within you, but that you have not looked to a guide that shows you your wholeness. Look now, and you will see.

Miracles come naturally to those who know their worth. Life is not an exercise in addition, but in recognition — the recognition of your goodness as God created you. That goodness has never been diminished, although it has been forgotten. The remedy, then, is not change, but remembering and awakening.

Ask to see, and you will be shown. Ask to know, and you will understand. Ask to be free, and you will see that you were never bound. And ask to touch others with the power of your love, and you will be healed. This is the promise of the One Who loves you because She knows who you are. Join in that knowledge, and all Heaven and earth will lay their gifts at your door.

The Case for Forgiveness

Living without forgiveness is worse than death.
                                        - Mr. Miyagi, *The Karate Kid II*

"The morning the case was due in court, I was at a loss as to how to handle it," confided Michael Rembolt, a young attorney in Spokane, Washington. A dozen of us had gathered to share in a spiritual support group meeting, and we wanted to hear more.

"This divorce proceeding was a long and bitter battle," Michael told us, "and I could see no way that my client and her husband were going to reach an agreement. Feeling that I had come up against a stone wall, I sat in meditation one morning and prayed for guidance.

"*'Only forgive,'* spoke a voice of inner knowing.

"Yes, that made more sense to me than any other way that I had considered," Michael confided. "I began to think about the ways I was judging or limiting the people involved in the case. I realized that I was feeling put off by my client's husband for making such strong demands. So I started to look past the things I did not like about him, seeking the spark of the Divine within him. Within a short time I saw that all of his outer irritability was actually a disguised call for love. The truth was that he loved his wife, and he felt very hurt by the divorce. His large demands were not really an expression of hatred, as I had thought, but actually a plea for love.

"When I saw this it was easy to see the light in him. I was able to bless him and actually pray for his happiness and well-being. I offered him, his participation in this divorce, and his whole life up to the Light.

"That felt so good that I wanted to look further to see who else I needed to forgive. I discovered that I was a little annoyed at my client as well, for she could have been more flexible in her counter-demands. I released her, too, and I felt the same sense of peace and relief that I did when I prayed for her husband.

"Soon this process of forgiveness became uplifting and actually ex-hilirating! I began to feel free and light, and I realized I had hit on something extremely powerful, a redemptive secret that was hidden only by my own fear of love.

"I decided to forgive and release everyone and everything associated with the case. I thought of the opposing lawyer, whom I had feared because of his reputation as one of the most ruthless and uncompromising attorneys in the city. I blessed him, the judge, the witnesses, and everyone in the courtroom; all the other litigants, attorneys, clerks, and anyone connected with the case in any way.

"Then I realized there was still one person I needed to forgive — *me*. I became aware that I had been judging myself for being put off by the other people in the scenario and for feeling inadequate about how I was handling the case. It seemed to follow naturally that if I could bless and wish the others well, I certainly deserved the same love myself.

"I knew that I had hit on the perfect approach for facing the situation. Gratefully I arose from my meditation, confident that with the help of the Holy Spirit I could face the case and the day. I didn't know how it would all work out; I just knew that because I had invited God into the situation, the case would somehow be handled in everyone's best interest."

Michael leaned forward on his chair, resting his elbows on his knees. The entire group was rapt with his account.

"When I arrived at the court I could not find my client. Nor the opposing lawyer. Nor the husband. For that matter I could not find anyone in the courtroom — not even the judge! I looked at my watch and checked my calendar; they confirmed I was in the right place at the right time. But where was everyone? Puzzled, I walked into the lobby to telephone the opposing lawyer.

"'Oh, yes, Mr. Rembolt, I'm glad you called,' answered the secretary. 'I've been trying to get in touch with you all morning. I wanted to tell you that our client has decided to settle out of court; he instructed us to give you anything you want. Just draw up the papers, send them over to us, and we'll get them signed.'"

A spontaneous chorus of "Wow's" and "Yay's" went through our audience. But Michael had more to tell.

"'Amazing!' I remarked to myself — 'Forgiveness really works!'

"I went back to the courtroom to tell the judge, but to my surprise neither he nor anyone else had arrived. 'Strange,' I thought, 'nine-thirty, and still no court.' I went back to the pay phone and called the judge's office.

"'Michael,' answered Judge Hillman, 'the most *miraculous* thing has happened!' (Those were his exact words.) 'We had thirty-two cases on the docket this morning, and every one of them has *settled out of court!*"'

Every one of them. The first lesson of *A Course in Miracles* is that there is no order of difficulty in miracles, and here is a most exciting example of the power of one man's prayer to heal his own mind and the lives of everyone he touches. Michael is no different than you or me, nor does he have any spiritual power that is not available to all of us. Michael simply *put into action* the energy that lives in every divine being. This true story is a cogent testimony for the fact that thoughts are things, and we can make our thoughts work *for* us to bring love, harmony, and real peace into any situation, no matter how bleak it may seem.

There is one message of this story, this book, my life, and all lives:

Any hardship can be undone, transformed, and healed to reveal a shining star where once there was but a dark night. The most powerful way to accomplish this miraculous transformation is through **forgiveness.**

The Sin that Had No Effect

One summer afternoon when I was doing a series of workshops in Washington, a thoughtful masseuse offered me a complimentary massage. Thankful for the opportunity to unwind during a busy week, I gratefully accepted. A friend gave me a ride to her studio on the outskirts of the city. Eagerly I stretched out on the table, laid back, closed my eyes, and began to drift.

The next sound I remember was that of the masseuse's voice calling to me, "It's five o'clock, Alan."

"Five o'clock?!" I awoke with a start; at five o'clock I had an appointment on the other side of town, half an hour away. There my friend Alden was waiting in his car to pick me up to give me a ride to another engagement. Upset, I wondered how I could possibly make it in time to meet him.

Frantically I scurried off the table, threw my garb together and bolted out the door (not exactly the best way to complete a massage!). When we reached the appointed meeting place I was quite late. Alden had given up waiting and left.

I felt terrible. Here this thoughtful man had volunteered to give me a ride, and I stood him up because I nodded out on a massage table. Not a very nice thing to do, I thought. I felt guilty, and shuddered at the thought of facing Alden later that evening.

Sure enough, there he was at the lecture; nervously I thought about what I would say to him. When he approached me after the workshop I immediately apologized to him: "Gosh, Alden, I'm so sorry I didn't show up for our appointment this afternoon; I kept you waiting so long. Could you possibly forgive me?"

There was a pregnant moment before Alden spoke. I felt that my soul was in his hands. I waited for some kind of of chastisement or retaliation.

But it never came. Instead of attempting to punish me, Alden's words sailed to me on a gentle smile: "Would you like a ride home tonight?"

Wow! I felt like a condemned man pardoned from prison. I felt that Alden could have justifiably condemned me, yet he treated me as if I had not wronged him at all. I was free and just as lovable as if I had not done the "sin" with which I perceived I had hurt him. My "sin" had no effect — in fact, it contributed to a miracle of love — and we were both free!

Real Forgiveness

The key to real forgiveness is to understand that forgiveness has nothing at all to do with overlooking a sin or crime that has been committed against you. It is to know and demonstrate that no real harm has been done.

You are in danger nowhere in the universe. There is no person or force outside of your own mind that could ever hurt you. Indeed you have never really been hurt, no more than you are wounded in a dream that dissolves the moment you awaken.

There is very strong agreement in the world that we are vulnerable and subject to the attack thoughts and actions of those around us. Because we have been heavily trained in this way of looking at life, it is very real *in our experience. But experience is not always the same as reality.* Our experience of vulnerability seems real not because this is God's truth, but because we have created it to be so with our faulty perceptions based on an erroneous original premise. *Our opportunity in life is to reverse our own thinking that we are weak or hurtable in any way, and to serve others by knowing that they are equally whole.* From this awareness we will demonstrate with our actions that all pain springs from faulty thinking, and suffering need not be.

The Message of Healing

One of the greatest teachers of forgiveness was Jesus. The whole of his ministry was dedicated to teach one lesson: all is good, all is God, and *there is no other force in the universe.* Hell is simply the belief in it. And we discover, too, that even that belief was part of our ascension. *Nothing is outside the picture of our good.* Paint a picture of evil with your mind and you will smudge the portrait where a blessing was meant to be seen. You can make a movie of any idea you generate. But you can't leave the theatre until you see all the credits. You wonder why you have to stick around until the end of the film, and then in the last frame you discover that you are the producer!

Jesus saw the whole picture, and that is why he was able to teach that forgiveness, or looking beyond error into the light, is the way to Heaven. He had no sense of attack, and that is why he said, "Forgive them, Father, for they know not what they do." He recognized that the Father had *already* forgiven them, and he was sharing his Father's freedom in knowing that there was no need for punishment. Both he and his Father — our Father, too — knew that all is forgivable because *there was no real loss.*

What those who crucified Jesus needed was not blame or punishment, but love and understanding, for their error was to believe that the Christ could be killed, and that is a problem in perception that calls not for punishment, but awakening. If they knew who they were, they would have known who Jesus was, and that would have been the end of the drama. Then they could have celebrated their freedom in not needing to change the outer world to gain peace. Jesus was not desirous of revenge, but of sharing with them the understanding — the good news — that they were as invulnerable as he was, and is, as we are. Anyone who knows that he is invulnerable has no interest in killing or hurting anyone, because he realizes that that is impossible. Our purpose in life is to practice and celebrate our spiritual invulnerability, and teach it to others by the very joy we exude as we live with dignity in that truth.

251

The End of Crucifixion

Many people believe that the purpose of Jesus' life was the crucifixion. The symbol of Christianity has become the crucifix, we glorify the blood of the lamb, and many of us live our lives in a state of crucifixion, an unnecessary emulation wrought of a mistaken understanding of the mission of one who came to teach only love. Even if you believe that Jesus' crucifixion is to be imitated, you will have to admit that the many days, months, or years that you have lived in crucifixion far exceed the three hours that he underwent the cross. And if you believe that his crucifixion did indeed atone for the sins of humanity, what an unnecessary repetition it is for any of us to relive it!

Suffering is not necessary. You can learn from suffering, but you can easily learn the same lessons with joy and celebration. Give up your misery. Once you have seen that there is another way, all misery is self-indulgence. And there is another way. I saw a marvelous bumper sticker that proclaimed: *Misery is Optional.* And so it is. Every moment is a choice between life and death, between celebration and crucifixion, between wonder and despair. What do you choose? It does not matter in the least what you have chosen in the past. It matters only what you choose *now.* Choose the peace of God now, and it is yours for eternity.

Personal Resurrection

It is time for you to come out of the tomb. You have lived in darkness and misery for too long, and none of it was necessary. You could have been dancing in the light, and you still can. All you need to do is forgive yourself. When you truly forgive yourself it is easy to forgive all those around you, for you realize that you were but crucifying them for your sins. And *you have no sins.* You have but made errors in consciousness, and those errors are rectified the moment you see them for what they are. You were not bad; you were just learning. The remedy for error is not punishment, but practice. And you have been practicing a great lesson.

If you are reading this, you are ready to give up your value on suffering and punishment. This may seem like a quantum leap for you, and it is. Yet you are ready for it. When you carry a heavy sack on your shoulders for a long time, you must either release it or fall under it. You have fallen long enough, and now you are ready to arise and walk in dignity.

Join me in the light. There is room for all of us here, for the light knows no boundaries or smallness. Together we can show the world that life is good, that there is nothing to fear, and that we are capable of living in a state of love all of the time. You have come a long way to arrive at this point, and it would be rather foolish to turn back now. And there is no turning back — there is only delay.

Come, for all things are now ready. There is nothing you need do further but say, *"Yes, Father, I am willing to love."* With that invitation the Holy Spirit will come streaming into your mind and you will wonder why you ever resisted love. Child, your pain is over. Forgive yourself and join the ranks of those who have gained Heaven, even while on this earth. You are blessed.

*The holiest place on earth is where an ancient hatred has become a present love.**

---

*T, p. 522

The Lover's Gift

Seeing is believing in the things you see;
Loving is believing in the ones you love.

- *Unicorn Song*[1]

Bill sat back in the couch and faced his therapist. There was something he had to know, and now was the time to ask.

"Tom, I've been with you a long time, and now I want your advice on something that's very important to me."

"Sure, Bill, what's on your mind?"

"I've been with my wife for nineteen years now. When I married her she was like a queen to me — I loved her so much, and everything she did pleased me. But something's happened, Tom. Somehow over the years she's turned into a shrew. I tell you, she's not the same woman I married. She's cranky, she doesn't take care of herself, and she doesn't do half the things for me that she used to do. She's hurt me too much and frankly, I've had it. Can you tell me what to do that would really hurt her?"

Tom sat back. He folded his hands, and thought. A minute went by, but it seemed like an hour.

"Why, yes, Bill," he responded. "I do have an idea you might be able to use. It's up to you whether or not you will try it, but here it is: When you go home tonight, bring Stephanie a bouquet of her favorite flowers. This weekend take her out to her favorite restaurant. Next Tuesday night tell her, 'Sweetheart, if you would like to go out with your friends tonight, I'll be glad to watch the kids.' For one month treat her like that beautiful, wonderful, lovable person you married. Then, after a month of showering gifts and attention on her — leave her. That will really get her!"

Bill sat up in his chair with a look of amazed excitement on his face. "That's great!" he exclaimed. "Tom, you're a genius — I never would have thought of that! That'll really do her in!"

Bill stood up, shook Tom's hand vigorously, and walked briskly out the

---

[1] M. Adam, *The Unicorn Song*

door, on his way to the nearest flower shop.

Several months passed before Tom saw Bill again. Then one night they ran into each other at a party.

"Well, Bill, how are you doing? — I'll bet you're having the time of your life going out with lots of women!"

Tom looked astonished. "Me? Go out with women? — Not me! — I would never do that to my wife."

"But I thought you were leaving that shrew."

Tom smiled.

"Leave her? Shrew?...She's the most wonderful wife in the world! Bill, I must thank you for your advice; the most amazing thing happened! I did exactly as you told me — I brought her flowers, watched the kids, took her out — the whole bit, all with the intention of leaving her. But after the first week of being nice to her, something amazing happened to her. One night when I came home she was dressed up so gorgeous, just like she used to dress when we first were together. And she said it was just for me! Then, the night she came home after going out with her friends she told me, 'Thanks a lot for watching the kids, honey — if you want to go out with the guys Thursday night, I'll be happy to stay home.' I tell you she's a new person — and so am I. It's like starting all over — but better! How can I ever thank you enough, Tom — that was the best advice anyone ever gave me!''

We Create Our World

We create our world by the way we look at it and act in it. Every situation into which we enter is a product of our thoughts. And because the persons around us are sensitive receivers of psychic information (whether they realize it or not), they respond to our vision of them and the actions that follow from that vision.

The good is already there. Perfection already is. Wholeness is wholly created. But it needs your help to bring it forth. Positive thinking does not mean trying to create something that is not there. Real positive thinking acknowledges that good already exists—indeed it is *all* that exists. Your vision and affirmation draw it forth into expression.

It is supremely important to remember that every situation, event, and experience in life springs from your vision of it. In relationships, you will create and recreate situations based upon your vision of who the two of you are. The key to success in relationships is to hold to a vision of the perfection of everyone involved. This means consistently seeing the best in yourself as well as the other person. *A Course in Miracles* tells us, "it is impossible to overestimate your brother's value," and "the only response worthy of your brother is appreciation." This is why you must affirm your vision of beauty in everyone you meet.

Seeing Good Creates Miracles

Dr. Nelson Decker wrote a marvelous book[2] on the Native American ways of healing. One of the most important steps to happiness, the Native Americans teach, is to find something in every situation that you can appreciate.

Dr. Decker relates an experience that changed his life. When he was a young chiropractor in Englewood, New Jersey, a very shabbily dressed man came into his office. The man was dirty, unkempt, and he emanated an unpleasant odor. He had no money, but he asked for treatment. Dr. Decker was reluctant to see him, but he did so. While Dr. Decker's initial reaction was an aversion to the man's appearance, he remembered that a lesson of happiness was to find something you can appreciate in every situation. He scanned the man's appearance, and he could find nothing that he appreciated. Then he looked down at the man's shoes, and he noticed that they were neatly tied. This was the one thing about the man that he could honestly say he liked. So he focused on the tidiness of the man's shoelaces as he treated him. Over the course of the treatment he developed a nice rapport with the fellow, and the man went on his way happily.

A few days later the man returned in significantly better condition. He told Dr. Decker that he owed him a great debt of thanks. Several days earlier he felt that he was at the end of his rope. He walked from New York City to the George Washington Bridge with the intention of jumping off the bridge. When he got to the bridge he decided to give himself one more chance. So he kept walking over the bridge, hoping to find some kind of help on the other side. The first place he saw on the other side was Dr. Decker's office, and so he walked in the door.

"I want to thank you for being so kind to me, Doctor," the man shared. "I think that if you had turned me away I might have gone back to the bridge and jumped. But you didn't, and I am encouraged to live because of your kindness."

---

[2] Dr. Nelson Decker, *The Great Mystery in the Sky*, Benu, Inc., P.O. Drawer 4367, E. Lansing, Michigan 48823

The Beauty in the Beast

If you remember the fable of Beauty and the Beast, you may recall that the young maiden was forced to live in the woods with a beast. At first she was repelled by his appearance, but over time she discovered that he was a kind and gentle creature. After spending more time with him she began to truly love him. Finally she saw so much good in him that she chose to be with him of her own free will. When she kissed him he was revealed to be a handsome prince, upon whom a spell had been cast. Within the beast, there was beauty.

The lesson here is *not* that she learned to put up with his beastliness, but that she discovered his beauty. The moment she accepted the good in him, that became reality. And so it is with our lives. We must see beauty *first*, and then we can be certain it will be manifested.

The Desire to See

If you are seeing pain, ugliness, or emptiness, it is because on some level, probably unconsciously, you have chosen to see these images. And there may in fact have been value in your seeing them, for they are the signposts that you are travelling in the wrong direction. If they help you to return to your proper course, they have served you. But if you have had your fill of hurt and you are ready to see differently, you will see differently.

There is a very simple prayer that always leads to healing. If you pray it with sincerity, you are sure to be released from the limitations that you feel in any situation. Say these words, but mean them, and you will be free:

"I would like to see this differently."

If you make this request sincerely, quickly the situation will be shown to you in a different light. That light will include the way out. The inability to see the way out means that you have been looking in the wrong place. You must see differently before you can find your way to the door.

You may be surprised to find that you do not need to make any or many changes in the outer world to step through the door. You may need but to see the situation in a different light. One correct thought of love and acceptance can transform hell into Heaven.

The Healing Power of Vision

I had a friend who had a ten-year-old boy. When I visited their home, I found the boy to be rather selfish and annoying to me. I judged him as being something of a spoiled child.

One day I was sharing my feelings about the child with another friend of the family. "I don't know what to do about Jason," I told her; "every time I visit the family he gets on my nerves."

"Jason? You mean that sweetie Jason? He's one of the most lovable kids I know! Whenever I go to his house we have a great time together! I love to be with him!"

Hmmm. I had never thought about him like that before. Could it be that the friend was seeing something in the boy that I was missing?

The next time I visited the boy's house, I remembered my friend's words. I tried her perspective on for size. I considered the possibility that Jason was actually a sweet kid. And do you know what I discovered? He *was* a sweet kid. That day he was so kind and loving to me! I wondered how I could have ever thought otherwise.

I needed to hear that woman's perpective as a correction to my own. All she did was see him differently, and I began to see him differently, too.

Who was Jason actually? He was the best we saw him as being.

Who are you, actually? If "the only response worthy of your brother is appreciation," the same must be true for you. Perhaps your problem has not been that there was something wrong with you, but that you temporarily forgot who you are.

Are you so sure that you are weak, lacking, or afraid? Where did you get these ideas from? Who told you that there was something wrong with you? And why did they tell you that? Trace these ideas back in your mind as far as you can, and you may find that your notions of impoverishment are learned. Babies do not have a problem with self-image. They do not beat themselves when they fall down while learning to walk. They do not berate themselves as being weak for wanting and needing momma's breast. They do not see people as old, young, black, white, handsome, or ugly. They are ecstatic about the opportunities that life is offering them to play, discover, and grow. Maybe they are on to something!

Look clearly at what you believe you are, and what you believe you are not. The greatest mistake you have ever made is to stop believing in yourself. You stopped believing in yourself when you adopted a self-image that said you were less than lovable. You made a decision that there was something you had to do to earn love, and you have been trying to buy peace ever since. And of course you have failed. But be thankful that that decision is revokable, and you have the power to undo it entirely by making a new decision now.

The Lover's Gift

Why do we feel so happy in the presence of someone who loves us? They see the good in us, and they remind us that we are lovable. In our heart we know that we are lovable, and we want to live in the love that we deserve. This is why a life that does not reflect the love that we know we deserve is so painful. When someone loves us they help awaken us to the beauty within us. They have discovered the treasure in us, and we want to share in it. They act as a mirror for the best in us, and we want to be with them so we can see it, too. Truly it is an act of love to accept love, for in so doing we acknowledge that we are lovable. We *do* love ourself — that is our greatest purpose — and we want to live in the presence of our own wonder.

The greatest service that we can perform for another, then, is to see their beauty. If you see the good in others, you will experience three major benefits: (1) you will experience tremendous success in all of your endeavors, and enjoy the kind of rewarding relationships that you have dreamed of; (2) you will empower and support those you touch to be successful and happy; and (3) you will love yourself and find phenomenal wonder in your own being.

Surely we can only gain from focusing on the good. It is our most important gift to ourself.

The Final Vision

One of the clearest examples of the transformative power of vision comes in *The Return of the Jedi* movie. In this episode Luke Skywalker, who has mastered the Force, realizes that Darth Vader is his father. Actually, his father is Attikin Skywalker, but Attikin has become enamored by the dark side of the Force, and he has put on an intimidating mask, to become known as Darth Vader. But the man behind the mask is not the one who has created havoc. He is actually a being of radiant light. This is the man that Luke recognizes as his father.

Luke goes to the very core of the Empire's headquarters and confronts Darth Vader with the fact that he knows he is his father. But Vader has become so hardened in the ways of darkness that his response is to attempt to influence Luke to join the dark side of the Force with him. He even threatens Luke's life.

But Luke, a true Jedi Knight, is undaunted. "You cannot fool me, father," he tells Vader, "I know who you are. I know that you belong to the light."

Though Vader's mask is expressionless, we can feel the inner transformation taking place as his heart begins to awaken. The layers of armor begin to dissolve around him.

Vader brings Luke to the Emperor — the very monarch of the dark Empire. There, when the Emperor realizes that he cannot persuade Luke to join the dark side, he begins to electrocute him with lightning bolts of anger.

Darth Vader stands by and watches. But his heart has been opened. Finally he can stand it no longer. He makes the decision to honor the light. He picks up the evil Emperor and hurls him into a bottomless chasm.

But Vader is wounded in the process. He is dying. He asks Luke to take off Vader's mask. Finally, after years of fear, pain, and terror, Darth Vader's true face is revealad — it is the original countenance of Luke's father, Attikin Skywalker.

In the final scene of this saga we see Ben (Obi-Wan Kenobe — Luke's first teacher) and Yoda (Luke's elf-like guru) standing together in Spirit, blessing the celebration of the victory of the light over the darkness. And standing with them, in fully glory, is another figure: it is the spirit body of Attikin Skywalker, known in life as Darth Vader. But now he shines brightly, with the same radiant dignity as Ben and Yoda. We see a vision of his true being as a master of light. The nightmare is over.

It was Luke's willingness to see the light in Darth Vader that set the transformation into motion. Luke walked directly into the lair of the Empire to face Darth Vader with the truth of his being. Vision preceded victory. And so it always is.

You and I must have the same kind of vision to effect true transformation in our lives. The world is hungry for the vision of perfection. You can break the agreement of limitation by seeing freedom. You can transform ugliness by acknowledging beauty. You can awaken love by seeing it where hatred now seems to rule.

You must have the faith and the courage to act upon your vision. Luke walked into the center of the Empire because that is where he had the most power to transform it. The Empire that you and I must penetrate is not a place, an institution, or a country, and it is not founded on the actions of other people. The Empire that you and I must conquer is the fortress of fear that has been erected in our own mind. We have allowed a dark perception to cast a shadow in the land of light. We have accepted the idea that evil has power. We have believed in a force outside our own divinity.

Yet correction lies within the same mind that led us astray. And that correction begins with vision. Begin now to see yourself in a new light. Begin to affirm, empower, and celebrate the greatness in you. Naturally your enthusiasm will spill over onto those you contact, and you will become a miracle worker. You will be astounded at how far your vision will carry you.

And you will not be alone. You will see for many, for many are in need of your sight. Do not belittle this responsibility, for it is the one you were born to accomplish. And it will be the easiest task you have ever mastered, for One will walk with you Who will see with you. And that One will affirm that all you see is born of goodness. You must believe that you are entrusted with the power to heal, for so you are.

The Letter

If, while you are presenting your offering upon the altar,
You remember that your brother has a grievance against you,
Leave your offering there upon the altar,
And go and make peace with your brother.
Then come back and present your offering.

                                                    - Jesus the Christ[1]

One Christmas a group of us gathered at a friend's house to create our own Christmas pageant. We celebrated song, laughter, prayer, and feasting. It was a wonderful day that we created according to the spirit of devotion in our own hearts.

At one point someone read from the Bible. Randomly he chose a passage that contained the verse, "If, while you are presenting your offering upon the altar, you remember that your brother has a grievance against you, leave your offering there upon the altar, and go and make peace with your brother. Then come back and present your offering." In other words, to have a clean slate with God you must have a clean slate with your brothers.

"Do I have a clean slate with my brothers?" I wondered.

I searched my mind for any grievances. I did not find any, but I did not feel totally peaceful. "Father," I asked God, "Is there anyone against whom I am holding a grievance?"

Immediately into my mind flashed the face of a fellow named Ronald. Ronald was a man I met many years ago at a professional conference. At this workshop Ronald attacked me verbally and physically for something I had said that he did not like. The thought of our relationship was a painful emotional memory for me. During the ensuing eleven years, whenever I thought of Ronald or my experience with him, I felt anxious. If I would even hear his name, I would lose my peace. I realized that I had been stuffing, or repressing my feelings about Ronald for a long, long time. And now the entire experience was ready for healing.

---

[1] Matthew 5:23

"If you remember that your brother has any grievance against you, go and make peace with him, and then come to the altar." I have fancied myself to be a pretty good meditator. I have often closed my eyes and dived into peace for long periods of time. Yet if I harbored feelings of resentment toward Ronald - or anyone - could I truly say that I have been peaceful? I realized that before I could come wholeheartedly to God, I would need to do something to heal my relationship with Ronald.

I sat down and wrote Ronald a letter. Upon reading it when I was done, I decided it was too stiff, and I tore it up. I wrote him another letter. This one was too sappy. I tore it up and tried again. The next one, I felt included a tinge of laying guilt on him. Into the wastebasket it went, with the others. I went on with draft after draft. Some were not completely honest; others, too honest. Some were bravado, others fawning. I kept going until I felt that the words on the paper said what I wanted to say.

Finally I held a sheet of paper in my hand and read, in my handwriting:

Dear Ronald,

I don't know if you remember me. We met at a professional meeting about ten years ago. There we had a bit of a confrontation.

I am writing to you now to let you know that I have not felt peaceful about that for all these years. I have come to a point in my life where my relationships are very important to me, and more than anything else I want all of my relationships to reflect love. I would like to bring my feelings about us into the light of peace.

I want you to know that if I offended or upset you in any way, I am sorry for that. I respect you as a person and a professional, and it was never my intention to interfere with the work that you are doing.

I would now like to count you among my friends. I know that we have not been in touch for a long time, but perhaps we could consider our friendship like a fine wine that took a long time to mellow.

Please know that my love and support are with you.

Yours truly,
Alan

That felt right.

I signed, sealed, and stamped the letter, said a prayer over it, and took it to the mailbox.

As I was about to drop it into the slot, my mind began to wriggle with all kinds of hesitations and warnings.

"He's going to think you're a real jerk," one voice in my mind warned me.

Another thought threatened, "What if he comes to see you and he hits you again?"

Yet another voice questioned, "What if he doesn't answer?"

But quickly I saw that those voices were all the ego, disguised as different characters. I have learned not to heed such ravings. I dropped the letter in the box.

When the letter dropped out of sight a feeling came over me that was so beautiful! I was a free man. *Eleven years* of hurt and anger and fear were dumped that day. And I was proud of myself for doing it!

It didn't matter if he thought I was a jerk, or if he got angry, or if he didn't answer. I did what I had to do, and the relationship was healed in *my heart.*

"It is the destiny of all relationships to become holy," *A Course in Miracles* tells us.[2] That was the day for that one.

I went home and sat down to meditate. How sweet it was.

---

[2] M, p. 7

Love Always Answers

A miracle is never lost. It may touch many people you have not even met, and produce undreamed of changes in situations of which you are not even aware.

- A Course in Miracles*

There was a woman who was married to a very cold and emotionally insensitive man. For many years the man did not show his feelings or acknowledge his wife's love for him. Often over the years she thought about leaving him, and at times she almost did. But each time she was about to walk out the door, a voice within her heart told her to stay. And so she did.

Many years passed. Still the man showed little appreciation for this devoted woman. She wondered where it was all leading to.

Then the husband passed away. The wife went to the family safe deposit box to collect their valuables, and there she found a letter that her husband had written to her some time before he passed away. The letter said,

> *Dear Betty,*
>
> *I want you to know how much I love and appreciate you. As you know, I am a man who does not show his feelings very much or very well. But that does not mean I do not feel. It has been very difficult for me to express appreciation, and perhaps that is why I am writing this letter to you instead of speaking what I want to say.*
>
> *Betty, I have been aware of all the kindnesses and thoughtful acts you have done for me over all these years. You have been a wonderfully devoted and giving wife, and I want to acknowledge you for it. Please do not ever feel that what you have done with me and for me has gone unnoticed or unappreciated. I am thankful for all of it. Please know that I love you, I value you, and I am very grateful for our years together.*

---

* T, p. 4

God bless you for being such an angel in my life.
                                                    Always,
                                                    John

Do you have any idea of the power of your loving acts? Perhaps you do not. Every act of kindness, yea, every *thought* of loving creates a wave in the ocean of the universe, and ripples out to touch, affect, and heal everything everywhere. The value of your love can never be overestimated. Your simple caring deeds are supremely important, and you must never underestimate how you can help someone in gentle ways that may seem to go unnoticed. In reality such acts have healing power of unbelievable magnitude.

Sometimes, when I think of the people in my life who have had the most profound and transformative effect on me, I realize that some of these beautiful souls have no idea how they have contributed to my life. Two of the people whom I think of as my most important guides are individuals that I spent just a few minutes with. I am certain that neither of them is aware of how valuable those few minutes were to me.

One summer, when I was thirteen years old, my Cousin Ethel invited me to spend a few weeks with her and her family at her home in the suburbs of Wilmington, Delaware. As I was raised in the city, the experience of spending a vacation in a country setting was a special gift. I accepted.

One afternoon Ethel took me to the community pool just down the street from her house. There she introduced me to a man named Mr. Simmons. Mr. Simmons was a schoolteacher, I believe. I don't really remember much else about him, except for one very important and, for me; unusual feeling: I felt happy in his presence. During our time together he asked me questions about my life and my interests, and he really listened to what I was saying. He was the first and perhaps the only person in many years, who I felt loved me unconditionally. The significance of our interaction was life-changing for me, and I was with him for no more than about half an hour. But in those thirty minutes I felt loved, cared for, and listened to. I felt like I was a worthwhile person, and that was a very important feeling for me at that time of my life.

Another person who touched me deeply was a man named Bill, a rather jovial fellow whom I met at a Unity retreat in Allentown, Pennsylvania. The gift that Bill gave me was that he hugged me very warmly. At retreats such as that one, many people share hugs. But when Bill hugged me, I felt that he was really giving me all of himself; he was not just wrapping his arms around me and squeezing;—he was really hugging! I felt that his heart was wholly with me, and that he was communicating *all* of his being in that hug. In short, he meant it and I felt it. Bill's hug encouraged me to share myself like that with others in my life, and more and more I have been doing so. Bill ignited within me the desire to give the gift that I had been given. And as we receive what we give, I have gained much.

I never saw Bill again; I do not even know his last name. I am certain that he does not know how much he gave me in one strong and genuine hug. But I have been passing it on, and I know the blessings are returning to Bill thousands and thousands of times over.

How many times I have heard a lecture, read a book, or studied with a teacher from which I gleaned one sentence, one word, one idea, or one feeling, and then taken the idea into meditation and found new and wondrous avenues opened to me! Most of these speakers or authors have no idea how they have touched me. To many I was just a face in an audience. If I was not smiling, perhaps they wondered if they were reaching me at all. Yet all the while inside my soul wheels of fire were churning. Insights and healings were coming. Doors were opening. All of these important changes were invisible to the world the eye sees. Yet they were indeed real and magnificent in the realm of the spirit.

Does it not stand to reason, then, that you and I must be affecting other persons without our knowing it? Could it be that our love is more powerful than we see? Let us know the value of every kind word, caring touch, and encouraging deed. Every act of love goes a long way, and though it may not be acknowledged openly, the heart knows. "What is essential," the Little Prince learned, "is invisible to the eye."

When Negativity is a Blessing

Sometimes we may seem to be affecting a person negatively, while actually they are undergoing an important positive transformation. Once I received a letter from a woman who complained vehemently about the content of one of my seminars. She objected to my emphasis on meditation, the sharing of my personal experiences, and my references to *A Course in Miracles*. This was rather surprising to me, as I have found these methods to be among the most powerful and well-received of the material I present. Yet she was disturbed enough about these ideas to write an emotionally-charged letter protesting them.

I took the letter into meditation, and the answer I received was a very important one. My guidance told me that actually the seminar touched a sensitive chord within her. I perceived that she had a lot of repressed anger and resistance to spiritual awakening, and the mention of these ideas set off deep issues within her, issues that were ready to be resolved.

My reasoning further told me that her response was actually a very positive one, for her experience was forcing her to bring these issues into the light and look at them. Looking at the things that press our sensitive buttons is healthy, for they are hidden fears seeking healing. Her response also got me to look at how I was presenting my materials; I had to ask myself if I could find a way to offer these ideas in a form that would reach more people.

Thinking about our interaction even more, I wondered if perhaps she had actually gotten more than some persons in the seminar who listened politely and took notes without filtering the material through their thoughts and feelings.

I also remembered that some of the people and groups that have been the most important in my life are those to whom I initially had an emotionally adverse reaction. Later I became deeply involved with these persons and organizations, and I ultimately learned and gained much through my participation with them. Sometimes when we meet a person or group that has come into our life to offer us an important healing, the ego steps in, and in its effort to resist healing it makes the situation out to be the exact reverse of what it is. But that is only temporary. Sooner or later we must accept our next step to the light. Our destiny is happiness.

I wrote this lady a letter telling her that I was sorry she found the material so unacceptable, and I offered to get together with her for lunch to chat some more if she liked. She did not take me up on the invitation, but she did send me back a lovely letter of thanks for my personal response to her.

The Perfect Timing of Love

Spirit never leaves us comfortless. Sometimes when things seem to be going all wrong, an angel of comfort will come to make our way easier and give us the strength to carry us over the bumps and move us up to the high country. Angels do not always appear with wings, halos, or wands. Sometimes they come in letters, animals, or sunsets.

A musician friend of mine told me that an angel once came to him when he most needed it. Peter was experiencing what seemed to be the end of his rope. His girlfriend had left him, and when he went to work that night at the club at which he had a standing engagement, the manager told him that his band had been discontinued at the club.

Peter felt that he had nothing. On his way home he became so overwhelmed with his difficulties that he stopped on the sidewalk, laid down his guitar, fell to his knees, and began to weep. "Where can I turn, now?" he wondered.

At that moment a little puppy dog crawled under Peter's arms and began to lick the tears off his cheeks. Peter had never seen this cute little fellow before, and you can imagine his joy at having this friend come to him at this time of his greatest need. He felt that someone cared about him, and he decided to carry on. He brought the dog home with him, and had it sit on the porch while he went inside to get him some food.

When Peter got in the door, his girlfriend was there waiting for him. She told him that she did not really want to leave him. She also told him that he had received a phone message about some wonderful new musical opportunities for him. His whole direction had been reversed in those few minutes.

When Peter went outside for the puppy dog, it had vanished. Peter reasoned that the little guy was an angel.

And I must share for myself that sometimes I wonder if I am doing anything worthwhile in this world. I wonder if my writing or workshops are the most powerful things I could be doing. Sometimes I wonder if maybe I should make candles for a living, or something like that.

Then, it seems to never fail, just as I start to doubt, someone calls, writes, or visits me and tells me quite specifically (without my asking), "When is your next book coming out? You must keep writing! What you are saying and doing is touching many more people than you realize."

I feel sort of ignorant for a minute. Then I sit down at my typewriter.

What's in the Minutes

I recently saw a wonderful film called *Vision Quest*. It is the captivating story of a high school wrestler who devotes nearly all of his time — and life — to training for a big match in which he intends to win the state championship from an undefeated and a seemingly invulnerable champion.

The young man, Louden, becomes obsessed with winning this match, and his friends accuse him of insanity in his passion to prove himself. He agrees that he may indeed be crazy, and he carries on with his training program of unbelievable intensity. He occupies nearly every moment exercising, jogging, dieting, visualizing, studying his opponent, and demanding top performance of himself at every turn.

The night before the match Louden's girlfriend leaves him, and he is crestfallen. He is so downhearted that he changes his mind about competing, and he goes instead to visit his friend Elmo. Elmo is an older man that Louden works with, who has become like a big brother to him. To Louden's surprise he finds Elmo dressed up nicely, fixing his tie as he is ready to go out. Elmo tells Louden that he has taken off from work this evening to go see Louden win his match.

Feeling rotten and trying to find a way to tell Elmo that he has copped out of the match, Louden asks, "Why would you want to take off work and lose money to see me wrestle? — It's just a lousy six minute match."

Elmo stops tying his necktie and asks Louden, "Have you ever heard of Pele?"

"Yeah, I think he's a soccer player, right?"

"I was sitting here alone one night," Elmo tells Louden, "and I discovered this soccer game on the Mexican channel. In that game I saw Pele flip his entire body into the air in a somersault, and then kick the ball into the goal while he was upside down — and backward. The ball was in the net before the goalee had a chance to think about it.

"You know, Louden," the older man says, "I'm sort of a tough guy — you know me. But when I saw that, I began to cry."

Elmo begins to weep even as he speaks to Louden.

"I began to cry because I knew that there were millions of us little people watching him, and most of us have not had our lives amount to anything. But when Pele made that goal like he did, for one shining moment he lifted me and everyone else into a higher place. It was as if he was saying, 'Look what a person can do if he puts his mind to it.' In that one glorious moment he was showing everyone that there is nothing that is impossible to someone who sets his mind and heart on something. In that moment he saved me and the millions who were watching him. We were small, and he made us great.

"No, Louden..." Elmo tells him, "It does not matter that the match is only six minutes long — It's what happens in those six minutes that is important."

Louden is touched. He got it. He dashes down to the high school and gets into the match just before he is about to default for being absent. And he wins.

The Sure Investment

Loving is an investment that always pays off. But do not dictate the how and the when of the payoff. You do not know. You cannot know. You may never know. But there is one truth of which you may be assured: God's payment plan is the best insurance in the world — you are guaranteed to always have what you need when you need it.

Always keep putting your love out there. This does not mean you need to be a doormat, a martyr, or a fool. All it means is that you keep on loving, and you trust that your love is working, even when you do not see the results on *your terms*. Your terms are based on an extremely limited picture. There is One who sees a bigger picture. Entrust your vision to Him, and you cannot lose.

Do not be attached to seeing the results of your giving. An act of love may go unacknowledged, but this does not mean that the effect has not occurred. All it means is that you did not see the effect. You must know that what you are doing is very much appreciated on some level, and it is improving the world significantly.

The real reward of giving is in the act of loving. The results in the outer world are the icing on the cake. The feeling of joy in truly giving love far exceeds the need to see a response. If you need a response, you have confused giving with getting, and that is a poor bargain to strike. Your love is real, it is felt, and it is working. Never doubt this. When you doubt, you begin to devise silly games to find proofs that you are loved, and those proofs are never satisfactory, even when they come. The real proof lies within your heart, where you feel peace when you give love.

Your faith is your greatest asset in this world of shadows and illusions. It will not fail you when all else is falling away. Your faith will tell you that nothing is taken away that you need, and nothing is given you that you cannot use. The gifts that you are given are based not upon your achievement, but upon your identity. Your identity is the heir to the Kingdom of God, and surely such a noble child would not be cast to the winds of fate. You make your own fate by believing that you deserve love, and you prove your destiny by accepting only good. Thus you go far beyond the meager property of time and space. You find the answer to your love in giving it.

My Beloved Son

Behold, this is My Beloved Son, in whom I am well pleased.
- Matthew 3:17

The crisp winter evening nipped at my ears as I approached the door of the laundromat. It would be good to get inside and feel the warmth. I emptied my laundry into the first available machine and, realizing I had half an hour to fill, I decided to stroll down the mall to Bradlees to return some Christmas gifts.

Heading toward the department store, my tummy told me it was dinnertime. Suddenly I felt a deep craving for eggplant parmesan. Instantly I conceived a whole menu of thought-forms about that savory dish, and in my mind I was quickly transported to an astral pasta palace.

As the divine plan would have it, there just happened to be an Italian restaurant right between the laundromat and Bradlees (It is not a random universe!) and I set my tastebuds on course toward Tony's.

As I approached the restaurant my mind began to generate all kinds of reasons why I shouldn't have an eggplant parmesan sandwich.

"You know," said the mind, "the bread will probably be made of white flour, and you should eat only whole wheat."

"Hmmm," I began to ponder, "maybe that's true."

Given an opening, the mind continued: "And don't you remember that radio program that said, 'Watch out for tomatoes — they are nightshades'?"

"Maybe this is a test of temptation!" I speculated.

In hot pursuit, the mind waged its final assault: "Just think: the cheese will not be organic!"

I stopped with my hand on the knob of the restaurant door. There I found myself at the crossroads of indecision, stymied at the intersection of the gulley of guilt and the freeway to freedom. It was an old familiar position of attempting to decide what to do to be good, how to please God, how to avoid the punishment that comes of being bad.

Then an inner guidance came, a voice nudging me in a direction I had not before considered.

"Alan, imagine you had a child, a little boy about five years old."

O.K., I could do that.

"Now imagine that you loved this child with the depth and breadth of your being, to the point that this child's happiness was more important to you than anything else in the world."

That was quite a feeling.

"Now, Alan, if you were out shopping with this son of yours one winter evening around dinnertime and your beautiful little boy, holding your hand, looked up into your eyes and asked, 'Daddy, I'm hungry...Could you please buy me an eggplant sandwich?' what would you do?"

The answer was easy, and so obvious. I would take the deepest delight in taking that child to the nearest Italian restaurant, sitting down with him at a table with a red and white checkered cloth, and ordering him the biggest eggplant parmesan sandwich on the menu — with ice cream for dessert! And I would sit with him and be thrilled by his enjoying it.

"Why, then, would you expect that I would want any less for you? For you are My Beloved Son, in whom I am well pleased."

Upon hearing those words a feeling came over me that was totally fulfilling and complete, unlike anything I have known in this world. It was the simplest and yet most profound feeling of being loved by God. For so long I felt that I was unworthy and punishable. But in just a few moments of feeling what I would do for a child that I loved, I became the child that God loved.

Then I received a garland of words I had read and heard many times before, but as I heard them that day I heard them anew. I understood the meaning of these words, for I heard them from the mouth of the One Who spoke them:

> *If a man's son asked him for a loaf of bread,*
> *would he give him a stone?*

I realized, as if for the first time, that God wants only for us to be happy, and He would never hurt us. I knew that God is a God of only love, the source of everything that is good. The idea of God punishing us or giving us something we didn't ask for is inside out (and it has been the cause of our doing some very crazy things!). I knew that my relationship with God is not one in which He is a demanding authority figure requiring me to prove my worth, but a loving Father taking delight in seeing me happy. I further reasoned that one of the purposes of our having children is to feel how much joy God derives from giving us what makes us happy. We can use the best of our relationships on earth to see what our relationships in Spirit are really like.

As Thyself

Once I was visiting some friends who had a little child. As her mom and I were conversing in the kitchen, the little girl tugged at her mom's dress and asked her for some orange juice. Mommy gave her the juice in a glass with a straw, and within a few seconds the child had imbibed the entire glass. She concluded her drink with a symphony of delightful slurping sounds indicating that the straw was vacuuming the bottom of a nearly empty glass.

"She sure did a quick job on that one!" mom commented. We both smiled, as we enjoyed the child's joy in drinking the juice and her playfulness.

Then it occurred to me that if I had drunk the juice that quickly, I probably would have considered myself a glutton. Sometimes when I have been very thirsty I have drunk something quickly, and I have judged myself for it. But I had no judgement for this child in my heart — I loved watching her enjoy it.

I wondered, then, why could I not extend the same freedom to myself? Jesus' most often quoted teaching is "Love thy neighbor as thyself," and we usually interpret this to mean that we should be as kind to our neighbor as we would like them to be to us. And this is surely true.

But perhaps there is another meaning to this great teaching. Perhaps we are being reminded to extend the same forgiveness to ourself that we offer our neighbors. We are much harder on ourself than we are on others. How often do we forgive a neighbor for something for which we would judge ourself harshly? If so, we are loving our neighbor *more* than ourself, and we need to love ourself just as much.

Years ago when I was in college I would sometimes go to x-rated movies. I felt rather guilty about this, as I judged myself for it. One evening when my roommate was out I decided to go to the local art cinema. I slinked into the theatre, feeling strange about being there. I took a seat and waited for my eyes to adjust to the darkness. After a few minutes I looked down the row, and who did I see sitting there, but my roommate!

Now here is a great lesson that I learned: Upon seeing him my initial reaction was, "I must not let him see me — he will think I'm weird." It was fine with me that he was there; I did not judge him for it — lots of college guys go to x-rated films, and he was just out enjoying himself one evening. I certainly did not love him any the less. Perhaps I even loved him more, knowing that he was like me. But I felt that I was bad for being there. Even when confronted with the truth that I and my brother are one, my ego found a way to fabricate a separation between myself and my brother. I let him know I was there, and we had a good laugh together. "All sin ends in laughter."

That night I learned to love my neighbor as myself, or should I say, to love myself as much as my neighbor.

Forgiveness Clears the Way

We need to forgive ourself before we can make progress with any challenge. At a workshop a woman approached me and told me that she was having a very hard time quitting smoking pot. "I've been smoking every day for ten years, and I have tried everything to help me stop. I've been hypnotized, I've asked my friends to hide my joints, — I even went to Pot Smokers Anonymous — yet I haven't been able to stop. I just don't know what to do!"

"Who says you have to stop?" I asked her.

She was startled. "But it's a terrible habit!"

"Here's my suggestion," I offered. "Don't judge yourself or make an issue of smoking. Just love yourself. If you smoke, you smoke; if you don't smoke, you don't. Learn that smoking pot has nothing to do with your worthiness or lovability. But do this: Go for the light. Do the things that really bring you peace. Meditate, pray, sing, come to my workshops or others — do whatever brings real joy to your heart. Don't curse the darkness; light a light. Then you will see exactly what pot smoking is all about."

Several months later the woman came to me, ecstatic. "It's amazing!" she raved. "I haven't smoked pot in months — for the first time in ten years!"

"Tell me more!" I encouraged her.

"Well, I did just as you said. I decided not to let smoking or not smoking be a big deal. I decided to love myself no matter what. I did more of the things that bring me real peace.

"Then one night I went to a party and before long a joint came my way. I took one toke, and it was nothing — I tell you, *nothing!* It wasn't good, it wasn't bad — it just wasn't interesting. I passed it by, for the first time in all those years. The same situation came up once or twice since then, and my experience was the same. I think I am done with pot."

I am happy to report to you that I have seen this woman often since her report and she has not smoked in years. In fact, she is an entirely new person — all because she was willing to forgive herself and love herself just as she was.

When we hate ourself, we energize the thing we hate. Hatred is a powerfully creative emotion, for it feeds the object of our wrath and causes it to loom even larger in our mind. Ironically, we tie ourself to that which we resent. Thoughts are targets, and emotions (e-*motions*) are the fuel that moves us toward those targets. To hate anything we do, therefore, is to cause us to do it more. The only antidote to a bad habit is to love yourself for what you are, and then to cultivate the habit we do want. Love and hate both move us toward their objects. We must choose what we really want.

Good and Truth

One of the ways that we violate ourselves is by trying to prove that we are good. To try to prove that you are good is to affirm that you are not already good. So in a sense you are trying to fill in a hole that does not exist. No wonder your life has been bumpy!

The Indian saint Neem Karoli Baba said, *"Truth does not come from good; good comes from truth."* When you tell the truth, much good comes, but if you try to attain truth by doing what you believe is good, you may not gain truth, but confusion. It is very difficult to know exactly what good should come of any particular situation. To attempt to manipulate circumstances so *your* idea of good can come about, is to let the ego play God — and that, as you know, can and does backfire. "You cannot be your own guide to miracles, for it was you who made them necessary."[1]

I first learned about the pitfalls of being a do-gooder several years ago when I was invited to visit the home of Maurice B. Cooke, the author of the *Hilarion Series*,[2] a powerful collection of spiritual teachings. I had respected

[1] T, p. 277
[2] M.B. Cooke, *The Hilarion Series*, Marcus Books

279

and admired Mr. Cooke's work for a long time, and I considered it a great honor and opportunity to be with him and his family.

The first evening of our visit we shared a lovely dinner, and after some intriguing conversation the dishes from the main course were collected. Now, what would any self-respecting do-gooder do at that moment? The dishes, of course! I arose and went straight for the sink. "They'll really appreciate this," I subconsciously thought; "I'll do all the dishes, and they'll see what a good person I am! Then they'll like me and invite me back." So, while everyone else was sitting at the dinner table enjoying apple pie, Dudley Do-Right was in the kitchen washing away. (I whistled occasionally to let them know that I was on the job.)

The final piece was the wok in which the Chinese vegetables had been stir-fried. "What an oily wok!" I remarked to myself. "This needs a real scrubbing...I'll clean it up, and then I will have done really good!" Out came the Brillo, and away I scrubbed.

Soon Maurice's wife Christine came into the kitchen to see what had happened to me. With great pride I held up the shiny scrubbed wok, and like a little boy showing his mom the finger-painting he made in kindergarten, I proclaimed, "Look, Christine, how clean the wok is!"

Christine's jaw dropped about six inches. (With a remarkable amount of self control) she exclaimed, "It took me three years to season that wok!"

What I didn't know was that you're not supposed to scrub a wok until it shines. Woks, I learned (quickly) are better when they are seasoned. But I was busy doing good — which is not always so good!

Christine was a good sport and we had a good laugh. It was a priceless lesson to me. If I had listened to my inner voice, I probably would have stayed in the dining room and enjoyed dessert with my friends. Then perhaps several of us would have gone into the kitchen together and played through the cleanup in song and laughter. And saved the wok. That was the last time I did good.

Stand Up and Be Counted

One of my most important lessons of this life has been that is it more important to *be* myself than to prove myself. I have gotten into all kinds of trouble in relationships, business, and communications because I wanted to be nice at the expense of telling the truth. I was afraid that I would be rejected or somehow lose if I said something that another person would not like to hear. Yet time and time again I have found that people value the truth more than sugar-coating. Loving honesty is much more productive in the long run.

The only thing more frustrating than being a nice guy is to be with a bunch of nice guys trying to make a decision. It doesn't happen!

Several years ago I was spending a day in New York City with some friends. As evening approached we were deciding whether to go to a movie in the city or return home.

The driver of the car turned to the rest of us and asked, "Well, folks, what would you like to do tonight?"

"Anything's fine with me!" Charley answered.

"I'm flexible!" we heard from Susan.

"I will go with the flow!" responded Artie.

When the poll got around to me, I answered, "Whatever you like!"

"Now wait a minute!" the driver retorted. "No one is saying anything that will help us decide! We really need to have some opinions here. This is just one of those situations where everyone is going to have to be honest about what they want. Let's go around again, and everyone please take a stand."

As it turned out, none of us really wanted to go to the movie, and so we went home. But we could have said that the first time.

Love Proves Itself

Love requires no defense and bears no need to prove itself. It knows that it is lovable, and all that comes from love must be lovable, too. You, who are love, need no method to demonstrate your worth, for your value speaks for itself before you even say a word or begin a deed. You accomplish far more by allowing your true goodness to shine than by attempting to neurotically demonstrate that you are valuable. Any attempt that you make to convince another that you are good will interrupt the One who stands with you to speak on your behalf, and you will demonstrate to the contrary. There is nothing you can do to make yourself more worthy, but you can, and *must*, awaken to your own greatness.

God needs no proof of who you are. Why should you? The fact that you do not remember your Origin is not a statement about your Source, but about your memory. One day you will learn that you have always been whole, despite your lapses in recollection. Thank God that your perfection is not dependent upon your recall.

Imagine for a moment that everything you do, that you have done, and that you will do is good. Imagine that you could not possibly do any bad if you tried. Can you get a taste of the feeling of forgiveness and release? That is how God sees you now. God has not been fooled in the least by your facade of unworthiness. The only difference between God and your self-image is that God always remembers how much you are loved, while you have sometimes forgotten.

You are lovable not because of what you do; you are lovable because of what you *are*. And that can never change. Your true nature as a loving being is *invulnerable and inviolable*. Spirit knows this about you now, and this is how you will learn to see yourself. When you see yourself as God sees you, you will have become God. And that is very possible indeed. In fact, you will not be finished with your wondrous journey of consciousness until you have claimed the vision of yourself as healed.

My Beloved Son

At an intensive healing retreat my roommate Lou sat in the center of a circle of supportive friends, describing the most important transformational events of his life. After painfully describing many years of challenge, hardship, and feelings of unworthiness, his face lit up as he described his experience of being at his first son's birth. Immediately he burst into tears, calling the child's name, "Andrew! My God, Andrew! How beautiful you are! How blessed I feel that you have come to be with me as my son! I have never felt so much love in all my life!"

The group of listeners began to weep with him, for the depth of his appreciation struck a chord deep within all of us. Here was a man who was totally grateful for the gift of his child.

After hearing Lou's entire story the facilitator began to offer her insights and counsel him. She encouraged him to know above all else his worthiness and beauty in the eyes of God. At the end of her sharing with Lou she stopped, thought for a moment, and told him: "And if there is one thing I would like you to remember the next time you do not love yourself, it is this: The way you felt when Andrew was born is the way God felt when you were born, multiplied ten thousandfold, and lasting unto eternity."

Story of a Soul

Nothing you can do can change Eternal Love.
- A Course in Miracles[1]

There are some experiences in life that come to us as gifts of grace. Sometimes we receive blessings that clearly do not bear a relationship to anything we have done. They are bestowed upon us to remind us that we are lovable not for what we do, but for what we are.

A blessing such as this was given to me during a planetary healing pilgrimage that I undertook to the European continent. Thirty of us gathered to find and explore the ancient mystical healing sites of the continent. It was during this journey that I had one of the most treasured and transforming experiences of my life, and I would like to share it with you now.

One of the shrines we visited was the Church of St. Theresa of Lisieux, who was affectionately known as "The Little Flower." St. Theresa was a little-known nun who lived in the late nineteenth century. Her devotion as a child was so compelling that she obtained the Pope's permission to enter a Carmelite convent at the age of thirteen. For seven years she served in the order, seeking to emulate the innocence that she found exemplified by the Child Jesus.

During her stay in the convent Theresa often underwent criticism and blame from the elder sisters. Once Theresa loaned her last favored possession, a water pitcher, to a sister in the convent. When it was returned with a crack in it, Theresa thanked God for removing the last barrier to peace from her heart. Such was the gentle willingness of Theresa to find Heaven above all else.

Around the age of twenty Theresa became ill. When it became apparent that she would not be living in this world much longer, her elder sister asked her to write the story of her life and her devotion to the way of simple loving. Theresa did so, more out of obedience than desire, and left the *Story of a*

---

[1] M, p.84

Soul [2] as a tender, shining legacy of her short but meaningful life. Theresa promised that she would "spend my Heaven doing good on earth," and "let fall a shower of roses to all who need love."

When the book was published after Theresa's passing, it became a sensation, selling out almost as fast as it could be printed. Theresa's readers discovered an immense spiritual power in her uncomplicated words and childlike devotion. The unassuming strength of her conviction won the hearts and souls of readers throughout the world. Soon Theresa began to appear in visions and accomplish miracles for many persons in need of help. The healings were often accompanied by the sweet fragrance of roses. Sometimes a rose would be found at the site of a miracle.

I was told the story of a woman who prayed to St. Theresa for help for her mother, who was undergoing a surgical operation. After the daughter waited for a long time in the anteroom of the surgical suite, a doctor emerged from the operating room, exhibiting a sweaty brow and a half-smile.

"It looks like your mother is going to be alright," he comforted her, "...but I don't know how I could have done it without the guidance of that nun."

"What nun?" inquired the daughter.

"The nun who came into the operating room and gave me directions during the surgery — Didn't you see her?"

"No, I didn't," answered the young woman "...and I was sitting here the whole time."

At that moment the two of them looked down, and found a rose at their feet.

It was with great anticipation and devotion that the thirty of us bussed toward Lisieux on that rainy September morning. How light we became as we sang songs and told miracle stories woven about our love for The Little Flower! The bus seemed to lift a few inches off the highway as we rode through the French countryside. What a reason to "arise at dawn," as Kahlil Gibran wrote, "and give thanks for another day of loving!"

Can you imagine our delight to learn upon arriving in Lisieux that this, the one day that we would be there, was St. Theresa's feast day! We joined thousands of pilgrims scaling the sloping hill to the pastel basilica high atop the picturesque little town. Gratefully we gazed upon the patchwork countryside of Brittany, a soft mirror of the gentleness that Theresa lived to extol.

---

[2] *Story of a Soul: the Autobiography of St. Theresa of Lisieux*, ICS Publications, Institute of Carmelite Studies, Washington DC 1972

As I entered the church I saw a thousand candles burning a thousand prayers into the high archways of the basilica. The contoured ceilings were elaborately yet tastefully decorated with painted roses, portraits of St. Theresa, and quotes from her brief but eternal lifetime. My gaze was drawn to the high altar, hundreds of feet away yet nearer than my breath. There I beheld a score of white-robed, hooded priests chanting hymns to God and celebrating the virtues of their dear patroness. Love filled the air; it was a moment of pure adoration. The service that followed was a touching communion of souls. We held hands with the elderly ladies who had come many miles to attend this mass. They appeared to be peasants, but I saw that they were queens. We hugged them warmly as the celebration concluded. The fact that we spoke no French did not matter; we were united in love, and that language transcended all apparent differences. It was a moment orchestrated by angels.

Exiting from the mass I noticed a sign pointing "To the Crypt." The word "crypt" has never had a great appeal to me, as I have always associated it with maudlin tales of sardonica *a la* Edgar Allen Poe. Yet today I felt guided to step inside this place to see what was there.

What I found was a blessing of the highest Light. The feeling in this sanctuary was sweet, nourishing, and deeply healing. Slowly, reverently I made my way beneath the painted arches to the golden altar at the front of the sanctuary. I sat down for a minute to listen to the music and feel the peace. What happened to me then I shall never forget.

As I settled into my seat a feeling of the deepest serenity enfolded me. It was as if I was being bathed in a pool of tenderness. Glued to my seat, I felt myself washed over and healed in a golden light. I looked at the gold of the altar and I realized that it was but symbolic of the wealth of the healing energy emanating from the crypt. There was no death in that crypt, only eternal life in the most magnificent testimony of its own reality. There I knew with all my heart that Spirit is the only reality; that love and service are the real essence of life; and that this physical plane is not even like unto dust covering a lamp. Everything physical, everything of this world seemed as nothing compared to the peace flowing over and through me.

There I felt a *living presence* — not just an idea or a belief — it was the essence of a living being, created and creating of love itself. If I could give it a voice, it was saying, *"My Child, God is real; Love is real; all the teachings of the Christ and the saints are true. Nothing you do in this physical world can touch the power of the presence of God, Who is Love and Love alone."*

Then I understood the meaning of the *Course in Miracles* teaching, *"Nothing you can do can change Eternal Love."*

I wanted to sit there forever; there was nothing more I wanted, nothing I needed, nowhere to go, nothing to do, not a thing to say but, "Thank you, I love you." I felt comforted in a universal womb, safe and sure of my protection, nourished to my depths. I felt that I could have stayed there for eternity. Perhaps I did. It was a taste of Heaven, one that remains imprinted in my heart like the soft warmth of the first spring rain. It was a true gift from God.

Realizing at some point that it was time to go, I arose a changed man. A saint had taken my hand and shown me the lawns of Heaven. I was told very directly that God is with me and all of us all the time, and there is nothing to fear in all the universe, for all there is, is the love of God.

As I made my way out of the church I saw a lifesize statue of The Little Flower standing by the door. Posted beside it was a sign promising that "Those who sign the book at St. Theresa's feet are assured of her protection." I signed the book, including my name and those dear to me.

As I laid down the pen, my eye was drawn to a collection of plaques from persons who had received answers to their prayers in the name of The Little Flower. Most of them said simply, "Thank you, St. Theresa," gently meaningful testimonies that I know she appreciated and offered to her Lord.

I thought that I, too, should like to offer The Little Flower a plaque of thanks for blessing me so richly. I would like to designate this testimony as my plaque of appreciation to my Little Flower. I want to say publicly, St. Theresa, that I believe in you; to me you are more real than this physical world, and if, as a result of reading this, others are inspired to seek and find help through your intercession, I will celebrate with you the shower of roses that you have sent to a world pining to know the joy of true love. You have taught me that the path of the pure of heart is the straightest road to God, and that the simplicity of a child is the way to find the peace you discovered. Thank you, St. Theresa, for spending your Heaven doing good on earth. I should like to join you in your noble cause

Saint Theresa

The HEALING of the PLANET EARTH

Now, Voyager

We are on the verge of the new age, a whole new world.
Human consciousness, our mutual awareness,
is going to make a quantum leap.
Everything will change...
All this is going to happen just as soon as you're ready.
                                        - Paul Williams, *Das Energi*[1]

One night I had a most symbolic dream. In the dream I was in an airplane flying from New Jersey to Hawaii. En route I experienced incredible delays. First, the plane landed in Kansas City where I had to make a connection. But the airplane landed in an old, rundown baseball field, as if I had gone into a time warp — it was back in the 1950's! Then the plane had to go to another airport in the city to make the connection. But instead of flying to the airport, the plane drove on the highway with the automobiles — and it was rush hour. It seemed like it was taking forever to get there!

When I asked the steward when my next flight was scheduled to leave, he answered, "That flight is scheduled to depart in one year, sir." *One year!* Then I noticed that I was the only one on the plane. And it was not the airline I had originally scheduled. Finally, when the flight was airborne, the stewardess announced, "We are scheduled to arrive in New Jersey in two hours." After all that, I was back where I started!

Finally I got disgusted with this dream, and I decided to wake up. And do you know where I woke up? In Hawaii, where I had gone to sleep the night before.

It can be very frustrating trying to get where you already are. If you are already home, you can be sure that any attempt to get there will cause delays, and ultimately will not work. You need but realize you are already home.

I had another experience which also had to do with airplanes and

---

[1] Paul Williams, *Das Energi*, Warner Books, 1978, p. 50

airports, but this time it was in a waking dream.

Last spring I went to North Carolina to participate in a healing conference. It was a long weekend of travelling and workshops, and when Sunday came I looked forward to returning home, stretching out on my couch, and relaxing. My plane touched down to the Newark runway at 9 o'clock on Sunday night, and I was glad to be home. My friend Anne would be waiting for me at the gate, and it would be good to see her.

When I reached the lobby, Anne was not there. I waited five, ten, fifteen minutes, and still there was no sign of her. Where was she?

I phoned the house, and to my surprise Anne answered.

"Where are you?" I asked. (Actually, it was a rhetorical question. I already knew the answer, but it was not the one I wanted to hear.)

"I'm home," she brightly replied. "Where are you?"

"I'm at Newark Airport."

"Noooo!"

"That's what this sign here says."

"But you're not coming in until tomorrow night."

I looked at my ticket. "The ticket says I'm here tonight."

"The message from your office says Monday night."

"I think the pilot didn't get that message."

"O.K...Hang in there — I'll be right there." Right there meant at least forty-five minutes. I felt annoyed. "Why is this happening, God? What am I going to do in Newark Airport for almost an hour?"

The Voice came loud and clear: *"Why not practice being happy?"*

"Yeah, that's easy for You to say," I retorted. "You get to hang out on some celestial cloud, listening to harp music and watching sunsets — You don't have to sit in Newark Airport on a Sunday night."

"What makes you think Newark Airport is outside of Heaven?"

"Now, really, God, You're stretching it on that one."

"Am I?"

"Of course You are. If You're so great, why didn't You have Anne here on time?"

"Listen, Son," the Big Air Traffic Controller went on, *"It's really up to you. You can be bugged, or you can have the greatest hour of your life. You can choose to be upset or you can be in love. That's the power I gave you. Don't you remember all those books you wrote telling people that happiness is available at any moment?"*

(Why is it that God always has to hit you with the truth when you're upset?)

"Sure, I remember."

"Well, here's your chance to practice. Imagine that you are in Heaven now."

"You sure do have a great imagination."

"I know — that's how I created the entire universe! Not a bad production, wouldn't you agree?"

I had to agree. I had my assignment.

So I decided to play a game while I waited. I decided to imagine that I was in Heaven, and everything I saw happening before me was actually happening in Heaven. I saw that the porters were smiling as they were ticketing luggage. "Wow," I exclaimed to myself, "...they are ticketing suitcases in Heaven — what a great job!"

Then I saw families greeting their children at the baggage carousel. "What a wonderful scene," I remarked to myself; " — families reuniting in Heaven!" My heart felt warm.

Then I noticed several people standing at the rent-a-car desks, making arrangements to pick up transportation. "How beautiful!" I considered. "These folks have arrived in Heaven and they are going to tour or find their new homes!"

As I continued to play the game, I found myself in a state of deep tranquility. The flight attendant had said, "Welcome to New Jersey," but I was beginning to see that that was but a part of a bigger picture.

Sitting there in what seemed to be Newark Airport, I went into an exquisitely beautiful meditation — with my eyes open. Why would I need to close my eyes to find Heaven, if I were seeing it all around me?

My reveries were interrupted by Anne's hand on my shoulder. "Hi!" she smiled.

Had it been forty-five minutes?

"Ready to go?" she asked, car keys jingling in her hand.

"Sit down," I invited her. "This is a wonderful place!"

"What are you talking about?"

"This is Heaven!" I told her.

"Noooo!"

Anne sat down, and I explained to her what had happened. She loved the idea; she was happy to be in Heaven, too.

Then came the icing on the cake. A rather harried fellow came up to us and asked us if we would mind watching his bags for a few minutes while he went to make a phone call. Already in Heaven, we had no place to go; so we were happy to tell him "sure." A short while later he returned and thanked us profusely for our help.

Then it occurred to me that we had just brought Heaven to earth. Because we were in a heavenly state of consciousness, we served our brother and made his life easier. (George Eliot said, "What do we live for if not to make life less difficult for one another?") If we were in a state of fear or impatience, we might have said no or acquiesced begrudgingly. But we were at peace, and in that consciousness it was our joy to bring him peace.

I saw that we had actually *created* Heaven in Newark Airport, and we saw it manifest in a very material, practical, and grounded way. So I learned that Heaven begins with our thoughts.

This is It

At a workshop I attended, the leader taught a strong lesson about the power of the now. "This is it," he stated, "and it doesn't get much 'itter' than this!"

There is just as much love, God, peace, and healing in the room in which you are now reading, as there is or ever will be anywhere in the universe. There is a great ocean of love, which includes every kind of fulfillment you have ever dreamed of, inviting you to swim in it. But you have to step into it. And it is even easier than that — you don't even need to know how to step into it; you just have to let go of the ways that you have devised to dam it away from you. *"The course does not aim at teaching the meaning of love, for that is beyond what can be taught. It does aim, however, at removing the blocks to the awareness of love's presence, which is your natural inheritance."*[2]

One of the ways we deny love's presence is by placing it in the future or the past. We see Heaven as being in the future, like a carrot on a stick which we will get a bite of if we are good between now and then. But *there is no "then."* All there will be in the future is here now. We deserve good not by earning it, but by accepting it.

The concept of future peace actually works against peace, for if there is no peace now, there is no peace. Jesus was not a pie-in-the-sky teacher, although many who claim to teach in his name use the carrot of Heaven as a tool of fear. Jesus taught, "The Kingdom of Heaven is at hand," and "It is within you." He was a teacher of love in the present moment. Indeed this moment is the only one in which we will find true love.

---

[2] T, Introduction

In a way similar to misplacing our trust in the illusion of a future Heaven, we hurt ourselves by believing in a Heaven that existed in the past. "If only I could go back to the good ole' days," we think, or "if I could just recapture that moment." But what we need to realize is that the joy of those moments came from being in those moments, and if we would be willing to be in the present moment, we would find the same wonder waiting for us to enjoy it.

Even in new age teaching, we may tend to glamorize our "former" innocence or the heavenly realm from which we came to earth. This, too, is a trap, for the way we lose that innocence is to wander into thoughts about it being in the past. The same innocence and light are available to us here, now, in a body, on the earth. "On earth as it is in Heaven," prayed Jesus. He wouldn't have declared it if it weren't possible and true. We have *not* lost our innocence, except in our thoughts, and our thoughts alone. Paradise has not been removed from us. But we have removed ourselves from It by believing it was there or then, and not here and now.

One afternoon when I was in Olympia, Washington, I was riding in a car with Unity minister John Wingfield and his lovely five-year-old daughter, Leanna. Somehow our conversation got around to where we came from.

"I know where I came from, Daddy!" Leanna offered.

"Where's that, sweetheart?" Daddy inquired.

"Heaven!"

John and I looked at one another and we smiled. It was, of course, a perfectly cute answer.

Then John turned to Leanna and added something quite profound to her response:

"That's right, Leanna...And you are still in Heaven!"

That got me. John's words put it all in perspective. His statement was the missing link, the truth that bridged the supposed gap between the Heaven that we came from and the Heaven that we are taught we will go to (if we are good). We *are* good, and we are good *now*. This knowledge is the key that unlocks the door to the Heaven that we deserve, now and always.

The Invitation

Life is not a delicatessen where you have to take a number and wait until your turn is called. It is an always alive and fully exciting gift of total love.

Many times Jesus likened the Kingdom of Heaven to a great banquet to which everyone is invited. The table is set, and all are free to partake. But if you believe there is something you have to do first, you will delay your homecoming and you will be hungry. Not because the food is kept from you, but because you had something you believed was more important.

That something may be a job or a marriage or a new car, or any of the glittering things of this world. Or it may be a thought that you need to suffer first or do something to earn Heaven. Suffering has no place in the Kingdom, and the idea of earning God's love is as preposterous as an infant earning his mother's adoration or proving himself worthy to be sheltered by his father. A child receives love because she is lovable. That lovableness has nothing to do with what she does, but it has everything to do with what she *is*. *Is* is a present tense verb. Because you are always in a state of *is*ness, you are always in the Kingdom. Any concepts that you harbor about what you have to do first to deserve Heaven are roadblocks which you have erected between yourself and your happiness. They push Heaven away from you by exactly the distance of the width of your fear of It.

The Door to the Light

Even a little consideration of the possibility that you are already healed will begin to undo the tight ball of knotted fears which has bound you, and set into motion the dynamics of mind that will open the door to the Light. Real healing in your life is possible only now, and it is up to you to accept it or delay it. Please accept it all now. You have no karma to pay off, no more tests to face, and no further lessons to learn. All of those ideas are products of past, future, and separation thinking. If all there is, is now, from when could you have incurred a karmic debt? If you are one with God and there is no power outside your own Self, who could test you? And if your mind is one with the Mind of God, Whose knowledge of the whole of the cosmos is imbued in your soul, what lesson would further be required of you?

These concepts of salvation in time may have served you to bring you to the point at which you now stand, but beyond this moment they will act only as an encumberment. *Be free now!* This moment is the only one in which liberation can be found. *Future salvation is no salvation.* You have allowed thoughts of past and future Paradise to edge you out of eternity. This need not be. The same eternity that was available to you before you chose to step out of it is available to you now, as it always has been, and always will be. That step was taken in thought only, and not in reality. You are free to think with

God or against Her, but you are not free to be outside Her love. Peace is here for you to choose, but the only moment in which you are free to choose it is the present one.

Who would wander into past guilt or future fear if he knew that he could have all the peace he has ever dreamed of, now? Who would make a plan for her liberation if she knew that plans were the ego's tools to avoid freedom now? Who would preach the way to escape from a future hell unless he were in hell already? And how clearly do you think one in hell can see the way out?

But one who walks with God at this moment can show you the way to healing. You are not a body, but an idea, and ideas are alive only as you think them. Think another, and the original idea is gone. Return to the original one, and what you interposed between its inception and your return was but a dream. No matter how long you have dreamed of loss, only a moment's awakening is required for you to realize that all is quite intact.

Celebration, not Anticipation

To attempt to act to create a new age in the future is to fall into the subtle trap of denying that it is already with us. To manufacture a future Heaven is to judge the present One, and the present One is all there is. In so judging you will see separation, find people who are wrong, and feel that you are a victim — none of which are true.

The Millenium that you rightfully seek lives within you even as you read these words. But it needs your assent to be made real on earth. God has done His part to create it, and now your part is but to accept it.

Do not delay your healing by doubting, questioning, or waiting. You are never farther than one thought away from peace, and if you choose to think a peaceful thought, the Kingdom of Heaven is at hand. Every great sage has taught this truth, and if you are willing to accept it, you may count yourselves among those who see God.

> *Do you not say, "There are yet four months, then comes the harvest"? I tell you, lift up your eyes, and see how the fields are already white for harvest!*
>
> - Jesus the Christ[3]

---

[3] John 4:35

The Day After the Prayer

Someday, after mastering the wind, the waves, and the tides,
We shall harness for God the power of love,
And then, for the second time in history,
Man will have discovered fire.

- Teilhard de Chardin

God, what can I do to heal the earth?'' I asked as I sat in the quiet of my room late that Sunday evening. Thirty of us had gathered to watch the television docudrama "The Day After," and though I had expected the movie to be grimly depressing, I found myself more inspired than despairing. Deeply I yearned to be guided to know the way I could contribute to eliminating any possibility of the horrific scenes I beheld on the television screen.

There was one scene in particular that stood out in my memory. It was a scene in which a young woman was about to give birth to her child in a musty, dimly lit hospital. This was after the bomb had dropped, and she and her doctor were discussing the possibility of her child growing up healthy. The possibilities were slim.

"This did not have to happen," she said. "We knew about nuclear power for forty years. We knew its dangers and what it would do to the earth. But nobody cared. If someone cared enough, this would not have happened."

I thought about it, and I cared. I cared enough to want to do something about it. Perhaps if there were more people like me, we could make a difference.

Then came to me a thought, the kind of inspired awareness that is bestowed as a graceful gift, delivered by angels of the kindest intention. I remembered a project which a friend had told me about, in which American and Russian families were exchanging photographs and keeping one another's pictures in their living rooms as constant reminders of our abiding sameness. To me this was a guiding vision that there is nothing to fear of one

299

another, that we are all children of One God.

A voice of inner guidance blended with the memory. *"This project is symbolic of the way that the healing of the planet will be born, through overcoming fear with genuine love. The people of the world can create peace simply by finding peace within each one's own heart. As that happens — and it is happening, now — the governments of the world must follow suit. The politics of the world are nothing more or less than the reflection of the consciousness of the people. Make peace with the Russian people. Pray for Soviet families. Let there be a healing within your heart and mind, and the strength of your love will be the cornerstone upon which the temple of peace on earth will rest."*

Of course, it made so much sense. I began to see the wisdom of this way. As the outer world is but a mirror of my own mind, if I want to make a change in the world I see, I must first transform, or re-create, my pattern of thinking. If I seek to build a bridge of peace between nations, I must first find unity within my own self. This is the law of mind, love, and life, a principle I have seen demonstrated thousands of times in my own experience. And because the world I see is a reflection of my own self, what heals my own life must also heal the planet.

With the firmest confidence in the power of my intention, I began to radiate love and genuine caring to the people of Russia. As I did so I realized so clearly that they are just like me, appreciating life, enjoying their children, and yearning for peace and good will on our garden planet. Mentally I enfolded the Soviet people in my arms and told them that they need not be afraid of me. I let them know that I cared for them, that I would never do anything to hurt them. In a flash I saw the insanity of fear and the futility of casting anyone out of my heart. It was a vision of how easily love can transform our world.

As the power of the prayer increased, my relationship with the Soviet people became a reality. The thought occurred to me that I would love to visit the Soviet Union, to get to know the Russian people, to celebrate the truth that we are not really different after all. I imagined meeting Russian families, embracing them as my own, and sharing my books with them as an expression of our real unity. As I visualized these scenes I felt a warm glow in my heart, as if God was confirming to me that my desire was aligned with Divine Intention. I felt not so much that I was praying to God, but that God was praying through me.

Divine Appointment

The next morning I found myself in the USAir waiting room at Toronto Airport, en route to Newark, hardly able to think of anything but the destruction my eyes had beheld the night before. I watched the smiles of the families greeting one another at the gates. Light was dancing in the eyes of the children with their noses pressed against the viewport windows. I noticed the gaily-colored wall murals with scenes of international celebration, a striking contrast to the charred grey rubble of the razed, radioactive Kansas City depicted in the movie.

I wanted to see what effect the movie had had on the people of the world. Half-anxiously, half-eagerly I peered over some shoulders to catch a glimpse of the morning headlines. I hoped to read, *"'The Day After' Births New Efforts Toward World Peace."* Instead I found, *"Nuke Film Stirs Debate."*

"Debate?" I exclaimed to myself, "The last thing we need more of is debate — Didn't that film wake everyone up, as it did me? Didn't it make any difference?"

At that moment my reflections were interrupted by the sound of a mother reading a children's story to her little daughter, sitting just a few inches to my right. I couldn't make out the words she was reading, so I scanned the book. It looked like *"Babar,"* but I couldn't understand the characters of the writing on the page.

"Excuse me," I carefully interrupted them, "Could you please tell me what language that is you're reading?"

The mother lifted her head, and with the kindest smile she answered, "Russian."

My heart soared like a sailing star. The previous evening I had prayed with the deepest fervor to meet and make peace with Russian families, and now, *less than twelve hours after the prayer,* I found myself seated next to a lovely Russian family.

Silently I said a prayer of gratefulness. The night before I had seen the grim vision of our holy planet reduced to a mound of burning cinders because the American and Russian people forgot our mutual divinity, and this morning I found myself with another chance. It was as if I had awakened from a grievous nightmare, and here I was given the ability to personally stop the horror from becoming a reality.

"How to make contact, now?" I deliberated. I wanted to approach them in a way that would be comfortable for both of us. (There is a bumper sticker that advises, *"Expect a Miracle Today,"* and what a marvelous counsel that proved to be on that special day!) I reached into the pouch of my parka and there found a multicolored strip of heart stickers, the kind that children love to collect.

"That's it!" I silently celebrated. I tore off a section, held it firmly between my hands, and silently prayed, *"God, I'm going to give this little girl these hearts, and I ask you, Father, to imbue these hearts with Your Heart. Let this act of sharing symbolize the healing of the planet. With these hearts I offer all the love and understanding that will renew the truth of the real brotherhood and sisterhood of the American and Soviet peoples. Let this gift heal the earth of all separation, fear, and warfare forever. Let Your Light be shared now. The fate of the whole world and all humanity rests in my hands, and I ask You to use this act for your healing purposes. Let your blessing ripple out like waves on the ocean of eternal love. Thank you, Father, for I know You have heard and answered."*

With full confidence that what I had just done may have been one of the most important acts of my life, I turned to the little girl and asked her, "Would you like some hearts?" Though she had not been paying much attention to me, her eyes instantly lit up. Her mom, humbly grateful, asked her if she could say "thank you" in English. Shyly she did her best. As I gave her the strip I peeled off one heart, the color of the sun, and gently pressed it onto the page she was reading.

The girl's father, having watched our meeting, walked over to thank me, and we began to converse.

"What kind of work do you do?" he asked.

"I write books...some for children."

"Oh, really?" mom perked up, "On what subjects?"

"On themes like making friends."

An idea lighted in my mind. "Say, I have a book called *Have You Hugged A Monster Today?* If you'd give me your address, I'd love to send one to your beautiful daughter."

"Isn't that kind of you!..." the father began to respond, and just then we were shuffled onto the plane. As I took my seat about ten rows behind the family, I wondered if he was just being polite, or if I would have the joy to complete my offer. I sat and beamed prayers of thankfulness nearly the whole flight, tears welling up in my eyes at the thought of the immediacy with which last night's prayer was answered. Earnestly I hoped that more good would come of our meeting.

A few minutes before the plane was about to land, the burly man with a kind face rose from his seat and walked toward me with a slip of paper in his hand.

"Here is our address...You must come and visit us for dinner sometime!"

My joy at his invitation was exceeded only by the amazement that welled up within me as I read what was written on the paper. The girl's name was "Shlomit," which means "Peace." She was born in Jerusalem, which in Hebrew means "The City of Peace." The icing on the cake, the real cosmic giggle, however, was their address: Einstein Drive, Princeton. That is where Albert Einstein developed the formula for atomic energy. The symbology of the meeting is awesome: Peace is growing up on the street that Einstein paved.

A Formula for Planetary Healing

As this lesson was received for all of us, I would like to share with you some of the very important principles I gained from this miraculous experience:

WE CAN USE OUR THOUGHTS TO CREATE PEACE ON EARTH.

Thoughts are things, and every thought is a prayer. Our thoughts are very powerful, and we attract to ourselves that which we think upon. The Law of Mind is perfectly consistent, and it can be focused upon any chosen goal. The formula for healing ourselves, one another, and our planet is:

$$C + B = A$$

CONCEIVE + BELIEVE = ACHIEVE

I *conceived* of the idea of making peace with Russian families. (Mental conception, like physical conception, requires two partners. In this case God impregnated my mind with an idea, and I accepted it; thus was consummated the marriage of God and man.) Then I *believed* that such a marvelous healing could take place. A feeling of joyous completion vibrated through me. Finally, the idea was *achieved* as it was realized on the physical plane.

This incident is a dramatic example of how the Law of Mind works, a ubiquitous principle that governs all of our thoughts and their subsequent manifestations. The divine promise of the Law of Mind is that *we can change our life by changing our thoughts.* If we seek to change our planetary life, we must begin by

visualizing, feeling, and *accepting*

the reality of a peaceful, healed world. All actions that stem from these thoughts work instantaneously and dynamically to create peace.

Peace is an Idea
Whose Time Has Come

Since my vision, I have seen many indications that others have been inspired by the same lofty idea, and they are acting on it. Within a week after my prayer I saw a newspaper headline proclaiming, *"New York Town Launches First Strike for Peace."* The city of Saratoga Springs, New York has been matched by the Ground Zero Pairing Project[1] with a city in the Soviet Union, Kashin, U.S.S.R. (It is interesting to me that the USA and USSR both start with *US.*) The sister cities were chosen for similarities in climate, geography, population, industry, and in this case a special interest: both cities are known and celebrated for their natural spring water. The people of Saratoga Springs sent the Russian townspeople a three-pound love package, called a "Community Portrait," containing a scrapbook of items that are personally meaningful to the Saratogans, and it was arranged that the Kashin people do the same.

In Seattle, Washington, three thousand miles from where the idea came to me, I was given a flyer entitled "Send Your Heart to Russia," announcing the *Earthstewards Network* [2], a group without any particular religious, secular, or political affiliation, bound together only by their desire to make contact and share understanding with the Soviet people. The group organizes personal good-will tours of the Soviet Union (exactly my idea!).

---

[1] Ground Zero Pairing Project, Community Portrait Exchange, PO Box 19049, Portland, Oregon 97219

[2] Earthstewards Network, 6330 Eagle Harbor Drive N.E., Bainbridge Island, WA 98110

Besides inviting people to make a personal statement by visiting Russia, some of the Earthstewards were collecting small hand-made gifts from regular American people like you and me, to be personally delivered to Russian people like you and me, along with hugs and arrangements for pen-pal relationships. The trip includes a meeting with the Peace Committee of Moscow, visits to the sister cities, and sharing circle dances with the Russian people in the parks of Crimea, Georgia, and Muldavia. What a wonderful way to make contact!

Since that time I have learned of many other citizen diplomacy groups, each offering a unique and creative method of making human contact. "Play for Peace"[3] joins American and Russian people for frisbee throws and other light-hearted activities. One sculptor has proposed a Soviet-American "clay stomp," in which Russian and American persons of all ages come together, stomp a huge vat of modeling clay into mouldability, and then create ceramic ornaments to share and display in the spirit of mutual support. Other groups include volleyball tournaments, musical collaboration, and clowning. The possibilities for healing through creativity are endless! And many of them are being explored. Last year there were seventy-three citizen diplomacy groups scheduled to visit the Soviet Union from the *Seattle area alone*. Surely we are awakening to our own power to build bridges of love, no matter what the distance that seems to separate the shores. Love knows no distance or limitation.

The Way Out

As I was meditating after watching "The Day After," all I could see in my mind's eye were the two nuclear bombs bursting over Kansas City. Though in the movie they were red, in my field of vision I saw two dark masses, expanding into a nightmare of death and destruction. Then I remembered that a friend with whom I had watched the film had suggested the affirmation, *"The love of God is now pouring through the whole earth."* I began to repeat this affirmation, asking my Heavenly Father to show me the truth of these words. Then I saw a great beam of golden light coming down from far up in the heavens. This light was like a wonderful shaft of healing power pouring through the clouds. This wondrous ray shined down right where the bombs had burst, and the golden light began to dissipate the darkness. Like a horror film vanquished by a bright dome light switched on

---

[3] Play for Peace, PO Box 8910, La Jolla, CA 92038

in a theatre, this bright beam completely outshined the black mass of the bombs, until there was only golden light where the bombs had been. With this healing vision came these words:

The power of God is far greater than nuclear power.

This message of encouragement was followed with this explanation:

Atomic power is not even an eyelash compared to the arsenal of love that is God. The Power of the Divine, given cooperation, can free you from the seeming nuclear dilemma in a thousand ways that you haven't even begun to think of.

In other words, *God has a way out*, and indeed God is the *only* way out. God always has a way out, and just because we haven't discovered it yet, doesn't mean that it isn't there — it just means that we haven't approached it from the right angle yet. God's power begins where thoughts of limitation leave off. A miracle is simply something that God does as easily and naturally as anything else, except that we didn't think He could. The miracle, then, is not a reflection of God's ability to transcend law, but a statement of our willingness to accept the Law of Love as the only law.

In my lifetime I have seen many miracles, wondrous healings that have left me with the firmest conviction that God can indeed do anything. I have seen the lifetime crippled arise and walk at the touch of a healing hand; I have friends who have had seemingly inoperable cancers disappear in a matter of minutes; and I know of Padre Pio, the twentieth-century saint who prayed for a man with no corneas in his eyes, and the man had his sight restored. These are not supernatural occurrences, but natural expressions of God's Healing Love shining through the door of the opened mind. *A Course in Miracles* teaches that ''Miracles are natural. When they do not occur, something has gone wrong.''[4] Our problem is not that miracles are not available to us, but that we do not live in the expectation of miracles. The key to transforming our lives is to gladly *let go of our attempts to change other people, and use that energy to expand our expectation of what God can do for us.*

As the ancient orientals taught, every crisis equals danger plus opportunity. Where there is apparent danger, you can be sure there is a lesson, really a precious gift, waiting to be learned. When we accept the gift, our life

---

[4] T, p. 1

is infinitely enriched. Indeed the whole nuclear dilemma is actually our first planetary lesson, a cause for rejoicing, for through solving it we shall be firmly established in the great awareness that we live, breathe, and love as one family on this one planet — under one God.

Love's Way of Transformation

Nuclear power seems fearful — as does anything — only when we forget that God is in charge of the universe. *A Course in Miracles* reminds us, "The presence of fear is a sure sign that you are trusting in your own strength." The belief that we are lost, helpless, and unloved children is the source of all of our problems, and the nuclear situation is a magnification of our self-image as being outside of God. Who that believes God is present would need an atomic bomb? And who that believes God is not present could possibly secure his safety with ten thousand atomic bombs?

Whenever we act on a false idea, only more confusion can result. And so our world has become a nuclear porcupine, the natural result of unnatural thinking. We are like a family of children feeling deserted by a father who would gladly embrace us if we would only drop our defenses long enough to let a hug in. The only way out of the confusion is the memory that there is indeed a Divine Order to the universe, no matter how confused it may *seem* to be. The truth is that if we are willing to love, we shall surely discover we *are* loved.

The Heart is the Real Peacemaker

President Eisenhower said that

> *"One day the people of the world will want peace so much that the governments are going to have to get out of their way and let them have it."*

This is exactly what is happening on our planet now, and you and I have the great privilege to participate in this miraculous transformation and watch it unfold before our eyes. We are the channels through which a new age is being delivered upon the earth. The new age will not happen *to* us, but *through* us. There is no use in waiting for a savior. The savior is within each of us, patiently awaiting our expression.

We have now come to the moment in planetary evolution at which we must allow destiny to be delivered through us.

We are all expressions of the Mother Principle, and we can now all participate in the birth of a safe and healed world — a holy child that belongs to all of us.

Peace Needs Your Belief

It is possible that the only wall remaining between us and the complete healing of the planet is the *belief* that war is an inevitable part of life on earth. If this is so, then you and I can make a major contribution to the healing of our earth by simply understanding and knowing that war is *not* a necessary part of anyone's life, and certainly not of our collective lives. In fact, peace is what life on earth was intended to be about, and indeed *will* be about, as soon as we cease to believe that war is necessary. The course of human evolution involves shifts — sometimes radically rapid shifts — in what we *believe* to be so, and consequently what *is* so on the planet.

Until about a hundred years ago slavery was an accepted common practice in life on earth. Yet now slavery has almost entirely disappeared, and it is certainly unthinkable to us. The idea of slavery seems so outlandish that we can hardly conceive of it at all. Yet only a hundred years ago millions of human beings were indentured as slaves.

Although the idea of complete — *complete* — peace on earth may seem impossible, we need to look at planetary healing from the point of view of *the possible*. The first principle of miracles is that *there is no order of difficulty in miracles*. There is no reason to believe that healing the world of nuclear arms is any harder or needs to take any longer than the shift of one thought in your mind or mine, which are one. If we can see one possibility in a million for peace, it will surely come, for the mind works in terms of *possibilities*, and *it is only a matter of time until that which we can see to be possible becomes real.*

Peace Begins with Me

The most powerful way to bring about peace on the planet is to create peace in our personal relationships. Because the world is a manifestation of many small relationships, *we can create global peace by initiating interpersonal peace.* The fate of the world literally rests on our daily interactions with our husbands, wives, children, parents, roommates, friends, and co-workers. The politics of the world are simply a magnified reflection of the way we handle our daily personal politics. How can we expect the earth to be healed of separation if we are operating our individual lives under the illusion of personal separateness? And how can all the pain of the world but be healed, as we exchange our idea of being alone for the truth of being all one? Spake Paul, "When I was a child, I talked like a child, I thought like a child, I reasoned like a child. When I became a man I put childish ways behind me." [5]

There is one truth upon which we can found all of our precious work toward the healing of the planet earth:

Peace in the physical world can be built only upon the corner-stone of peace in each of our hearts, and as we heal our sense of interpersonal separation, peace on earth is sure to follow.

Metaphysicians tell us that all of the bullets, bombs, and nuclear warheads in the arsenals of the nations are the manifestations of the collective fear and anger thoughts of the people of the world over all of history. And now, we are told, we are facing the results of our thoughts. This may at first seem intimidating, but actually it is a cause for celebration, for if we created weapons with our thoughts of hatred, *we can dismantle them with our thoughts of love.* As we begin to think, feel, speak, and live in harmony with our treasured goal of peace, so must peace surely come.

This is Grace, which far supercedes karma. Grace means that no matter how big of a mess we seem to have made, it can all be erased, eradicated, and undone by correcting the way we *think.* No error, personal or global, is so great that a transformation of thinking cannot accomplish its complete

---

[5] Corinthians 13:11

correction. When our intention changes, so do our results.

*The most significant contribution you and I can make toward
world peace is to be peaceful ourselves, to give peacefulness to
those whose lives we touch daily, and to forgive ourselves for
our errors, to the point at which we love ourselves no matter
what we have ever done.*

When we find no sin in ourselves we will find no sin in the world, and
thus, after our long, thirsty trek through the desert of human separation, we
find ourself at the holy gate of New Jerusalem, key in hand.

> *If the people lived their lives*
> *As if it were a song!*
> *For singing out the light*
> *Provides the music for the stars*
> *To be dancing circles in the night.*

- Russian folk song

If we can build great bridges
Across the mighty waves, between the distant ridges
Is it a task too great
To build a bridge across the depths of hate?

For now more than ever
What the world needs more of
Is to reach for each other
With bridges of love [1]

If we can reach so far
To send men up to the moon and rockets to the stars
Why are we still so far apart?
Why can't we find the way from soul to soul,
From heart to heart?

For now more than ever
What the world needs more of
Is to reach for each other
With bridges of love

Bridges of steel reach from shore to shore
Bridges of love reach so much more
They link our common hopes, our common ground
Joining one and all, the whole world round

We all can build bridges of love each day
With our eyes, our smiles, our touch
With our will to find a way
There is no distance we cannot span
The vision is in our hearts
The power is in our hands

For now more than ever
What the world needs more of
Is to reach for each other
With bridges of love [1]

---

[1] Steven Longfellow Fiske and Jai Michael Josephs, "Bridges of Love," Fiske Music, 1983

Bridges of Love

In a gentle way, you can shake the world.

- Mahatma Gandhi

It was no surprise to me, then, that several months after my encounter with Shlomit and her family, I received a telephone call from a friend in Washington who was also committed to building bridges of love between nations. "Would you like to come to Russia with us in May, Alan?" she asked.

Think you not the goal itself will gladly arrange the means for its accomplishment?[2]

When I asked about the details, I was thrilled to learn that some of the people I most admire would be joining us: visionary woman of integrity Barbara Marx Hubbard, the great Swami Satchidananda, who has touched and inspired millions through his way of living yoga, and Patricia Sun, one of my favorite healers and teachers of love. I was also impressed to know that some well-known people from the entertainment industry would be with us, such as Dennis Weaver, Mike Farrell, and Shelly Fabares. The entire group was to be comprised of eighty spiritually-oriented teachers, business leaders, physicians, and artistically talented people, all dedicated to making a personal contribution to world healing. I took a deep breath in, and as I breathed out I realized I was about to undertake a great adventure.

Laughter and Sorrow

We arrived in Helsinki, Finland, where we spent three days undergoing an intense orientation to prepare us for our entry into the Soviet Union. Amidst the backdrop of a beautiful resort on the shores of the Baltic Sea, we got to know one another and learned much about Soviet history, the Russian people, and their culture.

---

[2] T, p. 340

Many of us brought gifts for the Soviet people, which we distributed among our group for each of us to give to individuals that we met in our travels. The first evening we came into our meeting room to find a glittering display of one hundred quartz crystals laid out on a table in a mandala geometric pattern. We filed up to the table and each of us chose a crystal that called to us vibrationally.

The next morning Patch Adams gave a lecture on the healing power of humor. Stunning the audience with his outrageous clown outfit, Patch revealed a table with one hundred rubber noses of all shapes and sizes, laid out in a mandala pattern. Each of us was invited to file up to the table and choose a nose, program it with our vibration, and give it to a Russian! (And we did. We "nosed" policemen, teachers, diplomats, children, shopkeepers, and anyone to whom we felt guided to give one. Without exception the noses were received joyfully, in the spirit of fun and sharing with which they were given. Long live nasal diplomacy!)

When the time came for our orientation about Soviet history, I learned some facts about Russia that stimulated a very deep process of transforming my attitude and understanding of Russia and her people.

The Russian people have had a horribly painful history. The country has been invaded and plundered over the centuries. From the Turks, to Napoleon, to Hitler, ambitious moguls have sought to overrun Russia, against which the Russians have taken up resistance. It is no wonder they are an isolated and defensive people.

Until 1917, the Russians were essentially a kingdom of peons. At the beginning of the twentieth century two percent of the population controlled eighty percent of the nation's wealth, and there were gross injustices in the dichotomous standards of living. We visited the Czar's Summer Palace in Pushkin, a staggeringly beautiful and glamorous estate with a thousand rooms embodying unbelievable wealth. One room had walls covered with pure gold; the next, malachite; and the next, ebony. Phenomenal treasures! We were told that eight of the royalty lived here, and they were staffed by three thousand servants! Artisans and craftsmen were paid next to nothing for their work. So in 1917 the people got fed up, they overthrew the Czar, and established a country where the ideal, at least, was for everyone to have an equal share of ownership and control of the country. Now that ideal has certainly not been realized, but an understanding of this history gives us a perspective on where the Russian people have come from in the brief space of seventy years.

Another very astounding fact was that the Soviet Union lost twenty million of her people in World War II. Ten million were killed through the war with the Nazis, and another ten million were lost to Russia's own Stalin. This is a rarely publicized fact. In all of the wars the United States has been involved in, from the American Revolution through Vietnam, this country has lost one million of our citizens. So you may begin to appreciate the kind of challenges the Russian have had to face. As so many families were touched by the war, there is still a strong memory of it. I would say that the Russian people have an extremely high value on peace — perhaps even more than our generation in America — for they have seen war, and they do not want to see it again. Be assured that all of their armaments and bravado arise from their feelings of insecurity; that they need to protect themselves from what they consider to be outside aggressors.

These facts gave me a great deal of insight into the life and genetic psyche of the Russian people. The purpose of our journey was to learn how to make contact with the hearts of the Russians, and knowing more about their history certainly helped me to do so. Here would be an important point to remember Longfellow's statement, "If we could look into the secret history of our enemies, we would find sorrow and suffering sufficient to disarm all hostilities."

Vicki's Tears

In Leningrad we were taken to the War Memorial, where nearly five hundred thousand Leningrad citizens — half of the city's population lost in World War II — are buried in mass graves the size of six football fields. At the head of the park stands a huge statue of Mother Russia, looming with the solemn dignity of a people who feel. The Mother holds a great granite wreath lain across her open arms, a symbol of respect and life. Somber music stirs in the background as Russian citizens lay rare, expensive flowers at the feet of the mass graves, not knowing exactly where the ones dear to them lie. There is the feeling that all are dear to them.

Our tour guide, Vicki, guides us to the head of the memorial, under the arms of Mother Russia, where she recounts to us the story of the war. An entire generation was lost from the body of the nation. The Russian people remember.

Vicki, I am told, is a KGB agent, a party member, an avowed atheist. And Vicki, in the midst of her canned discourse, stops and breaks into

315

tears, a striking contrast to her otherwise controlled presentation.

"Please forgive me for digressing," she mutters through the mascara running down her round cheeks.

"I want you to know how grateful I am that you have come here...Our countries must unite...We cannot go on like this...For the sake of our children...there is no other way."

We weep with her. There is a moment of spontaneous silence, deeper and firmer than the granite from which Mother Russia herself is hewn.

Behind Vicki we hear a munchkin-like *babushka* explaining that four men from her family are buried here. We think, we feel, we begin to see.

Vicki returns to her lecture, slightly disarrayed, yet still professional. She points out the age of some buildings, the style of the architecture, the method of construction. To walk past us now one would not know, except perhaps for a few undried mascara lines just below the eyes, that just moments before this one all the borders on the planet were erased, fifty thousand nuclear warheads disarmed, hearts opened as they never had before, and the people of America and the Soviet Union united as one on a healed planet.

But I would know. I would know that behind the most threatening facade, underneath the most terrifying mask, is but a frightened child, calling desperately for the love he feels he has lost. I would know that a huge aggressive bear acts ornery only because he has felt wounded; that there is no real distance between hearts; that the pain of the planet's past is shared by all of us; and the healing of that pain lies within our very hearts, now. I would know.

Gorgi's Gift

While standing in a bookstore in Leningrad one afternoon, I felt a hand on my shoulder as I heard a voice ask, "Do you want to sell your pants?" (There is a big black market for blue jeans in the Soviet Union.) When I turned my head I saw that it was a fellow from our group, playing a little trick on me.

But with him was a Russian man, Gorgi, a handsome young fellow with deep-set dark eyes and a sort of early-Beatle-ish crop of raven-black hair sweeping across his forehead. Gorgi spoke almost impeccable English. We chatted amiably for a while, and then he invited us back to his apartment. It felt right, and we decided to go.

He guided us up the back stairway of a shabby apartment building and cautioned us to please not speak English in the halls. We understood. Stepping into his apartment, we were appalled. One wall of Gorgi's living room was completely covered with picture post cards of the United States. This panorama was composed of most of the great sights of this country, from the Statue of Liberty to the Golden Gate Bridge. The adjacent wall displayed a collage of peace posters and buttons, similar to ones you might find in a young person's room in this country: pictures of doves, olive leaves, flags with peace symbols, and buttons with bombs crossed out by x's. The only difference was that the lettering was in Russian. Another wall contained a stereo cassette player. He put on a Michael Jackson tape.

Gorgi invited us to sit down at his little kitchenette table, and he put up water for tea. Then he went to his refrigerator and took out a luscious chocolate cake that looked as if it had been decorated by Michelangelo.

"What are you going to do with that cake, Gorgi?" we asked.

"Serve it to you!" he answered. " — It may be another fortnight before I meet some more American friends."

We enjoyed the cake and conversation immensely. None of us were as interested in discussing politics as we were enthusiastic about getting to know one another.

After some very vibrant conversation, we realized we needed to get back to our hotel. We thanked Gorgi for his warmth and hospitality. On our way out, Gorgi called, "Oh, wait a minute — I have something for you!" He went to his cabinet and took out a beautiful shawl, woven of cotton and printed with red roses. Humbly Gorgi handed it to me, and I did not know what to say. As I was admiring the shawl he dashed to the kitchen and brought me a jar of caviar. I did not even know what it was. Later I learned it was worth about eighteen dollars — a lot for a Russian tailor.

I thought for a moment, and I gave him my Sony Walkman — He was visibly touched. (I knew I would not come home with that Walkman.) I threw in some tapes.

"One more moment, please," Gorgi requested as we were about to step out the door. "Would you like some of these?"

He opened a cardboard tube and took out a thick pile of large printed posters. As he unfurled one for us to see, I could hardly believe the picture — it was an illustration of a little naked child, holding the earth close to his/her heart. At the top of the poster there were two words in Russian.

"What does that mean, Gorgi?" I asked.

"Embrace peace," he answered.

317

I was almost at the point of tears. He is not different than us. We love the same things. We want peace. We have been afraid of our brothers. We have been afraid of our self. We have been ignorant. That will change.

"Gorgi, is there anything we can do for you?" we wanted to know. "Can we send you anything or help you in any way?"

Gorgi smiled politely and shook his head, pushing his hands away from him as if to stop the idea.

"Thank you, no," he answered. "They read the mail, and packages do not always get through. It would not be a good idea."

We were disappointed.

"But there is something I would like."

"Please tell us."

"You can send me a picture post card every now and then!"

Gorgi's message: "Protect Peace"

Heart to Heart

On the evening of Ascension Thursday Swami Satchidananda was invited to address the Baptist Church in Moscow. (If you have any doubt that we have entered the new age, that invitation should dispell any question!)

It was raining in Moscow as the eighty of us dashed from our busses into the stone church, which was marked only by a small sign. We were ushered with great hospitality up to a lounge adjoining the balcony of the church, where we huddled together and enjoyed the flavored mineral water and tasty cookies put out by our hosts. There we presented the minister of the church with many hand-made dolls for his congregation, which we delivered as love gifts from a church in Washington. Each of the dolls contained a photo of the family that made it, a copy of the Silent Unity Prayer, and a love letter from the maker, stuffed into the doll's clothing. The minister and the elders of the church were delighted to receive these special gifts, and their faces lit up as they accepted them.

We filed into the balcony, but it seemed as if we were going into another world. In contrast to the gray concrete starkness of the streets of the city, here was warmth and wood and people gathered to sing to God. Most of the people in the sanctuary were *babushkas,* elderly women who had nothing to lose in the society by coming to church and celebrating their spiritual nature. They greeted us with their humble smiles, and made us feel welcome. It felt as if we had arrived home to grandma's house.

Our group stood and sang the One World Anthem, a song of international peace. It is sung to the tune of "My Country 'Tis of Thee," the melody of which is used as the national anthem of four countries on the globe. But instead of glorifying one nation over another, the One World Anthem glorifies the unity of all people everywhere.

Then we sang the anthem in Russian. Hardly any of us knew the Russian language, but we had rehearsed the song phonetically, and here was our chance to see if anyone would understand us. To our amazement, they did! Their faces lit up as we sang, and we were happy to see them elbowing their neighbors to listen carefully to what we were singing. There is something very touching about singing to someone in their own language.

Then Swami rose to offer his address. There are not many swamis in Russia, and to have a yogi give a spiritual address in Russia is quite a phenomenon. The congregants were leaning over the edge of the balcony to see and hear the man in the flowing robes.

And what an address he delivered! His words were simple, universal, and sincere. Swami spoke about the strength of our spiritual unity with the Soviet people. He said that Spirit is the Father of all of us, and the Earth is our Mother. That makes us all Children of the same Parents, brothers and sisters of one family. He even made a few jokes that the people enjoyed, even in translation. It was a perfect speech for the event.

After Swami's discourse it was time for us to leave. Everyone in the church had been emotionally moved, and we could feel the electricity in the air. The church choir rose, and to the accompaniment of the stirring tones of a pipe organ, they sang a Russian hymn that resonated deep within us. It sounded like "God Be With You 'Til We Meet Again," and it had the haunting flavor of the old Russia in which the soul of the people flourished like deeply-rooted flowers waving in the wind. It was a key to the real spiritual nature of the people.

As we began to file out of the church all of the *babushkas* rose to their feet, took white hankies out of their pockets, and began to wave them high in the air. They called, *"Mir, mir,"* ("Peace, peace") over and over again, in a chorus that shook the very bastions of the edifice.

I think there was not one dry eye in the house. Nearly every person in the church was moved to tears. We hugged and kissed and held the hands of many of the *babushkas* on our way out, and gave them our personal blessings as we received theirs. It was a holy moment.

When we arrived back at our bus, there was hardly a word spoken or heard. I sat in silence, wanting to bathe in the feelings of that magnificent experience. An awesome feeling of confirmation rolled through me; it was as if God was saying, *"This is surely the way to peace — from heart to heart."*

Vessels

The Russian people have a very high value on the exchanging of gifts. They do not take giving or receiving gifts lightly, and you can be sure that if a Russian gives you a gift or receives one from you, it means a lot to them.

One couple in our group took one of the homemade dolls on the subway, and gave it to a little girl they met there. The little girl's parents could hardly believe this was happening, and they were deeply moved. After accepting the doll they put their hands over their hearts, and bowed their heads toward the couple who gave their daughter the gift. The Soviet family's gratefulness was the best gift they could have given to the American couple.

Jim Barlow, a beautiful businessman with a huge heart, went to visit some Soviet dissidents, or peaceniks. There is a small group of peace activists in the Soviet Union who stage various forms of demonstrations and make statements for disarmament, ecology, and peace initiatives. Many of them dress in late-sixties garb, and one of their greatest heroes is John Lennon (an interesting variation on "Lenin"). To come out as a peacenik in Russia is quite a step, for although the government has become much more lenient than it used to be, those in power do not have as much patience for dissidence as do western governments, and those who rock the boat too much lose privileges. The man whom Jim visited had been demoted from a computer programmmer to an elevator operator. But, as Jim described him, "the light shined in his eyes very brightly indeed."

Upon the conclusion of Jim's visit with this couple, the wife went into the bedroom and brought Jim a gift. "Do you love God?" she asked Jim. "Yes, very much." he answered.

"Then we would like you to have this." Jim saw that it was a silver-plated Bible in the Russian language. "It is over a hundred years old," the woman explained. "We have treasured it, and now we would like you to have it as a symbol of our appreciation for your visit and your love."

A woman from our group, Dulcie, is a make-up artist for movies in Hollywood. Her dream was to visit a Russian movie set and learn about their make-up techniques. As this was a rather unusual occupation, the organizers of the trip were not able to arrange such a contact before the journey. But Dulcie was determined.

While we were in Moscow Dulcie learned that *Peter the Great* was being filmed there, and it was in the last few days of shooting. This, Dulcie reasoned, would be a marvelous opportunity to make contact. She found her way to the studio, but now the question was, "How to get in?" She had heard that one of the make-up artist's name was Tania, but that was all she had to go on. She had brought with her an American pictorial book on popular make-up techniques that she could show to someone who would be interested.

Dulcie began to nonchalantly walk through the security gate when she was stopped by a guard. He asked her in Russian, "Where are you going?" Dulcie knew no Russian, but she held up the make-up book and pointed to the cover, on which was a picture of one of the Ape-Men from *Planet of the Apes*. The guard looked at the photo, laughed, and began jumping up and down, scratching his sides, imitating an ape. Then he waved her into the studio.

Once inside, Dulcie still had no idea how to make contact. "Looking for a Tania on a movie set in Russia would be like walking into Universal

City and asking for Susan," she explained. After making several inquiries she did not find Tania, but she was directed to a very kind and hospitable make-up artist who spent hours sharing and discussing make-up techniques and movie production with Dulcie. "That, in itself, was quite a gift," Dulcie told our group. "To give an uninvited visitor even a few minutes during the last three days of a shoot in Hollywood would be unheard of. But this lady gave me her full attention and the gift of her time, which was very valuable indeed!"

And what about our friend Patch? Patch was a little disappointed, because although he is a doctor, he went on this pilgrimage as a clown, and he wanted to meet a Russian clown. On our last evening in Moscow we attended the Moscow circus, at which we saw an excellent clown. After the circus Patch went backstage to meet the man. Patch came out glowing. "Look what he gave me!" Patch announced, pointing to his feet. We looked down and there we saw some funny-looking clown's shoes, about two feet long. "He has been wearing these shoes in his act for twenty years!" Patch told us. "They were his first clowning shoes — and he told me he wants me to take them home as a gift from him!"

It is said that the only function of the things of this world is to communicate love. A gift of a material object is a vessel through which love and caring and encouragement are communicated. Through sharing gifts with the Russian people we discovered the highest purpose of the things of this world.

Star Peace

It was arranged for us to visit the Canadian-American Institute where, we were told in advance, the Russians observe and analyze our political, economic, and social trends. "I've never before been to a place where they study me," I joked as we walked through the large doors of the old yet stately building.

Several of the Soviet political analysts who staff the institute entered and sat at the head of a horseshoe of meeting tables. These men were more casually dressed than we expected, but they were neat and dapper.

They began our meeting with a brief description of their purpose, their work, and some of their methods. It was clear that they were not into propagandizing or giving any speeches. They were, however, very open and receptive to answering questions, which is what we preferred, as well. (As our hosts concluded their introduction, someone in our group told me that these people had the ear of Premier Gorbachev. I later saw one of the advisors on television during the news reports of the summit meetings.) Several of our group asked more probing questions about their methods. I wondered how much these men actually knew about us and our country. Did they just read propaganda literature? Had they ever visited our country? What were their sources? As I wondered, they answered all of our questions cordially. They seemed to be glad we were there. I sensed that these people were truly interested in communicating.

Some of the people in our group began to challenge the Russians on political issues such as the Soviet invasion of Afghanistan and the "Star Wars" militarization of outer space. I cringed a little bit, as political debate seemed so out of context with the goal of our visit. The people in our group who were asking the questions got a little hot under the collar, but the Russians handled the challenges in a cool, dignified, and respectful way. Our people looked a little foolish by contrast.

Then someone in our group asked them what they felt were the reasons that Ronald Reagan had won the American presidency.

"What kind of question is that?" I wondered to myself. "Why would you come to Russia and ask something like that?"

The answer took all of us by surprise. The gentleman who responded was a genius. A soft-skinned twenty-seven-year-old fellow with a boyish face, he gave an astute, unbiased, and enlightening discourse on the dynamics of the election. His explanation was so fascinating, in fact, that all of us were on the edge of our seats as we listened. In just a few short minutes he explained the economic conditions in the United States at the time, the influence of the fundamentalist Christians, an analysis of the strengths and deficits of Jimmy Carter's campaign, and several other insights which exemplified a deep working knowledge of how the American people think, act, and react. This fellow had lived in Washington for a number of years, and he put our newscasters to shame. His analysis was so well-integrated, interesting, and nonjudgemental that our entire group broke into a wave of spontaneous applause when he had completed his observations.

A little while later, as we concluded our session with this group, one of their members called out, "I would like to say just one more thing before you leave."

This gentleman had been stting quietly and doodling while he was listening to the discussion.

323

"Here is what I would like to share about my feelings and reaction to your group and today's meeting..." he stated.

He held up the paper on which he had been doodling. On it was drawn a gold star next to a red star.

"The symbol for both of our countries is a five-pointed star," he explained. "Meeting your group and feeling what you stand for, confirms to me that we are indeed more alike than we are different."

We looked at the picture. Above the stars he had written in bold letters, *"Star Peace — not Star Wars."*

Helen's Response

Helen was our tour guide, and to me she appeared to be tough. From the moment she greeted us at the train station in Leningrad, my feeling was that this woman was not to be messed with. She marched us from the train to our bus like a bunch of cub scouts on their first camp-out (maybe Patch Adams in his clown outfit told her something).

As she conducted the first day's tour Helen was rather authoritative, and it was clear that while she was very efficient she also seemed mechanical. I respected Helen, but I kept my distance.

One afternoon I was the first to return to the tour bus after a walking tour. There I found Helen alone, sitting and reading a book. I noticed a lovely softness in her face, a lightness I had not seen before. Helen was relaxed and her eyes were gentle, and it made me happy to see her in a peaceful way. She showed me the book; it was an American book about Samantha Smith's visit to Russia. Samantha was a twelve-year-old American girl who made international headlines when she wrote to then-Premier Breznhev telling him that she knew very little about the Soviet Union, and that she would like to get to know the Russian people herself. Both nations were shocked when the Premier replied and invited Samantha and her family to come to Russia as guests of the Soviet government. The book was the pictorial account of Samantha's journey in which she, in her own way, opened the door to citizen diplomacy. I looked at the page to which the book was opened, and there was Helen's picture — she had been Samantha's tour guide.

(Since that time, Samantha has become something of a heroine to the Russian people. After she and her father were killed in a private airplane crash in Maine, the Russian government issued a Samantha Smith commemorative stamp, and they named several streets after her.)

Still, I felt a little leery about Helen. Could I trust her? I had brought a bunch of my pamphlets, *"If We Only Have Love"* (printed in this book as *The Day After the Prayer*). I had had them translated into Russian, and I gave them to persons whom I felt would be receptive. I had given one to Vicki, our other tour guide, but I was still reluctant to give one to Helen. I had been told that she was KGB, and as some of my like materials had been seized at the border, I wondered if it would be wise to give it to her. I played it safe and said nothing.

Then one afternoon Helen approached me and told me quite sincerely, "Alan, Vicki told me you gave her a pamphlet which she liked very much. Why did you not give me one? I would love to read it and show it to my children." I felt a little embarrassed, but more grateful than anything else. I was glad that Helen reached out to me. *A Course in Miracles* tells us that if one person in a relationship remains sane, it will help both to be sane. I was glad that Helen was sane.

Helen softened and unfolded as the tour progressed. The real miracle, however, came at our closing luncheon, at which each person in our group stood and shared what they had gained from our journey. When the microphone came to Helen, she rose and began to speak with tears streaming down her cheeks. "I have grown to feel that I am one with you...And I want to tell you that I love you very, very, very, very much." All of us were deeply moved. Helen received a long standing ovation.

We Will Always Be with You

One evening we were invited to something of a new age party in Moscow. Our group piled into several little cars and taxied to a rather large apartment of a Belgian journalist living on the outskirts of Moscow.

And what a party it was! For me it was a momentous evening, for I had the opportunity to be with some of the people I most admire. In one room Swami Satchidananda was leading chanting. In the living room, Patricia Sun was offering her healing sounds. In the next room Barbara Marx Hubbard was discussing a satellite space bridge with several Russian geniuses.

Elsewhere in the house a talented Russian icon painter was describing how he tunes his mind to serve as a channel to paint beautiful holy pictures, into which he imbeds crystals for healing. A little later a tiny Greek fellow showed up at the door, offering a concert on this nifty little cello-like musical instrument he carried with him. We accepted, and he found himself a place on the couch, where he droned on for the remainder of the evening. Like I say, it was quite an evening.

At this party was a young man with a shining face. He was an accomplished artist, and his specialty was etching. He showed us some of his work, and we were astounded. He had taken birch bark, rolled it into a flat canvas-like medium, and into pieces of the bark he had etched exquisite scenes of the Russian countryside, concentrating mainly on churches. All of us were taken aback by the beauty and the craftsmanship in these renderings.

This young man was especially touched by the presence of Swami Satchidananda. He had never seen a yogi before, and to this young man, Swami represented God (to us, too!). The young man watched Swami from afar for most of the evening, and when we left to get a cab back to the hotel, the man followed us to the parking lot of the apartment building. The man approached Swami and gave him one of his portraits. Then he took Swami's hands and kissed them, and almost tearfully asked him, "You're leaving now?" It was a very moving scene to behold.

Swami took the young man's hands, pressed them to his own heart, looked the fellow in the eyes, and answered, "No — we will never leave you — our hearts will always be with you."

How the Forest Answers

When we arrived back in Finland to get our plane to the states, our tour guide joyfully told us, "I heard your tour was very successful." We all assented. "Yes," she went on, "there is an old Finnish saying: *'The forest answers you the way you call into it.'*"

And indeed that is how the forest answered us. We went with a clear purpose: to build bridges of love between the American and Russian peoples, and to make a personal statement that we are ready to have peace in our world. And because our statement was honest and simple and undisguised, it was heard and reflected back to us in the spirit in which we gave it.

We learned the power of unconditional love and communication from the heart. We saw the importance of valuing peace above all other goals. We found that the way to real communication is to focus on how we are alike, instead of analyzing our differences. We learned that the Russian people want peace as much as we do, and that they are one with us in so many ways. We discovered that the real menace is not nuclear weapons, but fear. If we as a people knew more about the Russian people, we would not be afraid of them, and we would feel no need to be pointing nuclear weapons at them. We would want to be with them more and seek to learn from them as they have learned from us.

A long time ago someone said, "We have met the enemy, and he is us." This is so, and now I would add, "and we have loved him, and in discovering his beauty, we have unveiled the doorway to peace."

For now more than ever
What the world needs more of
Is to reach for each other
With bridges of love

Power, Peace, and Pedestals

There remains but one lesson for the Children of God to master to enter into the Age of God: the reclaiming of personal power to be used in the service of Love, free of guilt, and dedicated to the celebration of light in human experience.

This is not a power *over*, but a power *for*. We cannot afford to misuse our power, and neither can we afford to deny it. Both errors, actually forms of fear, can be rectified only by knowing ourselves. There is but one reason that a being of light would lose the power to be happy, and that is that such a one does not remember who he or she is. Yet in the regaining of that precious awareness is the entire world restored to the soul to whom it rightfully belongs.

Let us now discover the process by which that error can be undone.

Shadows

Many times and in many ways we have spoken of the shadow that stands between you and your own light. Now we must focus on it so clearly and with such keen determination that you will be able to see clearly, without any question, how you have divested yourself of joy by the denial of your power.

The Dark Shadow

When we become appalled at the evil we *believe* is in us, one of the ways that we attempt to get rid of it is to project what we do not like about ourself onto the outside world. By seeing the unwanted trait in someone else instead of ourself, we believe we have relieved ourself of the "sin." Once the feared trait is "out there," we identify with the opposite "good" quality, and then engage in obvious or hidden attack against the negative trait that we have projected outward. Sometimes, for example, we may find

329

newspaper stories about persons who are well-known for their personal combat against some kind of evil, who are discovered to be engaging in the very evil they are fighting. This is because we only fight ourself, and if someone has a personal vendetta against any cause, you can be sure that within themself they are harboring some kind of guilt or fear over the same issue, or a variation of it. If they had made peace with that issue in their own heart, they would feel only compassion for persons still struggling with that situation, and they would treat the problem not as an attack, but as the call for help that it is.

It is impossible to project a shadow and not engage in a war against it. Inherent in our view of the outer shadow is the self-hatred that caused us to project it originally. Hence we see the most important dynamic that *all attack is a statement of self-hatred*, and thus a *desperate plea for healing*. But because the entire dynamics of shadow-making are veiled from conscious awareness by the ego (like the greater part of an iceberg under the surface of awareness), no one in a state of war is aware that it is himself that he is attacking.

While all of us have engaged in shadow war in our personal life, perhaps the clearest and most dramatic example of shadow-making is Adolph Hitler and Nazi Germany. During the time of that regime an entire culture projected a shadow of unprecedented proportions and then attempted to get rid of it by annihilating the persons onto whom they had projected it. The Nazis took every trait and weakness that they hated in themselves, projected those characteristics onto the Jewish people, and then attempted to purge themselves by getting rid of the Jews.

Seen on such a massive scale, the insanity of such a plan and its utter hopelessness is obvious. What we need to see, little though we may be willing to admit it, is that *we engage in the same type of "windmill-warfare" each day*. Every time we feel angry or judgemental of someone, we are fighting our own shadow. We may not rally a nation around us to support our insanity, but we certainly blame and attack others for the faults that we are not willing to look at within ourself. (And then we solicit agreement to support our attack on ourself.)

The answer to the dark shadow is obviously not in attempting to attack or destroy the screen onto which we have projected our fear. Imagine a motion picture theatre in which a beautiful movie is marred by a huge, ten-foot fly crawling all over the the screen. Then imagine the audience becoming so fearful and irate that they throw objects at the big black bug and ultimately tear the screen apart in an effort to get rid of the intruder. How mistaken they would find themselves to be as they discover that the problem was not a ten-foot fly on the screen, but a quarter-inch fly on the lens of the projector! The answer was not at all to attack what they were seeing, but to examine and purify its source.

The mind is the source of all that we see in the "external" world. No matter how many years or lifetimes we may spend trying to purge the outer world of problems, the only path to real healing is to return our attention to the great projector of our mind and polish the mirror that reflects the Light that illuminates all that we see.

Our analogy becomes even more striking when we remember that it was a beautiful movie that was intended to be projected onto the viewing screen. To attack or destroy a brother or sister is to remove the one field on which we could behold the beatific image of Itself that Spirit projected into the world. We *need* one another to see the God in this world.

The understanding that the person "out there" is *not* the cause of our problem is a major first step toward the healing of any relationship. Acting upon this understanding offers a gift to your brother and the world that cannot be measured in any way except in the depths of the heart.

Correction versus Attack

The question may occur to you, "Does this mean that I am not to correct anyone? People certainly do make mistakes that I do not do." This is quite true.

There is one sure way to know if you are fighting with your shadow, or offering useful help: *Do you have an emotional charge when offering the correction?* If you feel in any way upset or less than peaceful when pointing out a problem to someone, you can be sure that it is yourself that you are attempting to correct. At such a time, your most productive step would be to stop for a moment, perhaps take a deep breath, and ask yourself, "Will the way I am about to speak to my brother or sister bring about healing, or more separation?" or "What do I really want to create in my life?" But a brief moment's consideration of this question will reveal the way that you can be most helpful to your friend and yourself.

The Healing of the Dark Shadow

The healing of the dark shadow involves a process which, if followed with sincerity, is certain to create most rewarding transformations in your relationships and your entire life. Life is made of relationships, and your sense of peacefulness in all that you do is directly related to how you see your sisters and brothers.

The first step to healing is releasing the person "out there" from the responsibility for your pain. It is a major premise of miracles that *no one and no thing can cause you pain except your own thoughts*. Every time you ascribe your suffering to a source outside your mind you not only perpetuate your hurt, but you divest yourself of the power that God gave to you to create a loving and rewarding life. You do not stand a chance to be truly healed until you own everything that happens to you as your own creation.

The second step to undoing the shadow is to acknowledge that you believe you do the same thing for which you find the other party guilty. You may not see yourself as doing it in exactly the same form, or you may not find yourself doing it now, or you may have done it in thought but not action. This attribute may not even be true about you, but you may believe it is true or harbor fears that it may be true. Your sense of guilt may disguise itself in any one of a thousand forms. But of one thing you may be sure: if you see it in another, you see it in yourself. You would not have needed to cast it onto another if you had not first found it too overwhelming to accept in yourself.

The third step is a joyful and liberating one: Forgive yourself. You may rejoice in the knowledge that you were wrong about being guilty. You have not sinned. You may have made an error, but that is not the same as a sin. Sins require punishment, but errors require only correction. Your judgements about yourself were too heavy. God has found no sin in you, and now it is for you to align your vision of yourself with God's, which is always merciful. You must transform your attitude about this so-called sin; you must cease to see it is evil, and begin to see it as a call for healing, which you deserve. Such a perspective will bring great peace to your heart, for now you can use your experience as a springboard to greater love. Thus, with just a slight change of mind, you have transformed your "sin" into a blessing, and you see yourself as God sees you, which is totally lovable.

Then you can turn the whole situation over to God. It is not your job to heal yourself. Your job is but to see yourself clearly. Looking at yourself in this light, constructive change must flow naturally. Problems are not a call for condemnation, but vision. When you see yourself as innocent you defuse the need for punishment which you have called upon yourself by your sense of guilt. And you are innocent. You deserve only good. You are here to reflect only peace. This awareness will take you all the way Home.

If you follow this healing process whenever you feel angry, victimized, afraid, hurt, or rejected, you will quickly reclaim the power that you have given to fear. You always had the power, but you gave it away because you believed that someone else could be the source of your experience. In so believing, you reversed the sequence of cause and effect in your life. *You* are the cause, and your experience is the effect. To see the world as the cause is to make yourself helpless; to know that your mind is the cause is to make yourself helpful. The time has come for you to reclaim power over your life.

The White Shadow

Many teachers, psychologists, and consciousness trainers have intelligently and productively identified the dynamics of the dark shadow. But there is one aspect of shadow-making that has rarely been illuminated: the white shadow.

The dark shadow is projected when we are unwilling to accept our faults. The white shadow is projected when we are unwilling to accept our beauty. If we are afraid of being beautiful we hurt ourself as much as we do when we are afraid of being ugly. We cannot afford to be afraid, and the most direct way to disarm the fear in our life is to undo the fear of ourself.

In some of my workshops I ask the participants to take a sheet of paper and list their positive traits in one column, and their negative traits in another. Then I ask each person to stand up and share their list with the members of the class.

You would not believe the length of the negative lists, and the brevity of the positives! Most people have little difficulty describing what is wrong with them, but when it comes to reading the list of their wonderful attributes, they inject a symphony of "uh"'s, "sort-of"'s, and screwed-up faces. Most of us are embarrassed to be beautiful, and that is a great problem indeed! The white shadow is projected when we are afraid to own our goodness. Feeling unworthy to accept holiness as a part of our real being, we throw it off of ourselves, create someone out there to be wonderful in the ways that we are not, and then we worship them. This is a terrible disservice to ourselves, and in the long run it hurts the other person as well, because sooner or later their humanness becomes obvious, and when we realize that they are not who we thought they were, we may tend to blame them for defrauding us or leading us to believe that they are something they are not. The problem is not that they misrepresented themselves, but that we made them out to be something they never could be. We gave our power away and blamed them for stealing it. All because we didn't love ourself in the first place.

White shadow-making has destructive ramifications to an astonishing degree. It has been a part of nearly every marriage and relationship, as many of us are attracted to the persons that we believe are the things that we are not. When we enter into any relationship with the premise that we are empty and the other person will fill us in, we are sure to fail. We can win only when we proceed from wholeness. A relationship in which two halves seek to become whole will be extremely disappointing, for you bring to the relationship only what you believe you are. To see both of you as incomplete is a very debilitating gift to offer to a marriage or relationship.

This does not mean that such a marriage or relationship is doomed; in fact, the reversal or transmutation of the white shadow releases healing energy that can build a real and nourishing relationship. When the two halves realize they are *already whole*, the relationship ceases to be a litany to emptiness and becomes a celebration of perfection. Two persons agreeing on their mutual innocence makes them quite invulnerable and opens the door to a cornucopia of miracles which only continue to surpass themselves. The energy generated in such a relationship is an example of the power of joining. So, you see, the thought that we are empty must ultimately lead to the discovery that we are whole. And therefore our adventure into shadow-land is actually a steppingstone to the joy of self-realization.

Real Teachers

Another example of white shadow-making that is especially ripe for understanding in our time and culture occurs in cults and guru-worship. Cult members are especially prone to divest themselves of the responsibility for their wisdom, strength, and independence, and place their own magnificence in the lap of the leader. Here it is easy to see that just as we cannot afford to ascribe our pain to a source outside ourself, neither can we place our salvation in the hands of another person.

If the leader in such a situation does not have a high degree of integrity they will play on the followers' sense of lack and unworthiness, and use the power that their followers have given them for spiritual tyranny. We do not have to go into the details or offer many examples of teachers who have led disciples into darkness or students who have hurt themselves by offering their power to someone who was not worthy of it.

If, on the other hand, the leader is a true teacher, they will take advantage of the disciples' attention to teach them that the power they would like to give away rightfully belongs within themselves. It is said that a real teacher is one who makes himself or herself progressively unnecessary. A good guru teaches the disciples to go beyond his or her form. Hilda used to tell us that the best compliment we could give her would be for us to graduate from her teachings and become our own teacher. One of the lessons in *A Course in Miracles* tells the students to "forget this course."[1] And Jesus said, "Even greater things than I, shall you do."

The word "guru" means "from darkness to light." If a guru guides his or her disciples to the light, they are fulfilling their function in a powerful way. If they keep the disciples in darkness, they may not be called a guru. Beware of teachers or groups that threaten you with evil things that will happen to you if you leave the organization. Some students of certain cults are told that if they leave they will go to hell, lose their spirituality, or be cursed in one form or another. I was told by one ex-cult member that he was told that if he left the organization he would be reincarnated as a cockroach. Well, maybe that would be an improvement over his current situation. There is no curse worse than fear, and if you allow fear to motivate you on the spiritual path, you are already cursed. But that can all be undone instantly as you choose love as your guide instead of fear.

The desire of a disciple to stay with his or her teacher should be born of love for the teachings, a feeling of increasing strength, and the manifestation of real healing in the student's life. The student should have little patience for healing that is promised just around the corner, after death, or after obtaining a high rank in the organization. It may be said that the presentation of a threat at the suggestion of leaving the organization is a clear sign to leave the organization. The purpose of any guru, church, therapy, or consciousness organization is to teach that God is everywhere. If Spirit is purported to be only in this group, it is a poor spirit indeed, and one that is not worthy of

---

[1] W, p. 350

learning more about. If you are told that you are too weak to leave, you must respond with the knowledge that you are too strong to stay.

The Right to Power

The bottom line, of course, is that no teacher, therapist, cult-leader, or guru can hurt you or hold power over you unless you first give him or her that power. The tendency to project blame can and must be transmuted to appreciation for a valuable lesson in personal responsibility. The moment you are ready and willing to reclaim the power you gave away, you are free. If you know how to think with God, you will bless the leader for having played an important role in the lessons that ultimately lead to your liberation.

Thus we see the wisdom in the *Course in Miracles* teaching that "all things, events, encounters and circumstances are helpful."[2]

From Pedestals to Power

We can no longer afford to hold idols before the face of God. To be afraid of our power is to be afraid of God, and in turning our back on our source of Light we create shadows. In so doing we severely limit who we are and what we can do, and such a way of walking this world is very much out of context with the purpose of our life.

But the awareness of our misunderstanding is the perfect prelude to understanding. We must learn that God is a God of only love, and knows nothing of the punishment that we fear. The awareness of God's unfailing knowledge of our innocence is enough to dethrone our idols and place us on equal footing with our Self, where we belong.

Placing one who is equal with us on a pedestal is not to raise him or her up, but to lower ourself. All of us are equal Children of Perfect Spirit, and to deny our perfection in any way is to suffer. Pain would not be possible if we knew without a doubt that only good dwells within us, regardless of what we may seem to see to the contrary. In Spirit's eyes there is no contrary, and it is for us to see ourselves through those uplifted eyes. To love ourself in the same light in which Spirit holds us is to live free of judgement, purified of fear, and confident in the knowledge that we may walk in poise and dignity.

---

[2] M, p. 9

From Power to Peace

Power and peace are one and the same. Any dichotomy that we hold between the two is a function of a split mind, born of the fear of our own being. When we trust our feelings, our intuitions, our love, we honor the power that we have been given to find our way Home and know ourself. There is no greater gift in all the universe than discovering our own beauty, and we do have the power to do it. But we must accept it. When you are asked to surrender, you are not asked to surrender to death, but to life. You are not asked to become weak or subservient, but to accept your own strength. You are not summoned to give up your joy, but your lack of confidence in your ability to be grand. You already are grand. And so you are asked only to know yourself.

You cannot know yourself as long as you see others as shining brighter than you or lesser than you. You must love yourself so much that you are unwilling to deny your own wonder by seeing it in another instead of you, or in yourself to the exclusion of another. You must enfold everyone you meet in that same dignity, or else your dignity is lost. It is not only possible to hold all in the highest esteem — it is imperative. There is room at the top for everyone, and none of us are Home until all of us are Home. And all of us *are* Home.

You must appreciate yourself with such integrity that your heart beats a blessing to you and the world every time it pumps. Each breath you take is an affirmation of God's need for you. Do not fear, deny, or misappropriate your greatness — it is what you came to know and live.

Peace *is* power, and all of it has been given to you. It is now for you to take what you have been given and use it. The world rejoices at your peace.

There is a hush in Heaven, a happy expectancy, a little pause of gladness in acknowledgement of the journey's end...No illusions stand between you now. Look not upon the little wall of shadows. The sun has risen over it...No more can you be kept by shadows from the light in which illusions end. Every miracle is but the end of an illusion. Such was the journey; such its ending.[3]

---

[3] T, p. 381

What One Can Do

The pure, unadulterated love of one person can nullify the hatred of millions.

- Mahatma Gandhi

Your personal power is as unlimited as you would have it be. You are under no restriction of age, gender, education, or experience. The only thing that can bind you is your mind, and that is something over which you have total control. You are a free soul, and if you do not allow fear to stand between you and your vision, you will walk with dignity upon the earth and bring healing to the world.

The world cannot defeat you. Only you can defeat yourself. There have been many persons who have caught a glimpse of their personal power, and moved with that vision. One morning they woke up and realized that they were not small. They understood that those who told them that they couldn't make it were seeing but their own illusions of limitation. And then they went out and did something about it.

The difference between an ordinary person and a saint is that the ordinary person dismisses his dreams as fantasies, and a saint takes a step to making them realities. Never underestimate the power of your vision. Your dreams are your fuel, given to you to lift you out of the mire of small thinking and power your way to the stars. Your vision of who you can be and what you were born to do is a gift from a loving God, to help you find your way home. You are not meant to live in the mud — your home is in the heavens. Your dreams will carry you past obstacles that would otherwise defeat you. You were not born to be defeated. You were born to triumph.

At times your vision may be your only window to God. If you do not look through it, all you will see is limitation and despair. But lift up your eyes and you will see a golden destiny that is sure to bring healing to your heart and to all that you touch. This is God's promise of success, and you have every right to claim it.

You have sometimes, perhaps often considered how much you need

God. Now you must consider how much God needs you. There are certain questions that you must ask, for you are now ready to receive the answer: Does God want you to succeed? Does God want you to be happy? Does God want you to make a special contribution to the healing of this planet?

If you believe that Spirit wants anything less than total joy for your life, you have allowed guilt to cast its shadow upon the light that burns within you and yearns to be expressed as you. The shadow cannot take away the light, but it can hide it from your awareness. This is tragic, not because you could lose who you are, but because time in life is given you to celebrate your beauty, and every moment that you do not see yourself is literally a waste of time.

Make time your friend by finding a cause for joy in every moment. If you look, you will find. Spiritual enlightenment is not a matter of finding the right answer in one place, but discovering God in *all* places. The journey is complete when you see God everywhere. And because God *is* everywhere, such a vision will be profusely rewarded.

In Your Own Way

There are no standards in the outer world to which you must adhere. If you attempt to live your life to fulfill external pressures, you will prolong the illusion of death, you will not create anything new, and you will be miserable. But there is a standard to which you must be true, and that is to do what is personally meaningful to you. Whether or not it is meaningful to anyone else does not matter. But that it is meaningful to you matters a great deal. Your destiny lies at the end of that path, as well as in every step of the way. If you follow that path, you will be at peace and your acts of integrity will change the world. To be at peace with yourself is to make the greatest contribution to life.

Stepping into Your Own Shoes

One who succeeded gloriously in living her truth was a remarkable woman known as Peace Pilgrim.[1] After years of contemplation about what is required to bring personal and planetary healing, Peace Pilgrim renounced her past, possessions, and name, and walked for over twenty-five thousand

[1]Peace Pilgrim Center, 43480 Cedar Avenue, Hemet, California 92344

miles in the name of peace. Owning only the clothes she wore, including a tunic that said *PEACE PILGRIM* on the front and *25,000 MILES ON FOOT FOR PEACE* on the back, this courageous lady crossed America for nearly three decades, sharing with anyone who had ears to hear the simple principles for which she walked and lived:

Overcome evil with good,
falsehood with truth,
and hatred with good.

Peace Pilgrim placed herself entirely in the hands of the Lord; she would not eat unless offered food, she did not seek shelter unless invited, and she solicited no money for her work. In spite of her renunciation Peace Pilgrim became something of a celebrity. She was sought after as a speaker and teacher, and she was invited to speak on radio and television and in schools nearly everywhere she went. She sought no personal glory, and yet her influence was so profound that many articles and books have been written about her life.

I saw a video and several photographs of Peace Pilgrim, and the clarity of the light in her eyes was a teaching of tranquility. Here was one person who made a stand for what she believed in, and many hearts were opened as a result of the purity of her love.

We do not all need to renounce our homes and literally walk for peace as Peace Pilgrim did, but we do need to live for it. Peace Pilgrim was guided to serve in her own way, and if you are willing to listen to the Voice of Truth within your own heart, you will be given clear, unfailing direction toward the discovery and fulfillment of your destiny.

We do not need to be statesmen or diplomats or revered celebrities; we do not need to demonstrate the riches of royalty or the sacrifice of martyrs; neither need we be lauded, applauded, or acclaimed. All we need to be is real. There is but one requirement to feel the peace of God in every activity of life: We need to live our lives according to the integrity that we know, and love ourself and our life just as it is.

The Power of Giving

One man who has touched my life is "Highrise Joe," a blind man who attended one of my workshops near Minneapolis. What a contribution he made to our class! Joe was a positive, inspiring, and dynamically alive giver in our group. During one session someone in our group asked Joe how he has come to shine so brightly, and he told us this story:

"One day I became so frustrated that I was about to pack it all in. I felt that I had had it, and I didn't think I wanted to live any longer. Then the telephone rang; it was a caller who had the wrong number. He was in desperate need. It was a teenager who was contemplating suicide. My heart opened as I talked to the boy, and after a long conversation he changed his mind. I decided at that time that if there is one person out there who needs me, it is worth it for me to be here. I can make a useful contribution to the world, and that gives me great joy."

Joe's life has changed quite a bit as a result of that experience. He has since become a one-man hotline for teenage crisis intervention, and now he receives calls from all over the country, from teenagers who need help. Joe has developed remarkable relationships with many of these young people, which have continued over the years.

Another experience that has shaped Joe's life occurred when he tripped over some packages of groceries that were left in the hallway of his apartment house. As he picked himself up he was feeling clumsy and upset. At that moment he heard the sobbing of a woman. He followed the sounds into an apartment near the groceries, and there he found a neighbor in deep despair. Upon returning home from shopping she had received a telephone call that her husband had been taken to the hospital, and suddenly he had passed away. The woman was sitting at her kitchen table weeping, in something of a stupor.

Joe sat with this woman and comforted her. He gave her loving support and helped her make some necessary telephone calls. Joe spent four hours being fully with her, and when she was in a better frame of mind and in a position to act more effectively he left her in greater peace.

How God uses us when we are willing to be of service! Joe's tripping over those bundles was not an accident at all, and he was not clumsy. He was in his right and perfect place, and he was actually an angel in that situation. How appropriately he is called "Highrise Joe"!

You, too, are in your right and perfect place. When you seem to be tripping up or clumsy, you need but shift your focus slightly, and you will find that God is right where you are. Never forget this. It can make the difference between despair and great triumph.

Be a Lighthouse

Another person who has changed the world in his own way is Willie, a shining soul in a nursing home in New Jersey. Willie is diagnosed as a paraplegic, but he is not a disabled person. After speaking with Willie for just a few minutes the first day I met him, I saw that he is a bright light in that hospital. There his positivity and his love have worked wonders. He is like a beacon in the halls. Many patients approach Willie for moral support and counseling, and I have seen doctors and nurses come to him to renew and energize themselves. Sitting in the hall with Willie, it is difficult to have a continuous conversation, for so many people, from the custodians to the hospital director, stop to talk with this man. He has a smile, a joke, and an encouraging word for everyone who passes him.

When I had originally gone to the hospital to conduct a weekly yoga class, I felt put off by the pain and limitation that I saw. But Willie showed me that happiness goes far beyond circumstances; it is really a state of mind.

Not Afflicted

Willie is not the only one to make a stand for joy in the hospital. During one of our classes I instructed the group to "Raise your arm like this..." One fellow, Earl, called out, "I can't see what you're doing — I'm blind."

A woman down the row responded abruptly, "Well, we all have our afflictions."

"I'm not afflicted," answered Earl, " — I'm just blind."

Perhaps we can learn from this man's willingness not to see himself as a victim. I learned so much from the hospital patients, and I honor them as my teachers. I had thought that I was going there to teach them something, and I did. But along the way I learned a great deal from them.

To Feel Full Inside

There is a young woman in a Unity church who has won the hearts of the entire congregation. In the world of appearances Wendy is a paraplegic. Some may see her as a limited victim of a disease. But that is not how she sees herself! And therefore that is not who she is. Wendy is a vibrant, energetic, loving being, and she is an inspiration to all who meet her. I have never met Wendy in person, but someone gave me her card, by which I feel I know her totally. Her wallet-sized card shows a sun, a rainbow, and a pot of gold at the rainbow's end, colored with beautiful water-colors painted by Wendy, with a brush that she directs by holding it in her mouth.

The card says,

> *My belief is that life is like a rainbow.*
> *At the beginning you struggle uphill,*
> *But at the end, if you make it,*
> *You find the "Pot of Gold."*
> *I found the gold in all of you here.*

I found it in true friendship and love.
To me you shine just like gold.
I found out what God's plan and gift to me is:
The ability to help other people.
*I feel full inside! Love is **everything**.*

Wendy

How Wishes Come True

As I was sitting and writing this on the patio of my back yard, the wind blew a piece of newspaper into the yard. My friend Anne, who had been assisting, picked up the paper, read it, and handed it to me. The title of the article was, "Wishes Can Come True." It was a story about the Make-a-Wish Foundation[2], which has been created to grant wishes of children suffering with life-threatening illnesses.

The organization was founded when a seven-year-old Phoenix boy who was dying said his dream was to become a policeman. The State Department of Public Safety became aware of his vision and made him an honorary policeman for a day. On his day they gave him a custom-made helmet, a badge, and a glorious helicopter ride. The boy passed on a few days later, but before he did, he had an adventure he had always dreamed of.

Other examples of the work of the Make-a-Wish Foundation have included arranging a leave of absence and paying the salary of a working woman whose fifteen-year-old daughter's last wish was for her mom to be able to spend more time with her; sending a group of forty children with cancer to Disney World; and providing children with cassette players, VCR's, and computers to make their time in bed more comfortable and stimulating.

The heart of the Foundation, the article reports, is the volunteer staff, a cross-section of persons with all kinds of occupations and interests, who are described as being generous, compassionate, and "giving two hundred percent." "When something reaches way down inside you and grabs at your heart," Jane Martens (a high school teacher and founder of one chapter) describes, "you just know you have to help in some way."

---

[2] Make-A-Wish Foundation, 4601 North 16th St., Suite 205, Phoenix, Arizona 85016

The Best Teacher

Perhaps the miracle change agent closest to me is a beautiful and sensitive man named Lou. At an early age Lou found in himself a degree of sensitivity which the persons around him did not understand or appreciate. As a result he entered a long struggle with his identity, and he went through a very challenging and difficult adolescence and early adulthood. Eventually Lou entered a monastary in hopes of escaping from the harshness of the world. But there he found monks flagellating themselves and being surprisingly unkind to their fellows.

As Lou grew he learned not to look outside himself for solace. He discovered that to be happy he would have to find worth in his own self, just as he was. He made a decision that gentleness and sensitivity are gifts and not deficits, and that suffering and separation are not necessary. Lou worked his way through all kinds of questions, fears, and doubts, and ultimately Lou's sensitivity made him a healer in his own right.

As a teacher, Lou established a new program in his high school. The course, called "Humanities," is an elective for seniors in which the students are offered a full semester to explore themselves and discover who they are and what they would like to do with their life. Lou employs methods such as inviting each student to sit with him in two director's chairs in front of the class, where he interviews them about their ideas, their feelings, and their aspirations. His goal is for the students to learn to see themselves as whole persons, and to love and accept themselves in the process. And it works. The kind of rapport that Lou develops with his students is one that every teacher has dreamed of, for he inspires them to open their minds and hearts to a greater vision of themselves and the possibilities for their life. They appreciate his gift in the deepest possible way. During the three years that I shared a home with Lou, he received many phone calls and loving letters from students and former students who wanted to stay in touch with him. "Please tell Mr. Chalupa that Gary Carlson called...I am in the Air Force now, and I just wanted Mr. Chalupa to know that I am doing great." One day Lou took the day off from work to go canoeing with a former student who had just lost his father unexpectedly. Another time I saw a copy of a teacher's evaluation form lying on our kitchen table. It was an evaluation made by the school vice-principle who sits in on classes unannounced, and grades each teacher on various kinds of performance. Curious as to what the school administration thought of Lou, I picked it up and read, "Mr. Chalupa did not seem to be scientifically organized, and I didn't really understand what he was talking about; but it should be noted that once again the students have voted Mr. Chalupa the best teacher in the school, and therefore I recommend him to continue." Largely as a result of Lou's quality of inspired teaching, two other full-time teachers have been hired to teach the same course, and last semester so many seniors signed up for the class that even though six hundred of them were able to take it, many were turned away.

Lou's latest triumph was gaining the approval of the Board of Education to allow senior citizens to join the high school students in his classes. In an unprecedented project, the senior citizens come to class every day and participate with the younger students in dialogues, sharing, and study. Lou reports that the results are phenomenal; the wisdom of the seniors' experience is melded with the vitality of the teenagers. During a Halloween costume contest, the teens voted one of the golden agers as having the best costume as a sailor. (Another student came to school dressed as Mr. Chalupa.) The Board is so impressed with the quality of what is happening in this project that they are planning to expand it to the entire high school. What one man can do.

The Power of Willingness

As we can see through the example of all of these courageous people, it is not your position in society that allows you to become an effective change agent, but your willingness to shine where you are. The number of people that you seem to affect is not as important as the quality of the effect that you have on those you do touch. Some of us have chosen to touch large numbers of people, and some have chosen to work intensively with a few. Both are equally important, and both serve the entire universe profoundly. Never be fooled into believing that you are judged on the number of people you help. God is impressed by a loving heart more than pure volume. More is good, but it is not always better. A mother who gives one child unconditional love is making an enormous contribution to the universe. A friend of mine, a young mother who used to be very active in social, political, and spiritual organizations, wrote me a letter describing her life with two infants. "Most of my time is occupied with feeding, cleaning, and diapers," she wrote, "but it's the strangest feeling; I feel like I am accomplishing less in the world than I ever have, but I feel more rewarded and content within my self than ever before." And no one could ask for more.

The Most Effective Healer

There is but one further awareness that all who would serve the world must accept: It is not up to you alone to do it all. Remember that the real healer is Spirit, and that Spirit will work through you if you are willing to listen with a quiet mind and a receptive heart.

The first step in changing the world is to change the way you see the world. You must acknowledge God's presence in the world before that presence can be made manifest. If you proceed with a picture of victimization, injustice, fear, or anger, your work will largely be ineffective. Wrath is a vicious temptress, and if you fight under her bloodied flag, your losses will most surely outweigh your gains.

Love will afford you your most powerful position, and draw to you all manner of strength and support. The energies that you make available to yourself when you are at peace will enfold you with a mantle of comfort and protection that cannot be violated by any sense of fear or loss. When your goal is to be truly helpful, you are literally invulnerable. Being truly helpful means that you seek only the solution in which everyone wins. If anyone loses, everyone loses. The only real victory is one which brings peace to everyone involved. To understand this kind of victory you must see with your heart, and not your eyes.

This shift absolutely requires that you know who you are and Who is your Source. If you believe that you are your own source, you are doomed to failure and you will wither behind the walls of your self-imposed loneliness. But to know that there is a higher power that is acting though you, and in fact needs you to accomplish its great goal, is to find your full strength. You don't have to go it alone, do it alone, or be it alone. The knowledge that God is with you is the strength that will carry you over the hurdles at which lonely warriors falter. Everything you need to succeed is already within you, and it has been but awaiting your assent to pour forth in creative healing.

The Healing Vision

Like you, the world already has what it needs to be perfect. Some have feared the healing of our world because they have equated healing with ending. But this could not be so. All healing is a beginning. The resurrection of our life will come not through destruction, but through transformation. The caterpillar does not die; it becomes something entirely new and more wonderful. To hold our world in the willingness to have it continue to live, and to acknowledge that such a world already lives within our hearts, is the greatest gift that you and I can offer to our planet.

Thus we arrive at the ultimate awareness of the spiritual warrior, a joyful renunciation which only the stoutest of heart can embrace: the world is already saved. The healing of the Planet Earth has already been accomplished by God, and you are free of this awesome burden. Spirit does, however, vitally need one contribution from you, something that only you can choose to offer: *your vision.*

You will not see a perfect world until you see a perfect world. This is the first and final element of healing, the part that you came here to play. You may delay it, but you cannot change it. Nor would you want to. Who but an insane person would focus on chaos when he or she could create healing through a vision of perfection? You are not insane, but you have been asleep. The world does not need your manipulation, but it is desperate for your awakening. With your arising to the truth within you, you will carry all who have slumbered to their healing, as well. You are not separate from the world. Heal your mind, and you will transform your world. Thus you have the key to the healing of the Planet Earth.

Offer, then, this gift with me. We need each other to share in this vision. Joined, our minds are an unstoppable force. Jesus said that "the gates of hell shall not prevail against the Son of God," and we join him in his identity as a peaceful warrior. He came as a harbinger of what we have come to accomplish. And we shall not fail. We cannot fail because we act in the name of the One Who sent us. And I assure you that we are sent in the name of Love.

> *What one man can do is change the world*
> *And make it new again*
>
>   - John Denver

349

The Healing of the Planet Earth

Children of Light,

The time of the great awakening is come.
You who have chosen to lift your eyes from
the darkness to the light are blessed to see the
advent of a new day on the Planet Earth. Because
your heart has yearned to see real peace where war
has reigned, to show mercy where cruelty has domin-
ated, and to know love where fear has frozen hearts,
you are privileged to usher real healing to your
world.

The Planet Earth is a blessing to you. She
is your friend and your mother. Always remember
and honor your relationship with her. She is a
living, loving, breathing being, like unto yourself.
She feels the love that you give as you walk upon
her soil with a happy heart.

The Christ has chosen your hands to reach the
lonely, your eyes to see innocence in the guilty, and
your lips to utter words of comfort to the wounded.
Let pain be no more! You have wandered in dark
dreams for too long; now you must step into the light

and stand for what you know is true. The world has suffered not from evil, but from the fear of the acknowledgement of good. That fear must be ended now, forever, and it is within your power to do so.

No one can find yourself but you. All of your answers are within. You must now teach the lessons you have learned. Your understanding has been given not only for yourself, but to guide a sore and tired world to a place of rest in a new consciousness.

Here before you is your vision come true. Here is your answer given you, a song to soothe a weary soul and make it new again. Here is the bridge that joins you to your brothers and sisters. Here is your Self. Look gently upon your Self, and allow yourself to be filled by the Light you have been seeking. True love comes from your Self, and with such a power your every thought is a blessing to the entire universe.

All areas of your life will be healed. You will shine with a golden splendor that speaks of the One Who created you in wisdom and glory. The past will dissolve like a dark dream, and your joy will be so brilliant that you will have no recollection of the night.

Go forth, then, and be a messenger of hope. Point the way to healing by walking in gratefulness. Your brothers and sisters will follow, and as you pass beyond the portal of limitation you will be united and reunited with all who seem to be lost. There is no loss in God. Choose the path of forgiveness, and you will weep tears of joy for the goodness you find in all.

Go forth and live the life of the radiant soul that you are. Glorify God in your every deed. You are important, you are needed, and you are worthy. Never allow the dark cloak of fear to hide the light from your view. You were not born to fail; you are destined to succeed. The hope of the world has been planted in your breast, and you are assured of success as you stand for the One who sent you.

This, then, is the healing of the Planet Earth. All of your doubts and fears can be set aside as you know that the healing will come through the love in your heart.

All blessings are with you. Go in Peace. All is well.

One day, you will sit on a plateau and the wind will blow through your hair, and you'll have a simple cloak on. And you will sit there and you will contemplate your life and you will realize the magnificent creature that you really are. And you will have not done one thing that would have ever harmed you or hurt you or would have disrespected you in any way, because, above all, it was your respect that you upheld and no one else's. That is when you can sleep and slumber at night and rejoice during the day and love what you are. Then you are a happy entity and, indeed, a happy God.

- Ramtha

By Alan Cohen
BOOKS

The Healing of the Planet Earth
A golden gift of empowering ideas, an excellent guidebook to give you the courage to release all fear and allow yourself to be lifted naturally to the next stage of personal and planetary transformation. Introduction by Barbara Marx Hubbard, with magnificent photographs by Awakening Heart Productions.

The Dragon Doesn't Live Here Anymore
A bestselling book of encouragement and joyful self-discovery. This warm, open-hearted, and inspiring journey through spiritual growth sheds loving light on self-acceptance, healing, and the power of positive living. A steppingstone and companion to many hearts.

Rising In Love
A touching guide to healing our relationships in the light of love. In a personal, comfortable, and captivating way, Alan offers important, practical insights on how to create fulfilling relationships by believing in ourselves and those we love.

Companions of the Heart
An attractive hard cover volume of the above three popular books. This collection is perfect for those who love to read and re-read these inspiring ideas and to offer as a gift to friends.

The Peace That You Seek
A deeply inspiring and moving collection of channelled messages of guidance, offered as gifts to the Children of Light on the threshold of a New Age. These messages offer great strength, wisdom and caring, shared to serve as healing reminders of the wonder that shines within us. A special gift for the spirit.

Have You Hugged A Monster Today?
A delightful story that teaches how to discover the hearts of the meanest monsters and make friends with the friendless. Shared through clever, laughable cartoons and captions, this is an entertaining course in human relations for children of all ages. Illustrations by Keith Kelly.

Setting the Seen
A series of fascinating guided visualizations for deep relaxation and stress management. Written with instructions for use by teachers, counselors and those in the healing profession, this is a practical guide to physical, emotional and spiritual tranquility. (Companion to cassette *Peace*)

CASSETTE TAPES

Peace
A soothing tapestry of guided images, excellent for meditation, relaxation and personal growth. Useful for spiritual growth, awakening creativity and mental clarity. Alan Cohen's voice blends with Steven Halpern's music to create a deep harmony of being that will touch you in a most important way.

Deep Relaxation
A one-hour program of exercises to relax, renew and reinvigorate. Excellent for those who would like to practice yoga at home; this tape guides the listener through a basic series of yoga postures, guided deep relaxation, breathing exercises and meditation. Gentle background music by Dr. Steven Halpern.

Miracle Mountain
A live recording of one of Alan's workshops, in which he invites the participants to become themselves and celebrate their own strength. These tapes capture the essence of Alan's teachings, including many powerfully inspiring moments. Themes include: keys to healing, loving relationships and believing in ourselves. Tapes include songs and music, guided meditations, group interactions and joyous laughter.

I Believe in You
An orchestral journey of self-affirmation, including inspiring, empowering songs by the popular minstrel, Stephen Longfellow Fiske, and a marvelously uplifting guided meditation by Alan. A very moving and practical gift to encourage healing for yourself or others.

★★★

Personal Orders:

For a free catalog of Alan Cohen's books, tapes and workshop schedule, write to:

Alan Cohen Publications and Workshops
P.O. Box 450, Kula, Hawaii 96790

Bookstore Orders:

New Leaf
5425 Tulane Drive S.W.
Atlanta, Georgia 30336

(1-800) 241-3829
toll-free number for stores only